ESSEX COUNTY DEEDS
1639–1678

ABSTRACTS OF VOLUMES 1–4
COPY BOOKS
ESSEX COUNTY
MASSACHUSETTS

ESSEX SOCIETY OF GENEALOGISTS, INC.

HERITAGE BOOKS
2010

HERITAGE BOOKS
AN IMPRINT OF HERITAGE BOOKS, INC.

Books, CDs, and more—Worldwide

For our listing of thousands of titles see our website
at
www.HeritageBooks.com

Published 2010 by
HERITAGE BOOKS, INC.
Publishing Division
100 Railroad Ave. #104
Westminster, Maryland 21157

Copyright © 2003 Essex Society of Genealogists, Inc.

Other books by the author:

*Essex County Deeds, 1639-1678, Abstracts of Volumes 1-4
Copy Books, Essex County, Massachusetts*

CD: The Essex Genealogist, Volumes 1 and 2 (1981-1982)

The Essex Genealogist, Volumes 1-25 (1981-2005)

The Essex Genealogist, Index to Volumes 1-15 (1981-1995)

The Essex Genealogist, Index to Volumes 16-20 (1996-2000)

The Essex Genealogist, Index to Volumes 21-25 (2001-2005)

All rights reserved. No part of this book may be reproduced or transmitted in any form or by any means, electronic or mechanical, including photocopying, recording or by any information storage and retrieval system without written permission from the author, except for the inclusion of brief quotations in a review.

International Standard Book Numbers
Paperbound: 978-0-7884-2441-0
Clothbound: 978-0-7884-8306-6

With special thanks to:

Essex County Registry of Deeds

And volunteers:
Alice Bonney
Elizabeth Frost
Marilyn Fitzpatrick
Rosalie Godfrey
Nancy Hayward
Norma James
Shirley Learned
Marcia Lindberg
Shirley Orr
Catherine Piemonte
Virginia Ryan
Marie Scalisi

Although every effort has been made for accuracy by the volunteers, any deed of interest should be verified by consulting the original copy books.

Essex Society of Genealogists, Inc.
P.O. Box 313
Lynnfield, MA 01940
www.esog.org

ESSEX COUNTY DEEDS Book 1

"RECORDS OF SALEM 1640"

THOMAS DEXTER to SIMON BRADSTREET (mortgage) – (1:1) Thomas Dexter of Lynn (yeoman) by his deed dated [22nd of October] 1639 hath mortgaged his farm in Lynn, containing about [ ] acres with all his houses, meadows and broken ground thereon for 2 oxen & 2 bulls, upon condition of payment to Simon Bradstreet of Ipswich [ ] 90 pounds the 1st day of August next following [with] a reservation upon the sale…to give the said Dexter the overplus above the debt and damage of the said 90 pounds.

JOHN HUMPHREY to EMANUELL DOWNING – (1:1) John Humphrey of Salem, Esq. By his writing dated 6 September 1638, has granted to Emanuell Downing of Salem, Esq., the 2 ponds and as much high ground about the ponds as is needful to keep the duck coye private from the disturbance of plowmen, herdsmen [or others] passing by that way which he may enclose, so as he take not in above 50 acres of the upland round about the same.

JOSEPH ARMITAGE to RICHARD RUSSELL (mortgage) – (1:1) Joseph Armitage of Lynn, by his writing dated the 10th of December 1640 has sold unto Richard [Russell] of Charlestown, the house wherein the said Joseph now dwells with the land lying in the pales by [the west] sides…?…and the foot of land lying from the E side of the pale of the said house together with [ ] of meadow and [ ] acres of upland [100 pounds].

JOHN PRIDE to WILLIAM WALTHAM (mortgage) – (1:2) John Pride of Salem, in consideration of 4 pounds 8 shillings 6 pence by his deed dated 23rd of the 10th month last 1640 hath mortgaged unto William Waltham of Weymouth, for 4 pounds 8 shillings 6 pence his house wherein he dwelleth with 1½ acres of ground enclosed near Mr. Holgrave's stage in Winter Harbor with power of redemption upon payment of the said 4 pounds 8 shillings 6 pence by the latter end of May which shall be in the year 1641.

WILLIAM PESTER to CHARLES GOTT (mortgage) – (1:2) William Pester of Salem (merchant) hath mortgaged unto Charles Gott & John Horne, 1 house and the ground adjoining to it for security of 19 pounds, 2 shillings, 6 pence per bill dated 20: 8ber: 1641, being bound therein in 40 pounds for further security of the said deed 19 pounds, 2 shillings 6 pence. **Recorded**: 20 October 1641.

SAMUEL SKELTON to RICHARD DAVENPORT – (1:2) Samuel Skelton sold 4 acres of land lying on the back side of Mr. Ruck's dwelling house in Salem unto...Lieut. Richard Davenport. **Recorded**: 21: 12th month: 1643.

JOHN PEASE to RICHARD INGERSOLL – (1:3) John Pease sold to Richard Ingersoll one house and 75 acres of land being the one-half (or moytye) of the farm which the town of Salem granted unto Frances Weston which 75 acres lyeth next unto the farm wherein the said Richard now dwelleth, as by the deed dated 13: 4: 1644.

JOHN ELDERKIN to SAMUEL BENNETT – (1:3) John Elderkin by his deed dated 16: 7 month: 1643, sold unto Samuel Bennett the newly built watermill at Lynn for 100 pounds. **Recorded**: 15: 5: 1644.

ADAM OTLEY (for JOHN HUMPHREY, Esq.) to RALPH FOGG – (1:3) Adam Otley (on behalf of John Humphrey, Esq.) sold to Ralph Fogg of Salem, a farm of a dwelling house & cellar, with ¼ acre of land near the common pound in Salem for 3 pounds, 6 shillings, by writing dated 11: 2nd month 1644. The records to this purchase were certified to the recorder of Boston. **Recorded**: 25: 5: 1644.

GEORGE HAWKINS to WILLIAM DODGE – (1:3) George Hawkins (shipwright) of Boston, by power of attorney from George Richesson (mariner) of Wapping, bearing date of 1 May 1641, has sold unto William Dodge & his heirs forever, 200 acres of land in Salem, near the head of Bass River, lately in possession of Peter Palfrey, for the sum of 40 pounds as by his deed appeareth bearing date of 28: 7ber: 1644. **Recorded**: 27: 8ber: 1644.

THOMAS DEXTER to RICHARD LEADER – (1:4) Thomas Dexter of Lynn (yeoman) sold for 40 pounds sterling to Richard Leader for use of the Iron Works, all that land, which by reason of a dam (now agreed to be made), shall overflow, and all sufficient ground for a water course from the dam to works to be erected, and also all land between the ancient water course and the new intended watercourse, together with 5½ acres of land in the corn field most convenient for the Iron Works, and also the convenient cartways on each side of the premises as by a deed bearing date the 27th of January 1645. **Recorded**: 25: 1: 1646.

CHRISTOPHER FOSTER to DANIEL KING – (1:4) Christopher Foster sold to Daniel King of Lynn, 1 house with 25 acres of land; also 8 acres of land called Sagamore Hill, also 10 acres of land called Parker's land, also one farm of 60 acres lying between Mr. Clark's and Mr. Humphry's farms, as by his deed appeareth bearing date of the 10th day of the 1st month 1645. **Recorded**: 10: 1: 1645.

EDWARD RICHARDS to DANIEL KING – (1:5) Edward Richards sold to Daniel King, a parcel of land called the Windmill hill in Lynn, as by his deed thereof dated 30: 2nd month: 1646. A caveat entered by Daniel King for all the land about Windmill Hill as is now enclosed and in his own possession and by him purchased. **Recorded**: 30: 2: 1646.

TOWNSEND BISHOP to RALPH FOGG – (1:5) Robert Moulton and Michael Shafflin, agents for Mr. Townsend Bishop sold unto Mr. Ralph Fogg of Salem the new messuage or dwelling house of the said Mr. Bishop's by the rocks, near Captain Hathorn's house in Salem for 3 pounds, 10 shillings, as by a writing bearing date xith: 1st month: 1645/6 (more at large appeareth). **Recorded**: 27:3: 1646.

TOWNSEND BISHOP to RICHARD ADAMS – (1:6) Robert Moulton and Michael Shafflin, agents for Mr. Townsend Bishop have sold unto Richard Adams one old house with 1 acre of land within the common field and about 1½ acres of land next to the common enclosed by itself, for 3 pounds, 10 shillings as by a writing thereof made dated the xith of the 1st month 1645/1646 appeareth. **Recorded**: 27:3:1646.

JOHN ELDERKIN to MARY KINSLEY – (1:6) John Elderkin mortgaged unto Mary Kinsley his half part of the sawmill in Reading in consideration of 10 pounds as by the writing dated the 27th of June 1646 as more at large appeareth. **Recorded**: 5th of the 6th month 1646.

SAMUEL SHARPE to JOHN PORTER – (1:6) Samuel Sharpe sold unto John Porter his farm lying on the N of Mr. Skelton's farm deceased with all thereto belonging for the sum of 110 pounds. **Recorded**: 12th of 7ber 1646.

JOSEPH ARMITAGE to NATHANIEL HANDFORD – (1:7) Joseph Armitage of Lynn sold unto Nathaniel Handford of London (haberdasher) one new house in Lynn adjoining to the Common with 3 acres of ground adjoining to said house, shooting down towards the brook, and 2 acres of meadow ground in the marsh before the town for the sum of 27 pounds as by the said deed more fully appeareth bearing date the 6th of September 1638. **Recorded**: on the 7th of the 5th month 1647.

RICHARD STILEMAN to SAMUEL SHARP – (1:7) Richard Stileman of Salem granted to Samuel Sharp, Elder of the church at Salem and Elias

Stileman, Sr. ffeofies in trust, all the messuage or tenement in Salem lying between the dwelling house of Phillip Cromwell and the shop of Benjamin Felton with the old house by the water side, and 1 acre of ground whereon the two houses stand, for the use of his son Samuel Stileman, the said Richard reserving his dwelling house therein for 18 years at the rent of 5 pounds a year, provided if by casualties of fire, the houses be destroyed, the rent to be abated accordingly, and in case the said Samuel dies before he be at age 21 years, then the whole estate to return to the said Richard...as by the said deed bearing date 9 August 1647 more at large appeareth. **Recorded**: on the 11th of the 6th month 1647.

ROBERT NANNY to Capt. WILLIAM HATHORNE and Mr. WILLIAM BROWNE – (1:8) Robert Nanny of Dover in the county of Norfolk (planter) has granted in mortgage one house and 1 acre of land thereto adjoining and 20 acres on the back river, to Captain William Hathorne and to Mr. William Browne of Salem (merchants) as by a deed dated the 22th of the 10th month, more at large appeareth. **Recorded**: on the 25th of the 10th month 1647.

JOHN KITCHEN to THOMAS SCUDDER the Elder – (1:8) John Kitchen of Salem (cordwinder) sold on the 28th of the 12th month 1647, unto Thomas Scudder the elder, 1 house and ¼ acre of land by Capt. Trask's house near the new mill, for 13 pounds.

EDWARD GILMAN to THOMAS SAVAGE (mortgage) – (1:8) Edward Gilman has sold his farm and house thereon with all thereto pertaining as was in the possession of Richard Smith his father-in-law, with 8 cows and 2 mares, unto Thomas Savage of Boston, upon condition of repayment of 100 pounds in money, beaver, or fish, before the last day of May next as by a deed dated the 20th day of December 1647 more at large appeareth.

ELIAS STILEMAN the Elder to RICHARD HUTCHINSON – (1:9) Elias Stileman the elder sold to Richard Hutchinson his farm containing about 150 acres for 15 pounds as by deed dated the 6th day of the 4th month 1648. **Recorded**: on the 6th day of the 4th month 1648.

WILLIAM HAYNES to JOHN PORTER – (1:9) William Haynes of Salem (husbandman) sold to John Porter of Salem (yeoman) 4 score acres of upland, 8 acres of meadow, for 5 pounds, as by the writing more at large appeareth dated 28th of the 4th month 1648. **Recorded**: 28:4:1648.

JOHN PORTER to WILLIAM HAYNES – (1:9) John Porter of Salem (yeoman) sold to William Haynes of Salem (husbandman) 4 score acres of upland and 4 acres of meadow for 5 pounds...dated the 28 of the 4th month 1648 as more at large appeareth. **Recorded**: 28:4:1648.

SIMON BRADSTREET to JOHN PORTER – (1:9) Simon Bradstreet of Andover (gentleman) sold to John Porter of Salem (yeoman) for 15 pounds in hand paid, his 3rd part of the farm which was Mr. Bishop's containing about 100 and 4 score acres of upland and meadow lying in Salem, as on 29: 4month: 1648 appeareth. **Recorded**: 29:4:1648.

WILLIAM & RICHARD HAYNES to JOHN PORTER, Sr – (1:10) William Haynes and Richard Haynes of Salem (husbandmen) sold to John Porter, Sr of Salem, for 30 pounds...their true and third parts of the farm which was lately Mr. Bishop's containing about 104 acres of upland and meadow, as by a deed dated 29: 4th month: 1648. **Recorded**: 29: 4th month: 1648.

JOHN LUFF to FRANCIS SKERRY – (1:10) John Luff of Salem (weaver) sold to Francis Skerry of Salem (husbandman), 3 acres of land near the ferry between Wallers' and Edwards' lots for 50 shillings, as by his writing dated the 6th of the 4th month last past appeareth. **Recorded**: 3: 5th month: 1648.

ROBERT ADAMS to WILLIAM GERRISH – (1:10) On 18: 2nd month: 1649, Robert Adams of Newbury (tailor) sold to William Gerrish, for 30 pounds, one house and 1 acre of land, lying between Mr. Batter's & Henry Cook's houses in Salem, as by his deed dated day and year above written.

PERCIVAL LOWELL to WILLIAM GERRISH – (1:11) Percival Lowell of Newbury (gentleman) sold to William Gerrish, 1 barn and 6½ acres of arable land thereto belonging...in Newbury, as by his deed dated 6: Nov 1648 more fully appeareth. **Recorded**: 1: 3rd month 1649.

JOHN HUDSON to WILLIAM HATHORNE – (1:11) John Hudson of Jeffries Creek (now called Manchester) sold to William Hathorne of Salem, half his house and half of 25 acres of land at Manchester, whether it be upland or meadow, for 18 pounds paid by said William to said John, and also a great sow and 2 iron pots as by a writing dated 11: 4th month: 1649, more at large appeareth. **Recorded**: 26: 4th month: 1649.

JOHN INGALLS to DANIEL KING – (1:11) John Ingalls of Lynn sold to Daniel King of Lynn for 17 pounds 10 shillings, a house & 6 acres of ground adjoining, 4 acres of meadow, whereof 1 is in the town marsh and 3 in Rumney Marsh; also one 10-acre lot, amongst the town lots; also 1 parcel of upland lying by the plain beyond Capt. Bridges' house; also 4 acres of meadow in the fresh marsh, as by a deed indented bearing the date 6th of the 12th month 1648 appeareth. **Recorded**: 27th of the 4th month 1649.

HENRY COMB to FRANCIS JOHNSON (mortgage) – (1:12) Henry Comb mortgaged to Francis Johnson, for 3 pounds, 6 shillings, 9 pence, his house and ground which he bought of Samuel Corwin & John Northy, as by 6th March 1648 appeareth.

RICHARD HAYNES to SIMON BRADSTREET (mortgage) – (1:12) Richard Haynes of Salem hath sold unto Simon Bradstreet of Andover, all his house & 12 acres of land – meadow and upland, with the proviso for the sale to be void upon the payment of 4 pounds 5 shillings in good wheat, as by a writing dated 29: 4th month: --- appeareth.

WILLIAM GERRISH to EDWARD NORRIS – (1:12) William Gerrish (gentleman) of Newbury sold to Mr. Edward Norris, for 30 pounds, 1 house with 1 acre of land, lying between Mr. Batter's and Henry Cook's houses, as by deed dated the 7th of the 6th month 1649 appeareth. **Recorded**: 8th of the 6th month 1649.

JOSEPH ARMITAGE to THOMAS SAVAGE (mortgage) – (1:12) Joseph Armitage of Lynn mortgaged unto Thomas Savage of Boston, his now dwelling house and stall with 2 acres of land on which the house stands and 6 acres of marsh in Rumney Marsh in consideration of 35 pounds, as by his deed dated the 8th day of the 4th month 1648 more at large appeareth. **Recorded**: 5th of the 8th month 1649.

JOHN BAYLES to WILLIAM PAINE and to EDWARD EASTWICK – (1:13) John Bayles (tailor) of Salem sold to William Paine (shoemaker) of Salem 1 shop adjoining the shop of Alexander Field in Salem for 9 pounds 10 shillings as by his deed dated the 8th day of 8ber 1649 more at large appeareth. **Recorded**: 8th of the 8th month 1649.

John Bayles (tailor) of Salem sold to Edward Eastwick (mariner) of Salem, 2 acres of land on the south River between Elias Mason and Richard Raymond's lots for 4 pounds 5 shillings, as by his deed dated the 8th day of the 8th month 1649 appeareth.

WILLIAM HAYNES to RICHARD HUTCHINSON & NATHANIEL PUTNAM – (1:13) William Haynes, in consideration of an engagement unto Richard Hutchinson and Nathaniel Putnam, made over unto them all his right and interest to 150 acres...being ½ of the farm which was formerly John Pease's as by a writing dated the 21st of February last, more at large appeareth. **Recorded**: the 14th of the 9th month 1649.

ELIZABETH EDWARDS (wife of THOMAS EDWARDS) to DAVID CORWITHIN, Sr and JOSEPH YONGES to DAVID CORWITHIN – (1:14) Elizabeth Edwards, wife of Thomas Edwards (shoemaker), by virtue of a power of attorney, sold unto David Corwithin, Sr. for 3 pounds 1 shillings, 10 acres of land near Darby Fort hill, lying between said David's and Joseph Grafton's land, as by a deed dated the 9th of July last appeareth. **Recorded**: the 14th of the 9th month 1649.

Joseph Yonges of Salem (mariner) has sold unto David Corwithin for 17 pounds, a dwelling house with 1 acre of land thereto adjoining in Salem, as by a deed dated the 4th of Sept last, more fully appeareth.

JOHN COYT to WILLIAM PITT – (1:14) John Coyt sold to William Pitt all his houses, his 3rd part of the stages with the land adjoining, 2 acres of marsh, 8 acres of upland on the neck, for 11 pounds, as by a writing dated the 9th of February 1647 appeareth. **Recorded**: on the 28th of the 9th month 1649.

THOMAS WHEELER to JOHN BURTON – (1:15) Thomas Wheeler of Lynn (yeoman) sold to John Burton of Salem, 1 house and 2½ acres of land in the North field in Salem between Thomas Buxton & William Nichols' lands, for 10 pounds, as by his deed dated 11 Dec 1649 appeareth. **Recorded**: on the 11th of the 10th month 1649.

HENRY COOK to HENRY BIRDSALL (mortgage) – (1:15) Henry Cook (butcher) of Salem, for 10 pounds, mortgaged his house & shop and 1 acre of ground adjoining in Salem, to Henry Birdsall, as by his deed, dated the 10th of 10ber 1649 appeareth. **Recorded**: on the 11th of the 10th month 1649.

JAMES HINDS to JOHN GETCHELL – James Hinds sold to John Getchell a 5-acre lot on Darby fort side, between said Getchell and Mr. Button's lots and one other 5-acre lot between Goodman Williams' and Oliver's lots for 45 shillings, as by his deed dated the 5th of the 8th month 1649 appeareth.

JOSEPH ARMITAGE to WILLIAM BARTHOLOMEW – (1:15) Joseph Armitage of Lynn, for security of 15 pounds, bound over his bay mare to William Bartholomew, as by his bill dated the 15th of February last appeareth. **Recorded**: the 4th of the 1st month 1649.

JOSEPH ARMITAGE to THOMAS SAVAGE (mortgage) – (1:16) Joseph Armitage of Lynn, mortgaged to Thomas Savage, for 75 pounds sterling, his dwelling house & 2 acres of land where his house stands, and 6 acres of meadow in Rumney Marsh, as by a writing dated the last day of December 1649 appeareth. **Recorded**: the 17th of the 1st month 1649.

JEREMY MEACHAM to JAMES HAMPTON – (1:16) Jeremy Meacham sold to James Hampton for 19 pounds 10 shillings, his dwelling house with 1 acre of land, except 2 rods sold to John Smith, as by a writing dated the 8th of the 2nd month 1650. **Recorded**: on the 15th of the 2nd month 1650.

JOHN GEDNEY to THOMAS SPOONER – (1:16) John Gedney sold to Thomas Spooner a parcel of ground which was given to old Norman, & 1¼ acre of meadow in the south field, for 3 pounds, 10 shillings as by a writing dated the 16th of the 1st month 1649 more at large appeareth. Recorded on the 15th of the 3rd month 1650.

JAMES HINES to RICHARD MOORE – (1:16) James Hines of Salem (cooper) for 22 pounds 10 shillings sold to Richard Moore, a dwelling house on the south river side with ¾ acre of land adjoining, and 10 acres of upland in the south field, as by a writing dated the 3rd of Oct last appeareth. **Recorded**: the 15th of the 3rd month 1650.

HENRY HARWOOD to WILLIAM STRATTON – (1:17) Henry Harwood of Salem (shoemaker) sold to William Stratton for 8 pounds, 10 acres of land near Throgmorton's Cove, as by a writing dated the 10th day of July 1649.

PHILLIP CROMWELL to DOROTHY KENNISTON – (1:17) Phillip Cromwell, before he married his now wife Dorothy Kenniston did covenant to give her 10 cows and for her security thereof did make over to said Dorothy his dwelling house & grounds and the house the said Dorothy then lived in, as by a writing dated the 10th day of the 2nd month 1649 more at large appeareth. **Recorded**: the 22nd of the 3rd month 1650.

SAMUEL BENNETT to ROBERT MANSFIELD – (1:17) Samuel Bennett (carpenter) sold to Robert Mansfield, 4 acres of salt marsh in Lynn for 4 pounds, as by his writing dated 20: 3rd month last appeareth. **Recorded**: the 25th of the 4th month 1650.

RALPH FOGG – (1:17) Ralph Fogg's caveat against all bargains made since his troubles (without his consent) of any of his lands or houses. **Recorded**: the 2nd of the 5th month 1650.

JOHN FOGG to GEORGE ROPES – (1:18) John Fogg, with consent of his mother, sold to George Ropes, 1 acre of salt marsh in the south field, adjoining the marsh of Richard Raymond for 25 shillings in ready money as by a deed dated the 20th of the 12th month 1648. **Recorded:** the 9th of the 7th month 1650.

JOHN FOGG to JEREMY VAILE – (1:18) John Fogg sold to Jeremy Vaile, one swamp joining his own land in the south field as by a writing dated 20th of the 12th month 1648 appeareth. **Recorded:** the 9th of the 7th month 1650.

RICHARD LEADER to Capt. WILLIAM HATHORNE – (1:18) A caveat recorded of the sale of the slitting mill in Lynn by Richard Leader for 10 pounds to Capt. William Hathorne.

SAMUEL SKELTON to JOHN PORTER – (1:18) A caveat was recorded of the sale of 1 neck of land in Salem, between Crane River and Wooliston River by Samuel Skelton for 41 pounds to John Porter of Salem, reserving unto Samuel Skelton 3 score acres of the said neck lying furthest W as by a deed dated 8 March 1649. **Recorded:** the 3rd of the 8th month 1650.

DORCAS VEREN to FRANCIS PERRY – (1:19) A caveat was recorded of the sale of a farm with houses thereon by Dorcas Veren to Francis Perry in Salem, for 35 pounds, to be paid at certain dates yet to come, and for want of any of said payments the land to return to said Dorcas as by the deed dated the 3rd day of October 1649. **Recorded:** the 12th of the 9th month 1650.

(1:19) Dorcas Veren sold her farm with the houses thereon with 20 acres of land, formerly part of Mr. Batter's farm thereto adjoining, and 160 acres near cedar pond, for 35 pounds, whereof 10 pounds to be paid on the 1st of November 1649 and 10 pounds on the 1st of 9ber 1650 and 10 pounds on the 1st of 9ber 1651 and 5 pounds on the 1st of 9ber 1652, and for default of any of the payment, the land to return to Dorcas Veren as by a deed dated 3: 8ber: 1649. **Recorded:** 3: 11 month 1650.

WILLIAM KNIGHT to THOMAS FARRINGTON – (1:19) William Knight of Lynn...sold to Thomas Farrington of Lynn, for 27 pounds, 13 shillings, 4 pence. 200 acres of land with the meadow thereto belonging, lying on the S by Adam Hawks' land and on the W of the river that parts the Lynn Village from the town, also 8 acres of meadow lying near the lands of George Smith, and 5 acres of meadow in Rumney Marsh as by a writing dated the 17th of the 4th month 1650. **Recorded**: the 7th of the 12th month 1650.

JOHN KNIGHT to THOMAS ERINGTON – (1:20) John Knight of Lynn...has sold to Thomas Erington for 3 pounds, 2 parts of a 10-acre lot lying E and W on the town's common as by writing more at large appeareth dated 1: 9 month: 1648.

RICHARD ROOTEN to THOMAS ERINGTON – (1:20) Richard Rooten of Lynn has sold to Thomas Erington of the same town, for 14 pounds, 3 score acres of ground in Reading as by a writing dated the 1st day of the 8th month 1649.

PHILIP CROMWELL to THOMAS COLE – (1:20) Philip Cromwell of Salem (butcher) sells unto Thomas Cole, the 10-acre lot late belonging to Allen Keniston, lying in the north neck next to John Gedny's on the one side and Mr. Williams' lot on the other side, for 8 pounds and a calf of 3 weeks old, 3 pounds 9 shillings in cotton cloth; the remainder of the 8th in a milk cow or fat beast as by a writing dated 13: Feb 1650 appeareth. **Recorded**: the 14th of the 12th month 1650.

SAMUEL ARCHARD to EDMOND MARSHALL – (1:21) Samuel Archard sold to Edmond Marshall of Manchester, 60 acres of land with 2½ acres of marsh in Manchester as by a writing dated the 18th of the 12th month 1650 appeareth. **Recorded**: the 18th of the 12th month 1650.

JOHN HIGGINSON to JOHN PICKERING – (1:21) On the 1st of the 3rd month 1651, a caveat for John Pickering who bought from John Higginson, 150 acres of upland and meadow...lying near Mr. Gardener's farm for which he paid 13 pounds, as by his deed dated the 23rd of March 1651.

GERVASE GARFORD to HENRY BARTHOLOMEW – (1:21) Gervase Garford of Salem sold to Henry Bartholomew all the marsh, upland and meadow that was in his possession on Salem neck near Jeffry Massey's marsh, being in all about 7 acres as by a writing dated the 3rd of the 11th month 1650 appeareth. **Recorded**: the 26th of the 3rd month 1651.

FRANCIS PERRY to RICHARD WAY – (1:22) Francis Perry of Salem (wheelwright) sold to Richard Way, his farm which he bought of Dorcas Verin with 10 acres of land bought of Hilliard Veren, one acre of land bought of Edmond Batter and about 1½ acres exchanged with the town for 40 pounds, as by a writing dated the 12th of May 1651 appeareth. **Recorded**: the 28th of the 3rd month 1651.

SAMUEL ARCHARD to HENRY BARTHOLOMEW – (1:22) Samuel Archard of Salem (marshall) sold to Henry Bartholomew of Salem, ½ acre of the land which was land of Thomas Oliver, lying between land of the honored Gov. on one side and land of said Henry on the other side, for 3 pounds, as by a writing dated 26: 4 month: 1651 appeareth. **Recorded**: the 30th of June 1651.

JOSEPH and JANE ARMITAGE to SIMON BRADSTREET (mortgage) – (1:22) Joseph Armitage and Jane Armitage of Lynn sold to Simon Bradstreet of Andover, their dwelling house in Lynn called the Anchor with the home lot containing 6 acres and 6 acres of marsh in Rumney Marsh, and 5 acres of planting ground at the fresh marsh, with the dwelling house wherein the widow Blaisdell dwelleth, with the appurtenances…provided if the said Joseph shall pay Simon 30 pounds the 1st of May and 30 pounds the 1st of June, or if…Joseph shall pay…Simon 80 pounds in 4 years next, either half year 10 pounds until the 80 pounds be paid then this sale to be void as by a deed more fully doth appear. **Recorded**: the 5th day of the 5h month 1651.

ROBERT ISBELL to RICHARD NORMAN – (1:23) Robert Isbell of Manchester (carpenter) for 15 pounds, has sold to Richard Norman the elder of Marblehead (carpenter) his dwelling house and 49 acres of land with his portion of meadow thereunto pertaining, as by a writing dated the 29th of the 5th last appeareth. **Recorded**: the 4th of August 1651.

THOMAS ERINGTON to JOHN TURNER, Jr. – (1:23) Thomas Erington of Lynn mortgaged unto John Turner, Jr. of Hammersmith, his dwelling house and lot being 2/3 of a 10-acre lot near the Ironworks and 5 acres of marsh in Rumney Marsh for 16 pounds as by a writing dated the 16th 10th month 1650. **Recorded**: the 8th of the 6th month 1651.

NATHANIEL BISHOP to WILLIAM HOAR – (1:24) Nathaniel Bishop of Salem sold to William Hoar (fisherman) one house and 5 acres of land lying between Thomas Root's and Joseph Root's lands at Cape Ann side for 8 pounds, as by a writing dated this 10th of the 6th month 1651 appeareth. **Recorded**: the 11th of the 6th month 1651.

JEFFREY ESTY to HENRY BULLOCK – (1:24) Jeffrey Esty sold the herbage or after-feeding of the 5 acre lot to Henry Bullock the planting whereof was formerly granted to Nathaniel Bishop as by a writing dated the day and year above written. **Recorded**: the 23rd of the 6th month 1651.

HENRY COOMBS to THOMAS WEEKS – (1:24) Henry Coombs of Marblehead (fisherman) for 30 pounds mortgaged his dwelling house with one acre of land thereto adjoining in Marblehead with his 3rd part of his shallop (whereof John Clement and Peter Petford hath the other 2/3) as by this writing dated the year & day above, which appeareth unto Thomas Weeks. **Recorded**: the 15th of 7ber 1651.

JAMES UNDERWOOD to JOHN GETCHELL – (1:24) James Underwood of Salem (baker) for 3 pounds 15 shillings, sold to John Getchell of Marblehead (planter) one 10-acre lot on Darby fort side lying between Mr. Peter's farm and Forest River, as by a deed dated the 18th of this month appeareth. **Recorded**: the 29th of 7ber 1651.

JAMES UNDERWOOD (Attorney for Abraham Williams) to JOHN GETCHELL – (1:25) James Underwood (attorney for Abraham Williams) for 50 shillings, has sold to John Getchell of Marblehead (planter) one 10-acre lot (same as previous deed to month) of 7th appeareth. A caveat recorded 29th of 7ber 1651 by James Underwood for half an acre of salt marsh lying on Forest river to the which John Jackson pretends a title.

JEREMY VALE to RICHARD ADAMS – (1:25) A caveat recorded for Richard Adams who bought 4 score acres and a half of upland with a little swamp adjoining of Jeremy Vale who removed out of this plantation and jurisdiction the sale bears the date the 6th of this instant month of October. **Recorded**: 7th Oct 1651.

JEFFREY ESTY to WILLIAM DIXIE – (1:25) A caveat recorded for William Dixie who purchased of Jeffrey Esty, 30 acres of upland for 30 shillings in Mackerel Cove, as by a writing dated the 6th of October 1651 appeareth, "the said Esty being out of this jurisdiction and cannot yet be called to acknowledge the same."

JOHN STUDLEY to WALTER PRICE (mortgage) – (1:26) John Studley mortgaged to Walter Price, his house and 1 acre of land in Salem between the houses of Robert Strand & Thomas Tuck for 7 pounds, 14 shillings 1 pence, by the last day of July next as by a writing dated the 12th day of July 1651 appeareth. **Recorded**: the 3rd of the 9th month.

EDWARD NORRICE to EDWARD WOOLEN – (1:26) Edward Norrice (teacher of the Church at Salem) has sold his late dwelling house with land pertaining unto Edward Woolen for 25 pounds, whereof 10 pounds in hand paid, with a proviso for re-entry in case the 15 pounds resting be not paid by or before the 10th of 7ber next as by the deed of sale appeareth bearing date the 8th of 9ber 1651.

JOSEPH ARMITAGE to JOHN HATHORNE – (1:26) Joseph Armitage sold to John Hathorne for 105 pounds his dwelling house with 2 acres of land adjoining in Lynn, as by a writing dated the 31st of the 10th month 1651 appeareth. **Recorded**: the 15th of the 11th month 1651.

WILLIAM LORD to The Church at Salem – (1:27) William Lord of Salem (cutler) gave to Edward Norrice, Emanuel Downing, Capt. Hathorne, Henry Bartholomew, Robert Turner, Joseph Grafton & John Browne…his dwelling house with the barn and back houses belonging for and to the use of the church of Salem after the death of his wife or second marriage which shall first happen as per deed dated the 12th of the 11th month 1651 appeareth.

William Lord of Salem (cutler) has given…to Emanuel Downing, etc. (see above) all his lands in Salem bounds except his dwelling houses to be sold for the payment of his debts, legacies and funeral charges as per deed dated the 13th of the 11th month 1651 appeareth. **Recorded**: on the 16th of the 11th month 1651.

WILLIAM HORE to WALTER PRICE – (1:27) William Hore sold to Walter Price the house and 5 acres of land, which he bought of Nathaniel Bishop, with condition of redemption upon the repayment of 8 pounds to the said Walter as by deed dated the 13th day of the 12th month 1651. **Recorded**: the 14th of the 12th month 1651.

WILLIAM HORE to WALTER PRICE – (1:28) William Hore sold to Walter Price all the fish he shall take during this voyage for 15 pounds in hand paid as by a writing dated the 18th day of the 11th month 1651. **Recorded**: the 14th of the 12th month 1651.

ROBERT GUTCH to WILLIAM NORTON (mortgage) – (1:28) A caveat for William Norton who has the mortgage of Robert Gutch's house for 40 pounds payable in June and 7ber next as by a deed dated the 14th date of February 1651 appeareth.

ESDRAS READE (Executor of Christopher Young) to JOHN SULARD – (1:28) Esdras Reade (Executor of Christopher Young) has sold to John Sulard one house and 15 acres of land in Wenham which was Christopher Young's for 8 pounds as by a deed dated the 23rd of the 1st month 1651 appears. **Recorded**: the 23rd of the 1st month 1652.

WILLIAM RAYNER to SAMUEL FOSTER – (1:28) William Rayner sold to Samuel Foster of Wenham, half the upland that the said William bought of George Byam with 2 acres of meadow as by a writing dated the

30th of September 1651 appeareth. **Recorded**: the 23rd of the 1st month 1652.

ALICE JOHNS to SAMUEL FOSTER – (1:28) Alice Johns sold to Samuel Foster her house with 10 acres of land lying on the neck of Wenham for 7 pounds, as by a writing dated the 20th of April appeareth. **Recorded**: the 23rd of the 1st month 1652.

RICHARD PETINGILL to SAMUEL FOSTER – (1:29) Richard Petingill of Wenham sold to Samuel Foster all his houses and land in Wenham and also 19 acres of upland lying in Ipswich bounds, joining to Wenham, and also 1½ acres of a meadow lying in the great meadow as by a writing dated the 1st day of the 2nd month 1650 appeareth. **Recorded**: the 23rd of the 1st month 1652.

ALEXANDER FIELD to WILLIAM VENUS – (1:29) Alexander Field (cordwainer) of Salem sold to William Venus, one dwelling house with the shop and half an acre of land on which the house standeth, adjoining the shop of Thomas Rix in Salem, for 45 pounds…as per deed dated the 3rd of the 12th month 1651 appeareth. **Recorded**: the 24th of the 1st month 1652.

SAMUEL ARCHARD (Atty. to Capt RICHARD MARINER) to GEORGE WILLIAMS – (1:29) Samuel Archard of Salem (Attorney to Richard Mariner) sold to George Williams of Salem (cooper) one house and 1¾ acres of land in Salem for 5 pounds…as per deed dated the 29th of the 1st month 1652 appeareth.

ROBERT GOODHALL to DAVID CORWITHEN – (1:30) Robert Goodhall of Salem (planter) sold to David Corwithen, 3 acres of salt marsh on the Royall side for 6 pounds…as per deed dated the 31st of the 1st month 1652 appeareth. **Recorded**: the 31st of the 1st month 1652.

ALEXANDER FIELD to WILLIAM CHICHESTER – (1:30) Alexander Field of Salem sold to William Chichester of Salem, his house and ground about it and 5 acres out of his lot in the south field, and…Alexander is to make good a way from the said house to the street…writing dated the 16th of the 1st month 1650, the price paid…was 10 pounds in commodities and 6 pounds in mackerel. **Recorded**: the 12th of the 2nd month 1652.

JOHN PAINE to ROBERT PEASE – (1:30) John Paine sold to Robert Pease one house and one acre of land it stands on between Goodman

Rootes and Goodman Weeks lands in Salem and one 10-acre lot on Cape Ann side for 9 pounds. **Recorded:** the 16th of the 2nd month 1652.

JOHN PAINE to THOMAS WEEKS – (1:31) John Paine sold to Thomas Weeks for 4 pounds, 2 acres of land in Salem between Isaac Este's and Robert Pease's lands...as per deed dated 16th of the 2nd month 1652 appeareth.

PECKANANNQUIT (alias NED INDIAN) to HENRY BARTHOLOMEW – (1:31) Peckanannquit (alias Ned Indian) late servant to Zacheus Gould has for 30 pounds mortgaged unto Henry Bartholomew of Salem all his land, being about 8 miles square on the further side of Merrimack River, lying about 8 or 10 miles from Andover...as per writing dated the 17th of the 2nd month 1652 appeareth. **Recorded:** the 17th of the 2nd month 1652.

BENJAMIN SMITH to THOMAS JAMES – (1:31) Benjamin Smith of Boston (yeoman) sold to Thomas James (planter) of Salem, his farm in Salem joining Mr. Johnson's farm, as by a deed dated the 24th day of February 1651 appeareth. **Recorded:** 7th January 1652.

WILLIAM PAYNE to THOMAS RIX – (1:31) William Payne (merchant) of Salem sold his shop to Thomas Rix for 10 pounds, as per deed dated the 7th of June 1652 appeareth. **Recorded:** 8 June 1652.

JAMES FRIEND to EDWARD PRESCOTT – (1:32) James Friend of Salem (carpenter) for 10 pounds 10 shillings, sold half an acre of land in Salem adjoining the burying place, with sufficient highway for cart and horse to the street...deed dated the 15th of July 1652...unto Edward Prescott of London, Merchant, appeareth. **Recorded:** 16 July 1652.

WILLIAM LORD to JOHN FISKE – (1:32) William Lord of Salem (cutler) sold to John Fiske (pastor of the Church of Wenham) his farm of 3 score & 10 acres of upland and 7 acres of meadow near the great pond towards Ipswich, for 16 pounds...as by writing dated the 26th day of the 6th month 1651 appeareth.

HENRY COOK to WILLIAM FLYNT – (1:32) Henry Cook of Salem (butcher) sold to William Flynt 5 acres of land in the south field lying between John Reeves & Elias Mason's lot, for 3 pounds. **Recorded:** the 23rd of July 1652.

THOMAS JAMES to WILLIAM FLYNT – (1:32) Thomas James of Salem (husbandman) sold to William Flynt for 18 pounds, one house and one acre of land adjoining, and one other acre of land adjoining to Goodman Adams' land, near the brick kill, and 2½ acres of land in the south field, between Goodman Lord's and Goodman Adams' lots.

ALICE JOHNS to SAMUEL FOSTER – (1:33) Alice Johns of Wenham (widow) sold to Samuel Foster of Wenham, her house with 10 acres of land lying in the neck in Wenham for 7 pounds...indenture dated the 20th of April 1651 appeareth. **Recorded**: the 10th of the 7th month 1652.

RICHARD PETINGILL to SAMUEL FOSTER – (1:33) Richard Petingill of Wenham sold to Samuel Foster 1 dwelling house, one cow house, 5 acres of upland joining to the house and 19 acres of upland lying in Ipswich bounds adjoining Wenham line and 1½ acre of meadow lying in the great meadow as per a writing dated the 1st of the 2nd month 1650 appeareth. **Recorded**: the 10th of the 7th month 1652.

ALEXANDER FIELD to WILLIAM FLINT – (1:33) Alexander Field of Salem (shoemaker) for 8 pounds sold unto William Flint, 7½ acres of land and ½ an acre of salt marsh in the south field, as in writing dated the 14th of the 2nd month 1652 appeareth. **Recorded**: the 11th of the 7th month 1652.

WILLIAM BROWNE to THOMAS BUXTON – (1:33) William Browne of Boston (glover) sold to Thomas Buxton of Salem (husbandman) for a valuable consideration in hand paid, his home lot in the north neck, being 10 acres...and his late dwelling house standing on the said lot...as per deed dated the 7th of 7ber 1652 appeareth. **Recorded**: the 15th of the 7th month 1652.

THOMAS RUCK to JOHN RUCK – (1:34) Thomas Ruck of Boston (draper) for 40 pounds sold to John Ruck, his house and 9 acres of land and all the outhouses and wharfe pertaining & adjoining to Mr. Emery's land on the N, to the sea on the E, and the common on the W, as per writing dated the 9th of the 11th month 1651 appeareth. **Recorded**: the 6th of the 8th month 1652.

DORCAS VERRIN to MICHAEL SHAFFLYN – (1:34) Dorcas Verrin of Salem (widow) for 5 pounds 15 shillings sold to Michael Shafflyn of Salem (tailor) 25 acres of land on the E side of Mr. Downing's farm...as by writing dated 28 12th month 1649 appeareth. **Recorded**: the 19th of the 9th month 1652.

ROBERT PEASE to HENRY PERCY – (1:34) Robert Pease sold to Henry Percy, 10 acres of land on Cape Ann side lying between Mordecae

Crevett's and Robert Lemon's lands for 5 pounds 10 shillings, as per deed dated the last day of November last appeareth. **Recorded**: the 8th day of December 1652.

WILLIAM TOWN to HARRY BULLOCK – (1:35) William Towne of Salem (gardener) sold to Harry Bullock of Salem, 9½ acres of land between Goodman Waters land and the great cove, for 6 pounds...as in a deed dated the 19th of Nov 1652 appeareth.

ELIAS STILEMAN to JAMES SMITH – (1:35) Elias Stileman, Sr. of Salem, for 52 pounds in hand paid, sold to James Smith of Marblehead, his upland and marsh called Castle Hill lying on the South River and the land of Elias Stileman, Jr...as by a deed dated the 13th of December appeareth. Recorded the 13th of December 1652.

CHARLES GOTT (Atty. to Mr. HUGH PETERS) to JOHN HORNE – (1:35) Charles Gott of Salem (attorney to Mr. Hugh Peters) sold to John Horne of Salem for 40 shillings ¼ acre near the meeting house in Salem on the N side running along by the highway, being the land of Mr. Hugh Peters, provided if Mr. Peters shall return to New England in person and repay the said John all his charges of building or other ways, best owed upon, and that said Mr. Peters shall have the land again...as per writing dated the 28th of Dec 1652 appeareth. **Recorded**: 29 December 1652.

ROBERT GOOTCH to WILLIAM NORTON – (1:36) Robert Gootch of Salem mortgaged his dwelling house to William Norton for 40 pounds, to be paid said William at or by the 10th of June next as by...deed dated the 22nd day of Dec 1652 appeareth; this entry is by way of caveat. **Recorded**: the 24th of December 1652.

JOHN GEDNEY to RICHARD BISHOP – (1:36) On the 15th of January 1652, John Gedney of Salem sold to Richard Bishop of Salem, 15 acres of land...late the land of George Ingersoll, in the North field near Thomas Spooner & Thomas Gardner's lands...as by deed dated the 15th of January 1652 appeareth.

EDMOND BATTER to RICHARD WEIGH – (1:36) Edmond Batter of Salem sold to Richard Weigh for 20 pounds, 14 acres of upland lying near Thomas Goldthwait's land on the N the 10 acre lots on the E and a little below Wigwam rock, and a strip of land running down to the river containing about 2 rods, and 5 acres of meadow...as per deed dated the 19th of the 11th month 1652 appeareth. **Recorded**: the 20th of January 1652.

JOHN ROWDEN to EDMOND BATTER (mortgage) – (1:37) John Rowden of Salem mortgaged to Edmond Batter of Salem, for 45 shillings, 9 pence, his dwelling house and 5 acres of land adjoining, for the repayment, 45 pounds 9 pence were to be paid by the 24th day of the 5th month next...as per writing dated the 27th of the 11th month 1652. **Recorded**: the 27th of the 11th month 1652.

ELLINOR FELTON to WILLIAM MASTON – (1:37) Ellinor Felton of Salem sold to William Maston of Salem for 7 pounds sterling, a dwelling house and 20 rods of land near the North River in Salem...as per a writing dated the 28th of the 11th month 1652. **Recorded**: the 28th of the 11th month 1652.

JAMES STANDISH to WILLIAM DIXIE – (1:37) James Standish of Salem sold to William Dixie, his dwelling house with all his land and swamp adjoining, for 35 pounds as per a deed dated the 22nd day of December 1652. **Recorded**: the 3rd of the 12th month 1652.

THOMAS WEEKS to JOHN WILSON – (1:38) Thomas Weeks of Salem (turner) sold to John Wilson of Salem, for 16 pounds, a dwelling house with 2 acres of land adjoining in Salem, lying between William Lord's and Thomas Root's lands as by deed dated the 3rd of the 12th month 1652. **Recorded**: the 3rd of the 12th month 1652.

THOMAS RIX to DAVID TOMMAS, JOHN STONE & ROBERT STONE – (1:38) Thomas Rix of Salem (barber) sold to David Tommas, John Stone & Robert Stone, that part of a dwelling house wherein formerly dwelt William Cockerell, with ¾ of an acre of land adjoining and one 10-acre lot by Darby fort side, for 9 pounds...as by deed dated the 11th of November 1651. **Recorded**: the 3rd day of the 12th month 1652.

DAVID TOMMAS, JOHN & ROBERT STONE to ROBERT SALLOES – (1:38) David Tommas, John & Robert Stone sold to Robert Salloes for 9 pounds 10 shillings part of the dwelling house where William Cockerell lately dwelt, and ¾ acre of land adjoining...as per deed dated the 4th day of the 12th month 1652 appeareth. **Recorded**: the 4th of the 12th month 1652.

GUYDE BAYLEY to HUMPHREY WOODBURY – (1:38) A caveat for Humphrey Woodbury of Salem (fisherman) who purchased from Guyde Bayley of Salem (gardener) his dwelling house and 20 acres of land, as by a writing dated the 11th of October 1652 appeareth for 16 pounds in hand paid. **Recorded**: the 8th of the 12th month 1652.

JOSEPH HARRIS to OSMOND TRASK – (1:39) Joseph Harris of Salem (planter) sold to Osmond Trask of Salem, 40 acres of land on Royall Side, lying between Jacob Barnes' and Edward Bishop's lands, in Salem...for 3 pounds in hand paid...as by a deed dated 12th month 1652 appeareth. **Recorded**: the 9th of the 12th month 1652.

THOMAS VERRY to WILLIAM BROWN – (1:39) A caveat for William Browne, who, for 17 pounds 8 shillings due to him from Thomas Verry of Gloucester hath a mortgage for his house & land in Gloucester & Chebacco, and also his lot in Annisquam for the repayment of the said 7 pounds 8 shillings by the 15th day of June next...as in a deed dated the 2nd of November last. **Recorded**: the 3rd of the 1st month 1652.

JOHN HATHORNE to THOMAS PUTNAM – (1:39) John Hathorne of Malden in the county of Middlesex, sold to Thomas Putnam of Salem, for 45 pounds, his house and land in Salem, containing 214 acres of upland and meadow...as in a deed dated the 16th day of the 4th month 1651 appeareth. **Recorded**: the 3rd day of the 1st month 1652.

RICHARD HUTCHINSON to NATHANIEL PUTNAM – (1:40) Richard Hutchinson of Salem (yeoman) for 7 pounds 10 shillings sold to Nathaniel Putnam half the farm which was Mr. Stileman's consisting of 75 acres of upland and 4 acres of meadow in Salem, as in deed dated the 4th of December 1651. **Recorded**: the 3rd of the 1st month 1652.

WALTER PRICE & THOMAS COLE to THOMAS PUTNAM and NATHANIEL PUTNAM – (1:40) Walter Price & Thomas Cole of Salem sold to Thomas Putnam & Nathaniel Putnam, 140 acres of upland and 14 acres of meadow. This entry is by way of caveat, their writing being not yet acknowledged before a magistrate. Their writing bears date of the 3rd day of the 1st month 1652. **Recorded**: the 4th of the 1st month 1652.

GILES CORY to NATHANIEL PUTNAM (caveat) – (1:40) On the 4th day of the 1st month 1652, a caveat was recorded for Nathaniel Putnam who bought of Giles Cory, 20 acres of upland near Ipswich River as in a writing dated the 3rd of March 1652.

JOHN SWASY to DOROTHY KING – (1:41) John Swasy of Salem sold to Dorothy King of Salem (widow) his dwelling house with the land belonging...on the South River in Salem and 5 or 6 acres of land in the south field, lying between Richard Hide and Daniel Rumball's lands...as by a writing dated the 15th of the 1st month 1652 appeareth. **Recorded**: the 14th of the 1st month 1652.

ROBERT GOWING to RALPH ELLINGWOOD – (1:41) Robert Gowing sold to Ralph Ellingwood, his house in Wenham...with 8 acres of land joining to it and 10 acres of land in the neck and 2 acres of meadow in the great meadow near the island, and all the common which lies in Wenham which belongs to the same house...for 9 pounds...as in a deed dated the 24th of the iith month 1652. **Recorded**: the 30th of the 1st month 1653.

PETER PALFREY to FRANCIS SKERRY – (1:41) Peter Palfrey of Reading in Suffolk County, sold to Francis Skerry of Salem (husbandman), for 6 pounds, 2 acres of marsh lying near the ferry and abutting on the garden of John Luff in Salem...as by a deed dated the day and year last above written. **Recorded**: the 31st of the 1st month 1653.

ROBERT GOODELL to FRANCIS SKERRY – (1:42) Robert Goodell of Salem (planter) sold to Francis Skerry for 14 pounds 10 shillings, 4 acres of land in Salem neck, lying between Mr. Gedney's & Jeffry Massy's lands, as in a deed dated the 4th day of the 2nd month 1653 appeareth. **Recorded**: the 4th of the 2nd month 1653.

THOMAS HAWKINS, GEORGE INGERSOLL, JAMES OLIVER, EDWARD GUILLAM & ROBERT GUTCH (for WILLIAM NORTON) to NICHOLAS DAVISON (Atty. for Capt. JOHN ANDREWS) – (1:42) Nicholas Davison of Charlston (merchant and attorney unto Capt. John Andrews of London, merchant), as appears by a letter of attorney bearing date of the 3rd of May 1652, to receive from William Norton of Ipswich in New England, the sum of 160 pounds sterling, and having spoken with the said William Norton and informed myself of his estate, have thought it best for the advantage of the said Capt. John Andrews, to take such security as he by himself and friends presented to me for a full discharge of the said debt as follows: By Thomas Hawkins (baker) to pay in mackerel in September next 20 pounds & in flour and bisquit 70 pounds. By George Ingersoll, in fish and mackerel, 19 pounds. By James Oliver in 7ber in beef 13 pounds. By Edward Guillam, in boards 12 pounds, and by Robert Gutch of Salem in fish 26 pounds—all which sums amount to 160 pounds. In which consideration and also considering his low estate, do acquit...William Norton of the said sum of 160 pounds...as witness my hand 7 June 1653. **Signed**: Nicholas Davison; **Witnesses**: John Dudley and Thomas Hawkins; **Recorded**: 10 5th month 1653.

RICHARD PRINCE to ARTHUR KIPPING – (1:43) Richard Prince of Salem (tailor) sold to Arthur Kipping (fisherman) his late dwelling house with ½ acre of land, lying between Adam Westgate and Thomas Jegles' lands, for 27 pounds...as in a deed dated 23 June 1653 appeareth. **Recorded**: the 23rd of the 4th month 1653.

WILLIAM ALLEN to JOHN BRIDGEMAN – (1:43) William Allen of Manchester (carpenter) sold to John Bridgeman of Salem his late dwelling house with ½ acre of land adjoining in Salem, and 6 acres of land in the south field, for 14 pounds...as in a deed dated the 9th of the 4th month 1652 appeareth. **Recorded**: the 24th of the 4th month 1653.

WILLIAM VENUS to JOHN MILLAR – (1:44) William Venus of Salem sold to John Millar, for 45 pounds, his late dwelling house with half an acre of land adjoining, with the shop and cellar thereto, near the windmill field in Salem...as in a deed dated the 16th of the 12th month 1652 appeareth. **Recorded**: the 27th of the 4th month 1653.

RALPH ELWOOD to FRANCIS SKERRY – (1:44) Ralph Elwood of Salem (planter) sold to Francis Skerry of Salem (maulster) for 20 shillings one acre of land in Salem near Ipswich ferry...as in a deed dated the 22nd of June 1653 appeareth. **Recorded**: the 27th of the 4th month 1653.

DANIEL KING to TIMOTHY COOP – (1:44) Daniel King of Lynn sold for 12 pounds to Timothy Coop one house with 2 acres of land adjoining and 3 acres of land...in Lynn, as in a deed dated the 12th day of the 12th month appeareth. **Recorded**: the 27th of the 4th month 1653.

WILLIAM DODGE & HENRY BARTHOLOMEW (Agts for GEORGE TAYLOR) to RICHARD JOHNSON – (1:44) William Dodge & Henry Bartholomew (agents for Mr. George Taylor) late of Lynn, sold to Richard Johnson, a house and barn with land adjoining & 4 acres of salt marsh on the E of the town marsh...as in a deed dated 18: 1st month: 1652. **Recorded**: the 29th of the 4th month 1653.

JOSEPH GARDNER to JOHN PUTNAM – (1:45) Joseph Gardner of Salem sold to John Putnam for 15 pounds, 18 acres of meadow near Ipswich river...as in a deed dated the day & year above. **Recorded**: the 1st of the 5th month 1653.

EDMOND FARRINGTON to JOSEPH POPE and SAMUEL EBORNE – (1:45) Edmond Farrington granted to Joseph Pope and Samuel Eborne, 200 acres of upland and meadow in Lynn and 10 acres of meadow in the great meadow about half a mile from the 200 acres...as by a deed dated the day and year above. **Recorded**: the 4th of the 5th month 1653.

JOB HILLIARD to ISAAK ESTY – (1:45) Job Hilliard of Salem (fisherman) granted to Isaak Esty of Salem (cooper) a house and land adjoining, being near ½ acre, for 20 pounds, to be paid as follows: viz: 6 pounds the 15th of 8ber next in cod fish or caske, 8 pounds the 15th of 8ber in 1654 in fish or mackerel, 6 pounds the 15th of 8ber 1655 in fish or mackerel, or Job to have the house and land again as in deed dated the 19th of the 5th month 1653 appeareth. **Recorded:** the 22nd of the 5th month 1653.

ROGER SPENCER to JOHN & NATHANIEL NEWGATE (mortgage) (1:46) Roger Spencer of Charlestown (merchant), for 215 pounds, mortgaged to John & Nathaniel Newgate, one house in Charlestown, and ground thereto belonging, late in the occupation of Mr. Cooke, and the moiety (half) of a plantation in Kennebeck, the money to be repaid in Beaver or oyle [?] for it on the last day of 9ber next as by deed dated the day...above. **Recorded:** Xmo: 6: 1653.

ABRAHAM BELL to JEFFRY MASSEY – (1:46) Abraham Bell of Charlestown in the county of Middlesex (waterman) for 45 shillings (paid) unto Jeffry Massey of Salem (planter) one 2 acre lot in Salem, late in the possession of John Bulfinch, adjoining lands of Francis Skerry and George Ropes, as in deed dated the 24th of August appeareth. **Recorded:** the 24th of the 6th month 1653.

JOHN JACKSON to JEFFRY MASSEY – (1:46) John Jackson of Salem (mariner) for 9 pounds, 10 shillings, granted to Jeffry Massey of Salem (planter) a parcel of upland and meadow near Winter Harbor in Salem...as by a writing dated the 20th of the 9th month 1651 appeareth. **Recorded:** the 24th of the 6th month 1653.

JOHN HOLGRAVE to JEFFRY MASSEY and NICHOLAS WOODBERY – (1:46) John Holgrave of Salem...for 11 pounds, 15 shillings paid unto Jeffry Massey of Salem (planter) & Nicholas Woodbery of Salem (mariner), one farm containing 150 acres of upland adjoining on the E to the long hill called Mr. Alford's hill, unto the bound tree of Edward Bishop and from that tree S along the country way to Leeche's Hill and upon the W by the side of Jacob Barnes and Pascha Foot's land & N by the common & 15 acres of meadow in the great meadow in Wenham as in a deed dated the 14th of April 1652 appeareth. **Recorded:** the 24th of the 6th month 1653.

GERVASE GARFORD to ELIZABETH HARDEE – (1:47) Gervase Garford of Salem (gentleman) granted to Elizabeth Hardee of Salem (widow) for 80 pounds sterling, his dwelling house & 10 acres of arable land & 6¼ acres of meadow near Draper's Point on Bass River adjoining the house, and 80 acres of land between Lord's Hill & Birt's plain on Bass River side, within the precinct of Salem, as by a deed dated the 26th of 7ber 1653 appeareth. **Recorded**: the 25th of the 8th month 1653.

DOROTHY KING to THOMAS JOHNSON & THOMAS REYNOLDS – (1:47) Dorothy King of Salem (widow) granted to Thomas Johnson & Thomas Reynolds, for 28 pounds, a dwelling house with land adjoining lying between Timothy Lafkin's & Robert Gray's lots, which was late the dwelling house of John Swaysy, as in a deed dated the 21st of October 1653 more at large appeareth. **Recorded**: the 29th of the 8th month 1653.

PHILLIP & DOROTHY CROMWELL to JOHN PORTER – (1:48) Phillip Cromwell of Salem (butcher) and Dorothy (his wife) granted to John Porter, 200 acres of upland and 20 acres of meadow lying between the land of Daniel Ray & Richard Davenport, in Salem…for 40 pounds, as in a deed dated the 22 of the 8th month appeareth. **Recorded**: the 29th of the 8th month 1653.

NATHANIEL & JANE TYLER to PHILLIP KIRTLAND – (1:48) Nathaniel Tyler of Lynn (husbandman) and Jane his wife, granted to Phillip Kirtland of Lynn (shoemaker) all their lands and houses with appurtenances in Lynn…as by deed dated the 1st of Oct 1652 appeareth. **Recorded**: the 29th of October 1653.

JOHN BOURNE to HENRY COOK – (1:48) John Bourne of Salem granted to Henry Cook of Salem (butcher), his dwelling house with 21 acres of land, lying between Joseph Pope's and John Burton's lands in Salem, as in a deed dated the 29th of the 8th month 1653 appeareth. **Recorded**: the 29th of 8ber 1653.

JOHN BLACKLEICH to ROBERT GOODHALL – (1:49) John Blackleich of Boston (merchant) granted to Robert Goodhall of Salem, 50 acres of land between Mr. Higginson's and Mr. Alderman's lands in Salem, for 3 pounds, as in a deed dated the day above appeareth. **Recorded**: the 31st of October 1653.

DOROTHY KING to THOMAS BARNES – (1:49) Dorothy King of Salem (widow) granted to Thomas Barnes of Salem (blacksmith) for 7 pounds 10 shillings, 6 acres of planting land in the south field in Salem, between Daniel Romball & Richard Hide's lands, as in a deed dated the 8th day of October 1653 appeareth. **Recorded**: the 18th of November 1653.

WILLIAM MARSTON to EDMOND MARSHALL – (1:49) William Marston granted to Edmond Marshall of Salem (weaver) 5 acres of land between said Edmond Marshall's & John Bachellor's lands near Bass River in Salem, for 4 pounds, as in a deed dated the same as above appeareth. **Recorded**: the 28th of November 1653.

SAMUEL BENNETT to THOMAS WHEELER – (1:49) Samuel Bennett of Lynn (carpenter) granted to Thomas Wheeler of Lynn (miller) for 220 pounds sterling, one watermill in Lynn, with lands thereto belonging and 2 dwelling houses with 2 lots of land pertaining, containing in both about 11 acres, also 5 acres of marsh in Rumney Marsh, and the windmill standing in Salem, as in a deed dated the 1st of April 1653 appeareth. **Recorded**: the 29th of 9ber 1653.

PETER PALFREY to JOHN PORTER – (1:50) Peter Palfrey, late of Salem (planter) sold to John Porter of Salem (yeoman) half an acre of land lying between John Hornes and Captain Hathorn's grounds over and against Mr. Downing's house in Salem for 4 pounds, as by deed dated 10th of December 1653 appeareth. **Recorded**: the 11th day of 10ber 1653.

JONATHAN PORTER to OSMOND TRASK – (1:50) Jonathan Porter of Salem (planter) sold to Osmond Trask of Salem, the 2 late dwelling houses of himself and Edward Hornett, and 20 acres of land adjoining said houses, and also the 3rd part of 84 acres bought of Mr. Browne, and also 1 acre of salt marsh, 2 acres of fresh marsh, and also 20 acres of upland adjoining Thomas Brackett's land, as by a deed dated the 27th of the 10th month more at large appeareth. **Recorded**: the 27th of the 10th month 1653.

JOHN BARBOUR to ROBERT GOODHALL – (1:51) John Barbour, late of Salem (carpenter) sold to Robert Goodhall of Salem (husbandman) 30 acres of land in Salem for 9 shillings, as by deed dated the 26th of Oct 1653 appeareth. **Recorded**: the 4th of the 11th month 1653.

JOHN KELHAM to CHARLES GOTT – (1:51) John Kelham of Wenham sold to Charles Gott of Salem, his dwelling house in Wenham with 25 acres of upland adjoining, and 12 acres of meadow which was Austin Kelham's in the great meadow, as by deed dated the 14th of Nov 1653. **Recorded**: the 9th of the 11th month 1653.

JOHN GARDNER to JOHN PUTNAM – (1:51) John Gardner of Salem (mariner) sold to John Putnam of Salem (husbandman) for 40 shillings, 2 acres of meadow near Ipswich River, as by a deed dated the 6th of February 1653 appeareth. **Recorded**: the 6th of the 12th month 1653.

RICE EDWARDS to JOHN SALLARD – (1:51) Rice Edwards sold to John Sallard, his house and 10 acres of land lying on the neck in Wenham, for 8 pounds, as by a deed dated the 29th of 10ber 1652 appeareth. **Recorded**: the 16th of the 12th month 1653.

RALPH FOG to JOHN PUTNAM – (1:52) Ralph Fog of Salem sold to John Putnam, his farm of 4 score acres of land & 8 acres of meadow for 12 pounds, as by a deed dated the 14th of the 2nd month 1652. **Recorded**: the 3rd of the 1st month 1653.

THOMAS ANTROP to ROBERT GOODHALL – (1:52) Thomas Antrop of Salem sold for 30 shillings, to Robert Goodhall, 40 acres of land near the said Robert's land in Salem, by deed dated the last day of February 1653. **Recorded**: the 4th of the 1st month 1653.

CHARLES GOTT to JOHN PORTER – (1:52) Charles Gott of Salem, for 15 pounds, sold to John Porter of Salem, 118 acres of upland and meadow, lying between the land of Pasco Foot on the E and said John Porter on the W in Salem, as by deed dated the 4th of the 1st of March appeareth. **Recorded**: the 26^{d} of March 1654.

JOHN CLEMENTS to Capt. HATHORNE (caveat) – (1:52) A caveat for Capt. Hathorne, having a mortgage of John Clement's house with 2 acres of land and one cow about 3 years old, for the security of 46 pounds to be paid unto the Captain in manner and form following; that is to say: 6 pounds 13 shillings 4 pence by the 6th month next and 6 pounds 13 shillings 4 pence per year according to a former agreement, that then this mortgage to be void or else to stand in full force. **Recorded**: the 27th of March 1654.

JOSEPH ARMITAGE to JOHN SOUTHWICK – (1:53) Joseph Armitage of Lynn sold to John Southwick of Salem for 20 pounds, 21 acres of meadow lying in Mr. Willis' meadow in Lynn, as by deed dated the 4th of April 1654 appeareth. **Recorded**: the 4th of the 2nd month 1654.

HUGH LASKIN to ROGER HASKELL – (1:53) Hugh Laskin of Salem (planter) for 40 pounds, sold to Roger Haskell of Salem (husbandman), his dwelling house and four score & 18 acres of upland and 6 acres of meadow on Bass River side in Salem. **Recorded**: the 6th of the 2nd month 1654.

GEORGE BURRILL to JOSEPH JENKS – (1:53) George Burrill of Lynn sold to Joseph Jenks the younger, for 17 pounds, 6 acres of land lately purchased of Josiah Starborough, as by deed dated the 20th of September 1650. **Recorded**: the 10th of the 3rd month 1654.

JOHN GIFFORD to EDWARD RICHARDSON – (1:54) John Gifford assigned the deed and sale of 6 acres of land to Edward Richardson, which George Burrill sold to Joseph Jenks, the deed bears the date of the 20 of September 1650. The assignment endorsed on the deed is dated the 2d of the 2d month 1654.

JOSEPH JENKS to JOHN GIFFORD – (1:54) Joseph Jenks, for 20 pounds, mortgaged to John Gifford, his forge, working house and work, with all the appurtenances thereto belonging in Lynn...the said forge and all belonging to be free upon repayment of the said 20 pounds on the 10th of October 1651, as by deed dated the 9th of April 1651. **Recorded**: the 10th of the 3rd month 1654.

JOHN GIFFORD to EDWARD RICHARDS – (1:54) John Gifford assigned all his right to the forge and all thereto pertaining unto Edward Richards, as by writing dated the 25th day of the 2nd month 1654.

JOSEPH JENKS, Jr. to JOHN GIFFORD – (1:54) Joseph Jenks, Jr., for 20 pounds, mortgaged 6 acres of land (which he purchased of George Burrell) unto John Gifford, the 20 pounds to be repaid on the 10th of October 1651 or the land to be forfeited as by deed dated the 9th of April 1651 appeareth. **Recorded**: the 10th of the 3rd month 1654.

JOSEPH JENKS, Jr. to JOHN GIFFORD – (1:55) Joseph Jenks, Jr. stood bound of 40 pounds to John Gifford to make good to said John 2 bills of sale and all the covenants therein, which bear date of the 9th of April 1651; the bond dated the same. **Recorded**: the 10th of May 1654.

JOHN GIFFORD to EDWARD RICHARDS – (1:55) John Gifford assigned his right of the 6 acres of land unto Edward Richards, as by writing dated the 25th of the 2nd month 1654 appeareth. John Gifford assigned the bond of 40 pounds unto Edward Richards, the 24th of the 2nd month 1654.

JOHN TALBY to WALTER PRICE – (1:55) John Talby of Salem has sold unto Walter Price for 6 pounds, a 10-acre lot in the South field, which was formerly Richard Waters'. This entry is for a caveat until John Talby can be brought to acknowledge the deed.

RICHARD JOHNSON to WILLIAM CLARKE & RICHARD BLOOD – (1:55) On the 17th of May 1654, a caveat entered for William Clarke & Richard Blood who bought of Richard Johnson his whole accommodation in Lynn.

JOHN KELHAM to CHARLES GOTT – (1:56) Whereas John Kelham has sold to Charles Gott (late Deacon of Salem) 25 acres of upland and 12 acres of meadow in Wenham, now this record testifieth that Austin Kelham and Alice, his wife, did freely consent to the sale, and the said Alice did resign her interest of her thirds in the said land as by writing dated the 26th of the 3rd month under the Deputy Governor's hand appeareth. **Recorded**: the 26th of the 3rd month 1654.

CHARLES GOTT to JOHN BROWNE – (1:56) Charles Gott (late Deacon of the Church of Salem), sold to John Browne of Salem (merchant) his dwelling house, barn yard and garden with all appurtenances for 44 pounds, as by deed dated the 10th of March last past appeareth. The wife of Charles Gott released and surrendered her right and title to the 3rds of the above premises, as appeareth by writing under the Deputy Governor's hand. **Recorded**: the 26th of the 3rd month 1654.

PETER PETFORD to WILLIAM NECK (mortgage) – (1:56) Peter Petford of Marblehead mortgaged to William Neck of Marblehead, for 60 pounds, his stage and dwelling house and the house he bought of Mr. Browne, with 8 acres of land pertaining and joining to the two houses and stage, and one 10-acre lot lying on Forest River side near Gott's Point, and also 3 cows and one yearling, as by deed dated 13 June 1654, to be paid by June 1657, for which this mortgage is made. **Recorded**: the 13th of June 1654.

EDWARD RICHARDS to HENRY RHODES – (1:57) Edward Richards of Lynn (joiner) for 22 pounds, sold to Henry Rhodes of Lynn, the same 6 acres of upland and meadow being salt marsh, formerly in possession of Joseph Jenks, Jr. lying in Lynn between John Fuller's land and the salt creek, as by deed dated the 20th of the 4th month 1654. Edward Richards binds himself and heirs & executors unto Henry Rhodes in 40 pounds to secure the possession of the 6-acre lot unto said Henry Rhodes...in the record next above mentioned as by bond dated the 21st of the 4th month 1654. **Recorded**: the 6th of the 5th month 1654.

NICHOLAS DAVISON (Attorney for REBECCA CRADDOCK, alias GLOVER) to WILLIAM WALTON – (1:57) Nicholas Davison, attorney for Mrs. Rebecca Craddock, alias Glover, for 15 pounds, sold to Mr. William Walton of Marblehead, the house where said William now dwells with the ground...as by deed dated the 6th of June 1650 appeareth. **Recorded**: the 19th of the 5th month 1654.

EDWARD NORRICE to ELIANOR TRUSTLER – (1:58) Edward Norrice (minister and teacher to the church of Salem) for 12 pounds, sold to Elianor Trustler (widow) 100 acres of land and 10 acres of meadow in Salem; also 6 acres of meadow lying on the Ipswich River, all in Salem, by a deed dated 7 August 1654 appeareth. **Recorded:** the 11th of the 6th month 1654.

JOHN HOOD to WILLIAM CROFTS – (1:58) John Hood of Lynn (yeoman), for 30 pounds, sold to William Crofts of Lynn (yeoman) 3 dwelling houses or tenements with all belonging in Halsted in the county of Essex in old England, with a covenant for further assurance, and the said William is to pay 40 shillings apiece to the sisters of said John according to his father's will, the which appeareth in the bargain and sale by deed dated the 10th of December 1652. **Recorded:** on the 14th of the 6th month 1654.

JOHN & ROBERT BLOOD to WILLIAM CROFTS – (1:59) John Blood and Robert Blood of Concord in New England, for 53 pounds, sold to William Crofts, the moitye (half) of one tenement and half an oxe gang in Ruddington (county Nottingham), and ¼ part of a little cottage and ground…in possession of Edward Symple, as by deed dated the 1st of May 1649 more at large appeareth.

GABRIEL and JOHN WELDON to WILLIAM CROFTS – (1:59) A caveat for a sale of the close or inclosed land lying by the mill in Arnold in the county of Nottingham, and one parcel of land in tannell (?) field, one other parcel of land lying in Redhill field, and one other parcel lying in Swynehouse field, all which parcels…were sold to William Crofts of Lynn in New England (yeoman) by Gabriel Wheldon and John Wheldon his youngest son for 20 pounds in hand paid by said William unto said Gabriel and John with a covenant to make further assurance according to law, as by deed dated the 21st of October 1653 more at large appeareth. **Recorded:** the 14th of the 6th month 1654.

THOMAS REYNOLDS to THOMAS JOHNSON – (1:59) A caveat for a grant and deed of gift of Thomas Reynolds to Thomas Johnson of his part of the house lately purchased of Dorothy King as by writing dated 20th of February 1653 appeareth. **Recorded:** the 29th of the 6th month 1654.

THOMAS JOHNSON to ADAM WESTGATE – (1:59) Thomas Johnson, for 30 pounds, sold to Adam Westgate, his dwelling house with land thereto adjoining lying between Timothy Laskin and Robert Gray's lots in Salem, as by deed dated the 29th of the 6th month 1654 appeareth.

GEORGE KEYSAR to JOHN FULLER – (1:60) George Keysar of Lynn, for 14 pounds 10 shillings, sold to John Fuller, 27 acres of meadow in Rumney Marsh, between lands of Samuel Bennett and John Tarbox, as by writing dated 5: 1st month 1649 appeareth. **Recorded**: the 2nd of September 1654.

SAMUEL BENNETT to NICHOLAS POTTER – (1:60) Samuel Bennett of Lynn (carpenter) sold to Nicholas Potter of Lynn (bricklayer) 60 acres of land lying northwards from Adam Hank's [Hawk's?] farm adjoining land of said Nicholas Potter, as by writing dated the 25th of the 1st month 1644 appeareth. **Recorded**: the 2nd of September 1654.

GEORGE KEYSAR to NICHOLAS POTTER – (1:60) George Keysar of Lynn, for 5 pounds 4 shillings, sold to Nicholas Potter of Lynn, 12½ acres of meadow in Rumney Marsh, lying between John Gillo and Thomas Townsend's lands as by a writing dated the 3rd of July 1648 appeareth. **Recorded**: the 2nd of September 1654.

WILLIAM HOOKE to GEORGE KESAR – (1:61) William Hooke of Salisbury in New England, sold to George Kesar of Lynn, for 24 pounds 10 shillings, 7 acres of salt marsh in Rumney Marsh, late the land of Thomas Dexter, as by deed dated the 1st day of July 1647 appeareth. **Recorded**: on the 2nd of September 1664.

JOHN POOLE to GEORGE KEYSAR – (1:61) John Poole of Reading (yeoman) sold to George Keysar of Lynn (tanner) for 5 pounds, 16 acres of salt marsh in Rumney Marsh in Lynn...as by deed dated the 28th of the 3rd month 1650 appeareth. **Recorded**: the 2nd of September 1654.

EDMOND BATTER to THOMAS ANTHROP – (1:61) Edmond Batter of Salem sold to Thomas Anthrop, his farm at Brooksby, except what was sold to Richard Way, and excepting a parcel of meadow and land called Cranberry Pond, as by deed dated the 5th of the 2nd month 1653. **Recorded**: the 2nd of September 1654.

RICHARD WATERS to WALTER PRICE – (1:62) Richard Waters of Salem (gunsmith) sold to Walter Price for 6 pounds, one 10-acre lot in the South field in Salem, lying between lands of said Walter and Richard Moore, as by deed dated the 25th of the 11th month 1653 appeareth. **Recorded**: the 13th of the 7th month 1654.

SAMUEL HUTCHINSON to JOHN MANSFIELD – (1:62) Samuel Hutchinson of Lynn, for 30 pounds, sold to John Mansfield of Lynn, his dwelling house with 10 acres of land adjoining and 2 acres of salt marsh and 3½ acres of fresh marsh in Lynn as by a deed dated the 12th of July 1648 appeareth. **Recorded**: the 18th of the 7th month 1654.

THOMAS KENDALL to JOHN MANSFIELD – (1:62) A caveat for John Mansfield, who purchased of Thomas Kendall (carpenter) his house and lot which were Mr. South's 12 acres of upland and 8½ acres of marsh in Lynn, as by a deed the 25th of the 5th month 1654 appeareth. **Recorded**: the 18th of the 7th month 1654.

GEORGE & ELIZABETH KEYSAR to ANDREW MANSFIELD – (1:62) George Keysar of Lynn (tanner) and Elizabeth, his wife, for 16 pounds 10 shillings, sold to Andrew Mansfield, 8 acres of salt marsh in Rumney Marsh, as by deed dated the 14th of the 4th month 1653 appeareth. **Recorded**: the 18th of the 7th month 1654

ROBERT MANSFIELD to ANDREW MANSFIELD – (1:63) Robert Mansfield of Lynn sold to Andrew Mansfield, a house and 6 acres of land adjoining, with the rocky hill, also Sadler's Marsh and 12 acres of salt marsh in Rumney Marsh, as by deed dated the 10th of the 4th month appeareth. **Recorded**: the 18th of the 7th month 1654.

JONATHAN PORTER to JAMES CHICHESTER – (1:63) Jonathan Porter of Salem (planter) sold to James Chichester, his dwelling house with land adjoining being about 1¾ acres in consideration that…James shall freely allow and give meat, drink and lodging unto his wife Eunice Porter during her widowhood in case the said Jonathan shall die before her, as by deed dated the 2nd day of October 1654. **Recorded**: the 10th of October 1654.

JOHN PICKERING to JOHN WOODY & THOMAS FLINT – (1:63) A caveat for John Woody and Thomas Flint who bought of John Pickering his farm which he bought of Mr. Higginson, being 150 acres of meadow and pasture, as by deed dated the 18th of 8ber 1654 appeareth. **Recorded**: 19 Oct 1654.

JOHN JACKSON to JONATHAN PORTER – (1:64) John Jackson of Salem (mariner) sold for 3 pounds, ¾ acre of salt marsh in the south field between Goodman Ray's and Goodman Archer's salt marsh, to Jonathan Porter, as by a deed dated the 2nd of Oct 1654 appeareth. **Recorded**: the 27th of October 1654.

Jonathan Porter hath assigned all his right and intent to the three-quarters of an acre of salt marsh in the next record above mentioned unto Francis Skerry of Salem, husbandman. **Recorded**: the 27th of October 1654.

SAMUEL ARCHARD to JOHN BECKETT – (1:64) Samuel Archard of Salem (carpenter) sold, for 16 pounds, to John Beckett of Salem (shipwright) a dwelling house and 3 acres of land behind it between Edward Harnett & Richard Lambert, as by a deed dated 9 Apr 1655 appeareth. **Recorded**: the 9th of the 2nd month 1655.

NATHAN BIRDSALL to HENRY COOKE – (1:64) Nathan Birdsall of Salem, for a valuable consideration, sold to Henry Cooke of Salem, 5 acres of land, having Joseph Pope on the N side & Richard Bishop on the S as per a deed bearing date 16 Feb 1654.

THOMAS MARRINER to JOHN PHILLIPS – (1:65) Received by me, Thomas Marriner of Newfoundland, from Mr. John Phillips of Boston, 2 bushels of malt, 4 new nets, 2 dozen new lines & am to deliver same to said John Phillips…at all demands in the same condition I received them…in witness this 20 August 1650. **Signed**: Thomas Marriner [by mark]. **Witness**: by Paul Mansfield; copied as it was exhibited the 14th 2: month: 1655. Witness that I Thomas Marriner of Newfoundland, acknowledge to be indebted unto Mr. John Phillips of Boston…for the full sum of 38 pounds 2 shillings to be paid…in good merchantable salt; ½ at or before the 1st of next May, the other half at or before the 1st of July next, & the salt is to be delivered at the price of 12 shillings the hogshead & for payment whereby…I, Thomas Marriner do bind myself…for the sum of 60 pounds of lawful money of England. In witness…this 20: August 1650. **Signed**: Thomas Marriner [by mark]; **Witness**: John Phillips; **Testified**: John Gill. This is a true copy as it was exhibited the 14: 2 month: 1655.

JOHN SHEPLEY to WILLIAM FISK – (1:66) John Shepley of Wenham sold to William Fisk of Wenham, a dwelling house with an outhouse & 10 acres of ground adjoining, in Wenham, butting with a bound tree by the mill and so running up to the meeting house due North 116 poles wide to Robert Gowing's lot E…for a full sum in hand paid according to an agreement as appears 28: 2 mo: 1655. **Recorded**: the 28th of the 2 month 1655.

RICHARD GRAVES to JOHN PUTNAM – (1:66) Richard Graves sold to John Putnam, his grant of 40 acres of upland between land of John Ruck and William Hathorne & William Nichols in Salem, for 55 shillings as appeareth 12: 3 mo: 1655. **Recorded**: the 15th of the 3rd month 1655.

RICHARD GRAVES to JOHN GEDNEY – (1:67) Richard Graves sold to John Gedney 2 acres of land joining to Henry Cooke's on one side & Michael Ward on the other side, for 42 shillings 6 pence…as 1st January 1649 appeareth.

THOMAS & MARGARET RIX to JOHN GEDNEY – (1:67) Thomas Rix & Margaret his wife, for 5 pounds, sold to John Gedney, 4 acres of land next to the pasture of said John Gedney towards Ipswich ferry in Salem, as appears 15: 3m: 1655. **Recorded**: 16: 3: 1655.

ALICE VERNAZ to HENRY SKERRY – (1:67) Alice Vernaz (widow), sometimes of Salem, for 10 pounds in hand paid by Henry Skerry of Salem (cordwainer) sold 10 acres of land in the North Field between lands of Daniel Ray on the E and Thomas Watson and Thomas Tuck on the W butting on the North River; also 5 acres of meadow in Wenham meadow joining land given Henry Skerry & Francis Skerry by the town of Salem...as per deed dated 3:6 mo: 1655 appeareth. **Recorded**: the 3rd of the 6th month 1655.

ROBERT BRETT to GEORGE EMERY – (1:68) Robert Brett of Salem, for a valuable consideration, sold to George Emery, 1½ acres of meadow, between lands of Samuel Archer on the SE & the meadow of John Jackson on the NW, which meadow lies on both sides of the cross river that comes out of Forest River in Salem...as appeareth on the 6th of August 1655. **Recorded**: the 6th of the 6th month 1655.

WILLIAM LORD to ROBERT BRITT – (1:68) William Lord of Salem (cutler) for 20 pounds in hand paid, sold to Robert Britt of Salem, 2 acres of upland in Salem lying between lands of Nathaniel Pickman on the W and house of William Gott & John Miller on the E, butting on the burying place, then up to the street, as appeareth the 6th of the 6th month 1655. **Recorded**: the 9th of the 6th month 1655.

ROGER HASKELL to RICHARD DODGE – (1:69) Roger Haskell (husbandman) of Bass River in Salem, for 8 pounds in hand paid, sold to Richard Dodge of Salem (husbandman) 40 acres of land...with Beaver Pond on one side & the said Richard Dodge's bounds on the other side, 6 acres of meadow that lies within this compass & the said Richard is to have a watering place of said Roger for his cattle & this said land lies in the bounds of Salem, as per deed dated 28: February: 1654. **Recorded**: the 23rd of the 6th month 1655.

THOMAS & ANIS CHUBB to WILLIAM PITT & MOSES MAVERICK – (1:69) Thomas Chubb & Anis his wife of Manchester, for 12 pounds in hand paid, sold to William Pitt & Moses Maverick of Marblehead, a dwelling house with 50 acres of land...situated between the bounds of Manchester E & N and the meadow of said Pitt & Maverick, which they bought of John Horne, as per a deed on 17th of the 2nd month 1655 appeareth. **Recorded**: the 23rd of the 6th month 1655.

JOHN HORNE to WILLIAM PITT & MOSES MAVERICK – (1:70) John Horne of Salem...for 50 pounds in hand paid, does set over...unto William Pitt & Moses Maverick of Marblehead...85½ acres...viz: of Salt Marsh 10½ acres of upland and in the plain 25 acres, & of upland besides 50 acres, being bounded with land of Manchester on the NE, the farm land of Mr. John Blackleech on the SW...as appears at large by a deed dated 23: 2 mo: 1653.

JOHN LYON to MOSES MAVERICK – (1:70) John Lyon of Marblehead (fisherman) for 15 pounds in hand paid, has bargained...Moses Maverick his dwelling house, with half an acre of land...lying between Mr. Walton's orchard & Henry Stacy's house lot in Marblehead...as per a deed 17:6 month: 1653 appeareth.

WILLIAM HATHORNE (Atty. For LIDIA BANKS) to MOSES MAVERICK, ETC. – (1:70) William Hathorne of Salem, attorney of Mrs. Lidia Banks, late of Salem, for 123 pounds, doth give to Mr. Moses Maverick, David Corwithen, Arthur Sandin, William Charles, John Peach, the Elder, & other inhabitants of Marblehead, all that farm called the "Plaine's Farm" in Salem, adjoining Mr. Peter's farm, being 400 acres...with whatsoever, excepting 50 acres & 2 ponds, formerly granted to Mr. Downing, as per an instrument dated 24th of the 7th month 1645. **Recorded**: the 23rd of the 6th month 1655.

THOMAS PUTNAM – (1:70) Thomas Putnam took up a stray sow with 7 small pigs by her side the 9th of the 6th month 1655, appraised to be worth 22 shillings.

ROBERT & ELIZABETH MANSFIELD to ANDREW MANSFIELD – (1:71) Robert Mansfield of Lynn (yeoman) with Elizabeth his wife, in consideration of their son Andrew Mansfield living with them until the time of his marriage as a faithful & obedient child, has given Andrew forever as a child's portion a house and house lot of 6 acres with the enclosure adjoining to the N end of it the whole bounded E with land of Hugh Burt & the rocky hill of Andrew Mansfield, W with the house lot of Thomas Townsend & the street butting N on the country highway and S on the town highway & also the Rockie hill adjoining to said house lot on the E bounded with a close & house lot of the said Andrew Mansfield & the house lot of Hugh Burt & from the corner of Hugh Burt's lot by the descent of the hill near the highway to the swamp & so at the descent of the hill by the swamp we come unto the close of the said Andrew Mansfield & that without any division: also a parcel of fresh meadow at the head of the 2nd pond from the town, which runs to the watermill, lying upon a triangle usually called Mr. Sadler's marsh; also 3 acres of salt marsh lying in the salt marsh before the town bounded S with the marsh of Hugh Burt, N with the marsh of Mr. Handford, butting E on the land of Mr. Knowles; also one acre of marsh in the 1st division in Rumney Marsh, bounded E with the marsh of Capt. Bridges, W with the marsh of Mr. Burnall; also 3 acres of salt marsh in the 2nd division in Rumney Marsh, bounded E with the marsh of Capt. Bridges, W with the marsh of George Tayler; also 1 acre of marsh in the 2nd division in Rumney Marsh bounded E with the marsh lately in the tenure of Mathew West, & W with the marsh of old Winter; also 4 acres of salt marsh in the last division in Rumney Marsh, bounded E with the marsh of Edward Burcham, butting S on the river, N on the marsh of Edmund Farrington, all in the bounds of Lynn, and purchased of Mr. George Taylor, widower, by the said Robert, except one 3-acre lot in the 2nd division in Rumney Marsh & one 10-acre lot in the same division, & 2 acres of salt marsh before the town & 4 acres in the last division in Rumney Marsh, as per deed on the 10th day of the 4th month 1650 at large appeareth. **Recorded**: the 14th of the 2 month 1656.

ROBERT MANSFIELD to ANDREW MANSFIELD – (1:73) Robert Mansfield of Lynn gave to his son Andrew, one acre of fresh meadow up in the country, which he bought of Mr. Taylor of Lynn, which was formerly in the tenancy of Benjamin Panlly and by him sold to Mr. Richard Sadler, as by deed of 10: 4 mo: 1650 appeareth. **Recorded**: the 14th of the 2nd month 1656.

RICHARD GRAVES to JOHN GEDNEY – (1:73) Richard Graves of Salem sold to John Gedney for 42 shillings, 6 pence, 2 acres of land joining Henry Crook's land on one side & to Michael Ward's on the other side, with such land was sold by said Graves to said Gedney as per deed of the 1st of January 1649. **Recorded**: the 14th of the 4th month 1656.

THOMAS & MARGARET RIX to JOHN GEDNEY – (1:74) Thomas Rix (barber) of Essex county, with Margaret his wife, for 5 pounds in hand paid by John Gedney of Salem, sold to said Gedney 4 acres of land, which was the land of Michael Ward, the former husband of said Margaret, which said land is next to the pasture land of said Gedney towards Ipswich, ferry in Salem, as per deed of 15: 3 mo: 1655 appeareth. **Recorded**: the 14th of the 4th month 1656.

FRANCIS PERRY to THOMAS SPOONER – (1:74) Francis Perry of Salem (wheelwright) for a valuable consideration, sold to Thomas Spooner (weaver) 14 acres of land in the North field, bounded by the river S & joining Goodman Simon's land E & Mr. Gedney's land N & the highway W. as per deed of --- January 1651 appeareth; which said deed was consented to & all claims yielded up by Jane Perry, wife of Francis Perry before the worshipful John Endicott, Dept. Gov., 13: 1 mo: 1654. **Recorded**: the 23rd of the 4th month 1656.

Mr. DANIEL KING to THOMAS FARR – (1:75) Mr. Daniel King in New England & county of Essex, for 128 pounds 10 shillings in hand paid, sold to Thomas Farr of the same place, all of a parcel of ground in Lynn called by name of Sagamore Hill & also some part of the ground that was in the occupation of Christopher Foster, and another part of it in the occupation of Henry Walton & since in the occupation of Nathaniel Tiler, all of it amounting to 3 score acres…and 25 acres of meadow in Rumney Marsh in Lynn, bounded N & E with the common or highway that goes to Nahant & S & W with the lands of Mr. Edward Holyoke, as appears in a deed of 6 Nov 1654. Elizabeth King, his wife freely resigned her rights as appears on a deed dated 2: 2 mo: 1655. **Recorded**: the 24th of the 4th month 1656.

JOSEPH ARMITAGE to RICHARD JOHNSON – (1:76) Joseph Armitage of Lynn, for 5 pounds in hand paid by Richard Johnson, has bargained…six acres of meadow in Rumney Marsh, the first divident of it being to Thomas Townsend, bounded with lands of Joseph Redknap in the E and bounded S with a divident of lands of John Kirtland's & N butting on upland, as appeareth in a deed dated 22: December 1654. **Recorded**: the 26th of the 4th month 1656.

THOMAS MORE to MORDICA CRAFORD – (1:76) Thomas More of Southhold in New England, for 10 shillings in hand paid by Mordica Craford, sold to said Craford, half an acre of upland joining land of Mr. John Herbert on the point of land by Winter Harbor in Salem, as appears on a deed of 30th: 4: 1656. **Recorded**: the 30th of the 4th month 1656.

JOHN HERBERT to MORDICA CRAFORD – (1:77) John Herbert of Southhold on Long Island, for 10 shillings in hand paid by Mordica Craford, sold ½ acre of upland next to land of said Craford in the neck of land next to Winter Island in Salem, as appears in a deed dated 30: 4: 1656.

JOHN & KATHERINE GEDNEY to ADAM WESTGATE – (1:77) John Gedney and Katherine his wife, sold to Adam Westgate of Salem for 5 pounds in hand paid, 20 acres of land which was land of Senr Richard Hollingworth, situated next to land belonging to the watermill of Marblehead, lying beside thereof W toward the Forest River head, as appeareth in a deed dated 30: 4: 1656. **Recorded**: the 30th of the 4th month 1656.

GEORGE KEASER to PHILLIP CROMWELL – (1:77) George Keaser of Lynn has bound over unto Phillip Cromwell of Salem for security of a debt owed to said Cromwell of 50 pounds sterling, his dwelling house at Lynn with 6 acres of land, with his malt house and all other houses standing on said ground, and 14 acres of salt marsh at Fox Hill in Rumney Marsh, as appears on a deed dated 25: 4 mo: 1656. **Recorded**: the 30th of the 4th month 1656.

LUCIE DOWNING to JOSEPH GARDNER – (1:78) Lucie Downing of Salem, by advice and allowance of Emanual Downing, her husband, as appears by several letters under his hand, has given to Joseph Gardner (their son) a messuage or tenement in Salem on 4 acres of ground entire having the common on the E, the street or highway from the meeting house to the harbor on the S & a lane that goes to the North River on the W, which said premises, said Lucie gives unto said Joseph as his dowry & marriage portion with Ann, the daughter of said Emanuel & Lucie Downing, his wife, as appears by writing of 8 Aug 1656. This is entered by way of caution; witness to the deed: William Hathorn & George Norton. **Recorded**: the 12th of the 6th month 1656.

JOSEPH ARMITAGE to JOSEPH JENKS – (1:78) 12: Sept 1656: A caveat for Joseph Jenks, Sr. of Hammersmith, who bought of Joseph Armitage, all the company's part of a corn mill & forge situated at the tale of the forge & furnace for a valuable sum in hand paid as by a deed dated 12 Sept 1656 appeareth.

THOMAS & MARY WILKES to THOMAS HAYLE – (1:79) Thomas Wilkes of Salem (shipwright) and Mary his wife, granted to Thomas Hayle of Newbury, for 27 pounds, a dwelling house with 2 acres of ground by the North River, bounded by said river N & the ground of Widow Robinson on the S, the street on the E, and also 5 acres of upland on the other side of the North River, butting on said river on the S & the highway on the N & the land of Thomas Watson on the W, the land of Thomas Buffum on the E; also 1½ acres of marsh by Clay Brook, being between Thomas James & William Lord, Elias Stileman's ground at the head & pointing down to Clay Brook as by deed dated 1 Oct 1656 appeareth. **Recorded**: the 14th of the 8th month 1656.

RICHARD LEADER to JOSEPH JENKS – (1:79) An agreement between Richard Leader (agent for the company of undertakers of the Ironworks in New England) and Joseph Jenks (blacksmith): viz: that the said Richard Leader does covenant & agree with the said Joseph Jenks, that Joseph Jenks shall have liberty to build & erect a mill or hammer for the forging and making of scythes or any other iron ware by water at the taile of the furnace & to have full benefit of the furnace, water when the furnace goes, provided he damnify not any works that may hereafter be erected at the taile of the forge to have & to hold…to his proper benefit for the term of 21 years; also said Leader does promise to allow Jenks bar iron & cast iron for gudgins shafts and hooks for said mill, provided Jenks erect said mill & keep it in repair the said term Jenks to perfect the said mill by the 24th of June next & upon neglect of repair the grantor has liberty to re-enter as appears more at large by a deed dated 20 Jan 1647.

JOSEPH ARMITAGE to JOSEPH JENKS – (1:80) Joseph Armitage of Lynn (tailor) granted to Joseph Jenks of Lynn for a valuable consideration a slitting mill with all appurtenances & privileges at Hammersmith in the county of Essex which said mill was recorded by a judgment at Salem court the 24th of June 1656, as appeareth at large by a deed bearing date of 15 September 1656. **Recorded**: the 27th of the 8th month 1656.

JOSEPH ARMITAGE to JOSEPH JENKS, Sr. – (1:81) Joseph Armitage of Lynn granted to Joseph Jenks, Sr. of Hammersmith, for a valuable consideration, sold all right & title that the company of undertakers of the Ironworks had to a corn mill at the taile of the forge & furnace at the said works, which said premises was recovered out of the hands of the said undertakers upon judgment granted at Salem Court the which premises appear more at large by a deed bearing date of 12: 7 mo: 1656. **Recorded**: the 27th of the 8th month 1656.

PHILLIP CROMWELL to FRANCIS SKERRY – (1:81) Phillip Cromwell of Salem (butcher) with Dorothie his wife, granted to Francis Skerry of Salem, for a ewe lamb in hand paid & a ewe lamb to be delivered in 1654, 3 acres of land; 1 acre of it was Richard Leache, Sr.'s and 1½ acres was John Leaches and ½ acre Robert Leaches, situated between land of Robert Fuller & an acre of land of John Burrows on the W butting on the North River & from thence to the lane that goes to the old planters marsh; as by deed dated the 1: 9mo: 1656 appeareth. **Recorded**: the 2nd of December 1656.

Executives of THOMAS SCRUGGS to EDMOND PATCH – (1:81) Roger Conant, William Dodge, Benjamin Balch & John Rayment (planters), Executors to Thomas Scruggs of Salem, granted to Edmond Patch of Salem for 5 pounds, 10 acres of land, a part of their joint farm that lies next to Richard Dodge's farm, and the above said Conant, Dodge, Balch & Rayment, as does at large appear by a deed bearing date the 27th of the 9th month 1656. **Recorded**: the 2nd of the 10th month 1656.

ELIAS MASON to EDMOND PATCH & JOHN DODGE – (1:82) Elias Mason of the county of Essex, granted to Edmond Patch and John Dodge, son of Richard Dodge, of the same town, for 4 pounds, 40 acres of land next to land of Rice Edwards on the SW & bounded with the river on the NW & on the other 2 sides lying next to the common in Salem, as by a deed dated the 26th of the 9th month 1656. **Recorded**: on the 2nd of the 10th month 1656.

JEFFREY MASSEY to RICHARD DODGE – (1:83) Jeffrey Massey of Salem granted to Richard Dodge (planter) of Salem, for 20 shillings, 10 acres of land adjoining his own farm on the S & W sides & bordering on the N side with Rice Edward's land, lying next to the common as by a deed dated 27th day 9th month 1656 appeareth. **Recorded**: the 3rd of the 10th month 1656.

ROGER HASKALL to RICHARD DODGE – (1:83) Roger Haskall of Salem (planter) granted to Richard Dodge of Salem for 10 pounds, 3 acres of meadow in Salem bounded on one side by 6 acres of his own meadow & on the other side 6 acres of meadow of Benjamin Balch of Salem, commonly known by the name of Longham & is bounded on the NE by a common belonging to Wenham & on the other end upon a common belonging to Salem, as by a deed dated 27: 9mo: 1656 appeareth. **Recorded**: the 3rd of the 10th month 1656.

ROGER HASKALL to RICHARD DODGE – (1:83) Roger Haskall of Salem (planter) granted to Richard Dodge of Salem, for 8 pounds, 40 acres of upland in Salem, between his own farm & the pond commonly called Beaver Pond, bounded at one end with meadow of Rice Edwards & shrouting (?) with the other end toward land of Mr. Thorndikes of Salem, as by deed dated the 27th of the 9th month 1656 appeareth. **Recorded**: the 3rd of the 10th month 1656.

WILLIAM DODGE to RICHARD DODGE – (1:84) William Dodge of Salem granted to Richard Dodge of Salem, for 6 pounds, 40 acres of upland, part of 80 acres granted to them both, and 6 acres of meadow lying between a farm of said Richard Dodge & running up towards 3 acres that which was Roger Haskall's of Salem, commonly called Longham, as by a deed dated 27: 9 month 1656 appeareth. **Recorded**: the 3rd of the 10th month 1656.

HENRY & GERTRUDE PEASE to CHRISTOPHER CODNER – (1:85) Henry Pease of Marblehead, and Gertrude his wife, granted to Christopher Codner of Marblehead for 26 pounds, their dwelling house & outhouse with 3 acres of land, some of it without the fence, near land of

John Clements on the S with all other land & appurtenances belonging, in Marblehead, and the limits of same as by a deed dated 10 July 1656 appeareth. **Recorded**: the 24th of the 10th month 1656.

JOSEPH BOYCE to GEORGE BYUM – (1:85) Joseph Boyce of Salem (tanner) granted to George Byum of Salem (husbandman) for 16 pounds, 20 acres of upland with one dwelling house & barn or cow house upon said land, between lands of Nicholas Howard on the NW, & land of Edmund Marshall on the SE, butting on land of John Batchelor W & thence downto Bass River in Salem, as appeareth in a deed of 12: 1 month: 1655/56. Recorded the 3rd of the 4th month 1657.

ROBERT GOODALL to DAVID CORWETHIN – (1:85) Robert Goodall of Salem (husbandman) granted to David Corwethin of Salem, 6 pounds, 3 acres of salt marsh on Riall Side adjoining marsh that was Thomas Roote's on one side & the common on the other side as by deed dated 7: 5 month 1656. **Recorded**: the 4th of the 4th month 1657.

THOMAS & MARY WHEELER to GEORGE FRAILE – (1:86) Thomas Wheeler of Lynn and Mary his wife granted to George Fraile of Lynn for 9 pounds 10 shillings, 3 acres of upland, being part of his house lot, bounded E with the lane that goes out of Mill Street, to the house of said George Fraile, W with land of John Tarbox, lately in the tenure of Thomas Wheeler; S with the town common, N with land of said Thomas Wheeler, as appears by a deed more at large, expressing appurtenances & privileges, bearing date of 25: Jan: 1654. **Recorded**: the 30th of the 4th month 1657.

THOMAS & MARY WHEELER to JOHN TARBOX – (1:86) Thomas Wheeler of Lynn and Mary his wife granted to John Tarbox, for 10 pounds, 10 shillings, 3 acres of land, being part of the S end of the house lot of said Thomas Wheeler in Lynn, bounded E with land of George Fraile & west with land of said John Tarbox & George Keaser, butting S upon the town common, N on said Thomas Wheeler, as by a deed bearing date of 25: Jan 1654 appeareth. **Recorded**: the 30th of the 4th month 1657.

JOSEPH ARMITAGE to THOMAS WHEELER – (1:87) Joseph Armitage granted to Thomas Wheeler all his right in the sails, masts, roads & anchor and other appurtenances belonging to that boat which was cast away belonging to Thomas Wiggin & the said Joseph, which part was ½ of same, upon condition that if said Joseph pays said Thomas within 6 weeks, 3 pounds in bar iron & 4 pounds 12 shillings in English goods or bill to some corant shop, then the writing of none effect as appears more fully by deed dated 30: 4 mo: 1657. **Recorded**: the 30th of the 4th month 1657.

JOHN KITCHIN to JOB SWINERTON – (1:87) John Kitchin of Salem (shoemaker) granted to Job Swinerton of Salem (planter) for 8 pounds, 100 acres of upland, viz: 40 acres at upper end of the great swamp on the plain adjoining to the farm of Mr. John Endicott, Jr., & the other 60 acres next to a brook as specified in the deed, saving Thomas Read's 20 acres between as by deed dated 3: 5: 1657 at large appeareth. **Recorded:** the 6th of the 5th month 1657.

JOHN INGERSOLL to JOHN GARDNER – (1:88) John Ingersoll of Salem (mariner) granted to John Gardner of Salem (mariner) for 10 pounds, a dwelling house with ½ acre of land, between the house & land of Richard Ramonds E & Joseph Hardy on the W, butting on South River in Salem as by deed dated 9: 6th month: 1656 appeareth. **Recorded:** the 6th of the 5th month 1657.

SAMUEL FRIEND to SAMUEL PICKMAN – (1:88) Samuel Friend of Manchester, granted to Samuel Pickman of Salem, for 5 pounds 10 shillings, ½ an acre of land on the South River side, between George Keaser & Mr. Prescot, as by deed dated 24 December 1657 appeareth. **Recorded:** on 8: 11 mo: 1657.

JOSEPH JENKS, Sr. to SIMON BRADSTREET (mortgage) – (1:88) On 6: 5 mo: 1657, Joseph Jenks, Sr. of Hammersmith (smith) granted to Simon Bradstreet of Andover (gentleman) for 3 score pounds, his dwelling house & house lot in Hammersmith & all his corn mill, hammer mill & slitting mill with all utensils & appurtenances to every & each of them belonging, all in Hammersmith, provided Joseph Jenks shall pay said Simon Bradstreet the sum of 88 pounds in good English commodities, bar iron or nails at price current amongst merchants, in 4 years at 7 several payments, viz: 22 pounds on the 29th of Sept next and 11 pounds on 25 March after & 11 pounds every 6 months til the 88 pounds be fully satisfied. Then this bargain & sale be void…the payments to be at South Meeting House in Boston & in case Jenks fail of any payments, Simon Bradstreet may enter upon…& fully satisfy himself for debt and damages and restore the remainder to said Jenks as appeareth by deed dated 10 March 1656 appeareth more fully.

HENRY & FRANCIS SKERRY TO HENRY HERRICK – (1:90) Henry & Francis Skerry of Salem granted to Henry Herrick of Salem, 100 acres of upland lying in Birch plain, butting William Lord's farm, John Leach's, William Elliott's & William Haskell's in Salem; also 6 acres of meadow butting upon widow Mark's in Wenham great meadow as by a deed dated 1 July 1653 at large appeareth. **Recorded:** on 7: 5 mo: 1657.

THOMAS SPOONER to JOHN DENMAN – (1:90) Thomas Spooner, county of Essex (linen weaver) granted to John Denman of Munnados (taylor) for 5 pounds, 40 acres of upland in Wenham & 4 acres of meadow in the great meadow, as by deed dated 25: 6 mo: 1657. John Denman of the Munnados in the New Netherlands (taylor) for the full value & worth in hand paid, has sold unto Walter Price of Salem (shopkeeper) 6 acres of upland in Wenham adjoining Mark Bachelor W and land of Thomas Fiske N as by deed dated 25 Aug 1657. John Denman of Munnados in the New Netherlands (taylor) for 5 pounds paid by Walter Price of Salem (shopkeeper) 40 acres of upland in Wenham bounded by the farm of James Moulton together with 4 acres of meadow in great meadow of Wenham as appears by deed dated 25 Aug 1657. **Recorded**: 11: 11 mo: 1657.

JOHN LUFF to JOHN STONE, Sr. – (1:91) John Luff of Salem granted to John Stone, Sr. of Salem (husbandman) for 4 pounds, 14 acres of upland between land of Robert Hebert & William Dodge on Bass River side, as appears by deed dated 10: 12 mo: 1657. **Recorded**: 20: 12 mo: 1657.

EDWARD HARNET to THOMAS GOLDTHWAITE – (1:91) Edward Harnet of Salem granted to Thomas Goldthwaite of Salem (cooper) for 38 pounds, 20 acres of upland & meadow with a dwelling house & barn next to the highway towards Mr. Downing's farm & the house & land of Thomas Avery in Salem, as by deed dated 20: 12: 1657 more appeareth. Cecily, wife of Edward Harnet yielded rights on 16: 1 mo: 1657/8. **Recorded**: 25: 12 mo: 1657.

GEORGE EMERY to WILLIAM FLINT – (1:92) George Emery of Salem granted to William Flint of Salem, 6 acres of swamp land at Clay Brook which land was given to said Emery by the town of Salem as by deed dated the 16: 1 mo: 1657 appeareth. [no amount given] **Recorded**: 16: 1 mo: 1657/8.

DAVID CORWETHIN to JOHN SOTHERICK – (1:92) David Corwethin of Salem granted to John Sotherick of Salem for 13 pounds, 3 acres of salt marsh lying on Rial Side, Woollistones River bounding in on S & some marsh late in possession of Thomas Roots, as by deed dated 2 Nov 1657 appeareth. **Recorded**: 16: 1 mo: 1657/8.

THOMAS & SUSANNA AVERY to GEORGE CORWIN – (1:92) Thomas Avery of Salem (blacksmith) with Susanna his wife, granted to George Corwin (merchant) his dwelling house, shop, barn or other outhouses thereto belonging, with 16 acres of upland & 6 acres of meadow, all which upland & meadow except 1 acre of said meadow is bounded by the land of John Sutherick on the N & land of Thomas Goldthwait, formerly Edward Harnet Sr's on the E & land of Brigett Giles on the W & Brooksby River running through said meadow, the other acre of meadow is between the meadow land of said Brigett Giles & Thomas Goldthwait, near the dwelling house of Samuel Verry, hier in the river, as by deed dated 10 March 1657/8 appeareth. **Recorded**: 18: 1 mo: 1657/8.

LAURENCE LEACH to RICHARD LEACH – (1:93) A caution for Richard Leach who had given to him by his father Laurence Leach, his farm on Rial Side that joins Jacob Barney, both upland and salt marsh, only reserving for his particular use so much as is needful during his & his wife's lifetime, and after their decease, the said Richard Leach to have the same, as by a writing bearing date of 14 December 1643 doth appear. Nathaniel Felton was witness to the writing. **Recorded**: 18: 1 mo: 1657/8.

EDWARD HARNET (Atty. for JONATHAN PORTER) to JOHN BECKET – (1:93) Edward Harnet of Salem (tailor) attorney to Jonathan Porter, sometimes of Salem, granted to John Becket of Salem (shipwright) for 15 pounds, the dwelling house and 1¾ acres of upland of said Porter's which was formerly John Jackson's & is between the house & land of Thomas Smith E and Henry Harwood on the W; also Elizabeth Porter rendered her thirds, as by deed dated 26: 3: 1656 appeareth. **Recorded**: 19 March 1657.

WALTER & ELIZABETH PRICE to RICHARD ADAMS – (1:94) Walter Price (shopkeeper) of Salem and Elizabeth his wife, granted to Richard Adams of Salem, for 6 pounds 15 shillings, 10 acres of planting land in South field, part whereof was formerly Richard Water's since John Talby & part whereof was formerly the land of William King, Sr. as by deed dated 9: 12 mo: 1657 appeareth. **Recorded**: 20: 1 mo: 1657/8.

EDWARD & EUNIS HARNET to THOMAS SOLAS – (1:94) Edward Harnet of Salem (tailor) and Eunis his wife, granted to Thomas Solas of Salem (fisherman) for 13 pounds to be paid in English goods at Mr. William Brown's shop on demand, a dwelling house with 1 acre of land adjoining & about ½ acre with all the fencing belonging thereto, adjoining land of John Becket W and Joseph Swazey E. **Signed**: 20 July 1658 by Edward & Eunis Harnet; **Acknowledged**: 20: 5: 58; **Witnessed**: by Joshua Turland & Hilliard Veren.

JOSEPH ARMITAGE to Mr. THOMAS RUCK (mortgage) – (1:95) Joseph Armitage of Lynn (tailor) granted to Mr. Thomas Ruck of Boston, for 34 pounds...and sell in plain & open market in the town of Lynn have delivered, 1 mare colt, color bay, with a star in the forehead, 1 sow and a hog swing; 6 pounds sterling in the hands of the townsmen of Lynn, & 60 pounds sterling due...by execution from Mr. Adam Oatly, levied upon a farm of his at Windmill Hill in the tenure of Francis Ingolls, to have...Said mare colt, sow and hog swing with 60 pounds due by execution from Mr. Adam Oatley. But if Joseph Armitage pay 34 pounds to said Thomas Ruck at or before 28 September next ensuing, then sale to be void. **Signed**: 15th of February 1653 by Joseph Armitage; **Acknowledged**: 10: 1 mo: 1653; **Witnesses**: Nathaniel Souther & James Hill; **Recorded**: 21: 5: 1658.

ALICE BULLOCK to HENRY COOKE – (1:97) Alice Bullock (widow), with consent of her father William Flint, granted to Henry Cooke of Salem for 70 pounds, to be paid yearly, according to the tenure of the bond, her dwelling house & out houses with all land pertaining, 20 acres, the house stands near unto the general fence of the north neck, having Henry Bullock on the one side & William Robinson on the other, the land adjoining unto said house running from thence unto John Southwick, except the wood on half an acre of land & the pond which belongs to Henry Bullock for the term of his life, on paying 10 shillings per annum during the term of his life unto the said Henry Bullock; also all the lands that lie in the North field which belonged unto Henry Bullock, Jr. late deceased; also 6 acres of meadow in the broad meadow that is near John Hathorne's old house. **Signed:** 22nd of the 6th month 1657 by Alice Bullock [by mark]; **Acknowledged**: 1: 5: 1658; **Witnesses**: Nathaniel Felton & Jonathan Browne; **Recorded**: 22: 5: 1658.

JOHN SMITH to ROBERT GOODELL – (1:98) John Smith of Salem (planter) granted to Robert Goodell, in consideration of the house & 10 acres of ground sold him by his father-in-law Robert Goodell as by his deed; 55 acres of land adjoining a farm of said Robert on the E and bounded with some land of Thomas Flint on the W. I, the said John Smith do by these presents covenant....with my father-in-law Robert Goodell that I will not sell...above said house & 10 acres of land whereby to defraud Elizabeth my wife her right...in the same, which the said John do freely consent to be the same as was in the 50 acres of land above mentioned. **Signed**: 21: 5: 1658 by John Smith by mark; **Acknowledged**, 21: 5: 1658; **Recorded**: 21: 5: 1658; **Witnesses**: Joshua Turland & Hillyard Veren.

ROBERT GOODELL to JOHN SMITH – 1:100) Robert Goodell of Salem granted to John Smith, in consideration of 50 acres of land sold him by John Smith "my son-in-law" which land lies & is adjoining to my farm, being bounded with some land of Thomas Flint on the West; 10 acres of upland with an old house with what fence there is belonging lying near the great cove in a neck of land commonly called the north neck. **Signed**: 21: 5 mo: 1658 by Robert Goodell; **Acknowledged**: 21: 5: 1658; **Recorded** 21: 5: 1658; **Witnesses**: Joshua Turland & Hilliard Veren.

RICHARD & SUSAN STACKHOUSE to ISAACK PAGE – (1:101) Richard Stackhouse of Salem and Susan his wife, granted to Isaack Page of Salem (bricklayer) for 15 pounds, a dwelling house and 1 acre of land, bounded E with some land of John Marsh & land of Christopher Waler on the W. **Signed**: the 20th day of July 1658 by Richard Stackhouse and Susanna Stackhouse [by mark]; **Witnesses**: Samuel Corning & Hillyard Veren.

JOSEPH ARMITAGE to JOHN SOUTHWICK – (1:102) Joseph Armitage of Lynn granted to John Southwick, for 20 pounds to him secured, 21 acres of meadow in the meadow commonly called Mr. Willis's meadow in Lynn bounded by the meadow of Thomas Hucheson & by the meadow of Mr. Thomas Willis & by the meadow of Joseph Armitage & by the upland. **Signed**: the 4th of April 1654 by Joseph Armitage; **Acknowledged**: 4: 2 mo: 1654; **Recorded**: 4: 2: 1654; **Witnesses**: Thomas Marshall & William Cowdrey.

GEORGE NORTON to EDMOND FAULKNER – (1:104) George Norton of Salem, in consideration of a deed signed over by Edmond Faulkner of Andover, declared he fully acquitted & discharged Edmond Faulkner of all debt & demands of deeds of land. **Signed**: 30th of June 1658 by George Norton; **Acknowledged**: 30 June 1658; **Witnesses**: John Ruck & John Symonds; **Recorded**: 13 June 1658.

JAMES UNDERWOOD & ALEXANDER SEARS to THOMAS STEGGE – (1:104) It was agreed upon between James Underwood & Alexander Sears, owner & master of the good ketch called the *Dolphin* on the one part, and Thomas Stegge (hirer of the said ketch) on the other side; witnesseth that the said master & owner do on their side promise to sufficiently fit & rig the said ketch & sufficiently man the same, with all expedition to be at the use & command of said Thomas Stegge or his assignes, for 4 months certain or 6 months uncertain, in consideration whereof, the said Thomas Stegge doth oblige himself…to pay unto the said master Alexander Sears for the said vessel & merchants wages: 18 pounds 10 shillings per month, which is to be paid in Manhattan, 1/3 in money or beaver & the other 2/3 in commodities at the price current of tobacco, and the said vessel to enter into pay within 12 hours after said Sears shall give notice of his readiness, & that the said Alexander Sears shall for his advantage have 2 hogsheads freight from Virginia to Manhattan between which places the said vessel is to trade with all possible expedition…and further, the said Thomas Stegge doth oblige himself to fit & provide the said company of the vessel with good & sufficient provision to the true intent. **Signed**: the 2nd day of September 1658 in Boston in New England, by me James Underwood, Alexander Sears, Thomas Stegge, in presence of Mr. Sammond & John Conney.

JOHN & HANNA WILSON to THOMAS ROOTS – (1:106) John Wilson of Salem (mason) with wife Hanna, granted to Thomas Roots of Salem (weaver) for 18 pounds, his dwelling house & 2 acres of land adjoining, also all the fruit now growing without the garden fence, situated near the land of William Lord on the S & Thomas Rootes N, & the peaceable possession to give by the 10th of October next ensuing. **Signed**: the 1st of July 1657 by John Wilson [by mark] and Hanna Wilson; **Acknowledged**: 1: 5: 1657, with Hanna yielding thirds; **Witnesses**: Richard Harvey & Hilliard Veren; **Recorded** 1: 5: 1657.

SAMUEL FRIEND to JOHN PEACH, Jr. – (1:107) Samuel Friend of Manchester (planter) granted to John Peach, Jr. of Marblehead (fisherman) for 3 pounds, 10 acres of upland on the Darby Fort side in Marblehead, bounded E with John Legg of Marblehead, W with land of William Hunter of Salem (mariner), having the harbor on the N & shooting out on the S towards the common. **Signed**: the 3rd of the 10th month 1658 by Samuel Friend; **Acknowledged**: 2: 10: 1658; **Witnesses**: Edward Norrice & John Grafton; **Recorded**: 3: 10 mo: 1658.

HENRY INGALLS to ROBERT RAND – (1:108) Henry Ingalls of Lynn (batchelor) granted to Robert Rand of Lynn (husbandman) for 16 pounds sterling, a parcel of land in Lynn with a dwelling house on it, the land formerly being the house lot of Edward Ingalls, which land contains 6 acres bounded S with land of Robert Rand, N with land of Henry Collins, Sr., abutting W on the common & E on land of Henry Collins, Sr. **Signed**: by Henry Ingalls 1 June 1652; **Acknowledged**: 13: 11 mo: 1656; **Witnesses**: Andrew Mansfield & Robert Ingalls; **Recorded**: 12: 10: 1658.

THOMAS WHEELER to ROBERT RAND - (1:111) Thomas Wheeler of Lynn (yeoman), with consent of Mary his now wife, granted to Robert Rand of Lynn (husbandman) for 7 pounds, 10 shillings sterling, 4 acres of salt marsh in the last division in Rumney Marsh, bounded S with marsh of William Longley, N with marsh of Lieut. Thomas Marshall, abutting E on marsh of Mr. Knowles & W on the creek. **Signed**: the 1st of April 1657 by Thomas Wheeler; **Acknowledged**: 1: 10 mo: 1658; **Witnesses**: Thomas Marshall & Andrew Mansfield; **Recorded**: 12: 10: 1658.

THOMAS MARSHALL to ROBERT RAND – (1:113) On 15: 10 month: 1657, an indenture was made between Thomas Marshall of Lynn (Lieut. Of the Military Company) and Robert Rand of Lynn (husbandman) for 12 pounds sterling, for 8 acres of salt marsh in the last division in

Rumney Marsh, bounded S with the marsh of Robert Rand (lately in tenure of Thomas Wheeler), N with marsh of George Farr, E on the marsh of Mr. Knowles and W on the creek. Thomas Marshall's "now wife" (not named) surrendered thirds. **Signed**: by Thomas Marshall; **Witnesses**: Thomas Wheeler and Andrew Mansfield; **Acknowledged**: 1: 10 mo: 1658; **Recorded** 12: 10: 1658.

THOMAS COATS to ROBERT RAND – (1:115) On 27: 10 month: 1649, Thomas Coats of Lynn, granted to Robert Rand of Lynn, for 1 cow, 1 heifer, and 30 hundred weight of hay and six days work, the house which was lately Joseph Flud's with the orchard, garden and fencing, with 4 acres of ground the house stood on, lying between land of widow Ingalls and the land of Thomas Coats, bounded E by a swamp, W on the common; also 5 acres of ground for planting beyond the swamp adjoining the land of William Tilton. **Signed**: Thomas Coats [by mark]; **Witnesses**: Edward Burcham and William Edmonds; **Acknowledged**: 5th of 11 mo: 1649; **Recorded**: 15: 10: 1658.

RICHARD BLOOD to ROBERT RAND – (1:117) On 28 June 1658, Richard Blood of Lynn sold to Robert Rand of Lynn, for a consideration for which he was "fully satisfied and paid," 4 acres of meadow in Reedy meadow, bounded N with 9 acres of Thomas Smith, now in hands of Thomas Wheeler, S with 2 acres given to Jenckin Davis, now in hands of Thomas Wellman, W with the Saugus River, and E with the upland. **Signed**: Richard Blood; **Witnesses**: Garrard Spencer and Henry Silsby; **Acknowledged**: 29 June 1658.

CHRISTOPHER WALLER to JOHN MARSTON – (1:118) On 1 Jan 1658, Christopher Waller of Salem sold to John Marston of Salem, for 3 pounds, 30 pole of ground, the S end of Whitlocke's lot, abutting the highway that goes down to the North river, against the E end of Mr. Endecott's field, E and W four poles in breadth, butting N & E on the remaining part of the said Waller's ground, with fence upon which 30 poles of ground stands, now the dwelling houses of John Marston and William Marston, S upon the narrow highway that turns down to the grounds of Mr. Downing's field on the other side of highway. **Signed**: Christopher Waller [by mark]; **Witnesses**: Samuel Pickman and Eliah Stileman; **Acknowledged**: 11: 11: 1658; **Recorded**: 3: 10: 1658.

HENRY PHELPS to EDWARD GASKILL – (1:119) On 3 January 1658, Henry Phephs of Salem (husbandman) granted to Edward Gaskill of Salem, for 9 pounds, 10 acres of land within the north neck and the limits of Salem, bounded W with land of Isaac Bacons, N with land of Thomas Bishop, Sr., E with land of Thomas Gardener, S with land of Josiah

Southwick. **Signed**: Henry Phelps; **Witnesses**: Joshua Turland and Hillyard Veren; **Acknowledged**: 4th 11mo: 1658; **Recorded**: 12: 11: 1658.

GEORGE CORWIN to THOMAS BARNES – (1:120) On 25: 11 month: 1658, George Corwin of Salem (merchant) granted to Thomas Barnes of Salem (blacksmith) for 18 pounds, a dwelling house with half an acre of ground with all appurtenances, being in Salem, formerly in the possession of George Bridgman, and bounded N & E with the street or common highway, S & W with the land of Samuel Archer, Marshall, and Mr. Richard Moore. **Signed**: George Corwin; **Witnesses**: Thomas Cromwell, Daniel Rumboll; **Acknowledged**: 25: 11: 1658; **Recorded**: 25: 11: 1658.

JOHN SMITH to THOMAS HALE – (1:122) On 28 January 1658, John Smith of Salem (tailor) granted to Thomas Hale of Salem for a valuable consideration for which he was satisfied, a house and one acre of land at Salem bounded S by house and land of Mr. Endicott, E by land of John Symonds, N by Ruben Guppy, and W by the broad street that comes from the meeting house to the North river, with all appurtenances and privileges. **Signed**: John Smith; **Witnesses**: George Dean and John Kitchin; **Acknowledged**: 28: 11 month: 1658; **Recorded**: 3: 12: 1658.

JOHN PUTNAM, JR to ROBERT PRINCE - (1:123) On the 1st day of the 12th month 1658, John Putnam, Jr. of Salem (planter) granted to Robert Prince of Salem for 30 pounds, 20 acres of meadow in Salem, on the N of the river called Ipswich river, bordering on said river on the S and on the W with a spring which runs into the said river, and E with land of William Cantleburye of Salem, which he bought of Mr. George Corwin (merchant) and shooting up northward as far as the uplands. **Signed**: John Putnam; **Witnesses**: Edward Norrice, Jr and Joseph Hucheson; **Acknowledged**: 1: 12 mo: 1658; **Recorded**: 8: 12: 1658.

JEFFERIE MASSY to THOMAS PUTNAM – (1:124) On 31: 11 month: 1658, Jefferie Massy of Salem (planter) granted to Thomas Putnam of Salem (husbandman) for 7 pounds, 40 acres purchased of John Swazey, late of Salem, as appears by his bill of sale given to me, bearing date of the last day of June 1653, said land is bounded S by the farm of Mr. Price, N by the common, W on the great river; also 4 acres of meadow ground lying to the great river as near there unto, which said 40 acres of upland and 4 acres of meadow with all appurtenances, without let or molestation from the town of Rowley (Memorandum: It was agreed by the parties before the sealing and delivery hereof, that the warrantee against Rowly is only for 3 years, and that if any of the meadow shall be lost to Rowley, then said Massy shall allow said Putnam only 20 shillings per acre for so much as they recover (31: 11: 1658; witnesses: Jeffrey Massey; Thomas Putnam). **Signed**: Jeffery Massy; **Witnesses**: William Hathorne, Ann Hathorne; **Acknowledged**: 7: 12 mo: 1658; **Recorded**: 14: 12 mo: 1658.

JOHN PUTNAM to JOSIAH SOUTHWICK – (1:126) On 8: 1st month: 1659, John Putnam of Salem granted to Josiah Southwick of Salem, for "full satisfaction" ten acres of land lying in the North neck. **Signed**: John Putnam; **Witnesses**: Samuel Eborn and Edward Wharton; **Acknowledged**: 8: 1: 1659; **Recorded**: 8: 1st month: 1659.

JAMES UNDERWOOD to WILLIAM BROWNE (mortgage) – (1:126) On 15: 12 month: 1658, James Underwood of Salem mortgaged to William Brown of Salem, for 33 pounds, 8 shillings and 9 pence, a dwelling house in Salem by the South river, lying between Thomas Gegles and the house of Henry Trewe, with all the ground adjoining thereunto, to stand engaged for the payment of the above amount at or before the first of May next ensuing 1659. **Signed**: James Underwood; **Witnesses**: Abraham Browne and William Browne; **Acknowledged**: 21: 12 month: 1658.

WILLIAM TRASK to ROBERT PRINCE – (1:127) On 20: 10 month: 1655, William Trask of Salem granted to Robert Prince of Salem, for 20 pounds, 150 acres of upland in Salem, with 15 acres of meadow, being formerly the land of William Pester, lying between land of Thomas Putnam W and N and the land of --- on SE. **Signed**: William Trask; **Witnesses**: Samuel Archard and Elyas Stileman; **Acknowledged**: 14: 1: 1658/59; **Recorded**: 15: 1: 1659.

WILLIAM GIGGELES to NATHANIEL PUTNAM – (1:128) On the 7th day of the 12th month 1658, William Giggeles of Salem (ship's carpenter) granted to Nathaniel Putnam of Salem (farmer) for a valuable consideration paid in hand before the ensealing hereof, a farm of 50 acres of upland together with 2 acres and ½ of meadow, more or less, lying in the township of Salem, bordering on the N from the land of Job Swinerton of Salem and on the S by the land of Nathaniel Felton and Mr. Samuel Downing, having the land of Mr. John Endicot, Jr. on the E and the land of Isaac Bacon on the W. **Signed**: William Giggeles; **Witnesses**: Walter Price and Edward Norrice Jr.; **Acknowledged**: 7: 12: 1658; **Recorded**: 15: 1: 1659.

PHILIP CROMWELL to THOMAS and NATHAN PUTNAM – (1:130) On the 7th day of the 12th month, 1658, Philip Cromwell of Salem (butcher) granted to Thomas and Nathan Putnam of Salem (farmers) for a valuable consideration already paid, 150 acres of upland, with 10 acres of meadow, in Salem, lying on the west side of the Ipswich river, having the river for the bound westward, and on the east bordering on 50 acres of upland belonging to Thomas Putnam, which he bought of Mr. John Hathorne of Lynn and having land of Mr. Walter Price of Salem on the north, and on the S land of Giles Coree in Salem, now also in possession of said Thomas and Nathanie. Putnam, the meadow lying on the N of the river joining to 3 acres of meadow laid out to John Reeves of Salem, now in possession of said Thomas and Nathaniel Putnam, lying near also unto 4 acres laid out to Mr. Gardener's sons, now in hand of John Putnam, **Signed**: Philip Cromwell; **Witnesses**: John Marsh and Edward Norrice, Jr.; **Acknowledged**: 8: 1 month: 1658/9; **Recorded**: 15: 1 month: 1659.

JOHN REEVES to THOMAS and NATHANIEL PUTNAM – (1:131) On the 7th day of the 12th month, 1658, John Reeves of Salem (planter) granted to Thomas and Nathaniel Putnam of Salem (farmers) for a valuable consideration in hand paid, 20 acres of upland with 3 acres of meadow, lying in Salem on the S side of the Ipswich river, bordering on the north, and on the east adjoining land of Giles Core of Salem, now in possession of Thomas and Nathaniel Putnam, on the W bounded with land of George Corwin of Salem (merchant) and on the S with land of said Nathaniel Putnam and Edward Norice, Jr. **Signed**: John Reeves; **Witnesses**: Walter Price and Edward Norice, Jr.; **Acknowledged**: 7: 12: 1658; **Recorded**: 15: 1 month: 1659.

WALTER PRICE and THOMAS COLE to THOMAS and NATHANIEL PUTNAM – (1:133) On the 7th day of the 12th month 1658, Walter Price of Salem (merchant) and Thomas Cole of Salem (merchant) granted to Thomas and Nathaniel Putnam of Salem (farmers) for a valuable consideration already paid: This bill witnesseth that the town of Salem has granted to me, Walter Price of Salem, 100 acres of upland and 10 acres of meadow and unto Thomas Cole of Salem, 40 acres of upland and 4 acres of meadow, the upland lying on the S side of the Ipswich river, and having on the S land of Mr. Ruck, and E with land of said Thomas Putnam, which he bought of Jeffrey Massey, and adjoining W to the land of Mr. John Herbert, the meadow lying 10 acres on the N side of said river, bordering on the meadow of said Nathaniel Putnam on the W and the other 4 acres lying also on the N of said river, near the usual place of going over. **Signed**: Walter Price and Thomas Cole; **Witnesses**: John Marsh and Edward Norrice Jr; **Acknowledged**: 7: 12: 1658.

GILES COREY to THOMAS and NATHANIEL PUTNAM – (1:134) On 7: 12th month: 1658. Giles Corey of Salem (planter) granted to Thomas and Nathaniel Putnam of Salem (farmers) for a valuable consideration, 20 acres of upland in Salem, on the S side of the Ipswich River, having on the W the lands of John Reeves of Salem, now in possession of said Thomas and Nathaniel Putnam and the land of Mr. Phillip Cromwell of Salem and John Hathorne of Lynn on the E now in possession of Thomas and Nathaniel Putnam. **Signed**: Giles Corey [by mark]; **Witnesses**: Walter Price and Edward Norrice Jr; **Acknowledged**: 7: 12: 1658; **Recorded**: 15: 1: 1658.

WILLIAM BROWNE to SAMUEL SHATTUCK – (1:136) On the 13th of the 2nd month (called April) in 1655, William Browne of Salem (merchant) granted to Samuel Shattuck of Salem, for 36 pounds in hand, a dwelling house wherein formerly dwelt John Browne, with ¼ an acre of land between the house of Mr. John Halgrave E and the house of Robert Gutch on the W and abutting the street on the N, that comes from the neck direct to the meeting house in Salem. **Signed**: William Browne; **Witnesses**: Nicholas Potter and Richard More; **Acknowledged**: 27 Nov 1656; **Recorded**: 4: 2: 1659.

ANDREW and MARY WOODBERRY to DAVID CORWITHY – (1:137) On 2 July 1658, Andrew Woodberry (with wife Mary), of Salem, granted to David Corwithy of Salem, for 8 pounds paid in hand, one acre, bounded with some land of Francis Collins on the W and the common on the E. **Signed**: Andrew Woodberry and Mary Woodbury [by mark], who released dower rights; **Witnesses**: Philip Veren and Hillyard Veren; **Acknowledged**: 20: 5: 1658 by both before worshipful Major General Denison; **Recorded**: 8: 2: 1659.

EDWARD LUMMUS to LAURENCE SOUTHWICK – (1:138) On 22 March 1658/9, Edward Lummus of Ipswich (weaver) granted to Laurence Southwick of Salem for 7 pounds in hand paid, a dwelling house and 3 acres of land adjoining (with appurtenances), in Salem, bounded W with the common, E on the North river and S with land of said Laurence. **Signed**: Edward Lummus [by mark]; **Witnesses**: Joshua Tourland and Hillyard Veren; **Acknowledged**: 22: 1 month: 1658/9; **Recorded**: 8: 2: 1659.

JOSEPH GARDENER to RICHARD PRINCE – (1:139) On 28 March 1659, Joseph Gardener of Salem (mariner) granted to Richard Prince of Salem (tailor) for a valuable consideration paid, about half an acre of land, being part of the field that belongs to the house formerly in possession of Mr. Emanual Downing, in Salem, and this parcel of land being 6 pole in breadth at the end S against the street that comes from the meeting house, and 6 pole in breadth at that end, N that abuts against the narrow lane that goes to the pound, and the length of said land W is bounded with the highway that leads between Robert Grayes house and the said land to the North river, and the said length bounded E with land of said Joseph

Gardner. **Signed**: Joseph Gardener; **Witnesses**: William Hathorne and John Whiting; **Acknowledged**: 4: 2 mo: 1659; **Recorded**: 20: 2: 1659.

EDWARD NORRICE Sr. to JOHN MARSH – (1:141) On 31: 6th mon: 1657, Edward Norrice, Sr. of Salem (teacher of the church at Salem) granted to John Marsh of Salem, for a valuable consideration in hand paid, a dwelling house with 1 acre of land in Salem, standing by the North river, having the house and land of Isaac Page on the W and the house and land of John Williams on the E. (Written below: my bargain with Edward Waller was frustrated through non-payment according to the deed). **Signed**: Edward Norrice; **Witnesses**: Christopher Waller [by mark] and Edward Norice, Jr.; **Acknowledged**: 7: 12: 1658; **Recorded**: 20: 2: 1659.

RICHARD BISHOP to SAMUEL EBORNE – (1:142) On the 7th of the 2nd month 1659, Richard Bishop (husbandman) of Salem granted to Samuel Eborne of Salem, for 4 pounds, 10 shillings, four acres of upland, being the remaining part of a 10-acre lot; six acres of which was lately sold to John Pease, lying in the North neck of Salem, and this above 4 acres being bounded with some land of John Pease on the SW and some land of Henry Cook on the N & some land of Richard Bishop on the E. **Signed**: Richard Bishop; **Witnesses**: Sarah Batter & Hillyard Veren; **Acknowledged**: 7: 2 mo: 1659; **Recorded**: 20: 2: 1658/59.

JOSEPH and ANN GARDENER to SAMUEL GARDENER – (1:143) On the 13th of the 6th month 1656, Joseph Gardener (mariner) of Salem and Ann his wife granted to Samuel Gardener (mariner) of Salem, for 6 pounds in hand paid, ¾ of an acre of land being within the four acres of ground given them by their honored mother, Lucie Downing, with the house in Salem aforesaid, which said ¾ acres is to take such a breadth from the barn that is by the dwelling along by the street toward the E corner as may go cross through the ground to the lane on the N where the pound (pond?) standeth. Added at the end: Mrs. Ann Bradstreet, formerly the wife of Capt. Joseph Gardener did this 5: 2 mo: 1679, freely consent to the contents of this instrument before me. **Signed**: Simon Bradstreet, Dept. Governor. **Signed**: Joseph Gardener and Anne Gardener; **Witnesses**: Elias Stileman and Mary Stileman; **Acknowledged**: 22: 2: 1659; **Recorded**: 20: 2: 1658.

THOMAS ANTRUM to ISAACK BURNAP (Indenture) – (1:144) On 17: 11: 1658, an indenture was made between Thomas Antrum of Salem for 140 pounds and Isaack Burnap (son-in-law to the said Thomas), of the same town, deeding the farm and building with out houses, barne fences, which I the said Thomas Antrum bought of my brother Edmond Batter, lying in Salem, bounded E with land of Samuel Very, W with lands of

Thomas James and Mr. Johnson, N with land of Thomas Goldthwaite and S with the commons. The 140 pounds was to be paid as follows: on the 1st of May 1660, 20 pounds in beefe, pork, wheat, peas, barley, Indian & butter or English goods, to be paid at price current on or upon the 1st of May 1661, 20 pounds to be paid as is above expressed in the first payment, due at or before the 1st of May 12 months following; 20 pounds yearly the 1st of May, until the whole of the above 140 pounds be fully paid. The said Thomas Antrum only reserving unto myself and proper use while I live, the lower five rooms to the east of the dwelling house and the chamber over the parlor to the west. **Signed**: Thomas Antrum [by mark] and Isaack Burnap; **Witnesses**: Hillyard and Mary Veren; **Acknowledged**: 17: 11: 1658; **Recorded**: 20: 2: 1658.

WILLIAM ALLEN to SAMUEL GARDENER – (1:147) On 22 April 1659, William Allen of Manchester (carpenter) granted to Samuel Gardener of Salem (mariner) for a valuable consideration to me in hand, a parcel of land containing 8 poles of ground in Salem, near the meeting house, bounded N with the broad street that goes from the Meeting house down to the neck & the dwelling of Phillip Cromwell on the E, and the land of Richard Stileman on the S & W, the said 8 poles being in breadth next the street, 3 pole & running inward from the street the same breadth, that is to say 3 poles, so far as to make up the full measure of 8 poles. **Signed**: William Allen [by mark] and Elizabeth his wife [by mark] who released dower; **Witnesses**: Richard Gardener and Hilliard Veren; **Acknowledged**: 22: 2 mo: 1658; **Recorded**: 20: 2: 1659.

RALPH TOMPKINS to EDWARD GASKILL – (1:149) On 22 April 1659, Ralph Tompkins of Salem (planter) granted to Edward Gaskill of Salem (ship carpenter) for 9 pounds in hand paid, a dwelling house and about 1½ acres of land adjoining, with fences, appurtenances & privileges, being in Salem near the Tide mill, being the dwelling formerly of John Hart, bounded N with land of Joseph Boyce & rounded on the E, S & W with the town common, near unto drawn water brooke. **Signed**: Ralph Tomkins [by mark]; **Witnesses**: Joshua Turland and Hilliard Veren; **Acknowledged**: 22: 2: 1659; **Recorded**: 22: 2 mo: 1659.

JOSEPH GARDENER to SAMUEL GARDENER – (1:150) On 22 April 1659 Joseph Gardener of Salem (mariner) granted to Samuel Gardener of Salem (mariner) for a valuable consideration paid, about ¾ acre of land in Salem, being part of a field of 4 acres belonging formerly to Mr. Emanual Downing, the which ¾ acre lies at the E end of said field & bounded on the E with the town common, on the W with land of said Samuel Gardener (which was formerly bought also of said Joseph Gardener (as appears by a deed-at-large) & on the S bounded with the street that comes from the meeting house and against the land that goes from Daniel Rumball's to the south river & N with the land that goes from the pond to the common. **Signed**: Joseph Gardener: Mrs. Ann Bradstreet, formerly the wife of Capt. Joseph Gardener, freely consented 5: 2m: 1679; **Witnesses**: Richard Gardner, Samuel Shattock; George Gardener; **Recorded**: 23: 2: 1659.

THOMAS HALE to THOMAS WEST – (1:151) On 10 March 1658/9, Thomas Hale of Salem (glover) granted to Thomas West of Salem (planter) for a certain valuable consideration, a house and one acre of land which was by me bought lately of John Smith, being at Salem, bounded S by the house and land of Mr. Endicott, on the E by land of John Symonds, on the N by Ruben Guppi and on the W by the broad street that comes from the meeting house to the North river. **Signed**: Thomas Hale; **Witnesses**: Hillyard Veren and Phillip Veren; **Recorded**: 3: 3: 1659.

SAMUEL SHATTOCK to HANNAH SHATTOCK – (1:152) On 19: 3rd month: 1659, Samuel Shattock of Salem (feltmaker) appointed Hanna, his wife, his lawful attorney to do and act for me in my name in all matters case or cases whatsoever concerns me the said Samuel; to bye, sell, rent deed of sale, according to law, to ask, receive and recover by law, and to acquit and discharge…I give my said Attorney full power to make attorney or attorneys under her. **Signed**: Samuel Shattock; **Witnesses**: Richard Gardner, John Kitchin, Hillyard Veren; **Recorded**: 28 May 1659.

FRANCIS PERRY to WILLIAM BROWN – (1:153) On 26 June 1655, Francis Perry, now in the Island of Barbadoes (carpenter) do acknowledge to owe and stand justly indebted unto William Brown of Salem (merchant) the full and just sum of 7 pounds sterling to be paid at or before the 1st of June next…in good dry at muscovados sugar payable at some convenient storehouse near the Indian Bridge of Barbados at 3 pence per pound. **Signed**: Francis Perry; **Witnesses**: Nicholas Davison and William Brown, Jr.; **Recorded**: 28 May 1659.

HUGH PETERS (by CHARLES GOTT, Atty.) to GEORGE CORWIN – (1:154) On the 1st day of July 1659, Charles Gott of Wenham (having full power and authority given by Mr. Hugh Peters, sometimes pastor of the church of Christ in Salem, as his agent or attorney in these parts) granted to George Corwin of Salem (merchant) for 30 pounds sterling already paid in London, 4 acres of pasturage in Salem adjoining land of Mr. Ralph Fogg N and of Mr. George Emory S and E with the river and W with the highway. **Signed**: Charles Gott; **Witnesses**: Edward Norice Jr and John Hathorne; **Recorded**: 2: 5 mo: 1659.

HUGH PETERS (by CHARLES GOTT, Atty.) to GEORGE EMORY – (1:156-157) On the 1st day of July 1659, Charles Gott of Wenham (having full power and authority given by Mr. Hugh Peters, sometimes pastor of the Church of Christ in Salem, as his agent or attorney in these parts) granted to George Emory of Salem (chirurgeon) for 3 pounds in hand already paid, 1½ acres of salt marsh in Salem, on the other side of the river, over against & in sight of his now dwelling house, having the said river on the N and shooting up southwards toward the uplands. **Signed**: Charles Gott; **Witnesses**: Thomas Roote and Edward Norice, Jr; **Acknowledged**: 1: 5 mo: 1659; **Recorded**: 22: 5: 1659.

HUGH PETERS (by CHARLES GOTT, Atty.) to JOHN DEVEREUX – (1:157) On the 1st day of July 1659, Charles Gott of Wenham (having full power & authority given by Mr. Hugh Peters, sometimes pastor of the Church of Christ of Salem) granted to John Devereux of Marblehead (fisherman) for 100 pounds sterling in hand already paid, all the neck or parcel of ground at Marblehead containing 350 acres of ground, bounded W towards the forest River, Tinker's Island lying on the E, being bounded S towards the river head & Throgmorton's cove NW. **Signed**: Charles Gott; **Witnesses**: George Emery and Edward Norice, Jr.; **Acknowledged**: 1: 5: 1659; **Recorded**: 22: 5: 1659.

CHRISTOPHER WALLER to WALTER PRICE – (1:159) On the 7th of July 1659, Christopher Waller of Salem granted to Walter Price of Salem (shopkeep) for full value to me paid in hand, 16 acres of land in the field called North Field, being formerly a lot belonging to John Shipley, lying betwixt Francis Skerry's lot W and John Luff's lot, E. **Signed**: Christopher Waller [by mark]; **Witness**: John Croade; **Acknowledged**: 11: 5: 1659.

ROGER HASCOLL to OSMUND TRASK – (1:159) On the 29th day of the 4th month 1659, Roger Hascoll (Haskell) of Salem (farmer) sold for 3 pounds ten shillings (in hand paid) to Osmund Trask of Salem, (planter), half an acre of salt marsh situated on the Bass river side in Salem, bounded NW with land of Henry Herrick, SW with land of Robert Hibert, NE with land of Hugh Larkin, and bordering SE on the cove against Mr. Gaffeards (Giffords) point. **Signed**: Roger Hascall [by mark]; **Witnesses**: Edward Norice, Jr. and Robert Hebbert; **Acknowledged**: 30: 4: 1659; **Recorded**: 22: 5: 1659.

WILLIAM HASCALL to OSMUND TRASK – (1:161) On the 30th day of the 4th month 1659, William Hascall of Gloucester granted to Osmund Trask of Salem (planter) for 3 pounds to me in hand paid 20 acres of upland on the hither end of Birch plain within Salem, having land of Henry

Herrick & John Rayment E and land of John Weston S. **Signed**: William Hascall [by mark]; **Witnesses**: Edward Norice, Jr. & Robert Hibard; **Acknowledged**: 30: 4 mo: 1659; **Recorded**: 22: 5: 1659.

WILLIAM HASCALL to ROBERD HIBBIRD – (1:162) On the 30th day of the 4th month 1659, William Hascall of Gloucester granted to Roberd Hibbird of Salem (bricklayer) for 15 pounds 12 shillings in hand paid, 13 acres of upland in Salem, on the Bass river side, having said river on the W border & shooting up eastward to the rocks, next to the country highway & having land of Samuel Corning N and Nathaniel Marston S. **Signed**: William Hascall [by mark]; **Witnesses**: Edward Norice Jr. & Francis Skerry; **Acknowledged**: 30: 4: 1659; **Recorded**: 22: 5: 1659.

ROGER HASCOLL to ROBERT HIBBERD – (1:163) On the 29th day of the 4th month 1659, Roger Hascoll of Salem (farmer) granted to Robert Hibberd of Salem (bricklayer) for 6 pounds to me in hand paid, 1 acre of salt marsh on Bass river side within township of Salem, between land of Osmund Trask N and "my owne land" S and bordering E upon the upland & W upon the marsh of said Osmund Trask. **Signed**: Roger Hascall [by mark]; **Witnesses**: Elias Stileman Sr and Edward Norice Jr.; **Acknowledged**: 30: 4: 1659; **Recorded**: 22: 5: 1659.

RICHARD DODGE to EDMUND PATCH – (1:164) On the 20th of the 3rd month 1655, Richard Dodge of Salem granted to Edmund Patch of Salem (amount not given) 2 acres of upland in Salem being part of a farm granted unto him by Salem, said parcel butting on a parcel of land which Edmund bought of certain persons dwelling at the riverhead W and on a little swamp N and on the farm of Richard Dodge E and S. **Signed**: Richard Dodge and Edmund Patch [both by mark]; **Witnesses**: Thomas Fiske, Samuel Foster and Robert Lord; **Acknowledged**: 28 June 1659; **Recorded**: 27 July 1659.

JOHN ORMES to ROBERT FALLET – (1:166) On the 24th day of May 1659, John Ormes of Salem (carpenter) granted to Robert Fallet of Salem, for a valuable consideration in hand received, a house and 1½ acres of ground in Salem, bounded E by a house and land of said Robert Fallet, S by the river against Winter Is and, W by land of George Burch and N by the common. **Signed**: John Ormes; **Witnesses**: John Mascall & Hillyard Veren; **Acknowledged**: 29: 3: 1659; **Recorded**: 27 July 1759.

GEORGE and SUSAN BYAM to NEHEMIAH HOWARD – (1:167) On the 18th of the 3rd month 1657, George Byam and his wife Susan Byam of Salem, granted to Nehemiah Howard of Salem for 21 pounds to be paid as followeth: at or upon the 16th of the 8th month next ensuing 5 pounds; &

at as upon the 16th of the 2nd month 1658, five pounds & at or upon the 16th of the 8th month following, the remaining 11 pounds, his dwelling house and out houses with 20 acres of land, next to land of Nicholas Howard W and land of Abraham Warren E at the head of the Bass river, and also 4 acres of meadow in Wenham great meadow adjoining to the upland on the south. **Signed**: George [by mark] and Susan Byam [by mark], who released dower rights; **Witnesses**: Hillyard Veren and John Horne; **Acknowledged**: 2: 2 mo: 1659; **Recorded**: 9 August 1659.

HOLLINWORTH – CORWIN – EGGINTON (Account) – (1:169) On 14 May 1659, received by order of William Hollinworth for account of Mr. George Corwin, the net quantity of 3,700 pounds of Nusco: sugar for Jeremiah Egginton & myself. **Signed**: Robert Gale; **Recorded**: 13: 7 month: 1659.

EVAN THOMAS and ALICE KIRTLAND (Marriage Agreement) – (1:169) On the 14th of October 1659, Evan Thomas of Boston (vintner), being about to marry the widow Alice Kirtland of Lynn, agreed with said Kirtland not to sell or alienate her now dwelling house and land and appurtenances in Lynn, but to leave it to the disposing of the said Kirtland for the good of her children, according to the mind of her former husband Kirtland unless he the said Evan Thomas and widow Kirtland shall see further cause otherwise to dispose of it. **Signed**: Evan Thomas and Alice Kirtland; **Witnesses**: Nathanyell Kirtland, Richard Haven, John Hathorne; **Recorded**: 17 October 1659.

JOHN WILLIAMS to SAMUEL WILLIAMS – (1:170) On the 14th of December 1658, John Williams of Salem granted to Samuel Williams of Salem (cooper) for "a bill of 6 pounds to me now in hand, payable according to the tenor...by Samuel Williams & John Gedney of Salem & for other good causes and considerations," about one acre of land in Salem between land of John Gedney W and land of Daniel Rumball E, abutting on a common way towards the S and the other land of said John Williams towards the N. **Signed**: John Williams; **Witnesses**: John Marsh, Henry Skerry, William Howard; **Acknowledged**: 26: 1: 1659; **Recorded**: 25: 7: 1659.

RICHARD MOORE to HENRY SHRIMPTON – (1:171) On 20 September 1659, an indenture was made between Richard Moore of Salem (mariner) and Henry Shrimpton of Boston (brazier) for 95 pounds 6 shillings & 8 pence sterling, for his dwelling house with ¾ acre of ground...with the yard, warehouse & stable...bounded with ground of William Chichester SW, ground of Thomas Rix NE, bounded E & S with a creek, as also ½ part of the catch called the *Susan* with her sails, rigging &

all other furniture belonging to the said half part; Richard Moore to pay Henry Shrimpton 95 pounds 6 shillings 8 pence sterling money or good merchantable beaver at money price before the 1st of Nov ensuing date hereof but not immediately which will be in the year 1661 at the now dwelling house of Henry Shrimpton in Boston...sale to be void. **Signed**: Richard Moore and Henry Shrimpton; **Witnesses**: Ephraim Turner & Jonathan Negrus; **Acknowledged**: by Richard Moore, 20 Sept 1659; **Recorded**: 22: 7ber: 1659.

THOMAS TUCK and JOSEPH HARRIS to THOMAS HALE – (1:175) On the 8th of June 1659, Thomas Tuck and Joseph Harris, both of Salem, granted to Thomas Hale of Salem (leather dresser) for 4 pounds to said Thomas Tuck, 4 acres of land...in the north neck of Salem & bounded with the North river on the S, with land of Marke Searnayes W and land of Thomas Watson N and land of Henry Skerrie on E. **Signed**: Thomas Tuck and Joseph Harris [both by mark]; **Witnesses**: Henry Bayly & Hillyard Veren; **Acknowledged**: 13: 7: 1659; **Recorded**: 27: 7: 1659.

NICHOLAS BARTLETT to JOHN SOLLAS – (1:176) On The 16th of September 1659, Nicholas Bartlett of Salem (seaman) granted to John Sollas of Salem (seaman) for 9 pounds 10 shillings in hand to me, ten acres of land on Cape Ann side within limits of Salem, bounded with land of Robert Lemons E and of Mordecai Creford W and the sea S. **Signed**: Nicholas Bartlett [by mark]; **Witnesses**: Andrew Woodbery & Hillyard Veren; **Acknowledged**: 19: 7ber: 1659; **Recorded**: 26: 7: 1659.

EDWARD GASKILL to JOHN WILLIAMS – (1:178) On the 19th of 7ber 1659, Edward Gaskill of Salem (ship carpenter) granted to John Williams of Salem (fisherman) for 25 pounds, a dwelling house with outhouses, orchard, fences...with 20 acres of land adjoining...in the North neck within Salem...bounded with the N river, above the mill on the W and land of John Kitchin & Thomas Goldthwaite on the S & Henry Trask & Thomas Spooner on the N and land of above Edward Gaskill on the E. **Signed**: Edward Gaskill [by mark]; **Witnesses**: John Lambert [by mark], Hillyard Veren, Tobias Temple; **Acknowledged**: 19: 7: 1659; **Recorded**: 26: 7ber: 1659.

HENRY BARTHOLOMEW to ROBERT GRAY – (1:179) On the 13th of 7ber 1655, Henry Bartholomew of Salem granted to Robert Gray of Salem for 110 pounds, a dwelling house with 1½ acres of land adjoining, in Salem, bounded with land of Mr. John Endicott N and land of Mr. William Browne & Mr. John Gedney S...with fences, orchard, gardens & all other appurtenances. **Signed**: Henry Bartholomew; Mrs. Bartholomew yielded her rights of thirds; **Witnesses**: John Marston & Walter Price; **Acknowledged**: 10: 6 mo: 1659; **Recorded**: 26: 7: 1659.

ISRAIL TRUE to GEORGE GARDNER – (1:180) Before 22: 9 mo: 1659, Israil True, wife of Deceased Henry True, sometimes of Salem & now of Salisbury, for a valuable consideration to me in hand, granted to George Gardner of Salem (merchant) a dwelling house with ¼ acre of land...with apple trees, fences...and also a 10-acre lot...& ¾ acre of salt meadow, the house being in Salem, adjoining the house & ground of James Underwood N and the house & ground of Goodman Browning SE, the ten lying on the south field belonging to Salem, adjoining Mousers Cove W and Forest river S and land of Goodman Lord N; the marsh adjoining the said ten acres on the north, the river on the S & between some marsh of Samuel Archer & Goodman Skerry. **Signed**: Israil True [by mark]; **Witnesses**: Bridget Skerry & Hillyard Veren; **Acknowledged**: 22: 9 mo: 1659; **Recorded**: 23: 9: 1659.

JOHN SOUTHWICK to WILLIAM BURNELL – (1:182) On the 26th of the 9th month 1659, John Southwick of Salem (husbandman) granted to William Burnell of Pullen Point, Boston, for a valuable consideration to me in hand paid, a dwelling house & barn & outhouses...with 4 score acres of upland & meadow...in Salem, bounded with a highway which goes through the middest of the land & with land of widow Giles on the SW & of Mighill Shaflin on the NW & land of Henry Cook on the SE & Mr. Read's farm on the NE, as also all my stock of cattle & swine, viz: 3 cows, 2 steers of 3-years old, 2 yearlings, 6 oxen, 3 mares, 1 horse & 1 yearling horse colt & 6 small swine; also my plow & cart tacklin; also 11 acres of fresh meadow in a meadow called Williston's Meadow & bounded with meadow of Goodman Hart on the N & S & meadow of Goodman Townsend on the NW & upland of Samuel Hucheson on the SW & 3 acres of salt marsh adjoining marsh of Jeffrey Massey on the NW & bounded with Williston's river on the SW. **Signed**: John Southwick [by mark]; **Witnesses**: Joshua Turland & Hillyard Veren; **Acknowledged**: 26: 9: 1659; **Recorded**: 26: 9: 1659.

DANIEL SOUTHWICK to JOHN BLETHIN – (1:184) On the 28th of the 9th month 1659, Daniel Southwick of Salem granted to John Blethin of Lynn, for 40 pounds to me in hand paid, a dwelling house with a barn & outhouses with 3 acres of upland & 1½ acres of salt marsh...in Salem, bounded with the common on the W & with a brook called strong water brook on the S & land of Henry Trask on the N & some meadow of Captain Trask on the E; also 10 acres of land on the North Neck bounded with land of Anthony Needham on the W & Josiah Southwick on the E; also 2 acres of meadow lying by Ipswich river in Salem, bounded with the river on the E; some common upland on the W & some meadow of Job Swinerton on the N. **Signed**: Daniel Southwick; **Witnesses**: Thomas Rooten and Hillyard Veren; **Acknowledged**: 28: 9ber: 1659; **Recorded**: 28: 9: 1659.

SAMUEL RANDAL to WILLIAM BROWN – (1:186) On the 8th day of September 1659, I Samuel Randel now at Boston…bound for London in the good ship called the *Prudent Marye* do acknowledge myself to owe and to be indebted unto Mr. William Browne of Salem…the sum of 30 pounds, to be paid unto him…the 1st day of May next ensuing. **Signed**: Samuell Randal; **Witnesses**: Henry Webb & Elisha Huchinson; **Recorded**: 28: 10: 1659.

GILES COREY to JOHN NORTON – (1:187) On the 14th of the 8th month 1659, Giles Corey of Salem (planter) granted to John Norton of Salem (carpenter) for 44 pounds, 2 dwelling houses in Salem, one the now dwelling house of Giles Corey & is the corner house next to the bridge; the other being the house where Mr. Alderman formerly dwelt & is near adjoining Giles Corey's house…together with all land belonging, containing 1½ acres within the fence near unto the bridge; also 10 acres of upland in the North field, formerly in possession of Mr. Alderman of Salem. The 44 pounds is to be paid in the frame of a house to be finished & set up where Giles Corey shall appoint at or before the 1st day of March next ensuing, containing 20 foot in length, 15 in breadth & 8 foot stud; also 5 pounds…in goods at Mr. William Brown's of Salem…to be delivered, and the other 29 pounds to be paid in cattle; i.e. 4 milch cows of a reasonable age, & one mare colt, to be prized by any 2 indifferent men, except a butcher & to be delivered at or before the 1st day of May next ensuing…provided that if default of payments aforesaid shall happen either in whole or in part within 14 days after the 1st of May next ensuing, then it shall be lawful for the said Giles Corey to re-enter & take possession of the premises. **Signed**: Giles Corey [by mark]; **Witnesses**: Edward Norrice, Jr., Jonathan Corwin & Henry Kenys; **Acknowledged**: 15: 8 mo: 1659; **Recorded**: 15: 11: 1659.

RICHARD HIDE to EDWARD HILLYARD – (1:189) On the 26th of October 1657, Richard Hide of Salem (carpenter) granted to Edward Hillyard of Salem (seaman) for 19 pounds 10 shillings, a house and half the ground lying behind the house, containing ¼ acre in Salem, next to the house of Andrew Woodbery on the E. **Signed**: Richard Hide; **Witnesses**: Edward Norrice, Nehemiah Hayward; **Acknowledged**: 26: Oct: ---; **Recorded**: 18: 11: 1659.

CHARLES GOTT (agent for HUGH PETERS) to BENJAMIN FELTON – (1:191) On the 8th of the 12th month 1659, Charles Gott of Wenham (having full power & authority given him by Hugh Peters, sometimes pastor of the Church in Salem as his agent in these parts) granted to Benjamin Felton of Salem (turner) for 12 pounds, a dwelling house in Salem, with a parcel of ground adjoining, containing about ¼ acre...having land of Ralph Fogg on the S & W and bordering E upon the street, & N upon the lane, being the corner house, next to the now dwelling house of Mr. Edmond Batter. **Signed**: Charles Gott; **Witnesses**: William Hathorne & Edward Norice; **Recorded**: 8: 12 mo: 1659.

RICHARD WAYE to SAMUEL VERY – (1:192) On the 6th of October 1656, Richard Waye of Dorchester granted to Samuel Very of Salem, for 4 score & ten pounds (paid in part and the residue secured to be paid by Samuel Very of Salem) a farm or farm house...being near the farm house that is or late was Mr. Edmond Batter's of Salem, with 10 acres...adjoining which sometimes was in the possession of Joshua Veren & one acre of land fenced in...on this side of the water next to the town of Salem & 20 acres...which was part of Mr. Edmond Batter's farm, & 160 acres...lying at Cedar pond, with all the meadow belonging except about 2 acres of meadow which Phillip Veren, late husband of Dorcas Veren gave to his son Hillyard Veren, in his last will & testament, all which several parcels are contained in a deed of sale from Dorcas Veren of Salem, widow, unto Frances Perry of Salem, dated 3: 8mo: 1649; also 10 acres sometimes in the tenure of Hilliard Veren, the said farm on one side & land of Zacheus Cortes on the other side; & one acre of land sometimes Edmond Batter's where the house of Phillip Veren Jr (deceased) stood, & about 1½ acres exchanged with the town on the S side of the brook near the farm & also 14 acres bounded with a parcel of ground of Thomas Goldthwaite on the N & 10 acres on the E & to the S a little below a rock known as Wigwam rock & W on Thomas Antrum with a small strip of land running down to the river to the S containing about 2 rods. **Signed**: Richard Way & wife Ester Way. Hester Way released dower; **Witnesses**: Temperence Smith, Robert Howard, notary public; **Acknowledged**: 20: 8: 1656; **Recorded**: 16: 12: 1659.

RICHARD WAYE to SAMUEL VERY – (1:197) On 19 May 1658, Richard Waye of Dorchester, Suffolk County, with Ester Waye, granted to Samuel Very of Salem for a valuable consideration in hand received, 5 acres of meadow in Salem...lying over the brook next to Francis Johnson's, the remainder to begin from Thomas Antrum's meadow next to the beaver dam & so upwards to make the 5 acres...the said 5 acres of marsh which Richard Waye purchased amongst other lands of Edmond Batter of Salem...bearing date of 19: 11 mo: 1652, and which other lands

were since sold unto Very by the said Way...bearing date 6: 8 mo: 1656.
Signed: Richard & Ester Waye. Wife Ester Way yielded dower rights.
Witnesses: Jasper Rush & Robert Howard; **Acknowledged**: 19: 3: 1658;
Recorded: 16: 12: 1659.

BENJAMIN FELTON claim against **HENRY HARROD** – (1:199) On 27: 12th month: 1659, Benjamin Felton laid claim to 5 acres of land lying in the South field now in the possession of Henry Harrod and bounded with some land of Widow Jegles on the S, Henry Harrod on the N and the south Harbor on the E.

THOMAS WIGGINS to JOHN PORINGTON (Power of Attorney) – (1:200) 3: March: 1660. I, Thomas Wiggins of Rustport in the New Netherlands have 2 years since or upwards made unto my wife, then in Boston, a letter of attorney to demand, recover & receive all my debts within the jurisdiction of Boston...which my wife gave unto Thomas Wheeler of Lynn...in the presence of Capt. Thomas Marshall & John Hathorne; I Thomas Wiggin do appoint John Porington of mash page kills in the Netherlands to demand & receive of the said Thomas Wheeler, my attorney, all such debts recovered belonging unto me & do also appoint the said John Porington to receive power of my said attorney to recover all such debts as he has not recovered; I do...give unto said John Porrington my full power & lawfull authority to call my attorney to account & to receive on my behalf all those debts my attorney hath recovered belonging to me as if I myself were there personally. **Signed**: Thomas Wiggins [by mark]; **Witness**: Daniel Denton.

WILLIAM VINSON to JOHN ROE: - (1:201) On 28: 10 mo: 1651, William Vinson of Gloucester granted to John Roe of Gloucester, for 16 pounds in hand paid, his farm lying in Gloucester, which he bought of George Norton, & given by the town to said Norton, namely, 40 acres of upland & 12 acres of salt marsh...lying near little good harbour, bounded & laid out by the town measurers...as recorded in the towne booke, except a little amount of upland that adjoins to John Collins & Goodman Jackson's measure. **Signed**: William Vinson [by mark]; **Acknowledged**: 17: 7th mo: 1659, with wife Sarah yielding rights; **Witnesses**: Robert Tucker & Elizabeth Tucker [by mark]; **Recorded**: 11: 1: 1660.

THOMAS HALE to HILLYARD VEREN – (1:202) On 30 December 1659, Thomas Hale (leather dresser) of Salem granted to Hillyard Veren of Salem, for 4 pounds 10 shillings in hand paid, 4 acres of land lately bought by Thomas Hale of Thomas Tuck & Joseph Harris as by deed of sale, dated 8: June 1659, lying...in the north neck...within the limits of Salem & bounded with the north river on the S & some land of Mark Fermays on the W & some land of Thomas Watson on the N & some land of Henry Skerry on the NE and a cove on the E. **Signed**: Thomas Hale; **Acknowledged**: 20: 12 mo: 1659; **Witnesses**: John Lovett & Mary Lovett [by mark]; **Recorded**: 11: 1: 1660.

LT. THOMAS MARSHALL to FRANCIS BURRELL (Indenture) – (1:203) On the 14th of the 10th month 1655, Lt. Thomas Marshall, of the Military Co of the town of Reading in Middlesex County, granted to Francis Burrell of Lynn, for 8 pounds sterling paid by Francis Burrell, a parcel of meadow…in the 1st division in Rumney Marsh in Lynn, containing 4 acres, bounded E with the marsh of Thomas Marshall, which was lately in possession of Capt. Bridges, & W with the marsh of Francis Burrell, lately in possession of Andrew Mansfield, abutting N on the upland lot & S on the common that parts the 1st & 2nd division of lots. **Signed**: Thomas Marshall; **Acknowledged**: 1: 10 mo: 1658; **Witnesses**: Oliver Purchase & James Axey; **Recorded**: 11: 1: 1660.

JOHN HORNE to WALTER PRICE – (1:206) On the 1st day of the 10th month 1650, John Horne (carpenter) & Frances Horne, his wife both of Salem, granted to Walter Price (merchant) of Salem for 150 pounds already paid, a dwelling house wherein said John Horne lately dwelt, together with ¼ of an acre of land…in Salem, having the now dwelling house of the said Walter Price on the E, being the corner house in the same street near the meeting house. **Signed**: John & Frances Horne; **Acknowledged**: 21: 12 mo: 1659; **Witnesses**: William Hathorne & Edward Norice; **Recorded**: 25: 2 mo: 1660.

CHARLES GOTT (for Mr. HUGH PETER) to WALTER PRICE – (1:207) On the 9th day of the 12th month 1659, Charles Gott (agent) of Wenham, having full power given unto him by Mr. Hugh Peters of the Church of Christ at Salem, granted to Walter Price (merchant) of Salem for 9 pounds already paid, 5 acres of upland in Salem in south field, near the town, having the river on the W & the salt marsh now in hands of Mr. George Emory N, & bordering E on the land of Daniel Rumboll and S on [blank—no more description given]. **Signed**: Charles Gott; **Acknowledged**: 9: 12 mo: 1659; **Witnesses**: Edward Norice & John Corwin; **Recorded**: 15: 2: 1660.

JOHN CROAD to Mr. WALTER PRICE – (1:208) On the 6th day of April 1660, John Croad (merchant) of Salem granted to Mr. Walter Price of Salem for a valuable sum to him in hand paid, his full & whole interest of fish & traine oil, that hath been and shall be produced by three fishing shallops at Marblehead, kept there on fishing, at Mr. Moses Maverick's Island, from the beginning of October last past, until the last of May next ensuing... it is intended that the fisherman's wages together with the men that have worked ashore, in making the fish, be fully paid out of the said fish & traine. **Signed**: John Croad; **Witnesses**: Moses Maverick & Hillyard Veren; **Recorded**: 25: 2: 1660.

HENRY SKERRY, Sr. to ROBERT TEMPLE – (1:210) On the 23rd of April 1660, Henry Skerry, Sr. (cordwainer) of Salem granted to Robert Temple (tailor) of Salem for 10 shillings in hand paid, 8 pole of land lying in Salem, in breadth 2 pole E and W & in length 4 pole N & S, bounded on the N & W with some land of John Symonds, & on the S with land of John Endicott Esq. & on E with a lane. **Signed**: Henry Skerry; **Witnesses**: Hillyard Veren, Isaack Williams, Christopher Waller [by mark]; **Recorded**: 25: 2: 1660.

THOMAS MARSHALL to WALTER PRICE – (1:211) On the 25th of April 1660, Thomas Marshall of Lynn granted to Walter Price (merchant) of Salem, for a valuable consideration already paid, 40 acres of upland & meadows in Lynn, being part of his farm, formerly bought of Capt. Robert Bridges, lying within the field that is fenced in, at the S side of said field, adjoining some land of Allen Breed...20 acres of the aforesaid 40 acres is to be marsh. **Signed**: Thomas Marshall; **Acknowledged**: 25: 2: 1660 (by Capt. Thomas Marshall); **Witnesses**: Hillyard Veren & Anna Hathorne; **Recorded**: 25: 2: 1660.

WILLIAM ALLEN – (1:212) On 8 May 1660, William Allen of Manchester laid claim to a certain parcel of land containing 8 poles, lying in a field formerly in possession of Richard Stileman, upon which land the then dwelling house of the said Stileman was & situated near the meeting house in Salem.

EMANUEL CLARKE for EDWARD BARTON – (1:213) [no date & no signature] Emanuel Clarke, attorney of Edward Barton do in the main & stead of said Edward Barton lay claim to a certain parcel of land containing about ½ acre upon which there was a house lying in Marblehead, adjoining the waterside at leggs cove, so called, & also about 3 acres upon the necke side which land was formerly lawfully bought and possessed by said Barton of Richard Hide, shipright, but now illegally possessed & withheld by William Nicke.

HENRY KERRY to WILLIAM FLINT – (1:213) On 28 February 1659, Henry Kerry (husbandman) of Salem granted to William Flint of Salem for 35 pounds in hand paid, a dwelling house...together with 3 acres of ground adjoining...in Salem near the brickill, bounded with land of Richard Adams toward the S & SE, the land of said William Flint toward the NE &

the street toward the NW. **Signed**: Henry Kerry; **Acknowledged**: 28: 12 mo: 1659; **Witnesses**: Joshua Turland & Hillyard Veren; **Recorded**: 14: 3: 1660.

WALTER PRICE (Executor for FREEBORNE BALCH) to BENJAMIN BALCH – (1:214) On 20th of the 11th month 1658, Walter Price (executor & administrator unto Freeborne Balch) of Bass River, Salem, granted to Benjamin Balch of Bass River, Salem, for 20 pounds and ½ of the 5 acres of upland & meadow in the field called the planter's marsh, formerly belonging to John Balch; at Bass River, all that part of the farm…which John Balch deceased hath given by will unto Freeborne Balch. If Freeborne Balch appear to be alive, then this bargain to be void. **Signed**: Walter Price; **Acknowledged**: 26: 3: 1660; **Witnesses**: Hillyard Veren & Theodore Price; **Recorded**: 26: 3: 1660.

BENJAMIN BALCH to WALTER PRICE – (1:216) On the 20th of the 11th month 1658, Benjamin Balch (husbandman) of Salem granted to Walter Price (shopkeeper) of Salem, for value to him in hand paid, ½ of the 5 acres of upland and meadow lying in the field called the planters' marsh, lying between Francis Skerry on the S side & Mr. George Emory on the N side. **Signed**: Benjamin Balch; **Acknowledged**: 26: 3 mo: 1660; **Witnesses**: Hillyard Veren & Theodore Price; **Recorded**: 26: 3: 1660.

JOHN TURNER to JOHN BROWNE – (1:217) On 23 June 1659, at Barbadoes, John Turner acknowledged that he had received from Mr. John Browne, one Negro woman called Cate, for which he engaged to deliver unto said John Browne or his order, one choice young Negro woman, such as the said Browne or his assigns should accept of out of some ship that does shortly arrive at this island. **Signed**: John Turner; **Recorded**: 20: 4: 1660.

RICHARD COYE to SIMON BRADSTREET (mortgage) – (1:217) On 27 May 1660, Richard Coye (husbandman) of Wenham mortgaged to Simon Bradstreet of Andover, for 30 pounds in hand paid, his dwelling house, where he now lived…in Wenham, with the house lot or land adjoining, containing 4 acres…to said Simon Bradstreet…provided that if said Richard Coye…shall pay or cause to be paid to said Simon Bradstreet…the just & full sum of 40 pounds in good merchantable wheat at Ipswich at price current…or other payment that said Simon shall accept of, at 4 several payments, that is to say, 10 pounds on the 3rd Tuesday in May next…1661 & 10 pounds more upon the same day 12 months after…and so 10 pounds a year at the day & place & in kind before mentioned, until the aforesaid 4 payments be fully complete, that then this bargain & sale to be void & of no effect, otherwise to remain in force, the place of payment is to be at the meeting house at Ipswich or any other place within a half mile that the said Symond...shall appoint and the said Richard do hereby covenant & promise to pay or cause to be paid to the said Simon...the four payments... **Signed**: Richard Coye; **Witnesses**: Daniel Dennison & Samuel Archerd; **Recorded**: 30: 4: 1660.

GEORGE KEYSAR to NICHOLAS POTTER (indenture) – (1:219) On 3 July 1648, George Keysar of Lynn granted to Nicholas Potter of Lynn, for 5 pounds, 4 shillings, one parcel of meadow in Rumney Marsh on the old dividend, lying for 12½ acres in the town's book...the said lot lying E on land of John Gillow, S on land of Richard Johnson, W on land of Thomas Townsend, N on the upland. The said George Keysar did firmly by these presence, bind himself...in the full sum of ten pounds to defend and protect the aforesaid Nicholas Potter. **Signed**: George Keser; **Acknowledged**: 7 Feb 1656; **Witnesses**: Edward Burcham & Richard Mower; **Recorded**: 28 Aug 1660.

THOMAS BOWEN to ROBERT CODNER – (1:220) On 10 August 1660, Thomas Bowen (fisherman) of Marblehead granted to Robert Codner (fisherman) of Marblehead, for 20 pounds in hand paid, one dwelling house with about ¾ of an acre of ground in Marblehead, bounded with some land of John Stacy NE, land of Christopher Lattamore on the S, & Samuel Conde on the SW, the highway on the NE; & to be understood that the cow's lease which belonged to him the said Thomas Bowen, upon the town commons is not intended in the aforementioned sale. **Signed**: Thomas & Eliza Bowen [both by mark]; **Acknowledged**: 10: 6: 1660; Elizabeth Bowen, wife, released dower rights; **Witnesses**: Mary Veren & Hillyard Veren; **Recorded**: 20: 6: 1660.

THOMAS BROWNING & SAMUEL ARCHARD (appraisal) – (1:222) On 10: 10 month: 1660, the testimony of Thomas Browning (aged about 73 years) and Samuel Archard (aged 52 years) deposed that the said Thomas, being chosen by Henry True and said Samuel being chosen by Major Gibbons to apprize the house that some time was Mr. John Strattons & at that time in the hands or disposing of Major Gibbons & to be sold to the said Henry True, according as the above mentioned apprisers did value the said house...at 4 pounds together with the ground adjoining, both house and land in Salem, by the south river side, adjoining the house & land of said Thomas Browning (and this was about 15 or 16 years ago), taken upon oath by both the parties above mentioned before me William Hathorne.

HANNA SHATTOCK to Mr. JOHN GARDNER – (1:223) On 28 May 1659, Hanna Shattock, wife of Samuel Shattock & being lawful attorney of said husband, for a valuable consideration to her in hand paid, granted to Mr. John Gardner (mariner) of Salem, a dwelling house with a shop & about ¼ acre of land…in Salem…bounded with the broad street that comes from the meeting house on the N, with the dwelling of Richard Prince on the E & some ground of Nathaniel Pitman on the S, & adjoining to the dwelling of Richard Gardner on the W. **Signed**: Hannah Shattock [by mark]; **Witnesses**: Hillyard Veren & William Browne Jr.; **Recorded**: 20: 6: 1660.

THOMAS MARSHALL's mare – (1:224) There was taken up by Thomas Marshall of Lynn, a mare of an iron gray color & a bit cut out of the right ear, being prized by Mark Graves of Andover & Robert Burgess of Lynn at 12 pounds. **Recorded**: 12: 11: 1658.

THOMAS PUTNAM's mare – (1:224) There was a black mare with a white face taken up by Thomas Putnam of Salem about 2 months ago & "cried" in Salem 3 several lecture days & order taken for the "crying" of her…according to law & apprised by Richard Hucheson & Joshua Ray at 12 pounds. **Recorded**: 3: 10: 1658.

GOODMAN MARSHALL – (1:225) On 23: 10: 1659, Goodman Marshall of Lynn, took up a stray mare & colt & were apprized by Mathew Farrington & John Farrington at 16 pounds. **Recorded**: 28: 10: 1659.

Footnote - (1:225) 3 December 1874, at the Essex Registry of Deeds, Southern District at Salem, Mass.: The foregoing copy of the First Book of Records for Salem & vicinity was made in 1855 under the direction of the County Commissioners. It has now been examined and converted and is a true copy of the original. **Attested**: Ephraim Brown, Registrar.

***
Conclusion of Book 1 of Essex County Deeds
***

ESSEX COUNTY DEEDS Book 2

BRAY WILKINS and JOHN GINGION to RICHARD BELLINGHAM (mortgage) – (2:1) On 10: March 1659, Bray Wilkins (husbandman) of Lynn and John Gingion (taylor) of Lynn granted to Richard Bellingham, Esq. of Boston, for the securing of the payment of 225 pounds sterling with interest & forbearance at 8%, according to agreement: granted that parcel of land or farm, containing 700 acres, lying on the head of Salem to the NW from the said town and there being within the said place a hill where an Indian plantation sometime had been, & a pond, & about 100 or 150 acres of meadow; all which 700 acres of land being part meadow, we the said Bray Wilkins & John Gingion late purchased of said Bellingham & which the said Bellingham had by grant from the General Court of the Colony, as by an order of the said court bearing date the 6 day of September 1638. 25 pounds to be paid at or before the 29th day of September next ensuing & 100 pounds more of the said sum of 225 pounds...from the day of the date hereof at or before the 16th day of November which shall be in the year of our Lord 1661, and 100 pounds more residue of the said sum...from the day of the date hereof at or before the 16th day of November which shall be in the year of our Lord 1662, in such goods at current merchants price, as is agreed upon, according to the specialty thereof; made & bearing date the 9th day of this present month of March 1659. [Postscript] No use is to be expected for the 25 pounds, being the first payment before mentioned. The release or discharge is entered foll. 2d. **Signed**: Bray Wilkins & John Gingell; **Acknowledged**: 21 April 1660; **Witnesses**: Henry Phillips & Robert Howard not publ.; **Recorded**: 12: 5 mo: 1660.

BRAY WILKINS & JOHN GINGELL to RICHARD BELLINGHAM – (2:4) On 20 April 1660, in accomplishment of the bargain between Richard Bellingham of Boston, Esq. of the one part & Bray Wilkins & John Gingell, both of Lynn, on the other part, concerning a farm of 700 acres, as by deed bearing date 9 March 1659, style of England, Bray Wilkins & John Gingell...grant unto said Richard Bellingham, that in case they hereafter discover & use any mines or minerals so as they or any of them shall make 100 pounds per annum, they shall pay or deliver unto said Bellingham the full sum of 10 pounds sterling per annum which said grant should have been inserted in the afore recited deed. [paragraph after recording] We as Executors to the worshipful Mr. Bellingham's last will acknowledge ourselves satisfied concerning this mortgage & desire that it may be entered at the foot of the record. *Signed*: John Oxenbridge, James Allen & Anthony Stoddard. On 10: 2 mo: 1673, Mr. Anthony Stoddard agreed & owned the subscription to be his hand, & affirmed that the subscription of Mr. Oxenbridge & Mr. Allen were both of their own writing. **Signed**: Bray Wilkins & John Gingell; **Acknowledged**: 21 April 1660; **Witnesses**: Robert Howard (notary) & Mary Howard; **Recorded**: 12: 5 mo: 1660.

ANN WOODBERY to GEORGE CORWIN – (2:5) On the 1st day of the 6th month, 1660, Ann Woodbery (widow) of Salem granted to George Corwin (merchant) of Salem ¾ of an acre together with a small dwelling house formerly built upon it in Salem, near the meeting house, having the now dwelling houses of Mr. Walter Price W & of Isaack Williams E, & bounded N with land of John Horne & Mr. Gedney, & S with the street. **Signed**: Ann Woodbery [by mark] 1: 6th month: 1660; **Witnesses**: William Hathorne & Edward Norrice; **Recorded**: 6: 6m: 1660.

RICHARD RAYMENT to WALTER PRICE – (2:7) On 27 August 1660, Richard Rayment (mariner) of Salem granted to Walter Price (merchant) of Salem for valuable sums in hand paid, ¼ part of the good ketch *Hopewell* of Salem, of 30 tons burden, now riding at anchor in Boston Harbor, with the ¼ part of all her masts, sails, sailyards, anchors, cables, roades, ropes, cords, tackle apparel, boat & furniture belonging to said Ketch & all right & title & interest of the same...warrant & defend, against all persons, for 1 whole year & a day next after the date hereof, according to the laws of Oleron, perils of the seas, fire & enemies only excepted. **Signed**: Richard Rayment; **Witnesses**: John Croad & Theodore Price; **Recorded**: 28: 6: 1660.

ROBERT TEMPLE to THOMAS PUTNAM – (2:8) On 10 August 1660, Robert Temple (tailor) of Salem granted to Thomas Putnam (farmer) of Salem for 30 shillings in hand paid, a parcel of 8 poles in Salem, 2 poles in breadth to the E & W end & in length 4 poles N & S, bounded N & W with land of John Symonds & S with land of John Endicott, Esq., & on the E with a lane that leads down to the North River. **Signed**: Robert Temple [by mark]; **Acknowledged**: 9: 8: 1660; **Witnesses**: Hillyard Veren & Theodore Price; **Recorded**: 4: 10 mo: 1660.

JOHN RUCK to sons JOHN RUCK & THOMAS RUCK – (2:10) On 8 December 1660, John Ruck of Salem granted for love and affection to his sons John Ruck & Thomas Ruck 100 acres of land, partly in Salem and partly in Topsfield, adjoining land of the Putnams on W & lands of William Nichols on the NE and the meadow of Putnam on the [blank]. **Signed**: John Ruck; **Acknowledged**: 7ber: 15: 1660 by John Ruck, Sr.; **Witnesses**: Thomas Ruck, Sr. & John Richmond; **Recorded**: 4: 10: 1660.

JOHN ANDREWS to HENRY RHOADS – (2:11) On 14 September 1660, John Andrews (gentleman) of Lynn, with consent of Sarah his wife, who relinquished her thirds, sold for 39 pounds sterling, to Henry Rhoads (yeoman) of Lynn, 45 acres which the town of Lynn formerly granted unto Mr. Timothy Tomlins, bounced E by Thomas Wheeler's land, and W by land of the Iron Works, N on the creek that parts it and the Iron Works land, & S on town common. **Signed**: John Andrews; **Acknowledged**: 28: 9ber: 1660; **Witnesses**: Edmond Batter & George Keiser; **Recorded**: 10: 10 mo: 1660.

ELEAZER HOLYOKE to GEORGE KEYSER & JOHN ANDREWS – (2:14) On 19 June 1660, whereas Mr. Edward Holyoke lately deceased did by his last will & testament, declare that he had given to his son Eleazer Holyoke, upon marriage with Mr. Pinchon's daughter, all his lands in Lynn, I...for certain considerations...grant unto my beloved Brethren, George Keyser & John Andrews, of those lands, a certain portion of salt marsh in Rumney Marsh, in the 2nd division, 10 or 12 acres. They are to have it from the 1st of April next & so forever, and are to share it between them in 2 equal portions. [Added after signature] We, George Keyser & John Andrews both of Lynn, do assign & make over all our right in this deed unto Henry Rhodes & to his heirs...*Signed*: George Keyser & John Andrews (with consent of Sarah Andrews) 22 July 1660. *Acknowledged*: 28: 9ber: 1660; *Witnesses*: Edmond Batter & George Davis; **Signed**: Eleazer Holyoke; **Witnesses**: John Tuttle & John Mathews [by mark].

Corp. JOHN ANDREWS to Capt. THOMAS MARSHALL (mortgage) – (2:15) On 16 May 1660, Corporal John Andrews of Lynn granted to Capt. Thomas Marshall of Lynn, for 300 pounds sterling in hand paid, all that parcel of upland and marsh that joins together, on which the said John Andrews now dwells, with all buildings thereupon, which land & marsh is bounded with the county highway NW & W, and S with Rumney Marsh fence & land of Allen Breed & the near swamp, as the line stretches from the land of Allen Breed to a red oak tree, marked close by the country highway; and E with the River & a small parcel of salt marsh of Mr. Needham's, called by the name of Ferry Point; also 20 acres in the 1st division in Rumney Marsh bounded N with the fence as it now stands between it & the land of John Doolittle, & S with the marsh of Francis Burrell, W with the marsh of John Diven, E with the common that parts the 1st & 2nd division of lots; also 45 acres, at least, of upland & meadow which the town formerly gave unto Mr. Timothy Tomlins, bounded E with the land of Thomas Wheeler, W with land belonging to the Iron works, N with a little brook & S with the town Common; also half the fresh meadow that lies under the W side of the Rocks, that lie on the W end of said 45 acres, also 10 acres of upland which was formerly Capt. Walker's & is bounded with land of Mr. Edward Tomlins, S with land of Edward Baker, W with land of William Merriam, and N with the town common, all of which parcels of land & marsh lie in Lynn, on the W side of Lynn river...Nevertheless, if John Andrews shall pay to Thomas Marshall 300 pounds, 200 pounds before 29 Oct 1660 in corn, cattle and English goods, the corn or cattle to be paid at the house of said John Andrews in Lynn and to be paid in English goods either at Boston or Salem, and give said Thomas a month's warning how much he will pay in each payment, and 50 pounds more on 29 Oct 1661 & 1662, etc... this mortgage shall be void. **Signed**: John Andrews; **Acknowledged**: 17: 3 mo: 1660; **Witnesses**: Andrew Mansfield & Bethia Mansfield; **Recorded**: 1: 11: 1660.

Caveat: Thomas Marshall to Simon Bradstreeet: On 30 November 1660, Thomas Marshall "of Concord" set over unto Simon Bradstreet of Andover, all my right and interest in this mortgage or bill of sale, with all dues & demands now or hereafter due from John Andrews to satisfy a debt of about 100 pounds with just damages, the remainder of said debt being paid, to be resigned to said Thomas Marshall, giving full power to said Symon Bradstreet to re-enter upon said farm and do whatever I myself might do. **Signed**: Thomas Marshall; **Witness**: Walter Price; **Recorded**: 4: 11: 1660.

WALTER PRICE & RICHARD COOKE from JOHN CROAD (Receipt) – (2:19) On 1 January 1660, John Croad (merchant) of Salem received from Mr. Walter Price & Richard Cooke (merchants) full satisfaction for any engagement made by them for the payment of one half of my protested bills, as in an article in writing bearing date of 26 July 1659 & thereof do acquit the said Walter Price & Richard Cooke, provided this shall not debar nor disenable me for coming in with the rest of the creditors, according to a writing of Skidwell, annexed to a deed made by Mr. Thomas Broughton, to the said Price & Cooke, bearing date of April 1659. **Signed**: John Croad; **Acknowledged**: 1: 10: 1660; **Witnesses**: William Hathorne & Hillyard Veren.

WALTER PRICE & RICHARD COOKE to JOHN CROAD – (2:20) On 1 January 1660, John Wincoll of Watertown, being engaged unto Walter Price of Salem & Richard Cooke of Boston, to build or cause to be built and set to work, a saw mill or mills, on the Salmon falls of great Newickawanock River, in Pascataqua River, as appears by his engagement under his hand & seal, bearing date 30 December 1659, and therein stands engaged to allow ½ of the meat produce of said mill or mills unto the said Walter Price & Richard Cooke...We the aforesaid Walter Price & Richard Cooke, do make over & fully interest John Croad of Salem...to have as good a share or proportion as either of us in the premises, which is in consideration of a more full satisfaction of ½ of all the bills of exchange which were formerly drawn on him, on Mr. Peter Cole of London & for want of acceptance by the said Cole, protested against the said Croad, the true intent & meaning hereof is that the said John Croad is to have the 1/3 part of the produce above said, or so much as either of us have, & what composition or agreement may afterward be made with the said John Wincoll, the said John Croad is to be equally interested in it as above said, and by these presents we do hereby interest him the said Croad with ourselves, in the 1/3 part of what we shall have, of the produce of the mill or mills. **Signed**: Walter Price & Richard Cooke; **Acknowledged**: 1: 11 mo: 1660; **Witnesses**: William Hathorne & Hillyard Veren; **Recorded**: 4: 11 mo: 1660.

WILLIAM ROBBINSON to RICHARD RICHARDS & WILLIAM HOBBS – (2:22) On the 1st of January 1660, William Robbinson (tailor) of Salem granted to Richard Richards (planter) of Salem and William Hobbs of Lynn (planter), for a valuable consideration in hand paid, or secured to be paid, 80 acres both upland, meadow & timber in Salem, bounded SE with land of William Nichols, & N with a brook & joining the Topsfield common on the NE, & some land of Mr. Ruck to the SW, & with one corner of land of Thomas Putnam's to the W. **Signed**: William Robbinson [his mark] and Jane Robbinson [by mark]; **Acknowledged**: 2: 11 mo: 1660; **Witnesses**: John Putnam & Nathaniel Putnam; **Recorded**: 7:10: 166.

ROBERT LEMON (a claim against MATTHEW NIXON) – (2:23) On 28: 11 month 1660, Robert Lemon laid claim to a certain parcel of ground, now in the possession of Matthew Nixon and withheld by him from the said Robert Lemon; which land is about 2 foot in breadth & about 20 foot in length & lies adjoining the dwelling of said Nixon.

JOHN SOUTHWICK to WILLIAM KING & ROBERT STONE – (2:24) On the 4th of January 1660, John Southwick of Salem granted to William King & Robert Stone of Salem, for a valuable sum of money in hand already paid, 6 acres in Salem, bounded with land of John Southwick on the N and E and S; and land of Michael Shaflin on the W. **Signed**: John Southwick [by mark]; **Acknowledged**: 4: 12 mo: 1660, with wife Sarah yielding thirds; **Witnesses**: Hillyard Veren and Mary Veren.

RICHARD & JOYCE WATERS to GEORGE JACOBS – (2:25) On the 25th of the 9th month 1658, Richard Waters and (wife) Joyce of Salem granted to George Jacobs of Salem for 16 pounds fully paid, a house and a 10 acre lot with the orchard & all trees & fence now standing upon it, and hath lying W of it, the 5-acre lot of John Tomkins & on the E side the end of Henry Cook's lot, next to the water side, & another end of a lot of Thomas Gardener's & another end of a lot that was lately the lot of George

Williams, deceased, & so runs straight up to the end of John Small's lot and so has the S end butting upon the said John Small's lot & Ralph Tomkins lot & N to the river. **Signed**: Richard Waters & Joyce Waters [by mark]; **Acknowledged**: Richard Waters and his wife, 25: 9ber: 1658; **Witnesses**: William Hathorne & Henry Skerry; **Recorded**: 18: 12 mo: 1660.

THOMAS RIX to JOHN PUTNAM, Jr. – (2:26) On the 10th of January 1660, Thomas Rix (barber) of Salem granted to John Putnam, Jr. of Salem, for a valuable consideration in hand paid already, 30 acres which was formerly given by the town of Salem to widow Scarlett (deceased) situated in Salem, bounded with a farm formerly Capt. Davenport's to the W & the land of John Porter to the E…both upland & meadow. **Signed**: Thomas Rix; **Acknowledged**: 16: 11 mo: 1660; **Witnesses**: Hillyard Veren & Henry Kenny [by mark]; **Recorded**: 28: 12 mo: 1660.

NICHOLAS POTTER to ISAAC WILLIAMS Indenture – (2:28) On 21 February 1659, Nicholas Potter (bricklayer) of Salem granted to Isaac Williams (cordwainer) of Salem, a dwelling house with a barn, an orchard & yard, ¼ acre of ground adjoining thereunto, with fences…in Salem & bounded with land of Mr. George Corwin on the W, & the dwelling house & ground of Bethiah & Hanna Weekes on the E, & the street on the S, and land of Mr. Gedney on the N…provided always that if default of payment shall happen to be made, in part or whole, in any of the several four payments, above 20 days after the several payments are to be made that then it shall be lawful to & for the heirs of Nicholas Potter to re-enter again upon the premises…as his first estate & right, in consideration of fourscore pounds to be paid at 4 several payments to the heirs or assignes of said Nicholas Potter, after his decease, by said Isaack Williams…, 20 pounds, at or before the same month of the next year, ensuing after the day of the decease of Nicholas Potter, that is to be understood within one whole year after the death of Nicholas Potter, the first payment, 20 pounds is to be made; & so 20 pounds to be paid at or before the same day of the same month, every year successively, until the whole sum of 80 pounds be paid; & each payment is to be made, 1/3 part thereof, in half wheat and half Indian corn & the other 2/3 in English goods, linen & woolen, all which kinds of payments are to be made at price current…also Isaak Williams promises to pay Nicholas Potter 5 pounds 10 shillings and 1 pair of shoes yearly, so long as Nicholas Potter shall live, which is for & in consideration of the forbearance of the abovesaid 80 pounds, as is more fully expressed in a bill under his hand, dated the day & year above mentioned. **Signed**: Nicholas Potter; **Acknowledged**: 21: 12: 1659 by Nicholas Potter, with wife Mary Potter yielding thirds; **Witnesses**: Joshua Turland & Hillyard Veren; **Recorded**: 28: 12 mo: 1660.

RICHARD RICHARDS to JOHN POTTER – (2:31) On 26: 11 month: 1660, Richard Richards (yeoman) of Salem granted to John Potter (yeoman) of Salem for 11 pounds 10 shillings secured to be paid, 40 acres in Topsfield, joining lands of William Nichols, on one side & lands of William Hobbs on the other. **Signed**: Richard Richards [by mark]; **Witnesses**: Delivered & possession given to Joseph Potter to the use of said Potter in presence of John Sampson & Morgan Jones.

Mr. SAMUEL WHITING to JOHN BURRILL – (2:32) On the 1st of November 1659, Mr. Samuel Whiting (pastor of the church of Lynn) granted to John Burrill of Lynn, for 13 pounds, 10 shillings, one six-acre lot which was given to said Mr. Whiting by the town & was lately in the hands of Mr. Rhoades & is bounded S by the River, W by the lot of John Burrill, N by Thomas Browns & E by lot that was called Mr. Cobbitts which lies for the ministry. **Signed**: Mr. Samuel Whiting & Elizabeth Whiting; **Acknowledged**: last 3 mo: 1660; **Witnesses**: William Crafts & Joseph Whiting; **Recorded**: 8: 2 month: 1660/61.

WILLIAM SARGEANT to RICHARD WINDOW – (2:34) On the 18th of the 7th month 1652, William Sargeant of Gloucester sold to Richard Window of Gloucester, a dwelling house in Gloucester near Trunnel Cove with 3 acres of upland adjoining. *Item*: 4 acres of salt marsh adjoining to the said 7 acres of upland. *Item*: 7 acres of upland, lying on Beskett Island, lying on the SW end of the Island. *Item*: a cove of marsh on Beskett Island, about ¾ of an acre. *Item*: 2 small parcels of marsh lying by the side of the main [Maine?] river. **Signed**: William Sargeant; **Acknowledged**: 28 6 mo: 1660; wife Abigail yielded dower; **Witnesses**: Robert Tucker & Henry Walker; **Recorded**: 9: 3m: 1661.
I, Walter Price of Salem, in consideration of the full sum of 132 pounds, 9s. to me in hand paid by the wcrshipful Mr. Symond Bradstreet, do make over my full and whole interest in the within specified deed. **Signed**: 21th of the 3rd mo: Walter Price; **Witnesses**: William Gerrish, Nicholas Noyes; **Acknowledged**: 21: 3 mo: 1661.

JOHN PUTNAM the Elder to son THOMAS PUTNAM – (2:36) On the 3rd day of the 1st month 1653, John Putnam the elder (yeoman) of Salem granted to his son Thomas Putnam of Salem, one half of all his lands, meadow & pasture except what he had formerly granted to his son Nathaniel Putnam, being within the bounds of Salem…giving said son Thomas Putnam power to make equal division of such land & meadows as are yet undivided. & where division already made & bounds set, that those bounds shall stand for land marks between him & his brother. **Signed**: John Putnam [his mark]; **Acknowledged**: 13: 3d: 1661; **Witnesses**: Emanuel Downing & William Norton [no recording date].

PETER PALFREY to Mr. WILLIAM BROWNE – (2:37) On the 7th day of May 1661, Peter Palfrey (yeoman) of Reading granted to Mr. William Browne (merchant) of Salem for 42 pounds sterling, a dwelling house with ¾ of an acre of ground adjoining, in Salem, bounded W with house & ground of Mr. John Gedney, & N with house & ground of Robert Gray, & with the street or highway that comes down from the meeting house on the S & with a lane or highway also on the E. **Signed**: Peter Palfrey; **Acknowledged**: 8: 3 mo: 1661; **Witnesses**: Jeffery Massey & Nathaniel Pickman; **Recorded**: 22: 3: 1661.

EDMOND MARSHALL to ABRAHAM WARREN – (2:39) On 25 March 1661 Edmond Marshall (weaver) of Ipswich granted to Abraham Warren (planter) of Salem for 12 pounds in hand already paid, one dwelling house, with 10 acres of upland in Salem bounded E & W with land of John Bacheldor, N with land of Nicholas Howard & S with land of Abraham Warren, also another parcel of 10 acres of upland, together with ½ acre of meadow lying near the former 10 acres, having land of William King on the E, on the N with land of said John Bacheldor, W with land of John Bacheldor & Nehemiah Howard, and S with the river. **Signed**: Edmond Marshall [by mark]; **Acknowledged**: 25: 1 mo: 1661; **Witnesses**: Edward Norrice & John Pickman; **Recorded**: 22: 3: 1661.

HANNA MOORE to ERASMUS JAMES – (2:40) On 15 May 1660, Hanna Moore (widow) of Salem granted to Erasmus James of Marblehead, for a valuable consideration in hand already paid, 10 acres of upland on Darby fort side, so-called, & was formerly in Salem, & bounded with the South harbor on the N & some land of Richard Norman on the W & land of John Peach on the E, & Marblehead common on the S...unto the said Erasmus James, as heir executor of his father Erasmus, deceased. **Signed**: Hanna Moore [by mark]; **Acknowledged**: 24: 2 mo: 1661; **Witnesses**: Hillyard Veren, John Legg [by mark] & Edward Read; **Recorded**: 22: 3 mo: 1661.

PAUL MANSFIELD to SAMUEL ROBBINSON – (2:42) On 5 April 1661, Paul Mansfield (fisherman) of Salem granted to Samuel Robbinson (baker) of Salem, for 45 shillings in hand received, 12 poles of land lying in Salem, bounded N with the common or highway next to the pen so-called at which end it is 2 poles in breadth & so runs S 6 poles in length & bounded on the E with land of Christopher Phelps; & on the S & W with land of me, Paul Mansfield...with the fence...covenants...that: Forever hereafter, the said Samuel or his heirs...should sell or alienate the said land to any person or persons whatsoever, that is not of his posterity or not lawfully descended from his own body, or his now wife Constance, that then the sale shall be void and said land shall return to me...paying for the abovementioned sum of 45 shillings & also paying for what buildings or other charges said Samuel...may lay out upon the same as it shall be adjudged to be worth by indifferent men being equally chosen (at that time) unless I the said Paul or my heirs...shall see cause to consent to the said Samuel...their selling of it to any other person. **Signed**: Paul Mansfield [by mark] (with seizure & possession according to law); **Witnesses**: Thomas Barnes & Elias Mason; **Recorded**: 22: 3: 1661.

RICHARD STILEMAN to ELIAS STILEMAN – (2:44) On 12 April 1660, Richard Stileman of Portsmouth (county of Norfolk) granted to Elias Stileman of Portsmouth, for 50 pounds in hand paid, a dwelling house, wherein he sometimes dwelt, together with 1 acre of land, whereon the said house stands; also one old house at the lower end of the said land, wherein Hugh Laskin dwelt, all between the house and land of Mr. Phillip Cromwell on the E and the dwelling house of Edward Wharton, the warehouse of Mr. George Corwin & dwelling house & barn of William Lord on the W, the street on the N & the S end butting on the river, near the meeting house of Salem...here by promise to defend the title...& have for that purpose by one writing, obligatory, bearing even date with these presents of 100 pounds sterling indorsed with condition to perform these covenants...also promising to deliver up all writings that do concern the same fairly written & uncancelled, unto all & singular the premises I the said Richard Stileman do bind me.
[Paragraph after acknowledgement] I Elias Stileman, Sr. of Salem feofee in trust for the said house on behalf of Samuel Stileman, son of Richard Stileman, in consideration that it is yet above 5 years before the said Samuel Stileman be of age to enjoy the said house within mentioned, & for as much as the said house is likely forthwith to come to ruin, therefore I consent & agree to the sale of the said house, notwithstanding any act or thing, formerly done by the said Richard Stileman to his son, concerning the same. 9 May 1650 by Elias Stileman Sr.; Acknowledged 9: 3 mo: 1660. I Richard Stileman of Portsmouth, county of Norfolk, do acknowledge myself to owe & be indebted unto Elias Stileman the sum of 100 pounds sterling, to be paid unto said Elias Stileman...which payment...I bind me...dated in Portsmouth, 12 April 1666. The condition of this obligation is such that if Richard Stileman...do well & truly defend the title of the within mentioned house & land unto Elias Stileman...against all persons...or his son Samuel Stileman, & do well & sufficiently save...this obligation to be void. **Signed**: Richard Stileman; **Witnesses**: John Cutts & John Shipway; **Acknowledged**: 30 Apr 1660. **Signed**: Richard Stileman; **Acknowledged**: 30 Apr 1660; **Witnesses**: John Cutts & John Shipwaye; **Recorded**: 23: 3: 1661.

JEFFERY MASSEY and NICHOLAS WOODBERY to THOMAS FISK – (2:47) On 20 December 1655, Jeffery Massey of Salem and Nicholas Woodbery of Salem, granted to Thomas Fisk of Wenham for 10 pounds, 8 shillings already paid, 15 acres of meadow in the great meadow in Wenham, bounded S by George Ingersoll, N by Thomas Brackett, John Symonds, Jonathan Porter, John Bushnell, Frances Skerry & Widow Fermayes; & from E to W, from upland to upland. **Signed**: Jeffery Massey & Nichlas Woodbery; **Acknowledged**: 29: 4: 1659; **Witnesses**: Nathaniel Felton & Elias Stileman; **Recorded**: 23: 3: 1661.

DANIEL RUMBOLL, MARK BACHELDOR & THOMAS FISK – (2:48) On the 15th: 4th mo: 1661, Daniel Rumboll, Mark Bacheldor & Thomas Fisk laid claim to 12 acres of meadow now in the possession of Edmond Towne & Thomas Browning, lying in Topsfield, bounded by upland S, joining to a meadow, sometime Mr. Pembleton's, N only a little run that parts them.

JOHN PICKETT to JOHN SOLAS – (2:48) On the 18th of March 1660/1661, John Pickett (husbandman) of Stratford, Conn. & late of Salem, granted to John Solas (seaman) of Salem, for 19 pounds, 10 shillings in hand already paid, a dwelling house & an out house & 12 acres adjoining in Salem on the Cape Ann side (so called) & bounded with a highway to the E, on the S with land of Goodman Black, Zebulon Hill & Robert Lemons, & some land of said John Solas to the W & with the General fence on the N, next adjoining to Humphrey Woodbury's land, pointing up to the bounds of Thomas Pigden's lot; also a small piece of ground, containing 25 poles, lying at the highway by the gate, as it were lying with the land of Lieut. Lothrop. **Signed**: John Pickett; **Acknowledged**: 19: 1: 1661; **Witnesses**: Hillyard Veren & John Phelps; **Recorded**: 23: 3: 1661.

RICHARD & PENELOPE BELLINGHAM to BRAY WILKINS & JOHN GINGION – (2:50) On 9 March 1659, Richard Bellingham & Penelope his wife granted to Bray Wilkins (husbandman) of Lynn and to John Gingion (tailor) of Lynn, for 250 pounds, 25 pounds in hand paid before the sealing hereof, viz: 24 pounds in a tunn of bar iron, the other 20 shillings in money, the residue secured to be paid, land Richard Bellingham, Esquire, of Boston & Penelope his wife were long since granted by the General Court...700 acres of land, which by order of the General Court, on the 6th of the 7th month (September) in 1638, Mr. Hathorne, Lieut. Davenport, Lieut. How & Mr. Ballard, or any 2 of them, were to consider thereof & inform the said Court, & by a 2nd order of said court bearing date 22: 3rd mo (May) 1639, Mr. Timothy Tomlins instead of Mr. Ballord, with the other three...were appointed to set out the said farm...and by a third order of the said court, bearing date of 4 Sept 1639, the place desired by said Bellingham for his said farm, being on the head of Salem to the NW from the said town & there being within the said place a hill, with an Indian plantation & a pond & about 100 or 150 acres of meadow, all which being viewed by the said Mr. Hathorne & Richard Davenport, is granted unto the said Bellingham...The said 700 acres of land consisting of upland & meadow. **Signed**: Richard Bellingham & Penelope Bellingham; **Acknowledged**: 21 Apr 1660 by Richard Bellingham & 2 June 1660 by Penelope Bellingham; **Witnesses**: Henry Phillips & Robert Howard; **Recorded**: 23: 3: 1661.

JOHN BOURNE to HENRY HARWOOD – (2:53) On 24: 1st month called March 1661, John Bourne of Barbados, granted to Henry Harwood of Salem, 5 acres of land in the field of Salem town, called Southfield, between lands of Goodman Gegles on one side & the other side on land of Henry Harwood, of whom I John Bourne sold this land unto; & so to reach down to the water side as the other lots did & so reaching up to the land of Benjamin Felton Indian Corn Hills, that was in 1649 or thereabouts, & so going cross the breadth of this 5 acres & here unto I do acknowledge to have sold unto said Henry Harwood. (Barbados): The deposition of John Bourne age 49 yrs or thereabouts deposed & said he did sell unto Henry Harwood of Salem, 5 acres of land being bounded according to a deed of sale given Harwood, the bounds of land at the upper end from the river was to go unto Benjamin Felton's Indian Corn Hills, across the breadth of the 5 acres, it being half an acre or thereabouts belonging to said Felton: and further this deponent saith not. **Acknowledged**: 29 April 1661; **Signed**: John Bourne; **Witnesses**: Joseph Grafton & John Gardener; **Recorded**: 26 May 1661.

JOHN BROWN to MORDECAI CREFORD – (2:54) On 4: 5 mo: 1661, John Brown (merchant) of Jersey, England granted to Moredecai Creford (seaman) of Salem, for 55 qu. of merchantable codfish, whereof there is 30 qu. in hand received; the other 25 qu. said Creford is to pay at or before 20 June 1662. ½ of a barque or ketch, called the *Mary*, of Salem of about 15 ton burden, with ½ of her masts, sails, sailyard, anchors, cables, roads, ropes, cords, tackle apparel, furniture...and also the half of 20 hhds of salt & half of 22 cod lines...warrants and defends against all...for 1 whole year & a day next after the date hereof according to the law of Oleron: peril of seas, fire & enemies only excepted. **Signed**: Edith Creford [by mark], attorney of Mordecai Creford; **Witnesses**: John Bessell [by mark] & Hilliard Veren; **Recorded**: 10: 5: 1661.

JENKIN DAVIES to GEORGE CORWIN – (2:56) On 10: September 1660, Jenkin Davies (joiner) of Lynn granted to George Corwin (merchant) of Salem for security of the payment of 77 pounds sterling, all his visible estate in Lynn of 14 acres, together with 2 dwelling houses built on it, 10 acres being upland & meadow, together with one dwelling house built upon it adjoining land of Robert Driver on the W, and of Richard Rooten on the S & being bounded N with the town common, & also 1 acre of the same together with 1 dwelling house built on it, adjoining said 10 acres on the E and the other 3 acres of upland lying near the aforesaid 11 acres, the land of James Axy on the W & of Joseph Redknap on the S & E & bordering N on the Town Common; also right & interest to 1 blackish gelding, 4 head of cattle, viz: 1 red ox, 2 cows, 1 heifer, & 19 swine, little & great. Mortgage: If Jenkin Davies shall pay George Corwin 77 pounds sterling with interest & forebearance after 6 pounds percent within 2 years, that is to say, at or before the 10th day of the 7th month 1662, viz: in wheat, beef, pork & such bills as George Corwin shall accept of to be delivered in Salem; then this sale shall be void. **Signed**: Jenkin Davies; **Acknowledged**: 17: 5: 1661; **Witnesses**: Thomas Bishop & Edward Norrice; **Recorded**: 22: 5: 1661.

DANIEL KING to HENRY COLLINS, Sr. – (2:59) On 1 Sept 1654, Daniel King (gentleman) of Lynn with consent of Elizabeth his now wife in reference to her surrendering up her thirds, granted to Henry Collins, Sr. (husbandman) of Lynn 10 acres of fresh meadow, formerly Mr. Humphry's, bounded E with marsh of said Henry Collins, N with the 10 acre lot that was formerly in possession of Mathew West, S with the common, NE with upland; also 5 acres of upland, being a neck of land given to John Wing, abutting E on the highway that runs across the brook which runs out of the fresh marsh above mentioned, which lies NW from the dwelling house of said Henry Collins & the rest is bounded with the said fresh marsh, the planting lots of Timothy Cooper & George Taylor, & the rocky land of Henry Silsby, which was given to Mr. Flood for a 10-acre lot, also 6 acres which was given to William Andrews, by the town; bounded W with land of Henry Collins, S with the brook that parts between it & the house lots, E with the land of Henry Silsby, N with the brook that parts between it & the land of Thomas Chadwell, also a 10-acre lot which was olde Goodman Fitch's bounded E with the common & all the rest of it is bounded with the land of said Henry Collins; also 4 acres of fresh marsh, bounded E with the highway by John Collins' that was Smith's. **Signed**: Daniel King & Elizabeth King; **Acknowledged**: 27: 4: 1661; **Witnesses**: Andrew Mansfield & Ralph King; **Recorded**: 1 August 1661.

ROBERT MANSFIELD and JOHN MANSFIELD to BENJAMIN BRISCO – (2:62) On 6: 1 month: 1659/60, Robert Mansfield and John Mansfield of Lynn with consent of Elizabeth & Mary, their now wives, who surrendered their thirds, granted to Benjamin Brisco (shoemaker) of Boston for 20 pounds Sterling in hand paid, 1 dwelling house, barn & orchard, together with all the land within the fence…the whole containing half an acre & now in the terure of John Deakin, & is in Lynn, on the N side the brook in the Mill Street, & is bounded E with land of Matthias Farnsworth, W & N with land of Richard Haven & S with the country highway. On the 12th day of March 1659/60, Robert Mansfield & John Mansfield gave possession to Benjamin Brisco. **Signed**: Robert Mansfield [by mark] & John Mansfield; **Witnesses**: Andrew Mansfield & John Deakin. **Signed**: Robert Mansfield [by mark] & John Mansfield; **Acknowledged**: 20: 4 mo: 1661 by Robert & John & wives Elizabeth, wife of Robert & Mary wife of John; **Witnesses**: Andrew Mansfield, Bethia Mansfield & John Deakin; **Recorded**: 1: Aug: 1661.

DAVID CORWITHIN Sr. to RICHARD CORTICE – (2:65) On 16 Feb 1660, David Corwithin, Sr. of Salem granted to Richard Cortice of Salem, for a valuable consideration in hand paid, a dwelling house & ¼ acre of ground adjoining, as it is now bounded out, which house & ground was formerly in possession of Christopher Younges & is in Salem, bounded with land of Robert Lemon on the E, land of said David Corwithin on the W & land of Francis Collins on the N & abuts the South River harbor to the south. **Signed**: David Corwithin; **Acknowledged**: 18: 12: 1660; **Witnesses**: Hillyard Veren, Mary Veren & Henry Coombes [by mark]; **Recorded**: 12: 6: 1661.

JOHN KILLUM to CHARLES GOTT, Jr. – (2:66) On 11: 4 month: 1659, John Killum of Wenham granted to Charles Gott, Jr. of Wenham, for 6 pounds, 10 shillings paid in hand 10 acres of upland, viz: ½ of a parcel of land granted to Esdrass Reade & William Geer by the town of Salem…20 acres & is situated in Wenham in a place commonly called the neck, butting on Mr. Brown's meadow W and Edward Waldron's lot S & the swamp N and is to be equally divided. **Signed**: John Killum [by mark] & Hanna Killum [by mark], who released interest; **Acknowledged**: 28: 10 mo: 1660 [no recording date given].

JOSIAH ROOTES to HENRY KENNY – (2:68) On 26: 12: 1660, Josiah Rootes (planter) of Salem granted to Henry Kenny (planter) of Salem for a valuable consideration in hand paid, 60 acres in Salem, bounded with land of William Nichols N & land of John Putnam W, Robert Prince on the S and land of Job Swinerton on the E. **Signed**: Josiah Rootes [by mark]; **Acknowledged**: 17: 8 mo: --- [1660]; **Witnesses**: Hilliard Veren & Theodore Price; **Recorded**: 6: 9: 1661.

JOHN LAMBERT to EDWARD GASKOYNE – (2:69) On 28 January 1660, John Lambert (seaman) of Salem, granted to Edward Gaskoyne (ship carpenter) of Salem for 25 pounds in hand paid, his now dwelling house with out houses, fences, orchard and all the ground adjoining, which ground he formerly bought of said Edward Gaskoyne, except 10 poles of said ground, lately sold to John Loomis. John Lambert was to give Edward Gaskoyne possession of the said premises before the 8th of April next ensuing & until the time mentioned of delivery to stand to the adventure of the said housing in case of any casualty by fire. **Signed**: John Lambert & wife [both by mark]; **Acknowledged**: 28: 8ber: 1661; **Witnesses**: Hilliard Veren & John Hill; **Recorded**: 6: 9: 1661.

ROBERT SOLLAS to EDWARD HILLYARD – (2:71) On 20 October 1653, Robert Sollas of Salem granted to Edward Hillyard of Salem for 9 pounds, 10 shillings in hand paid, one dwelling house, being part of a house formerly bought of David Thomas, John & Robert Stone adjoining to the W to the other part, formerly Richard Hides now in possession of said Edward Hillyard, together with about ¾ acre of ground adjoining, being in Salem, & bounded NE with some land of John Peckett to the W with the house & ground of said Hilliard, to the NW with the common or highway & the SE with the South harbor. **Signed**: Robert Sollas; **Acknowledged**: 9: 5 mo: 1661; **Witnesses**: Phillip Veren & Hillyard Veren; **Recorded**: 8: 9: 1661.

ROBERT GRAY to JOHN INGERSOLL – (2:72) On 29 7ber: 1656, Robert Gray of Salem granted to John Ingersoll of Salem for 45 pounds in hand, one dwelling house together with the land that he had bought of Timothy Laskins. **Signed**: Robert Gray; **Acknowledged**: by Robert Gray; wife Elizabeth yielded thirds, 23: 4 mo: 1661; **Witnesses**: Christopher Waler [by mark] and Isaack Page; **Recorded**: 8: 9: 1661.

(2:73) *Notation*: See page 414 of volume 2 for entry omitted here. [See KEISER to CRAFORD - 2:414 on page 146 of this book]

ROBERT and ELIZABETH SANFORD to JOHN PORTER – (2:73) On the 2nd day of the 4th month commonly called June 1652, Robert Sanford of Boston and Elizabeth Sanford, his wife, granted to John Porter (yeoman) of Salem, for divers considerations and especially the sum of 12 pounds sterling in hand paid, 20 acres of upland and meadow lying in Salem between the land of John Endecott, Esq. on the S, John Putnam on the W, the lands of said John Porter on the N & abutting towards the sea E...to beholden in free & common soccage and not in Capite, nor by Knights Service. **Signed**: Robert Sanford and Elizabeth Sanford [by mark]; **Acknowledged**: 2d: 3 mo: 1651; **Witnesses**: William Halstone, John Maryon & Nathaniel Souther; **Recorded**: 10: 9: 1661.

JOHN DEACON to ROBERT MANSFIELD – (2:76) On the 23rd of the 11th month 1659, John Deacon (smith) of Lynn, with consent of his now wife, granted to Robert Mansfield (yeoman) of Lynn, for 30 pounds in sterling paid, ½ part of his interest in his dwelling house & all other of his buildings (except his shop) & half his interest likewise in the land, his buildings and orchard standing upon, with half the orchard (the other half of the said dwelling house…the said John Deacon hath sold unto John Mansfield upon the day of the date hereof) the land in whole containing ½ acre & is situated in Lynn, in the mill street, & is bounded S with the country highway, E with land of Matthias Farnsworth, & W & N with the land of Richard Haven; & also a planting lot of 3 acres lying in the neck upon the W side of the mill creek, near Edmond Farrington, his mill dam & bounded southerly with the land of Robert Mansfield & N with the land of John Ramsdell, abutting E on the salt marsh of John Fuller and W on land formerly in possession of Mr. Cobbitt; & also one 10-acre lot, which the town of Lynn gave to said John Deacon. **Signed**: John Deacon; **Acknowledged**: 28: 4 mo: 1661 with wife consenting; **Witnesses**: Thomas Marshall & John Lewis; **Recorded**: 12: 9: 1661.

JOHN DEACON to JOHN MANSFIELD – (2:79) On the 23rd of the 11th month 1659, John Deacon (smith) of Lynn, with consent of his now wife, granted to John Mansfield (taylor) of Lynn, for 40 pounds sterling in hand paid, ½ part of his now dwelling house & all other of his buildings except his shop, & half his orchard, & half the land about his house, the other half the said John Deacon hath sold unto Robert Mansfield the date hereof the land in whole (see previous deed) upon the W side of Mill Creek, bounded S with land of Robert Potter or his father Nicholas Potter & N with land of Richard Haven, abutting E upon the salt marsh, W on the Rockes; also a lot of wood in Nahant, which the town gave him; which is the 13th lot & lies in Bass neck, bounded S with the lot of Henry Collins Sr. & N with the lot of Richard Blood; also 2 acres of salt marsh lying in the 1st division in Rumney Marsh bounded E with the marsh lately in possession of Capt. Bridges & W with the marsh in, or lately in tenure of William Croft, butting N upon town common, S upon marsh, commonly called the Lady Moody's marsh; also 2 acres in the 2nd division in Rumney Marsh bounded E with marsh of Thomas Chadwell & W with the marsh of Matthias Farnsworth, butting S on marsh of Jonathan Hudson & N on the common which parts the 1st & 2nd divisions; also 2 acres in the last division in the same marsh, bounded W with marsh formerly in possession of Nicholas Batty, & E with little creek that parts it & the neck of marsh that was Joseph Howe's, butting S on the great creek & N on the meadow that was

Mr. Knowles. **Signed**: John Deacon; **Acknowledged**: 28: 4: 1661, with wife yielding thirds; **Witnesses**: Thomas Marshall & John Lewis; **Recorded**: 12: 9: 1661.

JOSEPH HUMPHRIES & EDMOND BATTERS (Administrators of John Humphries Esq. deceased) – (2:82) Mr. Joseph Humphries & Edmond Batters, administrators of the estate here in New England of John Humphries, Esquire, deceased, lay claim to 500 acres of land about a pond of fresh water near Salem bounds, granted by the General Court to said John Humphries about the year 1635, & confirmed with its bounds by a General Court held at Newton the 12th of the 1st month 1637 or 1638, and now in the tenure of Joseph Pope as by the courts order appeareth this 19: 9ber: 1661; **Recorded**: 9: 9: 1661.

(2:82) [same as previous paragraph] omitting "here in New England" layeth claim to parcel of meadow 6 acres in Lynn in Rumney Marsh & now in possession of --- Johnson of Lynn, this 19: 9: 1661).

JOHN WITT (Stray horse) – (2:83) John Witt of Lynn hath taken up a stray horse colt about 2 years old, of color bay, a star in the forehead, a white snip on the nose, one white foot behind & half the hoof black & 2 snips in the farther ear. 8: 11: 1661 appraised at 7 pounds by Robert Burges (constable) and Thomas Newall.

Capt. RICHARD DAVENPORT (Claim to Major Hathorn's farm) – (2:83) On 19: 9: 1661, Capt. Richard Davenport laid claim to 2 farms: one known by the name of Capt. Davenport's farm & the other known by the name of Major Hathorn's farm; each containing 270 acres, both in Salem, near about NW of the town & bounded as they were laid out by the town of Salem, & now in possession of Thomas Putnam, John Putnam & Daniel Ray.

EDMOND BATTER & JOSEPH HUMPHRIES (Claim to farm of John Humphries, Esq., deceased) – (2:83) On 18 March 1661/2, Edmond Batter and Joseph Humphries signed a statement, saying whereas John Humphries Esq. deceased was possessed of a farm of upland & meadow of about 800 acres between Marblehead & Lynn within the limits of Salem grant from the General Court, Edmond Batter & Joseph Humphries, administrators for the estate lay claim to said farm and further deny all persons to seed or occupy said farm or any part thereof without our order.

WILLIAM LORD Jr. to JOHN MASON – (2:84) On the 10th of November 1661, William Lord, Jr. of Salem granted to John Mason (brickmaker) of Salem, for a valuable sum in hand paid, a parcel of land 8 poles in length & 7½ poles in breadth in Salem, part of that acre of land of William Lord's adjoining to the dwelling house he now lives in, & is bounded N with ground of said William Lord, & S & W with land of Francis Lawes, & E with the highway. **Signed**: William Lord (wife Jane yielded thirds), **Acknowledged**: 10: 9ber; 1661; **Witnesses**: Hilliard Veren & Mary Vern Jr.; **Recorded**: 6: 10: 1661.

ROSE GILLOW to GEORGE FRAYLE – (2:85) On the 8th of July 1661, Rose Gillow of Lynn, attorney to her husband John Gillow, granted to George Frayle (wheelright) of Lynn, for 26 pounds, 18 shillings, 8 pence in hand paid, by authority given her by her husband, also in reference to her surrendering thirds in one parcel of meadow ground...8 acres of salt marsh in Rumney Marsh in the 1st division laid out to inhabitants of Lynn, which meadow is bounded S with marsh of John Witt, N with marsh of Thomas Newell, Jr., E on marsh of Thomas Browne & W with upland, which said meadow is in bounds of Lynn. **Signed**: Rose Gillow; **Acknowledged**: 10: 10: 1661; **Witnesses**: Robert Driver & Richard Hood; [no recording date].

SAMUEL CONDY to JOHN BRIMBLICOM – (2:88) On 10 December 1661, Samuel Condy of Marblehead granted to John Brimblicom of Marblehead, for 5 pounds in hand paid, 1 acre of land, Samuel's part of the land that he had in partnership with Richard Read (being 2 acres in the whole) in Marblehead, joining land of John Legg N, land of John Northy W & a highway E. **Signed** Samuel Condy; **Acknowledged**: 10: 10ber: 1661; **Witnesses**: George Emory & Robert Lord; **Recorded**: 18: 10: 1661.

SAMUEL ARCHARD to THOMAS PITTMAN – (2:89) On 8 June 1661, Samuel Archard (carpenter) of Salem granted to Thomas Pittman (seaman) of Marblehead, for 4 pounds in hand paid, 1 acre of marsh ground in Salem, on Marblehead side of Forest river, in the form of a triangle, abutting N on Forest river, & runs with a point against the upland S, & joins to marsh of Richard Rowland E, & marsh of Henry Harwood W. **Signed**: Samuel Archard; **Acknowledged**: 18: 10ber: 1661; **Witnesses**: Mary Veren & Hilliard Veren; **Recorded**: 13: 10: 1661.

DANIEL KING, Sr. to ALCE THOMAS – (2:90) On 13: 10th mo: 1661, Daniel King, Sr. (gentleman) of Lynn granted to Alce Thomas (widow & vintner) of Boston, having sold 8 acres, all his right to the 8 acres of land in Lynn, bounded W with lands of Allen Breed, Jr. & lands of Thomas Chadwell, E with land of Mr. Samuel Whiting & George Burrill, butting on the S with lands of George Keyser, & on N butting on the town common. King promised that his wife would yield up her thirds & give a free title for 38 pounds in hand paid. And it was excepted viz: a highway that goes through said lands & a dwelling house, 1 outhouse or barn, that King has liberty to take of the said land, within one year. **Signed**: Daniel King Sr.; **Acknowledged**: 13: 10 mo: 1661; **Witnesses**: John Hathorne & Hillyard Veren; **Recorded**: 19: 10: 1661.

JOSEPH JEWETT to JOHN BRADSTREET – (2:92) On 28 June 1658, Joseph Jewett (merchant) of Rowley granted to John Bradstreet (now of Marblehead) in consideration of 4 score acres of land lying in Ipswich, late belonging to Humphry Bradstreet, late of Ipswich (deceased) and by his will bequeathed to his son John Bradstreet, & by said John Bradstreet sold unto said Joseph Jewett by a deed of feofement, bearing date, 3: July: 1657, the cornmill in Marblehead with the housing, ponds, dams, stones & priviledges to the same appertaining or belonging with the profits, rents...to be paid by William Beale, unto said Joseph Jewett, Mr. William Payne or Mr. Richard Russell before & until the date hereof; also a lot of land, 10 acres granted by the town of Salem to Henry Harwood, and by him sold to Mr. William Stratton, by Stratton sold to Mr. William Payne & Mr. Richard Russell, & by Mr. William Payne & Mr. Richard Russell sold unto Mr. Joseph Jewett and by Joseph Jewett sold unto said John Bradstreet. **Signed**: Joseph Jewett, with Ann Jewett acknowledging consent; **Acknowledged**: 28 Jun 1658; **Witnesses**: Robert Lord & Humphry Griffin; **Recorded**: 19: 10: 1661.

ELIAS WHITE & MARY CODNER – (2:94) On 25 June 1661, Elias White (mariner) of Marblehead & Mary Codner, widow of Christopher Codner, late of Marblehead: whereas said Christopher Codner, dying intestate, leaving 2 children, namely: Christopher Codner & Joane Codner, which he had by said wife Mary: The court ordered said Christopher Codner, the son, to have out of his father's estate, 60 pounds at age 21, & Joane 30 pounds at age of 21 or her day of marriage, and whereas there is a marriage intended between said Elias White & said Mary Codner, grant unto John Deveroux & Christopher Lattamore, both of Marblehead, mariners, as feoffees in trust to & for said children, a dwelling house, with all lands belonging in Marblehead, bounded by land of John Gatchell S, with land of John Rhodes SE, lands of John Hudson E & lands of Thomas Taynor W, which house & land was formerly the estate of said Christopher Codner, deceased, & which he purchased of Henry Pease...provided that the said Elias White or Mary his intended wife, pay the said 2 children...shall be void. **Signed**: Elias White & Mary Codner [by mark]; **Acknowledged**: 27: 4 mo: 1661; **Witnesses**: Michael Smith & Samuel Gatchell (Attested by Robert Howard, Notary Public); **Recorded**: 19: 10: 1661.

RICHARD HUCHESSON and NATHANIEL PUTNAM to WILLIAM HAYNES (discharge of mortgage) – (2:98) On the 9th of April 1662, Richard Huchesson and Nathaniel Putnam discharged a mortgage made by William Haynes on 21: February 1648, a parcel of land as appears by that writing unto Richard Huchesson and Nathaniel Putnam, for security for payment of an engagement from Haynes to the said Huchesson & Putnam...we have received the full of the said engagement. **Signed**: Richard Huchesson [by mark] & Nathaniel Putnam; **Witnesses**: Joseph Huchesson & Hillyard Veren.

MORDECAI & (wife) JUDITH CRAFORD and JOHN PRIDE to Capt THOMAS SAVAGE (mortgage) – (2:98) On 27 December 1661, Mordecai Craford & John Pride (both of Salem) acknowledged a deed of Mordecai Craford (& wife Judith) & John Pride to Capt. Thomas Savage of Boston, for a valuable consideration in hand received, one dwelling house & barn, with all exterior houses with 18 acres of land on which the house stands, on a neck of land in Salem near Bass River, with 20 acres of land at Cedar stand, near Bass River on the Cape Ann side, with one barque, with all sails, masts, yards, anchors, etc. belonging to the said barque which the said Craford commonly goes in; also half the barque in which John Pride goes in with half her sails...with the whole produce of a fishing voyage which said Craford is now undertaking with 2 boats at Cape Newegin. The sum of 280 sterling in merchantable & refuse fish at money price at his warehouse at Boston...½ to be paid before the 16th of June next, the other ½ at or before the 16th of October next following. **Signed**: Mordecai Craford [by mark] & Judith Craford [by mark] & John Pride; **Recorded**: 16: 11: 1661.

JOHN & (wife) SUSANNA MARSH & NATHANIEL & (wife) MARY FELTON to JOHN PORTER – (2:100) On 18: 3rd month: 1655, John & Susanna Marsh and Nathaniel Felton acknowledged the following sale (Mary Felton acknowledged on 14: 9ber: 1659). For 20 pounds sterling in hand, John (& his wife Susanna) Marsh & Nathaniel (& his wife Mary) Felton granted to John Porter (yeoman) of Salem, 40 acres of upland and meadow in Salem, lying between lands of John Endecott, Esq. S & John Putnam W, & lands of said John Porter N, and butting towards the sea E., to be held in free & common soccage & not in Capite nor by Knights service. **Signed**: John & Susanna [by mark] Marsh & Nathaniel & Mary [by mark] Felton; **Recorded**: 11: 11 mo: 1661.

GEORGE CORWIN to JOB SWINERTON, Jr. – (2:103) On the 18th: 11 mo: 1661, George Corwin (merchant) of Salem, with wife Elizabeth Corwin yielding dower, acknowledged his deed to Job Swinerton, Jr. (yeoman) of Salem, for 105 pounds in hand paid, to 280 acres of upland in

Salem between land of Robert Goodell W, land of Thomas Putnam (formerly land of Phillip Cromwell) E, having land of Robert Britt & Job Swinerton, Sr. S & thence down to the great River, 30 acres of which was formerly land of John Bridgman; also 25 acres of meadow, 9 acres of which is on the other side of the great River, between the meadow of John Putnam W & Richard Hutchesson E; the other 16 acres of meadow bounded by aforesaid upland & river…except 1 acre lying between said river & lands of above said Goodell with all timbers, commons…**Signed**: George & Elizabeth Corwin; **Witnesses**: Hillyard Veren & Richard Prince; **Recorded**: 20: 11: 1661.

JOHN GEDNEY, Sr. to JOHN GEDNEY – (2:105) On 8 June 1661, John Gedney, Sr. (vintner) of Salem granted to John Gedney (mariner) of Salem, for love and natural affection which he had unto his son, one new dwelling house with ¼ acre of ground in Salem, bounded with land of Joseph Miles N & land of Nicholas Potter & Benjamin Feirmaies E & land of William Marston W, & S with a lane of highway that goes to the town pound. **Signed**: John Gedney and Katherine Gedney (wife Katherine yielded dower); **Recorded**: 23: 11: 1661.

JOHN GEDNEY to NICHOLAS & MARY POTTER & HEIRS – (2:107) On 12: 11 month: 1661, John Gedney (with Katherine Gedney releasing dower) granted to Nicholas Potter & Mary his wife and to their heirs lawfully begotten of her, the said Mary's body, for natural affection unto my son-in-law Nicholas Potter, Sr., & Mary my daughter, his now wife, a dwelling house with ½ acre of ground adjoining in Salem, near the town pound & is bounded N with ground of Joseph Miles, E with ground of widow Feirmayes (deceased) & of Mr. Beadle, & S with a highway or lane, & W with ground of John Gedney, Jr.; & also about 4 acres of ground on the neck in Salem, which ground was formerly land of Thomas Pigden, & is bounded with the sea or north harbor NW, & with the common E, S & W. **Signed**: John Gedney & Katherin Gedney; **Witnesses**: Hillyard Veren & John Gedney. [No acknowledgement or recording dates given.]

WALTER PRICE to MOSES MAVERICK – (2:109) On the 3rd of March 1661/2, Walter Price (merchant) of Salem granted to Moses Maverick of Marblehead all his right in the stock of copartnership with Moses Maverick & John Scottoway & John Croade (merchants) & now in the hands of said Moses Maverick as agent, together with every such sum…to the same stock belonging or owing, as also whatever & all those debts that are due & owing from the said stock to me said Walter Price, which said principle with the debts owing to me from the said stock amounts to about 1,100 pounds. I have put Moses Maverick in full & peacable possession of the premises, by the delivery unto him of a piece of money called 6 d fixed in the scale hereof. Consideration: Whereas I am endebted & do owe unto divers persons in England divers sums of money to the value of about 700 pounds, which I cannot satisfy or make payment of as my said creditors do desire, by the reason that many debts are owing unto me. And whereas my loving friend Moses Maverick of Marblehead, has undertaken to give satisfaction to my creditors for my said debts. **Signed**: Walter Price; **Witnesses**: Hillyard Veren & Edward Norice.

WALTER PRICE to JOHN GEDNEY, Sr. & JOHN GEDNEY, Jr. – (2:111) On 1 March 1661/2, Walter Price granted to John Gedney, Sr. and John Gedney, Jr. both of Salem, for a valuable sum in hand paid, all his right title & interest in the quarter part of the ketch *Hopewell* abovementioned, with all her quarter part of tackle & furniture, as in the deed above mentioned. This above sale or assignment have reference to a bill of sale to Mr. Walter Price for a quarter part of ketch *Hopewell* from Richard Rayment, recorded on page 3 of this book. **Signed**: Walter Price; **Witnesses**: Hillyard Veren & Robert Prince.

EDMOND BATTER, Executor for THOMAS ANTRUM, deceased, to ISAACK BURNAP – (2:112) [no date] Edmond Batter, Executor to the Last Will and Testament of Thomas Antrum, deceased, do hearby acquit & discharge Isaack Burnap from all payments referring to the farm purchased of his father Antrum for which payments being all accomplished, the mortgage is hearby void & of no effect.

JOHN MARSH to Mr. PHILLIP CROMWELL – (2:112) On 20 December 1660, John Marsh (cordwainer) of Salem granted to Mr. Phillip Cromwell of Salem for 27 pounds, 10 shillings, one dwelling house with about 1 acre of land adjoining, with the orchard, garden, yard, housing, fences...in Salem, bounded N by the North River, E with land of Mr. John Gedney & W with land of Nicholas Potter & of Joseph Miles. **Signed**: John Marsh; **Acknowledged**: 7: 1: 1661/2; **Witnesses**: George Corwin & John Browne; **Recorded**: 11: 1: 1661.

JUDITH COOK to JOSHUA REA – (2:114) On 21 May 1662, Judith Cook (widow) of Salem, with consent of children, granted to Joshua Rea (husbandman) of Salem, for 5 pounds, ¼ acre of land in Salem having on the N land of Mrs. Sharp (widow) S & E with lands of said Judith Cook, & bounded W with the lane or highway. It is further agreed between them concerning the other ¼ acre adjoining, that the said Joshua Rea shall have the first offer of it, if it is to be sold & the said Judith Cook or her children have the 1st offer of this ¼ acre, here mentioned to be sold, by these presents, if at any time he shall be minded to sell it (in the presence of the same witnesses). **Signed**: Judith Cook [by mark]; **Acknowledged**: 21: 3

month: 1662; **Witnesses**: Edward Norrice, Francis Skerry & John Mascoll; **Recorded**: 23: 5: 1662.

JOB SWINERTON to WILLIAM CANTLEBURRY – (2:115) On 18 January 1661, Job Swinerton (yeoman) of Salem granted to William Cantleburry (yeoman) of Salem for 78 pounds & 15 shillings already paid in hand to Mr. George Corwin (merchant) of Salem, ¾ of all that meadow & upland, which he lately bought of Mr. George Corwin as is expressed at large, with the bounds thereof in a deed bearing date this 18 January 1661, which contains in the whole about 305 acres. I have bargained & sold ¾…unto the said William Cantleburry (except 20 acres of upland out of the said ¾ reserved upon agreement for my own personal use, which said land, meadow & upland lies all on this side of the great river, as it lies divided between me the said Job Swinerton & the said Cantlebury by Nathaniel Putnam, Joseph Hutcheson, John Swinerton, Nathaniel Ingerson, being mutually chosen to divide the said land, & bound the same between them and lay out ways for their own conveniences, 1 highway over the river to the meadow that was formerly Joseph Pope's & 1 highway to the meadow of Job Swinerton, Sr. which is to say a pack & prime way for said Job & William which said premises is lying in Salem & bounded on W with a white oak tree next to the river, adjoining to Robert Goodell, E with land of Thomas Putnam. It is to be understood that there is several ways to be allowed for common use, over the land reserved by the town upon allowance, also it is understood that the bounds by the river side runs from bound tree upon a straight line to the bound tree, some distance from the river. **Signed**: Job Swinerton, Jr.; **Acknowledged**: 18: 11 month: 1661; **Witnesses**: Hillyard Veren & Richard Prince; **Recorded**: 12: 1: 1661.

JOHN BLACKLEACH, Sr. to JOHN WEST – (2:118) On 14 December 1660, John Blackleach, Sr. (merchant of Boston), with consent of wife Elizabeth, granted to John West (husbandman) of Salem for 350 pounds sterling, in hand paid, all messuage or tenement in Salem & all such uplands & meadow ground, as has been given & granted unto said John Blackleach by the selectmen of Salem, within the bounds of Salem or Manchester in New England, which messuage or tenement was formerly in the tenure of Laurence Leach and now is in the occupation of said John West, and all barns, orchards, gardens, buildings, etc. **Signed**: John Blackleach; **Acknowledged**: 25 Dec 1660; **Witnesses**: Joseph Bastor & William Pearse; **Recorded**: 12: 1: 1661/2

JOHN WEST to GEORGE CORWIN – (2:121) I, the within named John West, in consideration that Mr. George Corwin of Salem has given his bond in the sum of 400 pounds sterling for the payment, the sum of 350 pounds sterling, by the value thereof in specie, as by the said bond appeareth, bearing date with these presents, have assigned this present deed…to have & hold…until the said bond be fully satisfied & said Mr. George Corwin…be discharged, over & beside the said messuage…I do assigne my right & interest in 8 head of cattle, viz: 6 steers or oxen & 2 cows for the consideration above said. Added: I the within named for valuable considerations have assigned Mr. George Corwin all the use, benefit & advantage which may arise…by the present obligation. **Signed**: John West [by mark]; **Acknowledged**: 26 June 1661; **Witnesses**: Joseph Bastor, William Pearse & John Blackleach. This above assignment refers to a bond bearing the same date.

Monsieur PIPIN to Mr. WILLIAM CLEMENTS – (2:123) Cape Negra: 28 August 1661: 34 pounds 17 sterling. At 14 days after sight of this my bill of exchange, I pray you pay to Mr. William Clements or his order, the sum of 34 pounds, 17 shillings, for so much received by me of him in provisions. I pray you make good pay & place it to the account as per advice of yours To Monsieur Pipin aboard his ship in Boston. Rivedou.

RICHARD BLOOD to BENJAMIN BRISCO – (2:123) On 27 April 1660, Richard Blood (yeoman) of Lynn, with consent of wife Isabell, granted to Benjamin Brisco (shoemaker) of Lynn, for 29 pounds sterling, 6 acres of land in Lynn, bounded E with the house lot of said Richard Blood, W with the land of Thomas Ivory, S with land of or in the possession of William Bartrum, & N with the town common, which land, said Richard Blood bought of Hugh Burt, Jr. which land was part of Joseph Armitage's house lot & part of Francis Lytefoot's house lot, & also a small addition which the town gave to Richard Blood, which also lies in the same bounds, also a lot which the town gave to Richard Blood, which lies in Nahant on Bass Neck, being the 14th lot containing 4 acres & bounded S with lot of John Deakin & N with lot of John Burrill…**Signed**: Richard Blood; **Acknowledged**: 1 Nov 1661 by Richard Blood and on 15 Mar 1661 by wife Isabell, who gave up her thirds; **Witnesses**: Andrew Mansfield & John Evesome; **Recorded**: 17 Mar 1661.

WILLIAM CLEMENTS – (2:126) Cape Negra: 28 August 1661: 34 pounds 17 shillings sterling: At 14 days after sight of this my bill of exchange, I pray you pay to Mr. William Clements [repeat of page 123 in entirety]. By this public instrument of protest, be it known…that on 22 March 1661, Stilo: Angliae; at the request of Mr. William Clements of Boston (merchant) I, Hillyard Veren, Recorder in Salem…having in my hand the original bill of exchange, whereof the copy is above written, did go to the house where Monsieur Pipin was resident in Salem unto whom the said bill is directed, & there speaking to him & showing him the said bill of exchange, whose answer was, that he had no effects of the drawer of the said bill in his hands, yet notwithstanding for the good will & affection that he did bear unto him, should be willing to make payment of the said bill for him, but having not provision in his hands at present could not do it, and therefore I, the said Hillyard Veren, Recorder, did solemnly protest (at the request of aforesaid) as well against Rivedou, who have subscribed the said bill of exchange, as all others, whom it doth or may concern, of exchange and re-exchange, and of all costs, damages & interest for want of acceptation of the said bill, suffered & sustained, & hereafter to be suffered & sustained to be all recovered in time & place convenient. Hillyard Veren, Recorder: **Witness**: Richard Lord.

EDWARD RICHARDS to HENRY RHOADES – (2:127) On the 20th day of the 4th month 1654, Edward Richards (joiner) of Lynn granted to Henry Rhoades of Lynn for 22 pounds sterling, 6 acres of upland & salt marsh, joining together, formerly in the possession of Joseph Jenckes, Jr. in Lynn, bounded E with land of John Fuller, W with a salt creek, S on land of Edmond Farrington, & N on aforesaid creek, the lot being a house lot...and all the estate...of them the said Edward Richards & Ann his wife...**Signed**: Edward Richards [by mark] & Ann Richards; **Acknowledged**: 27: 4 mo: 1654; **Witnesses**: Andrew Mansfield & William Clark [by mark]; **Recorded**: 23: 2 mo: 1662.

(2:129) I, Edward Richards of Lynn, bind myself...in the full sum of 40 pounds sterling unto Henry Rhodes...for his securing & keeping harmless from all molestation & suits at law, about the lot the said Edward sold unto said Henry, which was Joseph Jencks, Jr., according to a deed of sale under hand & seal of said Edward Richards bearing date: 21: 4 mo: 1654. **Signed**: Edward Richards [by mark]; **Acknowledged**: 27: 4 mo: 1654; **Witnesses**: Andrew Mansfield & William Clark [by mark]; **Recorded**: 23: 2: 1662.

WILLIAM ROSWELL & JOHN PARTRIDGE – (2:130) On 17 May 1662, a list of debts (i.e. pounds of sugar) left in the hands of William Roswell & John Partridge: John Wilson & Isaack Lowell 7000 lbs; John Wilson & John Cother, 4000 lbs; Miles Colby & Thomas Beckeles, 695 pounds; Jacob Withers, 12000 pounds; Capt. John Berry, 5250 lbs; William Pearsehoull, 1545 lbs. Total: 19,690 pounds. All which bills unto as above, 19,690 pounds of muscovadus sugar, which we do here by promise to be accountable for, unto Mr. James Brice of Dublin, Merchant, or his assignes, as witness our hands dated as above, in the Barbados (casualties excepted per William Rosewell & co.) **Test.**: James Russell, Marke Rice. **Recorded**: 4: 7: 1662.

SIMON DELBOE to THOMAS BARNARD – (2:131) London, 6th December 1661. Mr. Thomas Barnard. – Sir. Your letters of the 29th & 31st October from Theneriff, I received, with an account of your outward-bound voyage, & of the death of Mr. Nicholas Holding; with God's will we must be content; & now I hope as you mention in your letters that you will be careful in discharge of the command of the said ship: which I hereby confirm, & desire you by all means to comply with Mr. George Needham, in what he shall desire, tending to the dispatch of the voyage, which God grant may end in safety. I suppose you will be employed for New England, where, in case you may want any provisions for the ship, I question not, but you may be furnished at reasonable rates: much I suppose you will not want, for by God's blessing I hope, you may be at home in May or June next, so wishing you success in your several voyages, commit you to the protection of the Almighty, resting your loving friend, Simon Delboe.

GEORGE NEEDHAM to Mr. THOMAS BARNARD – (2:131) 4th April 1662: Mr. Thomas Barnard. Sir: By virtue of the above order of Mr. Simon Delboe, I do require you to proceed on those voyages that shall be ordered you by Mr. Samuel Vener, & in case of your not performance, I have required the said Vener to protest against you; that all damages are for your account, & this you are to comply with, until any further order to the contrary, & for your so doing, this is your discharge. Your loving friend, George Needham. **Recorded**: 30: May: 1662.

GEORGE NEEDHAM to Capt. THOMAS BARNARD – (2:132) Barbados, 24 Apr 1662: Capt. Thomas Barnard. Sir: I wrote you by Capt. Venner at large; this only serves to confirm those orders I then gave you, & do again require you to comply with said Capt. Venner in presenting what voyages he shall propound to you. I do not at all doubt of your performance, & you may be confident, that while you have a care to see performed my orders, I shall not only save you harmless, but serve you in what lies in my power: So wishing you all happiness, I am your assured loving friend. **Signed**: George Needham; **Recorded**: 30 May 1662.

GEORGE NEEDHAM to Capt. THOMAS BARNARD – (2:132) Barbadoes, 4 April 1661: Capt. Thomas Barnard. Sir: *The Bearer*, Capt. Samuel Venner, will deliver you a letter from Mr. Simon Delboe, in the which you are required to follow my orders & to comply with me in all that I shall desire: now you will find that at the foot of the said letter, I have required you to follow the order of Capt. Venner & have given him the same power that Mr. Simon Delboe has given me, & notwithstanding when you left this Island, I did positively order you to return with deal boards, etc. from Discattoe hither, I have now altered my intention & do declare the said former orders are of no force. Therefore, pray deliver to Mr. Samuel Venner, all what salt you shall bring from the Saltatudos, or if you have sold it before this comes to your hands, then make over to him your sums that shall be owing you for it, the which I have ordered Venner to invest into such commodities as shall be fitting for the Maderas: Whether you are designed, & further you are to take notice that the reason why I have undertaken this design, is in respect that there are several ships arrived here, that freight is of no value, so I am out of hopes, until the latter end of the year to find any considerable freight, & you know I have no sugar of my own enough to load her and withal at the present, there is not one pipe of wine in the island to be sold. So I shall get extremely by the voyage; & to put the ship in fit condition to undertake this design, and to provide her a fitting cargo for the said voyage, I have sent by Mr. Venner several goods & shall send others after him & I do not doubt but by God's assistance, but it will be a design very profitable for us all. I do not question but you will on your part freely comply with my orders, but in case your men should be refractory, you must then take order to make them comply: God willing I intend upon your arrival here to pay your men their wages that shall be due to them, which pray tell them, and if you and they do consider well, it will be not above 2 months longer that you will be out. In conclusion, you may be confident in your compliance, you will much oblige me, & that it shall be my business to requite you for your dilligence therein: and withal, take notice, that if you should have taken in boards, or contracted for any, then you are to give an account thereof to the said Mr. Venner, & to follow his order for the disposing of them, again they being of no value in the Maderas & as little esteem here, therefore, as I have above said, I do require you in every respect to follow the order of Mr. Venner, & I will assure you that in the end you shall not lose by it. I have ordered Mr. Venner to furnish you with what you want, at all ports you shall arrive at, and so recommending you to God Almighty, I am your assured friend & servant. **Signed**: George Needham; **Recorded**: 30 May 1662.

JOHN CROAD to Mr. JAMES BRICE – (2:134) On the 1st of Sept 1662, This bindeth me John Croad of Salem (merchant) to pay unto Mr. James Brice, 167 pounds, which sum I do promise to pay in good dry merchantable sale fish, at or before the 20th day of October next ensuing, which fish is to be put aboard the ship *Hopewell* of London, whereof Capt. Samuel Clark is master, now riding at anchor in the harbor of Marblehead & bound for Bilbao: in witness whereof…the fish is to be paid at price current. **Signed**: John Croad; **Witness**: Walter Price; **Recorded**: 4: 7: 1662.

EDWARD BURT to JOHN PEARSON – (2:135) On the 6th of the 11th month, Edward Burt of Charlestown (yeoman) granted to John Pearson of Lynn (yeoman) for 102 pounds sterling, all his accommodation in Lynn, viz: one house lot of 4 acres, bounded N & W with land of Andrew Mansfield, S & E with the town highway that leads into the woods, & also the orchard & all the buildings upon it, also the 6-acre lot called "Churchman's Lot" bounded N on the rocks, S with the swamp that was given by the town to Hugh Burt, E with land of Richard Johnson, & W on the town highway; also the swamp adjoining to the S end of the lot above mentioned called "Churchman's Lot," bounded N with Churchman's Lot, S & W on the common & E with land of Richard Johnson, which swamp contains 1½ acres; also 4 acres of salt marsh, in the marsh below the town, 1 acre of which was lately in possession of Robert Burges, the whole being bounded N with marsh of Mr. Samuel Whiting & the great pond, S with the marsh of Thomas Newhall, Sr., & the creek & E with the marsh of Edmond Farrington; also 1 acre of salt marsh in the marsh before the town, bounded N with the marsh of Nathaniel Hanforth; S with the River, E with the marsh of Nathaniel Kirtland & W with the marsh of Andrew Mansfield; also 5 acres of salt marsh in the last division in Rumney Marsh, bounded N with the marsh of Henry Rhodes, S with the marsh of John Collins, E with the other range of lots & W with the great creek. **Signed**: Edward Burtt; **Acknowledged**: 14: 11 mo: 1661; **Witness**: Richard Price; **Recorded**: 24: 4: 1662.

DANIEL RUMBALL to JOHN UPTON – (2:138) On the 6th of April 1662, Daniel Rumball (blacksmith) of Salem granted to John Upton (husbandman) of Salem for 10 pounds sterling, 4 score acres bounded out by the town of Salem, it being a great lot formerly granted & laid out to said Daniel by Salem, which land is in Salem & is bounded S with land of John Upton's, formerly bought of Henry Bullock, on the W, N & E with the common (as it is taken). **Signed**: Daniel Rumball; **Acknowledged**: 6: 4: 1662; **Witnesses**: Hilliard Veren & Samuel Williams; **Recorded**: 24: 5: 1662.

Deposition of JOHN PORTER, Sr. concerning estate of LAURENCE LEACH – (2:140) The deposition of John Porter, Sr. who said that not long before the death of Laurance Leach, & seeing him weak, pressed him to make his will. He said he would write none, but he said he owed 30 pounds for the Mill, & his debts being paid, he gave all he had to his wife, & for his farm, he had given it to his son Richard, by writing already, 23: 4 mo: 1662. William Hathorne, taken upon oath before me the day & year above said. W. H. **Recorded**: 29: 5: 1662.

HENRY BULLOCK to JOHN UPTON – (2:141) On 26 December 1658, Henry Bullock of Salem (husbandman) granted to John Upton (sometime of Hammersmith) for 4 pounds to be paid with forebearance, as per John Upton's hand does express, 40 acres of upland in Salem, bounded with land of Daniel Rumboll on the N & some land of Thomas & George Gardner on the S. **Signed**: Henry Bullock [by mark]; **Acknowledged**: 6: 4: 1662; **Witnesses**: Hillyard Veren & Joshua Turland; **Recorded**: 24: 5: 1662.

JOHN BROWNE & Co. to WILLIAM STEVENS – (2:142) 6 June 1661: Articles of agreement between Mr. John Browne for himself & in behalf of Mr. Nicholas Balhack & Mr. John Balhack, all of Jersey (merchants) on the one part, and Mr. William Stevens of Gloucester in New England (shipwright) on the other part as follows, viz: The said William Stevens doth covenant & agree to & with the said John Brown & Company: to build one new ship of 68 foot long by the keel, & 23 foot broad from outside to outside, & 9½ foot in the hold under the beam, with 2 decks, forecastle, quarter deck & round houses, the deck from the mainmast to the forecastle to be 5 foot high, with a fale at the forecastle 15 inches & a raise at the mainmast to the quarter deck of 6 inches, the great cabin to be 6 foot high; and the said Stevens is to find timber and plank, trunnels, pitch, and tar & oakum, & to finish the hull & launch the said vessel, by the last of July 1662; and the said Mr. Brown & Co. is to find all ironworks, carved work & joiners in time convenient, so that the work be not hindered for want thereof. In consideration whereof, the said John Brown...doth covenant...to pay...said Stevens...the just sum of 3 pounds, 5 shillings, for every ton of the ship's burden, in such kind and manner as followeth: 50 pounds in hand in good goods at Mr. Brown's, Mr. Corwin's or Mr. Price's of Salem, or otherwise to content & 150 pounds in good Muscovadus sugar, at 2 pence by the pound, at Barbados, & 100 pounds in good New English money, and 2000 weight of half-weight & half black oakum at 18 shillings per pound & 15 hundred weight of resin at 14 shillings per pound, plus 700 weight of iron in bolts & spikes at 5 pence per pound of such several sizes according to directions given & 50 pounds worth of new rope, at 3 pounds per hundred in such sizes... & the rest to be paid in goods as the said Mr. Browne do sell at wholesale price; and for the true performance...John Browne & William Stevens, do bind themselves in 200 pounds bond; in witness whereof, the parties above mentioned...to three covenants all of this tenor & date the one being accomplished, the other two are void. (dated 6 June 1661.) It is to be understood that the sugar above mentioned is to be made at 3 payments, the first 50 pounds at or before the 1st of Sept. next ensuing, the 2nd payment at or before the 1st of December...& the last 50 pounds at or before the 1st of March...always provided it be demanded according to bills given. **Signed**: John Brown &

William Stevens; **Witnesses**: Hillyard Veren & John Gidney. Received of Mr. John Browne in severals, the sum of 50 pounds, & appears by account & is in part for the building of the new ship this 5th of the 5th month 1661 per me, William Stevens. (50: 00: 00). Received of Mr. John Browne in part payment for the new ship the 5: 5 mo: 1661, 3 bills of exchange to Mr. Lega at Barbados, containing 150 pounds whereof one bill of 50 pounds is paid to Mr. John Browne, for calking & pitch & tar, so there is 100 pounds received (100. 00. 00): per me: William Stevens. Received of Mr. John Browne the 3rd: 7 mo: 1662, as appears in particulars in an account of Mr. Browne's by divers persons the sum of 160 pounds & 9 d. (160: 00: 09). per me, William Stevens.

RICHARD RAYMOND to JOHN GARDNER – (2:145) On the 10th of August 1662, Richard Raymond of Salem (mariner) granted to John Gardner of Salem (mariner) for a valuable sum in hand paid, 2¼ acres of salt marsh in 2 parts, being divided by about ¾ of an acre of marsh of Ralph Fogg, which divides the said marsh, which is in Salem & bounded on either side with meadow of John Browne, Sr. to the S, the common to the W, the meadow of Elias Stileman, Jr. to the N & his upland to the E; also ¼ acre of salt marsh in the South field, in Salem, adjoining the Forest river, bounded on one side with some marsh of Samuel Belknap, and on the other side with some marsh of Samuel Archard Sen'r. **Signed**: Richard Raymond & Judith Raymond; **Witnesses**: John Sedgwick & Joshua Raymond; **Acknowledged**: 11: 6 mo: 62.

JOSEPH HARDY & JOHN GARDNER (Agreement) – (2:146) These presents witnesseth: that we, Joseph Hardy & John Gardner, mutually agree that there shall be a cart way between our house lots, from the end butting on the common, down all along the lot to the river, & is to be one pole in breadth, to lay wholly in Joseph Hardy's ground, in the side next to John Gardner's ground, & this we do mutually engage ourselves…the cart way shall never be sold or converted to any other use, but to lay in common between us both for our own private use, & for the use of any that shall live on either lot, and in consideration of said premises, John Gardner has given unto Joseph Hardy, 50 shillings to his content, and therefore Joseph Hardy has & does sell unto John Gardner…half a pole in breadth of his grounds, all the length of the lot & by these promises…deliver the half pole in breadth hereby promising & binding me…unto John Gardner…to make good the sale. **Signed**: 26 Sept 1661, by Joseph Hardy & John Gardner; **Acknowledged**: 16: 6 mo: 1662; **Recorded**: 4: 7: 1662.

DAVID CORWITHY & RICHARD CURTICE (and wife) to THOMAS DIXY – (2:147) On 26 June 1656, David Corwithy and Richard Curtice (and his wife) of Salem, granted to Thomas Dixy of

Marblehead (ferryman) for divers good & valuable considerations and 6 pounds, 10 shillings sterling, all their 10 acres of upland & meadow, in Marblehead, lying between lands of Joseph Grafton on the W & David Corwithy of Salem, on the E, & butting on Darby Fort Hill…to be held in free & common soccage, & not in Capite, nor by Knights service. **Signed**: Richard Curtis [by mark] & Sarah Curtis [by mark]; **Acknowledged**: 26: 4 month 1656 with Sarah consenting & acknowledging; **Witnesses**: Edmond Batter & Edward Norice, Jr.; **Recorded**: 15: 8: 1662.

DAVID CORWITHY to THOMAS DIXY – (2:150) On the 26th of June 1656, David Corwithy of Salem granted to Thomas Dixy of Marblehead (ferryman) for 5 pounds sterling, 5 acres of upland & meadow in Marblehead, between lands of said Thomas Dixy, which he bought of Richard Curtis of Salem on the W & lands of David Corwithy E, & butting towards the sea N, to be held in free & common soccage & not in Capite, nor by Knights Service. **Signed**: David Corwithy [by mark]; **Acknowledged**: 26: 4 mo: 1656; **Witnesses**: Edmond Batter & Edward Norice, Jr.; **Recorded**: 15: 8: 1662.

JOSEPH GRAFTON to THOMAS DIXY – (2:152) On the 30th of August 1658, Joseph Grafton of Salem (mariner) (with Mary wife) granted to Thomas Dixy of Marblehead, for 12 pounds to be paid, 4 pounds on 20 Sept next ensuing, in corn, peas & fish, at price currant, & 4 pounds paid the 20th of June 1659 in fish at price currant, & 4 pounds the 20th of September following in such pay as said Joseph Grafton & said Thomas Dixy can agree, 10 acres of ground at the ferry on the Darby Fort side, abutting against the harbour N & running up to the common on the S & bounded with land of Thomas Calyes W & land of said Thomas Dixy E, the particular bounds to the E next to the harbor…stone, & at the upper end next to the common E. bounded with a red oak stump, which is bounds between said 10 acres & 10 acres formerly Thomas Edwards' land & some land that was formerly in possession of Joseph Young; the bounds of the west next to common, between said lot & some land of Thomas Calies…post & rock… the bounds next to the harbor on the W…rock…within 1½ poles of the house of said Thomas Dixy. **Acknowledged**: 20: 10 mo: 1658; **Signed**: Joseph Grafton & Mary Grafton; **Witnesses**: John Whiting & Thomas Cromwell; **Recorded**: 16: 8: 1662.

DAVID CORWITHEN to THOMAS DIXY – (2:154) On 23 April 1662, David Corwithen of Salem granted to Thomas Dixy of Marblehead (ferryman) for a valuable sum secured, all his right, title & interest in a cow lease or cow pasture that he had in Marblehead common, formerly given by the town. **Acknowledged**: 18: 6 mo: 1662; **Witnesses**: John Archard & Hillyard Veren; **Recorded**: 16: 8: 1662.

RICHARD CURTIS to THOMAS DIXY – (2:155) On 18 August 1662, Richard Curtis of Salem (with wife Sara Curtis yielding thirds) granted to Thomas Dixy of Marblehead (ferryman) for a valuable sum, all his right, title & interest in a cow lease or cow pasture he had in Marblehead common, formerly given him by the town of Marblehead. **Signed**: Richard Curtice [by mark]; **Acknowledged**: 18: 6 mo: 1662; **Witnesses**: Hilliard Veren & David Corwithen; **Recorded**: 16: 8: 1662.

CHRISTOPHER WALLER to FRANCIS NURSE – (2:156) On the 4th of the 12th month 1661/2, Christopher Waller of Salem (with consent of his wife) granted to Francis Nurse of Salem, for 4 pounds 12 shillings already paid, ½ acre of salt marsh, with all fences belonging, in Rial's Side in Salem, bordering E on land of Thomas Robbins, N on the common & S and W with the river. **Signed**: Christopher Waller [by mark]; **Acknowledged**: 16: 6 mo: 1662, with wife yielding thirds; **Witnesses**: Edward Norrice & Elizabeth Pester; **Recorded**: 16: 8: 1662.

EDWARD RICHARDS to ALLEN BREED, Sr. – (2:157) 10: 6 mo: 1657. This witnesseth that I Edward Richards of Lynn fully & freely acquit & discharge Allen Breed, Sr. in behalf of his present wife & her predecessors of Lynn, of all debts that have been between us. **Signed**: Edward Richards [by mark]; **Witnesses**: Thomas Laughton & Thomas Marshall; **Recorded**: 29: 8: 1662.

EDWARD RICHARDS to ELIZABETH BREED – (2:158) On 8: May 1657, Edward Richards declared he had received from Elizabeth Breed (Executrix of the last will of William Knight, deceased, and of Allen Breed her husband) the full sum of the legacies bequeathed "to my wife and children"—that is to say, 26 shillings received by him, Edward Richards. **Signed**: Edward Richards [by mark]; **Witnesses**: John Fuller & Richard Blood.

THOMAS GAGE to ELIZABETH (___) KNIGHT BREED – (2:158) On 11 March 1655, Thomas Gage, husband of Joanna Knight, did acquit the wife of his father William Knight...forever from a legacy of 40 shillings, which was given to my wife, at my father's death, which is now duly paid unto me by my mother Elizabeth Knight. **Signed**: Thomas Gage [by mark]; **Witnesses**: Samuel Hart & Edward Hall.

THOMAS GAGE to ALLEN BREED, Sr. – (2:158) On 8 July 1657, Thomas Gage of Yarmouth, did acquit Allen Breed, Sr. & his wife...of all debts... **Signed**: Thomas Gage [by mark]; **Witnesses**: Samuel Hart & John Witt [by mark].

JOHN FARRINGTON to ALLEN BREED, Sr. and ELIZABETH BREED – (2:159) On the 10th of the 2nd month 1661, John Farrington of Lynn did fully acquit his father & mother, Allen & Elizabeth Breed, the sum of the legacy bequeathed to his wife, according to the will of his late deceased father William Knight. **Signed**: John Farrington; **Witnesses**: John Breed & Henry Wormwood [by mark]. Also: I Mary Knight of Lynn do fully & freely acquit my father Allen Breed of Lynn, Sr....of a legacy bequeathed to me by the last will of my father William Knight... 10th 2 month 1661. **Signed**: Mary Knight [by mark]; **Witnesses**: John Breed & Henry Wormwood [by mark]; **Recorded**: 29: 8: 62.

JOHN & NATHANIEL BALLARD to ALLEN BREED, Sr. – (2:160) On the 4th of February 1661, John & Nathaniel Ballard did acknowledge they had received the full legacy bequeathed to them by their father-in-law William Knight's last will & testament, being 40 shillings apiece and did fully acquit & discharge Allen Breed, Sr. **Signed**: John Ballard & Nathaniel Ballard; **Witnesses**: John Fuller & Joseph Jenckes, Jr.

WILLIAM HATHORNE to HENRY SKERRY – (2:160) On the 28th of the 1st month 1658/9, William Hathorne of Salem (gentleman) granted to Henry Skerry for 56 shillings, a parcel of salt marsh, upland & mowing ground in the north neck in Salem, called "old planter's marsh," one part or parcel thereof being in the occupation of Henry Skerry of Salem, containing 7 acres bounded by land of Francis Skerry on the N, land of George Emory S & abuts land of Daniel Rumball W & the sea on the E. The land had been granted to William Hathorne by the town of Salem on 2: 9 mo: 1658. **Signed**: William Hathorne; **Witnesses**: John Porter & John Gedney.

PHILLIP VEREN to RICHARD SIBLEY – (2:161) On 22 November 1662, Phillip Veren of Salem (wheelwright), with consent of wife Johanah, granted to Richard Sibley of Salem (tray-maker) for a valuable sum already paid, ¼ acre of land in Salem, being part of that land of Phillip Veren's where his dwelling house stands, bounded with the highway or street S & land of Capt. Davenport E & land of Phillip Veren N & W, which land is in breadth, next to the said street 8 poles, from the land of Capt. Davenport W & to run inward from the street about 4 poles. **Signed**: Phillip Veren & Johanah Veren [by mark]; **Witnesses**: with livery & seizon, by turf & twig according to law, Timothy Robinson & Hilliard Veren; **Recorded**: 22: 9ber: 1662.

PETER PALFREY to SAMUEL PICKMAN – (2:162) On the 15th day of April 1662, Peter Palfrey of Reading, Co. Middlesex (husbandman) granted to Samuel Pickman of Salem (mariner) for 60 pounds, his 10-acre lot in South field in Salem, with state point, with his marsh & mowing ground thereto adjoining, & all his salt marsh & upland in planters marsh, containing 7 acres. **Signed**: Peter Palfrey [by mark]; **Witnesses**: William Cowdry & John Smith; **Recorded**: 28: 8 mo: 1662.

THOMAS ANTRUM to ISAACK BURNAP – (2:164) On 18 January 1658, Thomas Antrum of Salem, let by the year, the term of his life, 4 oxen, 7 cows & 9 young neat cattle & 5 or 6 swine, to Isaack Burnap, his son-in-law, which cattle & swine are to be delivered to said Isaack Burnap the 1st of May next ensuing & then be apprized by 2 indifferent men, chosen by either party, which full value Isaack Burnap is to pay…to said Thomas Antrum…in cattle or other current pay at or before the decease of said Thomas Antrum, it being at the liberty of said Thomas Antrum when to call for the principle and for the yearly rent of said cattle…Isaack shall maintain the said Thomas Antrum with meat & drink & washing & also winter yearly a mare of said Thomas Antrum's, but if said Antrum see cause to remove from said Isaac, or die then said Isaac shall pay…yearly while the stock is in his hands, 10 pounds in current pay & to winter a mare as above; also Isaack Burnap may deliver up half the stock above mentioned to Thomas Antrum shall at 5 years end, receive at the farm, the place of his dwelling, ½ the stock & then to acquit Isaack of the same & also ½ of the above mentioned yearly rent. **Signed**: Thomas Antrum [by mark] & Isaack Burnap; **Witnesses**: Mary Veren & Hillyard Veren; [*Written below*:] This covenant is void & of no force, being fully satisfied & the stock returned, 23: 3: 1663. **Signed**: Hillyard Veren; **Recorded**: 24: 10: 62.

MARY GOULT (Administrator for WILLIAM GOULT) to SAMUEL PICKMAN – (2:165) On 12 June 1660, Mary Goult (administrator to her late husband, William Gould of Salem), granted to Samuel Pickman of Salem (mariner) for 24 pounds sterling, her dwelling house with all lands & all appurtenances…bounded N of Mr. Richard Prescott's land, now enjoyed by Mr. Richard Moore, S by Mr. George Corwin's land, E by Mr. Henry Bartholomew's land, W by Mr. William Hathorne's orchard. **Signed**: Mary Goult [by mark]; **Acknowledged**: 13: 8 mo: 1662.

Major HATHORNE & RICHARD DAVENPORT to JOHN PUTNAM, Sr., RICHARD HUCHESON & DANIEL RAY & Mr. JOHN HATHORNE – (2:166) Whereas there has been a sale made about the 15th of July 1647 between the Worshipful Major Hathorne of Salem & Capt. Richard Davenport of Castle Island on the one part & John Putnam,

Sr., Richard Hucheson & Daniel Ray of Salem & also Mr. John Hathorne of Lynn on the other part of 2 farms in Salem, to each of them an equal portion, the farms containing 280 acres apiece of upland & meadow, that is to say: 260 acres of upland & 20 acres of meadow of each, being bounded as followeth: one of said farms belonging to the Worshipful Major William Hathorne, butting S with a corner of the meadow of said Richard Hucheson, & the other corner on a brook running between land of Richard Hucheson & Major Wm. Hathorne & N on land of Phillip Cromwell & some land given to Mr. John Hathorne, on the E the land of Mr. John Ruck, adjoining the meadow within said land, & the land of Thomas Putnam & John Putnam, part of their meadow within the land and part without, & on the W bordering on the Run in the swamp, having the land of Nathaniel Putnam on the W, all this being contained within the bounds except [40 acres...as it is now bounded lying on the S end of the farm] & also excepting [the land which was given to Thomas Smith (seaman) lying about the N or NE of the hill], being both upland and meadow reserved to Capt. Richard Davenport, only 1 acre & 100 rod of meadow adjoining the land of said Richard Hucheson, which is reserved to Thomas Putnam: And the other of the said farms, belonging to said Capt. Davenport, containing the same proportion, adjoining S to land of Mr. Ralph Fogg & Lieut. Thomas Lothrop, N to the land of Mr. Bishop & the meadow of the Right Worshipful Mr. John Endicott, also Mr. Ralph Fogg partly & Mr. Peters, E to land of John Putnam, Jr. & Mr. Kenniston, & W on land of Capt. Trask, formerly Mr. William Pester's, & the land of John Putnam, Sr. & the 20 acres of meadow lying in the great meadow, butting on land formerly Mr. Bishop's, having Jacob Barnes' meadow NW, also bounding on Mr. Fogg's meadow, having the meadow of the Right Worshipful John Endicott, Esq. & some upland belonging to the same on the S. We, Major William Hathorne & Capt. Richard Davenport, for a valuable consideration...in hand already paid...sell both the said farms...unto the said John Putnam, Sr., Richard Hucheson, Daniel Ray & John Hathorne, this last day of Oct 1662. **Signed**: William Hathorne & Richard Davenport; **Witnesses**: Ralph King & Edw. Norrice, Sr.; **Acknowledged**: before me by Capt. Davenport and owned by me William Hathorne, 31: 8: 1662.

THOMAS & JOHN PUTNAM to NATHANIEL PUTNAM – (2:169)
On the 17th of the 2nd month 1662, Thomas Putnam and John Putnam of Salem (farmers & sons of John Putnam, Sr.), granted to their brother Nathaniel Putnam of Salem, for a valuable consideration already paid & with consent of their father, their shares, that is to say ½ of the lands called the plains, which was given & laid out to their father there & no other, in Salem, having land of John Porter, Sr. formerly given to Mr. Sharp on the NE, also land of said John Porter, formerly given to Mr. Skelton S, &

bordering on the other half of said land called the plains, given to said Nathaniel Putnam by his father. **Signed**: Thomas Putnam & John Putnam; **Witnesses**: Edward Norrice & Francis Nurse [by mark]; **Acknowledged**: 30: 8: 1662.

JOHN PUTNAM to NATHANIEL PUTNAM – (2:171) On the 2nd of the 1st month 1653, John Putnam the elder of Salem (yeoman) granted to his son Nathaniel Putnam of Salem, ½ of his land or plains in his possession & ¼ part of all upland & meadow which was Capt. Danfords, except only so much of the hill as was sold to William Bayley & Thomas Hobbs, lying within the fence, all in Salem, by the presents granting unto his said son Nathaniel Putnam, full power & authority to make equal division of such lands & meadows as are yet undivided, & where division is already made & bounds set, that these bounds shall stand for land marks between him & his brothers. **Signed**: John Putnam [by mark]; **Acknowledged**: 30: 8 mo: 1662; **Witnesses**: Em. Downing & William Norton; **Recorded**: 6: 9ber: 1662.

WILLIAM HATHORNE & WIFE to GEORGE KEYSER – (2:172) On 28: 8 mo: 1654, William Hathorne & Ann his wife granted to George Keyser of Lynn, for 16 pounds, ¾ to an acre of enclosed land between land of William Chichester E & land of John Horne & John Porter, Sr. on the N & down to the south river side, with free egress & regress through the highway laid out from the street down to his warehouse intended, & so to the river.. in which said grant is excepted a piece of ground in which there is a cellar, over which a warehouse is to be erected, the said ground to be square from the said cellar down to the riverside, with so much ground without said cellar & warehouse, as a ladder may conveniently stand for the repairing of said house. The remainder of the enclosed ground to remain to Keyser. **Signed**: William Hathorne & Anna Hathorne; **Witnesses**: Jeffery Massey & Thomas Rix; **Recorded**: 7: 9ber: 1662.

GEORGE EMERY to GEORGE KEASER – (2:173) On 23 Aug 1662, George Emery of Salem granted to George Keaser of Salem (tanner), for 20 pounds sterling, 10 acres of land formerly Samuel Archard, Sr.'s, in the south neck in Salem, bounded with land of Richard Price S & of James Underwood E & of George Ropes N & with a strip of salt marsh of John Horne's W. **Signed**: George Emery; **Acknowledged**: 1: 7 mo: 1662, with wife yielding dower; **Witness**: William Delly [by mark]; **Recorded**: 7: 9 mo: 1662.

JOB & MARY TYLER to GEORGE ABBOT – (2:174) On the 10th day of June 1662, Job Tyler (husbandman) of Andover and Mary Tyler his wife, granted to George Abbot of Andover (tailor) for 29 pounds 15 shillings, a house lot of 4 acres in Andover, bounded N with lot of Richard Sutton, S with lot of John Aslet, E with the common, W with the highway; also 2 acres in Andover bounded E with the highway, W with land of John Fry, Sr., S with land of John Aslet, both which houselot & parcel of land, they acknowledged to have sold to George Abbott, together with his dwelling house thereupon & orchard & all fences, reserving unto himself all privileges in all lands & meadows already granted, only said Job & Mary Tyler do hereby acknowledge to have sold to said George Abbot, together with said land, 1 acre privilege in the common not yet granted or laid out. Said George is to pay unto the minister 4 shillings by the year so long as this way of rating remain. **Signed**: Job Tyler & Mary Tyler [by mark]; **Acknowledged**: 11 June 1662, & Mary resigned thirds; **Witnesses**: Edmond Faulkner & Thomas Abbott; **Recorded**: 21: 9: 1662.

JOB & MARY TYLER to THOMAS ABBOTT – (2:176) On 10 June 1662. Job Tyler of Andover (husbandman) and Mary Tyler (his wife) granted to Thomas Abbott of Andover, for 10 pounds 10 shillings already in hand paid in a horse, all that 12 acres of land in Andover bounded NW with the highway going to Little Hope, on SW with lot of Steven Osgood, SE with the highway to Billerica; with 1½ acres of privilege in the common that is not yet granted, said Thomas paying unto the minister 6 shillings by the year, as long as this way of rating remain. **Signed**: John Tyler and Mary Tyler [by mark]; **Acknowledged**: 11 June 1662; Mary resigned her thirds; **Witnesses**: Edward Faulkner & George Abbott, Jr.; **Recorded**: 21: 9: 1662.

SAMUEL CONDEY to EDMOND BATTER (mortgage) – (2:178) On 24 May 1662, Samuel Condey of Marblehead (fisherman) in consideration of a debt due Edmond Batter specified by bill, mortgaged all his house, houses & land in Marblehead, being now under attachment, together with my person, to be at the said Edmond Batter's service & to faithfully serve until the said debt be satisfied, with sufficient satisfaction for the forbearance of the said debt, as 4 indifferent men shall judge, 2 of them being chosen by the one party & 2 by the other party & if the said Samuel should die or otherwise depart this jurisdiction; it shall be lawful for the said Batter to take possession of said houses & land, as his own proper goods, in part of payment & valuable consideration to which agreement, I bind me…unto Edmond Batter. **Signed**: Samuel Condey; **Acknowledged**: 27: 8: 1662; **Witnesses**: Richard Norman [by mark] & Lot Conant; **Recorded**: 21: 9: 1662.

SAMUEL PICKMAN to Mr. WILLIAM BROWNE, Sr. – (2:179) On 3 Oct 1662, Samuel Pickman of Salem (mariner) granted to Mr. William Browne, Sr. of Salem (merchant) for 70 pounds, every part & parcel of land pertaining to him, either 7 acres of land in the planters' marsh with the properties thereof, or in the south field; the 10-acre lot with stage point & all the meadow & mowing ground thereto belonging accordingly, as specified in a bill of sale given him by his father-in-law Peter Palfrey dated 15 Apr 1662. **Signed**: Samuel Pickman & Lydea Pickman [by mark]; **Acknowledged**: 4: 4 mo: 1662, with Lydea yielding thirds; **Witnesses**: Elias Stileman, John Beckett & William Browne, Jr.; **Recorded**: 22: 9: 1662.

SAMUEL CONDEY to JOHN SLATTER – (2:180) On 17 Feb 1661/2, Samuel Condey of Marblehead (fisherman) granted to John Slatter, the younger, of Marblehead, part of his lot before his dwelling house in Marblehead on the other side of the highway, 3 score & 5 foot thereof in length from the stone wall, next to Richard Read's house E and in breadth from the stone wall next to the highway to the stone wall next to Mr. Lattamore's meadow. **Signed**: Samuel Condey; Edm. Batter consented to sale 24 May 1662; **Acknowledged**: 24: 9ber: 1662 by Samuel Condey & Mr. Batter; **Witnesses**: William Pitt & Samuel Morgan; **Recorded**: 24: 9: 1662.

WILLIAM LORD, Jr. to JOHN MASON – (2:182) On 19 Apr 1662, William Lord, Jr. of Salem (husbandman) granted to John Mason of Salem (brickmaker) for a valuable sum, 8 poles of ground, being 2 rods in breadth & 4 in length, not 2 rods at the S but as much more than 2 rods at the N as it wants at the S end, in Salem, being part of that ground on which the dwelling house of said William Lord stands at the NE corner of said ground, bounded with the street on the N & E & to the S & W with the land of said William Lord…with the fence that is about it. It is to be understood that said John Mason is to maintain the fence on his own charge. **Signed**: William Lord; **Witnesses**: John Gedney, Samuel Williams & Hillyard Veren; **Acknowledged**: 8ber 1662; **Recorded**: 22: 10: 1662.

THOMAS MARSHALL to WILLIAM BROWNE, Sr. & WALTER PRICE – (2:183) On 18 Dec 1662, Thomas Marshall of Lynn (yeoman) granted to William Brown, Sr. & Walter Price of Salem (merchants) for a valuable consideration in hand paid, 9 acres of meadow as it now lies bounded, William Browne is to have 1/3 and said Walter Price 2/3, lying in Lynn in Wigwam meadow, bounded E with meadow of Thomas Wellman, S with meadow of Benjamin Smith, & N & W with the common. **Signed**: Thomas Marshall; **Acknowledged**: 18: 10ber: 1662; **Witnesses**: Hillyard Veren & Phillip Cromwell; **Recorded**: 22: 10: 1662.

ROBERT GOODELL to GEORGE CORWIN – (2:185) On 20 December 1662, Robert Goodell, sometime of Salem (planter) granted to George Corwin of Salem (merchant) for 8 pounds, 2 acres of salt marsh in Salem at the upper end of the great Cove, between a parcel of upland which the said Mr. Corwin bought of John Smith, and Mr. Peter's, his salt marsh, having a spring of water in it, with a small parcel of meadow adjoining to Mr. Gedney's above the common highway. **Signed**: Robert Goodell; **Acknowledged**: 20: 10ber: 1662; **Witnesses**: Thomas Putnam & Edward Norrice; **Recorded**: 23: 10: 1662.

THOMAS CARTER (Atty. for Mr. MATHEW WILLIAMS) to WILLIAM WALTON – (2:187) On 9: 10: 1662, Thomas Carter of Charlestown (attorney for his brother Mr. Mathew Williams) granted to William Walton of Marblehead for 3 pounds, all the land in Marblehead "which my said brother Mathew Williams was possessed of." **Signed**: Thomas Carter; **Acknowledged**: This discharge of a sale of land passed by Thomas Carter, by virtue of his attorney-ship (as above) was owned & subscribed on 9 Dec 1662; **Witnesses**: William Rosewels & Andrew Belcher; **Recorded**: 24: 10: 1662.

JOSEPH HARDY to JOHN CROMWELL – (2:187) On 16 June 1662, Joseph Hardy of Salem (mariner), with wife Martha yielding dower, granted to John Cromwell of Salem (seaman) for 5 pounds sterling, 40 rods of land in Salem, 5 poles in breadth inward from the common to the S & 8 poles in length across the said Joseph Hardy's ground, bounded on the N with the common highway next to the pen so called, E with land of John Gardner & S with land of Joseph Hardy & W with land of widow Jeggles, & also provided always that said John Cromwell is to leave out ½ a pole of ground in breadth from the pen to the said Joseph Hardy's on the side adjoining the land of John Gardner; and said Hardy does promise to leave out as much in breadth of his ground adjoining the same side & so down to the water side for a highway only for said Hardy's and Cromwell's use…and further if said Cromwell ever sells the above land, said Joseph Hardy is to have first refusal of it. **Signed**: Joseph Hardy and Martha Hardy [by mark]; **Witnessed**: with turf & twig by Daniel Rumball & Samuel Williams; **Recorded**: 12: 11: 1662.

THOMAS MARSHALL to ANDREW MANSFIELD – (2:190) On 20 January 1661, Thomas Marshall of Lynn (Capt of the military there), with consent of Rebecka his now wife, granted to Andrew Mansfield of Lynn (husbandman) for a valuable sum of money, 6 acres of salt marsh in the lower division in Rumney Marsh, lately in possession of John Lewis, bounded S with the marsh of Robert Burges, N with the marsh of John Lewis, W with the marsh of Allen Breed, Sr., & E with the creek that parts it and the marsh of John Witt. **Signed**: Thomas Marshall and Rebecka Marshall [by mark]; **Acknowledged**: 27: 10ber: 1662; **Witnesses**: Thomas Marshall and Abigail Marshall [by mark]; **Recorded**: 12: 11: 1662.

JOB TYLER to JOHN GODFREY – (2:192) On 28 Aug 1662, Job Tyler of Andover (husbandman) granted to John Godfrey all his lands, meadow & upland of 40 acres, with the orchard & all the buildings, in Andover, together with all other lands and accommodations that at any time hereafter shall or may be allotted unto Job Tyler…all said land & meadow already in possession of Job Tyler is bounded E by the common and likewise on the other 3 sides. **Signed**: Job Tyler; **Acknowledged**: 29 Aug 1662; Mary Tyler surrendered thirds 12 Nov 1662; **Witnesses**: William White & George Abbott, Sr.; **Recorded**: 14: 12: 1662.

JOSEPH YOUNGES to DAVID CORWITHEN – (2:193) On 24 Sept 1649, Joseph Younges of Salem (mariner) granted to David Corwithen of Salem for 17 pounds, 2 dwelling houses on the S river side in Salem, one of them now in possession of said David Corwithen, with ¾ acre of ground behind said house, and one dwelling house now in possession of William Curtice, adjoining said house, with ¼ acre behind said house; also 20 acres of upland on the E side of Darby Fort Hill, now in possession of said David Corwithen, lying between land of said David Corwithen & land of William Chichester. **Signed**: Joseph Younges; **Acknowledged**: 24: 7: 1649; **Witnesses**: Pascah Souden [by mark], William Golt & Richard Stileman, Sr.; **Recorded**: 23: 12: 1662.

JOHN NORTON to THOMAS WEST – (2:195) On 19 January 1662, John Norton of Salem (carpenter) granted to Thomas West of Salem (planter) for a valuable sum, a 10-acre lot, formerly in the possession of Mr. Alderman, lying in the north neck, Salem, bounded W with land of Edward Beachum & E with land of Thomas James. **Signed**: John Norton; **Acknowledged**: 23: 11: 1662; wife Mary yielded thirds 10: 12 mo: 62; **Witnesses**: John Ruck & Hillyard Veren; **Recorded**: 23: 12: 1662.

JOHN RUCK to MATHEW WOODWELL – (2:196) On the 3rd of the 8th month 1660, John Ruck of Salem, with consent of his wife, granted to Mathew Woodwell of Salem (seaman) for 19 pounds, 2 acres of upland in Salem, near the now dwelling house of said John Ruck, having the cove that lies behind his house N, being bounded E with the river that runs to Castle Hill, & S & W with land of John Ruck…said John Ruck promises to lay out a highway of 14 feet in breadth, extending from the common that lies before Goodman Laws' house, down to land of Mathew Woodwell, as may be best for his convenience, within 2 years after said Woodwell is living on his said land & that in the meantime, he shall have liberty to bring any cart or cattle through the open bars & so through the land of John Ruck near the place where the highway should be, not leaving any of his cattle to feed in said land. **Signed**: John Ruck & Hanna Ruck; **Acknowledged**: 3: 8 mo: 1660; **Witnesses**: Edward Norice & George Keyser; **Recorded**: 19: 1 mo: 1662/3.

HENRY COOKE to HENRY BULLOCK, Sr. – (2:198) On 14 December 1657, Henry Cooke of Salem, having purchased the house and land formerly in possession of Henry Bullock, Jr., deceased, joining land of Henry Bullock, Sr...do promise to maintain the partition fence between said Cooke & Bullock which begins at the great white oak by the highway next to north neck & runs to the fence of John Southwick, NW by W, being 56 rods...Henry Cooke does promise to keep & maintain said fence from time to time, belonging to the said land purchased of Alce, the late wife of Bullock, deceased, with sufficient fence against all sorts of cattle. **Signed**: Henry Cooke; **Witnesses**: Edmond Batter & Elizabeth Sharp [by mark]; **Recorded**: 6: 2 month: 1663.

GEORGE CORWIN to WILLIAM PHILLIPS (Receipt) – (2:198) On 17 Nov 1663, George Corwin received from Mr. William Phillips, in full of all debts, dues & demands, either by bill or book, due unto him from said Phillips...the receipt was acknowledged by Capt. George Corwin to be his act & deed.

JOHN KITCHIN & JOHN SANDERS to JOHN WILLIAMS – (2:199) On the 8th of the 5th month 1661, John Kitchin of Salem (shoemaker) and John Sanders, his son-in-law, of Salem (seaman) granted for a valuable consideration to John Williams of Salem (seaman), 10 acres of upland in Salem in north field, being bounded E with land of Robert Buffum, W with land of John Williams & bordering S on the marsh of Thomas Spooner, and N on the highway that goes through the 10-acre lot. **Signed**: John Kitchin & John Sanders; **Acknowledged**: 2: 1 mo: 1662/3 by both John Kitchin & John Sanders; **Witnesses**: Thomas Hale, John Putnam & Edward Norice; **Witness** to John Sanders assignment & delivery: Hillyard Veren.

JOHN GILLOW to ROSE GILLOW – (2:200) On the 12th of the 3rd month (called May) 1656, John Gillow of Lynn constituted his wife Rose Gillow to be his true & lawful attorney, and in his name, his wife Rose was to sell or hire out, all such houses & lands & other goods or estate...and also to ask & receive all debts belonging to him, and for payment thereof, to sue, arrest, attach, etc... **Signed**: John Gillow; **Witnesses**: John Gisboine & Thomas Gillow; **Proved upon oath**: 20: 3 mo: 1663.

JUDITH COOKE to ISAAC COOKE – (2:201) On 14 Apr 1663, Judith Cooke of Salem (widow) granted to her son Isaac Cooke, as the legacy of 22 pounds due Isaac out of the estate of Henry Cooke, late deceased, 5 acres of upland called the cow pen lot, in Salem in the north field, butted & bounded W with the general fence & having on the N & E side, land of Joseph Pope, & to the S, the land of John Pease. **Signed**: Judith Cooke [by mark]; **Acknowledged**: 20: 2 month: 1663; **Witnesses**: Hillyard Veren & Obadiah Antrum; **Recorded**: 20: 3: 1663.

JUDITH COOKE to ISAACK COOKE – (2:203) In 1663, Judith Cooke of Salem (widow) granted to Isaack Cooke of Salem, for 5 pounds secured to be paid, 6 acres of meadow in the broad meadow beyond Lieut. Putnam, having the meadow of said Lieut. Putnam on the W & the meadow of Henry Bullock on the E. **Signed**: Judith Cooke [by mark]; **Acknowledged**: 20: 2 mo: 1663; **Witnesses**: Hillyard Veren & Obadiah Antrum.

ROBERT & ANN BURNUP to WILLIAM EASTON – (2:203) On 18 January 1657, Robert Burnup of Reading and Ann his wife, granted to William Easton of Reading, for 30 pounds, secured to be paid, 100 acres of upland in Lynn, bounded N with Wigwam meadow, E with land of one Wellman, S with land of Adam Hawkes, & W with the river. **Signed**: Robert Burnap; **Acknowledged**: at Reading, 13: 9 mo: 1662, by Robert and Ann Burnap, with Ann consenting & releasing dower 13 (9) 62 & signing [by mark]; **Witnesses**: William Cowdry & Edward Michell.

JUDITH COOKE to ISAAC COOKE – (2:205) [Repeat of 2:201]

JUDITH COOKE to ISAAC COOKE – (2:206) [Repeat of 2:203]

ROBERT GOODELL to GILES COREY – (2:207) On 15 March 1659/60, Robert Goodell of Salem (husbandman) granted to Giles Corey of Salem, for 30 pounds to be paid by Corey as per bill under his hand bearing date of 2 March 1659/60, 50 acres formerly given by the town of Salem to Edward Giles & sold by him to Mr. Blackleech of whom said Robert Goodell lately bought said land in Salem, bounded with land now in possession of Thomas Flint NE & land now in possession of Giles Corey SW. **Signed**: Robert Goodell; **Witnesses**: Joshua Turland & Hillyard Veren; **Recorded**: 30: 10: 1662.

MATHEW EDWARD to WILLIAM RAINES – (2:209) On the 18th of the 12th month 1658, Mathew Edward of Reading sold to William Raines of Ipswich for 7 pounds sterling, 20 acres of upland and 2 acres of meadow in Wenham, the upland bounded by Mr. Newman's farm eastward, the great swamp northward, and 2 acres of meadow within the great meadow being part of 8 acres which was late of John Fairefields, butting upon the great swamp eastward, running by the side of Richard Kimball's meadow, butting upon Goodman Morgaines meadow westward, which upland and meadow Mathew Edwards had by the bequest of his uncle John Fairefield, deceased, as expressed in his last will and testament. **Signed**: Mathew Edwards and Mary Edwards [by mark]; **Witnesses**: Richard Kimball [by mark] and Thomas Fiske; **Acknowledged**: 27: 4: 61: Mathew Edwards.

THOMAS HALE to JOHN KNIGHT – (2:210) On 6 November 1661, Thomas Hale of Salem (glover) sold to John Knight, of Salem (mason) for 35 pounds, a dwelling house and barn with ¾ of an acre in Salem, bounded with some land of Ralph Fogg on the west, and North River on north, and street on east and some land of said Hales on the south; also 2 rods and a half square of ground, which the town granted to said Hale for a watering place, near the water side, before the house to the east with the frame of a working house upon the same. **Signed**: Thomas Hale, with wife Tamsen releasing dower; **Witnesses**: Hilliard Veren and Samuel Williams; **Acknowledged**: 8: 9: 61 by Thomas Hale and wife, who yielded thirds.

ALLEN CONVERS to JOHN ROWDEN and WILLIAM CANTLEBURY – (2:211) **Acknowledged**: 11: 3 mo: 1664. This is to certify…that I Allen Convers of Woburn, to my best remembrance did never sell to said John Rowden, but half my lot wherein he now dwells and the other half to William Cantlebury & so what I have sold to said William Cantlebury, my wife Elizabeth Convers does resign all her right and title thereto, she had set her hand. **Signed**: Allen Convers, Elizabeth Convers [by mark]; **Recorded**: 6: 4 mo: 1664.

SAMUEL EDSON to WILLIAM BROWNE – (2:212) On 24: 7 mo: 1655, Samuel Edson, late of Salem, sold to William Browne (merchant) for 38 pounds sterling, one dwelling house, a barn and 10 acres of upland on Cape Ann side, between land of Robert Lemon on the west and land and house of John Black on the east; also 25 acres of upland between snakehill and land of Humphry Woodbery; also 2 acres of meadow, between the meadow of William Dodge on the south and Mr. Roger Conant on the north; moreover 20 acres of upland which was Thomas Brackett's given by the town of Salem to John Ward, his predecessor, and is adjoining to land of Osmand Trask, which he bought of Jonathan Porter, with 2 acres of meadow belonging to it, butting upon meadow of Jeffrey Massey in the meadow called Wenham meadow; also 4 acres of meadow in Wenham, formerly meadow of John Bushnell, given him by the town of Salem, all of said parcels are in the township of Salem. **Signed**: Samuel Edson; **Witnesses**: Thomas Barnes and Joshua Rea; **Acknowledged**: 24: 7 mo:

1655; [written below: "I assign over this deed and right and interest to Zebulon and John Hills, both of Salem." William Browne of Salem set his hand 30 June 1659; William Brown acknowledged 11: 1 mo: 1662/3]

MATHEW WOODWELL to JOHN RUCK – (2:215) On 19 August 1663, Mathew Woodwell of Salem (brickmaker) sold to Mr. John Ruck of Salem (merchant) for a "valuable sum" 60 rods of land; being part of the land which he formerly bought of said Ruck, on the outside of his fence northward, between the fence and a creek that comes in out of the South River, and bounds said parcel of land to the north, with a highway to the upper end westward, and eastward with the river, and on the south with his fence as it now runs. **Signed**: Mathew Woodwell, and Mary Woodwell [by mark], who relased dower; **Witnesses**: Hillyard Verren and Bartholomew Gedney; **Recorded**: 24: 6: 1663.

JOHN RUCK to MATHEW WOODWELL – (2:215) On 19 August 1663, John Ruck of Salem (merchant), with Sarah his wife releasing dower, sold to Mathew Woodwell of Salem (brickmaker), for a "valuable consideration already paid," 60 or 70 rod of ground within the field of said Mathew Woodwell, adjoining to a little cove of the South river, to south, & runs up a narrow slip, near to the dwelling house of said Mathew Woodwell, and is bounded with aforesaid little cove to south and land of Obadyah Antrum to the west, and on the east and north with land of said Mathew. **Signed**: John Ruck and Sarah Ruck; **Witnesses**: Hillyard Veren and Bartholomew Gedney; **Recorded**: 24: 6: 1663.

SAMUEL SKELTON to JOHN PORTER – (2:216) 30 March the 15th year of Charles the second. Whereas John Porter, son of John Porter, Sr. of Salem (yeoman), about 14 years ago, by order of said John Porter, Sr., his father, did purchase the farm of the late Rev. Samuel Skelton (late pastor of the Church of Christ in Salem), the farm commonly called and known by the name of Skelton's neck, from Samuel Skelton, son and heir of said (Rev) Samuel Skelton, being 200 acres, with all his right, title, claim and demand…in consideration of the sum of 41 pounds, said John Porter, Sr., having also purchased the right and interest of the 3 daughters of said Samuel Skelton, Sr., in the said farm, for several considerations to them in hand long since paid…Samuel Skelton, son and heir of the late abovementioned Samuel Skelton, Sr., having received 20 pounds sterling money of England from the said John Porter Sr. by the hands of John Brackenbury of Charlestown (mariner), whom he appointed to receive the ame, as the last payment for the above-mentioned farm, does hereby acknowledge and quitclaim rights in the above-mentioned farm of 200 acres to said John Porter, Sr. and discharge the said John Porter Sr., together with John Porter, Jr. his son, that by his engagement or indenture bearing date of 13 May 1659, stood bound for payment of above mentioned remainder. **Signed**: Samuel Skelton; **Witnesses**: Henry Hayward, George Robinson. Richard Sprague took oath that he saw Samuel Skelton sign, 14: 6: 63 before John Endicott, Governor; **Recorded**: 27: 6: 63.

JOHN WILLIAMS to JOHN STEVENS – (2:218) On 27 Aug 1663, John Williams of Salem (fisherman) sold to John Stevens of Salem (fisherman) for 25 pounds, 12 shillings, 6 pence already paid or secured to be paid, a certain dwelling house newly built with about ¼ acre, being a parcel of land sold to him by the town of Salem, lying against Tuck's Cove in the town of Salem, bounded with said cove or creek to the north and land of widow Holingwood to the west and the street or highway to the south and a highway from the street to said cove to the east. **Signed**: John Williams [by mark]; **Witnesses**: Hillyard Veren, John Porter; **Acknowledged**: 27: 6 mo: 1663.

ZACHARIAH GILLUM and WILLIAM HOLLINGWORTH – (2:219) On 10 September 1663, this Charter part of an afraightment made between William Hollingworth of Salem (merchant) on the one part and Zachariah Gillum master of the good ship called *Visitation* of Boston, and now riding at anchor in the river at Boston, being burden 100 tons or thereabouts on the other part, witnesseth: That Zachariah Gillum let unto freight, unto William Hollingworth, one hundred hhs. of Virginia tobacco, which Hollingworth is to deliver on board the said ship in Potomac River in Maryland, at or before the 20th day of December next ensuing, the date hereof which said tobacco, the said ship being then ready to sail, is to be transported in the said ship, God permitting, unto Plymouth in Old England where the said master and ship is to stay 4 days at the pleasure of Hollingworth for his advantage for a market and to sail to the Island of Jersey, and to any one port in Holland if said Hollingworth upon advice had for his best market, the ship staying 4 days in the Island of Jersey, as Hollingworth sees cause to do: and further Gillum does covenant and promise to be ready with his ship in some convenient place in Potomac River, to receive on board his ship, said tobacco of Hollingworth at or by the last of October next, the danger of the sea excepted, and William Hollingworth covenants and agrees to and with Gillum to pay or cause to be paid unto Gillum, his executors or assignes, for every ton contained in the hundred hogsheads of tobacco, allowing 4 hogsheads to the ton, the true sum of 7 pounds sterling of lawful money of England, to be paid in 20 days after delivery of tobacco: Furthermore, it is agreed between said Gillum and said Hollingworth that all port charges in Virginia and elsewhere to be borne by Gillum and other duties for tobacco to be borne by Hollingworth: and moreover that Hollingworth will pay or cause to be paid unto Gillum for every day said ship shall stay at said ports, more than is above expressed, the true sum or 5 pounds except it be for unloading of said tobacco: to all and the covenants, articles and agreement as above expressed to be performed on the part of Gillum and Hollingworth, they bind themselves, heirs, executors, each to other, in the sum of 500 pounds sterling. **Recorded**: 12: 7: 1663; **Signed**: Zachariah Gillum; **Witnesses**: Andrew Woodbery, Elias Stileman.

10th of 7ber 1663. "This shall oblige me, Zachariah Gillum, or my assignes to pay or cause to be paid to Mr. William Hollingworth or his order, 5 shillings current money of England, for every 4 hogsheads of tobacco. He shall ship in Maryland on board the *Visitation*, not to exceed 100 hogsheads to be paid in England or Holland, or where we discharge the said tobacco." Zachariah Gillum teste Elias Stileman.

ISAACK BURNAP to THOMAS JAMES – (2:222) On 22 January 1662, Isaack Burnap (with consent of wife) assigned a deed to Thomas James (husbandman) of the same town, for 205 pounds already paid by bill, with all estate, right, title and interest in and to the within named farm, dwelling house with all hereditaments and appurtenances upland and meadow. This assignment has reference to a deed of sale recorded in the 1st book, page 57. **Signed**: Isaak Burnap; **Witnesses**: Edward Norice, Dorothy Norice; **Acknowledged**: 6: 8 month: 1663; **Recorded**: 6 October 1663.

JOSEPH ARMITAGE to NATHANIEL KIRTLAND – (2:222-225) On 22 October 1663, an indenture was made between Nathaniel Kirtland of Lynn (husbandman), with consent of wife Parnell, and Joseph Armitage of Lynn (tailor) for 11 pounds sterling in hand paid and of 20 pounds sterling that Joseph Armitage acknowledges himself to stand indebted unto Nathaniel Kirtland to be paid at or before the 29th Sept 1664, viz: in fat cattle alive and pork or else 17 pounds in current money, for a certain parcel of land, a dwelling house with 2 acres, with all fences, in Lynn, bounded E with house lot of Thomas Townsend, W with land of Nathaniel Kirtland, N with Mill Street and S with lands of Thomas Townsend and said Nathaniel Kirtland. If Joseph Armitage shall pay, then premises to remain to Joseph, otherwise Nathaniel is to re-enter as his own proper estate. **Signed**: Nathaniel & Parnell Kirtland [by mark] & Joseph Armitage; **Witnesses**: Jonathan Witt & John Longley; **Acknowledged**: 31: 8ber: 1663 by Joseph Armitage; **Recorded**: 4: 9ber: 1663.

Nathaniel Kirtland acknowledged and signed that Joseph Armitage did fully satisfy me for the house and land he now lives in many years since, according to the covenant made between us in 1663. **Signed**: Nathaniel

Kirtland; **Witnesses**: Walter Fairfield & Joseph Phippen, Sr., who made oath 1 Dec 1675.

JOHN HATHORNE to SARA HATHORNE – (2:225) On 2 November 1663, John Hathorne of Lynn, for good reason, has given, granted and set over unto Sara Hathorne, his wife, his now dwelling house, outhouses, garden, orchard, with a house lot adjoining 3 acres that she shall quietly and peacefully possess and enjoy the same, from time to time and at all times as her proper and peculiar and to dispose of the same at her decease as shall see cause. **Signed**: John Hathorne; **Acknowledged**: 10: 9ber: 1663; **Witnesses**: Richard Haven, John Hathorne, Jr.; **Recorded**: 11: 9ber: 1663.

SAMUEL CONDY to GEORGE PIKE – (2:227) On 5 December 1663, Samuel Condy of Marblehead (fisherman) with wife Annis yielding dower rights, sold to George Pike of the same town (fisherman) for 32 pounds already paid, one end of his now dwelling house—the new end adjoining to the south of the old end that he now dwells in, together with all land adjoining (about one quarter acre) being all the ground he has on that side of the highway in that place, excepting the yard before the door, next to the street which he reserves for himself, so far as the parting of the house, and so eastward, in Marblehead on the north side of the street or highway and bounded with land of John Brimblecom and Richard Reed to the northwest, and northerly and with common and street to the southeast and southerly and the town pound westerly. **Signed**: Samuel Condy; **Acknowledged**: 5: 10ber: 1663 & Anna yielded thirds; **Witnesses**: Robert Pike and Hillyard Veren; **Recorded**: 29: 10: 1663.

EDMOND BATTER to JOHN PICKERING and JONATHAN PICKERING – (2:228) On 10 June 1659, Edmond Batter of Salem sold to John Pickering and Jonathan Pickering (as they were and are successors of their father John Pickering [deceased]), between one and a half and two acres in Salem bounded on the west with land of said John Pickering, on south with common, and on north and east with land of Francis Lawes. **Signed**: Edmond Batter and Sara Batter; **Acknowledged**: 5: 11 mo: 1663; Sara, wife, yielded thirds; **Witnesses**: George Gardner, John Massey; **Recorded**: 12: 11: 1663.

JUDITH COOKE to Mr. WALTER PRICE – (2:229) On 13 January 1663, Judith Cooke of Salem (widow) sold to Mr. Walter Price of Salem (merchant) for a valuable consideration already paid, half an acre in Salem betwixt Mr. Edward Norrice's house and Mrs. Sharp's house, now by them inhabited. **Signed**: Judith Cooke [by mark]; **Witnesses**: Thomas Putnam, John Croad, John Price; **Recorded**: 15: 11: 1663.

CHRISTOPHER WALLER to ROBERT WILSON – (2:231) On 5 January 1663, Christopher Waller of Salem (traymaker) with Margaret his wife releasing dower, sold to Robert Wilson of Salem (planter) for 10 pounds already paid, 30 acres, being a great lot granted Waller by the town of Salem, within limits of town, to the northwest, near a cedar pond, and bounded north with land of John Ingersoll, east with land of John Hill, and George Ropes to the south corner, and Samuel Very's farm to the west, with all profits, timber, privileges and appurtenances. **Signed**: Christopher Waller [by mark] and Margaret Waller [by mark]; **Acknowledged**: 9: 11: 1663; **Witnesses**: Benjamin Felton, Allester Macmallen [by mark]; **Recorded**: 2: 12: 1663.

ROBERT GOODELL to THOMAS FLINT – (2:232) On 6 January 1662, Robert Goodell of Salem (farmer) sold to Thomas Flint of Salem (farmer) for 20 pounds sterling already paid, 50 acres in Salem near upon a square and bounded with land of Henry Phelps southerly, and a brook called Phelp's brook westerly, and with land of said Robert Goodell north and east. **Signed**: Robert Goodell; **Acknowledged**: 6: 11 mo: 1662; **Witnesses**: Hillyard Veren, Giles Coree [by mark]; **Recorded**: 2: 1 mo: 1663.

PHILLIP CROMWELL to Major WILLIAM HATHORNE and Mr. WALTER PRICE – (2:234) On 9 April 1664, Phillip Cromwell of Salem (butcher) granted to Major William Hathorne and Mr. Walter Price (deputed feofees in trust by Dorothy his wife) his dwelling house, shop, slaughterhouse, with the rest of outhouses adjoining, together with a close, containing about an acre of land, situated and being between land of Elias Stileman on the west and house of said Phillips, where in Lakes now lives, butting upon South river, so-called on the south and the street on the north, passing to the meeting house in town of Salem, said Phillip acknowledged to be given in trust and by these presents gave...Major William Hathorne and Mr. Walter Price, feoffees in trust to only use of Dorothy together with two acres next adjoining the dwelling house of Jeffrey Massey on the east, with an acre and a half of land, that was in possession of Allen Kenestone to be to only use of said Dorothy. **Consideration**: For divers considerations and good reasons but more especially for an agreement made and done between me and Dorothy my wife at and before the time of marriage to and with Dorothy, then widow and relict of Allen Keniston at which said time of marriage I, said Philip did then promise to and with said Dorothy that out of estate she was then possessed of and to be transmitted unto me, Dorothy was to have her own proper use and behoof, 10 cows with the yearly rent of said cows, to dispose of at her pleasure. **Acknowledged**: 9 Apr 1664 with seize & possession given; **Witnesses**: Thomas Ives, Elias Stileman; **Recorded**: 20 April 1664.

ELIAS STILEMAN to WILLIAM BROWNE, Jr. – (2:236) On 7 April 1664, Elias Stileman of Salem (as administrator to estate of Elias Stileman of the same place, deceased) for 26 pounds, granted to Mr. William Browne, Junior, of Salem (merchant) 2 acres of upland between land of John Archard and Hanna Weeks on the south, and a piece of swamp land given by the town of Salem to Mr. John Higginson on the north, butting on the common called the training common on the west and on a narrow lane that goes between two coves, and between Thomas Root's and the above bargained premises on the east, including the thirds of Stileman's widow, deceased. **Witnesses**: Signed, sealed & delivered and possession given by turf and twig in present of Phillip Cromwell and John Archard; **Recorded**: 20 April 1664.

MATTHEW WOODWELL to JOHN PICKERING – (2:237) On 27 May 1664, Matthew Woodwell of Salem (brickmaker) granted to John Pickering of Salem, for a valuable sum, a parcel of land containing about half an acre in Salem, part of that ground the house of Matthew Woodwell does stand upon and lies next to the South river side, partly within the fence and partly without, bounded north with a strip of land of Mr. John Ruck, that runs between it and a cove, and on the east and south land is bounded with South river and west with Matthew's own land. "Be it known by these presents, that I John Ruck of Salem (vintner) for a valuable consideration, sell to John Pickering of Salem (yeoman) a strip or front of land being all ground Ruck has lying without Matthew Woodwell's fence to the south containing about one quarter acre being in Salem, at the south side of the said Matthew Woodwell's land, bought lately of me, the said Ruck, and bounded with a bending in or cove of the South river and with the said South river south east and southerly and on the east with some land of the said Pickering's lately bought of said Woodwell and of the land of said Woodwell to the north." **Signed**: 2 June 1664 by John Ruck; **Witnesses**: Hillyard Veren & Bartholomew Gedney; **Signed**: Matthew Woodwell; **Witnesses**: Jon. Prince & Bartholomew Gedney; **Recorded**: 6 June 1664.

WILLIAM HATHORNE to WALTER PRICE – (2:239) On 30: 11 mo: 1665, William Hathorne of Salem sold to Walter Price of Salem, for good and valuable consideration, all that parcel of land containing 4 acres of land marsh and upland being between land of George Emory to the south, land of Frances Skerry to the southwest and the sea to the east & land of Daniel Rumboll to the west to have and to hold all that right which was granted him in this parcel of land by the town in the year 1658, to him the said Walter Price. **Signed**: William Hathorne; **Witnesses**: John Croad, William Lake; **Recorded**: 30: 11 mo: 1665.

JOHN RAYMENT to RICHARD DODGE, Sr. – (2:240) On 23 June 1663, John Rayment of Salem (yeoman) with Rachel his wife yielding dower, sold to Richard Dodge, Sr. of Salem (yeoman) for 12 pounds, a parcel of meadow containing 4 acres, bounded with land of said Richard Dodge on the north and a small brook on the south and meadow of Zachariah Herrick on the east. **Signed**: John Rayment & Rachel [by mark]; **Witnesses**: Hillyard Veren and Mary Veren; **Acknowledged**: 9: 7 mo: 1663; **Recorded**: 6: 4 mo: 1664.

BENJAMIN BALCH to WILLIAM & MARY DODGE – (2:242) On 15 January 1663, Benjamin Balch of Salem (yeoman) sold to William Dodge and Mary his wife, for divers good causes and considerations, especially for that good will and affection he bore to Mary, the late wife of his brother John Balch, late deceased and now wife of William Dodge the younger, 16 acres of land in Salem on Bass River side at the head of the railes towards Wenham on the west side of center highway that goes to said Wenham and is part of about 50 acres of land, upland and meadow which was lately of John Balch, deceased, and by a county court of Ipswich held 31 March 1663 ordered to him: also 3 acres of meadow, being part of said land he set over to Mary or her assignes, the time of her life, and after her decease to return to him, with 3 acres of meadow, is that part which is outside farthest from his own land. **Signed**: Benjamin Balch; **Witness**: Hillyard Veren; **Acknowledged**: 14: 11 mo: 1663; **Recorded**: 6: 4: 1664.

THOMAS CHANDLER to THOMAS JOHNSON – (2:243) On 25 December 1663, Thomas Chandler of Andover (smith) sold to Thomas Johnson of Andover (carpenter) for 7 pounds, six acres of meadow as it was granted by the town in Wades Meadow, one part of it lying at the east end of the meadow of Robert Barnard and bounded round with upland, an acre more lying at the west end of the meadow of John Aslett and two parcels more lying against the meadow of John Aslett, on the north side of the brook. **Signed**: Thomas Chandler, Hannah Chandler [by mark]; **Acknowledged**: 1: 11 mo: 1663 & Hannah gave consent; **Witnesses**: Steven Osgood, Edward Phelps; **Recorded**: 6: 4: 1664.

GEORGE ABBOTT, Jr. & SARAH his wife to THOMAS JOHNSON – (2:245) On 18 November 1663, George Abbott, Jr. of Andover (husbandman) and Sarah (his wife) granted to Thomas Johnson of Andover (carpenter) for a certain sum or sums of money, four acres situated in the town of Andover, on the east side of the home lot of said Thomas. **Signed**: George Abbott, Jr. & Sarah Abbott; **Acknowledged**: 18 Nov 1663 & Sarah gave consent; **Witnesses**: Symond Bradstreet, Dudley Bradstreet, Hannah Wiggin; **Recorded**: 23: 4 mo: 1664.

JOHN RUCK to EDMUND FEVERYEARE – (2:246) On 25 March 1664, John Ruck of Salem granted to Edmund Feveryeare of Salem (seaman) for a valuable sum of goods a parcel of land containing 33 poles and better, it being part of the same land said Ruck dwelled on, butting on the north upon the land or highway that lies on the north side of his now dwelling house, upon the south about the middle of the creek or cove that runs up next on the south side or end of his now dwelling house, butting on the west upon a certain parcel of land of John Alfords, containing in length from north to south on west side, 8 poles and 3 quarters, butting on the east side upon a certain parcel of land lying on the west side of his orchard, and in length on the east side containing 10 poles, now the whole breadth from east to west throughout being 3 poles and a half, to have all convenience of creek that runs on the south side of his dwelling house, for his and their transportation of wood, hay, goods, etc. by water, either in canoe, boat, shallop or lighter, to the said Edmund Feveryeare's land. **Signed**: John Ruck, Sarah Ruck; **Acknowledged**: 13: 3 mo: 1664 with wife Sarah yielding thirds; **Witnesses**: Samuel Pickman, George Emorye; **Recorded**: 24: 4 mo: 1664.

WILLIAM BALLARD to WILLIAM CHANDLER – (2:247) On 25 May 1663, William Ballard of Andover (husbandman) granted to William Chandler (husbandman), for divers good causes and considerations, especially for certain parcel of land William Ballard bought or exchanged with William Chandler for certain sums of money, all his house and barn with 4 acres of land and a courtyard [?] belonging thereunto, in Andover, bounded on the north and east by land of Nathan Parker, on the west by land of John Lovejoy and Andrew Foster, and by the highway on the south, together with all buildings, mounds and fences and also all the acre house lot in Andover, with Andrew Allen on the west and north, the land of William Chandler on the east and the highway or common on the south, all of which house lot and land William was in possession of…to have and hold the 4 acres and orchard together with profits of appurtenances belonging and 5 acre houselot. **Signed**: William Ballard [by mark]; **Acknowledged**: 25 May 1663, by William Ballard, with wife Grace giving free consent; **Witnessses**: Andrew Aslett, Timothy Stevens; **Recorded**: 24: 4: 1664.

THOMAS TUCK to WILLIAM BEALE – (2:249) On 25 November 1657, Thomas Tuck of Salem (smith) granted to William Beale of Marblehead, for 3 pounds 10 shillings, all his land on Darby Point side, 11 acres granted to him by the town of Salem, having the mill lot towards the west, the common towards the south, and other land of said William Beale's toward the east & Frogmorton's Cove toward the north. **Signed**:

Thomas Tuck [by mark]; **Acknowledged**: 25: 9ber: 1657; **Witnesses**: John Hathorne, Robert Lord; **Recorded**: 6: 5 mo: 1664.

JOHN HORNE to RICHARD MOORE – (2:250) On 13: 7 mo: 1655, John Horne of Salem, granted to Richard Moore of Salem for 24 pounds, one dwelling house with land adjoining about 1 acre, situated within the town of Salem, one half acre butting against Mr. Downing's house and running down to the dwelling house of John Horne, the other part of land running down to the Cove, having Thomas Rix's ground on the north side and the said Richard Moore's on the south side, together with all outhouses, fencing and what else stands on said land. **Signed**: John Horne; **Acknowledged**: John Horne and wife Frances, who yielded her thirds; **Witnesses**: Henry Bartholomew, Elizabeth Bartholomew.

HENRY BARTHOLOMEW to RICHARD MOORE – (2:251) On 11 July 1664, Henry Bartholomew of Salem, with Elizabeth his wife yielding up thirds, sold to Richard Moore of Salem, one dwelling house with land belonging to it, about 1 acre, situated next to the house and land of George Keiser on one side and next to the said Richard Moore on the other side, together with all other fences, trees or whatever else belongs or appertains to said house and land. **Signed**: Henry Bartholomew; **Acknowledged**: 11: 5 mo: 1664 by Henry Bartholomew; **Witness**: John Horne; **Recorded**: 12: 5 mo: 1664.

THOMAS OLIVER to JOHN BRADSTREET – (2:254) On 5 July 1658, Thomas Oliver of Salem (callender) sold to John Bradstreet of Salem, for 3 pounds 10 shillings, 10 acres of upland being on Marble neck, butting upon Forest river and having in the south end an old Indian fort. **Signed**: Thomas Oliver; **Acknowledged**: 5: 3 mo: 1659; **Witnesses**: Edmond Batter; Nicholas Bartlett [by mark].

CHRISTOPHER WALLER to JAMES BROWNE – (2:255) On 14 July 1664, Christopher Waller of Salem (traymaker) sold to James Browne of Newbury (glazier) for 85 pounds sterling, his now dwelling house, which he now lives in, together with all the ground adjoining, about one acre, as it now lies bounded in Salem, bounded on the west with a lane or highway, on the south with some land of John and William Maston, east with land of John Gidney, north with land of Mathew Price. **Signed**: Christopher Waller [by mark] & Margaret Waller [by mark]; **Acknowledged**: 15: 5: 1664, with wife Margaret yielding thirds; **Witnesses**: George Emery, Hillyard Veren; **Recorded**: 15: 5: 1664.

ADAM WESTGATE TO JOHN BRADSTREET – (2:255) On 2 April 1658, Adam Westgate of Salem (mariner) granted to John Bradstreet of

Marblehead (seaman) for 7 pounds, 20 acres of land which was land of Richard Hollingsworth, Sr. sold to Adam Westgate by Mr. John Gedney of Salem (vintner) which said 20 acres is situated next to land belonging to the water mill of Marblehead, lying by the side thereof westward towards Forest river head; and the said Adam Westgate. **Signed**: Adam Westgate, Mary Westgate [by mark]; **Witnesses**: Samuel Pickman, John Peach; **Acknowledged**: 15: 6 mo: 1664; **Recorded**: 8 September 1664.

CHRISTOPHER WALLER to MATHEW PRICE – (2:256) On 20 May 1662, Christopher Waller of Salem granted to Mathew Price of Salem (tailor) for 36 pounds, a dwelling house, with about 90 rod of ground, now bounded out with two stakes to the south adjoining the house, situated in Salem, bounded with the ground of said Christopher Waller to the south and the land of Joseph Miles to the east and a lane or highway to the west and the North river to the north. (It is understood that the ground abovesaid is not to the river, but is to the highway between it and the river.) **Signed**: Christopher Waller [by mark], Margaret Waller [by mark]; **Acknowledged**: 15: 5: 64 and Margaret, wife, gave up dower rights; **Witnesses**: Thomas Cromwell to the said Christopher signing, Hillyard Veren, George Emory to both parties signing and delivery and to clause of bounds; **Recorded**: 28: 5: 1664.

JOSEPH GARDNER to WILLIAM BROWNE, Jr. – (2:259) On 3 August 1664, Joseph Gardner (mariner) of Salem granted to William Browne, Jr. (merchant) of Salem for 70 pounds 4 shillings sterling, 170 rods or poles of land near ¾ acre lying in length N & S, 18 rods & in breadth E & W throughout, 6½ rods; in Salem, and is bounded N with a lane, by the town pound, & E with land of said Joseph; S with the street that comes from the meeting house, and W with land of Richard Prince. **Release of Dower**: 4 Apr 1679 by Mrs. Ann Bradstreet, formerly the wife of Capt. Joseph Gardner who freely resigned all her interests as to her thirds; **Acknowledged**: Hilliard Veren, who made oath that he saw this writing signed, sealed & delivered with seizin & possession given by turf & twig; **Witnesses**: Hillyard Veren & Richard Prince; **Recorded**: 11 Aug 1664.

JOHN RUCK to JOHN GEDNEY, Sr. – (2:262) On 20 June 1662, John Ruck of Salem (merchant) granted to John Gedney, Sr. of Salem (vintner) for 20 pounds sterling, an acre of land in Salem, part of land adjoining the dwelling house of John Ruck, to the west side of his dwelling house, bounded with a highway to the south, which highway goes between the said acre of land and the land of Matthew Woodwell from the water side to the common, called Lawses hill, and with said common on the west and with land of said John Ruck on the north and abuts a cove or creek that comes out of the South river, eastward, which said cove or creek the said Gedney...is to have the free use of, the whole breadth of said acre of land being bounded and is to bear its full breadth equally at each end, i.e. the full breadth of said land eastward to the channel of said South river with free liberty of landing goods, wood or timber or launching of vessels, ships or boats, or also to dig and make convenient for his use...by wharfing any part of the aforementioned breadth to the river ward, or by any other ways or means. (It is to be understood that the said John Gedney is to have free use of cove and down to the river, the breadth of the acre of land which is expressed above is excepted against and only granted the free use of said cove. From a stone at the upper end and a stone at the lower end, on the north side, so to extend in breadth southward full 58 feet and so down to the channel of said river.) **Signed**: John Ruck; Sara Ruck (wife) yielded dower and signed. On 8: 6 mo: 1664, John Ruck gave possession unto Mr. John Gedney by turf and twig; witnessed by Hillyard Veren & Robert Wilkes; **Witnesses**: Abigail Wood, Hillyard Veren.

HUMPHREY COOMES to Mr. WALTER PRICE – (2:266) On 11 July 1664, Humphrey Coomes of Salem (fisherman) granted to Mr. Walter Price of Salem (merchant) in consideration of a valuable sum, a dwelling house with a quarter of an acre of ground adjoining thereto, which house and ground is in Salem and bounded with a highway next to the pen or common so called on the north, with the ground of Sander Sears on the east, the land of Oliver Manning on the south and land of John Gardner and John Sanders on the west. [marginal note: Capt. Price] **Signed**: Humphrey Coomes; **Witnesses**: Seizin and possession of premises given in presence of Hilliard Veren & Theodore Price; **Release of Dower**: Barsheba Coomes, wife, resigned dower & signed [by mark]; **Recorded**: 11: 6: 1664.

JOHN WALDRON to JOHN WEBB (alias Evered & Co.) – (2:267) On 28 February 1660, John Waldron of Marblehead (fisherman), with wife Dorothy yielding dower rights, sold to John Webb (merchant and in company partnership) alias Evered & Co. of Boston, county Suffolk, for 100 pounds, 10 acres of land in Marblehead, bounded with the harbor or great water to the south easterly, and a cove coming in out of said great harbor to the east and with some land of Mr. Walton on the west and by south and some land of John Waldron to the north and more particularly is bounded and extends from a rock at waterside to a birch and to a stake west northerly, compassing the hill to a small oak marked and then south west by south to fence as staked out, to a rock. **Signed**: John Waldron [by mark], Dorothy [by mark]; **Witnesses**: John Devereux, John Siscom; **Acknowledged**: 1: 11 mo: 63. **Recorded**: 7: 7 mo: 1664 and 8: 7: 1664 [two recording dates].

JAMES BROWNE to SAMUEL BACH (mortgage) – (2:270) 6 September 1664, whereas James Browne of Newbury (glazier) about 3 years ago, by way of mortgage, made over his house at Newbury and 12 acres of land adjoining, to John Chickly of Boston for the securing of 45 pounds, do by bond, unto Mr. Robert Taynton of London, England, which mortgage or bond are overcast and not to be found, James Browne of Newbury (glazier) mortgaged to Samuel Bach of New Haven of Boston (Attorney of Robert Taynton) & to his use, according to his letter of procuration dated April 1663 for 45 pounds aforementioned, James Browne's dwelling house situated in Newbury, with all out housing, yards, orchards, gardens, etc., with 12 acres of land adjoining, with all fences, wood, waters, soils, rocks, etc. thereon and therein, standing, growing or being, bounded northeast on a highway, leading into Merrimack river, southeast on Roger Moss, southwest on the lands of Mr. Soell, and north west on lands of Daniel Peirce of Newbury. It is the intent and meaning that James Browne...shall make payment of the sum of 45 pounds sterling, in wheat, bread or money, or some of them...some convenient landing place or storehouse near Mr. Webb's wharf in Boston, on or before the 24th of June, next ensuing the date hereof. **Signed**: James Browne; **Acknowledged**: 7: 7 mo: 1664; **Witnesses**: Nathaniel Branker, Samuel Moore, Joseph Hill; **Recorded**: 12: 7: 1664.

JOHN BURNELL to JOHN BLETHEN – (2:273) On 16 June 1664, John Burnell of Salem, granted to John Blethen, for 5 pounds (whereof 40 shillings is to be paid in money by the 16th of August next ensuing and the other 3 pounds to be paid in merchantable wheat and pork at price current by the 25th of December ensuing), his piece of land, about an acre, which lay between John Blethen's and John Smith's; John Smith's lying on the east and John Blethen's lying on the west, the north side being bounded with Thomas Gardner's and Daniel Southwick's marsh, the south side being bounded with the common. **Signed & acknowledged**: 4th: 7ber: 1664 by John Burnell; **Witnesses**: William Trask, Daniel Southwick, Josiah Southwick; **Recorded**: 14: 7: 1664.

HENRY PHELPS to JOSEPH POPE – (2:274) On 18 July 1664, Henry Phelps of Salem sold to Joseph Pope of Salem (husbandman) for a valuable consideration already paid, all his farm, 100 acres of upland, 10 acres of meadow ground, together with a dwelling house and orchard upon the same, in Salem, not far from Ipswich river, and bounded on the south with a farm once belonging to Mr. Higginson, and part with the common and the brook, on the west with a farm in possession of George Gardner and of Daniel Rumboll at the foot of the wood hill, on the north with a pine swamp, and to a bound tree at the foot of Bald hill, and on the east by the bound tree at Mr. Higginson's farm, also 6 acres of meadow lying on

Ipswich river, said farm was formerly in possession of Ellenor Trusler (widow), wife of Thomas Trusler, deceased, of Salem. **Signed**: Henry Phelps. Hannah Phelps (wife of Nicholas Phelps, lately deceased, who was joint executor to said Henry) surrendered up thirds in memorandum between signature & acknowledgement; **Acknowledged**: 23 July 1664 [? 33 July 1664]; **Recorded**: 27 July 1664.

CHRISTOPHER LATTAMORE & MARY (his wife) to ROBERT HOOPER – (2:276) On 1 February 1663, Christopher Lattamore of Marblehead and Mary, his wife, granted to Robert Hooper of Marblehead (fisherman) for divers causes and the sum of 33 pounds 10 shillings, all Christopher's dwelling house in Marblehead, standing on the hill where John Goyte's house stood, which he sold unto Christopher's "father Pitt" and also a spot of ground about a quarter part of an acre, now fenced in, lying between a parcel of land of Henry Russell's and Christopher Lattamore's fish yard...(the said Robert Hooper maintaining all the fence between the said Lattamore and him). [There is an evidence recorded overleaf that refers to this deed, etc...] **Signed**: Christopher Lattamore [by mark]; Mary Lattamore [by mark]; **Acknowledged**: 10: 8 mo: 1664; Mary Lattamore yielded thirds; **Recorded**: 17: 9 mo: 1664.

NATHANIEL FELTON to JOHN SAMPSON – (2:278) Nathaniel Felton of Salem, granted to John Sampson of Salem, for a valuable consideration already paid, 40 acres of land within the limits of Salem on the farther side of the Ipswich river, having the brook that comes out of Cromwell's meadow on the north side, and the meadow adjoining to the great river on easterly side, and the common land on the west and south side. (The land within specified was delivered and possession given by turf and twig, upon part in the name of the whole in the presence of Mr. Roger Conant and Thomas Picton 26 Oct 1664). **Signed**: Nathaniel Felton; **Release of Dower**: Mary Felton, wife [by mark]; **Recorded**: 17: 9 mo: 1664.

MOSE MAVERICK, JOHN PEACH, Sr., RICHARD NORMAN & THOMAS PITMAN (Depositions) – (2:279) On 13 May 1680, Mose Maverick, John Peach, Sr., Richard Norman and Thomas Pitman acknowledged that the greatest part of the land, whereon Robert Hooper's house "now standeth," was the town's land, all of which land was given, granted, disposed of, unto the said Robert Hooper, and further that the greatest part of Edward Holeman's house, stands where the old coit's house was, and further said no. Mark Pitman also testified to the same. (Taken upon oath 2: 3 mo: 1677 by William Hathorne, Assistant, this testimony refers to Hooper's on leafe back.) **Recorded**: 13 May 1680.

WILLIAM MAPES to DANIEL RUMBOLL – (2:280) On 21: 9: 1664, an agreement was recorded stating that William Mapes sold to Daniel Rumboll 10 acres of land, lying at the foot of Baldhill to the east, the land of Nathaniel Stone to the north, the way to the north and east to the said Daniel Rumboll and his heirs forever. William Mapes had 2 pounds 20 shillings six pence in hand and Daniel Rumboll was to sell it at the best advantage and to pay the remainder to William Mapes or his assigns, before William Hathorne, or to be prised by indifferent men. **Signed**: 20: 7 mo: 1662; **Attested**: 18: 9 mo: 1664 by William Hathorne.

DANIEL RUMBOLL to ROBERT HIBBERT – (2:280) On 18 November 1664, Daniel Rumboll of Salem (smith) did set over and assign to Robert Hibbert, all right and interest (according to an instrument within specified) to that parcel of land on Cape Ann side, sold to said Daniel Rumboll. **Signed**: Daniel Rumboll; **Acknowledged**: 18: 9 mo: 1664; **Witnesses**: William Browne, Edmond Batter; **Memorandum**: William Mapes did likewise sell the same land to Robert Hibbert taken upon oath by Daniel Rumboll 18: 9 mo: 1664 before William Hathorne.

WILLIAM WATERS, Sr. and WILLIAM WATERS, Jr. to JOHN CROAD (Bond) – (2:281) On 29 November 1664, William Waters, Sr. of Boston (husbandman) and William Waters, Jr. of Boston (seaman) bound themselves to be indebted to John Croad of Salem (merchant) for 100 pounds. They were to pay in 3 years 20 pounds per annum in merchantable and refuse fish at price current, or mackerel at price current, and the other 40 pounds to be paid in 4 years after paying 10 pounds per annum in the like kind, and the time of this obligation to begin from the day of the date hereof, so that the first payment be made by the 29th day of November 1665, and for the true performance hereof, the above bounded William Waters Sr. and William Waters Jr. did by these presents bind themselves in the sum of 200 pounds. **Signed**: William Waters Sr. [by mark], William Waters Jr.; **Witnesses**: Mathew Price, Edward Woolen [by mark], taken upon oath before William Hathorne; **Recorded**: 13: 10: 1664.

WILLIAM LONGLY to THOMAS BROWNE – (2:282) On 17 June 1663, William Longly of Lynn (yeoman) (with wife Johana releasing dower) granted to Thomas Browne of Groton (dishturner) for 125 pounds sterling, 6 acres of land, it being his house lot, bounded E with land of Richard Haven, W with land of John Newhall, S upon mill street; N on town common; with his dwelling house and orchard; also one acre of salt marsh in the marsh below the town, bounded E with the marsh of Thomas Ivory, W with the marsh of William Bartrum, N with the marsh of Mr. Samuel Whiting and S with a creek; also 2 acres of marsh in the 1st div. in Rumney Marsh, bounded E with the marsh of Robert Mansfield and John

Witt, W with the marsh of John Witt, S with the other division, N with upland; also 2 acres of salt marsh in the 1st div. in Rumney Marsh, bounded E with John Newhall's land, W with Richard Hood's marsh, abutting N on the creek (the bounds between Boston and Lynn), and S with the river; also 6 acres of the lower division in Rumney Marsh, abutting east upon the marsh of Robert Burges, W upon the great river bounded S with the marsh of Mr. Rhodes; & N with marsh of Robert Rand with all ways, easements, commons, liberties and privileges whatsoever unto the said dwelling house and lands. **Signed**: William Longly and Joanne Longly [by mark]; **Acknowledged**: by both 1: 10 mo: 1664; **Witnesses**: Joseph Mansfield; Thomas Marshall; **Recorded**: 13: 10: 1664.

CHRISTOPHER LATTEMOR and MARY his wife to AMBROSE GALE – (2:285) On 16 December 1663, Christopher Lattemor of Marblehead (yeoman) and Mary (his wife) sold to Ambrose Gale of Marblehead (fisherman) for divers good causes and 11 pounds sterling, all the acre of marshland, which lay next to an acre of land of Arthur Sandies near said Ambrose Gale's house. **Signed**: 16 Dec 1663 by Christopher Lattamore [by mark]; Mary Lattemore; **Acknowledged**: 2: 7: 1664 & Mary yielded thirds; **Witnesses**: John Northy, George Bonfield [by mark], William Pitt; **Recorded**: 17: 10: 1664.

JEREMIAH BELCHER to GEORGE CORWIN (mortgage) – (2:286) On 1 June 1660, Jeremiah Belcher of Ipswich (merchant) mortgaged to George Corwin of Salem (merchant) for the security of the sum of 229 pounds, all his farm, containing 100 acres, with all houses, barn or other edifices that are or may be built upon the same, situated between the farms of Thomas Safford and the land of John Adams, and also 16 acres of meadow lying near Ensign Howlett's land in Ipswich, besides what meadow is in the farm before mentioned and also his dwelling house and ground lying in Ipswich on the W side of Mill river, having the river on the E side; the land of Elder Whipple on the W and on the N the town and mill and bordering S on land of Elder Whipple...the forenamed farm of 100 acres of upland and meadow, and 16 acres of meadow near Ensign Howlett's and the dwelling house and ground in Ipswich...the full sum of 229 pounds (to be paid) in merchantable fish at price current, at or before the 1st of June 1663 at Salem, Marblehead, or the Isle of Shoals. (The said Jeremiah Belcher, besides the present assignment or mortgage, bound over and sold for just considerations 4 oxen expressed by name: Buck and Golden, Duke and Darbye, and 2 cows named Black & Pye and one red yearling steer unto the said Capt. George Corwin.) **Signed**: Jeremiah Belcher; **Witnesses**: Thomas Putnam, Edward Norice, Samuel Gardner; **Acknowledged**: 30: 9 mo: 1664; **Recorded**: 20: 10: 1664.

WILLIAM HATHORNE to ELEAZER HATHORNE (son) – (2:288) On 28 Dec 1664, William Hathorne of Salem, granted to Eleazer Hathorne of Salem (his son) for 95 pounds, a dwelling house with half an acre of land, which the house stands on bounded with land of farmer Porter on the E, land of Samuel Pitman of the S, land of Capt. Corwin to the W, and the street on the N; also a small parcel of land abutting the South river within George Keiser's fence, within which is an old cellar. **Signed**: William Hathorn Sr.; **Witnesses**: Anna Hathorne, Samuel Gardner; **Recorded**: 11: 11: 1664.

PHILLIP CROMWELL to STEPHEN HASKETT – (2:289) On 2 January 1664, Phillip Cromwell of Salem, with wife Dorothy yielding dower rights, granted to Stephen Haskett of Salem (soap boiler) for 88 pounds sterling, a dwelling house with a soap house, 2 coppers set up in the same – with land pertaining thereto (adjoining) on which the house stands; the land containing 1 acre and a half – the house and land (late in the tenure of Samuel Readle, deceased), in Salem, bounded N with the highway that goes between the North river and said house and land, E with land of John Gedney, S with land that was one Burrows (a cooper) and later Benjamin Fermaies, and on the W with Joseph Miles. (Phillip Cromwell does further covenant to maintain right and title of all to Stephen Haskett...against Edward Woolland.) **Signed**: Phillip Cromwell & Dorothy Cromwell; **Witnesses**: Hillyard Veren, Thomas Ives; **Acknowledged**: 2: 11 mo: 1664; **Recorded**: 9: 11: 1664.

DANIEL RUMBOLL to JAMES MOULTON, Sr. – (2:291) On 16 Jan 1664, Daniel Rumboll of Salem (blacksmith) sold to James Moulton, Sr. of Wenham (yeoman) for 30 pounds sterling, a parcel of land containing 40 acres, formerly land of George Norton (deceased) by a grant of the town of Salem, situated in the bounds of Wenham, bounded on the E with land formerly of Mr. John Fisk, and in the tenure of John Bette, on the south with land of Richard Kimboll Sr., on the west and north with land of James Moulton. **Signed**: Daniel Rumboll; **Witnesses**: William Curtise, John Pickering, Hillyard Veren; **Acknowledged**: 17: 11 mo: 1664; **Recorded**: 24: 11: 1664.

ROBERT COTTER to JOHN WATERS – (2:293) On 11 November 1664, Robert Cotter of Salem (tailor) sold to John Waters of Salem (planter) for 50 pounds, all his dwelling house where he now dwells with all his land adjoining, both arable and mowing ground, 15 acres, as it lay bounded which said house and land was in Salem, on the north neck (so-called) and was bounded on the northeast with the river, called the Cow house river; and on the southeast with the land of John Tompkins, and on the northwest and west with the land of John Foster. **Signed**: Robert

Cotter; **Witnesses**: Walter Price, Hillyard Veren; **Acknowledged**: 15: 9: 1664 and Johannah Cotter yielded her thirds; **Recorded**: 24: 11: 1664.

THOMAS KEMBLE to HERLACKENDINE SYMONDS – (2:295) On 24 April 1664, Thomas Kemble of Boston (merchant) sold to Herlackendine Symonds of Boston (gentleman) for a valuable consideration in hand received, 500 acres of land situated on the western side of a river in the eastern parts, commonly known by the name of Damariscotta River, in New England, which said land is part of a tract of land which said Thomas formerly purchased of an Indian Sagamore called Wittawoies, as by his bill of sale under his hand and seal more at large appears. **Signed**: Thomas Kemble; **Witnesses**: Samuel Symonds, John Paine; **Recorded**: 2: 12: 1664.

JOHN KETTEL to HERLACKENDINE SYMONDS – (2:296) On 14 November 1664, John Kettel of Gloucester sold to Mr. Herlackendine Symonds of Ipswich for considerable value paid in hand being 100 pounds, his now dwelling house with all his parcel of land upland and meadow and orchard, all being estimated at 40 acres, together with 3 canoes, carts and wheels and plow, coulter & share, yoke & chains with copping, the land, one parcel where the house stands, with orchards, the said parcel being 8 or 9 acres, bounded on the N with Mr. Emerson's land, on the W with the highway, on the E side taken in the swamp, on the S as the fence runs, another parcel being 8 or 9 acres situated and bounded with the highway, the highway lying and running on the E side and on the N side bounded with the creek which lies near the meeting house, and on the W side bounded with the lots of Thomas Bray and Samuel Kent, and on the S end as the fence runs, and one parcel of Meadow given to Thomas Millett, Jr. (his marsh) lying near Smith's hill (so called), it being 12 acres, and the other parcel of meadow, lying by the marsh of Richard Window one side and the creek on the other, running under the side of a little island, given to Goodman Harden (his marsh) and 7½ acres of upland being on the neck called the eastern point, with all tackling abovesaid, fences, boards and timber of the old meeting house. Possession was given of the dwelling house (as part of the whole) upon 15 November 1664 in presence of Silvester Eveleigh and James Travis. **Signed**: John Kettel [by mark] and Elizabeth Kettle [by mark]; **Witnesses**: William Sargeant, Samuel Keat; **Acknowledged**: 17 Nov 1664 & Eliza, wife gave up dower; **Recorded**: 3: 12: 1664.

JOHN RUCK to ELEAZER GIDNEY – (2:299) On 20 Apr 1664, John Ruck of Salem (vintner) granted to Eleazer Gidney of Salem (shipwright), for 10 pounds sterling, one half acre of land in Salem, bounded E with Obadiah Antrum, "which he lately bought of me," and is to run in length from the land or highway that runs from the cove in the South river to the common called Lawses hill and abuts against a strip of ground of Jonathan Pickering's that lies to a cove of the South river on the S end & is bounded on the W with land of said John Ruck, the side fence between the said half acre of land. The land of Ruck is to be set up and maintained by Eleazer Gidney...unless Ruck sells the land adjoining the half acre to another person...and it is to be understood that the said ground is in length 23 pole and ¾ or thereabouts & 4 pole broad, so it contains about ½ acre. **Signed**: John Ruck and Sara Ruck; & Sara wife yielded her dower rights; **Acknowledged**: 13: 12: 1664; **Witnesses**: Hillyard Veren, John Gidney, Jr., Elias Mason.

JOHN HUDSON to MOSES MAVERICK – (2:301) On 1 Mar 1664/5, John Hudson of Marblehead and Mary his wife, sold to Moses Maverick of Marblehead, for divers causes and the true value thereof, all his dwelling house and land, which he bought of Frances Linsford of Marblehead, being 5 acres, lying on Marblehead side, in the planting field that lies near Darby fort and next to the westernmost fence of that field. **Signed**: John Hudson [by mark] and Mary Hudson [by mark]; **Acknowledged**: 14: 1 mo: 1664/5 & wife Mary yielded thirds; **Witnesses**: Samuel Ward, Nathaniel Grafton; **Recorded**: 29 Mar 1665.

JOHN and ELIZABETH KNOWLES to JOHN FULLER and MATHEW FARRINGTON – (2:302) On 11 Nov 1658, John Knowles & wife Elizabeth, of the city of Bristol in old England, heretofore of Watertown in New England (clerk) sold to John Fuller and Mathew Farrington, both of Lynn (yeomen) for divers good causes and 55 pounds in hand paid by Edward Rawson (attorney) unto John Knowles, in said John Knowles' name, secured to be paid by John Fuller and Matthew Farrington, ten acres of upland in Lynn, bounded by a swamp on the east between land of Nathaniel Tyler's and it, by lands of Joseph Redknap and Thomas Townsend, W by lands of Thomas Cobbit on the south, & salt marsh of William Knight and Nicholas Potter on the north; together with 6 acres of salt marsh, lying in Lynn's marsh, bounded by the end of above mentioned 10 acres on the E and a salt creek on the W, the marsh of Richard Johnson on the N and the marsh of Joseph Redknap on the S; the land was free and clear of all other incumbrences under Thomas Willis, late of Lynn, gentleman. **Signed**: John Knowles and Elizabeth Knowles; **Notarized**: Fra. Yeamans, Notary Public, Bristol, England; **Witnesses**: Francis Knight of Pemmaquid, Richard Gregson, Jr., sometime of New Haven, New England; **Recorded**: 30: Mar 1665.

JOHN CROAD to FRANCES WILLOWBY – (2:305) On 26 May 1664, John Croad of Salem (merchant) sold to Frances Willowby of Charlestown (merchant) for a valuable sum in hand paid, the whole warehouse at Marblehead, near the now dwelling house of Mr. William Walton, formerly built by Mr. Walter Price of Salem, with a press to pack fish standing before the door, together with all ground thereunto belonging, granted by the town of Marblehead. **Signed**: John Croad, Elizabeth Croad; **Acknowledged**: 11: 2 mo 1665; Elizabeth released dower thirds; **Witnesses**: Samuel Hammond, Mildmay Tarrey; **Recorded**: 28 Apr 1664.

JOHN STACEY Elder and Younger to ROBERT HOOPER – (2:306) On 26 Dec 1663, John Stacey (the Elder) and John Stacey (the younger, with Ellenor his wife) granted to Robert Hooper of Marblehead (fisherman) for 8 pounds sterling received at the hands of John Trebey one quarter of an acre in Marblehead, joining unto the house of Thomas Soutons, and W towards John Stacey's new house, according to the bounds already set up, provided that the said Robert maintain all the fence of the said ground between said Robert and the Staceys. **Signed**: John Stacey, John Stacey the Younger [by mark] and Ellenor Stacey [by mark]; **Witnesses**: John Trebey [by mark]; William Pitt, John Lattermore; **Recorded**: 29 Apr 1665.

ROBERT HOOPER to WILLIAM BROWN (Assignment) – (2:307) On 27 Oct 1664: Whereas Robert Hooper has bought of John Stacey the within parcel of land, has also sold the same to William Brown of Marblehead and have received full satisfaction, does, with Elizabeth, wife, assign over the same land unto William Browne. **Signed**: Robert Hooper [by mark] & Elizabeth Hooper [by mark]; **Acknowledged**: 7: 9 mo: 1664, with Elizabeth Hooper yielding thirds; **Witnesses**: Nicholas Merritt and William Pitt; **Recorded**: 29: 2: 1665.

ROGER PRESTON to Capt. GEORGE CORWIN – (2:308) On 9 Feb 1664/5, Roger Preston of Salem (husbandman) granted to Capt. George Corwin of Salem (merchant) for a valuable sum of money and goods in hand paid, all his visable estate in Salem, consisting of moveable goods; that is: corn, cattle, hay and household stuffs, or anything whereof Roger Preston was proprietor. The particulars are: cattle: 4 oxen, 4 yearling steers & 15 swine (young and old) and all the corn which said Roger shall plant or sow this year ensuing. **Signed**: Roger Preston; **Acknowledged**: 9: 12 mo: 1664, **Witnesses**: Edward Norice and Jonathan Corwin; **Recorded**: 29 Apr 1665.

JOHN GODFREY to EDWARD PHELPS – (2:309) On 19 Feb 1661/62, John Godfrey of Ipswich (husbandman) granted to Edward Phelps of Newbury (husbandman) (no consideration given) 40 acres: all his lands, meadow and upland, with the orchard and all buildings and edifices…lying in Andover, together with all other lands…may be alloted unto the said John Godfrey, bounded on the E joining the common land, and likewise on the other 3 sides. **Signed**: John Godfrey [by mark]; **Acknowledged**: 31: 1 mo: 1664; **Witnesses**: William White, John Phelps; **Recorded**: 20 Apr 1665.

ANN MOORE to NATHANIEL GRAFTON – (2:311) On 10 Mar 1664/65, Ann Moore of Salem (widow) granted to Nathaniel Grafton of Salem (mariner) for 13 pounds, a half acre of land, partly upland and partly marsh, in Salem, on south side against South harbor, bounded to the W & N with land of said Ann Moore, on the E with land of Mr. Joseph Grafton, Sr., on S with highway between said land and South harbor. (Signed, sealed & delivered with seizing & possession of premises given.) **Signed**: 10 Mar 1664/65 by Ann Moore [by mark]; **Witnesses**: Hillyard Veren, George Gardner, Samuel Gardner; **Recorded**: 29 April 1665.

RICHARD SIBLY to PHILLIP VEREN – (2:313) On 20 May 1665, Richard Sibly of Salem (traymaker), with consent of Hana, his wife, who released dower rights, sold to Phillip Veren of Salem (wheelwright) for a valuable sum in hand paid, a certain parcel of ground, 28 rod, being part of that ground formerly bought of said Phillip Veren, the whole being 40 rod or ¼ of an acre, which said 28 rod is in Salem, and bounded with the land of said Phillip N and W, and with the ground of said Richard to the E, and the street or highway to the S. **Signed**: Richard Sibly [by mark] & Hana Sibley [by mark]; **Witnesses**: William Dounton, Hillyard Veren; **Recorded**: 20: 3: 1665.

HENRY REYNOLDS to THOMAS WEST – (2:314) On 18 March 1664, Henry Reynolds of Salem (tailor), with wife Sara yielding right of dower, sold to Thomas West of Salem (planter) for 3 pounds, 15 shillings, ¾ of an acre of upland and 10 poles, in Salem, within the glass house field (so-called), to the west end of said field, bounded S and W with the common; N with land of Henry Reynolds and E by Samuel Eborne Jr. (The above land was delivered by Henry Reynolds to Thomas West in the presence of John Hill and Joseph Boyce.) **Signed**: Henry Reynolds, Sarah Reynolds; **Witnesses**: William Dounton, Hillyard Veren; **Recorded**: 29 April 1665.

PHILLIP VEREN to MARY VEREN – (2:316) On 15 May 1665, Phillip Veren of Salem (wheelwright) granted to Mary Veren of Salem (widow) for 50 pounds sterling in hand already paid, a dwelling house with 2 acres & almost ¾ of an acre of ground adjoining, being all the ground he had adjoining the said house, situated in Salem and bounded with land of Hilliard Veren on the W and the highway to the N, yet goes upon the bank between said land and the North river, & some land of Capt. Davenport to the E and Richard Sibly's house, with 12 poles of ground on the southeast corner and with the highway to the south. (to have and hold...with all fruit trees, fences, privileges...It shall be lawful to and for the said Mary...from the 15th day of Sept next ensuing, the date hereof peaceable & quietly to occupy...In case the said Phillip Veren has not by the said 15th of September gathered in the fruits and corn growing on the ground and cleared the house...he shall have liberty to do so without molestation... gather in and take away his crop now on the ground and take his goods out of the house). **Signed**: Phillip Veren; **Witnesses**: Signed, sealed & delivered with seizin & possession of premises give in presence of William Dounton and Hillyard Veren; **Recorded**: 20: 3: 1665.

JOHN SCUDDER to JOHN BACHELDOR – (2:318) On 14 July 1654, John Scudder of Southold, Long Island (currier) gave to John Bacheldor of Salem (tailor) for 15 pounds, according to agreement, in that behalf to him paid, all the dwelling house and ground on Ryall's Neck in Bass river in Salem, with all outhouses, edifices, buildings, yards, orchards, gardens, several allotments, meadows, marsh grounds, uplands, woods, underwoods, commons & common of pasture...formerly in possession of John Scudder and now in occupation and tenure of John Bacheldor. (Entered as a caution by Hillyard Veren); **Signed**: John Scudder; **Witnesses**: John Youngs, John Herbert; **Recorded**: 31: May: 1665.

ELIZABETH NICHOLSON & others to Capt. GEORGE CORWIN – (2:320) On 3 September 1664, Elizabeth Nicholson of Marblehead (widow and administratrix of Edmund Nicholson late deceased) together with Francis Simpson, brother of said Elizabeth, and Christopher Nicholson & Joseph Nicholson, sons of the said Edmund & Elizabeth, granted to Capt. George Corwin of Salem (merchant) for a valuable consideration in hand already paid, all right & title to 2 acres of meadow ground with 2 dwelling houses built thereon, and 2 out houses & cow houses & work house, with the outhouses, fences in Marblehead, bounded with the dwelling house of Joseph Bowen in the NW or N, and some ground of John Waldren to the SW & near to great harbor on the SE and the Town common & highway, part westerly & part easterly; also 4 pounds belonging to the said Edmund Nicholson by purchases in the farm bought of the Worshipful Major William Hathorne, which by grant from the country was Mr. Humphries and another 4 pounds belonging to the said Frances Simpson, by purchase likewise in the said farm, together with 1 cow lease and a half in the town commons belonging jointly to the said Edmund and Francis. (Elizabeth Nicholson [alias Browne] & Joseph Nicholson did own the above said deed by the delivery of turf & twig, witnesses by Moses Maverick and Christopher Nick.) **Signed**: Elizabeth Nicholson alias Browne [by mark],

Francis Simpson, Christopher Nicholson and Joseph Nicholson [by mark]; **Witnesses:** John Higginson, Moses Maverick; **Recorded:** 6 June 1665.

DAVID CORWITHIN, Sr. to WILLIAM HOLLINGWORTH – (2:322) On 16 June 1665, David Corwithin, Sr., late of Salem, granted to William Hollingworth of Salem (mariner) for a valuable sum in hand paid, all his dwelling house in Salem with all the ground adjoining, containing ¾ of an acre, bounded E by the ground of John Marsh, N by ground of Francis Collins, W with ground of William Hollingworth, & S abutting against the South Harbor (so-called). [The deed was assigned over to Mary Hollingworth & entered in folio 122.] **Signed:** David Corwithin; **Acknowledged:** 16: 4 mo: 1665; **Witnesses:** Hillyard Veren, Isaac Tappen; **Recorded:** 17: 4: 1665.

DANIEL KING to ALLEN BREED – (2:324) On 20 February 1653, Daniel King of Lynn (merchant & agent of James Hubbard of the New Netherlands in America, Gentleman) sold to Allen Breed of Lynn (husbandman) for 8 pounds sterling in hand paid for the use of the said James Hubbard by Allen Breed, 11 acres of land, part upland & part meadowland, lying in Lynn, in a swamp between lands of Mrs. Ivory (widow) on the E and the common highway leading into the Town marsh on the W, a cove leading to the marsh on the S and the common lands on the N, with all woods, underwoods, trees, timber, lying & growing & being in, upon & about the said premises. **Signed:** Daniel King; **Witnesses:** Symond Bradstreet, Edmond Batter, Elias Stileman; **Recorded:** 17: 4: 1665.

JOHN POOLE to ALLEN BREED – (2:327) On 20 February 1653, John Poole of Reading (miller) granted to Allen Breed of Lynn (husbandman) for divers good causes, especially the sum of 22 pounds, 10 shillings sterling in hand paid, a dwelling house, commonly called the Cow house, late in the possession of John Pool in Lynn, and 9 acres of upland, lying between lands of Mr. Samuel Whiting on the S and lands of Nathaniel Tyler, now in possession of Phillip Kirtland on the W, lands of Joseph Howe & Edward Hall on the E and lands of William Knight on the N; and 3 acres of meadow in the town marsh between lands of William Knight on the S and the creek leading to the sea on the N; and 2 acres of meadow in the town marsh between the lands of Mr. Samuel Whiting on the N, lands of Thomas Newhall on the S, lands of John Deacon on the E and lands of William Longly on the W, and 6 acres of upland and marsh lying in the Reeds, between lands of Mr. Thomas Cobbitt on the E and lands of Mr. Samuel Whiting on the W, with all woods, underwoods, trees, timber...to be holden in free and common soccage & not in capite or by Knights service. **Signed:** John Poole; **Acknowledged:** 12: 4 mo: 1655, with

Margaret Poole, wife, resigning thirds [by mark]; **Witnesses**: Samuel Haugh, Thomas Marshall.

WILLIAM BASSETT to ALLEN BREED – (2:330) On 23 February 1664, William Bassett of Lynn (husbandman) granted to Allen Breed of Lynn (husbandman) for 10 pounds sterling in hand paid, 2 acres of salt marsh in Lynn in the 2nd division in Rumney Marsh, bounded W by marsh of Thomas Laighton, E with land of Thomas Ivory, S by Jonathan Hudson and N by a salt creek. [In the description, Allen Breed is referred to as a "Junior."] **Signed**: William Bassett and Sarah Bassett [by mark]; **Acknowledged**: 3: 2 mo: 1665; Sarah Bassett (wife) yielded her thirds; **Witnesses**: John Hathorne, John Hathorne, Jr.

ROBERT KEAYNE to ALLEN BREED – (2:333) On 1: 8: 1648, Robert Keayne of Boston granted to Allen Breed of Lynn (yeoman) the farm of Mr. Benjamin Keayne, which he purchased of Mr. Thomas Cobbitt of Lynn (teacher of the church there)…on considerations hereafter mentioned, namely: that Allen Breed shall pay unto Robert Keayne of Boston the sum of 10 pounds in wheat, peas or barley, or part of it in all, at the current price or in the fall of that, to be paid in cattle as they shall be appraised by indifferent men, one of them to be chosen by Robert Keayne and if in corn, then to be paid in Charlestown to such as the said Robert appoint, if the pay be made in cattle, they to be delivered at the farm of Robert Keayne, at Rumney Marsh, and the 1st 10 pounds to be paid at or before the 1st day of the 2nd month 1648 when the time is to begin and he to pay Robert Keayne 20 pounds more… 10 pounds in merchantable corn or cattle, or good bills, that Robert shall accept of, to any of the shops in Boston, to be paid in such English goods as said Robert shall make choice of, at or before the 1st day of the 2nd month 1649 next following the date hereof: if the pay be in corn, then to be paid at current price, delivered at his house in Boston, or at the farm in Rumney Marsh; if in cattle, then to be delivered at the farm of Robert Keayne; if there shall be any difference in the prices to be valued by 2 indifferent men chosen between them—and the last 10 pounds to be paid at or before the 1st of the 2nd month 1650, according to terms above mentioned for former pay and whereas there is 50 pounds more to be paid unto Mr. Thomas Cobbett of Lynn, as the portion of Theophilus Skipon, when he comes to age 21 years and the said farm being engaged in the purchase by Mr. Benjamin Keayne, to be security with himself for the true payment of the 50 pounds unto Robert or unto Mr. Thomas Cobbett of Lynn, if Robert shall so appoint, according to the conditions mentioned in the said bill of engagement of Mr. Benjamin Keynes to Mr. Cobbett. Lastly, it is agreed that whereas William Clark of Lynn (thatcher) is also to enter upon the farm of Benjamin Keayne, and joint purchased with Allen Breed in the whole bargain only said William Clark has his liberty of free choice within 1 year's trial to refuse or accept the said purchase; it is agreed that if the said William Clark shall accept the purchase in partnership after this 1st year, that then he does hereby bind…unto Robert Keayne…to become security with Allen Breed, for the due performance. **Signed**: John Pearson [by mark] and William Clark [by mark]; **Acknowledged**: Whereas in several places…John Pearson is struck out, and Allen Breed of Lynn is put in, it is with the free consent and request of Allen Breed, who has bought Pearson's right…hereby stands engaged to Robert Keayne…Allen Breed [by mark], witnessed by Joseph How and Edward Hall 1: 16: 1648; **Witnesses to deed**: Phillip Kertland, Peeter (?) Mary; **Recorded**: 19: 4: 1665.

THOMAS COBBITT to BENJAMIN KEAYNE – (2:335) On 22 September 1641, Thomas Cobbitt (teacher of the Church at Lynn) granted to Benjamin Keayne, for 3 score pounds, 50 whereof is insured to be paid to Theophilus Shepard by his appointment, as by a bond of Mr. Benjamin Keayne's appeareth, the other 10 pounds secured to be paid in good commodities (that are as money) to him paid by Mr. Benjamin Keayne of Lynn (gentleman), the farm which was given unto Thomas Cobbitt by the gift of the Town, consisting of 200 acres, bordering on the farm given unto Mr. Whiting; and also 20 acres of fresh meadow adjoining; and 10 acres of salt marsh given by the town in the last division. **Signed**: Thomas Cobbitt; **Witnesses**: Richard Keayne, Elizabeth Cobbitt, John Dennison [by mark]; **Recorded**: 12 October 1665.

Capt. ROBERT KEAYNE to ALLEN BREED – (2:336) On 1 February 1653, Capt. Robert Keayne of Boston (for himself, his heirs…and by virtue of a letter of attorney from his son Benjamin Keayne, late of Lynn, for his heirs)…set over the deed of sale above written, together with his and their right of title…to the above mentioned deed of sale, and also in and to the lands, houses and premises, to Allen Breed of Lynn, for 4 score pounds. **Signed**: Robert Keayne; **Witnesses**: Mary Bridges, Katherine Hunt [by mark]; **Acknowledged**: 6: 12 mo: 1653.

NICHOLAS BROWNE to ALLEN BREED – (2:338) On 20 February 1653, Nicholas Browne of Reading (planter) granted to Allen Breed of Lynn (husbandman) for 19 pounds sterling in hand paid, a dwelling house and 8 acres of upland in Lynn, the said house lying between the lands late in possession of Mr. Benjamin Keayne on the E and the marsh lying before the said town of Lynn on the S, the lands of George Burrell on the W, and the commons of Lynn on the N—and 1 acre of meadow lying in the fresh marsh near Lynn, between lands of William Crofts S and land of Nicholas Potter on the N—and 4 acres of meadow lying in Lynn's town marsh abutting on the sea on the S and lands of George Burrell on the W and the above said dwelling house and 6 acres of land on the N, and the lands of Mr. Daniel King and George Keayser on the E, with all woods, ways, waters, watercourses, mines, commons, to be holden & free & common soccage and not in cappite nor by Knight;s service. **Signed**: Nicholas Browne; **Acknowledged**: 12 June 1655. Elizabeth Browne, wife, resigned thirds; **Witnesses**: Samuel Haugh, Thomas Marshall; **Recorded**: 12: 8: 1665.

JOHN and ELIZABETH KNOWLES to ALLEN BREED – (2:341) On 11 November 1658, John Knowles, lately of Watertown, now of Bristol in old England (clerk) and Elizabeth (his wife) granted to Allen Breed of Lynn (yeoman) for 35 pounds (to Edward Rawson, agent and attorney to John and Elizabeth) 9½ acres of upland in the neck in the town of Lynn, bounded E by land of Edward Hall, W by part of the town's common, S with lands of William White, and N by the highway that goes to the ferry that was…the same was free and clear…of any claiming by either of them or by Thomas Willis, late of Lynn (gentleman). **Signed**: John Knowles and Elizabeth Knowles; **Witnesses**: Francis Knight of Pemaquid, Richard Grigson, Jr. (sometime of New Haven), Francis Yeamans (notary public of Bristol); **Recorded**: 16: 9: 1665.

PASCA FOOT to JOHN PORTER, Sr. – (2:344) On 18 December 1665, Pasca Foot of Salem, granted to John Porter, Sr. of Salem (yeoman) for a valuable sum in hand paid, 40 acres of land at the head of Willistone's river in Salem, bounded S by land of Jacob Barney, Sr., N on land of John Porter, and W by Willistone's river. **Signed**: Pasca Foot; **Witnesses**: Hillyard Veren, Benjamin Woodrow; **Acknowledged**: 18: 10 mo: 1665; **Recorded**: 27: 10: 1665.

JANE JAMES to RICHARD READ – (2:345) On 16 June 1665, JaneJames, relict of Erasmus James, late of Marblehead, deceased, and also administratrix of the estate of Erasmus James, granted to Richard Read, the house and ground adjoining it containing 1 acre and ½, which her said husband in his lifetime sold to Richard Read of Marblehead (fisherman) and her said husband dying soon after, before a deed in writing was made for the house and ground, being fully paid…in consideration of what is above expressed, the above said dwelling house, with all ground belonging to it, in Marblehead, bounded NW with the highway, NE by a highway that goes down to the harbor, and SE by a swamp laid out in small parcels to several men and SW or W to the fence beyond the row of peach trees. **Signed**: Jane James [by mark]; **Witnessed**: with seizin and possession given of the premises by William Beale, John Legg and Thomas Greatian; **Recorded**: 29: 10: 1665.

WILLIAM HOLLINGWORTH and THOMAS SONE (agreement) – (2:347) On 9 August 1664, Thomas Sone convenanted…from the day of the date thereof until his first and next arrival at Boston in New England and after, for and during the term of 4 years, to serve in such service and employment as William Hollingworth or his assigns shall there employ him according to the custom of the like kind: in consideration William Hollingworth covenanted…to pay for his passing and to find and allow his meat, drink, apparel and lodging with other necessaries, during the said term, and at the end of the said term to pay him 2 pounds, 10 shillings and one suit of clothes, fitting for Sabbath days. **Signed**: Thomas Sone; **Witnesses**: John Frekes and Thomas Garner; **Acknowledged**: 9 August 1664, by Thomas Sone who acknowledged himself willing to serve above named master: William Hollingsworth and his assigns. **Signed**: Richard Mathew (clerk to Richard Abell Esq. one of his Majesty's Justice of Peace in the county of Middlesex); **Recorded**: 6 August 1665.

SAMUEL ARCHARD Sr. to JAMES BROWNE – (2:349) On 27 April 1665, Samuel Archard, Sr. of Salem granted to James Browne of Salem (merchant) for 9 pounds, 5 shillings in hand paid, a parcel of land about 17 rod of ground and in length N & S on the eastern side 5 rod and 15 foot 9 inches—and on the western side 5 rod & 10 foot & 3 inches, and in breadth, said ground is 3 rod at each end, said land is in Salem and is bounded on land of John Archard on the S and E on Mr. John Browne Sr. & N on Daniel Rumboll and W on Samuel Archard. **Signed**: Samuel Archard and Susana Archard; **Witnesses**: Isaac Tappen and Hillyard Veren; **Acknowledged**: 4: 8ber: 1665, with wife yielding thirds; **Recorded**: 9: 8 mo: 1665.

ELIZABETH JEGGLES to JAMES BROWNE – (2:351) On 30 September 1665, Elizabeth Jeggles of Salem (administratrix of William Jeggles, late deceased) granted to James Browne of Salem (merchant) for a valuable sum in hand paid, a parcel of land, about 33 poles or rod of ground on the east side 12 poles, 6 foot in length, and on the W side, 12 poles 7 inches, on the north end 1 pole, 13 foot & 6 inches and on the S end 3 poles 14 foot & 8 inches, in Salem, bounded N with the highway, E with a cartway belonging to said Elizabeth Jeggles, S with land of Elizabeth, and W with land partly of James Browne and partly of John Browne Sr. Thomas Jeggles freely yielded up his rights. **Signed**: Elizabeth Jeggles [by mark] and Thomas Jeggles; **Witnesses**: Hillyard Veren and Thomas Laurence; **Recorded**: 16: 8 mo: 1665.

JOHN CLEMENTS to EDMOND BATTER – (2:352) On 23 October 1665, John Clements of Marblehead, and Aphia, his wife, sold to Edmond Batter, for 96 pounds, 8 shillings in hand, a dwelling house with all the ground belonging thereunto, about 2 acres, lying in Marblehead, which John Clements was then in possession of. **Signed**: John Clements [by mark] and Aphia Clements [by mark]; **Witnesses**: Francis Skerry [by mark] and Hanna Weekes [by mark]; **Acknowledged**: 13: 9ber: 1665, with wife Aphia yielding thirds; **Recorded**: 16: 9: 1665.

JOHN WINSLADE to Capt. WALTER PRICE (mortgage) – (2:354) On 23 November 1665, John Winslade of Malden (Co. of Middlesex) (fisherman) mortgaged to Capt. Walter Price of Salem (merchant) for 8 pounds, 6 shillings 8 pence in hand received, 8 acres of land in Malden, bounded E on a highway, N with land or farm of Greene, S with land of Roger Kennecotte, and W on land of Michael Smith and Goodman Coate. John Winslad was to pay the sum of 8 pounds 8 shillings 8 pence at or before the 20th day of June 1667 in dry fish or mackerel, corn or neat cattle. **Signed**: John Winslade [by mark]; **Witnesses**: Hillyard Veren, Theodore Price, John Price; **Acknowledged**: 24: 9ber: 1655; **Recorded**: 24: 9: 1665.

WILLIAM DODGE, Jr. to WILLIAM WOODBURY – (2:355) On 27 April 1665, William Dodge, Jr. of Salem (yeoman) granted to William Woodbury of Salem (mariner) for 36 pounds sterling in hand paid, a dwelling house, with 5 acres of land with fences standing thereon on Cape Ann Side, in the limits of Salem, bounded E to land of Christopher Croe and Thomas Tuck, W with land of John Porter Sr., on S with the highway against the North river and N with a highway. **Signed**: William Dodge [by mark]; **Witnesses**: Hillyard Veren, James Browne; **Acknowledged**: 28: 9 mo: 1665 with wife Mary giving up dower rights; **Recorded**: 8: 10: 1665.

JOHN GIFFORD to Capt. THOMAS BREEDON (mortgage) – (2:357) On 3 October 1662, John Gifford of Lynn (gentleman) mortgaged to Capt. Thomas Breedon of Boston in Suffolk County (merchant) for 200 pounds sterling paid, all his 2 farms or parcels of upland, 260 acres, with the meadow or marshland to said farms, in Lynn, butting on lands of Adam Hawkes on the E and SE, and on lands of the township of Reading on the W end thereof, and bounded by the lands and commons of the townships of Lynn and Reading on the N and S sides thereof, with all rights, from the 30 Sept 1662, 200 pounds sterling to be paid to Capt. Thomas Breedon at or in the now dwelling house of Capt. Thomas Breedon in Boston at or before 29 September 1664. [The release of this mortgage is in Book 4, page 56.] **Signed**: John Gifford; **Witnesses**: Richard Cook, William Killcupp, William Pearse; **Acknowledged**: 22 December 1665 by Richard Cook and William Kilcup; **Recorded**: 23: 10: 1665.

JOHN GIFFORD to Capt. THOMAS BREEDON (acknowledgement) – (2:362) On 1 May 1663, John Gifford of Lynn acknowledged himself indebted to Capt. Thomas Breedon and Company, for 300 pounds, payable at or before 29: Sept 1665 in current money of New England or in merchantable goods and merchantable iron wares or other metals as shall be produced at the works to be erected in Lynn and to be delivered at Boston at ready money price...which sum of 300 pounds the said John Gifford received of Hezekiah Usher and Thomas Lake by order of said Breedon for the making up of his 2nd part of 600 pounds a first stock to be employed in Iron works, as per contract made with said Breedon and John Paine the 6th of January 1662. He assigned over to said Thomas Breedon and Company all his rights in half of the said iron works and declared that whereas he was by the said contract to have 150 pounds per annum for his salary, he did hereby...discharge said Breedon and Company from paying him...anything, for their 4th part of the said 250 pounds, until the said 300 pounds be fully paid. **Signed**: John Gifford; **Witnesses**: John Bellingham and Thomas Norman; **Acknowledged**: 22: Dec 1665 by Thomas Norman; **Recorded**: 23: 10: 1665.

JOHN KNIGHTS to Capt. GEORGE CORWIN (mortgage) – (2:364) On 27 December 1665, John Knights of Salem (mason) mortgaged to Capt. George Corwin of Salem (merchant) for the security of a debt of 27 pounds 15 shillings, 10 pence halfpenny, due by book, a dwelling house and barn with ¾ acre of ground adjoining, in Salem, bounded W with land of Ralph Fogg, N with the North river, E with the street, and S by land of Thomas Hale, sometime of Salem; also 2 rods and ½ square of ground, which the Towne granted to the said Hale, for a watering place near the water side before the house to the east, with the frame of a working house, together with 2 head of cattle, one being a black heifer with calf and the other a cow with a white face; the mortgage to be paid at or before the 24th of June next ensuing. **Signed**: John Knights; **Witnesses**: Ralph King, Edward Norice; **Acknowledged**: 28: 10ber: 1665; **Recorded**: 28: 10: 1665.

THOMAS SOLLAS to HENRY MOSES – (2:366) On 24 October 1661, Thomas Sollas of Salem (seaman), with wife Grace yielding up dower, sold to Henry Moses of Salem (seaman) for 20 pounds in hand, a dwelling house with half an acre of ground adjoining, in Salem, bounded N on a highway, W on land of John Beckett, E on the common or some land appertaining to Mr. Stevens, and S by the South harbor. **Signed**: Thomas Sollas and Grace Sollas [by mark]; **Acknowledged**: 27: 9ber: 1661; **Witnesses**: Bethia Weeks, Hillyard Veren.

JOHN KNIGHTS to WILLIAM LAKE – (2:367) On 18 January 1655, John Knights of Salem (plasterer), with consent of his wife, Eme, who yielded up thirds, granted to William Lake of Salem, for 35 pounds in hand paid, a dwelling house and barn with ¾ acre of ground adjoining, in Salem, bounded W with some land of Ralph Fogg, and N by the north river, E with the street, and S by some land of Serg't Thomas Hale, sometime of Salem; also 2 rods and ½ square of ground, which the town of Salem granted to the said Hale for a watering place near the water side to the northeast. **Signed**: John Knights and Eme Knights [by mark]; **Acknowledged**: 24: 11 mo: 1665; **Witnesses**: Edward Norrice and Samuel Gardner, Jr.; **Recorded**: 9: 12: 1665.

SAMUEL BELKNAP to EDWARD GASKIN – (2:369) On 20 February 1665, Samuel Belknap of Salem (joiner) granted to Edward Gaskin of Salem (ship carpenter) for 3 pounds in hand paid, a parcel of land containing 10 poles, 2 poles broad next to the street and so is to run backward north 5 poles, that is to say north and south 5 poles, and in breadth, 2 poles as above said, lying in Salem, bounded S by the street, E by land of Mr. Phillip Cromwell, N and W by land of the said Samuel Belknap. **Signed**: Samuel Belknap. Sara Belknap yielded up dower & signed; **Acknowledged**: 20: 12 mo: 1665; **Witnesses**: Hillyard Veren, Edward Humber; **Recorded**: 20: 12: 1665.

JOHN FOGG to WILLIAM TITHERLY – (2:370) On 1 August in the 17th year of the reign of Charles the second, John Fogg of Barnstable County of Devon (merchant) leased to William Titherly of Bideford County, Devon (mariner) for 30 pounds lawful money of England in hand paid and secured to be paid, 2 acres of land in Salem in New England, now or late in the tenure, possession or occupation of Ralph Fogg, father of the said John Fogg…reserving out 2 poles of land, a parcel of the premises in the front end next to the meeting house, in breadth and so far back as the fence that parts the garden from the said piece…in length, the breadth thereof to be taken from the cart way next to the house, sometime in the possession of the Lady Moody, towards that house sometime in the occupation of Mr. Felton. (From the day of the date of these presents for and during the full and whole term and time of 2000 years, from thence forth next ensuing, fully to be complete and ended, paying therefore yearly, one grain of Indian corn if the same be lawfully demanded. **Signed**: John Fogg; **Acknowledged**: 13 March 1665/6 by Richard Bragg, age 43 or thereabouts; **Witnesses**: Thomas Leach, John Tetherly, Richard Bragg; **Recorded**: 20 Mar 1665/6.
Additonal: delivery and seazin of premises given by Edmond Batten, Attorney unto Ralph Fogg, late of New England, 20 March 1665/6; **Signed**: Edmund Batten; **Witnesses**: Thomas Brattle, John Croad, Eleazer Hathorne, Nathaniel Hathorne.

GEORGE CORWIN to FRANCIS JOHNSON – (2:375) On 29 Nov 1665, George Corwin of Salem (merchant) (having been administrator of John Slaughter of Marblehead, fisherman, lately deceased) granted to Francis Johnson of Marblehead (fisherman) for a valuable consideration in hand already paid, all of the visible estate formerly in possession of John Slaughter and contained in the inventory of estate...that is to say, one dwelling house and ground in Marblehead between land of Richard Read and Samuel Condy, together with the household goods. **Signed**: George Corwin; **Acknowledged**: 1: 10: 1665 by Capt. George Corwin; **Witnesses**: Edward Norrice, John Higginson; **Recorded**: 23: 2 mo: 1666.

WILLIAM LAKE to Capt. GEORGE CORWIN (mortgage) – (2:376) On 8 February 1665, William Lake of Salem (set work coop.) with consent of wife, granted to Capt. George Corwin of Salem (merchant) for security of sum of 31 pounds 10 shillings due to Capt. George Corwin, a dwelling house and barn with ¾ of an acre of ground in Salem, bounded W with land of Ralph Fogg, N by the North river, E with the street, S by land of Serg't Thomas Hale, also 2 rods and a half square of ground which the town of Salem granted to Hale for a watering place near the waterside to NE. **Signed**: William Lake and wife Anna Lake; **Witnesses**: Edward Norice, John Higginson, Jr.; **Acknowledged**: 8: 12 mo: 1665; **Recorded**: 10th: 3 mo: 1666 [at top of deed]; 6: 2 mo: 1666 [at end of deed]; **Mortgage agreement**: William Lake shall pay or cause to be paid 30 pounds 10 shillings...15 pounds by his Uncle Mr. Elias Stileman, Sr. of Pascataqua, to be paid in such pay as Capt. Corwin and Elias Stileman shall agree upon, at or before the full end and term of ¾ of a year...and the rest in any merchantable pay at price current which Capt. Corwin shall accept...to be made within 12 months after the 1st payment is made.

RICHARD HUTCHESON to JOHN HUTCHESON – (2:378) On 16 May 1666, Richard Hutcheson of Salem (husbandman) granted to John Hutcheson of Salem (his son) for natural affection and fatherly love and also divers other good causes, all visible estate within Salem containing several parcels: his now dwelling house and barn, together with all land then in his possession, which was already manured and broken up in part, and in part unbroken (except the apple trees that were in his old orchard, which lies SE of his now dwelling house together with 2 trees in the orchard which is behind the house, all of which he had already given to his son Joseph Hutcheson...to be possessed...after his death as by his deed of gift to him, bearing date with this, more plainly appeareth) and was contained within the several bounds as follows: by a great white oak at the SE end, which is dividing line between him and his son Nathaniel Putnam, and extends to the E to the dividing line between himself and son Joseph Hutcheson, which began at the path...to a great rock on a small Island, at their ordinary place of going over the brook, then to Lieut. Thomas Putnam's bounds, to a great white oak, which is bounds between Robert Prince and himself, it lying to the NE from the forementioned bounds: the last mentioned is at a place called Beaver Dam, and from thence the brook is the bounds to the place where the 1st bounds are expressed; lastly he gave to his son John all his share of meadow which he purchased of Capt. Davenport, being part of a meadow called Mr. Hathorne's meadow—½ of the premises at the sealing and delivery of these presents and the other half after his decease, except orchards before expressed, which he reserved to his own use. **Signed**: Richard Hutcheson [by mark]; **Witnesses**: Edward Norrice and John Putnam; **Acknowledged**: 16: 3 mo: 1666; **Recorded**: 30 May 1666.

JOHN SYMONDS and JOB SWINERTON, Jr. to Lieut. THOMAS PUTNAM – (2:381) On 8 March 1665, John Symonds of Salem (joiner) and Job Swinerton, Jr. of Salem (husbandman and son-in-law to John Symonds), with consent of their wives, granted to Lieut. Thomas Putnam of Salem for a valuable consideration already paid, 3 score pole of land in Salem, bounded S with land of Worshipful John Endicott, Esq., the Honored Governor, N with Job Swinerton, Jr., W by Thomas West and E with the lane that goes toward Christopher Waller's, except one parcel of ground adjoining on the SE corner, containing 2 pole in breadth & 4 pole in length, being already in possession of said Thomas Putnam which he formerly bought of Robert Temple. **Signed**: John Symonds and Job Swinerton; **Witnesses**: John Horne, Edward Norice; **Acknowledged**: 22: 3d mo: 1666; **Recorded**: 30 May 1666.

ALLEN BREED Sr. to ALLEN BREED – (2:383) On 5: 2 mo: 1665/6, Allen Breed, Sr. of Lynn, acknowledged a deed of gift to his son Allen Breed of Lynn, for a piece of land bought of Nicholas Browne, butting N on the highway, E with land of Mr. King, W by Francis Burrell, with the marsh adjoining thereto; and land he bought of James Hubbard lying above and below the highway to the meeting house and adjoining to highway W and the land of one Croft's wife, lately called by the name of the widow Ivory on the E and Mr. King on the S & half the houselot, half the housing, half the orchard and all the marsh adjoining the same, to the sea and the great gate, 6 acres; and the other half of the housing, orchard and land, to the said Allen his eldest son after his decease; also one horse, one mare, one mare colt, one cow, a one-year-old heifer, 2 weaning calves, 2 ewes and 2 weather lambs; also all the linen his mother left him at her death. **Signed**: Allen Breed Sr. [by mark]; **Witnesses**: William Sergeant and Phillip Kirtland; **Recorded**: 30 May 1666.

JOSEPH BOWD to WILLIAM BARTHOLOMEW (mortgage) – (2:384) On 24 May 1666, Joseph Bowd of Marblehead (liquor stiller) mortgaged to William Bartholomew of Boston (merchant) for 100 pounds sterling in hand paid, one dwelling house with outhouses and lands, fenced in etc. now in the hands and occupation and possession of Robert Sweete in Marblehead, formerly in the hands of Emanuel Clarke; and also a dwelling house, stillhouse, garden, lands, etc. now in his possession in Marblehead, joining lands of Capt. George Corwin and Francis Johnson toward the SW and W, otherwise surrounded with common lands, etc. 100 pounds sterling was to be paid at or before 25 May 1668. **Signed**: Joseph Bowd; **Witnesses**: John Cleare, Sr., John Cleare, Jr.; **Acknowledged**: 25 May 1666; **Recorded**: 1 June 1666.

SAMUEL BELKNAP to EDWARD GASKIN – (2:387) On 11 June 1666, Samuel Belknap of Salem (joiner) granted to Edward Gaskin of Salem (ship carpenter) for 6 pounds in hand paid, a parcel of land containing 20 rod, adjoining unto another parcel bought of Samuel Belknap by Edward Gaskin as per deed dated 20 Feb 1665, the said 20 pole being in the form of an L, encompassing about the 10 pole, formerly bought on the W side and N end, it being in breadth at the S end, next to the street 2 pole, and so of that breadth, runs along adjoining to the other 10 pole, on the W side of it and so beyond to 7½ pole in length and then turns toward the end on the N, so the 10 pole formerly bought by Edward and this 20 pole now being laid in one piece, it is in breadth next to the street on the S 4 pole and runs backward of the same breadth, to 7½ pole in length bounded on the S with the street, E with land of Phillip Cromwell and N & W with land of said Samuel Belknap. **Signed**: Samuel Belknap & Sara (his wife) who gave up her thirds; **Witnesses**: Mary Veren, Hillyard Veren with seizin & possession given; **Recorded**: 11: 4 mo: 1666.

ELLENOR HOLLINGWORTH to MARY HOLLINGWORTH – (2:388) On 14 October 1672, Ellenor Hollingworth (lawful attorney of William Hollingworth, her husband) assigned daughter Mary Hollingworth, all the houses and lands within mentioned. [This assignment refers to the deed recorded in folio 104]. **Signed**: Ellenor Hollingworth [by mark] 14: 8 mo: 1672; **Acknowledged**: 14: 8 mo: 1672; **Recorded**: 14: 8: 72.

EDMOND FARRINGTON to MATHEW FARRINGTON – (2:389) On 22 May 1666, Edmond Farrington of Lynn (yeoman) granted to Mathew Farrington (his son) for divers and sundry considerations, ½ of his corn mill, with utensils and all profits, produce and effects arising therefrom, except the toll of son Fuller's grists, which is well and duly to be ground toll-free, during the life of his daughter Elizabeth, his wife;

likewise to his son Mathew Farrington, ½ of the mill house, houses, barn and half the upland and meadow that he bought of Nicholas Browne and half his salt marsh in the town's marsh; in consideration & condition, that his son Mathew shall from time to time and at all times improve the aforesaid mill and lands of upland and meadow, so that he and his wife may have comfortable maintenance and attendance both in sickness and in health during the full term of his life and of his wife's life, and that they by him to be honorably buried at their decease, and likewise pay to his son John Fuller...10 pounds sterling at his decease...but in case God took away his son Mathew Farrington by death or otherwise, before the decease of him and his wife, then the mill and lands to be at his and his wife's disposal. **Signed**: Edmond Farrington [by mark]; **Witnesses**: Joseph Armitage, Nathaniel Kirtland; **Acknowledged**: 9 June 1666; **Recorded**: 16: 4 mo: 1666.

LAWRENCE CLENTON to THOMAS WHITE – (2:391) On 16 June 1666, Lawrence Clenton of Ipswich, and Rachel, his wife, one of the daughters of Richard Haffield of Ipswich (deceased), granted to Thomas White of Wenham (husbandman) for 30 pounds in hand per bonds paid by or of Thomas White, all right, title and interest to the farm house and land in Chebacco, within the limits of Ipswich, now in the occupation of Robert Crosse, Jr. (assigne of Richard Brabrooke) as by right from the said Richard Haffield, late father to the said Rachel, or by virtue of any donation, gift or bequest from Martha Haffield, mother of the said Rachel. **Signed**: Lawrence Clenton [by mark]; Rachel Clenton [by mark]; **Witnesses**: Robert Howard (notary public), Mary Howard; **Acknowledged**: 16: 4 mo: 1666; **Recorded**: 10: 5 mo: 1666.

Selectmen of Salem to JOHN CLIFFORD – (2:393) On 28 February 1664, the Selectmen of Salem, namely: William Hathorne, William Browne, George Corwin, Walter Price, Edmond Batter, Henry Bartholomew and Thomas Lothrop (administrators of the estate of William Goose, deceased) granted to John Clifford of Salem (rope maker) for 32 pounds sterling to them secured to be paid as per bill under his hand, dated the day of the date of these presents, a dwelling house and about ½ acre of ground adjoining, being ½ on the E side of that ground that did belong to the said house, it being that house and ground that was the said William Goose's, deceased, and is in Salem, and is bounded W with land of John Goose, S with the other half of aforesaid ground belonging to said house, sold by us lately to the said John Goose, and NW on land of Joseph Swasy, and NE by land of William Hollingworth, and S with the highway, between it and the south harbor. **Signed**: William Hathorne, William Browne, Edmond Batter, Walter Price (the major part of the Selectmen in name of whole); **Witnesses**: William Dodge [by mark]; Abraham Bartholomew; **Recorded**: 24: 5: 1666.

HANNA MOORE to JANE JAMES – (2:395) On 23 July 1666, Hanna Moore of Salem (widow) granted to Jane James (widow; late wife and administratrix of Erasmus James, deceased) for a valuable consideration in hand already paid by Erasmus James late of Marblehead, deceased, 10 acres of land on Darby Fort side, formerly in the town of Salem and now accounted to be within the limits of Marblehead, bounded N with the south harbor, W with land of Richard Norman, E with land of John Peach, and S with Marblehead Common. **Signed**: Hanna Moore [by mark]; **Acknowledged**: 23: 5 mo: 1666; **Recorded**: 24: 5: 1666.

JOHN HATHORNE to HENRY SILSBY – (2:396) On 7 April 1660, John Hathorne of Lynn granted to Henry Silsby of Lynn, 3 acres of upland with an old house on it, bounded E with upland of John Lewis and W with land of Henry Silsby, butting S on lands of Robert Ingalls and N upon the rocks of George Farr. The house and land were formerly in the possession of Thomas Look. **Signed**: John Hathorne; **Witnesses**: Joseph Armitage, Richard Haven; **Acknowledged**: 26: 9ber: 1662; **Recorded**: 19: 7ber: 1666.

OBADIAH FLUD and THOMAS COATS to HENRY SILSBY – (2:397) On 16: October: 1651, Obadiah Flud of Boston and Thomas Coats of Lynn sold to Henry Silsby of Ipswich, for 38 pounds in hand paid, the dwelling house of Thomas Coates in Lynn, which was once in the occupation of Joseph Flud, with 6 acres of ground the house stood on, lying E next to a little river & W on the town's common, S on lands of Edward Ireson and N on lands of Robert Rand, with all barns, outhouses, fencings, gardens, orchards, commons, also 14 acres of ground lying N on lands of Mr. Daniel King and E on lands of William Witter and N on lands of William Tilton, also 2 acres of salt marsh lying in the marsh before the town, (bounded) W by lands of William Parker, E by lands of Richard Rooten, S by the salt sea, N by lands of Robert Driver next to it, and also 4 acres of meadow in the marsh by Henry Collins (bounded) N by Mr. Daniel King, E by 10 acres of rocky ground; also 10 acres of rocky ground, butting E by lands of Henry Collins, N by lands of Mr. Edward Holyoke, adjoining on 4 acres of meadow, here before mentioned. **Signed**: "the mark of Obadiah Flud (obeflud), attorney of Joseph Flud," and Thomas Coates [by mark]; **Witnesses**: Robert Lord, Nathaniel Stow; **Acknowledged**: 16 day of 8th mo: 1652; **Recorded**: 19: 7ber: 1666.

JOHN BALLARD & NATHANIEL BALLARD to THOMAS WHEELER – (2:399) On 26 October 1666, Nathaniel Ballard and John

Ballard of Lynn, signed that they owed and did stand indebted to Thomas Wheeler, late of Lynn, 400 pounds sterling to be paid half in cattle valuable at indifferent rates and the other half in English goods at the price of the market to be paid upon all demands. **Signed**: Nathaniel Ballard [by mark] and John Ballard; **Witnesses**: John Breed, John Hathorne. The condition of the obligation was such that if John Ballard and Nathaniel Ballard paid Thomas Wheeler the sum of 230 pounds as follows: viz: now in hand 10 pounds, & next 1st day of September, 70 pounds, the one part in money, namely 3 pounds and the other in English goods, either at Mr. Maverick's or at a shop in Boston, in linen or woolen cloth, at the merchant's price or current price, and 50 pounds next 1st of September anno: 1668, to be paid 3 pounds in money, and the rest in English goods at Boston, and the next payment to be made, being 60 pounds to be paid in September 1st 1669, 3 pounds in money of New England, and the rest in English goods, at a shop in Boston, in linen and woolen cloth, and the next payment to be 20 pounds upon the 1st of September 1670, 3 pounds in money...and the last payment 20 pounds...in 1671, 3 pounds in money...the above obligation to be void. **Signed**: Nathaniel Ballard [by mark], John Ballard; **Witnesses**: John Breed, John Hathorne; **Acknowledged**: John Ballard 31 Oct 1666; **Recorded**: 30 October: 1666.

Selectmen of Salem to JOHN GOOSE ~ JOHN GOOSE to JOHN CLIFFORD – (2:401) On 28 February 1664, The Selectmen of Salem; namely: William Hathorne, William Browne, George Corwin, Walter Price, Edmond Batter, Herry Bartholomew and Thomas Lothrop, administrators of the estate of William Goose, deceased, granted to John Goose of Salem (mariner), for a valuable sum in hand paid, half an acre of ground being one half of that ground that the dwelling house stands upon of said William Goose, deceased, the whole containing in length from the N down to the South harbor, southward, near 447 foot, in breadth at the N end 90 foot, and in breadth at the S end next to the water side, 114 foot, which being equally divided, the bargained premises is the one half on the western side, and to run through from the water side, to the northernmost end there of, just in the middle, said half acre will be bounded with the other half of said land, now sold, John Clifford on the E, northerly with the land of Joseph Swasy to the N, westerly the land of widow Smith to the W southerly, and to the highway between the south harbor and it southerly. **Signed**: William Hathorne, William Browne, Edmond Batter, Walter Price (Selectmen of major part of us in name of whole); **Witness**: John Clifford. On 23 July 1666, John Goose assigned over to John Clifford of Salem (rope maker) all right to within premises. **Signed**: John Goose; **Witnesses**: "with seizing and possession of the premises," by John Beckett and John Brewer; **Recorded**: 10: 9 mo: 1666.

SAMUEL BELKNAP to EDWARD GASKIN – (2:403) On 9 Nov 1666, Samuel Belknap of Salem (joiner) sold to Edward Gaskin of Salem (shipwright) for a valuable sum in hand paid, 21 pole of ground containing in length from the street inward to N, 7½ pole, and in breadth between land of said Gaskin and the land of Thomas Coale, which is the two side bounds, & on the S bounded with the street and on the N with land of said Samuel Belknap, lying in Salem. **Signed**: 6 Nov 1666 by Samuel Belknap and Sara Belknap; **Witness**: Hillyard Veren; **Acknowledged**: 9: 9ber: 1666, with wife Sara yielding right of dower.

DANIEL SALMON to JOHN HATHORNE (mortgage) – 2:404 On 23 March 1664/1665, Daniel Salmon of Lynn (husbandman) mortgaged "to John Hathorne, his now dwelling house;" and a parcel of land adjoining, bounded W with land of Theophilus Baily, and with town common on the other sides of it and two cows: a brown cow and a black cow. Daniel was to pay 12 pounds, 13 shillings, one penny—½ in fat beef and corn at or before 29 Sept next ensuing and the other ½ in corn or pork or both, at or before the last day of November next ensuing, all merchantable and at price current, to be delivered to said John Hathorne...at his now dwelling house. **Signed**: Daniel Salmon; **Witnesses**: John Archard, John Hathorne, Jr.; **Added**: 18 Sept 1666: I assign this deed or mortgage within written unto Mr. Ralph King; **Signed**: John Hathorne; **Witnesses**: William Bassett, Joseph Armitage; Edward Richard [by mark]; **Acknowledged** and **Recorded**: 12: 9 mo: 1666.

FRANCIS JOHNSON to Capt. GEORGE CORWIN – (2:406) On 30 Oct 1666, Francis Johnson of Marblehead (fisherman), with consent of wife, granted to Capt. George Corwin of Salem (merchant) for a valuable consideration in hand paid, a dwelling house and ground belonging thereunto in Marblehead, between land of Richard Read on one side and Samuel Condy on the other side, having formerly been in possession of John Slanther, (fisherman) lately deceased. **Signed**: Frances Johnson [by mark]; **Witnesses**: Eleazer Hathorne, Edward Norice, Sr.; **Acknowledged**: 31: 8 mo: 1666, Elizabeth Johnson [by mark] yielded thirds; **Recorded**: 19: 9 mo: 1666.

RICHARD RAYMOND to OLIVER MANNERING (indenture) – (2:407) On 13 October 1662, Edmund Batter and Judith Raymond, true and lawful attorneys of Richard Raymond, late of Salem (mariner), granted to Oliver Mannering of Salem (seaman) for 72 pounds to be paid according to agreement, a dwelling house with outhouses, orchard, garden, with about ¾ acre of ground adjoining, being all the ground adjoining said house which said Richard Raymond did formerly possess, except ¼ acre of said ground which was reserved for his own use, lying at the N end next to the Common in Salem, and was bounded on N with said land, ¼ acre, and on E with the house and ground of Sander Sears, and on W with the house and ground of John Gardner, & is abutting against the South river; also 10 acres of ground lying in South field, bounded N with some land of John Horne, S with land of Samuel Cutler, E with South harbor, and W by the head of South river. On 15 July 1663, Richard Raymond declared that Mr. Edmund Batter and wife Judith Raymond were lawful attorneys. **Signed**: Edmund Batter, Judith Raymond; **Witnesses**: with seizin & possession given, by Benjamin Felton, Hillyard Veren and George Salmon [by mark]; **Recorded**: 4: 10: 1666.

ELIAS STILEMAN to OLIVER MANNERING – (2:410) On 25: 2 mo: 1664, Elias Stileman of Salem granted to Oliver Mannering of Salem (mariner) for 8 pounds in hand paid, 2 acres of upland in the south field, and within the 2-rail fence of Mr. Henry Bartholomew, butting on the South river on the front of it, and on land of Mr. Bartholomew, which 2 acres was formerly in the occupation of Mr. Elias Stileman, deceased, and by him bought of Alexander Field...about the thirds of the deceased Stileman's widow "I bind me..." **Signed**: Elias Stileman; **Witnesses**: Hillyard Veren, Samuel William (with seizin and possession given); **Recorded**: 4: 10 mo: 1666.

(2:411) There is a stray taken up by Mr. Oliver Purchase, viz: a black steer or about 3 years old as Mr. Purchase said having been cryed according to laws and apprized at 5 pounds 10 shillings, about the beginning of December 1663.

THOMAS SMALL to BENJAMIN WOODROW – (2:411) On 30 April 1666, Thomas Small of Salem (husbandman) granted to Benjamin Woodrow, for 30 pounds sterling, which was given to Rebecka, the wife of Benjamin Woodrow and to her children by William Cantlebury, late deceased, a legacy in his last will and testament, I in full payment of the said sum above said; unto Benjamin Woodrow, for the uses aforesaid—a certain parcel of land, containing between 30 and 40 acres, being part of a farm, bought by William Cantlebury of Capt. George Corwin, and now appertaining unto the said Thomas Small, husband of Ruth, the daughter of the said William Cantlebury, and succession of John, son of said William Cantlebury, deceased, said land is situated in the bounds of Salem and is bounded NE by land of Job Swinerton, S by Robert Goodell, and W with the farm aforesaid, now in the possession of said Thomas Small, having a kind of a run or brook, that runs near in the bounds between...[trees] (only excepted a cartway that is to go through said land down to the river, provided in case said John Cartlebury be surviving and come in his own person according to the will abovesaid to enjoy and possess the abovesaid farm. **Signed**: Thomas Small [by mark]; **Witnesses**: Hillyard Veren, Isaac Topen; **Acknowledged**: 30: 2 mo: 1666; **Recorded**: 4: 10 mo: 1666.

KEISER to CRAFORD - (2:414) (Omitted in its place, page 73 of this book) [See page 80]
Dated 1:9ber: 1661, George Keiser acknowledged himself indebted to Mr. Mordecai Craford of Salem in sum of 3 score pounds in merchantable leather to be paid March next ensuing in consideration of plantation of 400 or 500 acres of upland & 100 acres of salt meadow & mowing ground & promised to pay in consideration of & for so much land above specified in Shipcott River. **Signed**: George Keiser; **Witnesses**: Samuel Archard & John Bessell. "The original was marked with crossed lines on the original Book of Records."

Footnote – Essex Registry of Deeds, Southern District, Salem, Mass. March 9, 1875: The foregoing Copy of the Second Book of Records of Deeds for Salem and vicinity was made in 1855, under the direction of the County Commissioners. It has now been examined and corrected and is a true copy of the original. **Attest**: Ephm. Brown, Reg.

***
Conclusion of Book 2 of Essex County Deeds
***

ESSEX COUNTY DEEDS Book 3

ABRAHAM TOPPEN to WILLIAM DOUNTON – (3:1) On 3 October 1666, Abraham Toppen (tailor) of Salem granted to William Dounton (carpenter) of Salem for 37 pounds, a dwelling house with an out house and about ¾ acre of ground adjoining with the fences, garden, fruit and corn that is growing or did grow last summer, in Salem, bounded with the street on the W, with the land some time of John Endicott Esq. S, some land of Joshua Rea on the E and the highway by the water side & some ground of Ruben Guppy on the N. **Signed**: Abraham Toppen; **Witnesses**: Hilliard Veren, Sr., Henry Renolds, John Robinston [Robbinson?]; **Recorded**: 20: 9 mo: 1666.

DANIEL DENISON to THOMAS FULLER – (3:2) Deed dated 26 December 1663. Daniel Denison of Ipswich, with Patience Denison, to Thomas Fuller (smith) of Woburn: at a General Court held at Boston 7 May 1662, granted to Major General Denison, 300 acres of land between the bounds of Salem, Andover & Rowley, to be laid out by Maj. William Hathorne and Ensigne Thomas Howlett, which was accordingly done by them and their act under their hands returned to the next session of the General Court in October 1662, and was by said court allowed and confirmed as may more fully appear by the records of said Court, and whereas said Major Daniel Denison has by his act and deed passed away part of the 300 acres to Bray Wilkins and John Gingell of Salem, in exchange for other lands, by them conveyed to the said Daniel Denison as may appear by their deed dated as 28 November 1662, this witnesses that Daniel Denison of Ipswich, for 6 score pounds to be paid to him as by a writing bearing the date with these presents sold to Thomas Fuller of Woburn the remainder of the said 300 acres of land granted to the said Daniel Denison and not sold to the said Bray Wilkins and John Gingell together with the said lands, upland and meadows, containing about 130 acres, which said Daniel had in exchange being about 300 acres of upland and meadow & is situated and adjoining to the bounds of Salem and Andover and the farm granted to Richard Bellingham, Esq., lately in possession of Bray Wilkins and John Gingell in manner following: 180 acres upland bounded on NW by land of said Bray Wilkins, on SW & in part by Price's meadow, NE by land of John Putnam & SW by the common; also a parcel of meadow containing about 30 acres bounded by the land of said Wilkins NE, E and on the other sides by the common, the rest of the land being upland and meadow containing about 100 acres adjoining to the bounds of Andover on the NW, to the lands of Bray Wilkins and John Putnam on the SE, beginning on the E end at the part of the brook, that runs through beachy meadow where another brook falls into it from the NE & a great rock lies in the midst of the brook & ending on the W end at a white oak marked on the W side of Beachy meadow. **Signed**: Daniel Denison & Patience Denison; **Acknowledged**: 28: 9ber: 1666 by Major Denison; **Witnesses**: Amos Richeson & Jon. Corwin; **Recorded**: 7: 10 mo: 1666.

ALLEN BREED, Sr. to ALLEN BREED, Jr. – (3:4) On 28 November 1666, Allen Breed, Sr. (yeoman) of Lynn, granted to Allen Breed, Jr. (husbandman) of Lynn for 5 pounds, 3 acres of fresh meadow in Lynn, in the meadow commonly called fresh marsh, and is next to the town, the said 3 acres runs through the said marsh and is bounded N on land of Richard Haven, S with the Town Common and the marsh of Nicholas Potter, E by the marsh of John Ramsdell and Alec Kirtland and W by the marsh of Nathaniel Kirtland and John Mansfield. **Signed**: Allen Breed [by mark]; **Acknowledged**: Allen Breed the elder, 29: 9 mo: 1666; **Witnesses**: Hillyard Veren & Robert Lord; **Recorded**: 7: 10 mo: 1666.

ALLEN BREED, Sr. to JOHN BREED – (3:6) Allen Breed, Sr. granted to his younger son John Breed 16 acres of upland and marsh in Rumney Marsh adjoining William Winter on the E, Nathaniel Kirtland on the W and land of Mr. Knowles, lately Mr. Willis, on the S; 9 acres called the Ferry piece, adjoining land of Capt. Bridges E and that part of Rumney Marsh belonging to the town on the S and the common swamp called noeman's swamp on the W and Capt. Bridges land on the N; son John to be possessed of them at the age of 21, but in case said Allen Breed his father die before John comes to age then son to be possessed of the land at his death. Son John also to have one heifer, one ewe lamb, one brass pot and the linen his mother gave him which is in his sister Miriam's keeping for his use. **Signed**: Allen Breed, Sr. [by mark]; **Acknowledged**: 5: 1 mo: 1665; **Witnesses**: William Sergeant & Phillip Kirtland; **Recorded**: 7: 10 mo: 1666.

SAMUEL HART to JOHN BREED (indenture) – (3:7) On 5 March 1665/6, Samuel Hart (blacksmith) of Lynn, with Mary (wife) yielding thirds, granted to John Breed of Lynn, a dwelling house with outhouses at Lynn, with about 14 poles of land bounded N with land of Allen Breed, Jr. and E, W & S on town common. **Signed**: Samuel Hart & Mary Hart [by mark]; **Acknowledged**: 5: 1 mo: 1665/66; **Witnesses**: Phillip Read, Robert Potter & John Hathorne; **Recorded**: 7: 10 mo: 1666.

ALCE JOHNSON to SAMUEL JOHNSON (Indenture) – (3:9) Indenture made 12 November 1666 between Alce Johnson of Lynn (widow) on the one part, and Samuel Johnson of Lynn, being the natural son of said Alce Johnson and John Collens of the same town, son-in-law to

Alce, both of the other part, witnesseth Alce in consideration of affection to two sons as also for other consideration, gave to Samuel Johnson all her housing, lands and meadow grounds left her by will of her husband Richard Johnson, lately deceased, except 2 acres of salt marsh, being ½ of a 4 acre lot in salt marsh before the Town of Lynn, to take possession after the death of said Alce Johnson. Samuel Johnson is to pay his sister Elizabeth Toleman 10 pounds upon his entry upon the premises. If Samuel Johnson shall depart this life having no natural heir surviving, then to her son Daniel Johnson, and he shall upon the same consideration pay unto the children of his sister Elizabeth Toleman 10 pounds, and in consideration that John Collins is son-in-law and other reasons does give 2 acres of salt marsh in the marsh before the Town of Lynn, being half a 4-acre lot left her by will of husband Richard Johnson, lately deceased, to take possession of at death of Alce, and if said Samuel Johnson shall depart this life without a natural heir surviving, then to the children of her son-in-law John Collins, 2 acres salt marsh in the marsh before the Town of Lynn, being the other half of a 4-acre lot, also being understood that if necessity require, she may sell all or any part of housing lands and meadow grounds. **Signed**: Alce Johnson [by mark]; **Acknowledged**: 27: 9: 1666; **Witnesses**: Thomas Laughton & Andrew Mansfield; **Recorded**: 24: 10 mo: 1666.

WILLIAM BROWNE, Sr. to WILLIAM FLINT – (3:11) On 10 December 1666, William Browne, Sr. (merchant) of Salem granted to William Flint (yeoman) of Salem, for 25 pounds, 15 acres lately bought by said William Browne of John Beckett and was formerly land of William Jeggles, deceased, in the south field so-called, in Salem, bounded with the Forest River S, with the south harbor E, with some ground formerly of Henry Harrod now in possession of said William Flint N, and some land of Richard Adams W, and some land of Elias Mason SW, having a white thorne next to the Forest River, by a spring of water for the bounds between said land, and Elias Mason at the lower end and a stump at a great pit side at the upper end from the water side, all within said bounds except near half an acre of salt marsh that lies at the head of a little cove, against said Forest River, of Thomas Jegells. **Signed**: William Brown; **Acknowledged**: 11: 10 mo: 1666 with wife Sarah yielding thirds; **Recorded**: 26: 10 mo: 1666.

SAMUEL FRIEND to AMBROSE GALE – (3:13) On 28 June 1666, Samuel Friend (planter) of Manchester granted to Ambrose Gale of Marblehead 20 acres in Manchester on the E front of land going into the creek, joining land of James Standish NE, the sea toward the S and the creek toward the NW. **Signed**: Samuel Friend; **Acknowledged**: 28: 4 mo: 1666; **Witnesses**: Moses Maverick, Samuel Maverick & John Harris [by mark]; **Recorded**: 30: 10 mo: 1666.

JAMES BROWNE to PHILLIP CROMWELL (mortgage) – (3:13) On 27 November 1665, James Browne (glasier) of Salem granted to Phillip Cromwell of Salem, for 20 pounds sterling, a dwelling house with ground adjoining he had lately bought of Christopher Waller. The mortgage was to be paid by the sum of 20 pounds in money of New England, or by merchantable dry codfish at price current before 20 June next ensuing. **Signed**: James Browne; **Acknowledged**: 28: 9 mo: 1665; **Witnesses**: Isaack William & Thomas Ives; **Recorded**: 3: 11: 1666.

GEORGE CORWIN to THOMAS SMALLE – (3:15) On 24 November 1666, George Corwin (merchant) of Salem granted to Thomas Smalle (husbandman) of Salem, for 4 pounds, ten acres of meadow or bushy ground in Salem, between lands of Lieut. Thomas Putnam & Robert Goodell, bounded on one side with the river and the other side with land which George Corwin sold to John Swinerton. **Signed**: George Corwin; **Witnesses**: Edward Norice and Jonathan Corwin; **Acknowledged**: Capt. George Corwin, 9: 11 month: 1666; **Recorded**: 15: 11: 1666.

AUGUSTIN WARNER to RICHARD MOORE – (3:16) Shipped in good order and well conditioned by me, Richard Moore, in good ship *Swan*, Master Timothy Prout, Sr., riding at anchor in port of Boston & bound for London, 11 hogsheads of Virginia leaf tobacco & makes for the proper account of Col. Augustin Warner of Virginia, being marked & numbered & are to be delivered in the like good order & well conditioned, at aforesaid port of London, the danger of the seas only excepted, unto Arthere Baily or to his assignes, he or they paying freight for the said goods after the rate of 11 pounds per ton, 4 hogsheads to the ton, with primary & average accustomed. The master or purser of said ship, hath affirmed to three bills of lading, all of this tenner & date of one of which three bills being accomplished the other two to stand void, and so God send the good ship to her desired port in safety Amen. Dated in Boston 4 December 1666, the contents I know not. **Signed**: Timothy Proute; **Recorded**: 24: 11 m: 1666.

NICHOLAS DANIEL to Capt. GEORGE CORWIN & Co. – (3:17) Bill of 31 December 1666. Nicholas Daniel of Port Royall, Jamaica, is to pay unto Capt. George Corwin & Company of Salem, the full sum of 6 pounds 15 shillings sterling money of England, to be paid at or before the 10th day of May next ensuing. Theodere Price (merchant) came before me, 16 March 1666/7 and made his corporall oath that he was present and saw Mary Daniel sign and deliver this bill as her act & deed. William Hathorn, Assistant in the Massachusetts. **Signed**: Nicholas Daniel [by mark]; **Witnesses**: John Hardick & Edward Haward; **Recorded**: 16 March 1666/7.

PHILLIP VEREN to JOHN SMALL, Sr. – (3:18) On 12 October 1665, Phillip Veren (wheelright) of Salem granted to John Small (husbandman) of Salem, for a valuable sum in hand paid, 40 acres of land, a lot lately granted to Phillip Veren by the town of Salem, land adjoining Francis Johnson's farm in Salem, bounded S with said land; E with land of Thomas James & N with the farm that was Mr. Emanuel Downing's and W with a 40-acre lot of Widow Cooke, as laid out and bounded, with all the timber...appurtenances thereto belonging. **Signed**: Phillip Veren; **Witnesses**: John Burton & John Foster [by mark]; **Acknowledged**: 20: 10th mo: 1680 by John Burton & John Foster & that seisen & possession was given to John Small, Sr.; **Recorded**: 5: 12 mo: 1666.

THOMAS READ to RICHARD RICHARDS – (3:19) On 2 January 1663/4, Thomas Read of Salem (planter), with consent of wife, for 11 pounds, granted to Richard Richards of Salem six acres of upland in the north field, belonging to the town of Salem, bounded N with head of the great cove, S with land of Job Swinerton, Sr., E with land of Robert Goodell and W with land of Mr. Henry Bartholomew. **Signed**: Thomas Read [by mark]; **Witnesses**: Edward Norice & John Browne; **Acknowledged**: 11: 12 mo: 1666; **Recorded**: 19: 12 mo: 1666.

ROBERT MANSFIELD to JOSEPH MANSFIELD – (3:21) On 28: 12 mo: 1666, a deed, dated 16 June 1652, was recorded that witnessed that Robert Mansfield (yeoman) of Lynn (father) granted to Joseph Mansfield (son) for love and affection and other good causes respecting his own good, his whole accommodation, consisting in houses and lands (except 6 acres of salt marsh, which said Robert had made over to his son Andrew Mansfield by deed of gift) to take possession of it at his & his now wife's decease, 2 of which lying in the salt marsh before the town, bounded with the marsh of Nathaniel Hanaford W, and the marsh of Andrew Mansfield E, butting N upon Mr. Willis's upland & S upon the river, 3 acres more in the 2nd div. of Rumney Marsh, bounded E with marsh of Capt. Bridges & W with marsh of George Taylor, N on the common & S on the marsh of Mr. Willis, and 1 acre more in the same division, bounded W with the marsh of William Winter and E with marsh of Mathew West, butting N on the Common, S on Mr. Willis's marsh, all of which he purchased of John Hall; but for all the rest of the lands & marsh, houses and orchards, viz: 9 acres for his house lot, bounded E with land of John Witt, W with land of Francis Burrell, butting S on the country highway, and N on the rocks, with all the buildings on it & orchard; also 7 acres of land bounded E with the fresh marsh of Mr. Hollyoke, & W with the planting lot lately in the tenure of Edward Burcham, butting N on the brook that runs into the fresh marsh, & S on the rocks; also a 10-acre lot promised & also paid for to Lieut. Walker, also 5 acres of upland marsh & marsh joining together, bounded N with land of John Deacon, W with land of Mr. Cobbitt, E & S with the river which land lies in the neck; 3 acres of salt marsh in the 1st division in Rumney Marsh, bounded E with the marsh of Capt. Bridges & W with the marsh of John Fuller, butting N on the upland and S on the common, 2 acres more in the same division, bounded E with marsh of George Burrell & W with marsh of Capt. Keyne, butting N on the common or creek, S on the marsh of Mr. King; 1 acre more in the 2nd division in Rumney marsh, bounded E with marsh of Thomas Laughton & W with the marsh of Thomas Newhall, butting N on the common & S on Mr. Willis's marsh, 1 acre in the same division of Rumney Marsh, bounded E with the marsh of Capt. Bridges, butting N on the upland or swamp & S on the marsh of John Witt, and also what other fresh marsh he had in the country—he bought 5 acres—he gave unto Joseph Mansfield (that is to say) the ½ present & the other half at the death of the said Robert, provided that the provisions afterwards made about the 3rds of the whole estate to his wife surviving, be in force upon his decease upon this consideration: that the said Joseph is to carry on the whole husbandry of the living, in such manner as may be most to the advantage of both parties, at his own proper cost, only having allowed him what personal help the said Robert comfortably can perform in his old age & whereas it cannot be expected from the said Robert to equalize the said Joseph in respect of bodily strength & said Robert at present doth give unto said Joseph 2 cows & half his team, with ½ the furniture as plow, carts, chains, yokes, & at his death & his now wife's death, the whole furniture he then has for his teams and likewise at both of their decease, the bed Joseph now usually lies upon—and it is the intent of the said Robert that the said Joseph, with each of their families should live together, to keep equal stock of cattle together and as either of them may have occasion to sell part of the same, it is to be with the consent of the other and be accountable to the other & in case said parties cannot comfortably live together, then Joseph is to carry on…if the wife of Robert shall survive Robert…in case Joseph shall die without an heir, then wife of Joseph surviving…her name being wife Elizabeth daughter of Edmund Needham. **Signed**: Edward Needham; **Witnesses**: Thomas Cobbitt & Andrew Mansfield; **Acknowledged**: 29: 1 mo: (53). **Recorded**: 28: 12: 1666.

WILLIAM BROWNE to BARTHOLOMEW GALE – (3:26) On 16 March 1662, Bartholomew Gale (fisherman) of Salem, granted to William Browne of Salem, for 76 pounds, 17 shillings, 2 pence, a dwelling house with ¼ acre of ground in Salem, bounded N by Edward Woolen's near the common, and S with a highway. **Signed**: Bartholomew Gale [by mark]; **Witnesses**: Benjamin Browne & Abraham Bartholomew; **Acknowledged**: 9: 12: 1666; **Recorded**: 26: 12: 1666.

EDMUND & SARAH BATTER to MICHAEL SHAFLIN – (3:27) On 17: 10th mo: 1665, Edmund Batter & Sarah his wife, granted to Michael Shaflin of Salem for good & valuable consideration, 2 acres of upland lying at the N end of a pond, being part of the said Batter's farm at the brook, adjoining said Shaflin's ground. **Signed**: Edmund Batter & Sarah Batter; **Witnesses**: Hilliard Veren, Sr. & Hilliard Verren, Jr.; **Acknowledged**: 16: 1 mo: _666/67; **Recorded**: 16: 1: 1666.

JOHN GEDNEY, Sr. to BARTHOLOMEW GEDNEY – (3:28) On 25 March 1667, John Gedney, Sr. (vintner) of Salem granted to Bartholomew Gedney (son) (shipwright) of Salem, for good will & natural affection, an acre of marsh lying near the great cove on the north neck in Salem, bounded N with land of Robert Goodell, E by a brook & W with land of John Horne. **Signed**: John Gedney & Katheren Gedney; **Witnesses**: Hillyard Veren & John Buttolph; **Acknowledged**: 25: 1 mo: 1667 with Katheren releasing dower; **Recorded**: 1: 2 mo: 1667.

JOHN GEDNEY to BARTHOLOMEW GEDNEY – (3:30) On 20 November 1664, John Gedney (vintner) of Salem granted, for love, etc., to son Bartholomew Gedney (shipwright) of Salem an acre of land in Salem, lately bought of John Ruck, the bill of sale bearing date of 20 June 1662; part of the land of said Ruck adjoining his dwelling house, said acre being bounded with a lane or highway to the S. with the common on the W & with land of John Ruck on the N and the cove or river to the E. **Signed**: John Gedney & Katherine Gedney; **Witnesses**: John Buttolph & Hillyard Veren; **Acknowledged**: with release of dower, 25: 1 mo: 1667; **Recorded**: 4 April 1667.

JOHN GEDNEY to BARTHOLOMEW GEDNEY – (3:32) On 6 December 1665, John Gedney (vintner) of Salem, granted, for love, etc., to son Bartholomew Gedney (shipwright) of Salem, 10 acres of land in the north neck, in Salem, bounded E with land of John Symonds, W with a highway that runs into the lot by Marshall's, N with land of John Neale, S with a highway that runs between said lot & land of John Symonds. **Signed**: John & Katherine Gedney; **Witnesses**: John Buttolph & Hillyard Veren; **Acknowledged**: 25: 1 mo: 1667; **Recorded**: 5: 2 mo: 1667.

THOMAS WAYMOUTH to MOSES MAVERICK – (3:33) Thomas Waymouth (fisherman) of Marblehead does owe & stand indebted unto Moses Maverick, the full and just sum of 14 pounds, 10 shillings to be paid unto said Maverick in fish, merchantable & refuse at or before the 20th day of June next at price current & for security of the payment of the above said sum or what else shall be due & the said Thomas Waymouth...does bind over and engage unto said Moses Maverick...his now dwelling house, with the land thereto adjoining and all that land he now possesses, which he bought of Robert Brookes with orchard and meadow and all appurtenances & privileges thereto belonging. **Signed**: 3 Jan 1666/67 by Thomas Waymouth [by mark]; **Acknowledged**: 1: 2 mo: 1667; **Witnesses**: Robert Burgess [by mark], Samuel Maverick, Thomas Phillpot; **Recorded**: 5: 2 mo: 1667.

ELIZABETH JEGGELLS to ROBERT GLANFIELD – (3:34) On 16 April 1667, Elizabeth Jeggells, administrator of William Jeggles (deceased) and with the consent of Thomas Jeggells (son) of Salem (mariner), granted to Robert Glanfield of Salem (shipwright) of Salem, for 11 pounds in hand paid before the ensealing & delivery of these presents, a parcel of ground containing 22 poles, being part of that land on which Elizabeth's house stands at the N and next adjoining a piece of land formerly sold to James Browne and bounded N with land of James Brown, E with a highway or lane left out for their particular uses, on the S with her land & W with land of John Browne, Senior; to have and hold said 22 poles or rods of ground so bounded with all privileges of said lane as a highway to said ground to Robert Glanfield. **Signed**: Elizabeth [by mark] and Thomas Jeggells; **Witnesses**: with seisin & delivery...by turf & twig, Hillyard Veren, Sr., Richard Charlescroft; **Recorded**: 17: 2 mo: 1667.

EDMOND BATTER to THOMAS GOLDTHWAITE – (3:36) On 29 April 1667, Edmond Batter (merchant) of Salem granted to Thomas Goldthwaite (cooper) of Salem, 30 or 40 acres of land, part of the farm given him by the town of Salem, bounded on land of Samuel Very and Isaack Burnap to the S with a round meadow belonging to the farm of Isaack Burnap SW, both which said side bounds run upon a straight line & from a swamp at the NW end of the said meadow, the bounds run to a little brook or springy swamp and up to a black oak tree, on which side it is bound with the land of Robert Stone and William King, and NW & NE with lands of Michael Shaplin and some land of Robert Stone, and E with land he lately gave to Hillyard Veren. **Signed**: Edmond Batter; **Acknowledged**: 29: 2 mo: 1667; **Witnesses**: Henry Renolds; Phillip Veren; **Recorded**: 30 April 1667.

ABRAHAM ALRED to EDWARD JOANES – (3:37) Gentlemen & honest friends be pleased to pay unto my friend Edward Joanes, the several sums of sugar which you owe me which each gentleman's sum is underneath mentioned & directed to you, & every of you severally, for your each particular sum or sums, taking the said Joanes his receipt for any sum you pay for my account and in so doing you will oblige him that is – y'rs to serve you to this power, Abraham Alred.

to Coll. Timothy Thornehill	p. 4574} sugar
to ditto for one tunn of cask	360}
to Tho. Hart for	155
to Elizabeth Smale	174 for acc' of Tho. Webb
to Mr. John Rawdon	1574 bill}
to Mr. John Coates	225 bill} pd. by account
to John Seddon	1000 bill}
to William Bragg	for 2 bbls of tar 600 bill)
	8437 lbs

A copy of this acco't or order, I have received of Mr. Abram. Alred & am to be accountable to him or order for what I shall receive of it witness my hand this 25: January 1666/7
    Edward Joanes; Recorded 20: May: 1667

Barbadus List of debts due Elea. Hathorne	
Edward Bradhourne p. Judgment in	sugar
Austins Court 7 mo: 64	2389
Ralph Parrott Judgment pt pd	2149
Richard Dickenson Judgment in St Mich' lbs Jan 64	1880
James Cars Judgment	0041
Richard Griffen Judgment Dav. Fogg's note	0478
John Jepson p accot	0204
George Tompson	0269
James Hayden	0600
Richard Abbot p bill	0365
Benjamin Cotterill p A	0273
Thomas Powdrill for Tho Dinsdaile	0000
Henry Odiarne	0221
Thomas Applewhite p acco't Rumb.	0733
John Sandeford p acco't	0207
John Langley for 2 barrells beef	0600
Richard Barry for James Barry	0250
Capt Samuel Tidcombe as p. gene'll release of	
Gregory Sallens to Alice his wife	10000

Received from Nathaniel Hawthorne the about said bill accoumptb &c for acco't of Mr. Eleazer Hawthorne & for which I promise to be accomptable, as witness my hand this 20 day September 1665.
Abra. Hawkins.

OLIVER MANNERING to WILLIAM FLINT – (3:39) On 30 April 1667, Oliver Mannering (seaman) late of Salem, granted to William Flint (yeoman) of Salem for 14 pounds in hand paid (Mannering binds himself in the sum of 25 pounds against all title of dower or any interest that his wife Hanna may have), 8 or 9 acres of land, lying in the South neck in Salem, bounded with the south harbor to the E and land of James Smith to the S with the salt marsh against Castle Hill to the W and land of John Horne to the N. **Signed**: Oliver Mannering [by mark]; **Acknowledged**: 29: 2 mo: 1667; **Witnesses**: Samuel Williams, Hillyard Veren Sr; **Recorded**: 26 May 1667/24: 3 mo: 67.

NATHANIEL MASTERS to JOHN LAMBERT, Sr. – (3:42) On 8 May 1667, Nathaniel Masters (tailor) of Salem, granted to John Lambert Sr. (fisherman) of Salem, for 35 pounds, all his dwelling house with all ground adjoining, containing 2 acres partly orchard within the fence and some arable ground without the fence with all fence belonging and all trees in both orchards (except) all those trees that stand not in rows according to proportion of about 20 foot square in ranck & file, with the nursery, which he reserves for himself to have liberty to take them up and carry them away, at or before the 15th of April next ensuing the date hereof, with said houseing & ground lying near the meeting house on Bass river side belonging to Salem, bound NW with the highway, NE and next to the meeting house, with some land of Samuel Corning's as presently lies as common & fence as it stands to be bounds SE with land of John Lovett at the S end and somewhat W with land of Samuel Corning or William Dixy running to a narrow at the end…also about 2 acres on the other side of the highway to the NW bounded with the Bass river to the NW end with land of William Hoare SW and of Josiah Rootes SE to Robert Hibbert NE. **Signed**: Nathaniel Masters and Ruth Masters [by mark], with wife Ruth releasing dower rights; **Witnesses**: Walter Price, Thomas Pickton, Hillyard Veren; **Recorded**: 26 May 1667.

JUDITH COOK to JOHN SMALL – (3:44) On 17 May 1667, Judith Cook (widow & adminstratrix of Henry Cook) of Salem, granted to John Small (planter) of Salem for "a valuable consideration," 10 acres of land in the north neck in Salem, bounded by Williston's river E, with the great cove S, by land of Thomas Bracket & Hugh Jones W, with a highway that runs down from the lot to the river N. **Signed**: Judith Cook [by mark]; **Acknowledged**: 20: 10 mo: 1680 by John Foster, Sr. & George Jacob; **Witnesses**: Edward Groves (with seisin…given), John Foster [by mark] and George Jacob, Sr. [by mark]; **Recorded**: 26 May 1667.

FRANCIS NURSE to GEORGE JACOB – (3:45) On 10 March 1666, Francis Nurse (tray maker) of Salem, granted to George Jacob (planter) of Salem, for 11 pounds 10 shillings, about 3 acres of neck of land, except for a small point of it to the SE, reserved to Nurse's own use to set a cock of hay on, said neck was called Towne's Neck, lying on Ryall's side in

Salem, bounds as agreed to by said Francis and George, viz: the river bounding it to the W and said Jacob's marsh N and some marsh of John Foster S—to be understood that said George Jacobs maintain all the fence next to the common so far as his own land goes. **Signed**: Francis Nurse [by mark]; **Acknowledged**: 11: 2 mo: 1666; **Witnesses**: Will Dountin & Hillyard Veren, Sr.; **Recorded**: 27 May 1667.

PARNELL BARTOLL to JOHN HOOPER – (3:47) On 6 July 1665, Parnell Bartoll (relique & executrix of John Bartoll) of Marblehead, granted to John Hooper of Marblehead, for 9 pounds, 10 shillings, half an acre of land on the hill formerly called "Goites Hill," between the house of Robert Hooper SW and the cove called Scott's Cove, toward the NE, to the sea towards the harbor on the SE, bounded by the path NW. **Signed**: Parnell Bartoll [by mark]; **Acknowledged**: 15: 2 mo: 1667; **Witnesses**: Samuel Maverick, Moses Maverick, John Peach [by mark]; **Recorded**: 27 May 1667.

GEORGE EMERY – (3:48) The deposition of Mr. George Emory who said that being at the running of the line about 3 years since between John Deveroux's farm and Marblehead common and also between the farm once Mr. Humphries', Jeffry Massy and many others being present, it was agreed and we began at a white oak near the place in John Deveroux's meadow, & from there to a tall pine in John Deveroux's corn field near the fence to a marked pine in the plain not far from the new bridge and from thence to a great stone set up by us at the head of the 10 acre lots and from thence to a white oak on the edge of rocks called Mr. Ruck's tree, and from thence on a straight line to a tree marked by consent at the stony beach called Webb's. Taken upon oath 7: 2: 1668. William Hathorne, Assistant. I also tesify...William Hathorne; **Recorded**: 27: 3 m: 1667.

CHRISTOPHER LATTAMORE to HENRY RUSSELL – (3:48) On October 1663, Christopher Lattamore and (wife) Mary Lattamore of Marblehead, granted to Henry Russell, for 11 pounds 10 shillings in fish, a parcel of land in Marblehead against Lattamore's house that Mr. Shakerly once lived in, being in length S with the great brier bush to the rock about 7 score feet and from the same bush E 3 score feet to the stone wall standing near the E cove. **Signed**: Christopher Lattamore [by mark] and Mary Lattamore; **Acknowledged**: by Mary, who gave up thirds, 14: 1 mo: 1666/7 & by Christopher 6: 2 mo: 1667; **Witnesses**: William Pitt, Elias Kendall [by mark], John Trebey [by mark]; **Recorded**: 3: 4: 1667, 17: 4: 1667.

THOMAS CALY to THOMAS WHITE – (3:50) On 17 June 1667, Thomas Caly (planter) of Marblehead, granted to Thomas White (fisherman) of Marblehead, for 14 pounds, 3 to 4 acres of land on Darby Fort side, in Marblehead, bounded N with Salem harbor, E with land of Thomas Dixy, W with land of John Peach the younger, S with land of Benjamin Parmiter on S side or end, the dividing line from an old fence that stood on the east side; from that fence runs W to an Apson stump to John Peach's land on the W of the said lands, to have and hold...with the liberty & privilege of a highway through the ground of said Thomas Caly to the common—provided that hereafter said White, his heirs or assignes shall make a sale of said parcel of land that said Caly have first refusal thereof. **Signed**: Thomas Caly [by mark]; **Acknowledged**: & Mary yielded her thirds; **Witnesses**: Richard Rowland [by mark] & Hillyard Veren; **Recorded**: 17: 4 mo: 1667.

JOHN SMITH to JOHN NEALE – (3:51) On 10 April 1666, John Smith (sowgelder) of Salem, granted to John Neale, for a valuable sum in hand paid, an acre of land in the north neck near the great cove in Salem, part of a lot which Robert Goodell (his father-in-law) sold him, contained in a long narrow strip, taken out of said land formerly sold, on the W thereof by a straight line & bounded W with a brook, and runs on that side as the brook runs, and is bounded S with land of said John Neale & part W towards that end, and E with land sold him by his father Goodell, now in possession or occupation of Capt. George Corwin, and NE with ground of said George Corwin. **Signed**: John Smith [by mark]; **Acknowledged**: 10: 5 mo: 1667; **Witnesses**: William Foster & Hillyard Veren; **Recorded**: 10: 5: 1667.

THOMAS HALE, Sr. to JOHN MILKE – (3:53) On 6 October 1666, Thomas Hale, Sr. of Newbury granted to John Milke of Salem, for 15 pounds sterling, ¾ of an acre, all within fence, part of it next to the street and an orchard, and the other part arable ground, in Salem, bounded with the street that goes from the meeting house to the North river to the E with land of Elinor Robbinson (widow) to the S, with land of William Browne Jr. (merchant) to the W, and some land of Ralph Fogg and William Lake's house and land to the N, there being about 4 or 5 feet in breadth of ground that runs into the bargained premises at the end of William Lake's house to the S, the breadth of his house & leanto only which he lately sold to said William Lake...with all fences belonging, all fruit trees, all profits and privileges, with interest in ½ the well that stands in the street. **Signed**: Thomas Hale; **Acknowledged**: 25: 4 m: 1667, with Thomasine Hale resigning all rights. 12 June 1667; **Witnesses**: with seisin & possession given, Hillyard Veren, Elias Mason; John Massey; **Recorded**: 22 July 1667.

EDMUND PATCH to RICHARD DODGE – (3:55) On 9 July 1667, Edmund Patch (husbandman) of Ipswich granted to Richard Dodge (yeoman) of Salem, for 40 pounds, 13 and ½ acres of land with a dwelling house in Salem near Wenham, bounded with land of Humphrey Woodbery W, land of John Woodbury N to land of said Richard Dodge E and S, also a 3rd part of a 40-acre lot that Patch had in partnership with Richard Dodge and now in possession of said Dodge. **Signed**: Edmund Patch [by mark]; **Acknowledged**: 10: 5: 1667; **Witnesses**: Hillyard Veren & Roger Conant; **Recorded**: 10: 5: 1667.

ALLEN BREED to WILLIAM MERRIAM & ELIZABETH (BREED) MERRIAM – (3:57) On 26 June 1666, Allen Breed (yeoman) of Lynn, granted to William Merriam and Elizabeth (his wife and daughter of Allen Breed), a parcel of land or farm, formerly given by the town of Lynn to Mr. Thomas Cobbett and sold by said Cobbett to Benjamin Keyne, as by a deed dated 22 September 1641 and sold by Robert Keyne (attorney of Benjamin Keyne) to said Allen Breed as per deed dated 6th February 1653 which farm contained 200 acres, 20 acres of such meadow adjoining and 10 acres salt marsh, all in Lynn; the said 220 of upland and meadow lying near a farm given to Mr. Whiting and said 10 acres of salt marsh lying in the last division as per above said appeareth. **Signed**: Allen Breed [by mark]; **Acknowledged**: 26: 4 mo: 1667; **Witnesses**: Joshua Ward and Hillyard Veren; **Recorded**: 13 July 1667.

MATHEW CLARKE to EDMUND GALE – (3:59) On 18 Feb 1663, Mathew Clarke of Marblehead granted to Edmund Gale (fisherman) of Marblehead, for a valuable consideration, a quarter of an acre joining land of Mathew Clarke NW, Lott Conant on the SE, the marsh of Mr. William Walton and Moses Maverick on the NE, the highway on the SW. **Signed**: Mathew Clarke [by mark]; **Acknowledged**: with Abigail yielding thirds; **Witnesses**: Phillip Harding and Robert Hooper [by mark]; **Recorded**: 22: 4 mo: 1667.

RICHARD HUCHESSON to JOSEPH HUCHESSON – (3:60) On 16 May 1666, Richard Huchesson (husbandman) of Salem granted to son Joseph Huchesson of Salem, for natural affection and fatherly love, all his visible estate specified: the whole tract of land…all bounds to said land, as first his now dwelling house, barn and land already broken up, which he had now in his possession; a quarter part of the land he had purchased of Mr. Stileman Sr. with all his meadows formerly possessed and 2½ acres of meadow within son Nathaniel Putnam's field, the meadow commonly called Pease's meadow with the meadows which he has at the meadow commonly called Bishop's meadow containing 5 acres and at the river commonly called the great river, containing 2½ acres, together with that which lies at the S end of that meadow, which formerly belonged to Capt. Price, containing 4 acres; also in addition to the land before mentioned, he gave to son Joseph and his heirs all the land hereafter expressed by its particular bounds...containing 200 acres, a parcel of land having on the NE corner on the dividing line...tree, marked upon the 4 corners & extending on a straight line...stump and from there to a great rock to the N of the NW and from there...tree being the cornerbound between Lieut. Thomas Putnam's land and that land purchased of the Worshipful Major William Hathorne and from thence to the bound tree, that is the dividing bound between Capt. Davenport's land, lying W & SE to a stake that is the bound dividing between Lieut. Thomas Putnam's meadow and his own meadow at the brook...to son Joseph Hutcheson & his heirs...all the said lands as well as uplands and meadows lying on the W side of the dividing line, beginning at the brook before expressed, at the bounds dividing his own land and the said Lieut. Putnam's meadow, so extending to the W bordering on the aforesaid brook to son Nathaniel Putnam's land, lying to the W and from the aforesaid brook or swamp to the dividing line of Nathaniel Ingersoll's land, which is to the S of the aforesaid swamp and so from the dividing line to E; at a bound tree..., which is the dividing bound between Mr. Stileman's farm & Goodman Pease, & this land now last expressed which is part of the land purchased of Mr. Thorndike; also a lot to said son besides the forementioned particulars, another parcel of upland containing by estimation 100 acres in Salem, bounded with a white oak tree upon a hill commonly called the great hill, which is a dividing bound between Nathaniel Ingersoll's land, & from thence SW to a great white oak which divides Job Swinerton's land & his, & from thence to a scrubbed white oak tree standing on a hill called Shermaid's hill, lying to the W at bounds before expressed, from these bounds it is bounded N with a red oak tree & from thence to bounds first expressed, also all meadow which he now improves & makes use of lying to the W of the said dividing line, also to son Joseph after his decease; lastly after decease all the apple trees that are in old orchard, which lies to the SW from now dwelling house with 2 apple trees that are in the orchard which is behind the house, which he promises to mark & set out for Joseph's use & that the said Joseph shall & may from time to time & at all times after his decease have liberty to fence the said orchard...and also that neither son John Hutcheson, his heirs...shall or may have liberty to put into said orchard any swine, calves, sheep...whereby the said orchard maybe damnified...every year from the middle of August to the last of October... **Signed**: Richard Huchesson [by mark]; **Acknowledged**: 16: 3 mo: 1666; **Witnesses**: Edward Norice and John Putnam; **Recorded**: 10: 5: 1667.

THOMAS WEST (agent for WILLIAM RANDALL) to JOHN GODFREY – (3:64) On 22 July 1667, Thomas West (agent for William

Randall of Newbury), and Elizabeth Randall (wife of William) granted to John Godfrey of Newbury, for 30 pounds, 9 acres of broke up land joining land of said William Randall and bounded with lands of Aquilla Chase, Edward Woodman and Robert Coker on the N, the common on the S and W and running to a point on the E along by the orchard fence of said William Randall, with the fences and appurtenances thereunto belonging (the crop now on said land is reserved for the use of said William Randall) as it is now fenced, respectively to the proper use of the above said John Godfrey and his heirs. Thomas West and Eliza Randall acknowledged this writing to be their act and deed, and reserving liberty to said Elizabeth to plant one acre of the land the next year; dated 7 Aug 1667. **Signed**: Thomas West [by mark], and Eliza Randall [by mark]; **Witnesses**: Anthony Somerby, Thomas Browne, and John Kimball; **Recorded**: 9: 6 mo: 1667.

RICHARD GARDNER to EDWARD MOULD – (3:66) On 25 Aug 1667, Richard Gardner (mariner) of Salem granted to Edward Mould (fisherman) of Salem a dwelling house with 9 or 10 rods of ground adjoining said house in yard and garden spot with all fences and appurtenances belonging thereto (except as excepted) the new shop with cellar under it, which Richard Gardner reserved for his own use, as it now stands upon, part of the land now sold as abovesaid or until I see cause to remove it upon my own land or otherwise the said Edward Mould shall see cause to remove the said shop upon my land next adjoining or build another of like dementions as good with a like cellar under it, at his own cost, the said house and ground lying in Salem is bounded with some land of Richard Gardner S, which he reserves to himself, being near half about the garden, the other half being part of the bargained premises and bounded on the W with the street and partly N with the ground and warehouse of Mr. William Browne and E and partly N with ground of Samuel Shattock...to have and hold said house and ground adjoining to say near about half the enclosed garden next adjoining, as it is bounded out, with the yard fenced, appurtenances (except the shop as above excepted. **Signed & Acknowledged**: Richard Gardner & Sara Gardner, Sara released dower rights; **Witnesses**: with seisin & possession given by William Downton and Hillyard Veren, Sr.; **Recorded**: 7: 7: 1667.

JOHN GEDNEY to son JOHN GEDNEY – (3:68) On 28 August 1667, John Gedney (vintner) of Salem granted to son John Gedney (mariner) of Salem, for natural love & affection, all his farm formerly given him by the town of Salem, containing 80 acres of upland and 9 acres of meadow, the upland bounded with land of Mr. Thomas Gardner, Sr. on the N, with land of John Marsh, Sr. on the E and with Mories meadow (on which end there stands a pine tree marked and it is bound between Mr. Gardner and the premises) on the W end and with common land (not lately laid out by the town) S the said 9 acres of meadow lying in the great meadow of said Gardner's being about 1/3 of the whole meadow & lies partly within or adjoining; also an acre of ground in the Town, bounded N with the highway, by the North river, and the E with land of Samuel and John Williams, on the S with land by the pound & on the W with land of Stephen Haskett and Capt. Benjamin Fermaies. **Signed**: John Gedney & Katherine Gedney; **Witnesses**: Walter Price & Henry Bartholomew; **Acknowledged**: 31: 6 mo: 1667 by John Gedney & wife; **Recorded**: 10: 7 mo: 1667.

BENJAMIN BRISCO to JOHN JOLIFFE – (3:70) On 9 August 1664, Benjamin Brisco (shoemaker) of Boston and Sarah his wife, granted to John Joliffe (merchant) of Boston for 70 pounds in hand paid, a dwelling house and orchard with all land within the fence, half an acre lying in the town of Lynn on the N side of the brook in the Milne street, bounded with land of Mathias Farnsworth E, with land of Richard Haven W and N, with the country highway S, and also all the commons, liberties, privileges unto said house, land and orchard belonging, which said Brisco purchased of Robert Mansfield and John Mansfield of Lynn; also 6 acres of land lying in Lynn, bounded with the house lot of Richard Blood E, with land of Thomas Ivory W, with land now or late in possession of William Bartrum S and with town common N, also all the wood and timber remaining, growing on 2 lots in Bass Neck at Nahant in Lynn aforesaid; viz: the 13th and 14th lot containing 8 acres, which said 6 acres of land with said woodland, the said Benjamin Briscoe had purchased of Richard Blood of Lynn and said John Mansfield as by deed, 27 April 1660, also one mare and a black colt and all moveables in the aforesaid house. **Signed**: Benjamin and Sarah Brisco. On 10 Aug 1664, slate seizin & possession given in presence of Samuel Hart & Daniel Knight. **Acknowledged**: 17: 6 mo: 1664 by Benjamin & Sara, who released dower rights. **Witnesses**: Robert Howard (Notary Public) & Mary Howard; **Recorded**: 16: 7ber: 1667.

JOSEPH GRAFTON, Sr. to NATHANIEL GRAFTON – (3:74) On 23 September 1667, Joseph Grafton, Sr. (mariner) of Salem granted to his son Nathaniel Grafton (mariner) of Salem for love and natural affection, an acre of salt marsh in Salem by the south harbor, bounded N with land of Job Hillyard, E with land sometime of Henry Harrod, S with the beach against the south harbor and on the W with land of said Nathaniel Grafton and with land of the widow Moore. **Signed**: Joseph Grafton; **Witnesses** (with seisin & possession): Samuel Shattock and Hillyard Veren; **Recorded**: 24: 7: 1667.

MARTHA ANTRUM to JOHN MARSTON the younger – (3:75) On 4 Sept 1667, Martha Antrum (now resident in Ipswich), late wife & administrator of the estate of Obadiah Antrum, dec'd, granted to John Marston, the younger, (carpenter) of Salem, in consideration of a valuable sum, a new dwelling house not finished as it now is, with ½ acre of ground adjoining which said Obadiah lately bought of John Ruck, lying in Salem, bounded S with a cove in the South river, W with land of Eleazer Gidney, N with the highway and E with land of Mathew Woodwell. **Signed**: Martha Antrum [by mark]; **Witnessed**: with seisin...by Eleazer Gedney, John Gould and Hillyard Veren; **Recorded**: 24: 7 mo: 1667.

WILLIAM MARSTON to ALLESTER MacMALLEN – (3:77) William Marston of Salem granted to Allester MacMallen of Salem, for 30 shillings, a parcel of land joining John Symonses on 2 sides thereof, and another side toward the North river and the other side abuts to the lane, the parcel of land so mentioned is 20 rods or thereabouts. **Signed**: William Marston; **Acknowledged**: 5: 2 mo: 1661; **Witnesses**: John Marston & Christopher Water [by mark]; **Recorded**: 24: 7 mo: 1667.

SUSANNA HOLLINGWORTH to HUMPHREY WOODBERRY – (3:78) On 2 Dec 1667, Susanna Hollingworth (widow) of Salem granted to Humphrey Woodberry (yeoman) of Salem for a valuable consideration, 10 acres of land on Cape Ann side belonging to Salem, bounded with some land of Mr. Thorndike E, land of Peter Woolfe W, with land of Humphry Woodbury and partly of Mr. Thorndike N, abutting the sea S & warrant...late husband Richard Hollingsworth. **Signed**: Susanna Hollingworth [by mark]; **Acknowledged**: 3: 10 mo: 1667; **Witnesses**: John Browne, Mary Woodbury [by mark] & William Hathorne; **Recorded**: 10: 10 mo 1667.

RICHARD BISHOP to JOSIAH SOUTHWICK – (3:79) On 10 December 1667, Richard Bishop (husbandman) of Salem granted to Josiah Southwick (husbandman) of Salem for a valuable consideration fully paid, meadow & about ½ acre of salt marsh above the mill in the North River in Salem by Strongwater brook, bounded with marsh of Mr. Thomas Gardner S and surrounded with said river on all other sides. **Signed**: Richard Bishop; **Acknowledged**: 11: 10 mo: 1667; **Witnesses**: John Higginson and John Bacheller; **Recorded**: 11: 10 mo: 1667.

ROBERT RAND to HENRY and JOHN COLLINS (indenture) – (3:80) On 6 November 1663, Robert Rand (husbandman) of Lynn, with consent of Elizabeth his now wife, in reference to her surrendering up her thirds according to law, granted to Henry Collins, Jr. and John Collins (his brother of Lynn), (both carpenters), for 50 pounds, 9 acres in Lynn, bounded N with land of said Henry Collins, S with land of Robert Rand, abutting E on a brook and W on the town common, and also a dwelling house with part of his orchard. **Signed**: Robert Rand [by mark] & Elizabeth Rand [by mark]; **Acknowledged**: 27: 9ber: 1667 & wife released dower; **Witnesses**: Andrew Mansfield & Joseph Collins; **Recorded**: 17: 10: 1667.

JOHN MARSTON, Jr. to ANKIAS HORSMAN – (3:82) On 26 Dec 1667, John Marston, Jr. (carpenter) of Salem granted to Ankias Horsman (seaman) of Salem for a valuable sum of money in hand already paid, a dwelling house with the ground it stands on, formerly granted by the town of Salem to the wife of William Chichester (for her use) lying between the house of William Lord, Sr. and Hillyard Veren near the waterside, and warrant against all persons laying claim under me or from the said William Chichester or his now wife. **Signed**: John Marston, Jr.; **Witnesses** with seisin: William Woodcocke & Hilliard Veren, Sr.; **Recorded**: 28: 10 mo: 1667.

ANKIAS HORSMAN to PHILLIP CROMWELL – (3:83) On 26 December 1667, Ankias Horsman (seaman) of Salem granted to Phillip Cromwell of Salem for 16 pounds 12 shillings (which he owed unto Phillip Cromwell), a dwelling house and the ground it stands on which house and ground he lately bought from John Marston, Jr., lying between the house of William Lord, Sr. and the house of Hillyard Veren, near the water side in Salem, provided that if Ankias Horsman or any in his name, shall pay unto the aforesaid Phillip Cromwell, the full sum of 16 pounds 12 shillings in good current pay of this country at current price at or before the 25th day of December next in the year of 1668, that then this sale shall be void and of no effect, provided that whatever the said house shall be sold for by said Cromwell, more than the sum above said (he paying himself all charges thereto belonging with interest) said Cromwell shall pay the remainder to said Ankias or his assigns. **Signed**: Ankias Horsman [by mark]; **Acknowledged**: 27: 10 mo: 1667; **Witnesses**: Hillyard Veren, Sr. and William Woodcock; **Recorded**: 28: 10 mo: 1667.

THOMAS ROBBINS to GEORGE JACOB – (3:85) On 22 Sept 1666, Thomas Robbins (husbandman) of Salem granted to George Jacob (planter) of Salem for a valuable sum already paid, ¾ of an acre on Ryall's side, as it is bounded E with the marsh of Goodman Massey, N on the common and with land of Francis Nurse SW and a part of it lying against the cove to the NE. **Signed**: Thomas Robbins; **Acknowledged**: 4: 9 mo: 1666; **Witnesses**: Hillyard Veren, Sr. and Bartholomew Gedney; **Recorded**: 9: 11 mo: 1667.

WILLIAM and ELIZABETH RANDAL to JOHN GODFREY – (3:86) On 19 November 1667, William Randall and wife Elizabeth of Newbury granted to John Godfrey of Newbury for 50 pounds in hand paid and received, all the messuage or tenement where they now dwelt in Newbury, with all housing, fences, garden, orchard, containing 16 acres near the great pine swamp, being bounded with land of Aquila Chase on one end on NW & NE, by land of Edward Woodman and Robert Coker NW and NE, and the street & common on the SE with all housing, fences and the crop of rye now on the ground. It was agreed that William Randall and his family should have liberty to dwell in the house until the 29th of September next. **Signed**: William and Elizabeth Randall [both by mark]; **Acknowledged**: 9 Jan 1667, and Elizabeth released dower; **Witnesses**: Anthony Somersby, Thomas David [by mark] and Abriell Somersby; **Recorded**: 15: 11 mo: 1667.

SOLOMON STODDARD to MOSES MAVERICK & RICHARD ROWLAND – (3:88) On 1 May 1667, Solomon Stoddard (gentleman) of Boston (fellow of the college of Cambridge) granted to Moses Maverick and Richard Rowland of Marblehead, for 50 pounds paid, 50 acres of upland and skirts of meadow in Marblehead with such pond or ponds or other liberties that to the same belong, as it was given & granted to him by the late Emanuel Downing, his grandfather, bounded with the farm which sometime was John Humfrey's Esq. SW with the land of Nathaniel Pickman in part with the commons of the town of Salem in part W, and with the marsh of said Richard Rowland and Capt. Smith N, and reserving all such mines now or hereafter appear to be on the 50 acres with liberty to Stoddard to search for & improve same, paying all damages any work shall do. Moses Maverick and Richard Rowland assigned over one half part of this deed of sale, for contra specified, viz: unto John Peach, Sr. one quarter and unto John Peach, Jr. one half quarter part and unto Samuel Ward one half quarter part. Witness our hand 20 January 1667 by Moses Maverick and Richard Rowland [by mark]; **Acknowledged**: 20: 11 mo: 1667. **Signed**: Solomon Stoddard; **Acknowledged**: 15: 3: 67; **Recorded**: 20: 11: 1667; **Witnesses**: Anthony Stoddard, John Wiswall, Sr. and Peter Beckett.

RICHARD MORE to EDWARD GROVE – (3:92) On 17 January 1667, Richard More (mariner) of Salem granted to Edward Grove (sailmaker) of Salem for a valuable sum in hand paid, ½ acre of land which was formerly Mr. John Prescott's bought by him of John Friend, deceased and received by me, by virtue of an execution upon the said Prescott, said parcel lying in Salem and is bounded N with land of Samuel Pickman and Mr. Eleazer Hathorne, E with land of Samuel and John Pickman, S with the South river & W with the common or burying place and land of Mr. Hen. Bartholmew; also with privilege of a highway, sufficient for cart and house, from said land to the street that goes straight to the meeting house. **Signed**: Richard More; **Acknowledged**: 18: 11 mo: 1667 by Capt. Richard More; **Witnesses**: Henry West and Hillyard Veren, Sr.; **Recorded**: 20: 11 mo: 1667.

RICHARD RICHARDS to ROBERT PEASE – (3:93) On 16 January 1667, Richard Richards (planter) of Salem, with consent of Elizabeth his wife, for 11 pounds, granted to Robert Pease (weaver) of Salem 6 acres of upland and meadow lying in the north field belonging to Salem, bounded N with head of the great cove, S with the land of Job Swinerton, Sr., E with land of Thomas Goodell & W with land of Mr. Henry Bartholomew or John Tompkins. **Signed**: Richard Richards and wife Elizabeth Richards [both by mark], wife Elizabeth yielded her thirds; **Acknowledged**: 17: 11 mo: 1667; **Witnesses**: Hillyard Veren, Sr. & William Dounten; **Recorded**: 23: 11 mo: 1667.

ROGER CONANT to LOTT CONANT – (3:95) On 20 November 1666, Roger Conant (yeoman) of Salem granted to his son Lott Conant of Salem for love and affection, his now dwelling house and all his land adjoining with the orchard and all appurtenances there, lying on Bass River, belonging to Salem, all the said land containing 20 acres and is bounded with a bridge in the highway and the brook to the S and land of Edward Bishop on the N, with land of Henry Herrick, Sr. on the brook side to the E, together with some land of Roger Conant's at the north end on the E & the highway to the W; also 12 acres adjoining on the E side, to the N end on the eastern side of the brook and further bounded with land of Henry Herrick, Sr. to the S and to the N with land of Benjamin Balch and E with land of the Woodberry's abutting to the W, against the 20 acres near the brook, also about 10 acres of meadow lying in the great marsh against Wenham river, bounded E and N with Woodberry's marsh, W with Benjamin Balch, and S with his land; also 60 acres of upland near Richard Dodge's farm, bounded with land of Humphry Woodberry E, and land of William Dodge W, and a highway on the N to the land of William Dodge, Sr. and Roger Hascall S; also 1 acre of marsh, bounded on the Milne river S, with Benjamin Balch E and N and the Woodberrys W; also 1 acre of marsh at the thatch pond, lying in the middle of it. **Signed**: Roger Conant; **Acknowledged**: 10: 5 mo: 1667; **Witnesses**: John Veren [by mark] and Hillyard Veren; **Recorded**: 10: 12 mo: 1667.

LOTT CONANT and ROGER and SARAH CONANT (Indenture) – (3:97) On 21 Nov 1666, Lott Conant of Salem leased to Roger Conant and Sarah his wife, of Salem, for a valuable consideration in hand paid, a dwelling house with an orchard or orchards and garden adjoining containing about 3 acres on Bass river side in the town of Salem bounded with a brook near the bridge S, the land of Henry Herrick, Sr. to the E, with land of said Lott Conant to the N and the way to the W, being the house and orchard formerly of the said Roger Conant, now in the tenure or occupation of said Roger Conant and also 1 acre of salt marsh, lying on the head of the Milne river and bounded S with the said river, the land of Benjamin Balch to the NE and land of the Woodberry's to the W. Roger Conant and Sara, for and during the time of their or either of their natural lives, yielding and paying therefore during the time or term of their or either of their lives, unto said Lott Conant or his assignes, one Indian corn at or on the 1st day of January, yearly, the same be lawfully demanded. **Signed**: Lott Conant; **Acknowledged**: 10: 5 mo: 1667; **Witnesses**: John Veren [by mark] and Hillyard Veren.

EDMOND BATTER to RICHARD HUD (Indenture) – (3:99) On 10 January 1667, an indenture was made between Edmond Batter (merchant) of Salem and Richard Hud (husbandman) of Lynn for good causes and consideration. Batter, administrator to the estate of the late John Humfries, Esq. (deceased), demised, granted, set & to farm let unto the said Richard Hud, & his assignes all that messuage or tenement of the said John Humphries, Esq. now in the tenure & occupation of said Richard Hud commonly called Mr. Humfries farm, in Lynn, near Nahant, together with all houses, buildings, yards, orchards, lands, meadows, pastures, feedings, commons, profits & commodities whatsoever, to the said messuage or tenements of rite in anywise belonging or to same appertaining in that place or thereunto adjoining; as also 9 acres of salt marsh, lying in Rumney marsh to the said messuage or tenement belonging; also 6 acres of salt marsh lying also in said Rumney marsh, which said 6 acres is the marsh lately recovered by law from Richard Johnson of Lynn; to have & to hold the said messuage or tenement, with all houses, buildings, yards, orchards, lands, meadows, pastures, feedings, commons, profits and commodities with their appurtenances, & fence upon the said land now standing together with 9 acres of meadow & also 6 acres of meadow lying in 2 distinct parcels in Rumney marsh unto the said Richard Hud...from the 29th day of September last past unto the full end & term of seven years, from thence next ensuing & fully to be compleat & ended, yielding & paying therefore yearly during the said term unto the said Edmond Batter or his assignes, the yearly rent of 9 pounds sterling and one good load of salt marsh hay, which the said yearly rent of 9 pounds sterling & one load of good salt marsh hay, is to be paid by the said Edmond Batter in Salem, in some convenient place where the said Edmond shall appoint within ¼ of a mile from the meeting house, the hay & also the said 9 pounds in beef, pork, wheat, pease and corn of any sort (except oats) proportionally what is raised of or produced, upon the said messuage or tenement to be paid every year successively (after the first year) at or before the 1st of November at price current at the several times of payments, and the said Edmond Batter doth covenant & grant that the said Richard Hud & his assigns shall & may cause to be made at his p'per cost all manner or reparations upon premises before by these presents granted, from time to time, when & as often as need shall require during the term of 7 years & so well & sufficiently repaired as sd Hud shall find premises when he enters & takes possession shall in the end of sd term or other sooner determination leave the same & it is agreed Hud shall have allowed him 15 pounds out of first years rent for the reperation of the premises & it is understood that with buildings or other reparations Hud shall add & doe more then to value of 15 pounds for the necessary use & commodity of same shall at end of term (so leaving of it) be paid & further shall have liberty granted at his or their own pleasure, to break up & improve for arable land, what & as much as he will of that pasture, situated & lying next to Daniel King's & John Lewis's. **Signed**: Edmund Batter, Richard Hud [by mark]; **Witnesses**: Henry West & Hillyard Veren.

ROGER CONANT to EXERCISE CONANT – (3:102) On 20 November 1666, Roger Conant (yeoman) of Salem granted to Exercise Conant (his son), for love & natural affection, 45 acres of upland in Salem, toward Wenham, bounded NE with a highway, SW with land of William Dodge, Jr, SE also with William Dodge & NW with land of said Roger Conant and about 3½ acres of fresh meadow in Wenham great meadow, bounded S with Wenham river, E with the meadow of Benjamin Balch, E with the Woodberry's, N with the upland; also 1¼ acre at the great pond marsh, as it now lies, bounded between Benjamin Balch's marsh on one side, & marsh of Peter Woodbery on other side. **Signed**: Roger Conant; **Acknowledged**: 10: 4 mo: 1667; **Witnesses**: John Veren [by mark] & Hillyard Veren; **Recorded**: 14: 12: 1667.

WILLIAM STEVENS to FRANCIS WILLOWBY (Indenture) – (3:105) On the 14th of January 1667, William Stevens of Gloucester signed an indenture with Francis Willowby (merchant) of Charlestown in Middlesex County, stating that the said William Stevens bargained and sold unto said Francis Willowby, all his now mansion place in Gloucester at the place commonly called the gut, containing one dwelling house with about 8 acres of ground adjoining, being partly marshland and partly upland, & the said gut or passage for boats running through, as they pass between Cape Ann Harbor & Annisquam and is bounded S with the highway anent the sea W by marsh lands & E with lands sometime of Ralph Parker on the east…without disturbance of William Stevens or Phillip Stevens provided always & it is true intent of the present deed that whereas Will. Stevens by deed of feofement bearing date 30 of December in year named above has granted to Francis Willowby all of his farm containing 500 acres that if

Francis Willowby...without lett denial or interruption of Phillip Stevens wife of William Stevens the above grant shall be of no power. **Signed**: William Stevens; **Acknowledged**: 25 Jan 1667; **Witnesses**: Laur. Hammond & Richard Waldry; **Recorded**: 19: 12: 1667.

WILLIAM STEVENS to FRANCIS WILLOUGHBY, Esq. – (3:108) On 30 December 1667, William Stevens (shipwright) of Gloucester (with consent of wife Phillip) granted in feofed to Francis Willoughby, Esquire (merchant) of Charlestown, for 320 pounds sterling, one messuage or tenement, situated in Gloucester containing one dwelling house, bake house, barn & outhouses, with 500 acres of land more or less thereunto adjoining, containing all the neck land, lying between the river of Annasquam & Chebacco and is bounded N with the sea, W on the Chebacco River; E by the Annisquam River, S on the town common, with an island lying in the said river containing about 2 acres, & rights to the common & commonage belonging to said farm. **Signed**: William Stevens; **Acknowledged**: 25 Jan 1667; **Witnesses**: Laur. Hammond & Richard Waldrey; **Recorded**: 19: 12: 1667.

WILLIAM STEVENS to FRANCIS WILLOUGHBY – (3:111) On 15 January 1667, William Stevens (shipwright) of Gloucester, for sundry good considerations & love & affection to wife Phillip Stevens, granted to 2 sons James Stevens & Isaac Stevens as feoffees, in trust for Phillip Stevens their mother, and to her only use, all his now mansion place in Gloucester, containing one dwelling house and about 8 acres of land adjoining & the gut therein that is the passageway between Cape Ann Harbour & Annisquam with all the privileges to the same provided whereas I have by an Indenture bearing date of the 14th of this instant mortgaged & bound over all said land with the gut therein & housing thereon unto Francis Willoughby, against all claims that the said Phillip Stevens may make to the thirds of the farm or the neck of land within the same town by me lately sold to said Francis Willoughby, in case the said Phillip Stevens shall at any time after my decease make any claim to her thirds or dower right of the said neck of land, by me sold to the said Francis Willoughby. This grant to Phillip (wife) & to sons in behalf...void. **Signed**: William Stevens; **Acknowledged**: 25 January 1667; **Witnesses**: Laur. Hammond & Richard Waldron; **Recorded**: 27: 12: 1667.

JOHN MASSEY to GEORGE JACOB, Sr. – (3:113) On 17: 12 mo: 1666/7. John Massey (husbandman) of Salem, with Sarah releasing dower, 25 December 1700, granted to George Jacob, Sr. (husbandman) of Salem, for 6 pounds sterling, ¾ acre of salt marsh, more or less, in Salem, butting N upon Ryal's neck; E on land of John Southwick, W on Nurse's neck, S with Towne's Cove, and said John Massey for himself & heirs, did covenant warrant & defend the title to said George Jacob. **Signed**: John Massey; **Acknowledged**: 17: 12: 1667; **Witnesses**: Nathaniel Felton & Anthony Buxton; **Recorded**: 23 Mar 1667/68.

JOHN GALLY & HENRY BAILY to JOHN HALE – (3:114) On 28 Feb 1667, John Gally & Henry Baily (planters) of Bass River in Salem granted to John Hale (pastor) of Bass River, for a valuable consideration in hand paid, about 45 poles of land lying on the N side of part of the acre of land the company of Bass River bought of them for a minister, which is now settled upon the said Mr. Hale, the 44 poles being added to Mr. Hale's house lot makes his outlet into the highway by Mr. Livermore's corner, a pole wide & thence runs to a stake now set up about 20 poles E from the said outlet, upon a straight line which is the bounds between Mr. Hale's land and ours. **Signed**: Henry Baily [by mark] and John Gally [by mark]; **Acknowledged**: 28: 12: 1667; **Witnesses**: Thomas Pickton & Ann his wife [by mark]; **Recorded**: 23: 1 mo: 1667.

THOMAS PICKTON to JOHN HALE – (3:115) On 28 February 1667, Thomas Pickton (planter) of Bass River (with Ann Pickton releasing dower rights) granted to John Hale (pastor) of Bass River, for a valuable consideration, half an acre of land bounded W by Robert Morgan's lot & S by the other part of his 10-acre lot, out of which it is taken & is 19 poles long and 4½ poles wide, running cross the head of his said lot, save that which he reserved 1 pole's breadth of the E end of it, to go into his own land which is its east bounds next to John Gally's land, on the N it is bounded by that acre of land he sold the company of Bass River for a minister, which is now settled upon Mr. Hale & where the house now stands where the said Mr. Hale dwells, save that the highway runs between them, which said land lying in Bass River in Salem, said Hale is to have & to hold with its appurtenances to him, his heirs, etc. **Signed**: Thomas Pickton & Ann Pickton [by mark]; **Acknowledged**: 28 Feb 1667; **Witnesses**: John Galley [by mark] & Henry Baily [by mark].

ANKIAS HORSMAN to WILLIAM & ABIGAIL LORD – (3:116) On 3 February 1667, Ankias Horsman (seaman) of Salem saving harmless against claim of wife Jane with relation to dower granted to William, Sr. & wife Abigail Lord of Salem, for 50 pounds in hand paid, all his dwelling house which he lately bought of John Marston, Jr. with the ground it stands on being a parcel of land formerly granted by the town of Salem to wife of Will Chichester for her use & the use of her heirs, lying between the house & ground of the said William Lord and the house and ground of Hillyard Veren, near the south river side, the said house to be finished according to a covenant drawn between Mr. Henry Bartholmew and John Norman,

Senior, bearing date of 12: 11 mo: 1663. **Signed**: Ankias Horsman [by mark]; **Acknowledged**: 21: 12 mo: 1667; **Witnesses**: Phillip Cromwell & Hillyard Veren; **Recorded**: 23: 1 month: 1667/8.

EDMUND BATTEN to JOHN NORTHY – (3:118) On 9 March 1667/8, John Northy (fisherman) of Marblehead acknowledging he stands indebted to Edmund Batten (merchant) of Salem for 77 pounds, 1 shilling sterling, assigned, set over & confirmed unto said Edmund Batten…all the dwelling house with the ground adjoining, containing about 3 acres, being partly an orchard & garden, all being within the fence & is situated & lying in Marblehead & is bounded with a line or highway that leads to the common or woods E, with a street S, with the land of William Nicke and some land of Greenfield NW; also a stage standing by the great harbor side between the stage of Richard Read to the W & the stage of Christopher Lattamore to the E, to have & to hold the said messuage or tenement to say said dwelling house with all the ground adjoining being 3 acres more or less with orchard, garden, fences, appurtenances & priviledges without disturbance of John Northy or Dorothy his wife…if the said John Northy, his heirs or assignes, or any in their name do pay or cause to be paid unto the said Edmund Batten the sum of 77 pounds & 1 shillings at or before the 1st of March next ensuing, in dry cod fish, merchantable & refuse at price current; that then this bargain & sale to be void and of no effect, otherwise to stand forever in full force & virtue. **Signed**: John Northy; **Acknowledged**: 9: 1 mo: 1657/8; **Witnesses**: Henry West & Hillyard Veren; **Recorded**: 2: 2 mo: 1668.

WILLIAM LORD to NICHOLAS MANNING – (3:120) On 20 February 1667, William Lord, Sr. of Salem (with Abigail his wife yielding dower) granted to Nicholas Manning (gunsmith) of Salem for 25 pounds sterling, a parcel of upland called "Friend's Lot," containing about 8 acres, being all upland adjoining his land in Salem in the South field, bounded SW with the marsh that runs to Forest river, being the marsh of said William Lord, with a brook that runs down to the said marsh S, which brook parts the bargained premises & some land that comes in with a strip of William Flint's & with the land of John Neale's that bounds on the S to the E & some land of William Flint northerly and somewhat easterly. **Signed**: William Lord [by mark] & the mark of------; **Acknowledged**: 21: 12 mo: 1667; **Witnesses**: Edmund Batten & Hillyard Veren: **Recorded**: 2: 2 mo: 1668.

WILLIAM NICHOLS to JOHN PORTER, Sr. – (3:122) On 24 February 1667, William Nichols of Topsfield granted to John Porter, Sr. (yeoman) of Salem for a valuable sum, 5 acres of upland & 3 acres of meadow lying within & being part of a farm formerly Mr. Townsend

Bishop's, now the farm of & in possession of said John Porter & bounded with the said farm on every side...8 acres of upland & meadow with all profits. **Signed**: William Nichols [by mark]; **Acknowledged**: 24: 12 mo: 1667; **Witnesses**: Hillyard Veren & Henry West; **Recorded**: 3: 2 mo: 1668.

DANIEL SALMON to JOHN HATHORNE (Indenture) – (3:123) On 17 March 1667/8, Daniel Salmon (husbandman) of Lynn granted to John Hathorne of Lynn, for 6 pounds, paid & secured to be paid a parcel of salt marsh or meadow in Lynn in Rumney Marsh containing 6 acres, sold to Salmon by the town of Lynn, three 2-acre lots being given by the town to Michael Spencer, Nathaniel Whiting & Jerard Spencer, bounded W with the land formerly of Capt. Keyne, abutting N on the 1st division in Rumney Marsh, & S on the Pine River as being some estate of inheritance in fee simple. **Signed**: Daniel Salmon; **Acknowledged**: 30: 1 mo: 1668; **Witnesses**: John Hathorne & William Hathorne.

ELIZUR HOLYOKE to JOHN COLLINS – (3:125) On 25 April 1665, Elizur Holyoke of Springfield on the Connecticut River, with consent of Editha his wife, granted to John Collins of Lynn, for 9 pounds, 6 acres of land in Lynn (with all profits, etc.), bounded NW with land of George Taylor, by said John Collin's own land & Goodman Silsby and SW and NE by land of Henry Collins. **Signed**: Elizur Holyoke & Editha Holyoke [by mark]; **Acknowledged**: 18: May: 1666; **Witnesses**: Thomas Day, Samuel Holyoke & William Warner; **Recorded**: 20: 2 mo: 1668.

HENRY HERRICK, Sr. to ANDREW ELLIOT – (3:126) On 26 May 1668, Henry Herrick, Sr. (yeoman) of Salem, with Edith Herrick consenting & then signing (by mark), granted to Andrew Elliot (cordwainer) of Salem for 4 pounds sterling, an acre of upland lying on Bass river side in Salem, bounded S with land of Edmund Grover, or the neck fence that parts the said bargained premises & Edmond Grover's land & bounded E with the highway or common road, W & N with land of said Henry Herrick. **Signed**: Henry Herrick; **Acknowledged**: 27: 3: 1668; **Witnesses**: Hillyard Veren & Nehemiah Grover; **Recorded**: 27: May 1668.

SAMUEL HARRIS to NICHOLAS VINSON – (3:128) On 2 March 1667, Samuel Harris (seaman) of Salem granted to Nicholas Vinson (planter) of Manchester, for 4 pounds paid, right he now has or of right ought to have belonging to all the land, meadows, pastures, feedings & commons in Manchester, that is to say, his 3rd part of about 25 acres of meadow and upland, lying in several parcels & lying in common or partnership with said Nicholas Vinson & now in his possession, joining the now dwelling house of said Vinson, containing about 1 acre of marsh and about 5 acres of upland on the neck before the town & about 19 acres more unlaid out or undivided, lying in common with the town, all which premises were formerly in the possession & of right belonging to Robert Cotta & by him sold to Samuel's father-in-law, Thomas Tuck, to hold the said premises being the 1/3 part of 25 acres of upland & meadow lying in several parcels. **Signed**: Samuel Harris [by mark]; **Acknowledged**: 10: 12: 1668; **Witnesses**: Hillyard Veren & Samuel Williams; **Recorded**: 12: 6: 1668.

WILLIAM BASSETT to ANDREW MANSFIELD (Indenture) – (3:129) On 1 June 1660, William Bassett (husbandman) of Lynn (with Sarah Bassett releasing her thirds), granted to Andrew Mansfield (husbandman) of Lynn for 4 pounds sterling, 3 acres of fresh meadow ground in Reedy meadow in Lynn, it being ½ of a 6-acre lot, formerly in possession of Henry Rhodes, bounded with the meadow of John Pearson E. and the meadow of Robert Rand W, on that side toward Beaver dam, abutting on Bassett's upland N & the property of John Pearson S. **Signed**: William Bassett & Sarah Bassett [by mark]; **Acknowledged**: 10: 6 mo: 1668; **Witnesses**: James Mills [by mark] & Robert Burgess [by mark]; **Recorded**: 12: 6 mo: 1668.

EDWARD RICHARDS to EZEKIEL NEEDHAM (Indenture) – (3:131) On 14 October 1667, Edward Richards (joiner) of Lynn and wife Ann Richards (who yielded dower 10: 5: 1668) granted to Ezekiel Needham (gentleman) of Lynn for 3 score & 10 pounds in hand paid, a dwelling house in Lynn with barn, outhouses, gardens, orchards, together with a parcel of land adjoining, with all fences, trees, wood, underwood, containing 9 acres, bounded E with lands of Mr. Thomas Laughton, S on the town common, W with lands of Samuel Johnson as the fence stands only at the upper end next to the rocks, it is bounded by a white oak stump that has a young tree growing out of it, standing about half pole within the stone wall of said Johnson and butting N on the rocks of town Common, the upper end of the land running from the corner next unto the aforesaid Johnson, to a cleft post standing towards the middle of the upper end fence & runs up the hillside towards the NE along the bryer bush to an old oak stump as the corner bounds S to old stump and to an oak tree unto the corner where land of Mr. Thomas Laughton & Mr. Holyoke, now in possession of Christopher Brewer meets. **Signed**: Edward Richards [by mark] & Ann Richards; **Acknowledged**: 10: 5: 1668; **Witnesses**: John Hathorne & John Lewis; **Recorded**: 18: 6 mo: 1668.

THOMAS WAYMOUTH to MOSES MAVERICK – (3:134) On 15 April 1667, Thomas Waymouth of Marblehead granted to Moses Maverick of Marblehead, for a valuable consideration in hand paid, a dwelling house and land bounded with land of James Smith & Richard Rowland NW, the land of Mr. William Walton SW & land of John Waldron SE; and common land NE, which land he bought of Robert Brooks, to have & hold said dwelling house, orchard, garden, meadow & land with cow commonage. Moses Maverick of Marblehead assigned over unto Thomas Rose of Marblehead, all his right, title, claim & demand unto this deed & of the house & land sold him, as witnesses his hand, 27: 6 mo: 1668. **Witnesses**: William Hathorne, Sr. & Anna Hathorne; **Acknowledged**: 27: 6 mo: 1668; **Signed**: Thomas Waymouth [by mark]; **Acknowledged**: 22: 2 mo: 1667; **Witnesses**: Nathaniel Grafton & John Hathorne, Sr.; **Recorded**: 1: 7 mo: 1668.

WILLIAM LORD, Sr. to RICHARD PRINCE – (3:135) On 14 April 1668, William Lord, Sr. (cutler) of Salem (with wife Abigail releasing dower), granted to Richard Prince of Salem for a valuable consideration, 10 acres of upland in the south field in Salem, bounded N & S with land of Joseph Hardy, W with the Deacon's marsh, E with the south harbor; also ½ acre of salt marsh called Waller's marsh, bounded W with Thomas Browning's 10-acre lot & N with said Browning's marsh; also ½ acre & ½ quarter acre of marsh bounded with the marsh of Thomas Browning S and of William Flint N, Elias Stileman's upland E, and the widow Spooner W. **Signed**: William Lord [by mark] & Abigail Lord [by mark]; **Acknowledged**: 24: 6 mo: 1668; **Witnesses**: Samuel Pickman & Henry West; **Recorded**: 8: 7 mo: 1668.

RICHARD HOLLINGWORTH to DANIEL MORGAIN – (3:138) On 20 October 1668, Richard Hollingworth (mariner) of Salem granted to David Morgain (merchant) of the Isle of Barbadoes, for a valuable sum, 1/8th part of the good Ketch called the *Hope* of Salem of the burthen of 70 tuns now being or riding at anchor in the harbor of Salem, with 1/8th part of all her masts, sails, sailyards, anchors, cables, ropes, cords, tackle, apparel, boat and furniture to the Ketch anyways belonging and by these presents do warrant & defend against all persons for one whole year and a day next after the date hereof according to the laws of Oleron (peril of sea, fire & enemies excepted). **Signed**: Richard Hollingworth; **Acknowledged**: 26: 8 mo: 1668; **Witnesses**: John Curwin & John Higginson Jr.; **Recorded**: 26: 8 mo: 1668.

JOB SWINERTON, Jr. to JACOB BARNEY, Sr. – (3:139) On the 29th of November 1667, Job Swinerton, Jr. of Salem, granted to Jacob Barney, Sr. of Salem for 10 pounds, 68 rods of land in Salem, having land of Lieut. Thomas Putnam on the S. & the land formerly possessed by John Smith on the W, and the land of said Job Swinerton between it & the North river and at the NE corner it joins to Allister Mackmallen's land & the E end joins to the land that leads to Waller's cove, being 17½ poles long & 4 poles broad, as it is butted & bounded by the aforesaid Jacob Barney & Job Swinerton, at the aforesaid lane it joins to the said Lieut. Putnam's land, which 68 rods of land as it lies butted & bounded with all the commons & privileges thereunto belonging. Ruth Swinerton, wife of said Job Swinerton, fully & clearly yielded up her rights, 27: 3 mo: 1668. **Signed**: Job Swinerton and Ruth Swinerton; **Acknowledged**: 27: 3 mo: 1668; **Witnesses**: Job Swinerton, Sr. & John Swinerton; **Recorded**: 5: 9 mo: 1668.

THOMAS CHUBB to JACOB BARNEY – (3:141) On 8 October 1668, Thomas Chubb (carpenter) of Salem acknowledged himself to be indebted to Jacob Barney (tailor) of Salem, for 8 pounds 10 shillings, to be paid at or before the 25th of March next ensuing the date hereof, & for the security hereof, & bound unto him 4 acres of land, next to his dwelling house, adjoining John Stone, Sr. The condition was that if the said Thomas Chubb paid unto Jacob Barney, Sr. the sum of 4 pounds 5 shillings in corn & cattle at money price at the now dwelling house of said Jacob, by the day above specified, the bond to be void & of no effect & for the performance herein, he set his hand & seal. Jacob Barney, son of the within Jacob Barney acquits & discharges Thomas Chubb from all debts or covenant bonds contained in the within writing. **Signed**: 20 Feb 1682 Jacob Barnie; **Witnesses**: Peter Marshall, Deborah Roundie; **Recorded**: 20 June 1684; **Signed**: Thomas Chubb [by mark]; **Acknowledged**: 20 Feb 1682; **Witnesses**: Andrew Elliott & Zachary Herrick; **Recorded**: 6: 9 mo: 1668.

GERARD SPENCER to GEORGE ROPES (Indenture) – (3:142) On 1: 5 mo: 1657, Gerard Spencer of Lynn, for a valuable consideration to him in hand paid, sold to George Ropes of Salem 10 acres of meadow ground in the common of Lynn near a pond called Dogg Pond. The said meadow was given by the town of Lynn to Timothy Tomlin, having a small pond on the SE side and a small island joining to the said pond. **Signed**: Gerard Spencer; **Acknowledged**: July 1, 1657.

JAMES SMITH to WILLIAM FLINT – (3:143) On 26 August 1668, James Smith (mariner) of Marblehead granted to William Flint of Salem, for 10 pounds, two half-acres of salt marsh in Salem in several places at some small distance near unto a place called the Forest River head, on both sides of Marblehead bridge, one half acre lying above the bridge as it goes over to Marblehead, extending to the one end, to the Coye Pond land and at the other end to the river and having on one side joining to the land of said William Flint, being salt marsh, and the other side to the salt marsh of Richard Rowland of Marblehead, and the other half-acre lying below the said bridge, bounded S & SW with the highway which goes through the Coye Pond land, E & NE with the salt marsh that belonged to Thomas Pitman of Marblehead, NW with the river; the latter being the land sometime belonging to Mr. Stileman, Sr. which he bought from Thomas Moore. **Signed**: James Smith; **Acknowledged**: 26 June 1668; **Witnesses**: William Hathorne, Sr. and William Hathorne, Jr.; **Recorded**: 16: 9 mo: 1668.

MATHEW WOOD to WILLIAM CASH – (3:144) On 20 January 1667/68, George Corwin & Jeremiah Booteman of Salem granted to William Cash of Salem for a valuable consideration already paid by William Cash, ¼ acre in Salem near the North river and between the houses of John Baldwin and George Hodges, together with a new dwelling house built upon the same, but not fully finished sometime belonging to Mathew Wood of Salem, through default of payment fallen into the hands of Capt. George Corwin (merchant) of Salem, who by order of Jeremiah Booteman (attorney for said Mathew) had full power to sell & dispose of same. This house and grounds delivered by turf, possession given on the day of the date hereof in the presence of those whose names were underwritten: Thomas Pickton, Edward Woodland [by mark], & Hugh Paske [by mark]. **Signed**: Jeremiah Booteman & George Corwin; **Acknowledged**: 26: 8 mo: 1668; **Witnesses**: Edward Grove & Edward Norice; **Recorded**: 16: 9 mo: 1668.

RICHARD RAYMENT to OLIVER MANNERING – (3:146) On 25 June 1668, Richard Rayment, late of Salem, now of Saybrook, Connecticut granted to Oliver Mannering of New London, for natural affection to his son-in-law, a parcel of land in Salem in the south field or neck near Stage Point and is bounded SE to land of Richard Hide & land of Mr. Henry Bartholomew about the NW & of Mr. William Browne near to the SW & NE with the South river, containing about 2 acres. **Signed**: Richard Rayment; **Acknowledged**: 26: 4 mo: 1668; **Witnesses**: Nathaniel Sharp & Hillyard Veren; **Recorded**: 17: 9mo: 1668.

NATHANIEL FELTON to WILLIAM BROWNE, Sr. – (3:148) On 26 November 1668, Nathaniel Felton of Salem acknowledged he sold in the year of 1643 to William Browne, Sr. of Salem for a valuable consideration in hand paid, the S end of Mr. Skelton's lot lying against the land that now was in the occupation of Mr. Philip Cromwell, with an old house on it, viz: all the ground from outside of the fence to the water side with the house on it. **Signed**: Nathaniel Felton; **Acknowledged**: 26: 9 mo: 1668; **Witnesses**: Benjamin Browne & John Appleton; **Recorded**: 1 Dec 1668.

EDWARD RICHARDS to WILLIAM BASSETT (Indenture) – (3:149) On 29 October 1667, Edward Richards (joiner) of Lynn, with Ann his wife yielding dower 10: 6 mo: 1668, granted to William Bassett (husbandman) of Lynn, for 50 pounds, 12 acres of land in Lynn, bounded SE with land of Mr. Joseph Humphrey, late in possession of Francis Ingalls, butting SW on the highway that goes to Nahant, bounded NW with the house lot of William Bassett, butting NE on the highway that goes to Mr. King's of Marblehead, only the eastmost corner buts upon an old stump that is about 4 lengths of rails within the great gate, adjoining land of Mr. Humphries, commonly called the Ox Pasture, from which it runs near as the fence now stands between lands of Mr. Humphrey & Edward Richards, with all the wood, timber, trees, & fences. **Signed**: Edward Richards [by mark] and Ann Richards [by mark]; **Acknowledged**: 10: 6 mo: 1668; **Witnesses**: Joseph Armitage & John Hathorne; **Recorded**: 15: 10 mo: 1668.

ELIZABETH BERRY (widow of Roger Haskell) to EDWARD BERRY – (3:152) On 10 November 1668, Elizabeth Berry of Salem (late wife & Executrix of Roger Haskell), granted to her now husband Edward Berry of Salem, for diverse good causes & consideration, all her part & interest in the house & land both upland and meadow, that was formnerly bought of Mr. Gafford, called Gafford's point which is ½ of the housing, orchards, uplands and meadow belonging to the said tenement & by said former husband Roger Haskell, given & bequeathed to her, the whole containing 18 acres, lying on Bass River side belonging to Salem, it being a point of land encompassed by the water only to the NE on which end it is bounded with some land of Osman Trask. **Signed**: Elizabeth Berry [by mark]; **Acknowledged**: 7: 10: 1668; **Witnesses**: Hillyard Veren & Elias Mason; **Recorded**: 20: 10 mo 1668.

EDWARD BERRY to ELIZABETH BERRY – (3:154) On 10 November 1668, Edward Berry (weaver) of Salem covenanted & agreed to & with wife Elizabeth Berry of Salem (wife of Roger Haskall deceased) for several conditions & for good affection, that ½ of all that messuage or tenement called Gafford's, on Bass river side of Salem which said Edward has & holds by right of marriage with the said Elizabeth and also by virtue of a deed of gift from her, ½ of the housing & land both upland & meadow with ½ of all appurtenances & priviledges thereto belonging to be to the use of his said wife for her natural life. **Signed**: Edward Berry; **Acknowledged**: 7: 10 mo: 1668; **Witnesses**: Hillyard Veren & Elias Mason; **Recorded**: 20: 10 mo: 1668.

ROBERT BURNAP, Sr., THOMAS BURNAP, ROBERT BURNAP, Jr., ISAACK BULLARD of Dedham & SARAH BURNAP to ELIAS PARKMAN – (3:155) On 1 September 1668, Robert Burnap, Sr. (with consent of wife Ann), Thomas Burnap (with consent of wife Mary), Robert Burnap, Jr., (yeoman) of Redding (with consent of wife Sara), Isaack Bullard (with consent of wife Ann) of Dedham and Sarah Burnap (spinster) of Redding, granted to Elias Parkman (mariner) of Boston & his assignes forever, for 117 pounds, 10 shillings, all their moiety (or half) of a farm containing 50 acres of both upland & meadow, with the messuage, tenement or farm house & other buildings standing, in the bounds of Salem, which was formerly in possession of the late deceased Isack Burnap or his assignes, bounded E by land of Samuel Verye, W partly by land of Jeremiah Meachy partly by land of Frances Johnson, & N by land of Thomas Goldthwaite & S by the town common. **Signed**: Robert Burnap, Ann Burnap [by mark], Thomas Burnap, Mary Burnap [by mark], Robert Burnap, Sarah Burnap [by mark], Isaack Bullard, Ann Bullard [by mark], Sarah Burnap; **Acknowledged**: 1:.7 mo: 1668; **Witnesses**: Isaack Woode & William Pease, Sr.; **Recorded**: 19 Jan 1668.

JOHN TURNER to JOHN TURNER – (3:160) On 9 January 1668, John Turner (mariner) of Salem granted to Capt. John Turner (gentleman) of Barbados, for a valuable sum, one quarter part of the good Ketch called the *Speedwell* of Salem, being newly built, of a burthen about 80 tuns, riding at anchor in the harbour of Salem, with ¼ of all her masts…warrant for 1 year & 2 days. **Signed**: John Turner; **Witnesses**: John Godfrey [by mark] & Hillyard Veren; **Acknowledged**: 8: 12: 1668; **Recorded**: 9: 12 mo: 1668.

ANN (ANNA) MORE to JOHN TURNER – (3:162) On 17 August 1668, Ann More (widow) of Salem granted to John Turner (mariner) of Salem for a valuable sum, all her messuage or tenement in Salem, containing one old dwelling house with all the ground adjoining, containing 1¾ acres of ground, an orchard & partly arable ground & is bounded S with the highway that runs between the premises & the south harbor & W with the house & land of Mr. Joseph Grafton, Sr., N with land of Edward Woolan & E with land & housing of Nathaniel Grafton, said Nathaniel Grafton being possessed of about ¼ an acre formerly bought of said Ann More & taken out of the SE corner parcel of the said land, the whole being before the parcel was taken out about 1 acres. **Signed**: Anna More [by mark]; **Acknowledged**: 9: 12 mo: 1668; **Witnesses**: Moses Maverick & Samuel Ward; **Recorded**: 9: 12: 1668.

JOHN TURNER (List of debts) – (3:165) list of debts rec'd from Mr. John Turner for account of Capt. Walter Price & comp[a] . viz: [column heading figures below] pounds of sugar, Stephen Banks, bills for 6274; John Killicott, bills for 3800; Samuel Aspare, bills for 540; Total 10644.

The above acknowledged to have been received 9 May 1668. **Signed**: Evan Morgan.

RICHARD READ to ERASMUS JAMES – (3:165) On 14: 12 mo: 1667, Richard Read (fisherman) of Marblehead granted to Erasmus James (ship carpenter) of Marblehead, for good cause and consideration, all the house Erasmus James then dwelled in with all the out houses belonging to it and all that parcel of land as it was set out by Mr. William Hathorne & Mr. Moses Maverick, containing about 40 rods from the outside of the barn or stable as it stands upon a straight line down to the swamp abutting land of Widow James SW, to the land of Richard Reed NE, the town highway NW the swamp SE. **Signed**: Richard Read; **Acknowledged**: 22: 1 mo: 1668; **Witnesses**: Anna Hathorne & Elizabeth Hathorne; **Recorded**: 23: 1 mo: 1668/9.

DAVID THOMAS to WILLIAM HOOPER – (3:166) On 13 February 1668, David Thomas (planter) of Salem (with Joane freely yielding all rights) granted to William Hooper of Salem for 32 pounds, 10 shillings in hand received, a tenement lying on the Bass River side belonging to Salem, containing 5 acres of land with a dwelling house, with all the fruit trees, fences, appurtenances, privileges, bounded with some land of William Dodge, Sr. E & S with land or Roger Haskell, deceased, NW with land late of Roger Hascall, and E S with a highway, also 10 acres of land on said Bass River side bounded E with land of Robert Stone, John Stone & Thomas Chubb, S with the common land & W with common land also & N with land of Edmond Grover. **Signed**: David Thomas [by mark]; **Acknowledged**: 12: 12 mo: 1668; **Witnesses**: Hillyard Veren & John Todd; **Recorded**: 13: 12 mo: 21668.

ESTER ESTWICK to ISACK HIDE – (3:168) On 23 February 1668, Ester Estwick (widow & administratrix of Edward Estwick of Salem, deceased) granted to Isack Hide (mariner) of Salem for a consideration in hand paid, about 24 and ¾ rods of land in Salem, bounded N by land lately sold to William Curtis, which end is by measure 4 and 2/3 rods, W with the land late of Alexander Seere, deceased, and on that side it is 5 and 1/3 rods, on the S 4 & 2/3 rods and on the E 5 & 1/3 rods on both which side it is bounded with land of said Ester also to have free regress & egress to his said land both from the common & so to the water side through the highway. She left on the E side of her land throughout & it is joint agreement of both parties that Isack Hide shall always set up & maintain a sufficient fence on E & S side on his own cost. **Signed**: Ester Estwick [by mark]; **Acknowledged**: 23: 12 mo: 1668; **Witnesses**: Hillyard Veren, Sr., Nathaniel Putnam & John Becket; **Recorded**: 23: 12 mo: 1668.

RICHARD RICHESSON to Sergt. WILLIAM BASSETT – (3:170) On 17 February 1668, Richard Richesson of Lynn (wood cutter), with consent of Amy his wife, granted to Sergt. William Bassett of Lynn (husbandman) for a valuable price, for 3 acres of land in Lynn, in the plain lying S of the new sluice pond which land said Richard bought from widow Rooten, lying near the now dwelling house of Robert Rand, and also his dwelling house upon it and also 2 cows, one of which he had of Joseph Armitage, and the other of Mr. Ralph King, and hereby acknowledged receipt of the whole pay as fully satisfied, and does discharge said William Bassett & his heirs forever. **Signed**: Richard Richesson [by mark]; **Acknowledged**: 11: 12 mo: 1668; **Recorded**: 3 March 1668/9; **Witnesses**: Joseph Armitage & Andrew Mansfield.

JOHN BLACK, Sr. to WILLIAM BROWNE, Jr. – (3:171) On 28: 8 mo: 1668, John Black, Sr. of Salem (planter) granted to William Browne, Jr. of Salem for 6 pounds, one acre of salt marsh lying in the north field & bordering on the North river, abutting against said river to the SE and some land of John Symonds to the NE & some land of John Simonds to the NW & some land of Thomas Meekes to the SW. **Signed**: John Black, Sr.; **Acknowledged**: 28: 1 mo: 1668/9; **Recorded**: 23: 1 mo: 1668/9; **Witnesses**: with seazon…John Symonds & James Simonds.

WILLIAM DODGE, Sr. to JOHN HALE – (3:173) On 28 January 1668, William Dodge, Sr. (husbandman) of Beverly granted to John Hale, pastor of the church at Beverly, for a valuable consideration, 20 acres of pasture land, lying on the N side of Richard Haines, adjoining a dwelling house of said Richard, which 20 acres is bounded E by the highway that goes from the meeting house, to the outlet into the common sd highway being taken out of sd land, N by little strip of common lying between that & general fence at sd outlet being about 4 poles from sd fence, NW & W by fence line running between it & Robert Hibbert's pasture, until it comes into Goodman Stone's corner bounds for part of sd land & then the line between sd land & Robert Hibert's pasture runs W until it meets with Robert Haines' land about to a great rock lying here half way between corner bound tree & the country highway to Ipswich then it is bounded SW by said Richard Haines, by straight line running over the rocks to head of Haines' orchard to walnut tree standing on the E side of the highway to the outlet within the fence of Henry Baily. **Signed**: William Dodge; **Acknowledged**: 28 Jan 1668, with wife Elizabeth yielding dower; **Witnesses**: Daniel Epps & Isak Hull; **Recorded**: 23: 1 mo: 1668/69.

THOMAS OLIVER to ROBERT GRAYE – (3:174) On 11 January 1668, Thomas Oliver of Salem granted to Robert Graye (seaman) of Salem for a valuable sum, 12 rods or poles of land in Salem, part of that ground where his dwelling house stands lying on the N of the house next to the street, next adjoining grounds of Mr. Endicott on the S & E and with the street to the west & to be 12 rod of ground beginning at Mr. Endicot's N & to run on a square S towards house of Thomas Oliver...to make up full measure 12 rods of ground 3 poles & 14 foot front...Robert Gray to set up sufficient new pole fence...own cost...maintain for 9 years & afterwards to bear charge of ½. **Signed**: Thomas Oliver and Bridget Oliver [by mark]; **Acknowledged**: 8: 12 mo: 1668, with Bridget yielding dower; **Witnesses**: Hillyard Veren & Will Dounten; **Recorded**: 23: 1 mo: 1668/9.

ROBERT FOLLETT to RICHARD WATERS – (3:176) On 9 April 1669, Robert Follett (fisherman) of Salem granted to Richard Waters (gunsmith) of Salem for 6 pounds 10 shillings, about 1¼ acres of land in Salem near Catt Cove upon the town neck, bounded by land of said Robert Follett and land of George Burch SE, a parcel of land of Humfrey Woodberry lying unfenced to NW, common land to the SW and abutting NE towards Catt Cove, said Robert Waters to maintain fences. **Signed**: Robert Follett [by mark]; **Acknowledged**: 9: 2 mo: 1669; **Witnesses**: Hillyard Veren & Edmund Galle; **Recorded**: 10: 2 mo: 1669.

SAMUEL BENETT to ROBERT RAND – (3:178) On 5: 3 mo: 1669, Samuel Benett (gentleman) of Rumney Marsh in Suffolk County granted to Robert Rand (husbandman) of Lynn [no amount given] 6 acres of upland in Lynn, bounded S with Robert Rand, formerly land of Mr. Holyoke, E with land of Richard Richardson, SE on the town common, butting N on the pond & W with the river. **Signed**: Samuel Benett; **Acknowledged**: 5: 3 mo: 1669; **Witnesses**: William Bartholomew & John Hathorne; **Recorded**: 16: 3 mo: 1669.

JOHN SOUTHWICK & Children of THOMAS FLINT – (3:179) This may certify to whom it may concern, that whereas there has been a difference between John Southwick and the children of Thomas Flint, deceased, concerning an estate left or willed by their mother, who was the late wife of John Southwick, and they conceiving they had a right to what was willed to them by their mother, and the said Southwick conceived that they had no right to it, his late wife had no power to make a will or give away any estate to the aforesaid parties...have mutually & lovingly agreed as follows: John Southwick shall pay children of his late deceased wife...then children to give general acquittance to John Southwick of all differences...concerning father's or mother's will excepting such legacy...between Southwick & late wife upon contract of marriage. **Signed**: John Southwick [by mark], Thomas Flint, John Leach, Nathaniel Putnam, William Flint [by mark] and Jobe Swinerton, Jr; **Acknowledged**: 25: 4: 1668; **Recorded**: 20: 4: 1669.

SAMUEL ROBINSON to MICHALL CHAPPELLMAN – (3:181) On 7 April 1669, Samuel Robinson (baker) of Salem, with consent of wife Constance Robinson, granted to Michall Chappellman (seaman) of Salem for 65 pounds, 12 poles of land in Salem with dwelling house, bounded N with the common or highway, at which end it was the breadth of 2 poles, southward 6 poles in length, bounded E with land of Christopher Phelps, S & W with land of Paul Mansfield. **Signed**: Samuel Robinson; **Witnesses**: Paul Mansfield [by mark] and Edward Norrice; **Signed**: Constance Robinson [by mark]; **Witnesses**: Isack Williams and Thomas Marshall. Paul Mansfield of Salem formerly owner of contents of this writing & having liberty of refusal...relinquished right and signed [by mark] 7 Apr 1669; **Witnesses**: Jonathan Corwine, Edward Norrice; endorsement with Jonathan Corwine, Esq. oath recorded 22 January 1700/01; **Recorded**: 16: 3: 1669.

RICHARD GARDNER to EDWARD MOLDE – (3:183) ON 5 May 1669, Richard Gardner, late of Salem, (mariner), (with wife Sarah releasing dower) granted to Edward Molde (fisherman) of Salem for a valuable sum, all his dwelling house with the outhouse or shop together with all the ground adjoining, about 16 rods or poles in Salem, containing the yard & garden all within the fence, bounded N with the warehouse of Mr. Will Browne, Sr.; N & E with land of Samuel Shattock, W & S by the street and common land. **Signed**: Richard Gardner & Sarah Gardner; **Witnesses**: Samuel Shattuck, Sr. and Hillyard Veren; **Recorded**: 16: 3: 1669.

ROBERT GUTCH to WILLIAM NORTON to RICHARD GARDNER – (3:185) On 22 December 1652, Robert Gutch of Salem granted to William Norton of Ipswich, for 40 pounds, his dwelling house, provided if said Robert shall pay unto said William on or before the 10th day of June the sum of 40 pounds in money or merchantable codfish, deed void. **Signed**: Robert Gutch; **Witness**: Emmanuel Downing. William Norton set over this deed of mortgage of Robert Gutch to Nicholas Davisson, for 26 pounds, 6 June 1653. **Signed**: William Norton; **Witnesses**: Elias Stileman & Samuel Archard. I, Nicholas Davidson, for 22 pounds, sell & set over all my rights to Richard Gardner, 26 Nov 1656. **Signed**: Nicholas Davisson; **Witnesses**: Elias Stileman & Samuel Archard. 25 May 1669, abovesaid sale, assignment & mortgage was acknowledged in court 26: 9 mo: to be act & deed of Nicholas Davisson to Richard Gardner. Warrant to Richard Gardner. **Signed**: Nicholas Davisson.

JOHN FOSTER to NATHANIEL PUTNAM – (3:187) On 14 April 1669, John Foster of Salem granted to Nathaniel Putnam of Salem for a valuable consideration, all his right & title in 30 acres of land in Salem formerly granted to him by the town of Salem, near the Ipswich River. **Signed**: John Foster [by mark]; **Acknowledged**: 1: 3 mo: 1669; **Witnesses**: Hillyard Veren & John Phippen.

THOMAS OLIVER to ROBERT GRAYE – (3:188) Thomas Oliver of Salem granted to Robert Graye (seaman) of Salem for a valuable sum, 12 rods or poles of land in Salem, part of the ground whereon the dwelling house of said Thomas Oliver stands on the N of the said house next to the street next adjoining the ground of Mr. Endicott to the S; Endicott bounds parcel N & E, and by the street west. **Recorded**: 27: 3: 1669 ("this being recorded before").

DAVID THOMAS to WILLIAM HOOPER – (3:189) Joane Thomas acknowledged her free consent to sale of land sold by her husband David Thomas late of Salem unto William Hooper of Salem, the parcel of land lies at Bass River. Plimouth 1– July 1669. The deed of sale...is recorded in foll: 50 in this booke & Jeane wife of said David Thomas being in Plimouth acknowledged sale there...entered 3: 6: 69.

JOHN WESTON (WESSON) to JOSIAH ROOTES (the younger) – (3:189) On 3 May 1669, John Weston (or Wesson) of Reading, Middlesex County, with Sarah releasing dower, granted to Josiah Rootes the younger of Salem (mariner), for a valuable consideration, 30 acres of land in Salem on Bass River side alias Beverly, bounded by a marked tree E, a marked tree on S corner & on the N, on the W corner (each tree having letters I W cut in tree with ax) said land lying in Burch Plain. **Signed**: John Wessen & Sarah Wessen [by mark]; **Acknowledged**: 3: 3 mo: 1669; **Witnesses**: Hillyard Veren & Isack Williams; **Recorded**: 27: 3: 1669.

JOBE SWINERTON, Jr. and JOHN SWINERTON to THOMAS SMALL – (3:191) On 26 June 1667, Jobe Swinerton, Jr. and John Swinerton of Salem granted to Thomas Small of Salem, secured by bill bearing date with these presents, 20 acres of upland in Salem, having land of Robert Goodale on the W, said 20 acres being part of that farm which Capt. George Corwin sold to Jobe Swinerton, 4 score pole long, from said Goodale land lying S side of land of William Cantlebery, deceased, now in possession of said Small & from Cantlebury's line 40 poles broad having on S & E land of Jobe & John Swinerton. **Signed**: Jobe & John Swinerton; **Acknowledged**: 21: 8: 1667; **Witnesses**: Jobe Swinerton, Sr. and Benjamin Woodrow; **Recorded**: 27: 3 mo: 1669.

THOMAS SMALL to JOHN BUXTON – (3:192) On 17 March 1668/9, Thomas Small of Salem (farmer) granted to John Buxton of Salem, for a valuable consideration, 3 acres of upland adjoining 20 acres of land sold by him to said Buxton S, with land of Benjamin Woodrow W, with land of Small E & N...understood if hereafter John Cantleberry, son of William Cantlebery, deceased, came personally to make demand or lay claim, by his right by his father's will, sale shall be void. **Signed**: Thomas Small [by mark]; **Acknowledged**: 18: 1: 1668/9; **Witnesses**: Darcus Veren & Hilliard Veren; **Recorded**: 27: 3 Mar 1669.

THOMAS SMALL to JOHN BUXTON – (3:194) On 17 March 1668/9, Thomas Small (farmer) of Salem, granted to John Buxton (husbandman) of Salem for a valuable consideration, 20 acres of upland, having land of Robert Goodale on the W; said 20 acres being part of the farm which Capt. George Corwin sold to Jobe Swinerton, Jr. & by said Jobe lately sold to me, deed bearing date 26 June 1667 of said Jobe & his brother John Swinerton...lying by land of William Cantlebery deceased. **Signed**: Thomas Small [by mark]; **Acknowledged**: 18: 1: 68; **Witnesses**: Dorckos Veren, Hilliard Veren, Sr.; **Recorded**: 28: 3: 1669.

JOSEPH GRAFTON, Sr. to son JOHN GRAFTON – (3:195) On 15 September 1667, Joseph Grafton, Sr. (mariner) of Salem granted to his son John Grafton (mariner) of Salem for love & affection, 2 acres of land in Salem, lying against the South harbor, bounded N by the highway, E by land of said Joseph Grafton, W by land of Thomas Browning and by the highway by South harbor S. **Signed**: Joseph Grafton; **Witnesses**: Hillyard Veren & John Daye; **Recorded**: 28: 3: 1669.

WILLIAM BROWN to JOSEPH PHIPPEN – (3:197) On 8 July 1667, William Brown (merchant) of Salem granted to Joseph Phippen of Salem for 35 pounds, 1½ acres of pasture land in Salem, between the house and land of Edward Hilliard SW, and house and land of Henry Moses NE; also a parcel of salt marsh bought of John Beckett in the N neck of land between great cove and horse pasture. **Signed**: William Browne & Sarah Browne [by mark]; **Acknowledged**: 26: 5 mo: 1667, with Sarah yielding thirds; **Witnesses**: Phillip Cromwell & Edward Norrice; **Recorded**: 29: 3: 1669.

WILLIAM LORD, Sr. to HENRY COLBOURNE – (3:199) On 13 February 1668, William Lord, Sr. (cutler) of Salem (with wife Abigail yielding thirds), granted to Henry Colbourne (mariner) of Salem for 80 pounds sterling, a dwelling house with 3 rods of ground joining the back side of the house E, the house in Salem near the meeting house, adjoining his own dwelling house, at the end of his dwelling house to the N next to the meeting house, containing one lower room and one upper room a lower & a chamber brick chimney & ground that lies between house & Capt. George Corwin's warehouse from back of lower chimney on outside

& upon a straight line E as house stands upon a square to a little yard of Capt. George Corwin's on the E side of his warehouse about 2 foot of ground to S end of the warehouse & S with house of William Lord on E with warehouse & NW with street or land about meeting house. **Signed**: Abigail and William Lord, [both signing by mark]; **Acknowledged**: 15:12 mo: 1668; **Witnesses**: Hilliard Veren, Sr. & Henry West; **Recorded**: 2: 4: 1669.

JOHN STONE to WILLIAM DODGE – (3:201) On 22 November 1662, John Stone, Sr. (husbandman) of Salem, with wife Elener releasing dower granted to William Dodge (farmer) of Salem, for a valuable sum, about 7 acres of land on the Bass river side, so-called, and bounded W by land of Richard Haines, and Robert Hibberd N and William Dodge S and the common on the E. Note: Stone had the right to cut timber from the lot. **Signed**: John Stone; **Acknowledged**: 8 April 1669; **Witnesses**: Mary Veren [by mark] & Hilliard Veren.

ESTER ESTWICK to WILLIAM CURTICE – (3:203) On 23 February 1668, Ester Estwick, widow & Administratrix of Edward Estwick (deceased), granted to William Curtice of Salem for a valuable sum, about 46 rods of ground on Bass river side, the ground within the fence as now the fence of said William Curtice stands bounded with land formerly of Alexander Sears, deceased W, on which side is by measure 10 rods 4 foot on N with common highway & on that end 5 rods 12 foot E with land of said Ester left for private way on which side is in length 8 rod & 14 foot & S with land formerly of said Ester but lately sold to Isack Hide which end is 4 pole 12 foot. **Signed**: Ester Estwick [by mark]; **Acknowledged**: 23: 12: 1668; **Witnesses**: Hilliard Veren, Sr. and Isack Hide.

MATHEW DOVE to JOSEPH GRAFTON, Jr. – (3:205) On 24 Oct 1661, Mathew Dove (planter) of Salem (with wife Hannah yielding rights) granted to Joseph Grafton, Jr. (mariner) of Salem for a valuable sum, about 25 rods of ground ½ of all land of Mathew…adjoining said Grafton's land, half the length as it lies N & S & so right crosses to E & bounded in Salem adjoining land of Goodman Browning E, & highway W, & land of Dove's & land of Grafton N. **Signed**: Mathew Dove & Hannah Archer; **Acknowledged**: with Hannah yielding thirds; 12: 4: 1669; **Witnesses**: Richard Culleven & Abigail Kippin; **Recorded**: 13: 4: 1669.

WILLIAM BROWN to NICHOLAS FOX – (3:206) On 26 June 1669, William Brown (fisherman) of Marblehead granted to Nicholas Fox (fisherman) of Marblehead, for a valuable consideration, ¼ of an acre in Marblehead, adjoining the house of Thomas Souden W & John Stacy's new house E, formerly sold by John Stacy, Sr. and John Stacy, Jr. to

Robert Hooper, and by Robert Hooper to William Brown. **Signed**: William Brown; **Acknowledged**: 26: 4: 1669; **Witnesses**: Hilliard Veren & Nicholas Merritt; **Recorded**: 7: 5: 1669.

JOHN MASON to JOHN TAPLEY, ROBERT BRAY & JOHN WEBB – (3:207) On 28 June 1669, John Mason (brickmaker) of Salem granted to John Tapley, Robert Bray & John Webb (fishermen) of Salem for 6 pounds sterling, ¼ of an acre of land, formerly bought from Francis Collings & situated in the neck of Salem against a cove coming out of the North River, bounded S & W with the highway & common land & N with the cove. **Signed**: John Mason & Hanah Mason; **Acknowledged**: 28: 4 mo: 1669, with Hanah yielding thirds; **Witnesses**: Hilliard Veren & John Marsy; **Recorded**: 10: 5: 1669.

JOHN PEARSON to ANDREW MANSFIELD (Indenture) – (3:209) On 18 March 1666/7, John Pearson (yeoman) of Lynn, with consent of Mawdlin Pearson (his wife) granted to Andrew Mansfield (husbandman) of Lynn for 33 pounds, a dwelling house, barn & other outhouses together with orchard with 5 acres of land bought of Mr. Robert Burt in Lynn, bounded S with the land that parts said land & land in tenor of Samuel Johnson, usually called Churchman's lot, W & N with land of Andrew Mansfield. **Signed**: John Pearson [by mark]; **Acknowledged**: 29: 4: 1669; **Witnesses**: George Taylor & Ebenezer Taylor. On 19 Apr 1668, John Pearson acknowledged receipt of 33 pounds. **Signed**: John Pearson [by mark]; **Witnesses**: John Townsend & Mary Townsend [by mark]; **Recorded**: 14: 5: 1669.

JOSEPH ARMITAGE – (3:211) On the 19th of 1 month 1656, Joseph Armitage of Lynn (tailor) with consent of wife, granted to the inhabitants of Lynn, for so much wood as grows on 6 acres of land in Nahant, delivered unto Thomas Wheeler and Andrew Mansfield (appointed by said town to lay out and deliver wood to Joseph Armitage); 6 acres formerly given by the town of Lynn to John Poole in said town in plain next unto Hugh Burt's house lot, bounded with Fresh pond & land of Mr. Hollioke & land of Richard Rooten & by town's common. **Signed**: Joseph Armitage; **Acknowledged**: 29: 4: 1669; **Witnesses**: Thomas Wheeler, Andrew Mansfield & Katheran Lewis [by mark]; **Recorded**: 19: 1st mo: 1656.

ARTHUR KIPPEN to JONATHAN AGER – (3:213) On 19 July 1669, Arthur Kippen (seaman) of Salem granted to Jonathan Ager (ship carpenter) of Salem for a valuable sum, 14 rods of land adjoining his house, about ½ acre, bounded with land of said Kippen S, with the highway by water side W, & of Mathew Dove N, and Thomas Browning E. **Signed**: Arthur Kippen [by mark] and Abigail Kippen; **Acknowledged**:

19 July 1669; **Witnesses**: John Ingerson [by mark] & Richard Hide; **Recorded**: 21: 5: 1669.

JAMES BROWN to EDMOND BATTER – (3:215) On 22 June 1669, James Brown (glasier) of Newbury, with Sarah releasing dower, granted to Edmond Batter (merchant) for 36 pounds sterling, 15 acres of salt meadow in Newbury near Plum Island, bounded E on land of Herculus Woodman, S with land of William Kitcum, W with land of Samuel Moody and Widow Brown N. If James Brown pays 36 pounds, 18 pounds in wheat & mault at the monie price at or before 25 December next & 18 pounds in wheat & mault…at or before 25 of December in year next immediately following 1670 sale to be void. **Signed**: James Brown; **Acknowledged**: 3 July 1669; **Witnesses**: Hilliard Veren, Sr. & John Smith; **Recorded**: 18: 5: 1669.

ROBERT BRIDGES to ANDREW MANSFIELD – (3:217) On 9 August 1655, Robert Bridges (gentleman) of Lynn, granted to Andrew Mansfield (husbandman) of Lynn, for 12 pounds, 10 shillings sterling, 5 acres of salt marsh in the 2nd division of Rumney Marsh in Lynn, bounded S with marsh of said Andrew now in possession of Robert Mansfield his father & N with marsh of Robert Mansfield, which he bought of said Robert Bridges, abutting E upon the last division of lots, W upon common & parts the first & that second division. **Signed**: Robert Bridges; **Acknowledged**: 7: 6 mo: 1656; **Witnesses**: Thomas Marshall & John Mansfield.

MANASSEH MARSTON to ROBERT WILKES – (3:219) On 29 July 1669, Manasseh Marston (blacksmith) of Salem (with consent of Mercy Marston, who signed [by mark]) granted to Robert Wilkes (ship carpenter) of Salem for a valuable consideration in hand paid, 38 or 40 rods or poles in Salem, bounded W with a parcel of land of Daniel Rumball, S with the common or highway, N & E with common land called the pen. **Signed**: Manasseh Marston; **Witnesses**: Hilliard Veren, Sr. & Ephraim Marston; **Recorded**: 29: 5 mo: 1669.

JEFFREY MASSEY & NICHOLAS WOODBERY to JOSHUA RAY – (3:221) On 1 January 1656, Jeffrey Massy & Nicholas Woodberry of Salem granted to Joshua Ray, for a valuable consideration, 150 acres in the bounds of Salem, bounded by Long Hill E and the country highway on the S, by Jacob Barney W and near Burchin plaine N. **Signed**: [This deed was written with no signatures or witnesses & then rewritten with signature of Jeffrey Massey & Nicholas Woodbery]; **Acknowledged**: 20: 5 mo: 1669; **Witnesses**: John Porter & John Thorndike; **Recorded**: 10: 6 mo: 1669.

NICHOLAS MERRITT & MARGARETT SANDY to WILLIAM BROWNE – (3:222) On 21 June 1669, Nicholas Meritt & Margarett Sandy of Marblehead, administrators of the estate of Arthur Sandy (deceased), granted to William Browne (fisherman) of Marblehead, for a valuable sum, part of a dwelling house of late said Arthur Sandy, 2/3 part westerly of the said dwelling house, containing 2 lower and 2 upper rooms, the other third part eastward containing 1 room being lately sold to John Merritt; also an outer house with ¼ acre of land adjoining the said out house W of said dwelling house, bounds to run from West of dwelling house to a stone wall, SW to land of Nicholas Merritt, NW to land of Nathan Walton; SE with the highway to the highway to the harbor & NE with third part of dwelling house. **Signed**: Nicholas Merritt [by mark] and by Margaret Sandy [by mark]; **Acknowledged**: 26: 4: 1669; **Witnesses**: Hilliard Veren, Sr., Nicholas Fox, John Merritt, James Merritt; **Recorded**: 19: 6: 1669.

BARTHOLOMEW GEDNEY to Capt. WALTER PRICE & Mr. JOHN GEDNEY, Sr., JOHN CORWIN & JOHN GEDNEY, Jr. – (3:224) On 7 Sept 1669, Bartholomew Gedney (shipwright) of Salem granted to Capt. Walter Price, Mr. John Gedney, Sr., Mr. John Corwin and Mr. John Gedney, Jr., for a valuable sum, the hull of a ship called *John Adventure* with mast, yards, boat and all other appurtenances of carpenters thereunto belonging, each ¼ of said vessel. **Signed**: Bartholomew Gedney; **Acknowledged**: 7 Sept 1669; **Witnesses**: Theoder Price & John Price; **Recorded**: 10 Sept 1669.

JOHN LEACH to JOHN DODGE, Jr. – (3:225) On 2 September 1669, John Leach (miller) of Salem granted to John Dodge, Jr. (husbandman) of Beverly, for 250 pounds, land now belonging to his mills, 10 acres on the Beverly side, land called Bushnell lot, and 2 acres on the other side of the river in Salem, with dwelling house...mills, bounded S with land of Osmund Trask, E on Edward Grover, N on Henry Herrick, Sr. **Signed**: John Leach [by mark]; **Acknowledged**: 22: 7 mo: 1669; **Witnesses**: Andrew Elliott & Isaack Hull; **Recorded**: 5: 8 mo: 1669.

DAVID CORWITHY to ANDREW WOODBERY & ISAACK WOODBURY – (3:227) On 15 September 1664, David Corwithy, Sr. (gentleman) of Boston granted to Andrew Woodbery and Isaack Woodbury (mariners) of Salem, for 25 pounds current money in hand paid in part & the residue secured, one acre of land in Salem, bounded E on the highway, S by land of Edward Hilliard in part & land of Andrew Woodbery in part, W land of Mathew Nixon in part, land of Robert Lemon in part W and land of Francis Collins NW and again with land of Andrew

Woodbury N. **Signed**: David Corwithy; **Witnesses**: Robert Howard & Robert Howard, Jr.

JOHN MILLER to GEORGE CORWIN – (3:229) On 29: 6 mo: 1657, John Miller (tailor) of Salem granted to George Corwin (merchant) of Salem for 50 pounds, all his dwelling house with ½ acre, between land of Mason Hathorne on E, William Golt on S, Mr. William Bartholmew on W and the street on the N. **Signed**: John Miller; **Acknowledged**: 31: 6 mo: 1657; wife Elizabeth yielded thirds; **Witnesses**: Samuel Archard & Nathan Hathorne; **Recorded**: 7: 8 mo: 1669. On 19 March 1668/9, the within named George Corwin (merchant) of Salem assigned to Edward Grover (sailmaker) of Salem for a valuable consideration, contents of writing. **Signed**: George Corwin; **Acknowledged**: 20: 5 mo: 1669; Witnesses: Phillip Cromwell, Jonathan Corwin & Edward Norice; **Recorded**: 7: 8 mo: 1669.

JAMES PECKER (Deposition) – (3:231) Deposition of James Pecker aged 18 years that Mathew Price did buy a mare of Richard Fellies of Hartford Connecticut about the year 1657 & gave bill for the pay & after the bill was given, I being present at Price's house at Charlestown did understand by Fellies' words that he had then received his pay for the mare, for he promised to bring him his bill or else cancel it. Taken upon oath. **Recorded**: 25: 12 mo: 1669.

JAMES SMITH to WILLIAM FLINT – (3:231) On 13 Sept 1669, James Smith (mariner) of Marblehead granted to William Flint (husbandman) of Salem for a valuable sum in hand paid, 10 acres of upland in Salem in the field commonly called Southfield, bounded E with the harbor, W with the river that goes up to Castle hill, N with land of John Horne, Sr. & S with land formerly belonging to old Goodman Auger. **Signed**: James Smith; **Acknowledged**: 13: 7 mo: 1669 by Capt. James Smith; **Witnesses**: Henry Skerry & Joseph Phippen; **Recorded**: 7: 8 mo: 1669.

JOB HILLIARD to THOMAS MAULE – (3:233) On 7 August 1669, Job Hilliard (mariner) of Salem, with consent of wife, granted to Thomas Maule (tailor) of Salem for 7 pounds, a parcel of land in Salem on the South river side near the harbor & being part of land belonging to Job Hilliard there containing about 5 pole or 71 foot in length & 18 foot in breadth bounded E with land belonging to the widow Hollingworth, W & S with land of said Job Hilliard & N with land or the highway together with a barn standing upon ground at price of 5 pounds over said 7 pounds. **Signed**: Job Hilliard; **Acknowledged**: 13: 7: 1669 with wife Mary yielding thirds; **Witnesses**: John Ruck, Isaac Williams & Edward Norrice; **Recorded**: 7: 18 mo: 1669.

JEREMIAH BOOTEMAN to MICHAELL COMBE – (3:234) On 13 August 1668, Jeremiah Booteman (fisherman) of Salem, with consent of his wife, granted to Michaell Combe of Salem, for 55 pounds, the dwelling house wherein he now lives with land belonging thereto: ¼ acre & an out house in Salem bounded N with the street or highway, W with land of widow Hollingworth & on the other sides with land of John Beckett & is near the harbor or South river. **Signed**: Jeremiah Booteman [by mark]; **Acknowledged**: 18: 9 mo: 1669 & wife Hester yielded thirds. **Witnesses**: Edward Norrice & George Ropes; **Recorded**: 27: 9 mo: 1669.

JOHN FISK to CHARLES GOTT & DANIEL GOTT – (3:236) On 30 November 1665, John Fisk (carpenter) of Wenham, with Remember Fisk resigning right, granted to Charles Gott & Daniel Gott of Wenham, for 32 pounds in hand paid by bill, 50 acres in Wenham in part (or near about) the line that runs between Salem & Wenham bounded N upon Mr. Osband's farm & S upon land of said John Fisk; W upon Leach's meadow & E upon land of Phineas Fisk. **Signed**: John Fisk & Remember Fisk; **Acknowledged**: 30: 9 mo: 1669; **Witnesses**: March Bachelor & John Bachelor; **Recorded**: 7: 10 mo: 1669.

EDMOND BATTER to DANIEL ANDREWES – (3:237) On 13 December 1669, Edmond Batter (merchant) of Salem granted to Daniel Andrewes (bricklayer) of Salem, for a valuable consideration in hand paid, 30 rods of land on the front next to the street that goes to the meeting house in Salem, 7 rods wanting 3½ foot on the E, 5 rod & 10 foot & on W 3 rod & 10½ foot & is bounded on E, N & W with land of said Edmond Batter & on S with the street or highway aforesaid. **Signed**: Edmond Batter; **Witnesses**: with seisen possession by turf & twig, Hillyard Veren, Sr. & Henry West; **Recorded**: 14: 9: 1669.

EDMOND GALE to RICHARD THISTLE – (3:238) On 28 June 1669, Edmond Gale (fisherman) of Marblehead, with consent of wife Sara, granted to Richard Thistle (fisherman) of Marblehead, for 4 score pounds 9 shillings in money current in New England, his messuage tenement dwelling house with land whereon it stands with yard & garden & orchards; ½ acre on SE of Lott Conant or thereabouts belonging as it is now fenced being on the land of Mathew Clarke's lot on the NW & on the NE of marsh of Mr. William Walton & of Mr. Moses Maverick & in the highway on the street of Marblehead SW according to ancient butts & bounds. **Signed**: Edmond Gale & Sara Gale; **Acknowledged**: 31: 5 mo: 1669 & wife Sara yielding thirds 2: 8 mo: 1669; **Witnesses**: Robert

Bradford [by mark], Thomas Smith [by mark] and Samuel Leache; **Recorded**: 5: 8 mo: 1669.

BRIDGET VARNEY to GEFFERY PARSONS – (3:241) On 6 May 1669, Bridget Varney of Gloucester granted to Geffery Parsons of Gloucester, for 5 pounds, her 2 parcels of meadow & upland containing 11 acres; one parcel of 7 acres of marsh situated & lying the meadow of said Jeffery on S & W, bounded by creek on the N; the other parcel lying next to the land of said Jeffery on the SW & land of John Bryares on the E this parcel of upland being in Fisherman's field so called & both parcels in Gloucester. **Signed**: Bridget Varney [by mark]; **Acknowledged**: 9: 9 mo: 1669 by widow Bridget Varney; **Witnesses**: John Emerson & Phillip Staneswood; **Recorded**: 30: 9 mo: 1669.

THOMAS PUTNAM & NATHANIEL PUTNAM (Agreement) – (3:242) Whereas there is about 500 acres of ground together in one parcel & also several other parcels of meadow which have been held in partnership between Lieut. Thomas Putnam and his brother Nathanial Putnam both of Salem, now by mutual consent they have made division between them. It is agreed, 1. That the 500 acres of meadow & upland the whole parcel being bounded with the Ipswich river so called on the N with land formerly called Jeffery Massey's, NE with land of John Ruck & land of said Thomas Putnam SE, with land of said Nathaniel Putnam S & land Jonathan Walcott W, said parcel is divided by a divisional line beginning at said river from…trees…near the river side at the lower end of the island & from thence SE to an oak, which should stand outside bounds of 500 acres adjoining land formerly of Major Hathorne & some land formerly Philip Cromwell's…the land to the NE of said division line to belong to said Thomas Putnam & land to SW to belong to said Nathaniel Putnam. 2. The meadows in partnership lying on the N side of the river are also divided: to Thomas Putnam's meadow adjoining to N side of the river lying from the bridge to the lower end of a piece of upland of said Thomas Putnam of about 15 acres. 3. To Nathaniel Putnam the meadow called Price's meadow bounded S with some land of said Nathaniel Putnam & Thomas Putnam. 15 acres aforesaid beginning where the former parcel of meadow ends belonging to said Thomas Putnam; also bounded with the river E & N & with Thomas Fuller's upland upon the N & some meadow of said Nathaniel Putnam E. 4. To Nathaniel Putnam also the pond called Massey's Pond lying within the upland of Robert Prince. 5. The parcel of meadow formerly called Cromwell's meadow also is divided: the brook that runs through said meadow is to be bounds between them & the SW side to belong to Thomas Putnam & the NE side to belong to Nathaniel Putnam. 6. To Thomas Putnam a small parcel of meadow ¾ acre lying on both sides of the brook or run about 30 or 40 rods distance from the upper end of aforesaid last mentioned said parcel both upland and meadow divided as abovesaid by mutual consent. **Signed**: 20 December 1669 by Thomas Putnam & Nathaniel Putnam; **Witnesses**: Hillyard Veren, Sr., Thomas Maule and Edmond Batter; **Recorded**: 21: 10: 1669.

SUSANNAH (ARCHARD) HUTCHINSON to WILLIAM BROWNE, Sr. – (3:245) On 5 July 1669, Susannah Hutchenson (late wife of Samuel Archard, deceased & now wife unto Richard Hutchenson) granted to William Browne, Sr. of Salem for a valuable consideration in hand paid, all her housing & lands that former husband Archard died possessed of: the house & ground lying between Joshua Ward's & Samuel Archard's & a small piece of land lying over the way against it & 8 acres of upland & about 5½ acres of salt marsh in south field. **Signed**: Susannah Hutchinson and Richard Hutchinson, now husband, who consented; **Acknowledged**: 5: 5 mo: 1669; **Witnesses**: Richard Walker, Daniel King & William Browne, Jr.; **Recorded**: 18: 11: 1669.

ELIZEBETH HARWOOD to JEREMIAH BUTTMAN – (3:246) On 1 November 1669, Elizebeth Harwood of Salem (widow & administratrix of Henry Harwood deceased) & William Hathorne, Assist. & William Browne, Sen'r & Edmond Batter (selectmen) in name & by order of the rest of the selectmen of Salem, being joined with said William Hathorne together with said Elizebeth Harwood as per order of court at Salem, 29: 9: 1669, for a valuable sum in hand paid for the use of Elizebeth Harwood...granted to Jeremiah Buttman (fisherman) of Salem a dwelling house with 1 acre of ground upon which the house partly stands with all outhousing, garden & fencing that to house & ground belongs which was house & land of said Henry (deceased) & lying by South harbor in Salem, bounded W with land now of Richard Flinder formerly of said Henry's (deceased) on N & E with land of John Beckett. **Signed**: Elizebeth Harwood, William Hathorne, William Browne & Edmond Batter; **Witnesses**: Edward Humber & John Beckett; **Recorded**: 18: 11 mo: 1669.

JOHN WILLIAMS to JOHN LOOMES – (3:247) On 10 January 1669, John Williams of Salem (seaman) (with wife Elizebeth yielding dower) granted to John Loomes (seaman) of Salem for a valuable sum already paid, all land of his lying in North field near Capt. Trask's mills in Salem, 30 acres, 20 acres of which he bought of Edward Gaskin (shipwright) & the rest being about 10 acres he lately bought of John Ketchin & John Saunders & lay adjoining together with land of widow Buffam & land of Thomas Goldthwaite on the E & land of Job Swinerton partly on the N & land of Samuel Gaskin W & mill pond of aforesaid mill to SW...with all fruit trees, timber, woods, housing, fences... **Signed**: John Williams [by mark]; **Acknowledged**: 11: 11: 1669; **Witnesses**: John Lambert [by mark] & Hilliard Veren, Sr.; **Recorded**: 18: 11: 1669.

JOHN RUCK to MANASSEH MARSTONE – (3:249) On 7 January 1669, John Ruck (merchant) of Salem (with wife Sarah yielding dower) granted to Manasseh Marstone (blacksmith) of Salem for a valuable consideration in hand paid, ½ acre in Salem being in breadth at either end 4 poles, abutting to E against a creek & to W upon common land & to N with some land of John Ruck & to S with land of Mr. Bartholmew Gedney. It is understood that Manasseh is to set up & maintain upon his own cost all the middle fence between Ruck's land and premises so long as the land adjoining remains in Ruck's hand. **Signed**: John Ruck & Sarah Ruck; **Acknowledged**: 15: 11: 1669 & Sarah yielded thirds; **Witnesses**: Bartholomew Gedney & Daniel Bacon; **Recorded**: 18: 11: 1669.

WILLIAM BROWNE, Sr. to WILLIAM BROWNE, Jr. – (3:251) On 31 January 1669, William Browne, Sr. (merchant) of Salem granted to William Browne, Jr. (merchant) of Salem for a valuable consideration in hand paid, 8 acres of upland in South field so called in Salem bounded N with land of Jonathan Auger & Joseph Hardy & W to salt marsh, S with lands of Nathaniel Pickman & E with land of John Archard, & also one acre of salt marsh lying in South field aforesaid bounded NW with marsh of Thomas Reves, SE with marsh of said William Browne & so runs from upland to upland; also 1 acre more of salt marsh lying within fence of said South field & bounded NW with marsh of Mr. Edmond Batter formerly Thomas Antrum's (deceased) on SE with marsh of Mr. George Emmory & so runs from upland on NE to upland on SW & also ¾ acre of salt marsh more lying in South field aforesaid bounded with W end of it with marsh of Mr. George Emmory & with creek to S side & with E end & N side to upland of Lieut. George Gardener; all said parcels of land formerly land of Samuel Archard, Sr. (deceased) & by consent of Susanna Archard alias Hutcheson & Samuel Archard, Jr., formerly administrators to estate of said Samuel (deceased) & said estate committed into my hands together with their power of administration & confirmed by order of county court held at Salem 29 4th month 1669. **Signed**: William Browne, Sr.; **Acknowledged**: 28: 12: 1669; **Witnesses**: Edward Mowle & Hilliard Veren, Sr.; **Recorded**: 3 Mar 1669/70.

MEMORANDUM – (3:253) Whereas there is a well dug in John Gally's ground & new stoned by Mr. John Hale (minister) in town of Beverly, this is to declare to all men that John Hale shall quietly possess & enjoy said well with free egress…& said John Hale doth engage to make good all damages that shall arise…dated 18 Mar 1669. **Acknowledged**: John Gally [by mark] and John Hale 18: 1 mo: 1669.

ROGER CONANT, JOHN RAYMENT & BENJAMIN BALCH to ISACK HULL – (3:253) On 23 March 1670, Roger Conant, John Rayment & Benjamin Balch of Bass river side or otherwise Beverly planters, granted to Isack Hull (cooper) of the same place, for 9 pounds, 9 acres, part swamp & part upland near his now dwelling house bounded by John Woodbury, Sr. NE, John Woodbury SE & the country highway NW. **Signed**: Roger Conant, John Rayment & Benjamin Balch; **Acknowledged**: 23: 1 mo: 1669/70; **Witnesses**: William Dodge & Peter Woodbury; **Recorded**: 13: 2: 1670.

WILLIAM DODGE (& others) to ISAAK HULL – (3:254) On 7 June 1664, William Dodge, John Rayment, Roger Conant, Benjamin Balch & Peter Woodbury of Bass River in Salem granted to Isaak Hull (cooper) of Bass river upon considerations moving them, each of them, one acre in the whole 5 acres near to the SE corner of great pond & adjoining unto a parcel of land of Rayment with condition that Isaac Hull leave his habitation at Bass river & go elsewhere, he…shall not sell said 5 acres to any stranger but the aforesaid proprietors shall have liberty to redeem it if they please upon such terms as shall be judged by indifferent men chosen on both sides. **Signed**: Roger Conant, William Dodge, John Rayment, Benjamin Balch & Peter Woodbury; **Acknowledged**: 23: 1: 1669/70; **Witnesses**: Zachariah Herrick & Exercise Conant; **Recorded**: 13: 2: 1670.

JOHN WILLIAMS to EPHRAIM SKERRY – (3:255) On 17 June 1668, John Williams (cooper) of Salem granted to Ephraim Skerry (cordwainer) of Salem for a valuable consideration in hand paid, 56 poles of land in Salem, abutting S against the common called the penn & the other end to N bounded with land of John Williams being breadth E & W 3½ poles & in length 16 poles & side to E bounded with land of Thomas Watson & to W with land of John Williams & it is agreed that Ephraim Skerry is to make half the side fence & all the end between his land now bought & land of said John Williams. **Signed**: John Williams; **Acknowledged**: 27: 7: 1669; **Witnesses**: Samuel Williams & Nathaniel Beadle; **Recorded**: 13: 2: 1670.

EDMOND BATTER to JOHN MARTIN – (3:257) On 3 December 1669, Edmond Batter of Salem (merchant) granted to John Martin of Salem (fisherman) for a valuable consideration in hand paid, one dwelling house, outhouses & all land belonging to same…which according to a deed received from John Clements is expressed bearing date 3 Oct 1665. **Signed**: Edmond Batter; **Acknowledged**: 31: 10 mo: 1669; **Witnesses**: Philip Veren & Mary Veren.

JOHN NORTON to JEREMIAH MECHAM – (3:258) On 8 April 1670, John Norton of Salem (house carpenter) granted to Jeremiah Mecham of

Salem (weaver) for 80 pounds, a dwelling house with 1½ acres of ground adjoining with orchard fences...in Salem near the now bridge or causeway at the W end of town bounded with the highway by the North river side to the N & the highway that goes to said causeway to the SW & with land of Robert Nelson SE & land of Widow Buffam E. **Signed**: John Norton; **Acknowledged**: 8: 2 mo: 1670 & wife Mary yielded thirds; **Witnesses**: Hilliard Veren, Sr. & George Gardner; **Recorded**: 14: 2: 1670.

WILLIAM HOOKE to GEORGE KEASER – (3:261) On 1 July 1647, William Hooke of Salisbury granted to George Keaser of Lynn, for 24 pounds 10 shillings, 70 acres of salt marsh meadow in Rumney Marsh which was lately in the hands of Thomas Dexter & in case there fall short of 70 acres or any other way Thomas Dexter should disappoint George Keaser of meadow above mentioned then George Keaser is to repair to Thomas Dexter for to make up the sum of 70 acres of meadow. Further William Hooke engages himself to defend George Keaser...from his father, brother Robert Knight... **Signed**: William Hooke; **Acknowledged**: 3: 9 mo: 1648; **Witnesses**: Samuel Bennett & Henry Roades; **Recorded**: 2: 4 mo: 1670.

EDMUND BRIDGES to JOHN RUCK and JOSEPH BIGSBY – (3:262) On 3 February 1669, Edmund Bridges of Salem granted to John Ruck (vintner) of Salem and Joseph Bigsby (carpenter) of Rowley Village for 4 pounds 5 shillings, 2 parcels of land: 20 acres each of them, according as they lie in each division in the town of Topsfield, 1 parcel in the 1st division the 25th lot lying near Wheele brook & between Francis Peabody & John How's lot & 1 parcel of the second division being the 9th lot whereof Sticky meadow is part & between Ensign Howlett & John How's lot. **Signed**: Edmund Bridges & Sarah Bridges; **Acknowledged**: 11: 4: 1670 with wife Sarah yielding thirds; **Witnesses**: John Norman & Edward Flint; **Recorded**: 12: 4: 1670.

JOHN DEACON to JOHN PICKERING – (3:264) On 5 April 1670, John Deacon (blacksmith) of Boston granted to John Pickering (yeoman) of Salem for a valuable consideration in hand paid, 2 acres of salt marsh formerly Thorn's neck in the marsh called the Town Marsh within marsh of Lynn bounded N with marsh of Nathaniel Kirtland & SE & W side with creek. **Signed**: John Deacon & Ann Deacon [by mark]; **Acknowledged**: 5: 2: 1670; **Witnesses**: Hillyard Veren, Jr. & John Munjoy; **Recorded**: 21 June 1670.

GEORGE THOMAS to ROBERT BRONSDON – (3:265) On 9 September 1669, George Thomas of Salem granted to Robert Bronsdon (merchant) of Boston, for a valuable sum of money & current pay of New

England in hand paid, 20 rods of land in Salem between shop and land of William Curtice towards the E & house & land of Humphrey Coombes W & a common way reserved by Mary Sears as by deed appears E, abutting upon a common street N & extending toward house and land of Mary Searle the ½ of the extent of said parcel towards S. **Signed**: George Thomas: **Acknowledged**: 24: 4: 1670; **Witnesses**: Joseph Armitage, Edward Richards [by mark] & William Howard; **Recorded**: 25 June 1670.

WILLIAM BROWNE to WILLIAM FLINT – (3:268) On 2 May 1670, William Browne of Salem (merchant) granted to William Flint (yeoman) of Salem for 20 pounds sterling, 30 rods of land in Salem belonging formerly to the house of Samuel Archard (deceased) now in occupation of William Oxman, bounded N with the house & ground formerly Archard's now in occupation of said Oxman & S with house & land of Joshua Ward & W with house & land of Mr. Richard More on which W end parcel is 36 foot in breadth & on E bounded with a lane that goes to South river side on which E end parcel is in breadth 21 foot. **Signed**: William Browne; **Acknowledged**: 27: 4: 1670; **Witnesses**: Edward Norrice & John Appleton; **Recorded**: 27: 4: 1670.

WILLIAM BROWNE, Sr. to WILLIAM FLINT – (3:270) On 2 June 1670, William Browne, Sr. (merchant) of Salem granted to William Flint (husbandman) of Salem, for 20 pounds, all his share of a certain parcel of meadow with some upland which had been divided & enjoyed between them of late years but was formerly in possession of John Hardy, containing in whole 5 acres in Salem by Forest river on the S side of the common or Forest river neck of land N & bounded E by some marsh ground of Mr. Joseph Grafton, Sr. **Signed**: William Browne; **Acknowledged**: 2: 4: 1670; **Witnesses**: Edward Norris & John Appleton; **Recorded**: 27: 4: 1670.

GEORGE CORWIN to WILLIAM WOODS – (3:271) On 7 August 1669, George Corwin (merchant) of Salem granted to William Woods (fisherman) of Marblehead, for 70 pounds, 2 acres of meadow with such dwelling house or out houses that were then standing upon with the outhouse fences in Marblehead bounded with a dwelling house of Mr. Joseph Bowd on the NW or N & some ground of John Waldren to SW & near the great harbor on the SE & town common & highway part W & E together with 1½ cow's lease & in the town commons, all this having formerly been in possession of Edmund Nicholson of Marblehead lately deceased. **Signed**: George Corwin; **Acknowledged**: 14: 4 mo: 1670 by Capt. George Corwin; **Witnesses**: William Nick [by mark] & Edward Norrice; **Recorded**: 13: 4 mo: 1670.

MOSES MAVERICK to MATHEW CLARK – (3:273) On 18 February 1663/4, Moses Maverick of Marblehead granted to Mathew Clark (fisherman) of Marblehead, for a good & valuable consideration in hand paid, ½ acre of land joining land of Samuel Morgin on the NW, Lott Conant on SE, marsh of Mr. William Walton & Moses Maverick on the NE and the highway on the SW. **Signed**: Moses Maverick; **Acknowledged**: 22: 4: 1670; **Witnesses**: Phillip Harding & Robert Cooper [by mark]; **Recorded**: 7 July 1670.

EDMOND BATTEN to HENRY WEST – (3:273) On 17 June 1670, Edmond Batten (merchant) of Salem granted to Henry West (sadler) of Salem for a valuable consideration in hand paid, 20 rods of ground in Salem, part of land adjoining his own dwelling house, bounded W with a parcel of land lately given to Hilliard Veren, Sr. & E with land of Edmond Batten & on the S with the street or highway, one end of said parcel abutting against said street is 40 foot broad & to run the same breadth to land of Mr. Noriss whose land bounds it to the North. **Signed**: Edmond Batten; **Witnesses**: Hilliard Veren, Sr. & Benjamin Felton, with seizen & possession; **Recorded**: 7: 5: 1670.

THOMAS CHADWELL to MOSES CHADWELL – (3:275) On 4 February 1668, Thomas Chadwell (shipwright) of Charlestown, with consent of his wife Abigail, granted to Moses Chadwell (shipwright) of Lynn for 20 pounds in money & other good merchantable pay, 3 acres of land in Lynn, butting E on land of George Keser & W on the river where formerly was the ferry & bounded N & S by land of Edmond Needham. **Signed**: Thomas Chadwell & Abigail Chadwell [by mark]; Abigail yielded dower; **Acknowledged**: 4 Feb 1668; **Witnesses**: Elias Maverick & William Pearse, Sr.; **Recorded**: 8: 15: 1670.

WILLIAM BARTRUM to MOSES CHADWELL – (3:279) On 1 April 166-, William Bartrum & Sarah his wife & Mary Burt & Sarah Burt, daughters of Hugh Burt, lately deceased, & William Bassett being chosen guardian by & for said Sarah Burt, all of Lynn, granted to Moses Chadwell (ship carpenter) of Lynn, for 10 pounds sterling, 2 acres of land in Lynn, bounded S with Mr. Hanford's land, N with land of Mr. Jolly & W with land of Nathaniel Curtland. **Signed**: William Bartrum, Sara Bartrum [by mark], Mary Burt [by mark] & Sarah Burt [by mark] & William Bassett; **Acknowledged**: 30 Oct 1666; **Witnesses**: Andrew Mansfield & Daniel Salmon; **Recorded**: 8: 5: 1670.

JOHN MARSTONE, Sr. to SAMUEL PICKWORTH - (3:281) On 20 May 1670, John Marstone, Sr. (carpenter) of Salem granted to his son-in-law Samuel Pickworth & Sarah "my daughter, his wife" for love & natural affection, 16 rods in Salem & is part of land adjoining "my" now dwelling house & in breadth abutting on the lane that leads down to the North river 2 rods & runs 2 rods in breadth E through my land from said lane to land of Mr. John Gedney & is bounded with said John Gedney's land E & S with land of John Marstone & some land of William Marstone & W with aforesaid lane & N with land of James Browne. **Signed**: John Marstone, Sr. & Alice Marstone; **Witnesses**: Hilliard Veren, Sr., James Chichester & Samuel Small [by mark] by seizin & possession given at premises; **Recorded**: 8: 5: 1670.

WILLIAM BROWNE, Sr. to FRANCIS PARNEL – (3:283) On 10 October 1669, William Browne, Sr. (merchant) of Salem granted to Francis Parnel (fisherman) of Salem for a valuable sum in hand paid, 10¾ pole of ground in Salem, bounded W with the lane that goes down to South river on which side it is in length 5 pole 4½ foot, bounded S with ground of John Archard at which it is 2 pole, bounded on E with ground of Mr. James Brown on which side it is 5 pole 7½ foot & bounded N with ground of Daniel Rumboll on which end it is 2 pole 10 inches. **Signed**: William Browne; **Acknowledged**: 7: 1: 1669/70; **Witnesses**: Edward Maule & Hilliard Veren, Sr.; **Recorded**: 8: 5: 1670.

(3:284) For our loving friends Capt. Edward Johnson, Lieut. John Carter & the rest of the committee of Woburn appointed to order & lay out the common lands there: Whereas Mr. John Hale has by some of his friends made application to you for consideration in the division of your commons with reference unto an ancient lot (belonging to his father deceased) now to him within your town which lot with others of like nature were at first belonging to Charlestowne but by them assigned over to your town with a parcel of common land for the accommodations of the said lot as we are informed & have seen some ancient writings to that effect, but it seems you have denied his request, therefore he hath made application to us, entreating our assistance, wherefore we thought it convenient for prevention of further trouble between you, hereby do desire you to give him satisfaction according to justice & equity & in the interim to suspend the division of that 500 acres of common lands lying on the E side of Samuel Richardson's farm, so with our love to you we remaine 4 July 1670 your loving friends, Daniel Gookin, Edward Collins, Committee of the General Court for settling matters of difference in Woburn. In case you apprehend there is no ground to warrant his claim, we shall readily attend some convenient time to hear your respective allegations in the case & give you our sense thereof. Thomas Danforth. **Entered**: 20: 5: 1670.

NICHOLAS POTTER to THOMAS WELLMAN – (3:286) On 17 twelfth month 1653, Nicholas Potter (deacon) of Lynn, with consent of his wife, granted to Thomas Wellman and John Knight of Lynn, for 26 pounds sterling, two 3-score acre lots joining together one of them lately in tenure of said Nicholas Potter, & the other in the late tenure of James Boutwell, bounded S with the farm of Goodman Talmage's & 3 acres of marsh lately belonging unto aforesaid Nicholas Potter & E with the common, W with the river that cometh out of Stone's meadow & N with the land of said Thomas Wellman & John Knight; and also 3 acres of meadow lately in tenure of said Nicholas Potter adjoining to aforesaid purchased land on S & also all ways & easements to commons…to said arable lands nor marsh belonging. **Signed**: Nicholas Potter & Em Potter [by mark]; **Acknowledged**: 27: 5 mo: 1670; **Witnesses**: Andrew Mansfield & Katherne Moore [by mark]; **Recorded**: 10: 6 mo: 1670.

(3:288) We whose names are hereto subscribed being appointed to lay out land & meadow on Castle hill to Richard Rowland which having done & bounded on the 23rd of July 1667, do also on the same day agree upon & appoint there shall be a highway of a rod or pole in breadth from the meadow of Richard Rowland which he had of Mr. Gott cross over the land of Capt. James Smith & is to be along under the hill by the barn to the land of said Rowland & from thence to go so far as the dwelling house the one half lying in said Rowland's land & the other in the said Smith's land until it comes so far as the house then to cross over the land of the said Smith by the house to the bridge which bridge we also do agree & appoint is to be repaired & maintained at the charge of the said Rowland & Smith proportionable to their land on Castle Hill. **Signed**: William Hathorne & Samuel & George Gardner; **Recorded**: 15: 6 mo: 1670.

MARY SEARLE to FRANCIS SKERRY– (3:288) On 30 July 1669, Mary Searle, wife of Stephen Searle & administratrix of Alexander Seares deceased, for 5 pounds sterling in hand paid by Francis Skerry (malster) of Salem to satisfy so much of a debt owing from said Alexander deceased to creditors: sold Francis Skerry an interest & propriety in a highway she had reserved for her own use which is part of land belonging to her now dwelling house to say 10 foot broad & to run between the house & land of Humfry Coomes on W & some lately sold to Henry Kemball now in possession of George Thomas on E, from the highway or common N, to run S toward the waterside to orchard of said Frances & to run 69½ foot further along by side of orchard on E side…late husband Alexander Sears. **Signed**: Mary Searle [by mark]; **Acknowledged**: 18: 5 mo: 1670; **Witnesses**: Hilliard Veren, Sr. & Samuel Archard; **Recorded**: 14: 7 mo: 1670.

MATHEW BARTON to WILLIAM DICER – (3:290) On 8 August 1668, Mathew Barton (shipwright) of Salem granted to William Dicer (fisherman) of Salem for a valuable consideration in hand paid, a dwelling house & ¼ acre of ground adjoining, in Salem, lately bought of John Marsh, formerly in possession of Richard Curtice, situated against South harbor bounded with land of Robert Leman E & land sometime of David Corwithy now of William Hollingworth W & land of Francis Collins N & abuts against South harbor to the S. **Signed**: Mathew Barton & Martha Barton; **Acknowledged**: 23: 7 mo: 1670 by Mathew Barton and Martha Barton who yielded thirds; **Witnesses**: Nicholas Waterland & Thomas Wilson; **Recorded**: 24: 7 mo: 1670.

BEZALIELL OSBOURNE to ANTIPAS NEWMAN – (3:292) On 24 May 1670, Bezeliell Osbourne of South Hampton, East Riding, Yorkshire (Attorney to Frizwid Mulford of East Hampton, of Riding aforesaid as per instrument bearing date 14 May 1670), granted to Antipas Newman of Wenham (gentleman & preacher of the word of God at Wenham) for a valuable sum of money in current pay of New England, a farm of 100 acres of upland and 10 acres of meadow according to a grant of the town of Salem many years ago unto William Osborne, then husband of said Friswid Mulford within bounds of Wenham, bounded by the farm sometimes in hands of Goodman Trusker S & the meadow of Joseph Porter W & otherwise the meadow being bounded by James Bette's meadow W & the bridge S & Byum's meadow E & SE & all other estate...of Friswid Mulford with John Mulford her present husband who did also impower Bezaliell Osborne & said Bezaliell Osbourne doth covenant...that he by virtue of his power & letter of attorney from Friezwood Mulford his mother & John Mulford her present husband had authority to give the premises... **Signed**: Bezaleele Osbourne; **Acknowledged**: by Bezaleele Osbourne before Gov. Richard Bellingham; **Witnesses**: Thomasin Collacut & Joseph Osbourne; **Recorded**: 12: 7 mo: 1670.

ANDREW WOODBERY & FRANCES COLLINS to EDWARD BUSH – (3:295) On 7 January 1669, Andrew Woodbery & Frances Collins of Salem (administrators to the estate of Elizabeth Cockerill, widow deceased) & Susanna, the late wife of Edward Clapp of Dorchester, deceased, joint administrator with Andrew & Frances, granted to Edward Bush (seaman) of Salem for a valuable sum in hand paid, a dwelling house with an outhouse with about ¼ acre of ground adjoining in Salem, bounded W with house and ground of Elias Mason, both said houses adjoining on the N with the highway or common & on the E with a strip of land said Bush lately bought of Paule Mansfield. **Signed**: Frances Collens, Hana Collens [by mark], Andrew Woodbery & Susanna Clapp [by mark] & Mary Woodbury [by mark]; **Witnesses**: Richard Hide & Jonathan Ayer; **Recorded**: 7: 8 mo: 1670.

Mr. FRANCES JOHNSON to Mr. THADDEUS RIDDAN – (3:297) On 29 Sept 1670, Mr. Frances Johnson (gentleman) of Boston, with the free consent of his wife Hana, granted to Mr. Thaddeus Riddan (merchant) of Lynn, for a certain sum of money in hand, one acre of land with trees, fruit trees or what else soever in it is or belongeth thereunto as it is now fenced in Marblehead & formerly in possession of Mr. Thomas Pittman & Walsing Chilson & according to ancient butts & bounds thereof was bounded NE by Mr. Walton & E unto Samuel Morgain, N to one street side, SW to the other street side...with a small old house upon the upper of said land next unto Samuel Morgaine's. **Signed**: Frances Johnson; **Acknowledged**: 29: 7 mo: 1670; **Witnesses**: Samuel Morgaine, William Pitt & Samuel Leach; **Recorded**: 20: 8 mo: 1670.

JOHN LEWIS to RALPH KING – (3:300) On 6 March 1667, John Lewis (husbandman) of Lynn, with consent of wife Hana in reference to her surrendering thirds, granted to Ralph King (gentleman) of Lynn for 23 pounds sterling, 4 acres of upland in Lynn bounded N & E with the highway that parts said land & land of Mr. King, which way leads towards Mr. King's house, W with land of said John Lewis, S with the sea, the NW corner is to be at the old Ox Pasture gate & whereas now the usual highway lies as above said, now the highway is to lie along the line betwixt them, only the highway is to be upon land of said John Lewis...Ralph King to pay unto John Lewis the value of ½ of it & also 3 acres (1 parcel) of salt marsh in Rumney Marsh in Lynn, bounded E with marsh of John Lewis, W with marsh of Andrew Mansfield abutting N upon the 1st division, S upon the lowest division of lots which marsh was formerly Mr. Knowles'. John Lewis gives free liberty to Ralph King to sell all hay he gets yearly on said 3 acres upon marsh of John Lewis adjoining in a convenient place to boat away. **Signed**: John Lewis & Hanah Lewis; **Acknowledged**: 19: 5 mo: 1669 with Hana yielding thirds; **Witnesses**: Andrew Mansfield & Bethiah Mansfield; **Recorded**: 20: 8: 1670.

WILLIAM HOARE to JOHN LAMBERT, Sr. – (3:302) On 10 August 1670, William Hoare (fisherman) of Beverly, granted to John Lambert, Sr. (fisherman) of Beverly for 10 pounds sterling, 5 acres in Beverly bounded W northerly with the river called Bass river, N easterly with land of John Lambert, on SE end with land of Josiah Rootes & on the SW side with land partly of Josiah Rootes & Richard Haines. **Signed**: William Hoare [by mark] & Dorcas Hoare [by mark]; **Witnesses**: with seizin & possession given, by Hilliard Veren, Sr., George Penney & John Price; **Recorded**: 25: 8: 1670.

RICHARD THISTLE to RICHARD HANOVER – (3:305) On 24 October 1670, Richard Thistle (mariner) of Marblehead granted to Richard

Hanover (mariner) of Marblehead for 4 score pounds in money, all his messuage tenement or dwelling house with the land whereon it stands with the yard, garden, and orchard thereto belonging, containing half an acre belonging to the said house as now fenced, in Marblehead, joining land of Mathew Clark and NE by marsh of Mr. William Walton and of Mr. Moses Maverick and the highway, and on the street SW. **Signed**: Richard Thistle; **Witnesses**: Samuel Morgan, Abraham Alling, Samuel Leach, Sr.; **Acknowledged**: 4: 9: 1670; **Recorded**: 15: 9 mo: 1670.

MATHEW NIXON to THOMAS SEARLE – (3:308) On 14 November 1670, Mathew Nixon of Salem (fisherman) granted to Thomas Searle of Salem, for 35 pounds, a dwelling house with 2 pole of ground adjoining, in Salem where he now lived, standing in front of his now dwelling house, only a yard between said house and ground, taking up the whole front of his ground, next to the water side to the south from the paved yard, except for common use for egress and regress of said Mathew Nixon and said Thomas his heirs, i.e., 8 foot in breadth to the E next to the land of Walter Whitford, and so from the water side, unto the yard, also 2 foot breadth of ground behind said house against the said oven; the said house and ground being bounded with said passage of 8 foot, reserved & before accepted E and the south harbor to the SE, with land or yard of said Mathew N; also a parcel of land N of his now dwelling house, being part of his now orchard, beginning at the new stake, about 37 foot from the end of his house, north, where it is 15 foot in breadth, and so taking in that one row of trees on that side adjoining land of Walter Whitford and in breadth at the N end adjoining land of Andrew Woodbery. **Signed**: Mathew Nixon [by mark]; **Recorded**: 15: 9: 1670; **Witnesses**: Walter Whiteford, Hilliard Veren, John Price.

JOHN ROBBINSON to Ens. THOMAS BANCROFT – (3:311) On 8 November 1670, John Robbinson (husbandman) of Exeter, granted to Ensigne Thomas Bancroft (husbandman) of Lynn, for 17 pounds, sixty acres of land, lying within the bounds of Lynn, not far from Beaver Dam, bounded NW with land of Mr. Holyoke, NE on land of Isaac Hart, SE with land of Goodman Collins, and SW on Redding's meadow, this having sometimes been the land of William Blote. **Signed**: John Robinson; **Acknowledged**: 8: 9: 70; **Witnesses**: Edward Norice, Sr. and William Hodge; **Recorded**: 16: 9: 1670.

Deposition of witnesses on ARON READ's death – (3:313) On 11: 9: 1670, John Foster, Sr. (aged about 52), John Tompkins, Jr. (aged about 25), Samuel Ebonne [or Aborn] (aged about 58), Robert Pease (aged about 41) and Martha Foster (aged about 34) deposed that they were with Aron Read when he died, when Samuel Eborne asked him whether Joseph Small did not shoot him willfully, he answered with great affection, Oh no no no. **Recorded**: 22: 9 mo: 1670.

DANIEL KING, Sr. to RALPH KING – (3:315) On 27 Oct 1670, Daniel King, Sr. of Lynn granted to Ralph King, for divers causes and considerations, his now dwelling house and homestead, being situated in Lynn, commonly called by the name of Swampscott, for home house, with the barns and all outhousing, fencing and orchards…the bounds being at the sea at the west end of Long Pond, and so upon a straight line, over his farm to a little red oak standing on a brow of a hill on the S side of a path going to his farm, where George Darling did live, which tree is marked with a D and a K on the N, and an R and a K on the W side, so this line to run to the line between Lynn and his farm, so along between Lynn and his farm to a running brook on the S end of John Farr's and Edward Richard's lot, so over to Swampscott Pond to a little walnut tree on the W of the pond marked with R.K. on the S side, N.E. on the N side; and so to run westerly to another walnut tree, marked with R.K. on the S side; and bounded on the N side with the land of Ezekiel Needham, so all along upon a brow of a hill W and so to the highway that goes to Lynn…further to son Ralph King half his neck of salt marsh called 20 acres lying in the town marsh, which half is to lie on the E side. **Signed**: Daniel King; **Witnesses**: William Cowdry, John Blaney; **Acknowledged**: 19: 9: 1670; **Recorded**: 22: 9: 1670.

ELEAZER HATHORNE to GEORGE KEYSER – (3:317) On 7 Oct 1670, Eleazer Hathorne (merchant) of Salem granted to George Keyser (tanner) of Salem, for a valuable consideration paid to him in hand, land bounded on the N and E with land of said Keyser, S with land of Eleazer Hathorne, W with the land next to John Pitman. **Signed**: Eleazer Hathorne; **Witnesses**: Philip Cromwell, Edward Norrice, Sr.; **Acknowledged**: 25: 9: 1670; **Recorded**: 25: 9: 1670.

EDMOND BRIDGES to JOHN GOOLD – (3:318) On 9 December 1670, Edmond Bridges (blacksmith) of Salem granted to John Goold (yeoman) of Topsfield, for a valuable sum, 8 acres of land with a dwelling house and barn on it, lying in Topsfield, bounded NE with land of Thomas Perkins, Sr. and E or SE with land of Jacob Towne; also a parcel more on the other side or S side of Ipswich River, containing 10 acres of meadow, swamp and upland, bounded NE with the river, to the common land of Topsfield on all the other side. **Signed**: Edmond Bridges: **Witnesses**: Thomas White, William Fairfield; **Acknowledged**: 10: 10: 1670; **Recorded**: 14: 10: 1670.

BARTHOLOMEW ROES to RICHARD MOORE – (3:320) 15 Jan 1665, Charlestown, in Carolina, Sr. ten days after sight of this my bill of exchange…pay unto Capt. Richard Moore, 673 pounds of good Muschouads sugar, the value rec'd hear of himself, please to make good payment & place it to account as per advice. To his honored father Mr. Bartholomew Roes in Barbadoes. Your most obedient son, Bartholomew Roes, Junior.

GEORGE THOMAS to HENRY KEMBLE – (3:321) On 7 Sept 1669, George Thomas of Salem (gunsmith) acknowledges to be indebted unto Henry Kemble of Boston (blacksmith) the full sum of 30 pounds current money to be paid Henry Kemble…by sum of 5 shillings in money & by value of 4 pounds 11 shillings in gunsmith work in & upon every 24th day of April annually & every year from & after the day hereof at or in the now dwelling house of said Henry Kemble, George Thomas do bind me…& also that my small piece of land with shop on part thereof standing containing ¼ part of an acre in Salem & is bounded by land & shop of William Curtice E and land of Humfry Coomes W & is the same small parcel & shop late purchased of Henry Kemball. Collaterally it is agreed between the parties that work termed gunsmith work is to be good sound substantial fire lock musgatts with good locks in every respect with worme, scourerer gunstocks, sockets & gunstickes all completely fitted. **Signed**: George Thomas; **Witnesses**: Edward Nailer, William Cotton, William Pearce, Sr.; **Acknowledged and Recorded**: 27: 10 mo: 1670. The above named William Pearce, Sr. that [sic] is was agreed…that the above mentioned musquetts shall be delivered paid & received in pay at 18 sh p. musket. **Signed**: William Pearce Sr.

SAMUEL BENNETT to WILLIAM BARTHOLOMEW – (3:323) On 12 March 1669/70, Samuel Bennett of Rumney Marsh, with Sarah "now wife" releasing dower rights, granted to William Bartholomew of Boston, for 220 pounds, his farm, being a tract of land, meadow and marsh belonging thereto, with messuage or farmhouse and other buildings, now in possession of John Greene and Henry Greene, bounded W with land now in possession of Austin Sindall and Benjamin Murry, on N with hills bounded plow plains…rocks, ponds, brook…also 6 acres of upland lying on the E of said Brook or an equal half of a meadow called Squire's meadow, lying within Malden bounds; also 14 acres of salt marsh in Rumney marsh, formerly purchased of Capt. Robert Bridges, called the 14-acre lot…bounded E by a salt creek, SE by lands of Thomas Newell, NE with land of Samuel Johnson, SW with lands of John Ballard. **Signed**: Samuel Bennett; **Witnesses**: Thomas Marshall and John Hathorne; **Acknowledged**: 7 Apr 1670; **Recorded**: 7: 11: 1670.

WILLIAM BARTHOLOMEW to JACOB and MARY GREENE – (3:327) On 9 Jan 1670, William Bartholomew of Boston (merchant), granted to Jacob Greene of Charlestown and Mary his wife for divers causes and in respect of love and entire affection for his daughter Mary Greene, wife of Jacob Greene of Charlestown (merchant) & to her children begotten of her body now in being & those she may hereafter have, the farm bought of Samuel Bennett, for their use but chiefly for said Mary Greene & children of her body as copartners & coinheritors. **Signed**: William Bartholomew; **Witnesses**: Richard Prince and Henry Bartholomew; **Acknowledged**: 12: 11: 1670; **Recorded**: 17: 11: 1670. There is a release or making null this above intaile to Mary Greene & her children which is recorded in book the 6th & folio the 6th.

HENRY COLEBORNE to WILLIAM LORD – (3:331) On 20 Sep 1670, Henry Coleborne (mariner) of Salem, with Sara his wife releasing dower, granted to William Lord (cutler) of Salem, for a valuable sum in hand paid, a dwelling house with 3 rod of ground adjoining to the backside of said house E, in Salem near the meeting house, land adjoining the house which said William Lord now lives in, at the N end of it next to the meeting house, containing one lower room with a single partition about the middle and one upper room with a leanto on the E side and one chimney below; some chimney in the chamber of brick, the said house and ground adjoining and bounded W and N with the street and E with the house & ground of Capt. Corwin and S with land of said William Lord, said house and ground being that which he lately bought of said William Lord. **Signed**: Henry Coleborne, and Sara Coleborne [by mark]; **Witnesses**: Hillard Veren, Sr. and John Cole; **Recorded**: 1: 12: 1670.

NATHANIEL PICKMAN to ANTHONY DIKE – (3:333) On 10 July 1670, Nathaniel Pickman (carpenter) of Salem granted to Anthony Dike (seaman) of Salem, for a valuable consideration paid, the carpenter's work of the dwelling house the said Anthony Dike now lives in and the plot of ground it stands on with the garden room and wood room as now it stands within the fence, and also 2 acres of upland in the south field, being 3 by 50 pole and ¼ in length and 6 pole in breadth, the bound marks on the W end being a great walnut tree on S side of said end, and 2 young black oaks that grow close together as that they came out of one root, on the N side of said end being bounded S with land of Thomas Browning, N and E on ground of Nathaniel Pickman, W with the salt marsh. **Signed**: Nathaniel Pickman; **Witness**: Samuel Pickman; **Acknowledged**: 15: 10: 1670; **Recorded**: 1: 12: 1670.

WILLIAM LAKE to THOMAS CALEY – (3:334) On December 1670, William Lake (cooper) of Salem, with Ann Lake his wife releasing dower, granted to Thomas Caley (netmaker) of Salem for a valuable sum, 10 acres of land on Darby Fort side, in Marblehead...bounded E with land of Thomas Dixy, S with common land, W with land of John Peach, Jr. and abuts N against the south harbor of Salem. **Signed**: William Lake & Ann Lake; **Witnesses**: Walter Price and Hillard Veren, Sr.; **Acknowledged**: 5: 10: 1670; **Recorded**: 2: 12: 1670.

RICHARD MORE to THOMAS PITMAN – (3:336) On 10 Jan 1670, Richard More (mariner) of Salem, with wife Christian yielding thirds, granted to Thomas Pitman (husbandman) of Marblehead, for a valuable consideration paid, 10 acres in Marblehead, bounded N by the south harbor belonging to Salem, E with land of Richard Read, W with Mr. Moses Maverick, S with common land. **Signed**: Richard More & Christian More [by mark]; **Witnesses**: John Price and Hilliard Veren; **Acknowledged**: 8: 22 [sic] mo: 1670; **Recorded**: 22: 12: 1670.

EDMOND BATTEN to THOMAS BAKER – (3:337) On 22 Feb 1670, Edmond Batten (merchant) of Salem, with wife Mary freely yielding her thirds, granted to Thomas Baker (yeoman) of Topsfield, for 5 pounds, 2 and ½ acres of meadow late in the tenure of William Prichett, now the said Edmond Batten's by an execution legally levied on said parcel and given to said Batten, the said parcel is in Topsfield and is bounded E and S with the meadow of Thomas Baker with Pie Brook running between, on the W and N with the meadow of William Prichet. **Signed**: Edmond Batten & Mary Batten; **Witnesses**: John How and John Smith; **Acknowledged**: 22: 12: 1670; **Recorded**: 22: 12: 70.

THOMAS BAKER to JOHN HOW – (3:339) On 22 Feb 1670, Thomas Baker of Topsfield granted to John How (yeoman) of Topsfield for a valuable sum, 1 and ¼ acres of fresh meadow, being one half of that parcel said Thomas Baker lately bought of Mr. Edmond Batten, bounded E & S with meadow of said Thomas Baker, with Pie Brook between, W & N with meadow of William Prichett. **Signed**: Thomas Baker; **Witnesses**: Walter Price and Hilliard Veren, Sr.; **Acknowledged**: 12: 22: 1670.

MARK PITTMAN to ROBERT KNIGHT – (3:342) On 20 January 1660, Mark Pittman (fisherman) of Marblehead, with full consent of his wife Sara, granted to Robert Knight (carpenter) of Marblehead, for 8 pounds in hand paid, a parcel of land in Marblehead, which was in the first place granted unto George Write, but now by purchase in the possession of the abovesaid Mark Pittman, the now right owner thereof, the said Mark Pittman bargains and sells unto Robert Knight one moiety of the said parcel of land, which said moiety lies on the S and NW side of the running brook, bounded from the middle of a rock which lies in the lot of Mr.

Williams, running SE towards the S corner of his now enclosed lot, to the water together with whatsoever land in the S side of the brook, provided that the said Robert Knight leave a sufficient ingress and regress for all cattle whatsoever, and that a sufficient cartway be left without bars or any fence whatsoever for which Mark Pittman acknowledges himself satisfied. **Signed**: Mark Pittman and Sara Pitman [both by mark]; **Witnesses**: John Bartoll and John Peach [by mark]; **Acknowledged**: 10: 4 mo: 1670 & wife acknowledged & yielded thirds; **Recorded**: 6 April 1671.

WILLIAM WOODBERY to NICHOLAS WOODBERY, Sr. – (3:343) On 23 September 1670, William Woodbery (weaver) of Beverly (with Elizabeth Woodbury releasing rights), granted to Nicholas Woodbery, Sr. (yeoman) of Beverly, for 57 pounds 10 shillings, the dwelling house he now lives in with all outhousing belonging with 14 acres of land adjoining & upon which said house stands, containing an orchard, garden and yard, with the uplands, the housing and land is in Beverly, bounded NE and SE and S with land of Nicholas Woodbery, NW with land of Richard Brackenbury and NE with land of John Lovett, Sr. and Robert Bradford; also 4 acres lying N from said house and land, disjoining about 40 rod and is bound SW with the highway, NE on the common land, NW with land of John Patch & John Lovett, on SE with land of Robert Bradford; also 6 and ½ acres of meadow lying partly in Beverly and partly in Wenham, bounded N with an island of upland being common land, W with land of Nicholas Patch & Samuel Corning, S with a parcel of upland called Mr. Conant's neck & NE with Wenham common. **Signed**: William Woodbery [by mark] & Elizabeth Woodbery [by mark]; **Witnesses**: Samuel Plummer and Richard Ober; **Acknowledged**: 13: 11 mo: 1670; **Recorded**: 10: 2 mo: 1671.

JOHN and WILLIAM HASKELL to NICHOLAS WOODBERY – (3:347) On 6 March 1667/8, John Haskell and William Haskell (husbandmen) of Salem, with Patience (William's wife) yielding thirds, granted for 75 pounds sterling to Nicholas Woodbery of Salem, 80 acres in Salem, near Wenham, bounded by land formerly of William Lord's NE, land of John Rayment SE, land of Zachariah Herrick SW, and land of John Leach...also 3 acres of fresh meadow, being ½ of 6 acres that was Roger Haskall's...also 2 acres of fresh meadow in Wenham great meadow, bounded W with the bridge, N with the meadow formerly Mr. Fisk's, E with meadow of Nicholas Howard, & S by William Osborn's; also 4 acres of fresh meadow in Bunker's meadow, bounded E with the meadow of William Dodge, S with the meadow of Edward Bishop, W of John Raiment, N by the great river. **Signed**: John and William Haskell; **Witnesses**: Hilliard Veren, Edward Grove and Thomas Rix; **Acknowledged**: 18: 2 mo: 1667; **Recorded**: 12: 2: 1671.

ELIZABETH LEACH, Sr. to JOHN DODGE – (3:349) On 26 November 1670, Elizabeth Leach, Sr. (widow) of Salem confirmed & ratified the sale (and yielded interest) by son John Leach to John Dodge of Beverly, for 17 pounds, 10 shillings, of a mill or mills, with housing, land and orchard. **Signed**: Elizabeth Leach [by mark]; **Witnesses**: Andrew Elliot and Isaac Hall; **Acknowledged**: 16: 3 mo: 1671; Elizabeth acknowledged & it was agree by both parties that no part of this 17 pounds 10 shillings shall be deducted out of purchase with John Leach.

ELIAS STILEMAN to TAMSEN BUFFUM – (3:350) On 18 April 1671, Elias Stileman (merchant) of Portsmouth, with Mary Stileman rendering her thirds, granted to Tamsen Buffum (widow) of Salem, for a valuable sum, 12 acres of upland in Salem also 1 and ½ acres near the bridge to Castle Hill, lying on both sides to the river or creek, bounded W by the common, S with the marsh of John Gardner, N with a strip of marsh of Richard Rowland's lying between the bridge and said parcel, E with the land of said Rowland's; also 1 acre of salt marsh, abutting E against the said 12 acres of said Stileman, W on the common land, N on the marsh of Mr. Edmond Batter, late of Thomas Antrum, late deceased, S by the marsh of Eleanor Robbinson; ¾ of an acre of marsh lying between the late or now William Lord's N and the marsh of Marblehead men S; also ¾ of an acre abutting upon the upland of Nathaniel Pickman & Mr. William Browne E, Joseph Handy's marsh N, the marsh of Thomas Browning, late deceased S, the creek W. **Signed**: Elias Stileman & Mary Stileman; **Witnesses**: Hilliard Veren, John Wilson [by mark] and Joshua Buffum; **Acknowledged**: by both, 17 May 1671; **Recorded**: 19: 2: 1671.

CHRISTOPHER WALLER to GEORGE KEASER – (3:354) On 16 January 1664/5, Christopher Waller of Salem, with Margaret his wife yielding her thirds, granted to George Keaser (tanner) of Salem for 3 pounds, a parcel of land in Salem, 8 poles in length and 2 poles, 12 foot in breadth, bounded by land of Mathew Price on the N, and James Browne (glazier) on the S, of Joseph Miles on the E with the lane or the highway on the W. **Signed**: Christopher Waller [by mark] & Margaret Waller [by mark]; **Witnesses**: Edward Norice & John Orne; premises delivered up & possession given with livery and seizure 19 Sept 1665; **Witnesses**: Edward Norice & Benjamin Felton; **Acknowledged**: 15: 3 mo: 71; **Recorded**: 15: 3 mo: 1671.

ZACHEUS CURTICE Sr. to JOHN ROBBINSON – (3:355) On 2 March 1664/5, Zacheus Curtice, Sr. (planter) of Rowley, with wife yielding her thirds, granted to John Robbinson (planter) of Salem, for 10 pounds 3 shillings, 2 parcels of upland near Obadiah Antrum's farm on the S side the river called Brooksby, 20 pole, bought of Joshua Yenen, with an old cellar in it, and 1 acre of upland joining to the said 20 pole, and all the meadow lying above Mr. Clark's meadow, on the S of Mr. Humphry's farm, and on the N of Mr. Clark's plaine, next to Dog pond. **Signed**: Zacheus Curtice [by mark]; **Witnesses**: Richard Croad, Joseph Porter; **Recorded**: 15: 3: 1671.

MARY SEARLE to STEVEN HASKETT – (3:356) On 27 March 1670, Mary Searle of Salem granted to Steven Haskett of Salem, for 40 pounds, a dwelling house, with ¼ acre of land, bounded by the widow Estikes land E, by the south harbour S, by land of Thomas Skerry W, by land of Henry Kimball N, only if the said Mary Searle shall repay to said Haskett the sum of 40 pounds which the said Haskett paid for this land, she paying of it in kind, according to the day or time mentioned in a bill bearing date 27 March 1670, which said Searle stands bound to pay the said Haskett by the 20th of July 1670, then the sale to be void and of no effect. **Signed**: Mary Searle [by mark]; **Witnesses**: Henry Skerry, Sr. and John Williams; **Acknowledged**: 23: 7 mo: 1670; **Recorded**: 6: 4 mo: 1671.

JOHN BECKETT to PHILLIP CROMWELL – (3:358) On 31 May 1671, John Beckett (shipwright) of Salem granted to Phillip Cromwell (butcher) of Salem, for the security of 81 pounds, 11 shillings, 1¼ pence due upon account by book to be paid by Becket in 5 years in merchantable pay at price current, 3 acres of upland in Salem, near the harbor on the South river, in a field called Job's field, bounded E with land of Joseph Swazy, W with land of Edward Wooland, S with land of Jeremiah Booteman and Richard Flinder, N with several lands belonging to Michael Coomes, the widow Hollingworth, and some land formerly in possession of Thomas Sallas, deceased. On 22: 3 mo: 1676, Mr. Phillip Cromwell did acknowledge this before me that he did receive satisfaction for this mortgage and did deliver up the same, and his wife freely did the same. **Signed**: John Beckett; **Witness**: Edward Norrice, Sr.; **Acknowledged**: 10: 6 mo: 1671; **Recorded**: 12: 4: 1671.

WILLIAM LORD, Sr. to WILLIAM SHAW – (3:360) On 7 February 1670, William Lord, Sr. (cutler) of Salem granted to William Shaw (husbandman) of Salem for 8 pounds sterling, land in Salem adjoining the farms formerly of Mr. Edward Batters, late in the tenure and occupation of Thomas Antrum, deceased, and now in the tenure and occupation of Elias Parkman, bounded S with land of Elias Parkman and land of William Shaw, W & N with Mr. Downing's farm, and N with land also of William Shaw and S & E on land of Robert Stone. **Signed**: William Lord and Abigail Lord [both by mark]; **Witnesses**: Hilliard Veren, Sr. and Henry West; **Acknowledged**: 8: 12: 1670 and Abigail (wife) freely yielded her thirds; **Recorded**: 15: 4: 1671.

ELIZABETH COOMES to FRANCIS GRANT – (3:362) On 4 May 1670, Elizabeth Coomes of Marblehead granted to Francis Grant, by a verbal free gift and dower to her "son-in-law" half an acre near Marblehead ferry within land of Elizabeth Coomes. Signed: Elizabeth Coomes [by mark]; **Witnesses**: Thomas Dixey, Benjamin Parminter, Edward Humphry & Samuel Leach; **Acknowledged**: 23: 3: 1671; **Recorded**: 24: 4: 1671.

WILLIAM LAKE to JOHN TURNER – (3:364) On 18 April 1671, William Lake (cooper) of Salem granted to John Turner (mariner) of Salem, for a valuable sum, half an acre in Salem, bounded E by land of John Milke, S with land of Ellenor Robbinson, W abutting by the highway and the North river side, and N with land of Ralph Fogg. Signed: William Lake & Anna Lake [by mark]; **Witnesses**: Hilliard Veren, Sr. and Samuel Williams; **Acknowledged**: 22: 4 mo: 1671, with wife Anna yielding her thirds; **Recorded**: 24: 4: 1671.

MARK & ELIZABETH GRAVES to SAMUEL BLANCHARD – (3:366) On 19 July 1665, Mark Graves (weaver) of Andover and Elizabeth Graves of Andover granted to Samuel Blanchard (husbandman) of Charlestown, for 20 pounds in hand paid & also in consideration that Samuel Blanchard...do and from time to time...forever bear & pay ¼ part of all such duties & rates...toward the ministry in Andover & toward the rates of said town in respect to the house lot which said Mark Graves now stands possessed of in Andover, containing 4 acres according to a grant made to said Mark Graves by the inhabitants of Andover, his part of meadow in Crane meadow within the town as it was granted to said Mark by the inhabitants of the said town, for 3 acres, abutting E on the meadow of Samuel Blanchard, W on the commons of Andover, N & NW partly by the land of Andrew Allen & partly the upland common, and S with the upland commons of the said town, with appurtenances...may acrew or be due & appertaining to 1 acre of houselot of 4 acres before mentioned ...Also released unto Samuel Blanchard all interest "to parcel in cove of meddow adjoining said meddow of Samuel Blanchard & granted by the inhabitants of Andover to one of them but not contained in the bounds above mentioned." Signed: Mark Graves [by mark] and Elizabeth Graves [by mark]; **Witnesses**: John Osgood, John Browne and Laurence Lacye [by mark]; **Witnesses** to release: Simon and Dudley Bradstreet; **Acknowledged**: 19 July 1665.

JOHN WOODBERY to JOHN WILLIAMS – (3:371) On 30 Apr 1670, John Woodbery (mariner) of Salem mortgaged to John Williams (merchant) of Bristol, for 60 pounds, 18 shillings in hand paid (64 pounds, 10 shillings to be paid 1 May 1671), 40 acres near Bass River, adjoining lands of Benjamin Balch of Salem on the E, and certain other lands in possession of Henry Herrick. The above mortgage is entered as a caution, the said John Woodbery not being present to acknowledge his act there in: 27: 4: 1671. **Signed**: John Woodbery; **Witnesses**: E. Cooke, Notary Public, Edward Hancock, servant to said Notary; **Recorded**: 27: 4: 1671. Therein said John Woodbery is become & standeth bound to said John Williams, in sum of 120 pounds with condition 4 pounds 10 shillings in manner before expressed.

SAMUEL BALCH to JOHN WILLIAMS – (3:376) Samuel Balch of Beverly, son of Benjamin Balch late of Salem & now of Beverly (aged 19 or thereabouts) testifieth & saith that on the 28th of June last past, John Foot of Boston, by virtue of a letter or attorney and a mortgage, which he showed them was forfeited to John Williams of Bristol by John Woodbery, took possession for the use of said John Williams, of about 40 acres of land near Bass river in New England & adjoining as Samuel Balch & William Jones informed him to certain lands of Benjamin Balch late of Salem & now of Beverly, on the E side & to certain other lands in possession of Henry Herrick of the same place, husbandman, on the W wide…and saith that the abovesaid John Foot drove a stake into the ground marked I W 1671 within or about 2 pole of a stake which bounds the land of his father Benjamin Balch…Zachary Herrick (carpenter of Beverly) cut down timber…29: 4: 71; **Recorded**: 30 June 1671.

MATHEW BARTON – (3:377) [same parcel of land in 2 previous statements] Mathew Barton aged about 32 years of Salem (mariner), testified that on 28 June last past, John Foot (merchant) of Boston…by virtue of a letter of attorney and mortgage, which he showed them was forfeited to John Williams of the city of Bristol, England (merchant) by John Woodbery, took possession for the use of said John Williams, all the parcel of land or wood ground, containing 40 acres…and the said deponent testified and said that the aforesaid John Foot drove a stake into the ground marked E W 1671 within about 2 pole of a stake that bounds the land of Benjamin Balch and the land aforesaid, which lie the said John Foot took possession of. Taken on oath. **Signed**: 29: 4: 1671 by William Hathorne, Assistant; **Recorded**: 30 June: 71; No. 120.

GEORGE CORWIN to WILLIAM PITT; NATHANIEL ROBBINSON to WILLIAM PITT; WILLIAM BROWNE to Mr. PITT – (3:378) George Corwin having had former dealings with William Pitt acknowledged that he had received from said Pitt full satisfaction for 2 bills of 16 pounds which he had in his hands, and all other debts, dues and demands from the beginning of the world to this 29 December 1671. **Signed**: George Corwin.

Nathaniel Robbinson received 6th of October 1669 of Thomas Sowden, 4 quintalls of refuse fish, being in full of all accounts, between Mr. William Pitt and himself. **Signed**: Mr. Nathaniel Robbinson; **Witnesses**: John Corwin, Mr. Eleazor Hathorne, Mr. Phillip Cromwell and many others and their wives.

William Browne acknowledged himself fully satisfied by Mr. Pitt for bill and all other debts and demands, unto this 5th day of September 1671 and said he was satisfied in full. **Signed**: William Browne.

This was entered underneath a bill of 30 pounds under Mr. Pitt's hands, being fully satisfied. **Attested**: Hilliard Veren, Recorder.

JAMES STANDISH to WILLIAM PITTS – (3:378) On 29 October 1657, James Standish of Manchester in behalf & for the use & by the order of William Everton granted to William Pitts of Boston for "full satisfaction" 6 or 7 acres...3 acres of which were bought of Benjamin Parminter and the other 3 acres...given him by the townsmen of Manchester, joining Abraham Whitter's land...did sell and resign up to the said William Pitt. **Signed**: James Standish [by mark]; **Witnesses**: Pasco Foot & William Allen [by mark]; **Recorded**: 3 July: 1671. William Everton ratified sale by James Standish being in all about 11 acres as town book of Manchester appeareth 14 Dec 1657. **Signed**: William Everton; **Acknowledged**: by Everton that sale of land on other side by James Standish was with his consent, 27 July 1665.

JOSEPH BOWEN to WILLIAM BARTHOLOMEW – (3:380) On 20th of May 1671, Joseph Bowen (yeoman) of Marblehead granted to William Bartholomew (merchant) of Boston, for 105 pounds, land and house in Marblehead, bounded towards the S and SE by land of William Wood and towards the NE with a common way, and towards the N & W with land of William Pote. **Signed**: Joseph Bowen; **Witnesses**: James Halsey and William Howard; **Acknowledged**: 27 May 1671; **Recorded**: 27: 4: 1671.

JEFFREY MASSEY to JAMES BROWNE – (3:383) On 13: 5: 1671, Jeffrey Massey granted to James Browne, for 20 shillings, 10 rods of upland adjoining land of James Browne, to run from the partition post on a straight line about 14 rod, as it is now staked out, and from thence as the fence now stands, to the water side. **Signed**: Jeffrey Massey and James Browne; **Witnesses**: William Hathorne and Isaac Hide; **Acknowledged**: 13: 5: 1671; **Recorded**: 13: 5 mo: 1671.

Capt. THOMAS MARSHALL to OLIVER PURCHASE (Indenture) – (3:384) On 24 April 1665, an indenture was made between Capt. Thomas Marshall of Lynn, with Rebecca, his wife, surrendering her thirds, and Oliver Purchase of Lynn, for a valuable consideration, for 2 parcels of

upland ground and a house in Lynn containing 40 acres, 20 in each parcel, one on which said house stands bounded by a highway that goes by Henry Collin's land to Marblehead, E by land once old Farr's (deceased), S by land of said Farr; W by land of Henry Collins, Jr. the other parcel lying unfenced, being 20 acres as it was formerly laid out, bounded S with land of Josiah Witter, E by a run or small brook, N with the common to Mr. King's land, W with the highway that goes to Marblehead. **Signed**: Thomas Marshall and Rebecca Marshall [by mark]; **Witnesses**: Nehemiah Jewett and John Bull; **Acknowledged**: 9: 6 mo: 1665. Edward Richards has paid unto Oliver Purchase 160 pounds for the land contained in the above writing, a good part of it in cash and the rest equivalent to cash.
"Oliver Purchase of Lynn, do assign and pass over unto Edward Richards of Lynn and his Executors and Assigns, this deed as it is made by Capt. Thomas Marshall unto me, and the land that is herein contained in every part, as witness by hand this 14th day of the 4th month 1669." **Signed**: 14: 4 mo: 1669 by Oliver Purchase; **Witnesses**: Nehemiah Jewett and John Bull; **Recorded**: 27: 4: 1671.

SAMUEL BENNETT to GEORGE KEASAR – (3:387) On 19: 1 mo: 1649, Samuel Bennett granted to George Keaser for 4 pounds, 5 shillings, ground that Samuel Bennett did buy of Joseph Armitage, from before Goodman Potter's door up to Goodman Newell's property on both sides of the Mill River…but Samuel Bennett is to have clay to make so much brick as will make a stack of chimneys for Samuel Bennett's house. Moreover, Samuel Bennet is to have all the propriety of the river for fishing and for the free passage of the water, and this 4 pounds to be paid in a heifer, but if Samuel Bennett does not build his chimney himself for his own use, then he is not to have the clay. **Signed**: Samuel Bennett; **Witnesses**: Richard Haven and Richard Greene; **Acknowledged**: 12: 5 mo: 1671.

MARY HILLIARD to THOMAS MAULE – (3:388) On 20 October 1670, Mary Hilliard of Salem (administratrix of Job Hilliard) granted to Thomas Maule of Salem (tailor) for a valuable sum, a parcel or strip of land, lying on the west side or adjoining to a parcel of land Thomas Maule formerly bought of Job Hilliard in Salem, said strip being 5 foot in breadth and seventy-one foot in length, and is bounded on the E with land of said Thomas, on S & W with land of said Mary on the N with the lane or street. **Signed**: Mary Hilliard; **Witnesses**: Henry Bartholomew, Henry Skerry, Sr.; **Acknowledged**: 17: 5: 1671; **Recorded**: 20: 5: 1671.

ANTIPAS MAVERICK to MOSES MAVERICK – (3:389) On 16 December 1663, Antipas Maverick of Kittery, York County, stood indebted to Moses Maverick of Marblehead, for 4 score and 10 pounds, to be paid in merchantable dry codfish, refuse fish, boards or barrel staves, to be paid at Marblehead at or upon the twenty-fourth day of June next after the date hereof...and for true performance of above, made over the house and land in Kittery in York County, and whereas Antipas Maverick has formerly made a deed of bargain and sale of said house and land bearing date of 8 August 1661, unto one Thomas Booth for 520 pounds to be paid according to the expressions of the deed that if said Booth doth hold the said house and land then said Antipas Maverick does promise to surrender the said deed unto said Moses Maverick...& it is also agreed between the parties that if it so fails out, that the said Moses Maverick doth sell said house and land, then said Moses is to pay himself with all damages.,.. what remains said Moses is to return unto said Antipas. **Signed**: Antipas Maverick; **Witnesses**: Francis Johnson, Samuel Ward; **Acknowledged**: 16: 10: 1663; **Recorded**: 25 July 1671.

EDMOND BATTER and ELLENOR ROBINSON to WILLIAM SHAW – (3:391) On 21 May 1669, Edmond Batter of Salem (Executor of the Last Will & Testament of John Robbinson deceased) & Ellenor relict of said John Robbinson, granted to William Shaw of Salem (planter) for 25 pounds sterling, a parcel of land containing 40 acres in Salem, bounded ENE with land of Michael Shaflin, W with the farm that was formerly Mr. Emanuel Downing's, S with the land of Robert Stone. **Signed**: Edmond Batter & Ellenor Robinson [by mark]; **Witnesses**: Hilliard Veren, John Porter; **Acknowledged**: 6: 5: 1671; **Recorded**: 28: 5: 1671.

WILLIAM LORD, Jr. to THOMAS MAULE – (3:392) On 7 August 1671, William Lord, Jr. of Salem (planter) granted to Thomas Maule of Salem (tailor) for a valuable sum, a parcel of land in Salem, containing 14 or 15 rod as it now lies, being part of the land adjoining to the dwelling house of said William Lord, bounded E with ground of John Mason, and butts N against the street where it is about 35 feet in breadth and runs backward to the south end of William Lord's now dwelling house, and from thence by a straight line to the land of John Neale which bounds it on the W & runs to a parcel of ground sold to Thomas Flint & a parcel sold to John Porter, Sr. which bounds that part of the premises N & Thomas Flint's parcel also partly bounding said bargained premises to the W. **Signed**: William Lord, Jr.; **Witnesses**: Hilliard Veren, William Downton; **Acknowledged**: 7: 6 mo: 1671; **Recorded**: 18: 7: 1671.

ABRAHAM COOK to WILLIAM NORTON (Letter) – (3:394) Falmouth in Cornwall, 2nd May 1652. Good Brother: You have I hope received my letter from the Canaries in November last, for advice [on] your bill upon Mr. Cooke for 175 pounds is paid & in my absence my man has paid me out of it that money which you did owe me per bond, & for 1 piece of mixed searge, which together does amount unto 150 pounds so I do remaine with 25 pounds of yours in my hand, which I shall pay for you to Capt. Andrews, so what you more owe him, you must take care of. I do here enclosed send you back your bill of exchange upon Mr. Stephen Estwick, who you know denied payment of it at your last being at London & so doth still with absolute refusal, saying that he neither hath nor expect to have the drawers estate in his hands for to pay with so that if you have not already, you must require satisfaction in New England with damages of 30 percent, a little enough for this forbearance. Myself and wife salute you & your wife. I have now a 3d son, so wishing you health & happiness & myself out of my trouble (which I hope for) I respt. your affectionate brother to serve you. Thomas Norton.

London, 5 May 1653. To my very lo. brother Mr. William Norton these present in Ipswich: New England. Mr. William Norton. Brother.
I wrote you in November 1651 from the Canaries & several letters since my return into England but of neither have I rec'd any answer, & in the first I advised of the acceptance of Mr. Abraham Cooke's bill for 175 pounds sterling & in the latter of the payment & at this time had not wrote, but by the entreaty of the said Mr. Cooke to advise you once more that the bill of 175 pounds is received by me & accordingly I have given you credit in your account currant & for the over plus which is in my hands more than what will satisfy me my debt, by your bond of 140 pounds 1 piece of searge, money paid Mr. Bond for you at as he & I have settled some difference betwixt us, which will suddenly be done, but take notice that the overplus will be but a small sum, thereof if (not already done) you must provide another way for his further satisfaction and in all the forementioned letters I informed that your 70 pound bill upon Mr. Stephen Estwick (now Alderman) was not accepted nor like to be, thereof I hope you have recovered the value with damages of the drawer, so with my kind salutations to yourself and my sister, I remaine, your very loving brother Thomas Norton. To my very loving brother Mr. William Norton, these dated in New England.

JOHN HIGGINSON, Sr. to Capt. THOMAS SAVAGE – (3:396) On 25 Nov 1670, John Higginson, Sr. of Salem, with wife Sarah releasing her thirds, granted to Capt. Thomas Savage of Boston (merchant) for 25 pounds sterling, a parcel of land containing 6 acres lying upon the neck so-called, adjoining and lying on the E of the town of Salem and given by the inhabitants of the said town to said John Higginson in 1661 as by the town records appears, and is bounded W and S with land formerly Mordecai Craford's now the land of Capt. Thomas Savage, E with the sea and N with common land. **Signed**: John Higginson, Sr. & Sarah Higginson [by mark]; **Witnesses**: Hilliard Veren, Nathaniel Higginson; **Acknowledged**: 2: 9 mo: 1671; **Recorded**: 11: 10: 1671.

THOMAS SAVAGE, Sr. to JOHN HALE – (3:398) On 21 September 1671, Thomas Savage, Sr. of Boston (merchant), with wife Mary Savage who released dower, granted to John Hale of Beverly (clerk) for 43 pounds, 20 acres of land in Beverly near the Cedar stand, bounded E by John Sallow's lot and N by another piece of John Sallow's land, where it meets Thomas Pigdin's side line and so on the W bounded partly by Thomas Pigdin's and partly by John Gally's and S by the river, which land was mortgaged and sold by Mordecai Craford (and Judith his wife) and John Pride (their son) unto Thomas Savage. **Signed**: Thomas Savage, Sr. & Mary Savage; **Witnesses**: Ephraim Savage, Perez Savage; **Acknowledged**: 21 Sept 1671; **Recorded**: 23: 7 mo: 1671.

ABRAHAM ALLEN to WILLIAM BROWNE, Sr. (Mortgage) – (3:400) On 30 June 1671, Abraham Allen of Marblehead (blacksmith) mortgaged to William Browne, Sr. of Salem, for 75 pounds 12 shillings, 11½ pence, payment to be well paid unto William Browne, Sr. of Salem on or before the first of June next ensuing 1672, in good merchantable dry codfish at Marblehead and for the good and sure performance hereof Abraham Allen does bind over and mortgage his now dwelling house and shop in Marblehead and ground belonging to them, standing near a new shop Mr. Riddan now possesses, and by Mr. Francis Johnson's dwelling house and by Mr. Samuel Ward's to the NE of it, but if the said Allen shall pay the sum of 75 pounds, 12 shillings, 11½ pence, according to the condition above written, then this mortgage is to be void. **Signed**: Abraham Allen; **Witnesses**: John Appleton, Nathaniel Mighill; **Acknowledged**: 30: 4 mo: 1671; **Recorded**: 26: 7 mo: 1671.

WILLIAM HATHORNE to JOHN ROADES – (3:401) On 16: 11 mo: 1664, William Hathorne of Salem, with wife yielding her thirds, granted to John Roades, for 21 pounds, 10 shillings, a house, orchard and garden with about 1 acre of land...which he bought of John Clement of Marblehead, bounded N with the lane, E and S with the common, W with the land of John Gatchell. **Signed**: William Hathorne; **Witnesses**: Moses Marverick, John (___): **Acknowledged**: 16: 11 mo: 1664; **Recorded**: 24: 8: 1671.

Mr. PEPIN (Invoice) – (3:402) On 27 August 1671, a Mr. Pepin recorded an invoice he had prepared consisting of what he had put aboard the ketch *Speedwell*, for his particular account: 8½ dozen hats at 48 pounds the dozen (408...), 6½ dozen hats at 36 pounds per dozen (234...) for the custom and charges of same (34...) Total: 676 pounds. For half a hundred of salt and the charges (153...) Total 829 pounds. In case there will be 14½ dozen hats, Mr. Turner will be discharged of the ½ dozen that Mr. Pepin has put more in this present account in the bill of lading. In case Mr. Turner come again in this country, I intreat him to make my return of the above goods in fish for Bilbo and in case he should undertake some other voyage, until the next summer with the said catch, I consent that he should carry the same goods along with him to advance it in the Marlen. **Signed**: 27 August 1671.

RICHARD MOORE to WILLIAM FLINT – (3:403) On 21: 7ber, 1658, Richard Moore of Salem (mariner), granted to William Flint of Salem (husbandman) for 6 pounds, a ten-acre lot, formerly John Talebyes, lying in the south field, butting on the harbor to the E and the salt marsh near Castle Hill to the W, the land of Henry Harwood to the S and land of Thomas Browning to the N. **Signed**: Richard Moore; **Witnesses**: William Hathorne, Anna Hathorne; **Acknowledged**: 5: 8 mo: 1671; **Recorded**: 30: 8 mo: 1671.

Capt. WALTER PRICE and JOHN TURNER – (3:404) On 9 May 1668, a list of debts received from Mr. John Turner for the account of Capt. Walter Price and Company: Stephen Bank's bill for 6274 pounds sugar; John Killecott's bill for 3800 pounds sugar, Samuel Aspane's bill for 570 pounds sugar. Total: 10644 pounds sugar. The above mentioned, acknowledged to have received, 9 May 1668, Evan Morgan.

RICHARD MOORE to WILLIAM BROWNE, Jr. – (3:404) On 27 September 1671, Richard Moore of Salem (mariner), with wife Christian yielding thirds, granted to William Browne, Jr. of Salem, for 30 pounds sterling, a parcel of land, half an acre, or 80 rod or pole of ground, lying in length N & S 20 rod, and in breadth E & W throughout 4 rod... in the town of Salem... bounded N by the street, W with land of Joseph Porter, S with land of George Keasar, and E with land of Joshua Ward, and land formerly of Samuel Archard, Sr. and land formerly Thomas Barnes'... only the said Browne does engage to and with said Moore that he shall have a sufficient way through the length of the ground for a cart to pass through. **Signed**: Richard Moore and Christian Moore [by mark]; **Witnesses**: Richard Prince, Edward Grove; **Acknowledged**: 2: 8 mo: 1671; **Recorded**: 1: 9: 1671.

CHRISTOPHER LATTAMORE to JOHN PETHERICK – (3:407) On 17 October 1673, Christopher Lattamore of Marblehead, with wife Mary freely giving her rights, granted to John Petherick of Marblehead (fisherman) for a valuable sum, 2 acres of land, on Marblehead neck, which 2 acres is part of the 8 acres of land bought by Mr. William Pitt from John Coyte, and is bounded W with the other six acres, E with common land, N with the harbour, at which end it is 10 pole broad, and so to run the same breadth 32 pole long. **Signed**: Christopher Lattamore [by mark] and Mary Lattamore; **Witnesses**: Hilliard Veren, Christopher

Walen, William Pitt, John Furbush; **Acknowledged**: 28: 6 mo: 1671; **Recorded**: 6: 9 mo: 1671.

JOHN ROBINSON to NATHANIEL INGERSON – (3:409) On 20 March 1670/71, John Robinson of Topsfield (husbandman) granted to Nathaniel Ingerson of Salem (yeoman) for 30 pounds sterling, a parcel of meadow containing 10 acres, lying in Rowley village...that piece of meadow lately bought of John Gould and bounded E with a white oak tree, and over to a stake that parts the meadow of John Gould and the 10 acres, and otherwise bounded with the upland of said John Gould. **Signed**: John Robinson; **Witnesses**: Hilliard Veren, Sr. and Samuel Williams; **Acknowledged**: 25: 1 mo: 1671; **Recorded**: 10: 9: 71.

ANDREW WOODBURY to WALTER WHITFIELD – (3:411) On 12 October 1668, Andrew Woodbury of Salem (mariner), with wife Mary yielding thirds, granted to Walter Whitfield of Salem (fisherman) for 50 pounds, a dwelling house with about ½ acre of ground adjoining, being enclosed, containing an orchard and garden in Salem...bounded S by the highway against the south harbour, E with land of Edward Hilliard, N with land of Andrew Woodbury and W with ground of Mathew Nixon. **Signed**: Andrew Woodbury & Mary Woodbury [by mark]; **Witnesses**: Hilliard Veren, Sr., Hilliard Veren, Jr.; **Acknowledged**: 14: 9 mo: 1671; **Recorded**: 15: 9 mo: 1671.

JOHN WEBB to JAMES FROUDE – (3:413) On 18 November 1671, John Webb of Salem granted to James Froude of Salem (seaman) for 45 shillings, a parcel of land containing ¼ acre...being 1/3 of that parcel of land of John Webb, John Tapley, and Robert Bray, lately bought of John Mason, as per deed of 28 June 1669, the said third not yet divided from the other two thirds, situated in Salem, at the entrance of the neck, bounded E with land of John Mason, S and W with the highway and common land and N with the salt water. **Signed**: John Webb and John Tapley; **Witnesses**: John Tapley, Hillyard Veren, Sr.; **Acknowledged**: 18: 9ber; 1671; **Recorded**: 21: 9 mo: 1671.

THOMAS WHEELER to JOHN BALLARD – (3:414) On 26 October 1666, Thomas Wheeler of Lynn (husbandman), with wife yielding up her thirds, granted to John Ballard of Salem (for the space of 3 years), for 230 pounds, a dwelling house in Lynn, with water, mill stones, wheels etc. and all the working gears...with a mill house, barns and outhouses, garden and orchard, with a lot of land adjoining...by estimation 5 acres...bounded W with land of George Keasar, E with the town highway on the lane that goes by John Newhall's, butting S on land of John Tarbox and widow Fraile, and N on the highway that goes to the mill and also a piece of land adjoining the mill and lane to the NW, being given by the town, bounded by the fence as it now stood, entered in the grant from the town or selectmen with all the fences, timber, wood, trees, on the said land with all dams, flood gates, sluices, water and water courses belonging thereunto. Added: This witnesses that Thomas Wheeler has granted to John Ballard, 2 lots of salt meadow in the lower division of Rumney Marsh for the space of 3 years from the day of the date hereof, as lying to this within lease or deed for so long being satisfied for, as witness my hand this 26 of Oct 1666. **Signed**: Thomas Wheeler; **Acknowledged**: 31: 8 mo: 1666. **Signed**: Thomas Wheeler; **Witnesses**: John Breed, John Hathorne; **Acknowledged**: 31: 8 mo: 1666 by Thomas Wheeler; **Recorded**: 12: 10 mo: 1671.

JAMES HAGG to JOHN UPTON – (3:418) On 22 November 1671, James Hagg of Salem (planter) granted to John Upton of Salem (farmer) for 20 pounds, 40 acres in Salem bounded W & N with lands of Lieut. George Gardner and the said John Upton and John Robbinson, Richard Hollingworth and John Tomkins, and E with the farm of Joseph Pope, deceased. **Signed**: James Hagg [by mark]; **Witnesses**: Hilliard Veren, Sr., John Procter; **Acknowledged**: 27: 9 mo: 1671; **Recorded**: 14: 10: 1671.

JOHN BUTTOLPH to THOMAS GARDNER – (3:420) On 14 September 1671, John Buttolph of Boston granted to Thomas Gardner of Salem and Hannah his wife, for 112 pounds, a parcel of land and dwelling house in Salem, of 14 poles, bounded S with the street or lane that goes from the meeting house to the field and training place, on the W and N with land of Joseph Gardner and E with land of Samuel Gardner. **Signed**: John Buttolph and Hannah, his wife, who released dower rights; **Witnesses**: John Higginson, Jr., Israel Porter; **Acknowledged**: 14 Sept 1671; **Recorded**: 16: 10 mo: 1671.

THOMAS PERLY to JOHN RUCK – (3:423) On 7 December 1671, Thomas Perly of Rowley (farmer) granted to John Ruck of Salem (merchant) for 60 pounds sterling, one-sixteenth part of the Bloomery or Iron Works, newly erected in Rowley village, with the 16th part of all the housing, buildings, water-works, dams, water courses, lands, woods, timber, tools, instruments, with all the stack of coal & provisions of every kind that belongs or appertaines to the said works...the said Bloomery or Iron Works now in the possession or occupation of Henry Leonard. **Signed**: Thomas Perly; **Witnesses**: Hilliard Veren, Sr., Dorcas Veren; **Acknowledged**: 8: 10 mo: 1671; **Recorded**: 30: 10: 1671.

HENRY HERRICK, Sr. to PETER WOODBURY & WILLIAM RAIMENT – (3:426) On 26 October 1668, Henry Herrick, Sr. of Salem (yeoman), with wife Edith Herrick, who yielded up thirds, granted to Peter Woodbury of Salem & William Raiment of Salem for 40 pounds sterling, about 12 acres of land, being all the parcel of land he lately bought or had of John Leach, by way of exchange, situated on the Bass River side, belonging to Salem, bounded S with land of said William Raiment, E with county highway, W and N by particular lands or highways. **Signed**: Henry Herrick and Edith Herrick; **Witnesses**: Hilliard Veren, Sr., William Dounton; **Acknowledged**: 10: 9 mo: 1668.

RICHARD WATERS to WILLIAM PUNCHARD – (3:427) On 4: 7: 1671, Richard Waters, Sr. of Salem, with consent of wife Joyce Waters, granted to Abigail, daughter, wife of William Punchard, as her jointure with him during her life, land and part of the hill toward the NW side of the hill of their grant, as it is now partly fenced & partly staked out unto them, beginning at a stake at the upper end of the cross fence between the said Richard Waters' to the said William Punchard running upon a straight line 3½ poles unto a stake that stands 13 feet from the S corner of the house of said William Punchard & SE and from the stake SW by W, to an old stump of a tree under the stone wale, which is about 3 pole & 4 feet from the last aforesaid stake & from the aforesaid old stump of a tree round about the fence NW next the common & of Humfry Woodbery's ground yet unfenced which is about 9 poles by 7 foot until it comes to the lower part of the cross fence between the said Richard Waters & William Punchard, being the NW end & so to run up to the stake where it began..."as her joynture unto her husband William Punchard & they both jointly to have forever liberty to fetch & draw water at our well, so long as they or any of them shall contribute to the charges of the well as others of our children provided that whensoever any fence shall be set up from my garden at the furthmost end of my brew house to the waterside, that then they shall come in at such a gate or stile & place as shall be thought most convenient for all out of that highway that we have granted unto them all, & so to return the same way again without doing any damage & if any damage be done by neglect of leaving open any such gate or breaking any such stile where the coming in or going out shall be, they that are the cause of the neglect shall make good the damage to said Richard Waters..." **Signed**: Richard Waters and Joyce Waters [by mark]; **Witness**: John Cromwell; **Acknowledged**: 4: 9: 1671.

RICHARD WATERS to EZEKIEL WATERS (3:430) On 24 October 1671, Richard Waters of Salem, with consent of wife Joyce Waters, granted to son Ezekiel Waters of Salem, "all the part of their house frame at the easternmost end, square from the back of our chimney and the ground it standeth on & adjoining to it, as is hereafter expressed, from the northernmost side of the highway next to water side entrance into our ground, to run to the end of the stone fence by the water side, which is 7 poles, 2 foot, and thence to turn and run one pole and a half to three foot westward by the rail fence and from thence back again to the outside of the chimney back of said Richard Waters' being about 4½ poles in length to the said back, thence straight along through the house by the chimney back, straight before the part of the house of said Ezekiel Waters, butting to the N side of the highway that I have laid out in my ground for common use of myself and my children. Excepted Ezekiel Waters nor any under him shall neither let or sell any part of the aforesaid...during the life of Richard or Joyce Waters without their consent...& liberty to draw and fetch water from the well as long as he contributes to the charges of the well...equally as other of our children, provided whensoever any fence shall be from my garden at the southernmost end of my brew house. Also, for his pains & work in helping us from the time that he was 21, my bellows belonging to the smith's trade, the anvil, the 3 vices and all the files and punches and hammers and all the smither tools I have with all the stoking tools belonging to that employment, only reserving my own free use for all of them as long as I shall live." **Signed**: Richard Waters & Joyce Waters [by mark]; **Witnesses**: Edward Hilliard, Christopher Babidge.

RICHARD ADAMS to WILLIAM BROWNE, Jr. – (3:432) On 3 November 1671, Richard Adams of Salem (planter) granted to William Browne, Jr. of Salem, for 7 pounds in silver, ¾ acre of salt marsh in the south field, abutting E the land of said Browne, and S with salt marsh of Joseph Hardy, W with the river and N with salt marsh of Mr. Joseph Grafton; **Signed**: Richard Adams; **Witnesses**: Richard Prince, John Turner; **Acknowledged**: 9: 11: 1671; **Recorded**: 16: 11 mo: 1671.

JOHN ROBINSON to SAMUEL EBORNE (or ABORN) – (3:434) On 16 May 1671, John Robinson of Topsfield (planter) granted to Samuel Eborn (or Aborn) of Salem for a valuable sum, one acre, 20 pole of upland, formerly a grant to Zacheus Curtice by the town of Salem, and the other 20 pole bought by said Curtice from Joshua Veren, there being an old cellar dug in the said 20 rod, the said one acre, 20 rod of land lying near the farm formerly Mr. Batter's and Mr. Johnson's farms, and is bounded W with the brooke (called Brooksby), N on common land, N with or near a parcel of land of Hilliard Veren; also a parcel more, being all the meadow that lies SW above land formerly Mr. Clark's meadow, now Mr. Gedney's, N with Dog Pond plaine and Mr. Humphry's farm or near SW, the said parcel of meadow or lowland being given to said Zacheus Curtice formerly by the town of Salem, containing about 20 acres. **Signed**: John Robinson; **Witnesses**: Walter Price, Hilliard Veren; **Acknowledged**: 17: 3: 1671; **Recorded**: 16: 11 mo: 1671.

THOMAS JEGGLES, Sr. to JOHN TURNER – (3:436) On 5 June 1671, Thomas Jegles, Sr. of Salem (mariner) attorney of Nathaniel Sharp (mariner) of Salem, with Rebecka Sharp yielding her thirds granted to John Turner of Salem (mariner) for 20 pounds, a parcel of land containing 106 and ½ pole of land belonging and adjoining the house of Nathaniel Sharp, bounded E with land of said Sharp, S on land of Hannah Sharp, W with the lane formerly called William's Lane and with land of Christopher Phelps. **Signed**: Thomas Jeggles; **Witnesses**: Philip Cromwell, Thomas Cromwell; **Acknowledged**: 11: 10: 1671; **Recorded**: 5: 12: 1671.

MOSES MAVERICK to RICHARD REETH (REITH) – (3:437) On 18 January 1668, Moses Maverick of Marblehead (merchant), with wife Eunice yielding thirds, granted to Richard Reeth of Marblehead (fisherman), for 9 pounds, one quarter of one acre of land in Marblehead between land of Mr. William Waltham and land of said Moses Maverick on the E, with land of Mr. Francis Johnson on the W, and said Waltham's land on the S. **Signed**: Moses Maverick & Eunice Maverick; **Witnesses**: Samuel Maverick and Samuel Leach; **Acknowledged**: 1: 1 mo: 1668/9; **Recorded**: 6: 12: 1671.

MATHEW WOODWELL to ROBERT NOWELL – (3:440) On 15 November 1671, Mathew Woodwell of Salem, with wife Mary yielding thirds, granted to Robert Nowell of Salem (shipwright) for 35 pounds, 5 shillings, a parcel of ground in Salem, on part whereof the dwelling house and outhousing of said Robert Nowell now stood, the said land being 16 pole long and 3 pole wide...bounded N on land of Mr. Eleazer Gedney, S with the mill cove pond, E on land of said Mathew Woodwell, W by land of said Mathew...with benefit and privilege of a highway to his house, egress and regress free forever...said Robert setting up and maintaining one half of the fence against the highway between the said Woodwell and him. **Signed**: Mathew and Mary Woodwell; **Witnesses**: Richard Croade, William Hathorne, Jr.; **Acknowledged**: 12: 9: 1671; **Recorded**: 7: 12: 1671.

MATHEW WOODWELL to JOHN ANDREWS – (3:442) On 30 January 1671, Mathew Woodwell of Salem (brickmaker) with wife Mary releasing dower, granted to John Andrews of Salem (shipwright) for 27 pounds, 5 shillings sterling, a parcel of land containing 70 rod, in Salem, near the corn mill, on the South river, bounded E and S by said river and mill pond, except a highway for the town's use to the said Mill and over the bridge into the south field, along by the water side, N by the land of Mathew Woodwell as the stakes now stand and W with land of Robert Nowell; also the priviledge of highway laid out of one pole broad on the N end of the land of said Mathew Woodwell and Robert Nowell's ground and so to turn at the NE corner of said Newell's ground, and to S with land of said John Andrews, which said highway is allowed by said Mathew for free use of him. **Signed**: Mathew & Mary Woodwell; **Witnesses**: Hilliard Veren, Sr., John Price, Robert Newell; **Acknowledged**: 5: 12: 1671; **Recorded**: 22: 12: 1671.

ELISHA KEBEE to ISAAC COOKE – (3:445) **Recorded**: 22: 12: 1671, Elisha Kebbee of Salem (joiner) granted to Isaac Cooke of Salem (husbandman) for a valuable sum, 20 acres in Salem, bounded E by land of John Smale, W by land of John Will, S by land of William Browne, N by the farm commonly called Mr. Downing's farm, 3 neat cattle, one house and 9 swine…[postscript]…3 acres of fresh marsh, bounded on one side with marsh of Thomas Robbins and Henry Reynolds on the other side. **Signed**: Elisha Kebee; **Witnesses**: Hilliard Veren, Sr., Samuel Williams; **Acknowledged**: 23: 12: 1671.

SAMUEL GARDNER to SAMUEL ROBBINSON – (3:446) On 26 February 1671, Samuel Gardner of Salem (mariner), with wife Mary releasing dower, granted to Samuel Robbinson of Salem (tailor) for a valuable consideration, 16 pole or rod of land on which stands the dwelling house of said Robinson, in Salem, bounded N with the lane that leads to the pound, W with land formerly sold by Samuel Gardner to Samuel Simonds, S and E with land of said Samuel Gardner now in his possession…to build a good and sufficient fence of 5 foot high either of stones, boards or poles, and so close that poultry cannot creep through, and in defect thereof more than 48 hours after warning given, the said Robinson…shall pay or cause to be paid to said Gardner one shilling a day for every day the fence shall be down or not be so maintained. **Signed**: Samuel Gardner and Mary Gardner; **Witnesses**: Samuel Williams, Hilliard Veren, Sr.; **Recorded**: 29: 12: 1671.

Major WILLIAM HATHORNE and JOHN PORTER to JOSEPH PORTER and ANNA HATHORNE (Agreement) – (3:449) On 2 January 1664, in a marriage contract between Joseph Porter (son of John) and Anna Hathorne (daughter of the Major), Major Hathorne promised to give in marriage, 50 pounds within two years after the day of his daughter's marriage. John Porter promised to give his son that farm known by the name of Downing's farm, consisting of uplands and meadow…with half an acre of land in the town, near to George Keaser's on the day of his marriage…also the said John Porter to give to his said son Joseph Porter, 50 pounds to be paid in horses, neat cattle, hides, cider, and some corn and some money, within one year after the day of marriage. Both children are to be satisfied with this agreement. **Signed**: William Hathorne and Joseph Porter. **Witnesses**: Edmond Batter, Hilliard Veren appeared bef. Samuel

Simonds & Daniel Denison 1 Dec 1671 and swore they were present and saw the agreement signed and delivered.

ROBERT STARR to RICHARD MOORE and PHILLIP CROMWELL – (3:451) On 30 September 1665, Robert Starr granted to Richard Moore and Phillip Cromwell (guardians to his three children), the dwelling house he lived in together with land belonging to it, which house and land was given him by his father-in-law Richard Hollingsworth as a portion with his wife. The house and lands were bequeathed to Capt. Richard More and Mr. Phillip Cromwell who were guardians to his three children—to have and hold the house and land for the use and benefit of his three children, Robert, Richard and Susanna...to be improved until they come of age according to law to receive it into their own hands & then they are to deliver the possession of it into hands of children, as long as they shall live & if any of them die before they be of age, then to those that do so long live...but if God should take them all away by death before they be of age...shall return to him. **Signed**: Robert Starr [by mark]; **Witnesses**: Francis Wainwright, Edward Woolland; **Acknowledged & Recorded**: 18 March 1671/72.

ROBERT STARR to MARY CONKLIN – (3:452) On 12 September 1669, Robert Starr of Salem (mariner) gave to Mary Conklin, his espoused wife, in consideration of marriage, all his household goods and moveables, with all that is now her own, which estate he freely gave unto her and to be at her disposal. **Signed**: Robert Starr [by mark]; **Witnesses**: James Smith, Nathaniel Felton; **Acknowledged**: 18 March 1671.

LOT CONANT to JOHN TREBBY – (3:453) On 20 March 1671, Lot Conant of Beverly (yeoman), with Elizabeth Conant yielding her thirds, granted to John Trebby of Marblehead (fisherman) for a valuable consideration, a dwelling house and ground adjoining and belonging to said house, containing about ¼ acre, containing the orchard and garden in Marblehead, bounded S by the highway, W on lands of Vinson Stilson, NW on land of Richard Hanaver, NE by marsh of Nathaniel Walton and SE by land of said Lot Conant. **Signed**: Lot Conant & Elizabeth Conant; **Witnesses**: Hilliard Veren, Sr., Francis Johnson; **Acknowledged**: 20: 2 month: 1671/2; **Recorded**: 20 March 1671.

JOHN BLACK, Sr. to JOHN BLACK, Jr. – (3:455) On 20 April 1670, John Black Sr. (husbandman), gave to his son John Black of Beverly, his house lot and orchard, lying in Beverly, on the W side of Capt. Lothrop's now dwelling house lot...except for 2 acres of land of the said lot he sets over to his son-in-law Isaac Davis...at the north end of his said lot next to John Sollace's ground, only the said John Black reserved for himself that his son and son-in-law should for his life, give him such rent as shall be thought convenient: proportionable to their parts of the said land ...further...John Black, Sr., set over to his son John Black, his 2 acres of meadow at Topsfield...in consideration whereof his son John Black was to pay him the full sum of 8 pounds in such things as said John Black, Sr. should stand in need of for his subsistence. **Signed**: John Black; **Witnesses**: John Sollas [by mark], Paul Thorndike, Mary Thorndike [by mark], Mary Woodbery [by mark]; **Acknowledged**: 20: 1 month: 1671/2; **Recorded**: 21: 1 month: 1671.

BRIDGETT VARNEY to BARTHOLMEW FOSTER – (3:456) On 6 May 1669, Bridget Varney of Gloucester (widow) granted to Bartholmew Foster of Gloucester, for considerable value, a parcel of land and house standing on it, the land containing about 3 acres...lying at the harbor, having the common on the NW side and the harbor and a neck of land on the SE in Gloucester. **Signed**: Bridgett Varney; **Witnesses**: John Emerson, Thomas Prince; **Acknowledged**: 9: 9 mo: 1669; **Recorded**: 10: 2: 1672.

ELEAZER HATHORNE to GEORGE CORWIN – (3:457) On 20 March 1671, Eleazer Hathorne of Salem granted to Abigail, wife, in consideration of a portion received with "my beloved wife Abigail, daughter of Capt. George Corwin," of Salem & also of a promise upon marriage made for a joynture, his dwelling house with ½ acre of land, bounded E with the town lane, S with land of Samuel Pitman, W with land of Samuel Pitman and Edward Grove, and N with the street; also a small parcel of land, bounded S with the river, E and N with the land of George Keaser, and W with Samuel and John Pitman's land; also 2 acres of land granted to him from the town, bounded S with land late of John Kenny (now in possession of one Holmes) E, N & W with the town common, all in Salem...and unto the children begotten betwixt them, their or either of their heirs for her joynture & dower. **Signed**: Eleazer Hathorne; **Witnesses**: John Corwin, Jonathan Corwin; **Acknowledged**: 25: 1 mo: 1672.

ISAAC DAVIS to JOHN BLACK – (3:459) On 6 December 1670, Isaac Davis of Beverly (husbandman) and Lidea Davis, who yielded her rights, granted to John Black, the younger, of Beverly (husbandman) for 8 pounds, 2 acres of land, part of that lot which John Black formerly possessed and lately alienated to John Black, the younger...bounded N on land of John Sallows, E with land of Capt. Lothrop, W with land of John Hill, and S with land of said John Black, to have and hold also the two acres of land alienated to him by said John Black, Sr. **Signed**: Isaac Davis and Lidia Davis; **Witnesses** Hilliard Veren, Sr., Henry West; **Acknowledged**: 12: 9 mo: 1671. **Recorded**: 15: 2: 1672.

SAMUEL ARCHAUD (for RICHARD WAIT) to RICHARD WAIT – (3:461) Samuel Archaud of Salem (Marshall) assignee of Richard Wait of Boston (Marshall) served an execution of Joseph Armitage against the estate of Mr. Adam Oatly, of 126 pounds, 10 shillings; the execution levied upon 3 acres of salt marsh in Lynn, on the house and land that Francis Ingalls lived in with all appurtenances, commonly called Sagamore Hill. It was levied in 1653 and for the valuation of house, land and appurtenances was chosen John Fuller, John Hathorne and Edward Richards, being sworn before Capt. Thomas Marshall. **Signed**: Samuel Archard, Marshall. "We, John Fuller and John Hathorne, being chosen to value a parcel of land, whereon Francis Ingalls lives, called Sagamore Hill, we say: the broken-up land at 40 shillings per acre, the unbroken land at 30 shillings per acre. As for the building and fencing, we understood that Mr. Dunsten was to allow Francis Ingalls that for what he erected, the rest was estimated in the land." **Signed**: 30 Nov 1658, John Fuller & John Hathorne. Samuel Archard, Marshall, when living, did declare to me that this was a real act and so did my brother John Hathorne; per me, William Hathorne, 2: 3 mo: 1670. **Recorded**: 16: 2 mo: 1672.

JOHN KNOWLES to JOHN BEX – (3:462) On 25 October 1651, John Knowles of Watertown granted to the Worshipful John Bex & Company for the iron works, for a good and valuable consideration, a parcel of land in Lynn containing by estimation 20 acres, adjoining the lands of Capt. Robert Bridges on the SE, and the ironworks and land belonging thereunto NE, formerly bought of Mr. Tomlins of Lynn. On 16 March 1655, John Gifford assigned the bill to Joseph Armitage, as his own proper estate forever, as being agent to Mr. John Bex and company; **Signed**: John Gifford; **Witnesses**: John Hathorne & Samuel Johnson. **Acknowledgement**: 24: 12 mo: 1671 by John Giffords. There is an assignment of the above bill by Armitage to Capt. Marshall, entered in the 4th book, page 261. **Signed**: John Knowles; **Witnesses**: William Osborne, William Aspinwall (Notary Public).

JOHN GRAFTON to THOMAS GARDNER – (3:463) On 22 August 1670, John Grafton of Salem (mariner) and Seeth his wife, granted to Thomas Gardner of Salem (cordwainer), for 10 pounds sterling, a parcel of land, containing about 26 rod or pole of ground, said parcel being 5 poles & 1 foot & half square on every side, lying in Salem, bounded with land lately sold by Christopher Babadge N, land of Thomas Browning W, land of John Grafton S, and the lane or highway laid out by Joseph Grafton. **Signed**: John Grafton and Seeth Grafton; **Witnesses**: Hilliard Veren, Sr. and Christopher Babadge; **Recorded**: 3 May 1672.

ISAAC and PASCA FOOT and ABIGAIL EARLY to ROBERT LEACH – (3:466) On 17 April 1672, Isaac and Pasca Foote and Abigail Early sold to Robert Leach of Manchester, for 30 pounds sterling, land in Manchester, which fell to them by virtue of their father, Pasca Foot, deceased, in his last will & testament, lying in several parcels, whether laid out or not, all whatsoever lands, uplands or meadows their said father died possessed of, or of right did belong to him, however it lies in Manchester. **Signed**: Isaac and Pasca Foot and Abigail Early; **Witnesses**: Dorcas Hicks and Hilliard Veren, Sr.; **Acknowledged**: 17: 12 mo: 1672.

ELIAS WHITE to THOMAS TAINER – (3:469) On 22 March 1671, Elias White of Marblehead (fisherman) granted to Thomas Tainer of Marblehead (fisherman), land in Marblehead which lay N or NE from Thomas Trainer's dwelling house, joining the cartway, said land about ¼ of an acre. Lane above named joined also Joshua Codner's house. **Signed**: Elias White; **Witnesses**: Henry Trevitt, Jonathan Gatchell, Jonathan Gatchell, Jr.; **Acknowledged**: 22 March 1671; **Recorded**: 4 June 1672.

JOHN GATCHELL, Sr. to THOMAS TAINER – (3:470) On 29 January 1671, John Gatchell, Sr. of Marblehead granted to Thomas Tainer (fisherman) of Marblehead, land in Marblehead, joining the east end of a parcel of land which John Gatchell, Sr. have now given to his son Thomas Gatchell (tailor), joining the back side of John's planting field. The land was surrendered firmly in the presence of Elias White, John Gatchell, Jr. and Jonathan Gatchell. **Signed**: John and Wibro Gatchell; **Witnesses**: John Hooper, John Clement [by mark], John Gatchell, Jr.; **Recorded**: 4: 4: 1672.

ELEAZER HATHORNE to RICHARD WHARTON – (3:471) Whereas by charter p'ty between Richard Wharton of Boston & Eleazer Hathorne of Salem bearing date 29 July 1671, Hathorne being owner of the catch *Unity*, let his catch *Unity* to freight to said Wharton for a voyage or voyages…the said vessel being not sufficiently calked and fitted according to the covenants of said contract, did in prosecution of her said voyage, spring a leak at sea, by occasion whereof, the merchants goods are much lost and damnified and the voyage diverted, the vessel by the occasion having met with such disaster as makes her without supplies and repairs unfit to proceed upon or perform the said voyage and where as by advice received from the master, and oath of the mate, one of the mariners, it is evident the said vessel is not utterly lost, but in a capacity to be repaired and proceed on her said voyage. The said Richard Wharton therefore demands of said Hathorne, in order to performance of said charter partly and for preservation of said vessel and such goods as remain of her lading, his speedy and effectual supply of carpenters and necessaries to refit the said vessel and preserve the goods, on order for said Wharton in this behalf who hearby tenders all needful supply and convenient dispatch for the preservation of said vessel and refitting her, to bring her to Boston and upon her arrival there said Wharton further tenders to fit her completely for the said voyage and freight her for the same or to discharge her utterly from said voyages and receive satisfaction for money already furnished upon the said voyage and for all supply of disbursements to be made in prosecution of this tender and damages sustained by any neglect or defect as judicious men independently chosen shall determine. **Signed**: Richard Wharton. Upon the request of Richard Wharton, the above written was published at the gate of Mr. Eleazer Hathorne, who stood in the street looking on but refused to hear attest. **Recorded**: 10 May 1672; **Signed**: Hilliard Veren and John Higginson, Jr.

BARTHOLOMEW GEDNEY to ANDREW BOWNE – (3:472) On 13 May 1672, Bartholomew Gedney (shipwright) of Salem granted to Andrew Bowne (mariner) of Stepney (co. Middlesex) London, England, now resident of Salem, for a valuable sum, the hull of a new ship called *Providence* of London, being of burthen about 140 ton, built and finished with all carpenters work according to the customs of builders in this country. **Signed**: Bartholomew Gedney; **Acknowledged**: 27: 3 mo: 1672; **Witnesses**: Hilliard Veren, Sr., John Higginson, Jr.; **Recorded**: 27: May: 1672.

ANDREW BOWNE to WILL ANTELBY – (3:473) On 16 May 1672, Andrew Bowne (mariner) of Stepney granted to William Antelby (merchant) & partner of London, for 197 pounds 11 shillings sterling, $1/8^{th}$ part of the ship *Providence* of London...of 140 ton...in the harbor of Salem...with $1/8^{th}$ part of her masts, sails, sailyards, anchors, cables, ropes, tackles, apparel, boat and furniture in any way belonging to the ship...to warrant and defend against all persons laying claim thereto, danger of the seas, fire and enemies only excepted. **Signed**: Andrew Bowne; **Acknowledged**: 3 May 1672; **Recorded**: 27 May 1672.

ANDREW BOWNE to GEORGE COLE – (3:475) On 15 May 1672, Andrew Bowne (mariner) of Stepney (Middlesex co.) England, granted to George Cole (merchant) of London, for 196 pounds 11 shillings, $1/8^{th}$ part of the ship *Providence* of London (same deed as previous one on page 473). **Signed**: Andrew Bowne; **Acknowledged**: 3 May 1672; **Recorded**: 27 May 1672; **Witnesses**: Hilliard Veren, Sr., John Higginson, Jr.

ANDREW BOWNE to EDWARD MERRYWEATHER – (3:477) On 15 May 1672, Andrew Bowne (mariner) of Stepney (Middlesex co.) England, granted to Edward Merryweather (merchant) of London, for 197 pounds 11 shillings sterling, 1/8th part of the ship *Providence* of London. **Signed**: Andrew Bowne; **Acknowledged**: 3 May 1672; **Witnesses**: Hilliard Veren, Sr., John Higginson, Jr.; **Recorded**: 27 May 1672.

ANDREW BOWNE to THOMAS BURCHETT – (3:478) On 15 May 1672, Andrew Bowne (mariner) of Stepney, granted to Thomas Burchett (merchant) of London for 197 pounds 11 shillings sterling, 1/8th part of the ship *Providence* of London. **Signed**: Andrew Bowne; **Acknowledged**: 3 May 1672; **Witnesses**: Hilliard Veren, Sr., John Higginson, Jr.; **Recorded**: 27 May 1672.

ANDREW BOWNE to GEORGE SHAW – (3:480) On 15 May 1672, Andrew Bowne (mariner) of Stepney, granted to George Shaw (merchant) of London, 1/8th part of the ship *Providence* of London. **Signed**: Andrew Bowne; **Acknowledged**: 3 May 1672; **Witnesses**: Hilliard Veren, Sr., John Higginson, Jr.; **Recorded**: 27 May 1672.

ANDREW BOWNE to THOMAS BODBY – (3:481) On 15 May 1672, Andrew Bowne (mariner) of Stepney, granted to Thomas Bodby (merchant) of London, for 197 pounds 11 shillings sterling, 1/8th part of the ship *Providence* of London. **Signed**: Andrew Bowne; **Acknowledged**: 3 May 1672; **Witnesses**: Hilliard Veren, Sr., John Higginson, Jr.; **Recorded**: 27 May 1672.

RICHARD WATERS to CLEMENT ENGLISH – (3:483) On 2 July 1671, Richard Waters of Salem, with consent of wife Joyce Waters, granted to Mary, their daughter, wife of Clement English as her joynture with him, during her life, all the land and part of the hill which their house now standeth on and so much as is contained within the bounds now staked out around their said house, viz: from the lower corner of the land to the fence of George Burch, next to the sea side adjoining unto it, 2 pole & 6 foot in length, lying next the seaside, & running N and W from the above said corner of the land to the fence of George Burch, and from the end of that 2 pole & 6 foot, it turneth upward one pole & a half and 8 foot from the hindermost corner of their house, and thence runneth 2 pole NW and S wanting 2 foot to another stake & from that stake it runneth with a straight line SW by S, 5 pole & 16 inches, being the utmost corner, and so turneth straight to the land of Robert Follett, being three pole in breadth, at that end & running SE and then turned again by the land of the said Robert Follett, 3 pole less 2 foot, NE to the land of George Burch & then strikes NW one pole & a half, by land of said George Burch, and then turned again by land of said George Burch & runs 4 pole wanting 2½ foot, ENE to the corner where it first began...liberty to fetch & draw water for their use at our well so long as they shall contribute to the charges...also they may use a gate or stile to enter the land and shall do no damage to the gate or stile or shall make good the damage. **Signed**: Richard Waters & Joyce Waters [by mark]; **Acknowledged**: 4: 9 mo: 1672; **Witnesses**: John Mascoll and John Steevens [by mark]; **Recorded**: 5: 4 mo: 1672.

JAMES SMITH to JOHN TURNER – (3:485) On 11 May 1672, James Smith (mariner) of Marblehead, with Mary Smith yielding her thirds, granted to John Turner (mariner) of Salem, for 50 pounds sterling, about 15 acres of upland and meadow in Salem at the head of the South river, called Castle Hill, bounded NE and E with land of Richard Howland, being at the SE end next to the widow Buffum at a red oak tree and from thence running NW nearest to a small walnut tree & from thence NE to a red oak stump and from thence NW to a white oak standing by the river side, bounded NW by the river over against Major William Hathorne's, SW partly with some salt marsh of Richard Rowlands and partly with the river, and to the SE with land of the widow Buffum. **Memorandum**: It is to be understood that the old house and barn standing on the premises is included in the above said bargain and sale and this entered before signing and sealing. **Signed**: James Smith & Mary Smith; **Witnesses** to John Smith's signing: Thomas Cromwell, Daniel Andrews, Hilliard Veren, Sr.; **Witnesses** to Mary's signing: Samuel Ward and Richard Reith.

ELIZABETH SPOONER to JOHN SIMPSON – (3:488) On 10 May 1672, Elizabeth Spooner of Salem granted to John Simpson for good causes and mature consideration, a piece of ground in Salem, upon which Simpson hath built a house and in which he now dwelleth, with the yard room and garden plot as it is now fenced in together, with the whole being about 12 pole of ground…that is to say 6 pole in length fronting to the street S, about 2 pole in breadth W, butting upon own land, about 6 pole in length N, likewise butting upon own land & 2 pole in breadth, E butting on land of John Durland. **Signed**: Elizabeth Spooner [by mark]; **Acknowledged**: 11: 3rd mo: 1672; **Witnesses**: Richard Croad, Hannah Ruck; **Recorded**: 5: 4: 1672.

ELIZABETH SPOONER to JOHN TRASK – (3:490) On 11 May 1672, Elizabeth Spooner (Administratrix of Thomas Spooner, deceased) of Salem granted to John Trask of Salem, for 7 pounds 10 shillings, 3 acres of land in the north field of Salem, bounded with salt marsh S and some land of said John Trask W, the land of said Elizabeth Spooner N and land of Samuel Gaskin E. **Signed**: Elizabeth Spooner [by mark]; **Acknowledged**: 11: 3 mo: 1672; **Witnesses**: William Hathorne, Jr., John Simpson; **Recorded**: 7: 4 mo: 1672.

ELEAZER GILES to JOHN SOUTHWICK – (3:492) On 22 May 1671, Eleazer Giles (husbandman) of Salem, with Sarah Giles who yielded thirds, granted to John Southwick (husbandman) of Salem, for 13 pounds sterling, 13 acres of land in Salem, bounded with land of John Giles N, land of Capt. Corwin E, land of said Eleazer Giles S, and with land of John King W...said John Southwick shall forever hereafter make and maintain ½ of the partition fence that parts the premises of the land of said Eleazer whether the said Southwick improve his land yea or no. **Signed**: Eleazer Giles and Sarah Giles [by mark]; **Acknowledged**: 22: 3 mo: 1671; **Witnesses**: Hilliard Veren, Sr. and Hilliard Veren, Jr.; **Recorded**: 7: 4 mo: 1672.

JOHN ROBBINSON to JOHN PORTER, Sr. – (3:495) On 20 February 1671, John Robbinson (husbandman) of Topsfield, with wife Dorothy yielding thirds, granted to John Porter, Sr. of Salem for a valuable sum, 70 acres of land in Salem, bounded on one side with land of George Gardner, on another side with land of Samuel Gardner, on another side with land of Richard Collinsworth, and the other side with land of John Rubton. **Signed**: John Robbinson [by mark] and Dorothy Robbinson [by mark]; **Acknowledged**: 21: 12 mo: 1671; **Witnesses**: Hilliard Veren, Sr., Henry Skerry, Sr. and William Rayment; **Recorded**: 7: 4: 1672.

JOHN PORTER, Sr. to JOHN ROBINSON – (3:497) On 20 February 1671, John Porter, Sr. (yeoman) of Salem, with wife Mary yielding thirds, granted to John Robinson (husbandman) of Topsfield, for a valuable sum in hand paid, 40 acres of land in Topsfield, late bought of Richard Richards, adjoining on one side to lands of William Nicholl, and on the other side to land of William Hobbs, and N with Topsfield land and S with land of Mr. John Ruck. **Signed**: John Porter, Sr., & Mary Porter [by mark]; **Acknowledged**: 21: 12 mo: 1672; **Witnesses**: Hilliard Veren, Sr., William Rayment and Henry Skerry, Sr. [no recording date]

THOMAS BOWING to WILLIAM ROBERTS and FRANCIS JOHNSON – (3:500) On 20 February 1671, Thomas Bowing of Marblehead, with wife Elizabeth yielding thirds, granted to William Roberts of Marblehead and to Francis Johnson of Marblehead, for a certain sum of money, all the house and orchard and 2 acres of land in Marblehead common near and adjoining unto the house and lands of John Norlay...as it now stands...bounded as aforesaid [no description of land]. William Roberts and Francis Johnson paid equal amounts and shared equally, and after decease of William Roberts and wife to Francis Johnson. **Signed**: Thomas Bowing [by mark] & Elizabeth Bowing [by mark]; **Acknowledged**: 17: 4 mo: 1672 & Elizabeth yielded thirds; **Witnesses**: Francis Johnson and Samuel Morgan; **Recorded**: 17: 4 mo: 1672.

MATHEW PRICE to GEORGE MAYE – (3:502) On 11 June 1672, Matthew Price (tailor) of Salem granted to George Maye (merchant) of Boston, for 10 pounds with other changes amounting to 20 shillings, all his dwelling house and garden of about 5 or 6 rods of land, upon part of which the house standeth, in Salem, bounded with the river near the cove N, with land of Joseph Miles E, with his own land S and with a lane or highway W…provided and agreed upon between said Price and said Maye that if said Matthew Price, his heirs and administrators do pay or cause to be paid to said George Maye, his executors, etc. the sum of 11 pounds current money of New England, at the dwelling house of said George Maye in Boston, at or before the 24th of June 1673, without fraud or delay, then this present deed shall be void…that until the said Mathew Price shall make default in payment of said sum of 11 pounds on the day & place for the payment his heirs and assignes may take and receive the rents and profits of the bargained premises…*Postscript*: it is agreed that the said Price shall pay 20 shillings for the said years forbearance over and above the aforesaid sum of 11 pounds and look what the said Price can get abated of the officers fees in point of execution, the said Maye shall abate out of said 20 shillings, in case the money be paid at the time abovesaid and further that the judgment is to continue & stand in force until the sum be satisfied. **Signed**: Matthew Price; **Acknowledged**: 10: 5: 1672 by Richard Bellingham, Governor; **Witnesses**: Robert Howard, Notary Public, and Mary Howard.

ABRAHAM WARREN to JOHN GREENS – (3:505) On 13 May 1672, Abraham Warren (husbandman) of Salem, with wife Mary releasing dower, granted to John Greens (husbandman) of Salem, for diverse good consideration and a valuable sum, one acre of land on the outside of the land of the said Abraham, at or near Bass river head in Salem, bounded SE with land of John Bachelor, NE, NW and SE with land of Abraham Warren; also ¼ acre of land on the outside of the land of said Abraham to the NW to the common land, to have the free liberty of a highway to the said ¼ acre for a cart at all times and also to the said acre of land from harvest that the fruits be taken in until seedtime and so from year to year, & liberty of a footway at all times. **Signed**: Abraham Warren [by mark]; **Acknowledged**: 18: 4: 1672; **Witnesses**: William Downton and Hillyard Veren, Sr.

JOHN GILES to JOHN TRASK – (3:508) On 11 Dec 1671, John Giles (husbandman) of Salem, with wife yielding thirds (11: 5: 1672), granted to John Trask of Salem, for a valuable consideration, 10 acres of upland in Salem, bounded NE and S with land of John Southwick. **Signed**: John Giles; **Acknowledged**: 11: 5: 1672; **Witnesses**: Edward Norice, Sr. and William Ropps; **Recorded**: 13: 5 mo: 1672.

WALTER PRICE to HILLIARD VEREN, Sr. – (3:509) On 9 July 1672, Walter Price (merchant and administrator of the estate of Theodore Price, deceased) granted to Hilliard Veren, Sr. of Salem for a valuable sum, the dwelling house in Salem in which the said Theodore Price dwelt in, with ½ acre of land adjoining, with barn or outhouses and fences …bounded with land of Joshua Rey W, land of Thomas Jigils N, house and land of Mr. Edward Norriss S **Signed**: Walter Price; **Acknowledged**: 9: 5: 1672; **Witnesses**: Hilliard Veren and John Price; **Recorded**: 13: 5: 1672.

JOHN HIGGINSON, Sr. to RICHARD RUSSELL – (3:511) On 18 August 1670, John Higginson, Sr. (Minister) of Salem, with wife Sara yielding thirds, granted to Richard Russell (gentleman) of Charlestown, for 30 pounds sterling, about 1 and ¾ acres of ground in Salem, near the common called the pen & is bounded with some land of Mr. William Browne SE, the common land on the SW, the land of Mr. John Gedney, Sr. on the NW and abutting against the cove that comes out of the North river NE. **Signed**: John Higginson, Sr. & Sara Higginson [by mark]; **Acknowledged**: 24: 6: 1670; **Witnesses** (to Mr. John Higginson): Mary Williams and Henry Veren, Sr.; **Recorded**: 28: 6: 1672.

JOHN COOK to THOMAS MAULE – (3:513) On 7 March 1671, John Cook (blacksmith) of Salem granted to Thomas Maule (tailor) of Salem for a valuable consideration, about 50 or 60 pole or rod of ground in Salem, bounded on the N with land of Joshua Rea, E with land of Theodore Price and W with the highway or lane…bounded on the S with land of Mr. Edward Norice. The premises were delivered by turf and twig 1:5:1672; **Witnesses**: William Lord, Sr. & Thomas Flint. **Signed**: John and Mary Cook [both by mark]; **Witnesses**: Hilliard Veren, Sr. and Dorcas Hicks; **Recorded**: 15: 5: 1672.

RICHARD HUCHENSON to NATHANIEL PUTNAM – (3:515) On 10 August 1656, Richard Huchenson (yeoman) of Salem granted to Nathaniel Putnam (yeoman) of Salem and Elizabeth, his intended wife, daughter of Hutchinson, for good will and natural affection, all the farm he had lately bought in partnership with John Putnam, Sr., deceased, and Daniel Ray, deceased, and John Hathorne of Capt. Davenport as per deed of sale appeareth…all his part which is ¼ part of said farm excepting and is reserved a certain parcel of land containing about 30 acres, upon the hill, then within the fence, to have and to hold all that 4th part of the said farm both upland and meadow. **Signed**: Richard Huchenson [by mark]; **Acknowledged**: 22: 1: 1671/2; **Witnesses**: Mary Williams and Hilliard Veren, Sr.; **Recorded**: 15: 5: 1672.

JOSEPH GRAFTON, Sr. to NICHOLAS BARTLETT – (3:517) On 6 September 1671, Joseph Grafton, Sr. (mariner) of Salem, with wife Mary yielding thirds, granted to Nicholas Bartlett (fisherman) of Salem for 10 pounds, 1/6th of an acre (or 26 poles or rods and about ¾ of a rod) of land in Salem...bounded W by a highway or lane, left for the use of several of the neighbors situated in the said lane, N with land of John Day, E with land of Edward Woolland and S with land of Venus Colefax. **Signed**: Joseph Grafton, Sr. and Mary Grafton [by mark]; **Acknowledged**: 15: 6: 1672; **Witnesses**: Christopher Babbids and Joseph Williams. [no recording date]

ELLENOR HOLLINGWORTH to PHILLIP CROMWELL – (3:519) On 1 June 1672, Ellenor Hollingworth (attorney to husband William Hollingworth) of Salem, granted to Phillip Cromwell of Salem for 250 pounds in money and goods, a dwelling house in Salem with all grounds thereunto, bounded E with lands formerly Corwithie's, now her daughter Mary's, N with land of Robert Starr; W with land of John Clifford; S with Salem harbor...with the dwelling house and all outhouses, stables, barns, orchards, gardens, fences...possession given by Elenor Hollingworth to Phillip Cromwell, both by turf and twigg, in presence of Thomas Ives and Daniel Andrews. Elenor Hollingworth owned this to be her act and deed, 14: 8 mo: 1672. Know all men by these presents, that I, William Hollingworth, do owne and allow of my wife's act and deed in this bill of sale; Recorded and possession given according to law. Signed: William Hollingworth; Attested: Thomas Ives and William Hollingworth, Jr. Thomas Ives came before me and made oath that he writt what was above expressed and that he saw William Hollingworth set his hand, and deliver it to Mr. Cromwell and his son William whose name stands as a witness, write his name in his sight before me 28: 7 mo: 72. William Hathorne, Assistant. **Signed**: Ellenor Hollingworth [by mark]; **Acknowledged**: 14: 8: 1672; **Witnesses**: Ele. and Thomas Ives; **Recorded**: 14: 8: 1672.

ELLENOR HOLLINGWORTH to PHILLIP CROMWELL – (3:521) On 6 June 1672, Ellenor Hollingworth (attorney to husband William Hollingworth, mariner) of Salem, granted to Phillip Cromwell of Salem for 200 pounds in money and goods, her husband's good ketch called *The Trial* of Salem, with all her masts, yards, sails, tackles, blocks, rigging, boats and all other appurtenances. **Signed**: Ellenor Hollingworth [by mark]; **Acknowledged**: 14: 8 mo: 1672; **Witnesses**: Ele. Hathorne and Thomas Ives; **Recorded**: 14: 8: 1672.

WALTER PRICE to WILLIAM FLINT : to DANIEL EATON – (3:523) On 17 March 1671, Walter Price assigned over unto William Flint of Salem, the within specified 6 acres of meadow, his part of the 9 acres sold to Mr. William Browne, Sr. and himself as per deed expressed. **Signed**: Walter Price; **Witnesses**: John Pickering & William Hathorne; **Acknowledged**: 17: 1 mo: 1670/1.

William Flint assigned and set over unto Daniel Eaton of Lynn, all rights in this deed to 6 acres of meadow, his part of the 9 acres, 6: 9 mo: 1672. **Signed**: William Flint; **Witnesses**: William Hathorne, Jr. and Elizabeth Hathorne. William Flint owned this to be his act and deed, 6: 9 mo: 1672 before William Hathorne, Assistant. The above written refers to a deed that is recorded in book 2nd foll: 61: per me. Hilliard Veren, Recorder.

RICHARD HOLLINGWORTH to PETER WELCUM – (3:524) On 19 August 1672, Richard Hollingworth (mariner) of Salem granted to Peter Welcum (mariner) of Boston for 5 pounds, a parcel of land on which said Peter Welcum lately built a dwelling house in Salem, and by estimation 12 rods…(as is separated from Hollingworth's land by a stone wall) or is bounded or lies between said Richard Hollingworth E or N, otherwise surrounded with the common land of Salem. **Signed**: Richard Hollingworth and Elizabeth Hollingworth (who freely gave up her thirds); **Acknowledged**: 2: 7 mo: 1672; **Witnesses**: Phillip Cromwell & Thomas Ives; **Recorded**: 14: 8: 1672.

THOMAS WATSON to JACOB PUDEATOR – (3:525) On 14 April 1668, Thomas Watson (tailor) of Salem, with wife Joane yielding rights, granted to Jacob Pudeator (blacksmith) of Salem for a valuable consideration, 24 poles of land in Salem…abutting S to the common called the pen, & the other end to the N bounded with land of Thomas Watson, the said parcel being in breadth E & W 3 poles, in length 8 poles, and that side to the E is bounded with the lane or highway & to the west side with the land that he late sold to Thomas Brackett, deceased. Jacob Pudeator was bound forever to make all the fence between his land now bought & the land of the said Thomas Watson. **Signed**: Thomas Watson; **Acknowledged**: 20: 1 mo: 1671/2; **Witnesses**: Hilliard Veren & Samuel Archard; **Recorded**: 30: 8: 1672.

(3:528) On 18 October 1672, an agreement that Jacob Pudeator shall forthwith take into his care & keeping & to maintain the said Thomas Watson & his wife the time of their natural lives; to provide for them in sickness & in health, with all necessaries suitable & convenient for food, raiment, for physick & all other things suitable for their condition, from time to time & at all times, the time of their lives & at the time of their deaths, to decently inter them & all upon the cost & charges of said Jacob…for and in consideration thereof, the said Thomas Watson does set over & confirm…unto said Jacob Puteator…all said Watson's whole estate, lands, houses, hereditaments, moveables, chattels, goods, debts, & all that of right does belong to him the said Thomas Watson, except his money, to occupy & enjoy & to have the present use and improvement of said estate... *Memorandum*: that whereas what moneys Thomas Watson have by him is before excepted, it is to be understood that it shall be at the disposal of the said Thomas Watson & his wife, for their necessary use only the time of their lives, but not to give or dispose of it to any other persons or use, & after their decease what moneys shall be remaining, to the use & behoof of the said Jacob & his assignes forever. **Signed**: Thomas & Joane Watson [by mark] & Jacob Pudeator [by mark]; **Acknowledged**: 21: 8 mo: 1672; **Witnesses**: Henry Skerry, Sr., Jonathan Ager, John Williams, Mathew Price, Hilliard Verren; **Recorded**: 30: 8 mo: 1672.

MOSES MAVERICK to WILLIAM BROWN, Sr. – (3:530) On 20 August 1672, Moses Maverick (merchant) of Marblehead, with wife Eunice yielding thirds, granted to William Brown, Sr. (merchant) of Essex County, for a valuable consideration all that island or point of land called Maverick's Island, containing by estimation, 2 acres of land with all the staging and housing thereupon the said island being situated in Marblehead & surrounded with the sea at high water; also ½ of a ware house standing near the orchard of Mr. Walton (deceased) to the S, the said warehouse being lately held in partnership between the said Moses Maverick & Samuel Ward & sold the ½ to the said William Browne by the said Samuel Ward. **Signed**: Moses Maverick & Eunice Maverick; **Acknowledged**: 29: 8 mo: 1672; **Witnesses**: John Appleton & Hilliard Veren; **Recorded**: 2: 9 mo: 1672.

JOHN INGERSON, Sr. to RICHARD ROSE – (3:533) On 30 October 1672, John Ingerson, Sr. of Salem granted to Richard Rose & his wife Ruth Rose, for the love and natural affection he bears for Richard Rose & Ruth his wife, his daughter, 5 or 6 poles of land (in Salem) on which there is a new dwelling house & is part of that land belonging to his now dwelling house, & the said parcel is about 42 foot in breadth, next to the street or lane which bounds it on the E & runs the same breadth backward against the land of Adam West's gate, which bounds it on the W, & is bounded on the S with his land & N with land of John Ingerson, Jr. ...that if the said Richard Rose & wife Ruth or either of them should at any time sell the said ground that they are here by ingaged to let the said John Ingerson have the first refusal of the premises, paying as much as any other will give. **Signed**: John Ireson [by mark]; **Witnesses**: Dorcas Hickes & Hilliard Veren.

JOHN GOOLD to JOHN RUCK – (3:535) On 22 October 1672, John Goold (yeoman) of Topsfield, with Sara Goold yielding thirds, granted to John Ruck (merchant) of Salem for a valuable sum in hand paid, $1/16^{th}$ part of the bloomery or iron works newly erected in Rowley Village with the 16th part of all the housing, buildings, water works, dams, water courses, lands, woods, timber, tools, instruments, with all the stock of coal & provision of every kind that now belongs to the said works & all appurtenances whatsoever of right is there unto belonging or appertaining to the said bloomery or iron works with the appurtenances now in the possession or occupation of Henry Leonard. **Signed**: John Goold & Sara Goold; **Acknowledged**: 8: 9 mo: 1672; **Witnesses**: Edmond Bridges & John Price; **Recorded**: 8: 9 mo: 1672.

ELEAZER HATHORNE to GEORGE KEASER – (3:538) On 12 November 1672, Eleazer Hathorne (merchant) of Salem, with wife Abigail yielding thirds, granted to George Keaser (tanner) of Salem, for 8 pounds 10 shillings, about 3 poles or rods of ground in Salem, bounded N with said George Keaser's land, lately bought of Eleazer Hathorne on 7 Oct 1670; & so runs S to the south river, so far as of right is thereto belonging, according to law, E with land of said George Keaser, formerly bought of Major William Hathorne, & W with highway that leads down to the river. **Acknowledged**: Hilliard Veren & Nathaniel Beadle, the two witnesses, gave oath that they were present as witnesses when Mr. Hathorne did seal, sign & deliver this writing with possession of the premises given to said George Keaser before us: 29: 11 mo: 1677 before Samuel Symonds (Deputy Governor) & Daniel Denison. **Signed**: Eleazer Hathorne; **Witnesses**: Hilliard Veren & Nathaniel Beadle; **Recorded**: 20: 9 mo: 1672.

MOSES MAVERICK to ERASMUS JAMES – (3:540) On 25 August 1672, Moses Maverick (merchant) of Marblehead granted to Erasmus James (carpenter) of Marblehead, for a certain sum of money, 9 acres of land on the neck belonging to the town of Marblehead, adjoining house & lands of John Alling & Andrew Tucker & butting NW & SE on the harbour & SE & SW on the town land. **Signed**: Moses Maverick & Eunice Maverick, his wife Eunice yielding rights; **Acknowledged**: 29: 8 mo: 1672; **Witnesses**: Hanna Leach, Samuel Leach & Martha Maverick; **Recorded**: 2: 10: 1672.

RICHARD BRABROOK to PHILLIP CROMWELL – (3:544) On 18 November 1672, Richard Brabrook (husbandman) of Wenham granted to Phillip Cromwell (slatherer) of Salem, 6 acres of salt marsh in Chebacco in Ipswich, part of the farms of said Richard Brabrook and is bounded with the marsh of Mr. Cobbitt N, a creek parting, or lying between & the marsh of Robert Cross, Sr., partly E with the marsh of said Brabrook & a creek on the S & W & partly E. [no amount of money given]. **Signed**: Richard Brabrook; **Acknowledged**: 18: 9: 1672; **Witnesses**: William Downton, Samuel Archer, & Hilliard Veren, Sr.; **Recorded**: 3: 10: 1672.

JOHN PEARSON to JOHN LINSEY (Indenture) – (3:546) On the 5th day of November 1672, John Pearson (yeoman) of Lynn with consent of Mauldin, his wife, who surrendered her thirds, granted to John Linsey (carpenter) of Lynn for 32 pounds 15 shillings, 3 acres of land in Lynn usually called Grave's lot, which was given for a house lot by the town and is bounded S with land of Mr. Holyoke, E, W and N with the town common with all fruit trees planted on it & all fences, together with all commons, liberty & privileges belonging thereto. **Signed**: John Pearson [by mark]; **Acknowledged**: 28: 9: 1672; **Witnesses**: Andrew Mansfield & Samuel Rhodes [by mark].

JOHN NORTHY, Sr. to SAMUEL MORGAN & JOHN FURBUSH – (3:548) On 25 February 1671, John Northy, Sr. (fisherman) of Marblehead granted to Samuel Morgan and John Furbush, both of Marblehead, for 50 pounds current coined money, all the stage, with a little house adjoining, with ½ acre of land in Marblehead, joining land of Mr. Christopher Lattimore N nearest & the highway up towards the house of Richard Reade NW with the highway between it & the said fence of Richard Reed and so running down in breadth to low watermark of the great harbor to the S, with a privilege of 1 shallop's mooring in the said cove. Agreed that there shall as always has been, a cartway between the stage and abovesaid land & the boat's mooring shall be wholly to them so far as said Northy has priviledge & not futher & the said Northy does not warrant it to them, no further than what right he has to it. John Northy & Dorothy, wife, owned this to be their own act & deed, 30: 9 mo: 1672. Within specified purchaser of the stage and land, Mr. Samuel Morgan & John Furbush do yield up all right, title & interest to the same deed unto Richard Reed of Marblehead. Witness our hands, 25 May 1672, Samuel Morgan [by mark] & John Furbush; Witnesses: John Chinge & Samuel Leach. **Signed**: John & Dorothy Northy [by mark]; **Acknowledged**: 30: 9: 1672; **Witnesses**: William Pitt, Robert Rowles [by mark] & Samuel Leach [no recording date].

MOSES MAVERICK to RICHARD ROWLAND – (3:552) On 25 August 1672, Moses Maverick (merchant) of Marblehead, with Eunice his wife, who gave up her rights, granted to Richard Rowland, for 50 pounds in money of New England coin, three 10-acre lots in Marblehead, butting on the SE of Master John Deverick's land & adjoining land of said Richard Rowland on the SW & the land of William Nick on the NE & the river on the NW. **Signed**: Moses & Eunice Maverick; **Acknowledged**: 29: 8: 1672; **Witnesses**: Hannah Leach, Samuel Leach & Martha Maverick; **Recorded**: 5: 10: 1672.

JOHN FISK to WILLIAM DODGE – (3:555) On 6 June 1667, John Fisk of Chelmsford granted to William Dodge of Salem for 115 pounds, all the parcels of lands granted by the inhabitants of Salem to John Fisk in Wenham, be it upland or meadow except several lots that before the 6th day of June, 1667, he had alienated from same, namely John Deanman, Thomas Fisk, John Fisk & Edward Kemp—these 4 lots, being formerly sold out of the aforesaid grant by Salem to John Fisk, unto these 4 persons & bounded to them by their several marks and bounds which the said John Fisk does hereby except in this sale to William Dodge, and all the remaining lands, upland or meadow, that was granted by Salem as upon record appears, unto said John Fisk, the land & every parcel thereof with the appurtenances thereto belonging, as houses, fences, trees growing thereon... **Signed**: John Fisk; **Acknowledged**: 30: 7 mo: 1672; **Witnesses**: George Biham [by mark] & Samuel Foster; **Recorded**: 14: 10: 1672.

JOHN NEALE to JOHN SMITH – (3:558) On 16 March 1670/71, John Neale (yeoman) of Salem granted to John Smith (seaman) of Salem for a valuable sum, ½ acre of land in Salem...and is part of the land whereon said John Neale lately built a new house, & is bounded with land or highway that leads down to the north river to the E & on the S with fence that separates between said half acre & land of said John Neale, reserved to the said new house & W & N with the land also of said John Neale, said half-acre being in breadth S & N 8 rods & in length E & W 10 rods. It is to be understood & agreed upon between both parties that on the W & N sides of the said half acre, John Smith, his heirs & assignes, is to set up & maintain the fence on his own cost, so long as John Neal keeps the adjoining land on those 2 sides in his own possession & afterwards he is to bear the charge of one-half, according to law. **Signed**: John Neale [by mark]; **Acknowledged**: 25: 2: 1671; **Witnesses**: Hilliard Veren, Sr. & John Price; **Recorded**: 25 December 1672.

JOHN BLACKLEACH & RICHARD LORD to Mr. BROWNE – (3:560) What fish or other goods my partner Mr. Blackleach shall buy at Salem or elsewhere, for the full loading of the ketch *Blessing* & shall give bill for upon our joint account, I underwritten, do oblidge myself shall be duly paid according the tenner thereof, as witness my hand & seal this 21: November 1672. **Signed**: Richard Lord.

John Blackleach, partner with Richard Lord, made oath that this is the act, hand & seal of Richard Lord before me, 30: 10 mo: 1672. **Signed**: William Hathorne, Assistant.

Mr. John Blackleach in reference to the present voyage of the ketch *Blessing*, desires you would endeavor to have been fitted as soon as can be, & what the charge amounts unto for your & my part, the halfe place to the account of stock & for the hiring of seamen, get them as cheap as you can, to be paid equally by yourself & me. At return of said ketch, and for victualling for the voyage, I leave to your discretion to lay in what you judge needful, buy as cheap as you can. Mr. Browne has provided me to deliver what bee your needs on my account at money price, he is indebted to me about 10 pounds what fish or other goods you see cause to buy or agree for (besides the fish we have already bought at Salem) to completing the full loading of the ketch, engage me equally therein with yourself, which I shall abide by & perform: my desire is that you should go with the said ketch for Bilboa & then dispose of her cargo & thence into some port of France, where it may be most advantageous to lay out the proceeds of the cargo in linen cloth & what else you judge may conduce to our best advantage & thence directly to Boston; but the whole voyage I leave to your good discretion to name or alter as you shall find the Providence of God directing which way you judge may be more profitable for us, & also what agreements or bargains you shall make, in any place where you shall come in reference to any future trade, interest me therein equally with yourself, which I shall perform & in all respects do for me as for yourself & for your pain & trouble in the management of this present voyage, according to our agreement you are to receive no wages, but to deduct 10% for my half of the cargo, as it shall sell at & 5% at Boston if you sell the cargo there at your return. So, wishing you a prosperous voyage. I remain your loving friend, Richard Lord. **Recorded**: 31: 10: 1672. John Blackleach partner with Richard Lord made oath...of Richard Lord, 30: 10: 1672.

MOSES MAVERICK to GEORGE DARLING – (3:562) On 24 February 1671, Moses Maverick (merchant) of Marblehead, with wife Eunice giving up thirds, granted to George Darling (farmer) of Marblehead, for a certain sum of money, all his quarter part of land called Coye ponds land, formerly purchased of Mr. Solomon Stoddard, as appears on Salem records, and ¼ of all the land that was purchased of Nathaniel Pitman by said Moses Maverick, which said land is in Marblehead, bounded with the farm that was John Humphrey's Esq. SW, with land of Nathaniel Pitman on part with the commons of Salem W & the marsh of Richard Rowland & Capt. Smith N. **Signed**: Moses Maverick & Eunice

Maverick; **Acknowledged**: 29: 8 mo: 1672; **Witnesses**: Richard Rowland [by mark], John Peach & Samuel Leach; **Recorded**: 16: 11: 1672.

JOHN PEACH to GEORGE DARLING – (3:565) On 24: February 1671, John Peach (gentleman) of Marblehead granted to George Darling (farmer) of Marblehead, for a certain sum of money, a quarter part of land, called the Coye pond land, formerly purchased of Mr. Solomon Stoddard, as appears on Salem records & ¼ of all that land was purchased of Nathaniel Pitman by said John Peach, which said land in Marblehead is bounded by the farm which sometimes was John Humphry, Esquire's SW, with land of Nathaniel Pitman in part with the commons of the town of Salem on the W, & with the marsh of Richard Rowland & Capt. James Smith N. **Signed**: John Peach [by mark]; **Acknowledged**: 29: 8 mo: 1672; **Witnesses**: John Peach, Jr., Moses Maverick & Samuel Leach, Sr.

JOHN GOOLD to JOHN ROBBINSON – (3:568) On 21 November 1670/71, John Goold (yeoman) of Topsfield granted to John Robbinson (husbandman) of Topsfield, for 40 pounds sterling, 6 to 8 acres of land with a dwelling house & barn on it in Topsfield, bounded NE with land of Thomas Perkins, Sr., E & SE by land of Jacob Towne & W or SW with land now in possession of said John Robinson, & S with land of Edmond Towne; also about 10 acres of land on the other side (S side) of the Ipswich river, containing meadow, swamp & upland, bounded on said river on the NE side & the common land of Topsfield on all other sides, the said messuage or tenement, or parcels of land & housing together with all rights, privileges & appurtenances that belonged to Edmond Bridges in Topsfield touching land, when the said Bridges gave possession to said John Goold of said house & land in 1668—all of which said John Goold bought of said Edmond Bridges as per deed of sale on the 9th of Sept. 1670, and by these presents have sold to said John Robbinson, his heirs & assignes, except 2 ten-acre lots, more or less, which the said Edmond Bridges has lately sold to Mr. John Ruck of Salem. **Signed**: John Goold; **Acknowledged**: 25: 1 mo: 1671; **Witnesses**: Hilliard Veren, Sr. & Samuel Williams.

GEORGE CORWIN to PHILLIP LOGEE – (3:570) On 13 January 1672, George Corwin (merchant) of Salem granted to Phillip Logee (fisherman) of Salem for 20 pounds in hand, about 8 or 10 acres of land in Salem, bounded E with land of Thomas Goldthwaite & John King, NW with the common highway adjoining to land of John Southwick (deceased), S or SE with a stone wall of his own, which fenced in his meadow & some upland & on the other side being about the SW with the land of Elizer Giles. **Signed**: George Corwin & Elizabeth Corwin; **Acknowledged**: 13: 11: 1672 by Capt. George Corwin & Elizabeth his wife who yielded her thirds; **Recorded**: 16: 11: 1672; **Witnesses**: William Bowditch & Edward Norice.

THOMAS TOWNSEND, Sr. to JOHN TOWNSEND (Deed of Gift) – (3:572) On 23 Nov 1668, Thomas Townsend (husbandman) of Lynn (with consent of Mary his now wife) granted to John Townsend (natural son of Thomas Townsend) in consideration that he had lived with him from childhood until marriage estate, 60 acres of upland & meadow in Lynn, which said Thomas Townsend bought of Edward Huchinson, which was formerly in the tenure of Mr. Edmond Needham of Lynn, with all way easements, liberty & privileges belonging thereunto, being bounded with a meadow called Mr. Willis' meadow E, with land formerly in tenure of James Boutwell (deceased) on the W, with land in or lately in tenure of Henry Walton on the S and with land formerly in tenure of Capt. Bridges on the N, & moreover said Thomas doth covenant & promise to said John that he has good right, full power & lawful authority in his own name. **Signed**: Thomas Townsend, Sr., & Mary Townsend; **Acknowledged**: 12: 12: 1672; **Witnesses**: Andrew Mansfield & Elizabeth Taylor [by mark]; **Recorded**: 19: 12: 1672.

DANIEL KING, Sr. to EZEKIEL NEEDHAM (Indenture) – (3:574) On 1 November 1670, Daniel King, Sr. (gentleman) of Lynn granted to Ezekiel Needham of Lynn and Sarah his now wife, daughter of Daniel King, in consideration of the marriage, 33 acres of farmland in Lynn formerly in possession of the Lady Moody, bounded S with a walnut tree marked on the S side with R.K. & N with E.N. which tree is about 6 or 7 poles S of the bark house, & so on a straight line to another walnut tree, with the same marks on both sides as the other which is about 18 poles distant from the other and upon a straight line to land of John Lewis W...S about 2 or 3 poles and W with farm land formerly Mr. Humfry's now in tenure of Richard Hud, upon a straight line...unto stump in old divisional fence between said farm land and land herein inserted, said stump being 2 paces S of ditch of John Lewis and N with said ditch unto brook and over brook unto range of old divisional fence between land and land of John Farr which divisional range of old fence is E bound while it extends S unto brook and then brook E bound until it extends unto range S bound as aforesaid. **Signed**: Daniel King & Elizabeth King; **Acknowledged**: 13: 2: 1671, and wife Elizabeth yielded thirds; **Witnesses**: Ralph King & John Burrill; **Recorded**: 25: Feb: 1672/3.

RICHARD MORE to WILLIAM FLINT – (3:576) On 21: 7: 1658, Richard More (mariner) of Salem granted to William Flint (husbandman) of Salem, for 6 pounds, a 10-acre lot formerly John Talby's in the south field, abutting on the harbor & to the E & the salt marsh near Castle Hill to the W, the land of Henry Harwood to the S & the land of Thomas Browning to the N. **Signed**: Richard More; **Acknowledged**: 5: 8: 1671; **Witnesses**: William Hathorne & Anna Hathorne.

WILLIAM FLINT to JOHN PICKERING – (3:577) On 1 December 1671, William Flint granted to John Pickering (yeoman) of Salem, for divers good causes and considerations [no land specified]. **Signed**: William Flint; **Acknowledged**: 11: 2: 1672; **Witnesses**: Abraham Reed & Elizabeth Hathorne.

RICHARD ADAMS to JOHN PICKERING – (3:578) On 16 November 1670, Richard Adams of Salem granted to John Pickering (yeoman) of Salem for 50 pounds sterling, about 20 acres of land containing upland & meadow, lying together in the south field so called in Salem (except & reserved one three quarters of salt marsh lying & disjoined from the aforesaid parcel…as it lies in one entire piece & is bounded W with land of William Flint, N with land & meadow of said John Pickering, Joshua Reye & Elias Stileman, E with land of William Flint & Elias Mason & S with a swamp of John Neel). **Signed**: Richard Adams [by mark] & Susanna Adams [by mark]; **Acknowledged**: 6: 3: 1672, with wife Susanna freely yielding her rights; **Witnesses**: Hilliard Veren, Sr. & John Higginson, Jr.; **Recorded**: 25: 12: 72/73.

WILLIAM FLINT to JOHN PICKERING – (3:581) On 25 January 1669, William Flint (yeoman) of Salem granted to John Pickering (yeoman) of Salem for 4 pounds, ½ of a parcel of land he lately bought of John Lewis of Lynn…as per deed of sale dated 29: 11 month: 1669, which land contained 10 acres & was situated in Lynn…bounded by Lynn common, commonly known by the name of Ingols his plaine, being 40 rods square. **Signed**: William Flint; **Witnesses**: Walter Price & William Hathorne.

WILLIAM FLINT to JOHN PICKERING – (3:582) On 28 February 1669, William Flint (yeoman) of Salem granted to John Pickering (yeoman) of Salem for 12 pounds, 10 shillings, about 6 or 8 acres of land lying on Jeggles point, so called in the south field in Salem, bounded N with land formerly Henry Harwood's, now land of said William Flint; also on the W with land of said William, where is laid heaps of stones for the bounds & to the E & S with water or harbor. **Signed**: William Flint; **Witnesses**: Walter Price & William Hathorne; **Recorded**: 25: 12: 1672/3.

NATHANIEL INGERSON to JOHN BUXTON – (3:584) On 20 January 1672/3, Nathaniel Ingerson (husbandman) of Salem, granted to John Buxton (husbandman) of Salem for a valuable sum, 5 acres of meadow, being ½ of 10 acres lately bought by said Nathaniel of John Robinson and by deed of sale, bearing the date of the 20th day of March 1670/1, the said parcel of meadow lying in Rowley village, half in the said 10 acres that lies W, according as it is divided, from a rock on the N to a stake set on the S of the said meadow, in the line between said meadow & some meadow now or lately of John Goold, the whole 10 acres bounded as in the said deed of sale above mentioned. **Signed**: Nathaniel Ingerson; **Acknowledged**:   20: 11: 1672; **Witnesses**: John Williams & Hilliard Veren; **Recorded**: 25: 12: 1672/3.

ROBERT GOODALL to JOHN BUXTON – (3:587) On 29 June…in year of Charles the second, Robert Goodall of Salem and Margaret his wife granted to John Buxton of Salem for 40 pounds, 44 acres of swamp & upland in Salem, having land of Lott Kilham on the W, bounded on the end next to the Ipswich River, with a red oak tree being a bound also for said Kilham & runs by the side of his land, 143 poles to a stake which is the other corner bound & is 50 poles broad from the said stake to a stake adjoining the land of Job Swinerton, Jr. & from the said stake it runs 143 poles by the side of the land of said Job Swinerton, John Buxton & Benjamin Woodrow, and is bounded near the said river with a great white oak being also a bound for said Woodrow. **Signed**: Robert Goodal & Margery Goodal [by mark]; **Acknowledged**:   30: 4: 1672, with wife Margery yielding thirds; **Witnesses**: John Foster, Jr., Samuel Inguls & John Tompkins, Jr.

WILLIAM REEVES to JOHN KITCHIN – (3:589) On 2 July 1672, William Reeves of Salem granted to John Kitchin of Salem for 60 pounds in current silver, all his house, housing and lands in Salem, bounded with land of Paul Mansfield S & the street on the N & with the land of Edward Bush on the W & land of Paul Mansfield on the E. **Signed**: William Reeves; **Acknowledged**: 24: 12: 1672; **Witnesses**: John Bunker & John Hayward, Sr.; **Recorded**: 24: 12 mo: 1672.

OSMUND TRASK to SAMUEL CORNING – (3:592) On 26: 11 month: 1658, Osmund Trask (planter) of Salem with consent of Mary Trask, granted to Samuel Corning of Salem, for a steer of about 4 years of age, 26 & ¾ acres of land, which is a 3rd part of 80 acres bought of Mr. William Browne formerly, by Jonathan Porter, Goodman Symonds & Samuel Corning & this 3rd part sold by Jonathan Porter unto Osmund Trask. This land lying on Cape Ann side near the N side of Bald Hill; also the aforesaid Osmund has sold unto the aforesaid Samuel Corning 20 acres of upland adjoining land of Thomas Brackett, near the former 26¾ acres. **Signed**: Osmund Trask [by mark]; **Acknowledged**:   22: 6 mo: 1659; **Witnesses**: Roger Conant, Nathaniel Stone & Joseph Bailey; **Recorded**: 2: 2 mo: 1673.

ANTHONY ASHBY to NATHANIEL BEADLE – (3:594) On 25 December 1670, Anthony Ashby of Salem granted to Nathaniel Beadle (cordwinder) of Salem for 110 pounds, a dwelling house and barn with 24 rods or poles of ground on which said dwelling house & barn stands in Salem, it being a parcel of ground lately bought of Mr. Samuel Gardner & afterwards of Samuel Symonds of Topsfield, & is bounded S with land of said Samuel Gardner, E with land of Samuel Robinson, W with land of Mr. John Gardner & N with the highway…the said Nathaniel, his heirs & assigns shall from time to time & at all times hereafter forever set up & maintain at his & their own cost all the middle fence to the S to the partition fence on the S between the premises & Mr. Samuel Gardner, according to the terms expressed in a deed made from Gardner to Symonds 6 June 1667. **Signed**: Anthony Ashby; **Acknowledged**: 10: 3: 1671, with wife Abigail yielding her thirds; **Witnesses**: Mathew Price, Samuel Beadle & Edward Norrice, Sr.; **Recorded**: 25: 12: 1672/3.

SARA BROWN to JAMES BROWN – (3:596) On 10 March 1672, Sara Browne, daughter of John Cutting of Newbury (mariner deceased), now wife of James Browne (glasier) of Salem, granted to son James Brown (glasier) of Charlestown, for divers good causes & love and natural affection, a dwelling house & 12 acres of land in Newbury, bounded E with the highway next to the Merrimack River, N with the land formerly Mr. Miller's, W with land of Mr. Lowell, S with land of Nathaniel Clark; also ¾ of 20 acres of salt marsh in the great meadow in Newbury, which upland & meadow was formerly purchased of Mr. Steven Dummer by said John Cutting, her father & given by him in his last will & testament to the said Sara Brown & to her lawful heirs forever; also a freehold, which was formerly given to said father John Cutting by the town of Newbury, & by him given to his wife Mary at his decease & by the said Mary, her mother, given & bequeathed to Sara at her decease. **Signed**: Sara Brown; **Acknowledged**: 12: 1: 1672/3; **Witnesses**: Hilliard Veren & Hilliard Veren, Jr.; **Recorded**: 12: 2 mo: 1672.

JOHN COPP to GEORGE CORWIN – (3:599) On 21 March 1673, John Copp of Marblehead granted to George Corwin (merchant) of Salem, for 82 pounds 10 shillings, a dwelling house with a small parcel of land adjoining, containing about 3 poles square…in Marblehead, between land of John Legg, Sr. & land sometime in possession of John Clemence, bounded NW with a highway, SE with the common between the dwelling house of John Legg & the highway; also on the NE & SW bounded with the common. There was a lawful surrender made, & quiet possession given of the house & land above, by John Copp unto Wm. Bowditch, on behalf & for the proper use of Capt. George Corwin, 21: 1 mo: 1672/3; **Witness**: Christopher Nick & William Nick [both by mark]; **Signed**: John

Copp; **Acknowledged**: 21: 1 mo: 1672/3; **Witnesses**: Isaack Williams, William Bowditch & Edward Norice; **Recorded**: 21: Mar: 1672.

LOTT CONANT to VINSON STILSON – (3:601) On 10 March 1669/70, Lot Conant (husbandman) of Bass River, granted to Vinson Stilson (cordwinder) of Marblehead, for 12 pounds in money current, all his messuage, tenement or dwelling house, with land whereon it stands, & land belonging, being ¼ acre, according as it is now fenced, in Marblehead, butting on house & land of John Trevye S & the house & land of Richard Thistle N & the street W. **Signed**: Lott Conant & Elizabeth Conant [by mark]; **Acknowledged**: 23: 6 mo: 1671 & wife Elizabeth yielded rights; **Witnesses**: Obediah Carter [by mark] & Samuel Leach [by mark]; **Recorded**: 1: 2 mo: 1673.

THOMAS MAULE to JOSHUA REA – (3:603) On 10 June 1672, Thomas Maule (tailor) of Salem granted to Joshua Rea (husbandman) of Salem for a valuable consideration, ½ quarter acre of upland, being ½ of that land he bought of John Cooke, lying in Salem…bounded N with land of said Joshua Rea, E with land of Mistress Ann Price, widow, S with land of said Thomas Maule & W with the land… **Signed**: Thomas Maule & Naomie Maule [by mark]; **Acknowledged**: 10: 4 mo: 1672, with wife Naomie Maule freely yielding her thirds; **Witnesses**: Jeremiah Neale & Edward Norrice; **Recorded**: 7: 2 mo: 1673.

BRAY WILKINS and JOHN GINGION to JOHN OXENBRIDGE & Co. – (3:604) On 31 March 1673, Bray Wilkins (husbandman) of Salem, and John Gingion (tailor) of Salem, granted to John Oxenbridge of Boston & James Allen (gentlemen) of Boston & Anthony Stoddard (merchant) of Boston, (executors of the Last Will & testament of Richard Bellingham, Esq. late of Boston, deceased) for 50 pounds current money, with interest & forbearance after 6 pounds percent at or before 1 April 1694, 2/3 parts of all the land or farm of 700 acres on the head of Salem to the NW from the said town, & there being within the said place a hill whereon an Indian plantation sometimes had been, a pond & about 100 or 150 acres of land, being part meadow, which said 700 acres said Bray Wilkins & John Gingion, late purchased from said Richard Bellingham, & which said Bellingham had by grant from the General Court of the Colony, as by order of said court bearing date 6 September 1638. **Signed**: Bray Wilkins & John Gingion; **Acknowledged**: 31 March 1673; **Witnesses**: Aaron Way [by mark] & William Ireland. There is recorded in book 4th follio 131 a recept of the money & a clearing of this mortgage; **Recorded**: 11: 2: 1673.

EDWARD RICHARDS to JOHN BURRILL – (3:607) On 11 June 1669, Edward Richards of Essex County granted to John Burrell of Essex county for 4 pounds 5 shillings, an acre of salt marsh in Lynn, where the aforesaid John Burrill makes choice of, either next to Benjamin Chadwell's marsh or any one side of said Richards' marsh so as that the said Burrill take it together. **Signed**: Edward Richards [by mark]; **Acknowledged**: 1: 5: 1670; **Witnesses**: William Crofts & Robert Burgess [by mark]; **Recorded**: 5 May 1673.

(3:608) Essex Registry of Deeds, Southern District, Salem, Mass. April 28, 1875: The foregoing copy of the Third Book of Records of Deeds for Salem and vicinity, was made in 1855, under the direction of the County Commissioners. It has now been examined and corrected, and is a true copy of the original. **Attest**: Ephm. Brown, Reg.

***
Conclusion of Book 3 of Essex County Deeds
***

ESSEX COUNTY DEEDS Book 4

BRAY WILKINS and JOHN GINGELL to AARON WAYE & WILLIAM IRELAND – (4:1) On 31 March 1673, Bray Wilkins of Salem and Anna his wife (who released dower) & John Gingell (husbandman) of Salem granted to Aaron Waye and William Ireland of Boston (husbandman) for a valuable consideration to them in hand already paid, a third part of a parcel of land commonly known by the name of Wills Hill in Salem, containing by estimation 700 acres, together with a third part of all the timber lying on said farm, a third part of the houses, barns, tenements, stables, dwelling houses, outhouses and also a third part of timber, trees & underwood on said farm, together with a third part of swamp, meadows, pastures & ponds lying on said farm. **Signed**: Bray Wilkins & Ann Wilkins [by mark] & John Gingell; **Acknowledged**: 19: 2 mo: 1673 with Anna yielding thirds; **Witnesses**: Richard Bennett [by mark], Thomas Cooper [by mark] and Joshua Holdsworth, Sr.; **Recorded**: 4: 8: 1673.

THOMAS WATSON to JOHN LEACH – (4:5) On 25 September 1672, Thomas Watson (tailor) of Salem granted to John Leach (yeoman & son of Richard Leach) of Salem for 10 pounds sterling, 10 acres of upland near the head of Willistone's river on the Ryall side in Salem & is bounded N with some land of Henry Bartholomew, E with land of Jeffery Massy, S by the common lands, & W with lands of Richard Leach. **Witnesses**: Hilliard Veren & Samuel Williams. "Whereas Jacob Pudeter (blacksmith) of Salem being the successor of the above Thomas Watson, late deceased in his lifetime did not give legal conveyance of the above said land to the said John Leach or deceased before he signed to the above deed, do by these presents owne the said sale & also of it as the said Thomas Watson & in his name & stead sign, seal & deliver the said deed as my act & deed to him the said John Leach, his heirs & assigns, this 22 of April 1673;" **Signed**: Jacob Pudeter [by mark]; **Acknowledged**: 23: 2: 1673 by Jacob Pudeter; **Recorded**: 9 May 1673.

EDWARD WOOLAND to PASCO FOOT – (4:8) On 28 September 1667, Edward Wooland (fisherman) of Salem granted to Pasco Foot elder (fisherman) of Salem for 4 pounds, 10 shillings to him in hand paid, 20 poles of land between the dwelling house of himself and land of Jobe Hilliard, being in length 10 rods from the street inward S & in breadth 2 rods, being situated in the town of Salem & bounded N with the street, E with land of Jobe Hilliard, S & W by land of himself Edward Wooland. [Name on side of deed on page 8 is Isaack Foot] **Signed**: Edward Wooland [[by mark]; **Acknowledged**: 23: 2: 1673; **Witnesses**: Hilliard Veren & Stephen Haskett.

CHRISTOPHER WALLER to RICHARD LEACH – (4:9) On 22 October 1669, Christopher Waller of Salem, with consent of his wife, granted to Richard Leach of Salem for 10 pounds in hand already paid, one acre of salt marsh lying in Salem in a place called Ryall Side, bounded NW with the river, E with the land of said Richard Leach & S by marsh of Capt. Thomas Lathrop, to have & hold said acre of salt marsh with all priviledges thereunto belonging. **Signed**: Christopher Waller [by mark] and Margaret Waller [by mark]; possession of land by turf & twig; **Witnesses**: Nathaniel Felton & John Hybert; **Recorded**: 10 May 1673.

NATHANIEL FELTON to RICHARD LEACH – (4:10) On 13 June 1670, Nathaniel Felton of Salem, with consent of wife, granted to Richard Leach of Salem, for 25 pounds in hand paid, 25 acres of land in Salem, with appurtenances, bounded S with the Wooliston River, NW by land formerly of Laurance Leach, E by land of Mr. Bartholomew. Possession given by turf & twig. **Signed**: Nathaniel Felton & Mary Felton; **Witnesses**: Christopher Waller [by mark] & John Hybert [by mark].

WILLIAM PITTS to CHRISTOPHER LATTERMORE – (4:12) On 2 February 1659, William Pitts (merchant) of Boston, with consent of wife Susana Pitts, granted to Christopher Lattermore (mariner) of Marblehead, for divers good & valuable causes & consideration of a valuable sum in hand paid, all his house, lying in Marblehead, together with all his several parcels of upland, swamp & marshland & stage with the land thereunto appertaining, which is lying in Marblehead. **Signed**: William Pitts; **Acknowledged**: 2 February 1659 by William Pitts & wife; **Witnesses**: Hope Allen, Abraham Hawkins & Richard Garnett; **Recorded**: 7 May 1673.

THOMAS PITMAN to THOMAS PITMAN – (4:14) On 4 November 1657, Thomas Pitman (carpenter) of Salem granted to Thomas Pitman (fisherman) of Marblehead, for 39 pounds to him in hand paid before the date hereof, one dwelling house & barn, with 30 acres of upland & 2 cows, the house & land being on Darby Fort side near Throgmorten's cove, between land of William Beale & Francis Collins. **Signed**: Richard Hide; **Acknowledged**: 4: 9 mo: 1657; **Witnesses**: George Emery, Thomas Cromwell & Edward Norrice, Jr.; **Recorded**: 7: 3 mo: 1673.

WILLIAM FLINT to THOMAS PITMAN – (4:15) On 16 March 1669, William Flint (husbandman) of Salem granted to Thomas Pitman of Marblehead, for good & valuable consideration to him in hand paid, ½ acre of salt marsh lying within a parcel of marsh in Marblehead not far from the bridge by the waye side having the river on the NW & N side & the land of said Thomas Pitman's salt marsh on the NE. **Signed**: William Flint;

Acknowledged: 16: 1 mo: 1669/70; **Witnesses**: Eleazer Hathorne & Anna Hathorne.

JOHN MARSTON, Sr. to EDMOND MARSHALL – (4:16) On 11 June 1673, John Marston, Sr. of Salem granted to Edmond Marshall (weaver) of Ipswich, for a valuable sum in hand paid, one dwelling house with 5 acres of land on which the house stands, being the half of a ten-acre lot held in partnership with William Marston & since bought by Edmond Marshal of the said William Marston, the said house & the whole of the 10 acres is at the head of Bass river in Salem & is bounded E & W with land of John Bachelor, N with land of Nicholas Howard & S with land of said John Bachelor; also another 10 acres of land with about ½ acre of meadow lying near the said 10 acres having the land of William King on the E, & N with land of John Bachelor & Nehemiah Howard, & bounded E with the river; also 2 small parcels of marsh, lying near the said 10 acres of land within the land of William King, to have & hold the dwelling house with 5 acres adjoining & also the 10 acres with the 3 parcels of marsh, & Alce wife freely yields up her right title & dower interest. *Memorandum*: Further, said John Marston do assign unto said Edmond Marshall together with above bargained premises a small strip of land containing about ½ acre being planted for an orchard adjoining the premises S, being a grant from the town of Salem to said John Marston & is included in & is part of the above said grant, bargain & sale. **Signed**: John Marston, Sr. & Alce Marston [by mark & seal]; **Acknowledged**: 11: 11: 1673; **Witnesses**: Timothy Hicks & Hilliard Veren, Sr.; **Recorded**: 12: 4 mo: 1673.

EDMOND MARSHALL to ABRAHAM WARREN – (4:19) On 11 June 1673, Edmond Marshall, having formerly granted by deed & writing, under hand & seal, & recorded the within bargained premises unto Abraham Warren, but because there was a neglect in getting a deed from the said Marston until the present day, according to the within date & the date of his deed to said Warren being several years before, know all men by these presents, that said Edmond Marshall does declare said deed to be just & right & does further assigne over unto said Warren. **Signed**: Edmond Marshall [by mark]; **Acknowledged**: 11: 11: 1673; **Witnesses**: Hilliard Veren, Sr., & Timothy Hicks.

WILLIAM FISK to JOHN DODGE, Jr. – (4:20) On the 15th of the 12th month 1667, William Fisk (weaver) of Wenham granted to John Dodge, Jr. of Salem for the full & just sum of 31 pounds already paid in hand by bill, 5 acres of land in Wenham, being part of that lot which he bought of his mother, lying in the general field near the pond brooke, joining John Sclare's land N & Jeremiah Watts land E & upon the highway S, together with apple trees thereunto belonging with all appurtenances belonging except houses...also Sara the wife of above said William Fisk relinquished her thirds. **Signed**: William Fisk; **Acknowledged**: 25: 1 mo: 1673; **Witnesses**: John Clark & Thomas Fisk; **Recorded**: 18: 4: 1673.

ZACHERY HERRICK to JONATHAN MOSS – (4:22) On 18 June 1673, Zachery Herrick (carpenter) of Beverly & Mary his wife who yielded up her thirds, granted to Jonathan Moss (tailor) of Beverly, for 6 pounds in hand paid, one acre of upland in Beverly, bounded E with land of Zachary Herrick, S with the highway or common road, W & N with land of Henry Herrick, Sr. **Signed**: Zachery Herrick & Mary Herrick [by mark]; **Acknowledged**: 18: 4: 1673; **Witnesses**: John Bennett & William Elliot; **Recorded**: 18: 4: 1673.

MOSES MAVERICK to EDWARD DIAMOND – (4:23) On 20 March 1671/2, Moses Maverick (merchant) of Marblehead, with consent of Unis his wife, granted to Edward Diamond (fisherman) of Marblehead for a certain sum of money to him in hand well & truly paid, one dwelling house in Marblehead, near to the house & land of Robert Knight on the N with one orchard & one garden plot with all & singular land thereto belonging which said house & land, orchard & garden plot was formerly in possession of George Bonfield of Marblehead, with all & singular appurtenances...and Unis the wife of said Moses Maverick freely & clearly yielded up her right & title of interest & dower. **Signed**: Moses Maverick and Eunice Maverick; **Acknowledged**: 26: 4: 1673 at court of Salem; **Witnesses**: Samuel Morgan & Samuel Leach; **Recorded**: 3: 5: 1673.

MOSES MAVERICK to THOMAS SMITH – (4:25) On 20 June 1671, Moses Maverick (merchant) of Marblehead, with free consent of Eunice his wife, granted to Thomas Smith (fisherman) of Marblehead, for a certain sum of money to him in hand, well & truly paid, 4 acres of land in Marblehead, near the Scotch pond, with all appurtenances...as it is now fenced. **Signed**: Moses Maverick & Eunice Maverick; **Acknowledged**: Moses Maverick 26: 4: 1673; **Witnesses**: Samuel Cheever & Samuel Leach; **Recorded**: 3: 5: 1673.

JEREMIAH BOOTMAN to Mr. PHILLIP CROMWELL – (4:27) On 11 July 1673, Jeremiah Bootman (fisherman) of Salem granted to Mr. Phillip Cromwell of Salem for a valuable sum of money in hand paid, a parcel of land containing 2/3 parts of an acre of ground, or 106 poles or rod of ground...as it lies bounded, the said parcel of land being part of the house lot formerly Henry Harrod's deceased, & is lying by the South harbor in Salem & is bounded with land of John Beckett E & N, with the harbor S & with the land of Richard Flinder W. **Signed**: Jeremiah Butman;

Acknowledged: 12: 5 mo: 1673; **Witnesses**: John Hathorne & Jacob Burton; **Recorded**: 12: 5: 1673.

SAMUEL BENNETT to JOSEPH JENCKES, Sr. – (4:29) On the 1st day of the 1st month 1672, Samuel Bennett (carpenter) of Boston granted to Joseph Jenckes, Sr., (smith) of Lynn, for 20 pounds sterling to him in hand paid, a parcel of land in the bounds of Lynn, bounded with a brook NE, which brook lies between land of said Samuel Bennett, which Thomas Stocker now holds & a brook on the NE side & the land called Mr. Knowles or Mr. Willowes' lands & on the SW side the land of John Ottway, which land contains 20 acres, with all ways, easements. **Signed**: Samuel Bennett, Sr.; **Acknowledged**: 6 May 1673; **Witnesses**: Oliver Purchase & Allester Duggles [by mark]; **Recorded**: 29: 5 mo: 1673.

GEORGE & REBECKA VICKERY to WILLIAM BROWNE – (4:31) On 17 July 1672, George Vickery & Rebecka his wife of Hull (alias Nantasket), Suffolk County, granted to William Browne of Marblehead, for 8 pounds 10 shillings of current money of New England to them in hand paid, 4 acres of land at Marblehead butted & bounded E with the Southworths, W with land of Henry Stacy & N with land of Moses Maverick, bounded by marked trees...to have & hold said 4 acres with all meadows, timber, trees...commonages, fishing & appurtenances thereto belonging. **Signed**: George Vickery & Rebecca Vickery [both by mark]; **Acknowledged**: 18 July 1672 by both George & Rebecca; **Witnesses**: Edward Little & John Hayward.

ROBERT HIBBERT, Sr. to daughter HANNA SWARTON – (4:34) On 1 February 1672, Robert Hibbert, Sr. (bricklayer) of Beverly, with wife Joane giving her consent, granted to their daughter Hanna, wife of John Swarton (tailor) of Beverly, freely & forever, 4 acres of land to them & their heirs to be occupied & enjoyed by them...without molestation or trouble. This land is bounded as follows: 1½ acre on the NE adjoining his land, on the S adjoining to son Joseph Hibbert's land, on the W to the new land of Osmond Trask; & the other 2½ acres in the 10 acres which was formerly called Mr. Emery's lot at Bass River, being bounded E with land of Josiah Rootes Sr. & on the W with Bass River, on the S with John Lambert's land & on the N with land of Joseph Hibbert Jr. **Signed**: Robert Hibbert & Joane Hibbert [by mark]; **Acknowledged**: 18: 4: 1673 by Robert Hibbert & Joane his wife freely yielding her thirds; **Witnesses**: John Hibbert [by mark], Hilliard Veren, Sr.

ARTHUR KIPPIN to LAURENCE MAUZUNE – (4:35) On 20 May 1673, Arthur Kippin (seaman) of Salem granted to Laurence Mauzune & Mary his wife of Salem, for divers goods, causes & considerations, especially for the good will & affection he bore for son-in-law Laurence Mauzune & daughter Mary his now wife, 12 rods or poles of land in Salem, part of the land on which his dwelling house stands, the said piece of land being in breadth next to the street W 9 yards & 2 feet & so runs backward E the same breadth & of length, E & W 43 yards, & is bounded with said street W & with his land N & with land of Joseph Williams E & land & dwelling house of Thomas Jegels S. **Signed**: Arthur Kippin & Abigail Kippin; **Acknowledged**: 21: 5: 1673 by Arthur Kippen & Abigail freely yielded up her thirds; **Witnesses**: Jeremiah Neale and Hillyard Veren, Sr.

NICHOLAS BARTLETT to THOMAS IVES – (4:38) On 7 March 1672, Nicholas Bartlett (fisherman) of Salem granted to Thomas Ives (hatherer) of Salem, for 75 pounds in hand paid, his now dwelling house with all ground said house stands on and is adjoining, being the same house & ground he formerly sold to Capt. Walter Price & now the day of the date of these presents sold again by said Capt. Walter Price to said Nicholas Bartlett, which said house & ground is lying in Salem & is bounded with land of John Day N, land of Edward Woodland E & land of Mr. Joseph Grafton S & land or highway W…containing the 6th part of an acre of ground or 27 rods of ground, as it lies bounded as aforesaid. Elizabeth his wife freely yielded up her right, title & dower. **Signed**: Nicholas Bartlett [by mark] & Elizabeth Bartlett [by mark]; **Witnesses**: Joseph Phippeny & Hilliard Veren.

NICHOLAS BARTLETT to WALTER PRICE – (4:39) On 24 October 1670, Nicholas Bartlett of Salem granted to Walter Price (merchant) of Salem for a valuable sum in hand paid, a new dwelling house with 26 rods of ground adjoining in Salem bounded W with the land or highway, N with ground of Edward Woolland & S with ground of Joseph Grafton, Jr. **Signed**: Nicholas Bartlett [by mark]; **Witnesses**: Hilliard Veren, Sr. & John Price, with seizin & possession. On 7 March 1672, Walter Price, for a valuable sum in hand paid, assigned over all right title and interest in or to within bargained premises to Nicholas Bartlett. **Signed**: Walter Price; **Witnesses**: Hilliard Veren & Joseph Phippeney.

JOHN STACY to ELLEN STACY – (4:41) On 23 April 1673, John Stacy of Marblehead, in consideration of his maintenance he had a long time from his son John Stacy now deceased, granted to Ellen Stacy, wife of said Stacy deceased, his whole propriety and interest in a lot in Marblehead, adjoining the house of said Stacy deceased which is now fenced in together with a cow's lease in the common provided said Ellen Stacy keep & maintain said John Stacy so long as he lives, & if Ellen should depart this life before said Stacy then said Stacy's part of the lot must be rented but not sold & rent to go toward maintenance of him. **Signed**: John Stacy; **Acknowledged**: 27: 4: 1673 by witnesses; **Witnesses**: John Legg, Jr. & Edward Humphry, Sr.; **Recorded**: 18: 6: 1673.

THOMAS MAULE to SAMUEL PICKWORTH – (4:43) On 14 August 1671, Thomas Maule (tailor) of Salem granted to Samuel Pickworth (carpenter) of Salem for a valuable sum in hand paid, all his dwelling house newly built, with all land adjoining belonging thereto, being about 5 poles or rods of ground, as bounded & lately bought of Jobe Hilliard, late deceased & Mary his wife, as per deed from them appeareth & situated in Salem, bounded N with the street or highway, E with land of widow Hollingworth, & on the S & W with land of said Jobe & Mary Hilliard, to have & hold said dwelling house, with said 5 poles of ground the said house stands upon & adjoining thereto with all right, titles, unto said Samuel Pickworth & to his heirs, and said Thomas Maule covenanted & promised...to bargain, sell & convey the same aforesaid & that it may and shall be lawful for the said Samuel Pickworth, his heirs & assignes, to have, hold, occupy...from the 1st of June next ensuing the date of these presents. **Signed**: Thomas Maule & Mary Maule [by mark]; **Acknowledged**: 25: 10 mo: 1671 by Thomas Maul & Mary his wife, who freely yielded up her thirds; **Witnesses**: Hilliard Veren, Sr. & Hilliard Veren; **Recorded**: 3: 7: 1673.

SAMUEL PICKWORTH to JOHN TURNER – (4:45) On 30 August 1673, Samuel Pickworth (carpenter) of Salem granted to John Turner (mariner) of Salem for 45 pounds sterling to him in hand paid, the receipt whereof he acknowledged, his dwelling house with all his ground adjoining thereunto, which he lately bought of Thomas Maule, situated in Salem, said ground belonging to said house containing about 6 poles & is bounded E with land of Mary Beckett, lately given to her by her father John Beckett & was late in possession of the widow Hollingworth & bounded S & W with land late of Job Hilliard deceased, & was in possession of Mary the administratrix of said Job Hilliard & now wife of William West, & bounded N with the street, to have & hold said dwelling house with all the ground adjoining, being about 5 or 6 poles of ground. Sara, wife of Samuel Pickworth freely yielded up her right, title, dower, etc. **Signed**: Samuel Pickworth & Sara Pickworth [by mark]; **Acknowledged**: 30: 6 mo: 1673 by Samuel Pickworth with Sara his wife freely yielding her thirds; **Witnesses**: Hilliard Veren, Sr. & John Price; **Recorded**: 10: 7 mo: 1673.

FRANCES JOHNSON to EDWARD HOEMAN – (4:48) On 23 February 1671, Frances Johnson (gentleman) of Boston granted to Edward

Hoeman (cooper) of Marblehead, one cow's lease of herbage in the common of Marblehead...& in case said Frances Johnson recovers his right in the town farm of Marblehead, then it shall be at choice of Edward Hoeman whether he will have said cow's lease in the farm with the land & timber belonging to said cow's lease or the cow's lease in common. **Signed**: Frances Johnson; **Acknowledged**: 1: 2 mo: 1672; **Witnesses**: Abraham Allen & Samuel Leach; **Recorded**: 27: 7: 1673.

WILLIAM TOWNE, EDMOND TOWNE & JACOB TOWNE to ISAACK EASTY – (4:49) On 15 February 1671, William Towne, Edmond Towne & Jacob Towne of Topsfield, granted to Isaack Easty (cooper) of Topsfield, for 26 pounds, several parcels of land as follows: 17 acres of upland in Topsfield bounded S with a particular highway or cart way belonging to said Edmond, Jacob, William Joseph Towne & said Isaack Easty & W with the country highway & N with some land of said Edmond & Jacob Towne & E with some land of Edmond & Joseph Towne; also an equal interest in said country highway & all other ways agreed upon by & between William, Edmond & Jacob Towne lying or being in said land; also 3 acres of land bounded N with land of John Robbisson W with aforesaid highway, S with land of Jacob Towne & E with land of Edmond Town; also 10 acres of land & swamp bordering upon aforesaid highway which bounds it E & SE and some land of William Town's S; some land of Jacob Towne SE & some land of John Robinson's & John Tod's W & NW. **Signed**: William Towne [by mark], Edmond Towne [by mark] & Jacob Towne; **Acknowledged**: 25: 4: 1673 by Edmond Towne in his own behalf & behalf of his father Jacob Towne (deceased); **Witnesses**: Thomas Perkins & John How; **Recorded**: 27: 7 mo: 1673.

WILLIAM TOWNE to ISACK EASTY – (4:53) On ---- 1663, William Towne of Topsfield granted to Isack Easty of Topsfield, 2 parcels of meadow land, 4½ acres in Topsfield, 1 parcel bounded by the Ipswich river towards S, Jacob Townes meadow NW, a way towards N & meadow of Edmond Towne SE, the other parcel by aforesaid river S, meadow of Edmond Towne NW, the way towards N & meadow of Jacob Towne E. **Acknowledged**: 4: 3: 1663; **Recorded**: 27: 7 mo: 1673.

FRANCES JOHNSON to ISAACK MEACHUM – (4:54) On 8 September 1663, Frances Johnson of Boston granted to Isaack Meachum (husbandman) of Salem for a valuable sum in hand paid, 4 acres of land being part of the farm of said Francis Johnson in Salem at or near the place called Brooksby & lying to the side of said farm N & is bounded N with common land, with Ipswich highway E & S & W the farm W...lying partly on N & partly on S side of the river or brook that runs through said farm, the said river being part of said 4 acres. **Signed**: Frances Johnson; **Acknowledged**: 18: 7 mo: 1673; **Witnesses**: Stephen Haskett, Samuel Archer & Hilliard Veren, Sr.; **Recorded**: 2: 8 mo: 1673.

HENRY BARTHOLOMEW to RICHARD LEACH – (4:57) On 10 December 1672, Henry Bartholomew (merchant) of Salem granted to Richard Leach of Salem for a valuable sum in hand paid, 10 acres of land on Royalls side in Salem, bounded W by a parcel of land lately bought of Thomas Watson S, land of Jeffery Massey E, common land N & land of Richard Leach W. **Signed**: Henry Bartholomew; **Acknowledged**: 23: 2 mo: 1673; **Witnesses**: Richard Walker & Thomas Putnam; **Recorded**: 2: 8: 1673.

GEORGE EMORY to JOHN GEDNEY, Sr. – (4:60) On 28 November 1671, George Emory (cherurgeon) of Salem with consent of wife, granted to John Gedney, Sr. (vintner) of Salem for valuable consideration in hand paid, 3 acres of salt marsh in Salem near the dwelling house of said George Emory on the other side of the river bounded N with the South river & S with south field. **Signed**: George Emory & Mary Emory; **Acknowledged**: 22: 7 mo: 1673; **Witnesses**: Edmond Batter & Robert Kitchin; **Recorded**: 2: 8: 1673.

PETER WOOLFE to THOMAS WOODBERY – (4:61) On 28 April 1670, Peter Wolfe (husbandman) of Beverly granted to Thomas Woodbery (mariner) of Beverly, 1½ acre of land in Beverly being part of a 10-acre lot he now dwells on as it was laid out & sold to his father by Mr. Googe; he sold the premises unto said Thomas Woodberry...after his decease & the decease of Martha his wife...reserving the use of it only for his life & that of his wife & then Thomas Woodbery to take possession. **Signed**: Peter Woolfe [by mark]; **Acknowledged**: 15: 7 mo: 1673; **Recorded**: 2: 8 mo: 1673.

MARY READE to JOHN PUDNEY – (4:62) On 23 April 1673, Mary Read, widow & administrator of the estate of her late husband Thomas Read of Salem, deceased, granted to John Pudney (husbandman) of Salem, for 3 pounds, 100 rods in Salem near the dwelling house & land of Samuel Eborne, Sr. bounded with the county road S, or runs between land of said Samuel Eborn's & premises & bounded on all other sides with common land, containing between ½ & ¾ acre. **Signed**: Mary Reade [by mark]; **Acknowledged**: 23: 2 mo: 1673; **Witnesses**: Hilliard Veren & Hilliard Veren, Jr.; **Recorded**: 2: 8 mo: 1673.

SAMUEL SKRIMPTON to RICHARD MORE – (4:64) On 1 December 1673 at Boston, Samuel Skrimpton, executor to the last will & testament of his father Henry Skrimpton, deceased, acknowledged to have received full satisfaction of Capt. Richard More of the within deed of mortgage. **Signed**: Samuel Skrimpton; **Entered**: 20: 11 mo: 1673 & entry of mortgage...Book first fol. 76; **Acknowledged**: 12 January 1673.

NATHANIEL KIRTLAND, Sr. to JOSEPH ARMITAGE – (4:64) On 13 October 1673, Nathaniel Kirtland, Sr. (yeoman) of Lynn granted to Joseph Armitage (tailor) of Lynn, for 30 pounds sterling, 2 acres bounded E with the house lot of Thomas Townsend, W & S with land of said Nathaniel Kirtland & N with mill street, with dwelling house standing upon said 2 acres in Lynn & is part of a 6 acre lot granted by the town of Lynn formerly & was late in possession of Richard Blood as also 1/3 part of common liberties. **Signed**: Nathaniel Kirtland; **Acknowledged**: 14: Oct: 1673; **Witnesses**: John Hathorne & Moses Chadwell; **Recorded**: 14: 9: 1673.

Joseph Armitage of Lynn assigned over unto James Russell of Charlestown rights...within bill of sale, 15 Oct 1673; **Witnesses**: Nehemiah Willoughby & Richard Austin; **Acknowledged**: Joseph Armitage, 15: 8 mo: 1673.

ABRAHAM ROBBINSON to STEVEN GLOVER – (4:67) On 10 April 1672, Abraham Robbinson of Gloucester, with consent of wife, granted to Steven Glover of Gloucester, for a certain sum in hand paid, all his house lot & orchard, a new house which he was then building & agreed with Mark Hascol to build for him, 4 acres lying next to the land of said Steven on ENE & common on NNW & adjoining to highway next to water side; this land lying in Gloucester & in case Abraham Robbinson pays Steven Glover 38 pounds in 4 years time after date hereof, which 38, 18 of it to be paid in good lawful money of New England & the other 20 pounds to be paid in either fish or English goods, namely Woolen or linen cloth or pork or cord wood or chattel or corn at price current, then house & land to be delivered to said Abraham again. **Signed**: Abraham Robinson [by mark] and Mary Robinson [by mark] and Steven Glover; **Acknowledged**: 23 July 1673 by Abraham Robbinson & Steven Glover and on 25 July 1673 by Mary Robinson (wife); **Witnesses**: William Sergent, Sr. & William Sergent, Jr.; **Recorded**: 17 Dec 1673.

JOHN PATCH & THOMAS PATCH – (4:69) Whereas there was a writing given unto Salem court held 26: 9: 1673 which was an agreement between John Patch & Thomas Patch, sons of Nicholas Patch (deceased) of the division of estate left them by their father...for a cleaner explanation of meaning...it is agreed upon as follows: First that John Patch shall have that 4 acres of meadow by Dodge's farm; also 2 acres of meadow by Longham's also that 1 acre of meadow joining to Capt. Thomas Lothrop by Samuel Corning's farm; also a dwelling house with orchard & 4 acres of land adjoining & belonging to said house (except 1 of said 4 acres lying at NE corner towards the river head); 2nd, Thomas Patch shall have 40 acres of upland with 4 acres of meadow belonging thereto, which 4 acres is lying at a place called the old house where said Thomas lives; also 1 cow & 3 young cattle & all household stuff & moveables (except about the value of 10 shillings worth which said John has already in possession & is still to enjoy it); also the above acre of land excepted out of the 4 acres adjoining to said house shall be to the use of said Thomas & Mary his now wife & their children…(for to build upon) the time of their natural lives or the longest liver of them & after their decease the reversion of said acre to John Patch…Thomas not to have use of said acre until they build upon it. **Signed**: 8 Dec 1673 by John Patch [by mark] & Thomas Patch; **Acknowledged**: 8: 10 mo: 1673; **Witnesses**: John Lovet, Sr. & Hilliard Veren, Sr.; **Recorded**: 26: 10: 1673.

WILLIAM KING to ROBERT STONE – (4:71) On 14 December 1665, William King (cooper) of Salem granted to Robert Stone (seaman) of Salem for 47 pounds sterling, 20 acres of upland & 1½ acre of salt marsh adjoining being ½ of his 40 acres of upland & 3 acres of salt marsh lying at the head of Bass river & bounded E with the river & with land of Abram Warren NW & W, on SW with the land of John Bachelor with ½ of all housing. **Signed**: William King & Katherin King; **Acknowledged**: Katherin King appeared 15: 11: 1673 and freely yielded up her thirds; also witnessed that she did know her husband did sell the land; **Witnesses**: William Dounton & Hilliard Veren; **Recorded**: 16: 11 mo: 1673.

WILLIAM KING to JOHN LEACH – (4:73) On 8: 9 mo: 1662, William King of Salem granted to John Leach of Salem for a valuable consideration in hand paid, 2 acres, all that parcel of land that was sometime in possession of John Friend (deceased) on which said Friend built one dwelling house lying next to Bass river on one side & running along by the land of said William King on the other side. John Leach shall make a fence between the land of William King & gives liberty to John Leach to cart wood or hay through his ground to his house. **Signed**: William King; **Witnesses**: William Hathorne & Henry Bartholomew; **Recorded**: 17: 11 mo: 1673.
Mr. Henry Bartholomew & myself wrote, ended & delivered it in time as the date of this & the bond show & they owned, signed & sealed as within. **Signed**: William Hathorne.

GEORGE JACOBS, Sr. to GEORGE JACOBS, Jr. – (4:75) This indenture was made the 12th of January 1673 between George Jacobs, Sr. (husbandman) of Salem & George Jacobs, Jr. his son. George Jacobs, Jun'r doth covenant with said George his father & undertakes to carry on & to manage his affairs viz: to plant, sow & reap his land & to provide for his stock of cattle & to do such employments as belongs to carrying on of affairs of family & be responsible for ½ of debts which said George Jacob, Sr. doth now stand indebted for: George Jacob, Sr. doth give unto George his son, ½ of all his land both upland and meadow with half the orchard & at the decease of said George Jacobs, Sr. and Mary his wife (who is to enjoy the other half during her life) said George Jacobs, Jr. is to enjoy the other half of the land now belonging to said George Jacobs, Sr., said George his son paying such legacies as said George, Sr. shall bequeath not exceeding the value of ½ the land aforesaid. *Item*: the said George, Sr. doth give unto George his son the ½ of all his stock…& said George Jun'r is to have half the profit & in case said George, Sr. shall depart this life & his wife shall change her name being married…it shall be liberty of said George Jun'r to divide land & stock. **Signed**: George Jacobs [by mark] & Mary Jacobs [by mark]; **Acknowledged**: 28: 11 mo: 1673 by George Jacobs, Sr. & Mary wife; **Witnesses**: Henry Skerry, Sr. & Hilliard Veren, Sr.; **Recorded**: 8: 11 mo: 1673.

ROGER CONANT to JOHN CONANT – (4:77) On 4 February 1673, Roger Conant (yeoman) of Beverly granted to his kinsman John Conant (carpenter) of Beverly for love and natural affection, 20 acres of land near Wenham great pond bounded with said pond NW & with the highway or country road S & round to NE as land lies & N with land of said Roger Conant & W with land of Benjamin Balch. **Signed**: Roger Conant; **Acknowledged**: 24 February 1673; **Witnesses**: Daniel Epps & Exercise Conant; **Recorded**: 27: 12 month 1673.

HENRY LEONARD & NATHANIEL LEONARD to SIMON BRADSTREET – (4:78) On 16 June 1673, Henry Leonard of Rowley Village (refiner) indebted to Mr. Simon Bradstreet of Andover, 20 pounds in money which should have been paid long since…for the security & true payment of said sum with just damages, granted his 16th part of the ironworks in said village…provided if said Henry…shall pay said sum of 20 pounds in money with just damages or shall deliver to said Simon…at Boston the just & full quantity of one ton + 500 weight of good conditioned & well wrought merchantable iron by or before the 16 day of July next coming…void; & Nathaniel Leonard covenanted promised to & with Simon for his further security that said money or iron should be delivered. **Signed**: Henry Leonard [by mark] & Nathaniel Leonard; **Acknowledged**: the same date; **Witnesses**: James Hanscombe & Thomas Leonard & possession given in part in name of whole; **Recorded**: 9: 1st month: 1673.

GEORGE CORWIN to JOHN HILL – (4:80) On 29 January 1658, George Corwin (merchant) of Salem, as feofee in trust by John Bridman & his wife & by the court, granted to John Hill (wheelwright) of Salem for a valuable consideration in hand already paid, a dwelling house with several parcels of land all in Salem, bounded as follows: 4 acres lying in 2 places, one of which being that whereon said dwelling house is situated beyond the mill plaine & is bounded NE with the lane that extends from said plain down towards strong water brook, NW with the town common & S with land of Henry Renolds; the other parcel being bounded N & E with land of said Renolds, W with land of Samuel Eborne & Samuel Gaskin & on S with the common near Snake Hill & is distant from the other parcel about 15 poles; also a 5 acre lot of upland lying in north field of Salem, bounded at one end with land of John Burton, at the other end with land of John Tompkins, Sr. & widow Spooner & having on one side land of Job Swinerton, Sr. & on the other side land of 5 several men & another parcel of upland of 5 acres lying by land of John Southwick (deceased) & having on one end thereof extending close to the SE side of Read's hill, the other end & one side bounded with the brook, all of which was formerly in possession of William Osborne. **Signed**: George Corwin; **Acknowledged**: 11: 12 mo: 1673 by Capt. George Corwin; **Witnesses**: William Bowditch & Edward Norrice; **Recorded**: 10: 1 mo: 1673.

THOMAS PICKTON to CHARLES KEMBOLL – (4:82) On 19 March 1674, Thomas Pickton (husbandman) of Beverly, with wife's consent, granted to Charles Kemboll of Hull (county of Suffolk) for 10 pounds money, 10 acres of land in Beverly bounded on the E with land of Jonathan Biles & on the S next to the common & on the W side with an oak formerly Pickton's bound & on the N corner with a maple in the swamp near a place called Long Hill. **Signed**: Thomas Pickton & Ann Pickton [by mark]; **Acknowledged**: 19: 1 mo: 1673/4 & wife Ann yielded dower; **Witnesses**: Moses Maverick & William Levermore [by mark]; **Recorded**: 19: March 1673/4.

CHRISTOPHER LATTAMORE to EDWARD HOLMAN – (4:84) On 2 October 1673, Christopher Lattamore (mariner) of Marblehead granted to Edward Holman (cooper) of Marblehead for 11 pounds already paid, a parcel of land in Marblehead near the water side together with privilege of a cove adjoining & that from high water mark to low water mark & bounded with a stone wall S adjoining to land of Henry Russell next to the cove, being 60 foot in breadth next to the cove & running with a straight line from the cove on the S or SW up to the old house & just beyond the house of Robert Hooper (only said Hooper and his wife are to enjoy the land his house stands upon during their natural lives) & running with a N line close to the back side of Holman's house to the end of the leanto &

running from the end of said house on a straight line to said cove on the NE excepting the liberty of a highway for the town through said ground by the end of said Holman's now dwelling house which is to be left in common. **Signed**: Christopher Lattamore [by mark] & Mary Lattamore; **Acknowledged**: 30: 1 mo: 1674 & wife Mary yielded thirds; **Witnesses**: Frances Johnson & Edward Norrice, Sr.; **Recorded**: 31: March: 1674.

JEREMIAH BELCHER to Capt. GEORGE CORWIN – (4:86) On 8 April 1674, Jeremiah Belcher (merchant) of Ipswich granted to Capt. George Corwin (merchant) of Salem for 229 pounds already paid, all his farm of 100 acres of upland & meadow with all houses, barns...in Ipswich, between the farm of Thomas Safford & land of John Adams; & also 16 acres of meadow near land of Ensign Howlett in Ipswich besides which meadow ground is in or belonging to the farm before mentioned; & also his dwelling house & ground in Ipswich on the W side of Mill River having said Mill River on the E side & land of Elder Whipple on the W & on the N the town & the mill & bordering S upon land of Elder Whipple...the premises were free from all manner of former sales...excepting 1 former mortgage of premises unto said Capt. George Corwin bearing the date first day of June 1660...& further it is to be understood that there are 16 acres of upland & meadow belonging also to said farm & comprehended within this bargain & sale lying about ¼ mile from said farm & bounded on N & W within land of John Safford, S with the town common & E with the highway. **Signed**: Jeremiah Belcher; **Acknowledged**: 8: 2 mo: 1674; **Witnesses**: William Bowditch & Edward Norrice; **Recorded**: 8: 2 mo: 1674.

WILLIAM EDMONDS to WILLIAM MERRIAM – (4:89) On 4 December 1673, William Edmonds (tailor) of Lynn granted to William Merriam (husbandman) of Lynn for a valuable consideration in hand paid, 4 acres of meadow in Lynn and in Rumney marsh near the dwelling place of Mr. Samuel Bennett, bounded by meadow of William Edmonds S & by meadow of Edward Baker, Sr. N & by meadow of Thomas Farrer E & by a little pond joining said William Edmonds W. **Signed**: William Edmonds; **Acknowledged**: 3 March 1673/4; **Witnesses**: Humphry Warren & Stephen Seargent; **Recorded**: 9: 2 month 1674.

Mr. SAMUEL BENNETT to WILLIAM MERRIAM – (4:91) On 26 February 1673, Mr. Samuel Bennett (yeoman) of Boston, with consent of Sarah his now wife, with reference to surrendering thirds, granted to William Merriam (husbandman) of Lynn for a valuable consideration in hand paid, a parcel of land lying on the N corner of the farm of said William Merriam, bounded between the line of said farm & the brook next thereunto & the brook is the bounds all along down to the brook that runs between it and John Ottorray. **Signed**: Samuel Bennett; **Acknowledged**: 7: 1 month 1673/4; **Witnesses**: John Hathorne & Benjamin Muzzy; **Recorded**: 9: 2 mo: 1674.

THOMAS GARDNER, Jr. to HUGH JONES – (4:93) On the day above mentioned, Thomas Gardner, Jr. of Salem granted to Hugh Jones of Salem for a valuable sum in hand paid, 5 acres of upland bought of Henry Skerry being ½ of said Skerry's lot lying in north neck & having a lot on one side that was George Williams' & on the other side that was old Goodman Towne's & at one end a lot that was Goodman Water's. **Signed**: Thomas Gardner & Elizabeth Bartholomew [by mark]; **Acknowledged**: 13: April: 1674; **Witness**: John Stone; **Recorded**: 13: 2 mo: 1674.

NATHANIEL KIRTLAND to WILLIAM MERRIAM – (4:94) On 14 May 1672, Nathaniel Kirtland of Lynn granted to William Merriam of Lynn in exchange of a parcel of land, 4 acres in Rumney Marsh in Lynn, bounded W on land of Moses Chadwell & E on land of John Breed, butting N upon land of John Fuller & S by land of Jonathan Hudson. **Signed**: Nathaniel Kirtland & Parnell Kirtland [by mark]; **Acknowledged**: 13: 3 mo: 1672 & wife Parnell yielded thirds; **Witnesses**: Edward Richards [by mark] & John Hathorne; **Recorded**: 9: 3 mo: 1674.

JOHN NORTHY, Sr. to CHRISTOPHER LATTAMORE – (4:95) On 30 March 1674, John Northy, Sr. granted to Christopher Lattamore (mariner) of Marblehead for divers good causes & considerations, a well that stood on his land which he sold to John Furbush & Samuel Morgaine, now in possession of Richard Read, with a passageway to said well which he sold to said Lattamore & received satisfaction of him before he sold the land to the proprietors abovementioned. **Signed**: John Northy; **Acknowledged**: 30 March 1673; **Witnesses**: William Pitt, James Smith & Christopher Nicke; **Recorded**: 13: 2 mo: 1673.

RICHARD HOLLINGWORTH to PHILLIP CROMWELL – (4:97) On 27 January 1673, Richard Hollingworth (mariner) of Salem granted to Phillip Cromwell of Salem for a valuable sum in hand paid, ½ acre of land in Salem adjoining the N side of land that belongs to the now dwelling house of said Richard Hollingworth & is divided by an old fence where it lately stood, all within a stone wall & is bounded NE & NW with common land, SE with land of Richard Hollingworth so far as the old fence stood that fenced in his garden & orchard, the bounds at the E end come to within a foot of the post that stands in a stone wall & so for the partition bound straight to a foot of the house of office & thence to a briar bush that stands just within the stone wall to SW at which end the parcel abuts against or towards the harbor & against the house & land lately bought of

Peter Welcom. **Signed**: Richard Hollingworth & Elizabeth Hollingworth; **Acknowledged**: 9: 12 mo: 1673 & wife Elizabeth yielded thirds; **Witnesses**: Hilliard Veren, Sr., Thomas Putnam & Thomas Gardner; **Recorded**: 14: 2 mo: 1674.

JOHN RAIMENT, Sr. to WILLIAM LEVERMORE – (4:100) On 25 May 1671, John Raiment, Sr. (yeoman) of Beverly, granted to William Levermore (planter) of Beverly, for 25 pounds, 15 acres of upland in Beverly, bounded on the E with Sawer's plaine, on the W with Snake hill, N with land of Jonathan Grover, S with Macrell Cove. **Signed**: John Raiment and Judith Raiment [by mark]; **Acknowledged**: 25 May 1671, wife Judith Raiment yielded dower; **Witnesses**: Andrew Eliott & Zachariah Herrick; **Recorded**: 14 April 1674.

Capt. THOMAS BREEDON to JOHN GIFFORD – (4:102) Capt. Thomas Breedon received the 6th of April 1670 of Mr. Gifford 100 pounds, by bill on Richard Waye of Boston, from Mr. Richard Russell of Charlestown, & also one bond of the said John Gifford, for 100 pounds, payable the 24th of June in the year 1671, in full payment & satisfaction to him and company for all former claims & demands from the said Gifford, & also for ¼ part of the Iron works at Cheswick in New England, which belonged to him & company aforesaid: as witness hand & seal this day...**Signed**: Thomas Breedon; **Witnesses**: Richard Waite, Marshall, & John Conney. Mr. John Conney & Marshall Richard Waite, testifieth...they did see Capt. Thomas Breedon signe...Taken upon oath 17 April: 74 before Edward Ting Asst. The above written entered this 20: 2 mo: 1674 as the release of two mortgages or obligations, entered in booke 2d. foll. 114 & 115.

JUDITH COOKE to sons ISAAC and JOHN COOKE – (4:103) On 10 July 1673, Judith Cooke of Salem granted to her 2 sons Isaac Cooke & John Cooke of the same town for 30 shillings to be paid to her son Samuel, for what is due him by legacy, and the overplus to be at her dispose, one acre of land in Salem at the lower end of the 20 acres formerly in possession of Henry Bullock bounded N & E & W ends with land of said Judith Cooke & on the S side next to John Southwick it is bounded with a brook & then with land of William Robbinson, the same side. **Signed**: Judith Cooke; **Acknowledged**: 19: 5 mo: 1674; **Witnesses**: Nathaniel Felton & Anthony Buxton with possession given by turf & twig; **Recorded**: 17: 7: 1674.

ARRABELLA BALDING to ELIZABETH & JOHN PRICE – (4:104) On 7 July 1674, Arrabella Balding, administratrix & relict to the late John Balding deceased, granted to Mrs. Elizabeth Price and John Price,

Executors unto Captain Walter Price lately deceased, for a valuable sum in hand already paid, a dwelling house with all ground adjoining, about ¼ acre, in Salem, bounded E with land of William Cash; W with land of Jeremiah Batman, only a highway left between, S with the highway, N with the common. **Signed**: Arrabella Balding [by mark]; **Acknowledged**: 7: 5 mo: 1674; **Witnesses**: Benjamin Gerrish & Nicholas Bartlett [by mark]; **Recorded**: 17: 7 mo: 1674.

JOHN GIFFORD to EZEKIELL FOGG (Memorandum) – (4:106) Ezekiel Fogg (merchant) of London aged 32 years came before me & took his oath that he being in London in the year 1673, & meeting with Mr. John Gifford of Lynn in New England, did then & there covenant & buy of said John Gifford ¾ part of all his interest whatsoever in all those lands & edifices herein expressed viz: 400 acres of land, 1 house 24 foot long, 20 foot wide with 6 acres of land within the fence & broken up with garden, orchard, cow house & stable, 1 house 26 feet long & 18 feet wide with 2 acres of land in fence, with a small orchard, a house 50 feet long & 16 foot wide for the potters to work in & another house 40 foot long & 20 foot wide & also a furnace to cast iron ware in, as pots, kettles, sugar roles, guns and the like, together with flumes, dams, water courses, flood gates, & utensils belonging together with all mines & minerals of what nature soever; also all woods, underwoods...lying between Lynn and Reading formerly called by name of Silver works. Ezekiel Fogg doth declare upon oath that he bought of said John Gifford ¾ part of premises as doth appear by deed of sale on record at Major Wright's office a Notary Public, situated by Royal Exchange in London in which said deed and recording said John Gifford doth acknowledge full satisfaction for the premises, but now said Fogg being here, desires this may be recorded in Salem as a caution to secure his interest, he alleges that his deed is mislaid and cannot be found. **Acknowledged**: 21: 2 mo: 1674; **Recorded**: as a caveat 21: 2 mo: 1674.

THOMAS PICKTON to Mr. JOHN HALE – (4:108) On 21 April, 1674, Thomas Pickton (planter) of Beverly granted to Mr. John Hale (minister of the Gospel) of Beverly for a valuable consideration in hand paid, 140 rods of land in Beverly, bounded E by an acre of land he sold to inhabitants of Beverly for a minister, which acre said people have on certain conditions settled on said Mr. Hale; bounded S by the highway, W by Morgan's lot, N by another parcel of land lying within Mr. Hale's fence. **Signed** and **Acknowledged**: 21 April 1674 by Thomas Pickton, with wife Ann yielding dower on 21 April 1674; **Witnesses**: Samuel Corning & Paul Thorndike. **Recorded**: 4 May 1674.

JOHN GALLY to Inhabitants of Beverly – (4:109) On 22 April 1674, John Gally (planter) of Beverly granted to the inhabitants of Bass River (now called Beverly) an acre of land in Bass River, which he sold about 15 years ago & which was now in possession of Mr. John Hale, minister of Gospel there, and lies within Mr. Hale's fence, bounded W by another acre bought of Thomas Pickton, and S & SW partly by another parcel of land lying within said fence and partly by William Hooper's land, and N partly by another parcel of land he sold to said Mr. Hale, and partly by a parcel of his land and SE by his land & the highway; the said acre of land being above 40 poles long, for which land he received 3 pounds, and he sold unto said inhabitants of Beverly and Mr. Hale as is or further may be by them confirmed unto said Hale. **Signed**: John and Florence Gally [both by mark]; **Acknowledged**: 22 April 1674; **Witnesses**: Samuel Corning & Thomas Pickton.

THOMAS PICKTON to Inhabitants of Beverly – (4:110) On 21 April 1674, Thomas Pickton confirmed sale to the inhabitants of Beverly, an acre of land in Beverly, bounded S on the highway, E by another acre of land bought of John Gally for the same use, N by another part of said Mr. Hale's home lot, & on the W by part of Mr. Hale's orchard which he sold to him and acknowledged to be fully satisfied, it being sold to said company 15 years ago, and by them stated upon Mr. John Hale, the present minister of the Gospel in the same place, according to a certain engagement of them to said John Hale, and where his now dwelling house now standeth. **Signed & Acknowledged**: 21 April 1674; **Witnesses**: Samuel Corning & Paul Thorndike; **Recorded**: 4 May 1674.

THOMAS BOWEN to RICHARD KNOTT – (4:111) On 28 July 1674, Thomas Bowen (planter) of Marblehead granted to Richard Knott (cherurgeon) of Marblehead, for a sum of money in hand paid, 1 cow's lease & land in commons of Marblehead, with an acre of low land, which commoners of Marblehead have already laid out to said Thomas Bowen, which belongs to abovesaid cow's lease, with all vegetation, mines or minerals thereto belonging. **Signed**: Thomas Bowen [Text and witness statements say wife Elizabeth signed, but there is no signature]; **Acknowledged**: 29: 9 mo: 1674 by both; **Recorded**: 30: 9 mo: 1674.

THOMAS BAKER to ISAACK ESTY – (4:113) On 28 March 1674, Thomas Baker (yeoman) of Topsfield and Priscilla his wife granted to Isaack Esty (cooper) of Topsfield, for just reasons & for a valuable payment in hand received already & secured to be paid, a parcel or allotment of land, formerly Francis Bates, by grant, bought of William Smith of Topsfield, 10 acres, according to the Town grant of Topsfield, in bounds whereof it lyeth, S of the great fresh river called Ipswich River, bounded W with the lot of Isaack Esty, E with land of William Bradstreet & S with land now farmer Porter's & N with land on cow common.

Signed: Thomas Baker and Priscilla Baker; **Acknowledged**: 3 Apr 1674; **Witnesses**: John Hunkins [by mark] & John How; **Recorded**: 8: 10 mo: 1674.

THOMAS PERKINS to JOHN ROBINSON – (4:115) On 30 October 1674, Thomas Perkins of Topsfield granted to John Robinson of Topsfield, for several good causes & especially 20 acres of land by way of exchange received by deed of John Robinson, about 6 acres of upland & swamp in Topsfield, bounded E with a stake on the N side of a brooke & from the stake to another stake on a straight line which stands at the corner of said Robinson's field, the said Perkins' land joining on the E, and lands of Robinson's joining on the S & on the W, with lands of John How on N, beginning at the NW corner of a birch tree on the S side of the brook to a stake on side of brook, which joins to Thomas Perkin's land, the Birch and the stake being the two corner bounds. **Signed**: Thomas Perkins; **Acknowledged**: 11: 9: 1674; **Witnesses**: Daniel Clark & John How; **Recorded**: 8: 10: 1674.

DANIEL CLARK to JOHN ROBINSON – (4:117) On 29 January 1672, Daniel Clark of Topsfield acknowledged that he granted to John Robinson of Topsfield for 20 pounds, 12 acres of upland in Topsfield, bounded with 3 stakes on the N & W and on the S with a rune and highway, and so home to the line of Edmund Bridges, and with a run of permit land of John How & said land & on the S & SE with land of Thomas Perkins & Edmund Bridges. Daniel Clark promised his wife would give up her right. Possession given by turf and twig. **Signed**: Daniel Clark & Mary Clark; **Acknowledged**: 29 January 1674; **Witnesses**: Daniel Wood & John David [by mark]; **Recorded**: 8: 10: 1674.

PHILLIP & HANNAH WELCH to ISAACK EASTY – (4:118) On 4 March 1673/4, Phillip Welch (planter) of Topsfield with Hannah his wife (Hannah also giving up dower), granted to Isaack Easty (cooper) of Topsfield, for a valuable consideration, also for a sufficient sum of current pay of New England in hand received & secured to be paid, 20 acres of land in Topsfield, which he had bought from Thomas Baker of Topsfield on the S side of the great fresh river called Ipswich river & lyeth in the 1st division of lots on the side of the river, containing 2 small lots, the one whereof was sometimes Mathew Stanley's, the other Anthony Carrell's lot, given them by the town of Topsfield, the one being the 13th and the other the 14th lots in that division, and the aforesaid parcel is bounded by the lands of Mr. Endecott W, the lands of farmer Porter S, and is flanked with Isaac Easty's land on the E & with the common land N. **Signed**: Phillip and Hannah Welch [both by mark]; **Acknowledged**: 31 March 1674;

Witnesses: Thomas Baker, Priscilla Baker, Phillip Welch [by mark] and Richard Smith [by mark]; **Recorded**: 8: 16 [sic] mo: 1674.

Mr. WILLIAM BROWNE, Sr. et al. to DANIEL ANDREWS – (4:121) On 18 February 1672, Mr. William Browne, Sr., Capt. George Corwin, Capt. Walter Price, Mr. John Gedney, Sr., Mr. Eleazer Hathorne, Mr. John Corwin and Mr. Phillip Cromwell, administrators to the estate of Mr. William Woodcock, late deceased granted to Daniel Andrews (bricklayer) of Salem, for a valuable consideration in hand paid, a dwelling house with all goods or estate: household goods, clothing, physic, drugs, vessels and potts, with a horse and whatever else is mentioned in the inventory of said deceased William Woodcock's estate (only excepting one feather bed and the great still) which dwelling house is standing upon or joining to a parcel of land in Salem, late bought of Mr. Edmond Batter, said land said house stands on, is bounded E N & W by land of Mr. Edmond Batter and with the street on the S…and they promise to defend premises against Hannah late wife. **Signed**: Wm. Browne, George Corwin, John Gedney, John Corwin, Phillip Cromwell, Eleazer Hathorne, John Price, as "executor to my father"; **Acknowledged**: 13: 9 mo: 1674; **Witnesses**: John Marston, Jr. & William Hollis; **Recorded**: 8: 10: 1674.

HANNA WOODCOCK to WILLIAM BROWNE, Sr. etc. – (4:124) On 12 September 1670, Hanna Woodcock, late wife of William Woodcock, deceased, resigned her right of the dwelling house (which was lately her husband Woodcock's deceased) to William Browne, Sr., Capt. George Corwin, Mr. John Gedney, Sr., Capt. Walter Price, Mr. Phillip Cromwell, Mr. Eleazer Hathorne and Mr. John Corwin (all creditors & appointed by the County Court, administrators to the estate) for a valuable consideration in hand received. **Signed**: Hanna Woodcock; **Witnesses**: Moses Maverick & John Gardner; **Recorded**: 8: 10: 1674.

GEORGE MAJEIRE to PETER VALLAT – (4:125) On 28 April 1674, George Majiere of the parish at St. Lora in the Island of Jersey in Hampshire, now resident of Newbury in New England, acknowledged he owed and was indebted unto Peter Vallat of St. Peters in Jersey (seaman) 8 bushels of good sound merchantable wheat which he promised to pay to said Peter Vallat at Peter Vallat's, according to the measure of Jersey at or before St. Michall's Day next ensuing. **Signed**: George Majeire [by mark]; **Witnesses**: George de St. Croix and Julian Vibert & Hilliard Veren, recorder in Salem; **Recorded**: 28: 2 mo: 1674.

EDMUND BATTER to JACOB PUDEATER – (4:126) On 15 May 1674, Edmund Batter (merchant) of Salem granted to Jacob Pudeater (blacksmith) of Salem, for a valuable consideration in hand paid, all the parcel of land late bought of the town of Salem and laid out to him as entered in the town book of record, ¼ acre, butting against land of John Neale to the N and bounded by common land on all other sides, being in breadth 3½ poles wide from John Neale's fence southward, and 12 poles in length from the corner of John Neal's to land of Mr. Joseph Gardners according as it was laid out by the town. **Signed**: Edmond Batter; **Witnesses**: Benjamin Gerrish & John Gedney, with seizin & possession of premises given; **Recorded**: 15 May 1674.

JOSEPH POPE and SAMUEL EBBORNE to JOHN WESTON – (4:127) On 23 April 1674, Joseph Pope and Samuel Ebborne, Sr. both of Salem (husbandmen) granted to John Weston (husbandman) of Reading, for 8 pounds, 10 acres of meadow in Reedy meadow in Lynn, bounded S with a thicket of upland called the dark swamp, N with upland of Ensign Bancroft, E with meadow possessed by Hannaniah Parker & with some meadow of Joseph Felch on the W side. *Memorandum*: Samuel Eborne, as he owed 5 acres of abovesaid meadow, sold as above to said Weston so to the warranting of 5 acres being ½ of above premises. **Signed**: Samuel Ebborne, Sr. [by mark]; **Acknowledged**: 22: 2 mo: 1674 by Ebborne; **Witnesses**: Hilliard Veren, Sr. & John Horne; **Recorded**: 25: 2 mo: 1674.

HUGH JONES to WILLIAM ROBINSON – (4:130) On 22 April 1673, Hugh Jones (planter) of Salem granted to William Robinson (tailor) of Salem, for a valuable sum in hand paid, all the parcel of land that the town of Salem formerly granted to him, 2 or 3 acres in Salem at or near a brooke or river that runs down to the mill and is bounded S with the highway, N with land of John Southwick (deceased), NE with land of Widow Cooke & SE partly with the common land or the said brook, and partly with land of said William Robinson. **Signed**: Hugh Jones [by mark]; **Acknowledged**: 29: 2 mo: 1674; **Witnesses**: Nathaniel Felton and Anthony Buxton; **Recorded**: 5 May 1674 [at top of page] and 21: 3 mo: 1674 [at bottom].

JOHN BULTEEL, etc. to JOHN GIFFORD (Indenture) – (4:131) On 30 April 1674, the following indenture was acknowledged: Indenture tripartite made 1 August 1673 between John Gifford of New England (merchant) on the 1st part, John Bulteele of St. Margarett's (Westminster), Esquire, on the 2nd part, Sir Richard Combe of Hemel hemsted in the county of Hartford (Knight), John Wright of Wright's Bridge, County of Essex, Esquire, Francis Allen of London, Esq., John Godfrey of Canterbury, Esq., John Williams of Bristow (merchant), John Eaton of London (mercer) and Ezekiell Fogg of London (merchant) on the 3rd part, witnesseth: that in consideration of 5 shillings good and lawful money of England to said John Gifford by said John Bulteel in hand paid, and 1500 pounds of like lawful money by said Sr. Richard Combe, John Wright, Francis Allen,

John Godfrey, John Williams, John Eaton and Ezekiell Fogg in hand paid, John Gifford doth acquit said Richard Combe, John Wright, Francis Allen, John Godfrey, John Williams, John Eaton and Ezekiell Fogg, and to the intent and purpose that said John Bulteele should immediately reconvey land and premises as by another deed bearing date the day next after date of these presents is intended to be mentioned; as also for other considerations said John Gifford at and by the direction and appointment of said Sr. Richard Combe [etc.] testified by their being parties to and signing, hath given, granted unto said John Bulteele 400 acres of land and also 1 house containing 24 foot long & 20 foot wide, with 6 acres of land in fence and broke up, with garden, orchard, cow house & stable; one other house 26 foot long and 18 foot wide, with 2 acres of land in fence, with a small orchard; one other house 50 foot long & 16 foot wide, for a potter to work in; one house 40 foot long & 20 foot wide, a furnace to cast iron ware in as pots, kettles, sugar roles, guns, shot or the like, together with all floods, waters, water courses, dams, floodyches in betwixt Lynn and Reading, formerly called silver works. **Signed**: John Gifford, Francis Allen, John Bulteele, John Godfrey, Richard Combe, John Williams, John Wright, John Eaton, Ezekiell Fogg; **Acknowledged**: 30 April 1674 at Boston by John Gifford and Ezekiel Fogg, presenting instructions of the rest of the company concerned bearing date of 15 Sep 1673; **Witnesses:** (to John Gifford) John Bulteele, Richard Combe, John Wright, Francis Allen & Ezekiell Fogg; Richard Stonehill (Notary Public), 1673 William Reynolds; (to John Godfrey): Wittingham Fogg, Thomas Turner, Jr.; (to John Eaton): Richard Weeden, Richard Stonehill, 1673; (to John Williams): Samuel Hunt & Charles Tate; **Recorded**: 5 May 1674.

JOHN BULTEELE to JOHN GIFFORD, etc. (Indenture) – (4:136) Indenture tripartite made 2 August 1673 between John Bulteele of St. Margretts (Westminster), Esq. on the 1st part, John Gifford of New England (merchant), Ezekiell Fogg of London (merchant), John Wright of Wrightsbridge (County of Essex), Esq. on the 2nd part and Sr. Richard Combe of Henelhemsteed (county of Harford) (Knight). Francis Allen of London, Esq., John Godfrey of Canterbury, Esq., John Williams of Bristol (merchant) and John Eaton of London (mercer) on the 3rd part, in consideration of 5 sh. lawful money of England to said John Bulteele, paid by John Gifford, Ezekiel Fogg and John Wright in pursuance of agreement between parties in deed, indented tripartite dated before these presents, John Bulteel doth sell to John Gifford, Ezekiel Fogg, John Wright [same as previous] in trust... **Signed**: John Bulteele, John Gifford, Ezekiell Fogg, John Wright, Richard Combe, Francis Allen, John Godfrey, John Williams and John Eaton... **Witnesses**: (to John Bulteel, John Gifford, Ezekiel Fogg, John Wright, Sr., Richard Combe & Francis Allen) William Reynolds, Richard Stonehill, notary public 1673; (to John Godfrey)

Whittingham Fogg, Thomas Turner, Jr.; (to John Williams) Samuel Hunt, Charles Tate; **Acknowledged**: Boston, 30 April 1674 by John Gifford, Ezekiel Fogg, presenting instructions of rest of company dated 11 August 1673 & 15 September 1673; **Recorded**: 5 May 1678; deed 5 May 1674.

JOHN GIFFORD, etc (Indenture) – (4:140) This indenture sexpartite, made 2 August 1673 between John Gifford of New England (merchant) Ezekiel Fogg of London (merchant) and John Wright of Wrightsbridge (County of Essex), Esq. on the 1st part, Sr. Richard Combe of Hemellhem Steed (county of Hartford) (Knight) on the 2nd part, Francis Allen of London, Esq. of the 3rd part, John Godfrey of Canterbury, Esq. on the 4th part, John Williams of Bristoll (merchant) on the 5th part and John Eaton of London (mercer) on the 6th part, whereas by indenture tripartite...said John Bulteele did for considerations in said deed sell to said John Gifford, Ezekiel Fogg, John Wright (description as previous), nevertheless it is declared said sale is upon special trust and to such uses as by one other deed sexpartite should be particularly mentioned and whereas 1 June now last past, said parties have agreed to enter into a partnership or company for digging, smelting, working and refining of certain mines or minerals of gold silver, lead, tin, iron, copper and other metals within the land in these presents mentioned, as also for the obtaining a grant or patent from his now majie [or poss. matie] for the settling upon them for such number of years as can best be procured, one moyetie and half part of his Majesty's interest reserved by his letters, patents, formerly made of the fifth part of all ore and all gold & silver within the bound and limits of certain places within New England, in said letters patents to be mentioned and comprised: all and every which said workes, as well of said mines or minerals within said land as said moiety of said 5th part so belonging to his Majestie, it is the true intent of all the parties, shall be equally and indifferently done and the charges thereof borne and the profits divided by said parties according to such shares and proportions as are hereinafter expressed, the whole adventure being divided into 16 parts: Sir Richard Combe to have 1/16 part; John Wright 2/16; John Godfrey 1/16; John Williams 2/16; Francis Allen 1/16; John Eaton 1/16; John Gifford 4/16; Ezekiel Fogg 4/16 and whereas for the carrying on of said works and adventures said several persons have already articled to advanced their several proportions 2,000 pounds according to the rate of 125 pounds to every share or sixteenth of which 1 moyetie is presently to be advanced, and the other moyetie at such times and by such proportions, as by said article is expressed; and whereas it is the true intent of all parties that said lands should always accompany said works and adventure and should not be divided from the same, but should always be united to said venture until by consent of said company they should be declared to be dissolved. **Signed**: at Boston, 30 April 1674 by John Gifford and Ezekiell Fogg, presenting, instructions of rest of company bearing date 11: Aug 1673 and 15 Sept 1673; **Recorded**: 5 May 1674; **Signed**: John Gifford, Ezekiel Fogg, John Wright, Richard Combe, Francis Allen, John Godfrey, John Williams, John Eaton; **Witnesses**: (to John Gifford, Ezekiel Fogg, John Wright, Sr., Richard Combe and Francis Allen) William Reynolds, Richard Stonehill (Notary Public, 1673); (to John Godfrey) Whittingham Fogg, Thomas Turner, Jr.; (to John Eaton) Richard Weeden and Richard Stonehil, 1673; (to John Williams) Samuel Hunt and Charles Tate.

RICHARD HOLLINGWORTH to THOMAS FLINT and GERTRUDE POPE – (4:146) On 11 May 1674, Richard Hollingworth (mariner) of Salem granted to Thomas Flint and Gertrude Pope (widow), both of Salem, for a valuable sum in hand paid, 30 acres of land in Salem, bounded N with land of Mr. Gardner, NE by a brook, named Ipswich River, E with land of John Tomkins and S with land of John Rubton, W with some land of John Porter, Sr., the several bounds being (trees). **Signed**: Richard and Elizabeth Hollingworth; **Acknowledged**: 11: 3 mo: 1674, with Elizabeth yielding thirds; **Witnesses**: Richard Flinder & Hilliard Veren, Sr.; **Recorded**: 22: 3 mo: 1674.

SAMUEL DOLIBER to JOHN WALDEN – (4:149) On 20 June 1651, Samuel Doliber of Marblehead granted to John Walden of Marblehead, for a certain sum of money in hand paid, all his dwelling house with 10 acres as it is now laid out in Marblehead, adjoining to Mr. Walton's land S and on NW adjoining to William Barbor's land and northward butting on the commons and toward the E facing to the great harbor. **Signed**: Samuel Doliber; **Acknowledged**: 2: 2 mo: 1674; **Witnesses**: Moses Maverick & Erasmus James; **Recorded**: 6: 3 mo: 1674.

THOMAS MAULE to DANIEL WELD – (4:150) On 12 May 1674, Thomas Maule of Salem (with wife Naomi yielding dower) granted to Daniel Weld (physician) of Salem for a valuable sum in hand paid, all the dwelling house of Thomas Maule that he now lives in, together with ground the house stands on and adjoining, 20 rods of ground, most part of it being within the fence in Salem, bounded with a lane or highway W, with the land of Joshua Rea N & E and with land of Mr. Edward Norrice S. *Memorandum*: It is agreed that said Daniel Weld is to maintain all the cross fence at the end of the premises to the E, which is 2 lengths of rails. **Signed**: Thomas Maule and Naomi Maule [by mark]; **Acknowledged**: 13 May 1674; **Witnesses**: William Bowditch and Hilliard Veren, Sr.; **Recorded**: 14: 3 mo: 1674.

JOHN HUCHESON to JOHN PORTER, Sr. – (4:153) On 30 November 1670, John Hucheson of Salem granted to John Porter, Sr. (farmer) of

Salem for a valuable sum paid, about 1½ acres of land in Salem, formerly fenced by said Porter and bordering on the meadow lying on the W side of the brook that comes from Beaver dam, being a part of father Richard Hucheson's farm that was given to him by the town of Salem, said parcel lies within the said fence of said John Porter, the fence being the bound between them. **Signed**: John Hucheson; **Acknowledged**: 25: 3 mo: 1674; **Witnesses**: Henry Bartholomew, John Putnam & Richard Leach [by mark]; **Recorded**: 30: May: 1674.

JOHN FOSTER, Sr. to son JOHN FOSTER – (4:155) On 18 April 1672, John Foster, Sr. of Salem (with wife Martha Foster yielding dower) granted to his son John Foster for good causes, especially natural affections and fatherly care and love, a parcel of upland, swamp and salt marsh in Salem on the N side of the north field, having land of Thomas Robbins on the W and down to the river that is on the N side of said field, and said river on the N side and the land of John Waters formerly Robert Cotta on the E and land of John Foster, Sr. on the S from said Waters land to land of said Robbins, it being part of land formerly belonging to Thomas Scutter, Sr. **Signed**: John Foster [by mark]; **Acknowledged**: 14: 1 mo: 1672/3; **Witnesses**: Mathew Woodwell and John Swinerton; **Recorded**: 1 June 1674.

SUSANNA FOGG to sons JOHN, EZEKIEL & DAVID FOGG (Indenture) – (4:157) On 28 May 1674, an indenture was made between John Fogg of the 1st part and Ezekiel Fogg on the 2nd part and David Fogg on the 3rd part, sons and all the children of Ralph Fogg (citizen and skinner) of London, formerly of New England and late of Plymouth (county of Devon) in old England, deceased, witnesseth: whereas by virtue of a letter from Susanna Fogg, mother to John, Ezekiel and David, widow and relict of said Ralph Fogg, bearing date of 21 March last, directed to said David Fogg, wherein gives an account of the decease of Ralph Fogg, about the 15 March last that in pursuance as well of will of said Ralph Fogg, whether by word or writing as her said Susanna Fogg's mind will and pleasure as a mother hath ordered that what land or interest said Ralph Fogg deceased hath in or about Salem, County of Essex in New England, should be & appertaine to said John Fogg at his dispose and also all the interest Ralph Fogg hath or can claim in Saggadahoc patent or any other estate to the eastward of Cape Ann in New England should belong to Ezekiel at his own dispose; and also all the interest the said Ralph Fogg hath or can claim in Plymouth patent in New England should belong to David Fogg at his own dispose, and whereas said John Fogg, Ezekiel Fogg and David Fogg, sons and only children are now together in Boston in New England at the receipt of said letter said John Fogg, Ezekiel Fogg and David Fogg have agreed in pursuance of the mind of their mother; 1st said

Ezekiel Fogg and David Fogg grant all right in the lands that did belong unto Ralph Fogg, their father deceased in and about Salem to John Fogg, and John Fogg and David Fogg grant all right in and to all lands in Saggadahoc Patent to Ezekiell Fogg; 3rd John Fogg and Ezekiel Fogg grant all right in lands in and about Plymouth to David Fogg. **Acknowledged**: 29 May 1674; **Recorded**: 1 June 1674.

JOHN KNIGHTS to THOMAS WELLMAN – (4:162) On 29 March 1662, John Knights (mason) of Salem (with wife Em yielding dower) granted to Thomas Wellman (husbandman) of Lynn, for 80 pounds, all his farm on which he lately dwelt, also all the meadow, ground, timber, which said farm or land is ½ of all that land said John Knight and Thomas Wellman late bought together of Nicholas Potter of Lynn, which was 2 three-score acre lots, with 6 acres of meadow lying in 2 separate parcels in the limits of Lynn and bounded as is expressed in the deed of sale, bearing date of 17 February 1653, and also 3 score acres lately bought by said John Knights and Thomas Wellman of Edward Richards of Lynn, with a certain parcel of meadow containing 2 acres and being bounded as appears in that deed bearing date 12 December' 1653; ½ of all the above mentioned land, both uplands and meadow. **Signed**: John Knights & Em Knights [by mark]; **Acknowledged**: 20: 3 mo: 1674; **Witnesses**: Hilliard Veren & Richard Harvey; **Recorded**: 10 June 1674.

GEORGE EMORY to SAMUEL WARD – (4:165) On 4 December 1673, George Emory (cherurgeon) of Salem granted to Samuel Ward (cooper) of Boston, for a valuable sum in hand paid, ¾ acre of salt marsh, being that parcel of marsh formerly granted by the town of Salem to said George Emory within the grounds of Salem, at the great cove in the north neck and bounded by water E & S and is near or adjoining upland of Thomas Brackett N. **Signed**: George Emory; **Acknowledged**: 17: 4 mo: 1674; **Witnesses**: William Price & John Porter, Jr.; **Recorded**: 18: 4: 1674.

RICHARD HUTTON, Sr. to JOHN WEST (Mortgage) – (4:167) On 1 May 1674, Richard Hutton, Sr. of Wenham mortgaged to John West 60 acres of land lying upon the neck in Wenham bounds, and bounded with White's farm on one side and with the cartway on the other, in consideration of all the right that John West of Beverly has by mortgage unto a parcel of land or farm in Wenham once in the possession of Thomas White now deceased or any advantage said John West had therein in lieu of the real or supposed right said John West had in or to aforesaid land or farm or any part thereof. Richard Hutton to pay John West 60 pounds in matter and manner as followeth: 20 pounds in 1674 to be paid in pork, corn & seed at price current, or cord wood at 4 shillings the cord, at said John West's beach near his house, and 20 pounds in 1675 in pork & 20 pounds in 1676 in pork and further said Richard Hutton to pay all the payments of pork, beef and corn at the now dwelling house of said John West in Beverly or at the ferry place in Beverly Side. It is agreed that said Richard Hutten shall have liberty to pay whole or any part of aforesaid payments in neat cattle, provided they are under 10 years of age. **Signed**: Richard Hutten; **Acknowledged**: 17: 4 mo: 1674; **Witnesses**: Andrew Elliott & Paul Thorndike; **Recorded**: 24: 4 mo: 1674.

MARY LEOMAN to JEFFREY THISTLE & RICHARD THISTLE – (4:170) On 7 March 1673/4, Mary Leoman of Salem, relict and executrix of Robert Leoman (deceased), with consent of her children, Sara and Hana (and their husbands Charles Knight and Samuel Beadle), granted to Jeffrey Thistle and Richard Thistle of Beverly (seaman), for 50 pounds sterling in hand paid or secured to be paid, all that parcel of land left her by the last Will and Testament of said husband, deceased, lying on Cape Ann side, within bounds of Beverly, at Plum cove, 30 acres of upland, bounded S with the sea, E with land of Nicholas Woodbery, N by common land, and some land of Richard Thistle partly and some land of Richard Ober the other part on W and somewhat S. **Signed**: Mary Leoman [by mark]; **Acknowledged**: 13: 5 mo: 1674; **Witnesses**: Hilliard Veren, Sr. & Thomas Searle; **Recorded**: 13: 5: 1674.

HENRY SKERRY, Sr. and Mr. ROBERT BUTTEN (Exchange of land) – (4:172) On 22 July 1674, Henry Skerry, Sr. (cordwainer) of Salem, for 10 acres of land in the north field of Salem by great cove, acknowledged that he divers years since [ago] exchanged with Mr. Robert Butten, then of Salem, 10 acres of Darby fort side, bounded N on the river, W on the lot of James Moulton, S on the way to Marblehead & E on the lot of James Hind or James Underwood; also 2½ acres in the south field. **Signed**: Henry Skerry, Sr.; **Acknowledged**: 22 July 1674; **Witnesses**: Hilliard Veren, Sr. & Robert Lord, Jr.; **Recorded**: 23 July 1674. Edward Hutchinson, Sr. of Boston, out of fatherly love to son-in-law Samuel Butten, having married his mother, who was sole executrix to the estate of his father Robert Butten, released any title he might have to said land by virtue of his father's will... **Signed**: day and year above written by Edward Hutchinson; **Acknowledged**: 22 Jul 1674 by Capt. Edward Hutchinson; **Witnesses**: Hilliard Veren, Sr. and Robert Lord, Jr.

MOSES CHADWELL to DANIEL NEEDHAM – (4:174) On 20 November 1671, Moses Chadwell (ship carpenter) of Lynn granted to Daniel Needham (husbandman) of Lynn, for 20 pounds sterling, 3 acres of land in Lynn, abutting E on land of George Keaser, W on the river where formerly was the ferry, N & S with land of Edward Needham (gentleman) which was formerly the house lot of Thomas Chadwell. **Signed**: Moses

Chadwell and Sara Chadwell [by mark]; **Acknowledged**: 14: 3 mo: 1672, with wife Sara yielding thirds; **Witnesses**: Andrew Mansfield and John Breed (whose wives surrendered thirds); **Recorded**: 23 July 1674.

DANIEL NEEDHAM (Assignment) – (4:176) On 10 May 1672, Daniel Needham of Lynn, son of Edmond Needham of Lynn (gentleman) made over and assigned unto his father, this deed on the other side of this paper, as his own proper estate as being purchased with his said father's estate, namely Mr. Needham's estate, the said deed should have been in his name, whereas it is in name of Daniel Needham son of Edmond Needham. **Signed**: Daniel Needham [by mark]; **Acknowledged**: 14: 3 mo: 1672; **Witnesses**: Joseph Armitage & Andrew Mansfield; **Recorded**: 23 July 1674.

JAMES ALLEN to ROBERT SANFORD (Mortgage) – (4:176) On 29 February 1671, James Allen (teacher of the First Church in Boston) and Elizabeth his wife, granted to Robert Sanford (husbandman) of Boston for 330 pounds secured to be paid, a dwelling house and 300 acres of land, containing that land that was granted by the towne of Salem unto Townsend Bishop and by him sold unto Mr. Chickering and by him sold unto John Endecott, Esq., late Governor, deceased, lying in Salem, bounded E and S with Zerrubbabel Endecot; the NE corner with a brook adjoining unto farmer Porter's land, from thence running 400 rods to the NW corner. James Allen was to pay 330 pounds, either in money or what shall be raised upon said land at money price within the space of 10 years next ensuing but if it happen that a considerable part of said 330 pounds be unpaid either by exchange of land or otherwise within the first 3 years of said 10 years, then 340 pounds instead of aforesaid 330 pounds in the like pay and in the same 10 year space; it is agreed that if said consideration be behind or unpayed, within the whole or any part thereof, at the expiration of 10 years, that within 3 months space after said bargained premises shall be apprised by indifferent men chosen, at true value in money or money's worth and for what is unpayed, either whole or part thereof shall be adjudged worth the purchase money that is then unpaid, shall be delivered by deed unto James Allen or else to pay a competent rent until the whole purchase money be paid. **Signed**: James Allen and Eliza Allen; **Acknowledged**: 26 March 1672; **Witnesses**: John Man & Richard Goulding; (Book 8; page 80; 1:2 entered and recorded 10 March 1672/3 as attested by Isaac Addington, Recorder); **Recorded**: 19: 6 mo: 1674.

WILLIAM BROWNE, Jr. to Lieut. JOSEPH GARDNER – (4:180) On 27 July 1664, William Browne, Jr. (merchant) of Salem granted to Lieut. Joseph Gardner (vintner) of Salem, for a valuable sum in hand paid, 2 acres of land lying between land of John Archard & John Pitman on S on a piece of swamp land given by the town of Salem to Mr. John Higginson and now land of said Joseph Gardner, butting on the common called the training place on W; a narrow lane that goes between 2 coves, and between land of Thomas Roots and the above bargained premises on E, it being lately bought by said William Browne of Elias Stileman, adminstrator of Elias Stileman, deceased. **Signed**: William Brown, Jr.; **Acknowledged**: 17: 6 mo: 1674; **Witnesses**: William Browne, Sr. & Hilliard Veren, Sr.; **Recorded**: 19: 6 mo: 1674.

THOMAS GARDNER, Sr. to JOSIAH SOUTHWICK – (4:182) On 6 December 1671, Thomas Gardner, Sr. (husbandman) of Salem granted to Josiah Southwick (husbandman) of Salem for a valuable consideration paid about 13 years before sealing of this bill of sale, 2 acres lying in the north field in Salem, bounding upon the SW adjoining meadow late in possession of Robert Buffum, on the NE joining land in possession of Robert Pease, the NE & SW upon land of Henry Trask. **Signed**: Thomas Gardner, Sr.; **Acknowledged**: 13: 1 mo: 1672/3; **Witnesses**: Robert Pease & John King; **Recorded**: 20: 6 mo: 1674.

RICHARD BISHOP to JOSIAH SOUTHWICK – (4:183) On 30 December 1670, Richard Bishop (husbandman) of Salem granted to Josiah Southwick (husbandman) of Salem for 38 pounds, 10 acres lying in the north field near to aforesaid town, bounding N on land of John Burton & Isaack Cook, E on land of Samuel Gaskin, S on land of John King & W on land of Samuel Eborne. **Signed**: Richard Bishop and Mary Bishop; **Acknowledged**: 29: 3 mo: 1671; **Witnesses**: John Kitchen & George Deane; [no recording date].

THOMAS REMINGTON to DANIEL WICUM – (4:184) On 17 April 1674, Thomas Remington of Rowley granted to Daniel Wicum of Rowley for 14 pounds, 1½ ox gate which formerly was Francis Parrott's which abovesaid Remington bought of John Tenney, which gate and a half lyeth in the northeast ox pasture in Rowley. **Signed**: Thomas Remington and Mehitabel Remington [by mark]; **Acknowledged**: 9 May 1674; **Witnesses**: John Acy & Thomas Remington, Jr. [by mark]; **Recorded**: 20: 6 mo: 1674.

JOHN SANDERS to JOSIAH SOUTHWICK – (4:186) On 27 July 1674, John Sanders (mariner) of Salem granted to Josiah Southwick (husbandman) of Salem for a valuable consideration in hand paid, ½ acre of salt marsh in Salem above the corn mill in the North River and bounded E with some upland of widow Buffum & S with some salt marsh of said Buffum N by some marsh of Richard Bishop & W by the river or mill pond. **Signed**: John Sanders; **Acknowledged**: 27: 5 mo: 1674; **Witnesses**: Hilliard Veren, Sr. & John Kitchen; **Recorded**: 20: 6: 1674.

JOHN KNIGHT Sr. to Lieut. THOMAS PUTNAM (Mortgage) – (4:187) On 9 July 1674, John Knight, Sr. of Beverly mortgaged to Lieut. Thomas Putnam of Salem for 20 pounds sterling in money, his dwelling house newly built with ground it stands on being 24 rods or poles, which, according to bill of sale from Jacob Pudeater, bearing date of 24 June 1674, appeareth, lying in Salem & is bounded S by town common land, E, N & W with land of Jacob Pudeater. Thomas Putnam, observing the conditions as relating to the maintaining the fence as is expressed in the deed of sale from said Jacob Pudeater. John Knights shall pay Thomas Putnam or his assignes or special order in England 20 pounds sterling, current money of England at or before 9 January next ensuing or in case said Putnam does not give order for receiving said moneys in England, then John Knight shall pay 20 pounds to said Thomas Putnam or his assignes at his now dwelling house in Salem in current money of England at or before 9 April next 1675. **Signed**: John Knight; **Acknowledged**: 9: 5 mo: 1674; **Witnesses**: Hilliard Veren, Sr. & John Price; [no recording date].

(4:189) Duplicate of previous deed.

JOHN BALLARD to HENRY ROADES – (4:191) On 8 July 1672, John Ballard of Lynn (with consent of wife Rebecca, who surrendered her thirds) granted to Henry Roades (yeoman) of Lynn for 125 pounds sterling, his now dwelling house together with all his outhouses with watermill, mill stones, wheels & gears belonging to said mill, also 5 acres of land on which said dwelling house stands, bounded E with the town highway or lane, by the dwelling house of John Newhall, Jr., W with land of George Keaser, S with land of Samuel Fraile & John Tarbox, & N on the highway that leads to the mill; also a piece of land on which the mill and barn stands, lying N of the highway that parts between aforesaid 5 acres and it, which was formerly given by the town of Lynn, according as it was fenced, or as it standeth entered in the grant of the town or of the Selectmen, with all fences... **Signed**: John Ballard & Rebecka Ballard [by mark]; **Acknowledged**: 8: 8 mo: 1673; **Witnesses**: Andrew Mansfield & John Burrill; **Recorded**: 17: 7 mo: 1674.

ROBERT INGOLLS to HENRY ROADES – (4:194) On 16 April 1673, Robert Ingolls (yeoman) of Lynn (with consent of wife Sara who surrendered her thirds) granted to Henry Roades of Lynn for 10 pounds current money, 1½ acres of salt marsh in Lynn in the marsh below the town which was formerly William Harker's, bounded E with marsh of

Henry Silsby, W with marsh of Eleazer Lindsey, formerly Richard Rootens, N on marsh of Robert Driver, Sr. and S on the sea. **Signed**: Robert Ingolls & Sara Ingolls [by mark]; **Acknowledged**: 24: 9 mo: 1673; **Witnesses**: Andrew Mansfield and Sarah Rand [by mark].

JOHN PEARSON to HENRY ROADES – (4:196) On 8 March 1666, John Pearson (tailor) of Lynn (with consent of Mauldin who surrendered her thirds), granted to Henry Roades (yeoman) of Lynn for 4 pounds, 1½ acres of salt marsh, being generally sedge low ground in Rumney Marsh in Lynn, bounded on one side with marsh of widow Thomas of Boston & the other side with land of Henry Roads which was part of a 5-acre lot which said John Pearson bought of Edward Burt. **Signed**: John Pearson [by mark] & Madelen Pearson [by mark]; **Acknowledged**: 30: 4 mo: 1674; **Recorded**: 20: 6 mo: 1674.

ABIGAIL LORD to EDMUND BERRY, Sr. – (4:198) On 1 October 1674, Abigail Lord, relict and administratrix of William Lord late deceased of Salem, with consent of the overseers of her husband's will, viz: Joseph Grafton & Mr. Richard Prince, granted to Edmond Berry, Sr. (weaver) of Salem, for 40 pounds sterling in hand paid or secured to be paid, all that part of the dwelling house adjoining to the row of houses he lived in, lying next to the meeting house in Salem so far as to take in the chimney belonging to that part and is next adjoining to the chimney & house of his that William Hollis now lives in, with the leanto on the E side of said house with all the ground belonging thereto to the E, the bounds between that ground and ground of his belonging to the tenement the said Hollis lives in, is the fence as it now stands, running from the corner of the leanto E to a stake that stands 3 foot S from the end of Capt. Corwin's warehouse, & takes in a strip of ground at that S end of said Capt. Corwin's warehouse of 3 foot breadth by the end of said warehouse, until it comes to the fence that parts Mr. Stileman's ground and his and the said house & ground is bounded with Capt. Corwin's warehouse to the E, only that strip of ground of 3 foot breadth that comes up to Mr. Stileman's ground at the S end of Capt. Corwin's warehouse, with street or market place to the W & N, to possess from 15 April next. **Signed**: Abigail Lord [by mark]; **Acknowledged**: 5: 8 mo: 1674 & by Joseph Grafton & Richard Prince [no date]; **Witnesses**: Deliverance Parkman & Hilliard Veren, Sr.; [no date of recording given]

BRAY WILKINS and JOHN GINGEON to Maj.Gen. DANIEL DENISON – (4:201) On 28 November 1662, Bray Wilkins and John Gingeon granted to Worshipful Major General Daniel Denison for a valuable sum in hand paid, 100 acres of upland near Salem on a plain SE of the farm granted by the General Court to Richard Bellingham, Esq. and now in possession of said Wilkins and Gingeon, bounded NW with said farm and NE with a brook that runs into Price's meadow and W with the common; and also about 30 acres of meadow bounded on the NE & E with the farm and SW & N with the common. **Signed**: Bray Wilkins and John Gingeon; **Acknowledged**: 29: 9 mo: 1662; **Witnesses**: George Corwin & Hilliard Veren; **Recorded**: 33: 8 mo: 1674.

JOHN NORTON to JOHN POMERY – (4:203) On 4 October 1674, John Norton (house carpenter) of Salem granted to John Pomery (mariner) of Salem for 8 pounds sterling a dwelling house with ½ acre of ground, being all the land of said John Norton…adjoining said dwelling house in Salem bounded E with the street and runs backward W beyond the W end of the orchard, formerly of widow Robbinson's now in possession of Mr. Edmond Batter and so runs with an elbow to the N, on the W end of said orchard to said Mr. Batter's land, that runs down with a strip W by the side of that strip to the land of Christopher Phelps, to the orchard of Mr. Batters bounds, the premises partly on the N, partly on the E and said strip of land bounds it on the part on the N and the land of Nathaniel Sharp bounds the premises partly on the S next to the street and runs in with an elbow and bounds it there W and at the end at the next turn or partly S at the western end…being all the land belonging to said John Norton as his part upon the division of Mr. Samuel Sharp's lot amongst the children, further agreed that said John Norton shall have the liberty to live in said house until the 1st of May next ensuing & John Norton is to secure the house from all damage until the 1st of May next. **Signed**: John and Mary Norton [by mark]; **Acknowledged**: 10: 9 mo: 1674, with Mary his wife yielding her thirds; **Witnesses**: William Pomerye and Hilliard Veren, Sr.; **Recorded**: 11: 9 mo: 1674.

WILLIAM BROWNE, Sr. to RICHARD REITH – (4:206) 23: 9 mo: 1674: Be it known that William Browne, Sr. of Salem does convey all my right and interest in this deed of sale, except the half ware house unto Richard Reith of Marblehead, to have and hold said island as specified in this deed, with the stage and housing, this 23 of November 1674; **Witnesses**: Benjamin Browne, William Browne and John Appleton; **Acknowledged**: 23: 9 mo: 1674. Mr. William Browne Sen'r owned… The above assignment does refer to a deed of sale entered in the 3rd book of records in folio 163.

ROBERT LEMON. Deceased (Division of Estate) – (4:206) On 16: 9 mo: 1674, Mary Lemon, widow of Robert Lemon (deceased), Executrix of his will, and Charles Knights (husband of Sara Lemon his wife) and Samuel Beadle (husband of Hannah Lemon) that was: the abovesaid Sarah & Hanna, being legatees by the will of abovesaid Robert Lemon deceased…

agree to divide and assigne over to each person a third part of a piece of the estate that remains of the abovesaid Robert Lemon (deceased) which in his will have agreed to the assigne over to each person in manner as followeth, as witness our hands...13: 9 mo: 1674. **Signed**: Mary Lemon [by mark], Charles Knight, Samuel Beadle; **Witnesses**: Joseph Phillen & Nicholas Manning; For the widow Lemon, half the dwelling house & land the barn valued at 40 pounds; a bed with all furniture belonging to it, 12 pounds and a trunk, 10 shillings; total value 105: 10: 10. Charles Knight's half of the house and land valued at 40 pounds, beds and bolsters 2 pounds 10 shillings; many other particulars, 10 pounds: total 52: 10: 00. To Samuel Beadle one 10-acre lot lying at Cedar stand 12 pounds, 1¾ acres of salt marsh, 5 pounds; many other particulars, 35 pounds, 10 shillings; total 52: 10: 00 pounds. The above mentioned persons that are concerned in the division of the estate of Robert Lemon deceased came before me and acknowledged 7: 9 mo: 1674.

JOHN RUCK to JOHN NORMAN – (4:208) On 7 February 1670, John Ruck (merchant) of Salem granted to John Norman (shipwright) of Salem (with wife Sarah Ruck releasing dower) for a valuable sum in hand paid, a parcel of land between 40 & 50 rods or poles in Salem, bounded E with land of said John Ruck, the lane or highway N, the land of Edward Feveryeare W, the creek S; said parcel being in breadth next the lane 4 poles & so running the same breadth to the same creek. **Signed**: John Ruck & Sarah Ruck; **Acknowledged**: 18: 9 month: 1674; **Witnesses**: Hilliard Veren, Sr. & Samuel Williams; **Recorded**: 18: 9 month: 1674.

JOHN RUCK to BENJAMIN ASHBY – (4:210) On 11 November 1674, John Ruck (merchant) of Salem granted to Benjamin Ashby (sawyer) of Salem for a valuable sum of money in hand paid, 60 or 70 poles or rods of land in Salem bounded S with land of John Pickering & E with land of Eleazer Gedney, N with land of said John Ruck & W with land partly of John Pickering & partly on the common land, to say 50 foot against the common, said parcel on the W side running said 50 foot N beyond the corner of John Pickering's fence to the land of said Ruck & from the NW corner bounds it runs down E upon a straight line to a place marked in the fence of the said Eleazer Gedney. Benjamin Ashby is obligated to set up & maintain all the partition fence at the N end of the premises between land of said John Ruck & said premises, so long as said Ruck or his heirs...do keep it in their own possession, the said land that adjoins to the N of said premises. **Signed**: John & Elizabeth Ruck; **Acknowledged**: 18: 9 month: 1674, with wife Elizabeth yielding dower; **Witnesses**: John Norman & Hilliard Veren; **Recorded**: 18: 9 month: 1674.

THOMAS BROWNE to JOHN WITT – (4:214) On 10 December 1653, Thomas Browne (turner) of Lynn granted to John Witt of Lynn 4 acres of meadow in Rumney Marsh once in possession of Capt. Bridges, being a part of his 30 acres, bounded both E & W with land of Nathaniel Kirtland & N upon land of Capt. Marshall & S on the last dividend in & for the consideration of the full payment of this meadow by him fully received. **Signed**: Thomas & Mary Browne [by mark]; **Acknowledged**: 14: 10 month: 1674; **Witnesses**: Thomas Newhall, Sr. [by mark] & Henry Rhoades; **Recorded**: 14: 10 month: 1674.

MICHAEL SHAFLIN to WILLIAM RUSSELL – (4:215) On 20 January 1673, Michael Shaflin (tailor) of Salem granted to William Russell (fisherman) of Salem for divers good causes with several conditions & provisions hereafter expressed, and good will and affection, a parcel of land between 1 or 2 acres lying to the W of land belonging or adjoining now dwelling & is bounded or is the strip of land lying between the highway and the brook...provided first that said William Russell shall upon his own cost set up or make & maintain forever a sufficient stone wall or fence for a partition fence between the land of said Shaflin & the premises from the highway down to the river or brook. Secondly, said William Russell is not to let or hire it to any other person or persons, provided said Michael Shaflin...will buy it, who are hereby to have first refusal thereof whenever said William Russell...shall sell the same & thirdly, that in case the said Russell...should in time come to sell the same to said Michael Shaflin...it is agreed that the stone wall aforesaid is not to be included in the value of said land or house & land, but the said Shaflin or assignes paying for the said land according to the due value thereof or as another will give (without the stone wall) said stone wall to be to the use of the said Shaflin... **Signed**: Michael Shaflin [by mark]; **Acknowledged**: 9: 9 mo: 1674; **Witnesses**: Samuel Williams & Hilliard Veren; **Recorded**: 15: 10 mo: 1674.

JOSEPH FISK to ELEAZER LINSEY – (4:217) On 7 March 1672/3, Joseph Fisk of Lynn granted to Eleazer Linsey (carpenter) of Lynn for 75 pounds sterling, a dwelling house and barn which was formerly James Axey's plus the lot on which they stand in Lynn, 6 acres bounded E with land of Thomas Ivery. W with the houselot which was formerly Jenkin Davis' and land of William Croft, abutting N on the town common & S on the lane that lies by the dwelling house of widow Rooten with all fences & trees... It is to be understood that the said Joseph Fisk does engage his house & land which he bought of Eleazer Linsey to be responsible unto said Eleazer Linsey, viz: if any form, by or under James Axey deceased shall recover this house & land herein sold to Eleazer Linsey by Joseph Fisk which house and land was formerly James Axey's. **Signed**: Joseph

Fisk; **Acknowledged**: 9: 5 mo: 1673; **Witnesses**: Andrew Mansfield & Daniel Johnson; **Recorded**: 24: 10 mo: 1674.

EDWARD WHITEERE to JOHN PRICE – (4:219) 18 December 1674. Be it known that whereas I Edward Whiteere of Beverly (seaman) do owe unto the estate of Capt. Walter Price, late of Salem (merchant, deceased) the sum of 20 pounds or thereabouts which may appear upon the account of book of the said Capt. Price, being due to him in his lifetime, for & in consideration of the said sum, for which I received goods & am truly indebted as abovesaid, I the said Edward Whiteere sell unto Mr. John Price of Salem, merchant & executor of the last will & testament of said Capt., Walter Price, deceased, all interest that I have of the land both upland & meadow which my father Abraham Whiteere gave & bequeathed to me by his last will & testament, which is the ½ of 25 acres of land of upland & meadow being all the land my father died possessed of which said lands is in the town or limits of Manchester to have as by the will & inventory of my said father given in at the county court held at Salem the 24th of November 1674 provided if I the said Edward Whiteere pay or cause to be paid the above said sum of 25 pounds, 10 pounds in merchantable or refuse fish at price current or current money, or in suitable goods at money price, at or before the 1st of November next ensuing & 10 pounds more as the full of the said 20 pounds aforesaid in the like pay & price as abovesaid at or before the 1st of November 1676 sale to be void. **Signed**: Edward Whiteere [by mark]; **Acknowledged**: 18: 10 mo: 1674; **Witnesses**: Hilliard Veren, Sr. & John Hathorn; **Recorded**: 2: 11: 1674. Know all men that I Walter Price of Salem (merchant) only son & heir unto the above-named Capt. John Price (deceased) have received of Isaac Whiteere, natural brother of said Edward Whiteere, 20 pounds being the full payment & dischard of the above mortgage. **Signed**: 11 Sept 1713 by Walter Price; Examined as per Stephen Sewall. 11 September 1713, this mortgage is null and void. **Attested**: Stephen Sewall.

JOHN SIMONDS to NATHANIEL STONE – (4:222) On 8 April 1663, John Simonds (joiner) of Salem, with consent of his wife, granted to Nathaniel Stone (planter) of Salem, for 27 pounds, 47 acres of upland in Bass River side of Salem, in the manner following: 27 acres of the same being that parcel of land which said John Simonds bought of Mr. William Browne (merchant) of Salem and adjoining E to the land of Samuel Corning & S to 20 acres of land belonging to John & Zebulon Hill & shoots out N to the common or to the end of Long Hill & is bounded W with Bald Hill, & the other 20 acres being a parcel given to the said John Simonds by the town of Salem & lies NW from the aforesaid 27 acres adjoining to the same. **Signed**: John Simons; **Acknowledged**: 8: 2 mo: 1663; **Witnesses**: Edward Norrice & Abraham Cole; **Recorded**: 2: 11: 1674.

ABRAHAM PERKINS to SAMUEL CORNING, Jr. & NATHANIEL STONE – (4:224) On 15 April 1673, Abraham Perkins (yeoman) of Ipswich (with wife Hanna yielding dower), granted to Samuel Corning, Jr. and Nathaniel Stone, both of Beverly, for 31 pounds sterling, 10 acres of meadow being part of the farm that formerly was by the town of Ipswich granted & to the farm left, for the term of 1000 years, to John Coggswell deceased, lying in Ipswich limits at Chabockoe & said 10 acres of meadow is bounded partly by a river & partly by a creek that does surround said 10 acres only on the SW or S side, on which side it is bounded with land of Samuel Coggswell, to have…from the date of these presents for & during the full & whole term of time of 975 years. Samuel or Nathaniel may have free liberty of a cartway to carry & recarry the freights & effects of said premises through some convenient place of said Abraham Perkins' land. **Signed**: Abraham Perkins and Hanna Perkins [by mark]; **Acknowledged**: 29 May 1673; **Witnesses**: Benjamin Marshall & Edmond Marshall; **Recorded**: 5: 11: 73.

JOHN EDWARDS to NATHANIEL STONE – (4:227) On 24: 11 month: 1669, John Edwards of Beverly (with wife Marah relinquishing rights) granted to Nathaniel Stone of Beverly for 11 pounds already paid by bill, ½ right in a parcel of marsh which said John Edwards together with John Nowlton bought of Richard Lee, the whole parcel being 6 acres in limits of Ipswich, bounded W by Goodman Sellowes' Marsh, SW & E by Chebocke River & N by John Choate's marsh & NW by Goodman Bragg's marsh, or 1½ acre as it lies in common with the rest. **Signed**: John Edwards; **Witnesses**: Thomas White & Thomas Fisk; **Recorded**: 5: 11 month: 1674. Entered as a caveat 5: 11: 1674.

ISAACK HART to BENJAMIN & DEBORAH PROCTOR – (4:229) On 17 January 1674, Isaack Hart (farmer) of Lynn, granted to Benjamin Procter & Deborah his wife, for divers causes & for good will & natural affection to daughter Deborah, now wife of Benjamin Proctor & also said Benjamin Proctor, son-in-law as in performance of promise to said Benjamin upon marriage, all his farm or parcel of land bought formerly of Capt. Robert Bridges, 200 acres of upland & 22 acres of meadow, also with a house, barn, orchard, fences…in Lynn & now in the occupation of Thomas Marshall & bounded, to say the upland, with the great meadow called Lynn meadow S, with the land of Isaack Hart W, with the farm called Willis' farm N & so the bounds running up to Mr. Willis' meadow & 16 acres of the meadow is bounded with some meadow of Edward Taylor to the SW & some meadow of said Hart or swamp W, northerly some meadow of John Pearson, S with said 200 acres of upland E & 4 acres of said 22 acres of meadow is bounded E with upland of said 250 acres, S with some meadow of Jonathan Poole, & W with the meadow of Joseph

Belknap & 1 acre more of it is within the fence & 1 acre bought of John Pearson lying in the great meadow called Lynn meadow. **Signed**: Isaack Hart [by mark]; **Acknowledged**: 7: 11 month: 1674; **Witnesses**: Samuel Peppin & Hilliard Verin, Sr.; **Recorded**: 8: 11: 1674.

THOMAS WATSON to JOHN BEST – (4:232) On 25 November 1671, Thomas Watson of Salem granted to John Best (currier) of Salem for a valuable consideration in hand paid already, 24 poles of ground, 3 poles in breadth & 8 poles in length in Salem, bounded NE with land of said Thomas Watson, W with land of Ephraim Skerry & on the S with the common. **Signed**: Thomas Watson; **Acknowledged**: 20: 1 mo: 1671; **Witnesses**: Samuel Williams, Nathaniel Beadle & Edward Norrice; **Recorded**: 18: 11: 1674.

JOHN & SARA GOULD to Capt. GEORGE CORWIN – (4:233) On 29 March 1674, John Gould and Sara his wife of Topsfield, granted to Capt. George Corwin (merchant) of Salem for a valuable sum in hand received, 4 or 5 hundred acres of upland & meadow in Rowley Village, bounded SE from a black oak on the hill near Pout Pond, then on a straight line to a hill, on an easterly course to a heap of pines, which is the boundry of Mr. Endicott's farm and John Putnam, and also of his own farm, and from thence quartering more northerly about 150 rods near the middle on the N side of Bald hill, to a heap of stones near Crooked pond & from thence quartering to a heap of stones S to Andover angle bounds over against the meadow from that heap of stones unto the six-mile bound oak between Andover, Topsfield & Rowley Village land, thence SE down to the mile oaks near the great rock in Beachy River thence to said rock in Beachy river & from that rock to a great forked white oak that is in the bounds between Thomas Fuller, Sr. of Wills hill & own land S & lastly from that oak unto a black oak that is boundery between the land of Corp. John Putnam, Bray Wilkins & own land, near unto Pout pond on the SE side, excepting only 15 acres of meadow ground belonging to John Robbins as described in his bill of sale under hand of said John Gould. **Signed**: John and Sara Gould; **Acknowledged**: 21: 11 mo: 1674 with Sarah yielding thirds; **Witnesses**: William Andrew, John Whiting, Jr. & Edward Norrice; **Recorded**: 2: 11 mo: 1674.

JOHN RUCK, BARTHOLOMEW GEDNEY, JOHN PRICE, JOHN HIGGINSON & HILLIARD VEREN, Jr. to JOHN FOOT (Agreement) – (4:236) 25: 11 month: 1674. Know all men by these presents…John Ruck, Bartholomew Gedney, John Price, John Higginson and Hilliard Veren, Jr., all merchants of Salem do own ourselves to stand justly indebted unto John Foot, resident of Boston in New England (merchant) for 348 pounds sterling for the true performance of payment...do hereby engage ourselves...to pay 348 pounds in good merchantable dry cod fish at prices current to be delivered at Winter Island or near Salem & to begin to deliver the said fish the first fair day of July next ensuing this above date, and so to continue delivering said fish in 6 fair fish days as weather permits till the whole be fully paid. The aforementioned sum is in consideration of a parcel of goods bought of said Foot for the account of Joseph Bateman (merchant) in London: further we engage ourselves jointly & severally in 100 pounds sterling to pay all such damages as shall accrue by default of payment as is above expressed. **Signed**: 26 November 1674 by John Ruck, Bartholomew Gedney and John Price, John Higginson, Jr. and Hilliard Veren, Jr...in the presence of Susanna Gedney and John Wards [by mark].

(4:237) 25: 11 month: 1674 at Salem in New England: Whereas there was an obligation under the hands of John Ruck, Bartholomew Gedney, John Price, John Higginson and Hilliard Veren bearing date of 26 November 1674 for 348 pounds sterling payable to John Foot or assignes, the said Foot sending over power to me ..for receiving of the same, I do by there presents, acknowledge to have received...the full sum of 348 pounds in merchantable fish in time as was expressed 9 August 1675. **Signed**: Benjamin Alford; **Acknowledged**: Benjamin Alford, 9: 6 month: 1675; **Recorded**: 9 August 1675. The letter of attorney by this bill received as recorded in this book on page 119.

JAMES BROWNE to mother SARA BROWNE (Transaction) – (4:238) On 10 March 1672, James Browne (glazier) of Charlestown granted to his mother Sara Browne, for divers causes & more especially in consideration of a dwelling house and certain lands granted and given to said James Browne by Sara Browne mother as per deed of sale bearing date with these presents do covenant to pay said mother 6 pounds 10 shillings per annum so long as she shall live in current money at or before 29 December from year to year successively during her natural life and at her decease to pay her executors 35 pounds sterling more, ½ in current money & the other half in corn at price current & neat cattle as they shall be apprized by 2 indifferent men chosen by the parties. **Signed**: James Browne; **Acknowledged**: 12: 1 month: 1672/3; **Witnesses**: Hilliard Veren, Jr. and Hilliard Veren; **Recorded**: 28: 11 mon: 1674.

GEORGE DEANE to THOMAS MAULE – (4:239) On 14 October 1674, George Deane (cordwainer) of Salem granted to Thomas Maule (tailor) of Salem for 40 pounds sterling, a house and about 20 poles of land upon which said house stands in Salem, as it is now fenced in, bounded W on land of Richard Croade, N on and of Thomas Robbins, E on land of George Deane, the house and land fronting upon the street S, together with the freedom of an inlet of 5 foot wide egress & regress between the housing of said Deane and the E part of said Thomas Maul's house now sold him for his convenience of going in & out to his own land & for importing or exporting such things as said Maule may see good to or from said land of his; provided said George Deane doth reserve unto himself a like & equal right in said let for his convenience into his land & the same so to be holden for the mutual benefit of said Maule & Deane without infringing upon each other. There is an evidence entered in Book 5:105 that refers to this bill of sale. **Signed**: George and Elizabeth Dean [by mark]; **Acknowledged**: 2: 12: 1674, with Elizabeth yielding thirds; **Witnesses**: Richard Croade & Ephraim Marstone; **Recorded**: 6: 12 month: 1674.

JOHN BECKET to THOMAS MAULE – (4:243) On 3 March 1672, John Becket (shipwright) of Salem granted to Thomas Maule (tailor) of Salem for a valuable sum in hand paid, a parcel or strip of land in Salem lying in length N & S 71 foot,and in breadth E & W 6 or 7 foot, bounded on S with land of said John Becket, on E with land of widow Hollingworth, on W with land of Thomas Maule lately bought of Job Hillyard deceased & on the N with the street or highway. **Signed**: John Becket; **Acknowledged**: 27: 9 mo: 1673 by William Buckley who gave oath that he saw said Becket sign & further said William Buckley & Thomas Buckly at the same day and date of these presents was present as witnesses when said Beckett gave said Thomas Maule possession; 27: 9 mo: 1673; **Witnesses**: William Buckley, Edward Fish, Thomas Buckly, with seizin & possession of premises given; **Recorded**: 6: 12: 1674.

JOSHUA REA to THOMAS MAULE – (4:244) On 2 July 1673, Joshua Rea (husbandman) of Salem, with consent of his wife, granted to Thomas Maule (tailor) of Salem, for a parcel of land 9 poles by 1 pole given in exchange as by his bill of sale, bearing date with these presents and adjoining to the said land at E end thereof, a small parcel of ground in Salem near the middle of the towne, adjoining to said 9 poles at the W end, being upland, containing 11 poles in length & in breadth 4 foot 7 inches at the front or W end & about 2 foot at the E end, being bounded on the N with some land of his owne, on the S with land of said Thomas Maule, E with said 9 poles & W with the land or highway. **Signed**: Joshua Rea; **Acknowledged**: 3: 5 mo: 1673, with Sara wife yielding thirds; **Witnesses**: Edmond Batter & Edward Norrice, Sr.; **Recorded**: 6: 12: 1674.

EDWARD RICHARDS to son DANIEL RICHARDS, Jr. – (4:246) On 14 January 1674, Edward Richards (husbandman) of Lynn, granted to son Daniel Richards, Jr. for a parcel of money in hand paid, 6 acres of salt marsh in Lynn in the town marsh by the 2 trees, bounded E & N on a creek

& the river, S on lands of John Gillow & W on lands of Nathaniel Hanford. **Signed**: Edward Richards [by mark]; **Acknowledged**: 16: 11 month: 1674; **Witnesses**: Benjamin Redknap & Daniel Johnson & possession given by turf & twig; **Recorded**: 25: 12 month: 1674.

JOHN LEACH, Sr. & SARAH LEACH to JOHN BACHELOR, Jr. – (4:248) On 18 May 1674, John Leach, Sr. of Salem and Sarah his wife, granted to John Bachelor, Jr. of Salem for 37 pounds 10 shillings secured by bill bearing date with these presents, 15 acres of land in Salem commonly called Ryalls side, having the common on the S and the SE corner bound with a black oak tree by the swamp side and on the W side the land of John Massey & a piece of common on the NW corner of which the bound is a stake, on the N it joins to 5 acres of land belonging to said John Leach on the E side to the land of said John Bachelor bounded with a stake at the NE corner...John Leach & Sarah covenant to defend right against any person laying claim under them and the heirs...of John Friend deceased & who was the former possessor of said land. **Signed**: John Leach & Sarah Leach [by mark]; **Acknowledged**: 25: 12: 1674; **Witnesses**: John Swinerton & James Symonds; **Recorded**: 26: 12 mon: 1674.

PAUL MANSFIELD to BENJAMIN SMALL – (4:250) On 15 February 1674, Paul Mansfield (fisherman) of Salem granted to Benjamin Small (sailmaker) of Salem for 10 pounds, 10 rods or poles in Salem, part of his ground adjoining now dwelling house & bounded W with a lane or highway, left by said Paul Mansfield, for particular uses, & is 2½ poles in breadth, abutting against said lane, and so runs the same breadth backward Easterly 4 poles, & is bounded S & E with land of said Paul Mansfield & N with land of William Reeves. **Signed**: Paul Mansfield [by mark] & Demaris Mansfield [by mark]; **Acknowledged**: 16: 12 mo: 1674 & Demaris Mansfield relinquished dower; **Witnesses**: Hilliard Veren, Sr. & Samuel Williams; **Recorded**: 26: 12 mo: 1674.

THOMAS BAKER to JOHN RUCK – (4:252) On 24 November 1674, Thomas Baker (yeoman) of Topsfield or near unto said Topsfield (and wife Priscilla Baker) granted to John Ruck (merchant) of Salem for a valuable sum in hand paid, one thirty-second part of blowery or iron works in bounds of Rowley Village, with one thirty second part of all the housing, buildings, waterworks, dams, watercourses, lands, woods, timber, tools, instruments, with the 32nd part of all the coal, stock, provisions... **Signed**: Thomas Baker & Priscilla Baker; **Acknowledged**: 15: 12 month 1674; **Witnesses**: Sarah Ruck, Hilliard Veren, Sr., John Ruck, Jr. & John Price; **Recorded**: 27: 12 month: 1674.

JOHN GOOLD to JOHN RUCK – (4:255) On 25 November 1674, John Goold (yeoman) of Topsfield (or near Topsfield) granted to John Ruck (merchant) of Salem, for a valuable sum in hand paid, one-eighth part of the blowery or ironworks, etc. [similar to previous deed]. **Signed**: John Goold and Sarah Gould; **Acknowledged**: 23: 12 mo: 1674 and Sarah yielded thirds; **Witnesses**: John Ruck, Sr., John Norman & Hilliard Veren, Jr.; **Recorded**: 27: 12: 1674.

WILLIAM STOUGHTON, Esq. & NATHANIEL DAVENPORT to JONATHAN CORWIN – (4:257) On 11 February 1674, William Stoughton, Esq. of Dorchester and Nathaniel Davenport of Boston (merchant & administrator of & upon the estate of Capt. Richard Davenport, late of Boston, Gentleman, deceased) granted to Jonathan Corwin (merchant) of Salem, for 140 pounds lawful money of New England, all the house lot or parcel of land (2 acres in Salem) which formerly belonged to said Richard Davenport, bounded on the NE & S sides by streets or highways & on the W side partly by land of Lieut. Thomas Putnam & partly by the land of Richard Sibley & also all the 10-acre lot which formerly belonged to Capt. Richard Davenport of Salem in the north field bounded on the N & E sides by land of widow Spooner, on the S side partly by land of Thomas Robbins & partly by land that was lately in the occupation of Richard Bishop, W partly by land of James Simonds & partly by land of Thomas Coale; together with all houses. **Signed**: William Stoughton & Nathaniel Davenport; **Acknowledged**: 25 February 1674/5; **Witnesses**: John Hubbard & Paul Dudley; **Recorded**: 1: 1 mo: 1674/5.

ABIGAIL LORD to SAMUEL & ABIGAIL GRAY – (4:262) On 1 October 1674, Abigail Lord of Salem (relict & Executrix of William Lord, deceased) as Executrix of the Last Will & Testament of late husband & for divers good causes especially the love & natural affection for Abigail, now wife of Samuel Gray, her kinswoman & to said Samuel her husband, granted to Samuel Gray and his wife Abigail, all the dwelling house she now lives in, that is to say, that part that stands fronting to the S & is adjoining to the N to the house or tenement that she let to Edmond Berry & which he now lives in, with all the ground adjoining to said house in Salem, near the meeting house, provided that said Abigail Lord do except & reserve to her own use & behoof for & during her natural life such part of said house & ground as is hereafter expressed: ½ of the dwelling house being that end to the E, containing the upper & the lower room with ½ of the cellar, with free liberty to have free egress & regress through the lower room to the W to come to the cellar, also the use of the old barn & all the ground from the front of the house on a straight line to the ground of Mr. Elias Stileman & so southward only the yard before the door & lying W of the barn, & also the well to be in common for common use of said Abigail Lord, together with said Samuel & Abigail his wife; the said houses & ground by these presents granted is bounded: said house adjoining on the N to aforesaid tenements that now said Berry lives in, & the ground belonging to the said bargained premises to the NE is grounded with some land of hers that she laid out for a garden belonging to the aforesaid tenement, the bounds on that side to run as the fence runs from the said tenement & so right to Mr. Stileman's ground to a stake by the fence side, which said cross fence which is to be the bounds there is 15½ foot in breadth, between said fence & back side of said house & said house & ground on the E is bounded with ground of said Stileman & on the S & W is bounded with some land of said Abigail Lord, in manner following: beginning at a stake next to the ground of said Stileman toward the lower end, which stake is 22 foot N from the ground of John Cole & from that stake, the bounds run upon a straight line to the northernmost post of the little garden belonging to the tenement Edward Winter lives in, & within to about 2 foot (as by a straight line) of the back side N of said tenement to the fence of another little garden belonging to the tenement John Guppy lives in, & so from that fence to run as the fence of the yard runs, N somewhat westerly to the westernmost gate post next to John Horms, which gate post as the bounds stands W southerly from the SW corner of said dwelling house…said dwelling house & barn & ground containing about 8 or 10 poles. In case said Samuel & Abigail have issue lawfully begotten upon the body of said Abigail, said premises remain and be to the heirs of said Samuel & Abigail & in case of want of issue, said Samuel shall not alienate the premises the time of natural life of Abigail. **Signed**: Abigail Lord [by mark]; **Acknowledged**: 5: 8 mo: 1674; **Witnesses**: Edward Berry, Edward Berry, Jr. & Hilliard Veren, Sr.; **Recorded**: 6: 1 m: 1674/5.

THOMAS & MARY BURT to WILLIAM RUSSELL – (4:266) On 13 February 1674, Thomas Burt of Salem and Mary his wife granted to William Russell of Salem for 20 pounds sterling (and a house of the same bigness built) 4 acres of land and a house in Salem being part of the land of widow Southwick, which John Southwick gave to his daughter Mary, bounded E with land of Thomas Cooper, S with the highway & W with land of Thomas Cooper & N with land of Robert Stone. **Signed**: Thomas Burt and Mary Burt [both by mark]; **Acknowledged**: 16: 12 mo: 1674 & Mary Burt released dower; **Witnesses**: Samuel Frayle & John Fuller; **Recorded**: 9 March 1674/5.

JOHN MASON to WILLIAM GODSOE – (4:268) On 13 March 1674/5, John Mason (bricklayer) of Salem granted to William Godsoe of Salem for 31 shillings, ¾ pole of ground lying square 12 foot every side in Salem &

is part of ground where his now dwelling house stands & bounded with John Cook's ground W to the street N & land of said John Mason E & S. **Signed**: John Mason and Hanna Mason [both by mark]; **Acknowledged**: 15: 2: 1674/5 with Hanna yielding thirds; **Witnesses**: Hilliard Veren, Sr. & Nathaniel Felton; **Recorded**: 15: March: 1674.

GEORGE KEASER and SARAH GILLOW to HENRY ROADES, Sr. – (4:270) On 28 January 1674, George Keaser (tanner) of Salem and Sarah Gillow (Executrix of the last will & testament of John Gillow late of Lynn deceased) granted to Henry Roades, Sr., of Lynn for a valuable sum in hand paid, 3 acres of meadow in the fresh meadow, on the N side of Lynn, bordering on the highway that goes to the ironworks which was the meadow of John Gillow deceased & is bounded S with the highway that goes to the ironworks, N with lands of Mr. Hollyoke, E and W with land of Richard More. **Signed**: George Keaser and Sarah Gillow [by mark]; **Acknowledged**: 11: 1 mo: 1674/5 by George Keaser and Sarah Gillow who yielded thirds; **Witnesses**: Eleazer Roades, Eliezer Keaser & Samuel Roads; **Recorded**: 17: 1 mo: 1674/5. The grantors promised to defend against all persons laying claime under them or heirs...executors of Thomas Gillow the elder or John Gillow the younger, deceased.

THOMAS TOWNSEND to ANDREW TOWNSEND – (4:272) On 1 January 1674, Thomas Townsend of Lynn granted to Andrew Townsend of Lynn, being the natural son of said Thomas Townsend, in consideration that he together with Mary his now wife, natural mother of said Andrew, both of them being disabled in a measure through age to carry on their affairs, for their comfortable livelihood, together with other good reasons, 2 acres of land in Lynn on the S side of mill street, it being part of the house lot of said Thomas Townsend, lying W of the town highway that leads through said field, the said highway being the easterly bounds, & also when the Lord shall take Thomas & Mary out of this life, all the rest of his living, consisting of housing, lands and meadows, together with all other of their estate they or the longer liver of them may die possessed of upon considerations: First, Andrew does promise that he will live with them as their child, & carry on all their businesses for their comfortable livelihood as hitherto he has done, viz: during the time he shall live a single person, so as that they shall not be infringed of any liberty to entertain their friends or do any duty of charity to them that may be in want, that for & during each of their lives. Secondly, that if the Lord so order that he shall marry, & that he with his wife together with his father & mother cannot live comfortably together, that then said Andrew will build him a house upon the aforesaid 2 acres & there dwell & carry on their affairs in every respect, with that assistance from themselves as they may comfortably extend & so as that his said father & mother shall not be restrained of any liberty or privelege they did or should have enjoyed when he lived with them as a single person & for their comfortable livelihood; & for that end doth hereby engage himself to do or cause to be done what may be judged meet & reasonable, by an indifferent persons who may be Godlywise. Thirdly, that he will carefully see to them during both their lives that they suffer not in any respect, neither in time of sickness or health & when it shall please the Lord to put a period to their days here, to give them honorable burial. 4thly, that what debts may ther be due he will pay them. And lastly that he will pay 10 pounds to his brother Thomas Townsend & 5 pounds to his brother Samuel Townsend as legacies so ordered by his father for him to pay; viz: in 3 years time after decease of said father & mother by 5 pounds a year in such pay as he can make, this being understood to be true intent of this writing that in case Andrew should die before his said father and mother then said housing & lands & other estate to return to said father & mother or the longer liver of them except aforesaid 2 acres only but if he shall die & leave a wife or a child, then what of said estate they shall not live to spend only for their comfortable livelihood shall be to his heirs & assignes forever. **Acknowledged**: 24: 1 mo: 1674/5 by Thomas & Andrew; **Witnesses**: William Clark [by mark] & Andrew Mansfield; **Recorded**: 24: March: 1674/5.

THOMAS JEGGLES, Sr. to JOHN CROMWELL – (4:275) Thomas Jeggles, Sr. of Salem binds himself to allow & warrant unto John Cromwell of Salem the full right & privileges belonging unto the abovesaid Jeggles of a small parcel of land lying between land of abovesaid Cromwell & Mr. Hardy on one side & Mr. James Browne on the other side & to hold from him all his right as a general highway or cartway for to have free & common egress & regress so far as the length of his own ground that now is, which is from the town street to land of Joseph Hardy. This condition to be understood that said Jeggles is to have with said Cromwell, free egress & regress on above said way. **Acknowledged**: 3: 3 mo: 1674; **Witnesses**: Robert Gaindfield & Timothy Lindall; **Recorded**: 3: 3 mo: 1675.

EZRA CLAP to GILES COREY – (4:276) On 24 July 1663, Ezra Clap (son of Edward Clapp) yeoman of Dorchester and Nathaniel Clapp (son of Nicholas Clap of Dorchester) granted to Giles Corey (husbandman) of Salem, for 50 pounds part paid in hand & remainder secured to be paid, a dwelling house & 2 acres of land adjoining, in Salem, bounded E with land of Robert Buffum, W with said Giles Corey, N abutting on North river, S the street; also 50 acres of upland, with meadow thereto belonging, in Salem, bounded SW or westerly with land of Robert Moulton, NE or N with land that was Robert Goodell's; also 10 acres of upland in north neck, bounded SE with land of Thomas James, NW with land of Josiah

Southwick; which said house & several parcels of land was given & bequeathed to them by the last will & testament of Mr. John Alderman, late of Salem, deceased. **Signed**: Ezra Clapp & Nathaniel Clapp; **Acknowledged**: 6 April 1675; **Witnesses**: Signed, sealed & delivered said Corey several years in possession (by agreement) before sealing, in presence of Edward Clapp & Nicholas Clapp; **Recorded**: 7: 2 mo: 1675.

JOSEPH WILLIAMS & ISAACK MEACHUM – (4:279) 17: 2 month: 1675: Whereas there are several lands that were given & bequeathed, by Thomas Browning, deceased, by his last will & testament unto Joseph Williams & Isaack Meachum his sons in law, which lands lay undivided; now the said Joseph & Isaack have mutually agreed in divisions of those several parcels of land as followeth, viz: the said Joseph Williams is to have for his part the 10-acre lot lying in the south field, between Nathaniel Pickman's & John Pickering's land, & one acre of salt marsh lying in Marblehead bridge, & one acre of Bastard marsh lying in the south field between some marsh of Richard Prince & Paul Mansfield's marsh & ¼ acre of marsh lying by said Deacon's marsh, by the mill pond, with the fence belonging to said 10-acre lot, lying at the field gate; & for the house & ground in the town, Joseph is to have for his part the ½ of the land with the house that was said Thomas Browning's being the S end of the land next to the water, he paying said Isaack Meachum…at the decease of Mary Browning (their mother-in-law) the sum of 12 pounds in current pay, & the said Isaack Meachum, for his part, is to have the 5 acres called Mowser with the fence that belongs thereto, also ¾ acre at salt marsh that lies between some marsh of Joshua Buffum and some marsh of Richard Prince, & ½ of the ground in the town, being that half that lies from the water to the N, the said Joseph paying or causing to be paid the said Isaack…12 pounds at their mother's decease, in consideration of the housing that stands on the said Joseph part as aforesaid…in witness…per current pay is to be understood goods at current price. **Signed**: Joseph Williams & Isaack Meachum; **Acknowledged**: 17: 2 mo: 1675; **Witnesses**: Hilliard Veren, Sr. & John Bachelor.

JAMES SMITH to SAMUEL LINDE – (4:280) On 4 February 1674, James Smith of Marblehead (mariner & co owner & partner of the ketch *Mary & Sarah* of Boston) granted to Samuel Linde (merchant) of Boston, for 108 pounds lawful money of New England, all his farm in or near Marblehead, between 90 to 100 acres of meadow & upland, being part of that farm formerly called Mr. Humphries farm, bounded SW with land of Thaddeus Riddan, SE butting to the sea, NE with land of James Dennis & NW on several small lots of particular men of the town, with the housing thereon, being at present in the tenure or occupation of Michael Bowden, sometime of Salem (husbandman) together with the utensils, cattle, sheep, horses, oxen & swine upon said farm...to have...unto him the said Simond Lind. **Mortgage**: 108 pounds of lawful money on the 6th day of February 1675 according to tenor of a bill obligatory, bearing date with these presents; **Signed**: James Smith; **Acknowledged**: 15 February 1674; **Witnesses**: James Meade, Samuel Measy & Nathaniel Lynde; **Recorded**: 3 May 1675.

GERVIS GARFORD to HENRY BARTHOLOMEW – (4:283) On the 3rd day of the 11th month 1650, Gervis Garford of Salem granted to Henry Bartholomew of Salem all the marsh ground, upland & meadow that was sometime in his possession, lying on Salem neck, next to a parcel of marsh of Jeffry Massey's where sometimes he dwelt, the marsh ground containing 3 acres, the upland about 4 acres. **Signed**: Gervis Garford; **Recorded**: 10: May: 1675. On 3: 8 mo: 1653, Henry Bartholomew assigned the bill of sale unto John Browne of Salem.

JOHN BROWNE, Sr. to son JAMES BROWNE – (4:284) On the 4th day of the 4th month 1673, John Browne, Sr. assigned over all his right and title of "this bill of sale" with all his right & interest unto son James Browne, only the parcel son John possesses. John Browne, Sen'r also gave unto son James Browne, liberty of free egress & regress in the part of land that now is called "my cart waye" for him to have the benefit of that land of his which now are known by the name of "his gardens"; & also on 10 May 1675 gave & bequeathed unto him land at the burying point that was given by the town as appears upon record. **Signed**: John Brown, Sr.; **Acknowledged**: 10: 3 mo: 1675; **Recorded**: 11 May 1675. [no witnesses given]

THOMAS JEGGELLS to JAMES BROWNE (Permission) – (4:286) On 3 May 1675, Thomas Jeggells, Sr. of Salem bound himself to allow & warrant & maintain unto James Browne at Salem full right & privilege belonging to abovesaid Jeggells of a small parcel of land lying between land of abovesaid & James Browne on one side and John Cromwell & Joseph Hardy on the other side, to have and hold all right & title as a general highway or cartway to have free & common egress & regress so far as the length of his own ground that now is, which is from the town street to the land of Robert Glandfell. The consideration above is that Thomas Jeggells is to have free egress & regress with said Browne in the way. **Acknowledged**: 3: 3 mo: 1675; **Witnesses**: Robert Glandfell, John Cromwell & Timothy Lindall; **Recorded**: 11 May 1675.

ELIZABETH GREENE to ROBERT GLANDFEILL – (4:286) On 10 May 1675, Elizabeth Green (widow) of Malden, with consent of Thomas Jeggells of Salem (mariner & administrator to estate of Elizabeth Jeggells, deceased) granted to Robert Glandfeill (mariner) of Salem for a valuable sum in hand paid, 28 poles or rods of ground, all part of ground she had or of right to have, as portion left of right belonging unto her out of mother's estate; viz: the said Elizabeth Jeggells, according to a right & equal division of a piece of land father William Jeggells left adjoining to his then dwelling house, at his decease in Salem, bounded N with land of said Robert Glandfeill, E with land of Thomas Jeggells; S with land of Job Hilliard (deceased), which was lately sold to John Browne, Jr. & W partly land of Mr. John Browne, Sr. & partly land of son John Brown, Jr. the said Elizabeth Greene promised to defend against all persons laying claim under her or Jonathan Web, her former husband. Thomas Jeggells consented. **Signed**: Elizabeth Greene [by mark] & Thomas Jeggells; **Acknowledged**: 10: 3 mo: 1675; **Witnesses**: Nathaniel Sharp & Hilliard Veren, Sr.; **Recorded**: 11: 3 mo: 1675.

THOMAS DEXTER, Sr. to JAMES OLIVER & RICHARD MOODY – (4:288) On 11 May 1675, Thomas Dexter, Sr. (yeoman) of Boston granted to James Oliver and Richard Moody (sons-in-law) for divers good causes especially for love he bore 2 sons James Oliver & Richard Moody, 350 acres of land in Lynn which was granted to him by the inhabitants of Lynn in 1638. **Signed**: Thomas Dexter; **Acknowledged**: 11 May 1675; **Witnesses**: Mary Manning & John Williams; **Recorded**: 24 May 1675.

JEFFERY MASSY to JAMES BROWNE – (4:290) On 20 April 1675, Jeffery Massy (of the county of Essex) granted to James Browne of the same county, for 21 shillings 3 pence, 10 poles, ½ of a pole & $1/8^{th}$ of a pole of salt marsh & thatch ground, beginning at a post of said Browne's fence & running down upon a straight line to a point of thatch to the W of a small cove that said Browne did before own, & being for length about 9 poles ½ & 3 foot now staked out to said Browne. John Massy did agree to the sale. **Signed**: Jeffery Massy and John Massy; **Acknowledged**: by John Massy, 31: 3 mo: 1675; **Witnesses**: Sarah Massy [by mark] & Hanna Wells [by mark]; **Recorded**: 31 May 1675.

JOHN WEST to THOMAS WEST – (4:291) On 25 May 1675, John West of Beverly (farmer) granted to his son Thomas West in consideration for son's faithful service to him from youth to this day, as also son's engaging & giving bond to pay Capt. George Corwin & his son John (both of Salem) all debts, dues & demands, which John owed unto them, whether for the farm or otherwise; also in consideration of son's building for him a suitable house & housing as shall be judged meet by indifferent persons, upon what part of third part of the farm which he shall appoint upon all demands & reasonable warning given him during any time of his natural life & for the 2/3 of land, stock or moveables, it shall be divided & allotted out to said son or heirs whenever either he or son or they shall see meet to desire it, & that by indifferent persons chosen by both parties equally; that whereas said farm is under engagement unto Capt. George Corwin abovesaid for security till he had repaid money disbursed for him in the purchase he assigned said son as to pay the money so to see to & reassume said deed of sale by taking off said engagement, now dwelling & 2/3 farm bought of Mr. Blackleech & Richard Gardner & 2/3 cattle. **Signed**: John West [by mark]; **Acknowledged**: 31: 3rd mo: 1675; **Witnesses**: Paul Thorndike & Exercise Conant; **Recorded**: 31 May 1675.

DAVID FOGG to JOHN GIFFORD (Transcription) – (4:293) 4: 7: 1675, Mr. David Fogg, Sr.: I do here enclose & send the conveyance or assignment of the land you know Mr. John Gifford has taken in part of payment of the 1/8th part of the estate he has sold the company in which I am concerned, this & the goods he has received will be in full for my said 1/8th part, so you may deliver over the assignment to him, he giving you for me a counter part, which pray let him give: he has an order to Mr. Sampson Sheafe of Boston, from Mr. Henry Allen to said Sheafe, with whom the original mortgage of John Woodberry's and other papers concerning the premises were left by said Mr. Allen. I desire your care in this & all other of the company's affairs, referring you to the general advice. I am your loving friend, John Williams. This is a true copy of the original word for word & compared therewith as witness: David Fogg, John Hayward. David Fogg owned this to be a true copy of his order from John Williams. **Signed**: William Hathorne.

BENJAMIN & ELIZABETH CHADWELL to WILLIAM BASSETT – (4:294) On 15 April 1675, Benjamin Chadwell of Lynn (husbandman) with consent of Elizabeth his wife, granted to William Bassett (husbandman) of Lynn for 40 pounds sterling, 8 acres of salt marsh in Rumney Marsh in Lynn, being on a neck of land called Howe's neck, bounded NW on marsh of William Bassett, John Newell, Sr. & Henry Collins, Jr. & N on 2 acres of John Breed, & E on the Pine River; & S on a little creek that comes out of said Pine River, which doth divide between the land of Daniel Gott and this said land. **Signed**: Benjamin & Elizabeth Chadwell [both by mark]; **Acknowledged**: 17: 2 mo: 1675, with wife Elizabeth yielding thirds; **Witnesses**: John Hathorne & Sarah Hathorne; **Recorded**: 2: June: 1675.

JOHN HOW to GEORGE CORWIN – (4:296) On 10 December 1673, John How (husbandman) of Topsfield, granted as security of a debt of 14 pounds, 14 shillings, 2 pence due by a book & bill unto Captain George Corwin (merchant) of Salem for the clearing of accounts between them, 6 acres within the bounds of Ipswich or Topsfield within 1½ miles of the meeting house, bounded N with a ridge of upland, S on land of John Hovy, W with Baker's pond & E with the common. Payment to be made at or before the 1st day of December 1674 in corn or porke or cattle at merchant's price. **Signed**: John How & Edward Norrice; **Acknowledged**: 28: 3 mo: 1675; **Witness**: Phillip Cromwell; **Recorded**: 2 June 1675.

JOHN & RICHARD GARDNER to SAMUEL CORNING – (4:298) On 2 May 1659, John and Richard Gardner (mariners) of Salem, granted to Samuel Corning (planter) of Salem for a valuable consideration in hand paid, 20 acres in Salem on Cape Ann, bounded S with land of Mr. John Thorndike; NE with the common & bounded in special according to town grant. **Signed**: John & Richard Gardner. Sara Gardner (wife of Richard) and Priscilla (wife of John) consented & resigned thirds & Sarah signed; **Acknowledged**: 2: 3rd month 1659; **Witnesses**: Hilliard Veren & John Kitchen; **Recorded**: 10: June: 1675.

JOSEPH HARDY to SAMUEL CORNING – (4:299) On 29 January 1658, Joseph Hardy (mariner) of Salem granted to Samuel Corning (husbandman) of Salem, for 45 shillings, 10 acres of land on Bass river side in Salem bounded W with Catt swamp; E with land of William Woodbery; N & S by the common. **Signed**: Joseph Hardy; **Acknowledged**: 29: 11 month: 1658; **Witnesses**: Hilliard Veren & Joshua Turland; **Recorded**: 10: June: 1675.

RICHARD MORE, Sr. to sons CALEB & RICHARD MORE & daughters SUSANA & CHRISTIAN MORE – (4:300) On 25 May 1675, Richard More, Sr. (mariner) of Salem granted to sons Caleb More & Richard More & daughters Susana & Christian More, for natural affection & love & also divers other good causes, all his dwelling house in Salem where he lives, with all outhouses & all the land adjoining, both gardens, yards, orchards, fences & all appurtenances with all goods, chattels, household goods, utensils, moveables etc. in whatever place or places. **Signed**: Richard More, Sr.; **Acknowledged**: 31 May 1675 by Capt. Richard More; **Witnesses**: Henry West & Hilliard Veren, Sr.; **Recorded**: 10: 4 month: 1675.

JOHN KNIGHT to ROBERT BRIMSDEN – (4:302) On 16 October 1673, John Knight of Salem granted to Robert Brimsden (merchant) of Boston for a valuable sum of money a house in Salem, 26 foot long & 18 foot broad with all the land pertaining. 24 poles of land bounded E with land of Jacob Pudeater, W with land of John Williams (cooper), N with land sometimes in the hands of Thomas Watson & S with the common lands. **Signed**: John Knight; **Acknowledged**: 19: 10 month: 1673 [wife referred to in text as signing but signature does not appear]; **Witnesses**: Mary Richard & William Howard, Sr.; **Recorded**: 15: 4 mo: 1675.

JOHN KNIGHT, Jr. to ROBERT BRIMSDON – (4:306) On 8 May 1675, John Knight, Jr. (husbandman) of Beverly granted to Robert Brimsden (merchant) of Boston for 50 pounds paid to his father John Knights & him John Knights, Jr. a 10-acre lot in Beverly with his house & land, orchard, barn, fencing & accommodations, the said 10-acre lot being bounded E on the common, W on land of Mr. Paul Thorndike, NW by a white oak tree, & SE on the highway on land of John Williams. **Signed**: John Knight; **Acknowledged**: 8 July 1675; **Witnesses**: Daniel Richards & John Paine; **Recorded**: 15: 4 month: 1675. 50 pounds money or the certain value thereof is to be paid at the now dwelling house of said Brimsden in Boston before the 8th day of May in 3 years from date of these presents or in May the 8 1678.

JACOB PUDEATER to JOHN KNIGHT – (4:308) On 24 June 1674, Jacob Pudeater (heir or successor of Thomas Watson), blacksmith of Salem, upon consideration that John Knight, Sr. of Beverly having formerly bought of Thomas Brackett etc. a certain parcel of land bought formerly of the said Thomas Watson in his life time who deceased before he had given a legal assurance, granted to John Knight 24 rods of land in Salem being 3 poles in breadth & in length from the common backward N 8 Poles & is bounded E, N & W with land of said Jacob Pudeater & SW with the town common land. It is agreed that said John Knight…shall set up and maintain all the partition fence at the inner end to the N & the partition fence on the east side of the premises unless if in time to come said Jacob shall see cause to sell the land next adjoining either on the W side or N end to any other person or persons. **Signed**: Jacob Pudeater [by mark]; **Acknowledged**: 29: 4 month: 1674 and John Knight assigned over right unto Robert Brimsden; **Witnesses**: Hilliard Veren, Sr. & John Cromwell; **Recorded**: 24 June 1675.

PAUL MANSFIELD to WILLIAM REEVES – (4:310) On January 1670/71, Paul Mansfield (fisherman) of Salem, with consent of his wife, granted to William Reeves (butcher) of Salem for 14 pounds, land in Salem 16 pole square by measure (4 poles on each side) or 4 poles in length & 4 poles in breadth & bounded N with the street or highway next to the common S & E with land of said Paul Mansfield & W with the ground of Edward Bush, only the said Paul allowing room for a sufficient cartway between said Edward Bush & this ground and provided said William Reeves maintain a sufficient fence on each side of the said square ground, also said Reeve to have benefit of the cartway so far as his ground goes. **Signed**: Paul Mansfield [by mark] with wife Damaris [by mark];

Acknowledged: 16: 12: 1674 with Damaris yielding thirds; **Witnesses**: Edward Norris, Sr. & John Ricessone; **Recorded**: 24: June: 1675.

WILLIAM REEVES to ROBERT STONE – (4:312) On 10 March 1675 (27 1674/5) William Reeves (butcher) of Salem granted to Robert Stone (seaman) of Salem for 70 pounds a parcel of land in Salem containing 16 poles square (4 poles in length & 4 poles in breadth) bounded N with the street or highway next to the common on the S & W with land of Paul Mansfield (of whom said land was bought) and on the W with the ground of Edward Bush, only said Paul is to allow room for a sufficient cartway between said ground of Edward Bush & this ground together with a new dwelling house built on the same & also an outhouse next to the street & fence & fencing. **Signed**: William & Elizabeth Reeves [by mark]; **Acknowledged**: 12: 4 mo: 1675, with Elizabeth yielding thirds; **Witnesses**: Edward Morrly & Edward Norrice, Sr.; **Recorded**: 24: June 1675.

GEORGE GODFREY to MOSES MAVERICK (Mortgage) – (4:314) On 2 January 1673, George Godfrey (fisherman) of Marblehead, with consent of wife Hanah, granted to Moses Maverick (merchant) of Marblehead, for 46 pounds, 13 shillings, 7 pence, his messuage or dwelling house, with the orchard, garden & land as it is now fenced, being a quarter of an acre in Marblehead adjoining Richard Herman's. Mortgage: the whole 46 pounds, 13 shillings 7 pence to be paid yearly til the whole be satisfied; the 1st payment to be made being 10 pounds at or before 20 October 1674 & the 3 next payments the 3 following years; 10 pounds per annum & the last being 6 pounds, 13 shillings & 7 pence, the last year without covene, fraud or further delay in fish at price current, merchantable & refuse. **Signed**: George and Hannah Godfrey [both by mark]; **Acknowledged**: 21: 10 mo: 1674 with Hannah yielding thirds; **Witnesses**: Thaddeus Riddan & Nathaniel Watson. Hannah Godfrey owned the hand & seal to be her free act. **Witnesses**: Lydea Roberts & William Bound; **Recorded**: 1 July 1675.

WILLIAM PORR to MOSES MAVERICK (Mortgage) – (4:316) On 21 January 1673, William Porr (fisherman) of Marblehead, with consent of wife Elizabeth, granted to Moses Maverick (merchant) of Marblehead, for 58 pounds, 17 shillings, his messuage or dwelling house with the garden & land being a quarter of an acre in Marblehead upon the highway over against George Godfrey. Mortgage: the full & whole sum of 48 pounds to be paid 17 shillings 10 pounds per annum, half in merchantable fish at the end of the spring voyage & half in refuse at the end of the fall voyage at price current, the first payment in the year 1674 & so until said sum be satisfied only 8 pounds 17 shillings in the last year. **Signed**: William &

Elizabeth Porr [both by mark]; **Acknowledged**: 21: 10 month 1674; **Witnesses**: Edward Woodman & Samuel Cheever; **Recorded**: 1 July 1675. Rec'd towards the 1st payment, 27 June 1673, 1 pounds 11 shillings, 10 pence more Mr. Batten promised to pay 5 quintalls of merchantable fish July 1674.

JOHN HARRIS to MOSES MAVERICK (Mortgage) – (4:318) On 2 January 1673, John Harris (fisherman) of Marblehead, with consent of wife Sarah, granted to Mose Maverick (merchant) of Marblehead, for 53 pounds, his dwelling house with the garden, land fenced or unfenced, being ¾ acre in Marblehead on the mill pond & adjoining the land & mill of Robert Knight. [although text indicated that wife was to sign, her signature not listed] Mortgage: The ful. & whole sum of 53 pounds to be paid: 10 pounds, 12 shillings per annum, half in merchantable fish at the end of the spring voyage & half in refuse at the end of the fall voyage at price current, the first payment in the year 1674 & so til the said sum be fully satisfied. **Signed**: John Harris [by mark]. **Acknowledged**: 2: 10: 1674; **Witnesses**: Samuel Cheever & John Furbish [by mark]; **Recorded**: 1 July 1675.

JOHN TOMPKINS to JOSEPH and BENJAMIN POPE – (4:320) On 16 June 1675, John Tompkins (husbandman) of Salem (and Mary yielded dower) granted to Joseph and Benjamin Pope (farmers) of Salem for 10 pounds sterling, 30 acres of land formerly granted him by the town of Salem, lying in Salem, bounded W with land late of Richard Hollingworth, E with land of said Joseph & Benjamin, S by land of John Upton & N by the Ipswich River. **Signed**: John Tompkins [by mark]; **Acknowledged**: 16: 4 mo: 1675; **Witnesses**: Abraham Martin & Hilliard Veren, Sr.; **Recorded**: 1 July 1675.

JOHN GODFREY to BENJAMIN THOMSON (Indenture) – (4:322) On 23 July 1670, an indenture was made between John Godfrey of Andover (planter) who for divers valuable consideration, sold to Benjamin Thomson of Boston (schoolmaster) all & singular of his goods, chattels, implements, debts, bonds, bills, specialties, sums of money, lands, houses & other things whatsoever as well as moveables in whose hands, possession in whatsoever places they may be found, even all his estate whether personal or real as well on this side and beyond the seas…to enter into the possession thereof immediately after the said John Godfrey's decease without any reckoning be made. **Signed**: 23 July 1670 by John Godfrey [by mark]; **Acknowledged**: July 29, 1670; **Witnesses**: John Wriglee, Ralph Fletcher & Hannah Kirtland; **Recorded**: 21 November 1674. On the 298th page of the notary records of Massachusetts in New England. [Date at top of page: 4: 6: 75].

JOHN RUCK, etc. to ROBERT BARTON (Indenture) – (4:324) 9: 6 mo: 1675. By this public instrument of procurement or letter of attorney, be it known that on the 10th day of the month of May 1675, before me, Robert Barton (Notary & tabellion Public), dwelling in London, in the presence of the witnesses after named appeared John Foot of Bristol (merchant) now in London, late resident in Boston in New England, who has made ordained & in his stead & place has put Benjamin Alford of Boston, aforesaid merchant, his true & lawful attorney giving him full power & in the name of him constituant but to & for the use of Joas Batement & Company of this said city, merchants, to ask & receive from John Ruck, Bartholomew, John Price, John Higginson, Jr. & Hilliard Veren, Jr. all of Salem (merchants) or any of them or of their heirs or goods wheresoever they shall be found, or of such other person or persons as it of right shall appertain the quantity of fish which they are jointly & severally obliged to deliver unto the said constituant for the use aforesaid as by a certain obligation dated 26 Nov past going herewith doth appear & thereof to give due acquittance & having recived the same fish therewith to do & thereof to dispose according as the said Joas Bateman & company shall by their letters direct & appoint & in case the said obligation be not duly complied with, then to prosecute by law until contents together with all costs be fully paid. This was done at London in the presence of Josiah Jones & William Nowell. **Witnesses**: John Foot, Ezekiel Twisleton, Sampson Chester, Josiah Jones, William Norrell. Ezekiel Twisleton & Sampson Chester appeared, xxii of July 1675…they saw John Foot sign. John Leveret, Governor, & Daniel Gookin, Sr. In testimonium, Robert Barton, Notary Public. 3: 10: 1675.

THOMAS WEST to Capt. JOSEPH GARDNER – (4:326) On 22 July 1675, Thomas West (husbandman) of Salem granted to Capt. Joseph Gardner of Salem for the security of 20 pounds, 10 acres of land in Salem, bounded E with land sometime belonging to Thomas James, W with land of Josiah Southwick, N with land of John Foster & S with land of John Hill (wheelright). **Signed**: Thomas West [by mark]; **Acknowledged**: 22 July 1675; **Witnesses**: Francis Johnson & Edward Norrice, Sr. (Secretary); **Recorded**: 24 July 1675. The money was to be paid within 2 months next ensuing. 4: 7 mo: 1675. Joseph Gardner acknowledged he had received in full the within mentioned sum. **Signed**: Joseph Gardner; **Witnesses**: Hilliard Veren, Sr. & Hilliard Veren, Jr.

JOSEPH GRAFTON to WILLIAM HATHORNE, Jr. – (4:328) On 20 June 1675, Joseph Grafton (mariner) of Salem granted to William Hathorne, Jr. of Salem for a valuable consideration in hand paid, one acre of salt marsh in Salem at or about a bridge that goes over Forest River on the side next to town, it being 2 parcels, one lying on the upper side of the bridge & joining to it on the E, the land that was formerly in possession of William Browne, Sr. on the W, the town common on the N & the river on the S, the other lying below the bridge is bounded on the E with land formerly of Thomas Browning with a great post mortised on 2 sides & stands near the outside fence, & a log set into the ground near the water, on the W with the landing place, on the N with the common & on the S with the river. **Signed**: Joseph Grafton; **Acknowledged**: 12: 4 mo: 1675; **Witnesses**: Thomas Flint & John Pickering, Jr.; **Recorded**: 1 August 1675. Sara Hathorne (relict & administratrix of Capt. William Hathorne, deceased) for & in consideration of 7 pounds paid by Lieut. John Pickering of Salem assigned the within mentioned acre of salt marsh 19 April 1679. **Signed**: Sarah Hathorne; **Acknowledged**: 2 Dec 1681; **Recorded**: 3 May 1684; **Witnesses**: John Ruck, Hilliard Veren & John Bullock.

JOHN GODFREY to Dr. DANIEL WELLS & RICHARD CROAD – (4:331) On 24 July 1675, in consideration of what Dr. Daniel Wells & Richard Croad had done for him & expended upon him during time of God's visitation upon him by sickness, John Godfrey granted them 2 oxen now running upon Salem common, which 2 oxen were formerly let out to William Randall, 2 oxen & 2 cows in the custody of Abraham Whittaker of Haverhill & 100 acres of land at Haverhill, lying above Mr. Ware's land bounded on Goodman Satchell's land on the S, on Goodman Eaton's on the N, bounded on the E & W with 4 marked trees, 2 on the corner next to the river, & the other 2 on the other corner. **Signed**: 24 July 1675 by John Godfrey; **Acknowledged**: 31: 5 mo: 1675 by Peter Cheevers & John Cooke; **Witnesses**: Peter Cheevers & John Cook; **Recorded**: 1 August 1675.

JEFFREY MASSEY to JOHN BACHELOR, Jr. – (4:332) On 3 October 1674, Jeffry Massey (yeoman) of Salem granted to John Bachelor, Jr. (husbandman) of Salem for 17 pounds (that is: 6 pounds already in hand paid & 11 to be paid at time of delivery of these presents) 10 acres of land formerly land of John Garrett, lying to the N adjoining on Ryall's neck, bounded E with a small parcel or strip of land supposed to be the land of Nicholas Potter to the S, with Ryals neck to the N with the land of John Greene, W with the land of John Leach. **Signed**: Jeffrey Massey; **Acknowledged**: 20 July 1675; **Witnesses**: Benjamin Gerrish & Hilliard Veren, Sr.; **Recorded**: 1 August 1675.

HENRY BARTHOLOMEW to WILLIAM TRASK – (4:334) On 4 September 1675, Henry Bartholomew of Salem (administrator of Elizabeth Scudder deceased, with consent of Hilliard Veren of Salem the other & joint administrator) granted to William Trask (yeoman) of Salem for a valuable sum in hand paid, 2 acres of land with the orchard & fences or whatever old buildings is thereupon in Salem, against the north river above the mill & is bounded with the common land S & SW, NW with the marsh & partly the north river & E with the land of said William Trask, it being all that messuage or tenement formerly of Thomas Scudder deceased that was lying in that place…to have & hold against all claims under him or heirs of the said Thomas Scudder or Elizabeth his wife, both deceased. **Signed**: Henry Bartholomew; **Acknowledged**: 6: 7 month: 1676; **Witnesses:** Thomas Putnam & John Massey. Hilliard Veren as joint administrator consented with Mr. Henry Bartholomew in the sale. **Recorded**: 6: 7 month: 1675.

BENJAMIN CHADWELL to his 3 children now living – (4:336) On 7 June 1674, Benjamin Chadwell (ship carpenter) of Lynn granted to his 3 children (now living & unto any other that the Lord shall be pleased to give him by his now wife Elizabeth), for a parcel of salt meadow that said Chadwell sold that came by his wife Elizabeth Chadwell, all his estate in Lynn, namely: his dwelling house & barn with 5 acres of land joining, with 6 acres more of land lying between Nathaniel Ballard & Joseph Hall's land, with 5 acres of salt meadow in the town marsh, next to Allen Breed, Jr. & also 3 acres of meadow lying at the 2 trees. The eldest son of said Chadwell to have a double portion & all the rest equal, & if it please God that said Benjamin dies before his wife Elizabeth then wife Elizabeth to have 1/3 part of the said estate so long as she shall continue a widow, but upon the day that she shall marry again, it shall be divided amongst the surviving children & Benjamin Chadwell does nominate & empower Thomas Newhall & John Newhall, both of Lynn, true & trusty friends as feofees in trust to take care that there be no wrong done by either party. **Signed**: Benjamin Chadwell [by mark]; **Acknowledged**: 17: 6 mo: 1675; **Witnesses**: John Hathorne & Richard More; **Recorded**: 23 August 1675.

ELIAS MASON to CALEB BUFFUM – (4:337) On 6 April 1675, Elias Mason of Salem granted to Caleb Buffum (husbandman) of Salem for a valuable sum in hand paid, 4 acres of fresh meadow as the town of Salem granted to him in Salem at or near the Ipswich River near the farm of Joseph Pope, deceased, said 4 acres is lying in several parts: one part of which is lying with some meadow of Thomas Robbins, yet undivided 1/3 part of which upon a division is & does belong to said bargained premises. **Signed**: Elias Mason; **Acknowledged**: 15: 2 month: 1675; **Witnesses**: Hilliard Veren, Sr. & Sarah Parkman; **Recorded**: 24: 6 month: 1675.

JOHN FOGG to brother EZEKIEL FOGG – (4:339) On 2 January 1674/5, John Fogg of Barnstable, county of Devon England, (Gentleman), son & heir to Ralph Fogg, (citizen & skinner) of London, formerly of Salem in New England & late of Plymouth old England, deceased, granted to his brother Ezekiel Fogg (citizen & skinner of London & now of New England), (merchant), for 30 pounds lawful money of New England, a small tract of land in Salem, encompassed on both sides & behind with land possessed by Mr. John Hathorne & formerly belonging to said Ralph Fogg, containing in front 33 foot facing towards the meeting house & extending itself backwards as far as the outward ditch beyond the orchard containing in length, or thereabouts, & now in occupation of Hilliard Veren; & also 1½ acres in Salem, bordering on the land of Mr. Lake at the E side & being the outside lots of the fields behind Mr. Sharp's & next to the ferry commonly called Simonds ferry, going over to the 10-acre lots in the North river at Salem; & also 1 small spot of land containing about 1 acre in the common commonly called Capt. Trask's plaine next to the water side, & a little above the mill over against Buffum's lot in the north fields; and also all other spots of land appertaining to said John Fogg either by will of his late father deceased or otherwise by donation given by any otherwise purchased by him in Salem. **Signed**: John Fogg; **Acknowledged**: 3 Sept 1675; **Witnesses**: John Hayward, Hugh Baker & Joseph Clement; **Recorded**: 4: 7 month: 1675.

JOHN SOUTHWICK to JOSIAH SOUTHWICK – (4:342) On 2 June 1668, John Southwick (yeoman) of Salem granted to Josiah Southwick (husbandman) of Salem for a valuable sum in hand paid, 10½ acres of meadow being ½ of 21 acres of meadow bought of Joseph Armitage as by deed dated 4 April 1654, the said meadow lying in that meadow commonly called Willis' meadow in Lynn & is bounded as expressed in said deed. **Signed**: John Southwick ("The above deed is entered as a caution"); **Witnesses**: Hilliard Veren & Henry West; **Recorded**: 13: 7 month: 1675.

RICHARD HOLLINGWORTH to PHILLIP ENGLISH – (4:344) On 15: 3 mo: 1675, Execution of Phillip English was levied on Mr. Richard Hollingworth on 3 poles of land all the land within the stone wall at his house above it, and the upper part of the orchard next to the hill and it was apprised as the specie is, and delivered it to Phillip English in full satisfaction of the execution and gave him possession by turf and twig, per Henry Skerry, Marshall. **Recorded**: 28: 7 mo: 1675.

BENJAMIN PARMITER to WILLIAM BROWNE, Jr. – (4:344) On 15 June 1675, Benjamin Parmiter of Marblehead granted to William Browne, Jun'r of Salem, for a valuable consideration, a dwelling house and outhouse with half an acre of land in Marblehead, bounded NE & NW by land of Thomas Dixy and Francis Girdler, SW & SE by land lately of Thomas Cawlye, with one cow's lease and half free commonage on Marblehead commons. **Signed**: Benjamin Parmiter; **Acknowledged**: 20:

7 mo: 1675; **Witnesses**: John Endecott, Charles Redford and John Gedney, Jr.; **Recorded**: 21: 7: 1675.

PHILLIP CROMWELL to PHILLIP ENGLISH – (4:346) On 23 September 1675, Phillip Cromwell of Salem granted to Phillip English (mariner) of Salem, for a valuable sum, a dwelling house with thirty rods of land in Salem that he formerly bought of Mr. William Hollingworth and is in the tenure & occupation of Thomas Clouteman, bounded S by the street, N by common land near a creek, E by land now or lately of William Buckley, W by house & land of Bartholomew Gale. **Signed**: Phillip Cromwell; **Acknowledged**: 24: 7 mo: 1675 and wife Mary yielded dower; **Witnesses**: John Cromwell and John Beckett; **Recorded**: 25: 7 mo: 1675.

JOHN GRAFTON to CHRISTOPHER BABBAGE – (4:348) On 22 August 1670, John Grafton (mariner) of Salem and wife Seeth granted to Christopher Babbage of Salem for 10 pounds, 25½ or 26 rods of land in Salem being 5 poles & 1½ feet square on every side, bounded S by land lately sold to Thomas Gardner, W by land of Thomas Browning, N by the street, E by a highway laid out by Mr. Joseph Grafton, Sr. and said John Grafton with the use of the highway. **Signed**: John and Seeth Grafton; **Witnesses**: Hilliard Veren, Sr., Thomas Gardner; **Recorded**: 12: 8 mo: 1675.

RICHARD WATERS to HANNA STRICKER – (4:351) On 26 October 1675, Richard Waters and wife Joyce of Salem granted to their daughter Hanna Stricker, as her jointure to her husband Joseph Stricker, land in Salem bounded SE by house and land of William Punchard, S by the garden plot of Richard Waters, with the use of the present well of said Waters. **Signed**: Richard and Joyce Waters [by mark]; **Witnesses**: Christopher Babadg and Hilliard Veren, Sr.; **Recorded**: 27: 8 mo: 1675.

NICHOLAS MANNING to SAMUEL BEADLE – (4:353) On 8 July 1673, Nicholas Manning (gunsmith) of Salem granted to Samuel Beadle (turner) of Salem for 8 pounds, half a quarter of an acre of land in Salem, being about 10 poles in length & about 2 poles in breadth near the now dwelling house of said Manning, bounded N by land of John Preist, S & W by land of said Manning, E by the street. **Signed**: Nicholas Manning & Eliza Manning [by mark]; **Acknowledged**: 14: 10 mo: 1674 & wife Eliza yielded dower; **Witnesses**: John Preist and Edward Norris, sec'y.; **Recorded**: 10: 10 mo: 1675.

MOSES MAVERICK to SAMUEL CHEEVER – (4:354) On 31 August 1671, Moses Maverick (merchant) of Marblehead and his wife Eunice, granted to Samuel Cheever (cleric) of Marblehead, for divers good causes, about ¼ acre of land in Marblehead whereon the dwelling house of said Samuel Cheever now stands, bounded S by the house lot of Mr. Ward, N by the highway which once adjoined Henry Stacy's orchard. **Signed**: Moses and Eunice Maverick; **Acknowledged**: 13: 11 mo: 1671; **Witnesses**: Samuel Maverick and Timothy Roberts; **Recorded**: 19: 11: 1675.

MOSES MAVERICK to SAMUEL CHEEVER – (4:356) On 22 April 1672, Moses Maverick (merchant) and wife Eunice of Marblehead, granted to Samuel Cheever (cleric) of Marblehead, for 17 pounds 10 shillings, 8 acres of land in Marblehead near Darby's fort, which was sometime in the possession of Henry Combs, deceased, bounded NW by land of Lott Conant & Thomas Dix, SE by land of Robert Bartlett, NE by the sea, and the upper end by the commons. **Signed**: Moses and Eunice Maverick; **Acknowledged**: 29: 8 mo: 1672; **Witnesses**: J. Barton and Peter Maverick.

WILLIAM BROWNE, Sr. to JOSEPH PHIPPEN, Jr. – (4:357) On 28 December 1674, William Browne, Sr. (merchant) of Salem granted to Joseph Phippen, Jr. (fisherman) of Salem for a valuable sum, a dwelling house with 52 rods of land and orchard in Salem, formerly of Samuel Archard, deceased, bounded E by the street, S by land of Joshua Ward, W by land of Mr. William Browne, Jr., N by land of Samuel Archard. **Signed**: William Browne; **Acknowledged**: 17: 11 mo: 1675; **Witnesses**: John Appleton and Hilliard Veren, Sr.; **Recorded**: 19: 11 mo: 1675.

JOHN CLIFFORD to GEORGE HACKER – (4:359) On 5 September 1674, John Clifford (ropemaker) of Salem granted to George Hacker (fisherman) of Salem, for a valuable sum, 14 poles of land in Salem against the south harbor, measuring 4½ poles on the E, 3 poles on the N, 5 poles on the W and 3 poles on the S, bounded N & W by land said of Clifford, S by house and land of John Elwell, E by land of William Hollingworth. **Signed**: John Clifford [by mark] and Elizabeth Clifford [by mark]; **Acknowledged**: 22: 10 mo: 1675; **Witnesses**: Hilliard Veren, Sr. and Robert Follett; **Recorded**: 20: 11: 1675.

ADAM WESTGATE to WALTER MOUNTJOY – (4:361) On 26 January 1675, Adam Westgate (mariner) of Salem and wife Mary (who released dower) granted to Walter Mountjoy (fisherman) of Salem, for 28 pounds, land in Salem near the now dwelling house of said Westgate and the harbor or South river of said town, bounded E by land of Richard Rose, W by land of Christopher Phelps, N by the highway, S by land of said Westgate. **Signed**: Adam Westgate and Mary Westgate [by mark];

Acknowledged: 29: 11 mo: 1675; **Witnesses**: John Browne, Richard Croade & Edward Norrice; **Recorded**: 31: 11 mo: 1675.

JANE JAMES to JAMES SMITH – (4:363) On 6 August 1660, Jane James of Marblehead (widow and administratrix of her husband [unnamed] deceased) granted to James Smith (husbandman) of Marblehead for 56 shillings, her now dwelling house and 4 acres of upland in Marblehead, bounded SE by land of William Barber and the other sides by the common. Signed: Jane James [by mark]; **Acknowledged**: 4: 2 mo: 1667; **Witnesses**: Edward Norrice, Elizabeth Pester & William Vane; **Recorded**: 1: 12: 1675.

JAMES SMITH, Sr. to WILLIAM GREENOUGH (Mortgage) – (4:364) On 16 February 1674/5, James Smith, Sr. of Boston and wife Mary Smith granted to William Greenough, Jr. of Boston, for 95 pounds, a dwelling house and 6 acres of land in Marblehead, which was purchased by James Smith, deceased, from Jane James on 6 Aug 1660, bounded SE by land of William Barber and all other sides by the common. If Smith pays Greenough 95 pounds at 8% interest within a year then the deed is void. Signed: James and Mary Smith; **Acknowledged**: 16: 12th mo: 1674; **Witnesses**: Edward Grant and John Moore.

ELIZABETH and JOHN PRICE to HENRY BARTHOLOMEW, etc. – (4:366) On 10 March 1675, Elizabeth and John Price (executors to the will of Walter Price, deceased) of Salem, granted to Henry Bartholomew, Joseph Grafton, George Gardner, Samuel Gardner, Sr., Elizabeth Price and John Price (all owners of the new mill) for a valuable sum of money, about ½ acre of said Walter Price's land in the south field, bounded N, E and S by his land, W by the mill pond. Signed: Elizabeth and John Price; **Witnesses**: John Higginson, Jr. and John Marstone; **Recorded**: 15: 1 mo: 1675.

JOHN COLE to ROBERT WILKES – (4:367) On 22 February 1675, John Cole (cooper) of Salem granted to Robert Wilkes (shipwright) of Salem, for 28 pounds, land and dwelling house, shop, wharf and other outhousing on the south river in Salem, which Cole bought 19 March 1662 from William Lord, deceased. Signed: John Cole; **Acknowledged**: 17 March 1675; **Witnesses**: Richard Croad and Frances Croad [by mark]; **Recorded**: 20: March: 1675.

BRIDGET GILES to ELIEZER GILES – (4:370) On 10 November 1671, Bridget Giles (widow) of Salem granted to her son Eliezer Giles (husbandman) of Salem, for natural affection, about 20 acres of land in Salem, formerly belonging to her husband Edward Giles of Salem, deceased, bounded E by land of Capt. George Corwin, which he bought of Thomas Avery & extending on both sides of the brook upwards to the farther corner of her son John Giles' now dwelling house, N by land of John King and said John Giles, W by land of said John Giles, S by the common. **Signed**: Bridget Giles [by mark]; **Acknowledged**: 29: 5 mo: 1675; **Witnesses**: Thomas Coldum and Timothy W [sic]; **Recorded**: 20 Mar 1675.

ANTHONY STODDARD to BRAY WILKINS and JOHN GINGELL – (4:371) On 27 March 1674, a receipt was received from Anthony Stoddard for 3 pounds paid by Bray Wilkins & John Gingell. **Recorded**: 15: 12 mo: 1676.

ANTHONY STODDARD to BRAY WILKINS and JOHN GINGELL – (4:372) Receipt from Anthony Stoddard for 3 pounds in money paid to him by Bray Wilkins and John Gingell. **Recorded**: 14: 2 mo: 1675.

RICHARD WHARTON to BRAY WILKINS and JOHN GINGELL – (4:372) On 25 January 1676, a deed of release of mortgage was recorded in book 3, foll:182 from Richard Wharton, as administrator to the estate of Richard Bellingham, Esq. and in behalf of Mr. Samuel Bellingham, to Bray Wilkins and John Gingell, for 56 pounds in money. **Acknowledged**: by Wharton; **Recorded**: at Boston, 25 Jan 1676.

SAMUEL WALTON to MOSES MAVERICK – (4:372) On 16 November 1671, Samuel Walton (fisherman) of Marblehead, and wife Sara Walton granted to Moses Maverick (merchant) of Marblehead, for a certain sum of money, ¼ acre of land with dwelling house in Marblehead on the hill by the marsh formerly called the little neck. **Signed**: Samuel and Sarah Walton; **Acknowledged**: 23: 11 mo: 1672, and Sarah yielded dower; **Witnesses**: Thaddeus Riddan, James Dennis and Samuel Leach, Sr.; **Recorded**: 25 March 1676.

ROBERT GOODELL to JOHN BUXTON – (4:375) On 29 December 1674, Robert Goodell and wife Margerett of Salem granted to John Buxton of Salem, for 20 pounds, 21 acres of land in Salem near the Ipswich river with commonage privilege, bounded E by land of Job Swinerton, Jr. and said Buxton, S by the common & land of Zachariah Goodell & Lott Killum & Mr. Norrice's brook, W by land of said Killum & Thomas Flint, N by said brook. **Signed**: Robert and Margrett Goodell [by mark]; **Acknowledged**: 3: 3 mo: 1675, & Margery yielded dower; **Witnesses**: Job Swinerton and John Cook; **Recorded**: 25: 1 mo: 1676.

MATHEW WOODWELL to RICHARD PAMER – (4:377) On 3 December 1673, Mathew Woodwell and wife Mary of Salem granted to Richard Pamer of Salem, for 11 pounds, 4 shillings, 13 poles of land in Salem, plus 1 pole on the N side for a highway being formerly land of Mr. John Ruck, as by deed of sale appears, bounded S by land of John Andrews, W by land of Robert Nowell, N & E by land of said Woodwell. **Signed**: Mathew Woodwell and Mary Woodwell [by mark]; **Acknowledged**: 20: 1 mo: 1675 & Mary yielded dower; **Witnesses**: John Swinerton and John Andrews; **Recorded**: 25 March 1676.

ALEXANDER LILLINGTON to HENRY BARTHOLEMEW – (4:379) On 3 August 1675, Alexander Lillington (planter) of Alabama County, Carolina, husband of Sara James, the only surviving child of Thomas James late of Carolina (deceased) formerly of Salem, granted to Mr. Henry Bartholemew (merchant) of Salem, for a valuable sum of money, 100 acres of land (inherited from said Thomas James) in Salem (with housing), formerly belonging to William Cleark, deceased, & more lately sold by Benjamin Smith to said Thomas James; also 40 adjacent acres granted by the town of Salem; 10 acres of the farm in Salem now in the possession of John Gedney near Cedar Pond; 1¼ acres of salt marsh in the south field in Salem near Clay Brook; also 2 or 3 acres of meadow in Lynn on the west side of Dogg Pond. **Signed**: Alexander Lillington; **Acknowledged**: 4: 6 mo: 1675; **Witnesses**: Samuel Beadle and Hilliard Veren, Sr.; **Recorded**: 25 Mar 1676.

THOMAS BEADLE to ROBERT STONE – (4:382) On 12 April 1676, Thomas Beadle (mariner) of Salem, granted to Robert Stone (seaman) of Salem, for 30 pounds sterling, 30 poles of land in Salem with the frame of a dwelling house so far as the carpenters work was now done to it, as it stands raised with all the clabords, boards & shingles that belongs to it…with 6 windows to be set up, bounded E by land of Peter Cheevers, W by land of Nathaniel Silsby, S by the street, N by common land. **Signed**: Thomas Beadle; **Witnesses**: Samuel Beadle and Hilliard Veren, Sr.; **Recorded**: 13: 2 mo: 1676.

THOMAS SAVAGE to SARAH and JOHN HIGGENSON – (4:383) On 26 Aug 1675, Thomas Savage (merchant) of Boston, granted to his daughter Sarah Higgenson and her husband John Higgenson (merchant) of Salem, for natural affection, land in Salem he purchased of Mordecai Craford on the N side of Winter harbor, and 6 adjoining acres he lately bought of Mr. John Higgenson, pastor of the Church of Salem, bounded E, S & W by the water, N by common land. **Signed**: Thomas Savage; **Acknowledged**: 21 Feb 1675 by Maj. Thomas Savage & wife Mary who yielded dower; **Witnesses**: Martha Tabutt [by mark] and Hilliard Veren, Sr.; **Recorded**: 18: 2 mo: 1676.

JOHN GOOLD to ZACHEUS CURTIS, Jr. – (4:386) On 10 December 1672, John Goold of Topsfield granted to Zacheus Curtis, Jr. of Topsfield [no consideration given] 42 acres of land bounded by land of Zacheus Curtis, Sr. and John Goold, and by Mr. Endicott's line; also a parcel of meadow near crooked pond, bounded S by upland, W by Thomas Perkins line, N by upland, leaving out a highway for a cart[way]—also an acre of land at the east end of crooked pond & beaver dam bounded by said Goold's land on every side. **Signed**: John and Elizabeth Goold; **Acknowledged**: 4: 7 mo: 1675; **Witnesses**: Thomas Andrews and Zacheus Curtis, Sr. [by mark]; **Recorded**: 18: 2 mo: 1676.

CHRISTOPHER LATAMORE to ANDREW TUCKER – (4:388) On 28 March 1672, Christopher Latamore (mariner) and wife Mary of Marblehead, granted to Andrew Tucker (fisherman) of Marblehead, for a certain sum of money, 1 acre on Marblehead Neck bounded NE by land of John Pedrick, SW by land of John Allen, & running down to the water side of the great harbor 5 poles in breadth & 6 upward. **Signed**: Christopher [by mark] and Mary Latimore; **Acknowledged**: 1: 3 mo: 1674 with Mary yielding dower; **Witnesses**: Erasmus James and Samuel Leach; **Recorded**: 24: 2 mo: 1676.

JOHN BECKETT to SAMUEL PHIPPEN – (4:390) On 15 September 1675, John Beckett (ship carpenter) and wife Margarett, of Salem granted to Samuel Phippen (blackmaker) of Salem for 25 pounds 5 shillings, 70 poles of land in Salem, bounded N by land of John Robinson, S by land of said Beckett, W by land of Job Hilliard, E by the highway, with the privilege of a cart highway unto said land. **Signed**: John Becket; **Acknowledged**: 22: 3 mo: 1676 (wife Margaret yielded dower); **Witnesses**: Hilliard Veren, Sr. and John Robinson; **Recorded**: 23: May: 1676.

JOHN BECKETT to JOHN ROBINSON – (4:394) On 2 July 1675, John Beckett (shipwright) of Salem granted to John Robinson (tailor) of Salem, for 15 pounds sterling, 45 poles of land in Salem bounded S by land of said John Beckett, W by land of Job Hilliard (deceased) now in the possession of William West & wife Mary, E by the highway, N by land of Michael Coomes and land of Mary Beckett, with the privilege of a cartway from the street to the land. **Signed**: John Becket; **Acknowledged**: 22: 3m: 1676, with wife Margaret yielding dower; **Witnesses**: Hilliard Veren, Sr. and Samuel Phippen; **Recorded**: 23 May 1676.

PHILLIP CROMWELL to JOHN BECKETT – (4:396) On 1 February 1675/6, Phillip Cromwell (butcher) of Salem granted to John Beckett (shipwright) of Salem for 56 pounds, ¾ of an acre of land in Salem which was heretofore the land of Henry Harwood & since the land of Jeremiah Bootman, bounded W by land of Richard Flinder, E & N by land of said Beckett, S by the sea – payment to be made in 4 annual installments of 14 pounds or deed is void. **Signed**: Phillip Cromwell; **Acknowledged**: 22: 3 mo: 1676 with wife [not named] yielding dower; **Witnesses**: William Bowditch and Richard Croade; **Recorded**: 23: 3 mo: 1676.

EZEKIEL FOGG to WILLIAM LONGSTAFE – (4:399) On 25 May 1676, Ezekiel Fogg, (citizen & skinner) of London & now of New England (merchant) granted to William Longstafe (cordwinder) of Salem, for 12 pounds sterling, 1½ acres of land in Salem next to the north river, formerly Mr. Ralph Fogg's and after Mr. John Fogg's by succession & lately sold by him to his brother Ezekiel, bounded in part by the river, the highway and land of James Simonds. Ezekiel binds 12 pounds to save harmless from any claim of dower thirds by his wife Anna. **Signed**: Ezekiel Fogg; **Witnesses**: Hilliard Veren, Sr. and Samuel Williams; **Recorded**: 25 May 1676.

WILLIAM GERRISH to JOHN DOLE – (4:402) On 20 April 1676, William Gerrish of Newbury granted to John Dole, son of Richard Dole, for the fatherly affection he bore to daughter Mary Gerrish [&] in consideration of a marriage to be consummated between her and said John Dole, & for 500 pounds received of said Richard Dole, 6 parcels of land with the privilege of a freehold – the first 2 in Newbury, being 4 acres with a house and 10 acres of plowland bounded S & E by land of Daniel Pearce, N by land of Mr. John Woodbridge, W by the highway – the 3rd and 4th in Newbury, being 20 acres of meadow near the mill and 12 acres of salt marsh, bounded W by land of John Knight, E by the creek; the 5th and 6th on Plum Island, being 14 acres of salt marsh which was sometime the lot of Anthony Morse & 6 acres of pasture land bounded S by land of said Morse, E by the highway, N by land of Widow Browne. (Mr. Dole's deed to Capt. Gerrish is recorded in folio 155). **Signed**: William Gerrish; **Acknowledged**: 22: 2 mo: 1676 by Capt. William Gerrish; **Witnesses**: Joseph Hills and Moses Gerrish; **Recorded**: 3 May 1676.

JOHN GARDNER to JOHN BARTON – (4:404) On 23 June 1676, John Gardner (mariner, sometime resident at Nantucket Island) of Salem granted to John Barton (chirurgeon) of Salem, for a valuable sum, 25 rods of land in Salem bounded N by land of John Sanders, E by land of Humfry Coomes, S by land of John Gardner, W by the highway. **Signed**: John

Gardner; **Acknowledged**: 5: 5 mo: 1676; **Witnesses**: Hilliard Veren, Sr. and John Sanders; **Recorded**: 17: July: 1676.

JOHN BROWNE, Sr. to son SAMUEL GARDNER, Jr. – (4:406) On 7 July 1676, John Browne, Sr. (mariner) of Salem granted to son Samuel Gardner, Jr., 50 acres of land which was given him by the town of Salem & laid out by Capt. Joseph Gardner & Francis Nurse, bounded W by Major Rainsbery's farm, N by land of John & Joseph Moulton, E by land of Jno. Pudney, S by the common. **Signed**: John Browne; **Acknowledged**: 8: 5 mo: 1676; **Witnesses**: Elezer Hathorne, Wm. Hathorne, Jr.; **Acknowledged**: 17 July 1676.

THOMAS ROBBINS to WILLIAM KING – (4:407) On 2 June 1676, Thomas Robbins (husbandman) of Salem granted to William King (carpenter) of Salem, for a valuable sum, 8½ poles and 17 feet of land in Salem, bounded S by land of John Kitchin upon which William King has lately built a dwelling house, E by the lane, W & N by the dwelling house & land of said Robbins. (Another deed is entered in folio 150 for some addition to N side of premises). **Signed**: Thomas Robbins [by mark]; **Acknowledged**: 3: 4 mo: 1676; **Witnesses**: William Hathorne, Jr. and Robert Stone.

NICHOLAS MANNING to SAMUEL BEADLE – (4:410) On 14 August 1676, Nicholas Manning (gunsmith) of Salem granted to Samuel Beadle (turner) of Salem, for 50 pounds, 20 acres of land in the north field of Salem, formerly called Goodell's lotts, bounded E by land formerly Mr. Peeters' now in possession of Deacon Home, W by land of Job Swinerton, N by land of Robert Pease, S by land of John Neal & Nicholas Potter. **Signed**: Nicholas Manning & Elizabeth [by mark]; **Acknowledged**: 14 August 1676, with wife Elizabeth consenting; **Witnesses**: John Hill and Frances Neale; **Recorded**: 27: 7 mo: 1676.

THOMAS BAKER to JOHN RUCK – (4:411) On 4 September 1676, Thomas Baker (yeoman) of Topsfield "or neer unto Topsfield," granted to John Ruck (merchant) of Salem, for a valuable sum, $1/16^{th}$ part of the bloomery or iron works in Rowley village and $1/16^{th}$ part of all the housing, buildings, water works, dams, water courses, lands, woods, timber, tools, instruments & all the stock of coal & provisions that belongs to said works. **Signed**: Thomas and Priscilla Baker; **Acknowledged**: 4: 7: 1676 with wife Priscilla yielding dower; **Witnesses**: Benjamin Ganson and Richard Mabee; **Recorded**: 27: 7 mo: 1676.

SAMUEL CROMPTON to the Town of Saybrook – (4:414) An agreement (was signed) between Samuel Crompton of Salem and the town of Saybrook (New London County) whereby Crompton promises to send at the first opportunity after 1 May 1675, a pair of colloures fit for the company, of double sarsinet red, with a white field to show the red cross, a flag staff & tassels suitable [measuring] 1¾ yards on the staff, 2¼ yards flourish, with a blue ball in said colors [for which] we whose names are underwritten [will pay] 5 pounds in peas and rye at 3 shillings per bushel at or before 1 October 1675. **Signed**: 30 Mar 1675 by William Pratt and Abraham Post. The underwritten [will pay] 4 pounds 6 pence in pails at 10 shillings a dozen, and half bushels at 20 shillings a dozen to be delivered at Middletown at the landing place by Goodman Seaseage at or before 30 September 1675. **Signed**: 27 Mar 1675 by John Wilcock; **Witnesses**: Israel Wilcock, William Connell [by mark]. The underwritten [will pay] 6½ bushels of Indian corn, to be delivered to the said Crompton or his order at Wethersfield landing place at or before 30 Sept 1675. **Signed**: 24 Mar 1674/5 by Samuel Butler; **Witness**: Nathaniel Graye. The underwritten [will pay] 6½ bushels of Indian corn, to be delivered to said Crompton or to his order at Wethersfield landing place at or before 30 Sept 1675. **Signed**: 24 Mar 1674/5 by Nathaniel Graye; **Witness**: Samuel Butler; **Recorded**: as a memorandum or caution, 23: 8 mo: 1676.

EDMUND BATTER to JOHN MASCALL, Jr. – (4:416) On 16 November 1676, Edmund Batter (merchant) of Salem granted to John Mascall, Jr. (gunsmith) of Salem for a valuable sum, 16 rods of land in Salem bounded W by land of Henry West, S by the street, N by land of Mr. Edward Norrice, E by hid land and dwelling house. **Signed**: Edmund Batter; **Witnesses**: Henry West and Hilliard Veren, Sr.; **Recorded**: 17 Nov 1676.

BENJAMIN PROCTER to JOHN HART – (4:418) On 17 April 1676, Benjamin Procter (yeoman) of Ipswich granted to John Hart of Lynn for 110 pounds, all his farm in Lynn, containing 200 acres of upland and 22 acres of meadow, that he received 17 January 1674 by deed of gift from his father-in-law Isaac Hart. **Signed**: Benjamin Procter [by mark] & Deborah Procter [by mark]; **Acknowledged**: 3: 9 mo: 1676 with wife Deborah yielding dower; **Witnesses**: Elizabeth Mackmallen [by mark] and Hilliard Veren, Sr.; **Recorded**: 22: 9 mo: 1676.

MARK GRAVES to JOHN and JOSEPH PEABODY – (4:420) On 17 April 1675, Mark Graves of Andover granted to John Peabody and his brother Joseph Peabody of Rowley village, for 15 pounds, 4 acres on the SW side of Read's meadow which was his 2nd division of meadow granted by the town to his house lot bounded N by meadow of John Aslett and John Johnson, E by some great islands, SE by meadow of Mr. Deane, SW & W by upland. **Signed**: Mark Graves [by mark] & Elizabeth Graves [by mark]; **Acknowledged**: 29: 9 mo: 1676 & Elizabeth yielded dower; **Witnesses**: Thomas Osgood and John Lovejoy; **Recorded**: 4: 10 mo: 1676.

FRANCIS JOHNSON to JOHN BROCK – (4:421) 16 November 1676. Deed of mortgage from Francis Johnson (fisherman) of Marblehead to John Brock (mariner) of Jersey, for 16 pounds sterling, 1 acre of land in Marblehead bounded NW by the swamp or mill pond & all other sides by the common. If Johnson pays Brock 16 pounds in merchantable dry cod fish at current price before 15 June 1677 then deed is void. **Signed**: Francis Johnson [by mark] and Elizabeth Johnson [by mark]; **Acknowledged**: 27: 9 mo: 1676; **Witnesses**: John Curwin and Samuel Ward; **Recorded**: 4: 10 mo: 1676.

ELEAZER HATHORNE to JOHN HOLMES – (4:424) On 4 December 1676, Eleazer Hathorne (merchant) and wife Abigail of Salem, granted to John Holmes (husbandman) of Salem for 18 pounds, land in Salem the town granted to Eleazer in consideration of land near his now dwelling house that he granted to the town for a highway, bounded S by land of John Holmes, W by the highway that goes towards Marblehead, N by a small bridge by a swamp, E by the way that leads to the dwelling house of said Holmes. **Signed**: Eleazer and Abigail Hathorne [by mark]; **Acknowledged**: 4: 10 mo: 1676 and Abigail yielded dower; **Witnesses**: Nicholas Hutchins and Edward Norrice, Secr'y.; **Recorded**: 12: 10 mo: 1676.

ANTHONY DIKE to JOHN HOLMES – (4:426) On 4 December 1676, Anthony Dike (mariner) of Salem granted to John Holmes (husbandman) of Salem, for 6 pounds 15 shillings, 2 acres of upland in the south field of Salem, bounded S by land of Joseph Williams, N & E by land of Nathaniel Pickman, W by the marsh. **Signed**: Anthony Dike & Margery Dike [by mark]; **Acknowledged**: 4: 10 mo: 1676 & wife Margery yielded dower; **Witnesses**: Eleazer Hathorne, Nicholas Hutchins [by mark] and Edward Norrice, Secr'y.; **Recorded**: 12: 10 mo: 1676.

RUTH SMALL to LIDEA SMALL – (4:428) On 26 October 1676, Ruth Small (relict and administratrix of Thomas Small) of Salem granted to Lidea Small (relict and administratrix of Joseph Small) of Salem, deceased, for 20 pounds, 20 acres of upland bounded S by land of Job Swinerton, Jr., E by land of Jonathan Walcott, W & N by land of said Ruth Small; also 7 acres of swamp land by the great river side, bounded E by said Walcott, S by said Ruth Small, W by a red oak. The parcels were previously sold by Thomas Small to Joseph Smale but both men died before a deed was written. **Signed**: Ruth Small [by mark]; **Acknowledged**: 30: 8 mo: 1676;

Witnesses: John Buxton and Hilliard Veren, Sr.; **Recorded**: 26: 10 mo: 1676.

SAMUEL BEADLE to JOHN HILL – (4:430) On 14 August 1676, Samuel Beadle (turner) of Salem granted to John Hill (cooper) of Beverly, for 8 pounds, 10 acres in Beverly which was formerly Robert [Semons?], bounded E & S by land of John Hill, W by the cedar stand, N by land of John Sallis. **Signed**: Samuel Beadle & Hannah Beadle; **Acknowledged**: 14 Aug 1676, with Hannah yielding dower; **Witnesses**: Nicholas Manning and Francis Neale; **Recorded**: 28: 10 mo: 1676.

ELEAZER GEDNEY to WILLIAM HIRST – (4:432) On 26 November 1676, Eleazer Gedney (shipwright) of Salem sold to William Hirst of Salem for a valuable consideration, the hull of one new ketch called the *Martha and Mary*, being of burthen 58 tons built & finished with all builders work according to the customs of builders in this country. **Signed**: Eleazer Gedney; **Acknowledged**: 20: 11: 1676; **Witnesses**: Edward Grove and Samuel Pickman.

THOMAS WOODBRIDGE to WILLIAM GERRISH – (4:434) On 1 September 1676, Thomas Woodbridge (merchant) of Newbury deeded to Capt. William Gerrish of Newbury, for securing of payment of 500 pounds, his land in Newbury with dwelling house and warehouse & all household goods & other goods incerted in return of an attachment served by Constable Joseph Pike resulting from a lawsuit of Gerrish at the county court held at Salem 27 June last & appealed to the Court of Assistants at Boston and also a tract of land in Haverhill & condition or obligation is such that Thomas Woodbridge & William Gerrish being desirous to come to an amicable composure consented to submit all their sundry pending lawsuits to the arbitration of the Hon. John Leveritt, Esq., Thomas Danforth, William Stoughton, Esq., Mr. Nathaniel Saltonstall & Mr. John Hubbert. If Woodbridge attends a meeting with the arbitrators at Boston, Wednesday, 27th September 1676, and abides by their decision, or any 3, to be made on or before 31 October 1676, the above written obligation will be void, otherwise to remain in force. **Signed**: Thomas Woodbridge; **Witnesses**: Nathaniel Oliver, John Noyce and Isaack Addington (Noyce & Addington made oath at Boston, 16: 11 mo: 1676); **Recorded**: 17 or 18: 11 mo: 1676.

GEORGE CORWIN and PHILLIP CROMWELL to JOHN MASSEY – (4:436) On 18 May 1669, Capt. George Corwin (merchant) & Mr. Phillip Cromwell (butcher), both of Salem granted to John Massey (husbandman), for 42 pounds, their right, title & interest in their shares of a 40-acre parcel of land in the north field of Salem called the horse pasture, bounded W by the great cove & land of Ralph Tomkins, E & N by Willistons river, S by land formerly in the possession of Thomas Watson. This land is jointly occupied & possessed by said Corwin & Cromwell, Mr. William Browne, Sr., (merchant) & Mr. George Emory (chirurgeon), both also of Salem, & is divided into 7 shares, Corwin & Cromwell each having 2½ shares, Browne & Emory each having one share. **Signed**: George Corwin and Phillip Cromwell; **Acknowledged**: 15: 11: 1676 by both; **Witnesses**: Henry Skerry, Jr., Jonathan Hart and Edward Norrice, Sec'y.; **Recorded**: 22: 11: 1676.

THOMAS GARDNER, Jr. to GILBERT TAPLEY – (4:439) On 15 March 1674/5, Thomas Gardner, Jr. (Attorney of Lieut. Thomas Gardner of Pemaquid) of Salem, granted to Gilbert Tapley (seaman) of Beverly, for a valuable consideration, ½ acre of land with dwelling house in Beverly that said Lieut. Gardner bought from Robert Stone on 13 May 1661, bounded E [not stated], W & S by land of Robert Stone, N by land of Thomas Chubb. **Signed**: Thomas Gardner, Jr.; **Acknowledged**: 8: 11 mo: 1676; **Witnesses**: Richard Mabee, Israel Porter and Thomas Gardner, Sr.; **Recorded**: 26: 11 mo: 1676.

SAMUEL JENSON to ROBERT BRIMSDEN & JOHN SMITH – (4:441) On 26 November 1676, Samuel Jenson (mariner) of Lynn, granted to Robert Brimsden (merchant) of Boston and John Smith (butcher) of Boston, for a valuable consideration of money, 50 acres of land in Lynn which was granted to his father Edward Jensen of Lynn, bounded by land of John Hawkes, land of Abraham Wellman & the land his said father gave to him. **Signed**: Samuel Jensen; **Acknowledged**: 28 Nov 1676; **Witnesses**: Nicholas White & Thomas Kemble. Assigned to Philip Knell, 21 Jan 1676; **Signed**: Robert Brimsden & John Smith [by mark]; **Acknowledged**: 27: Jan: 1676; **Witnesses**: James Taylor [by mark], John Endecott and Thomas Kemble; **Recorded**: 30: 11 mo: 1676.

THOMAS CHADWELL to HENRY COLLINS, Jr. – (4:444) On 14 January 1676, Thomas Chadwell (ship carpenter) of Charlestown (with his now wife yielding thirds) granted to Henry Collins, Jr. (carpenter) of Lynn for 30 pounds, 11 acres of land in Lynn bounded E & W by land of said Collins, S by the country highway leading to Marblehead, N by land of Henry Collins, Sr. **Signed**: Thomas Chadwell & Abigail Chadwell [by mark]; **Witnesses**: Samuel Severans and Samuel [blank]; **Recorded**: 12 Mar 1676/7.

EDWARD RAWSON to ISAACK HART – (4:446) On 31 December 1673, Edward Rawson of Boston, Suffolk County, agent & attorney to the Rev. John Knowles (as by Knowles' letters dated Bristol 23 Feb 1657 &

London August 14th 1672, empowering Ramson to receive debts & sell lands in special a farm of 500 acres as granted to the late Mr. Thomas Willis by the town of Lynn), heretofore of Watertown, Middlesex Co., lately & now in the city of London, clerk [sic], by virtue of letters in the name of John & wife Elizabeth heretofore in 1657 did sell to Isaack Hart of Lynn or Lynn village (now called Redding, for 80 pounds with some interest for what was then unpaid, & security by bond bearing date 29: August last – 500 acres of upland & meadow which said John Knowles then had by gift of his father-in-law, said Thomas Willis & has been ever since in occupation of Isaac Hart, bounded by the line between Salem & Lynn & land of the late Capt. Robert Bridges & Mr. George Corwin. **Signed**: Edward Rawson as atty; **Acknowledged**: 31 Dec 1673; **Witnesses**: Nathaniell Raymond and Paul Batt; **Recorded**: 12 Mar 1676/7.

HENRY SKERRY, Sr. to ABRAHAM READ – (4:449) On 8 October 1673, Henry Skerry, Sr. of Salem granted to Abraham Read, for a valuable sum, 6 acres of land on Ryalls side in Willistons river, being the two necks of land that lie below the stony cove, which was given him by the town of Salem, excluding the salt marsh that lies at the head of the cove between the two points which was not his land. **Signed**: Henry Skerry; **Acknowledged**: 26: 1 mo: 1677; **Witnesses**: Hilliard Veren, Sr. and Hilliard Veren, Jr. [no recording date].

GEORGE JACOBS, Sr. to GEORGE JACOBS, Jr. – (4:451) On 31 March 1677, George Jacob, Sr. (planter) of Salem promised to acquit, discharge & pass by all differences, abuses, etc. that his son George Jacobs, Jr. had offered to pay him or his estate or his wives, from the beginning of the world to this day, for which he bound himself with 100 pounds. **Signed**: 31 March 1677 by George Jacobs, Sr.; **Acknowledged**: 30: 2 mo: 1677; **Witnesses**: Henry Bartholomew and Benjamin Small.

Agreement between George Jacobs, Sr. (planter) of Salem, and Daniel Andrew, Jacob Barney, Sr. & Thomas Ives on behalf of his son George Jacobs, Jun'r, voiding an indenture of 12 January 1673, wherein George Jacobs, Sr. resigned his estate to his said son, half to be possessed immediately, half at the death of said George, Sr. & his wife, said son paying such legacies as his father should bequeath, not exceeding ½ the land by this new agreement, George Sr. shall possess all the former estate that his son now possesses, & George Jr. has a year to remove from the premises the house he has begun to build. **Signed**: Jacob Barney, Daniel Andrews, Thomas Ives; **Acknowledged**: 30: 2 mo: 1677 by George Jacob, Jr.; **Witnesses**: Henry Bartholomew and Benjamin Small; **Recorded**: 30: 2 mo: 1677.

SARAH BROWNE to JOSEPH HARDY, Jr. – (4:453) On 1 May 1677, Sarah Browne, relict & executrix of James Browne, late of Salem, (glazier) granted to Joseph Hardy, Jr. (mariner) of Salem, for 12 pounds 16 shillings, 32 poles of land in Salem adjoining the house she now lived in, bounded W by the street, E by land late of John Gedney, Jr., deceased, N by land of said Sarah Browne, S by land in the possession of said Sarah Browne which was bequeathed to Abraham Browne by the will of his father. **Signed**: Sarah Browne; **Acknowledged**: 2: 3 mo: 1677; **Witnesses**: Samuel Browne and Hilliard Veren, Sr.; **Recorded**: 2 May 1677.

THOMAS ROBBINS to WILLIAM KING – (4:456) On 11 May 1677, Thomas Robbins granted to William King, for a valuable consideration, 2¾ poles of land as an addition to land sold to him & recorded in this book, foll: 138 & 139. King is obliged to set up & maintain the middle fence between his land & Robbins. Entered as a caution by me Hillard Veren: above written refers to the first deed of sale for land bought of which this was a small addition afterwards and was so entered on the back side of that first deed. **Signed**: Thomas Robbins; **Witnesses**: Sara Parkman, Hilliard Veren, Sr. and Thomas Rix; **Recorded**: 12: 3 mo: 1677.

PETER BRACKETT to THOMAS MAULE – (4:457) On 12 May 1677, Peter Brackett of Boston and wife Mary granted to Thomas Maule of Salem, for 32 pounds, land in Salem which formerly belonged to Samuel Belknap, 1 acre with dwelling house and orchard, bounded E by land of Phillip Cromwell, N by the river, W by land of Thomas Cole, S by land of old Gaskin; 2½ acres bounded S by the north river, E by land of Widow Spooner, N by the rocks of Old Bishop, W by land of Widow Buffum. **Signed**: Peter and Mary Brackett [by mark]; **Acknowledged**: 12 May 1677; **Witnesses**: John Lake and Benjamin Smith, Jr.; **Recorded**: 12 May 1677.

EDWARD BERRY, Sr. to son EDWARD BERRY – (4:460) On 8 May 1677, Edward Berry, Sr. (weaver) of Salem granted to his son Edward Berry of Painton (county Devon) Old England, now resident in Salem, for love & affection, his dwelling house & land in Salem & his land in Beverly called Draper's Point with all other goods, chattels, lands, implements, debts, bills, bonds, specialties, necessaries, sums of money, movables & immovables on this side & beyond the seas upon condition said son shall the time of his natural life, provide for & maintain in apparel, meat, drink, washing & lodging, & with all things necessary in sickness & in health. **Signed**: Edward Berry; **Acknowledged**: 9: 3 mo: 1677; **Witnesses**: Samuel Dutch and Hilliard Veren, Sr.; **Recorded**: 16 May 1677.

THOMAS ROSE to NICHOLAS ANDREW – (4:463) On 5 March 1676/7, Thomas Rose (fisherman) of Marblehead granted to Nicholas Andrew (fisherman) of Marblehead, for 80 pounds, land with a dwelling house he lately bought of Mr. Moses Maverick, bounded as given in a deed of sale from Thomas Waimouth, NW by land of Richard Rowland & James Smith, SW by land of Mr. William Walton; SE by land of John Waldron, NE by the common. **Signed**: Thomas Rose [by mark]; **Acknowledged**: 18: 3 mo: 1677; **Witnesses**: Joseph Nicholson and Hilliard Veren; **Recorded**: 23 May 1677.

GEORGE HOLLARD to ROBERT STONE – (4:465) On 6 January 1676, George Hollard (mariner) and wife Sarah of Boston, granted to Robert Stone (mariner) of Salem, for 18 pounds, 18½ rods of land in Salem bounded W by land of said Stone & Benjamin Small, N by the highway, E by land of Thomas Ives, S by land of Paul Mansfield. **Signed**: George and Sarah Hollard; **Acknowledged**: 6 Jan 1676; **Witnesses**: William Pitman and John Hayward, Sr.; **Recorded**: 23 May 1677.

JOHN MASSEY to ROBERT STONE – (4:468) On 16 January 1676, John Massey (yeoman) & wife Sarah of Salem granted to Robert Stone (mariner) of Salem, for 98 pounds sterling, 40 acres in Salem called the horse pasture which said Massey lately bought of Mr. William Browne, Capt. George Corwin, George Emory & Phillip Cromwell, bounded W by the great cove & the meadow formerly belonging to Ralph Tompkins, E & N by Woolestons river, S by land formerly possessed by Thomas Watson. **Signed**: John and Sarah Massey; **Acknowledged**: 7: 3 mo: 1677; **Witnesses**: Abigail Veren and Hilliard Veren, Sr.; **Recorded**: 23 May 1677.

JOHN PEASE to ISAACK COOKE – (4:472) On 6 April 1672, John Pease and his wife of Salem granted to Isaack Cooke of Salem for 40 shillings, ¼ acre of land in Salem at the north field, bounded N by land of said Cooke, S by land of said Pease, W by the common highway, E by a heap of stones. **Signed**: John and Ann Pease [both by mark]; **Acknowledged**: 14: 3 mo: 1677; **Witnesses**: Nathaniel Felton and Sarah Pease [by mark]; **Recorded**: 24 May 1677.

MARY MILLER to SARAH BROWNE – (4:473) On 27: 3d mo: 1662, Mary Miller (with consent of husband Miller) granted to her daughter Sarah Browne, the freehold granted by the town to her husband Cutting & the share in Plumb Island that belongs to it. (Entered as a caution this 16: June 1677). **Signed**: John and Mary [by mark] Miller; **Witnesses**: Nicholas Noyce and Elizabeth Masse. Nicholas Noyce made oath that he saw John Miller and his wife sign and deliver the writing, 2: 5: 1674. Entered as a caution this 16: June 1677.

WILLIAM BEALE, Sr. to JOHN CLIFFORD – (4:474) On 18 June 1677, William Beale, Sr. of Marblehead granted to John Clifford (ropemaker) of Salem, for a valuable consideration, 70 acres on Darby fort side, bounded N by the mouth of Forest river, E by land of Thomas Pitman, W by land of George Bonfield, S by land of Mr. Devorix & land belonging to Marblehead common. **Signed**: William Beale; **Acknowledged**: 18: 4: 1677; **Witnesses**: George Hacker [by mark] and Laurance David [by mark]; **Recorded**: 18: 4 mo: 1677.

MARY RUSSELL to WILLIAM BROWN, Jr. – (4:475) On 15 May 1677, Mary Russell of Marblehead (executrix of her late husband Thomas Cawley, deceased), with consent of overseers Mr. Samuel Ward & Benjamin Parmiter, granted to Mr. William Browne, Jr. (merchant) of Salem, for 15 pounds, 5 acres of land in Marblehead ferry lots, being 8 poles wide and 100 poles long, bounded NW by land of Robert Bartlett, below by Salem harbor, "the upper end" by the commons, SE by her land. **Signed**: Mary Russell [by mark], Samuel Ward and Benjamin Parmiter; Delivered to Samuel Cheever on behalf of Mr. Wm. Brown, Jun'r; **Acknowledged**: 20: 4 mo: 1677; **Witnesses**: Moses Maverick and Thaddeus Riddan; **Recorded**: 13: 5 mo: 1677.

ABRAHAM MATHEWS to THOMAS GARDNER – (4:477) On 3 7ber 1677, Abraham Mathews (mate) gave a receipt for thirty quintalls of merchantable winter cod fish on board the *John Booneyventure* (Mr. Anthony Roope commander) paid to him by Mr. Thomas Gardner upon the account of Mr. Robert Oxe. **Signed**: Abraham Mathews; **Recorded**: 29 August 1677.

HENRY COLLINS, Sr. to ANDREW MANSFIELD – (4:477) On 14 March 1671/2, Henry Collins, Sr. (yeoman) of Lynn, granted to Andrew Mansfield (yeoman) of Lynn, for 16 pounds 10 shillings, 5½ acres in Lynn called Reedy meadow, bounded E by land of Jonathan Pickering, W by land of said Collins, N by Blotts upland. **Signed**: Henry Collins, Sr.; **Acknowledged**: 27: 4: 1677; **Witnesses**: John Collins and Joseph Collins; **Recorded**: 13: 5 mo: 1677.

JOHN DOLE to WILLIAM GERRISH, Sr. – (4:479) On 15 Aug 1676, John Dole of Newbury granted to William Gerrish, Sr. for 500 pounds, 7 parcels of land, the first 2 being 4 acres adjoining a house in Newbury & 10 acres of plow land bounded S & E by land of Daniel Pearce, N by land of Mr. John Woodbridge, W by the highway; the 3rd and 4th being 20 acres of meadow near the mill & 12 acres of salt marsh bounded W by land of John Knight, E by a creek; the 5th being 14 acres of salt marsh on Plum Island lately occupied by John Lunt & John Smith; the 6th and 7th being 4 acres of marsh on Plum Island sometime owned by Anthony Morse, together with 7 acres of pasture bounded S by said Morse, E by the highway, N by widow Browne, with the privilege of a freehold. (This deed refers to a deed recorded in follio 137). **Signed**: John Dole; **Acknowledged**: 16 July 1677; **Witnesses**: John Gerrish, Benjamin Gerrish; **Recorded**: 17 July 1677.

GEORGE EMORY to ELIZABETH and JOHN TALY – (4:481) On 1 May 1677, George Emory (chirurgeon) of Salem granted to his kinswoman Elizabeth & her husband John Taly (mariner) for good will & natural affection, his dwelling house and all his land & goods, chattels, implements, debts, bills, binds, specialties, necessaries [and] moveables & unmovables on condition that they maintain him the remainder of his natural life. Further, the above house and lands may not be sold during his natural life. **Signed**: George Emory; **Acknowledged**: 1: 12 mo: 1678; **Witnesses**: Hilliard Veren, Sr., John Lambert & Benjamin Ganson; **Recorded**: 8: 6: 1677.

THOMAS PUTNAM to TIMOTHY LINDALL – (4:484) On 25 Aug 1677, Thomas Putnam (yeoman) of Salem and his wife Mary (formerly the wife & relict of Nathaniel Veren, late of Jamaica, deceased) granted to Timothy Lindall (merchant) of Salem, for 14 pounds, their right, title & interest in the 3rd part of 18 acres of land near the Black Rock in the Island of Barbados which belonged to Nathaniel Veren, who bequeathed it to his said wife & 2 children, Nathaniel & Mary Veren. **Signed**: Thomas Putnam & Mary Putnam; **Acknowledged**: 27: 6 mo: 77 by Lieut. Putnam & Mary yielded dower; **Witnesses**: John Cobbett and Nathaniel Adams; **Recorded**: 28: 6 mo: 1677.

DANIEL CLARK to JOHN ROBBINSON – (4:487) On 10 October 1676, Daniel Clark of Topsfield granted to John Robbinson of Topsfield, for 8 pounds, 2 lots of 20 acres of land in Topsfield on the south side of Ipswich river, bounded W or NW by land of John Goold, S by said river, E by land of Mr. Bradstreet, N by land of farmer Porter. **Signed**: Daniel and Mary Clark; **Acknowledged**: 19: 1 mo: 1676; **Witnesses**: John How and John Prichett; **Recorded**: 3: 7 mo: 1677.

JOHN GIFFORD to RICHARD RUSSELL – (4:488) On 8 April 1670, John Gifford (gentleman) of Lynn, granted to Richard Russell of Charlestown (Middlesex co.), Esquire, for 100 pounds in New England silver, 100 acres of land in Lynn with the green dwelling house which the said Gifford lately erected on part of his land which he bought and purchased of William Kilcup & Richard Cook, being 26 foot long and 18 foot wide, with a 50-foot warehouse, outhouses & $\frac{1}{4}^{th}$ part of his iron furnace, bloomeries, forges, tools & implements, bounded N by the river in front of the dwelling house of said Gifford, S or SW by commons which the town of Lynn gave as for feeding land to the town of Redding. If Gifford paid Russell 8 pounds of New England silver on 8 April 1671, 1672 & 1673, & 100 pounds on 9 April 1673, then the deed would be void. **Signed**: John Gifford; **Acknowledged**: 8 Apr 1670; **Witnesses**: Edward Rawson and William Webb, Jr.; **Recorded**: 3: 7ber: 1677.

THOMAS IVES to WILLIAM HENFIELD – (4:492) On 27 June 1673, Thomas Ives (slaughterer) of Salem (and wife Martha who yielded dower thirds) granted William Henfield (mariner) of Salem, for 80 pounds, 27 rods of land in Salem adjoining said Henfield's land, with a dwelling house that he formerly bought of Nicholas Bartlett, bounded N by land of John Day, E by land of Edward Wooller, S by land of Mr. Joseph Grafton, W by the highway. **Signed**: Thomas and Martha Ives [by mark]; **Acknowledged**: 26: 4 mo: 1673; **Witnesses**: Phillip Cromwell and Daniel Weld; **Recorded**: 17: 7 mo: 1677.

JOHN BROCK, Jr. to RICHARD KNOTT – (4:494) On 3 September 1677, John Brock, Jr. (son & attorney to John Brock, Sr., merchant in Jazey) granted to Richard Knott (chirugeon) of Marblehead, for a certain sum of money, 1 acre of land in Marblehead, bounded NW by the mill pond & all other sides by common land. **Signed**: John Brock, Jr.; **Acknowledged**: 13: 7 mo: 1677; **Witnesses**: Richard Oliver and Phillip Parson; **Recorded**: 24: 7 mo: 1677.

WILLIAM BEALE to JOHN HUDSON – (4:496) On 28 March 1673, William Beale (husbandman) of Marblehead, granted to John Hudson of Marblehead, for a considerable sum, that piece of land which formerly said Hudson sold to Peter Greenfield. **Signed**: William Beall; **Acknowledged**: 1: 2 mo: 1673; **Witnesses**: Arthur White and Benjamin Parmiter; **Recorded**: 24: 7 mo: 1677.

THOMAS WALKER to JOHN WILLIAMS – (4:497) On 9 March 1675, Thomas Walker (brickmaker) of Boston, Suffolk County, and his wife Susanna, granted to John Williams (butcher) of Boston, for 20 pounds, $\frac{1}{4}^{th}$ of an acre of land with a small shop in Salem bounded E by land of William Curtice, W by land of Humphrey Coomes, N by a common street, S by land of Humphrey Searle and wife Mary, reserving unto Mary Searles the wife of Stephen Searle of Salem, a common way of 10 foot in breadth to remain to her & their owne particular use & behoof forever. **Signed**: Thomas and Susanna [by mark] Walker; **Acknowledged**: 9th mo: 1675; **Witnesses**: William Cogswell, Samuel Bishop and John Hayward, Sr.; **Recorded**: 28: 7ber: 1677.

WILLIAM BARTHOLOMEW to JOHN WILLIAMS – (4:500) On 9 October 1676, William Bartholomew of Boston granted to John Williams (butcher) of Boston, for 50 pounds, land with dwelling house in Marblehead which said Bartholomew formerly purchased of Joseph Bond, bounded S & SE by land of William Wood, NE by a common way, N & W by land of William Pote. **Signed**: William and Anna [by mark] Bartholomew; **Acknowledged**: 24 Oct 1676; **Witnesses**: Jeremiah Cushing and Mathew Barnard; **Recorded**: 28: 7: 1677.

JOHN PARKER to JOHN VEREN – (4:503) On 17 December 1661, John Parker (fisherman) of Sagadahoc, with consent of wife Margaret, granted to John Veren (planter) of Sagadahoc for a valuable sum, his right, title & interest in land on the west side of Sagadahoc River, bounded & butting on the NE side with the Maine river down to a point of land commonly known & called by the name of John Veren's high head, & bounded by a cove on the SE side to the mouth of a creek which comes from a fresh water fall, & from the mouth of said creek NW to a swamp, commonly known & called by the name of Colley's swamp & from thence NE to Thomas Humphries head bounds, said Humphrie's head bounds runs SE to the E side of a ledge of rocks, which runs to the head of John Veren's marsh & from said Humphry's head bounds under the eastern side of the ledge of rocks NNE to the Maine river. **Signed**: John Parker [by mark]; **Acknowledged**: 17 Aug 1676; **Witnesses**: Ichabod Wiswall and John Selman; **Recorded**: 28: 7: 1677.

JOHN PARKER to JOHN VEREN, Jr. – (4:505) On 17 December 1661, John Parker (fisherman) of Sagadahoc, with consent of wife Margaret, granted to his godson John Veren, Jr. for divers causes, land called Colley's swamp. (Entered as a caution on 28: 7 mo: 1677). **Signed**: John [by mark] and Margaret Parker; **Witnesses**: Ephraim Marston and Thomas Humphrey.

JOHN BURNELL to EDWARD RICHARDS - (4:506) On 19 September 1677, John Burnell of Lynn gave discharge to Edward Richards of Lynn, of 1 acre of salt marsh that Richards mortgaged to Burnell on 11 June 1669 as security for a debt of 4 pounds 5 shillings. Now debt is paid & mortgage is discharged. **Signed**: John Burnell; **Acknowledged**: 1: 8 mo: 1677.

THOMAS CLARK to EDWARD BERRY, Jr. – (4:507) On 18 October 1677, Thomas Clark (tailor) of Salem granted to Edward Berry, Jr. (seaman) of Salem, for 56 pounds sterling -- 10 pounds to be paid in 50s. money, 50s. wood, 50s. dry fish & 50s. provisions to Abigail White, on order for the account of said Berry on or before 31 March 1678 & the same on or before 31 March 1679, 6 pounds money & 6 pounds dry fish to be paid to said Berry on or before 31 March 1680, 1681 & 1682. As security Clark binds himself with all the house & ground he lately bought of Berry. **Signed**: Thomas Clark; **Acknowledged**: 19 Oct 1677; **Witnesses**: John Swinnerton, Edmond Bridges and Hilliard Veren, Sr.; **Recorded**: 22: 8 mo: 1677.

EMANUEL DOWNING to JOHN PORTER – (4:509) On 15 April 1650, Emanuel Downing of Salem granted to John Porter (yeoman) of Salem, for 3 score & 10 pounds & one firkin of butter, his farm of 500 acres in Salem, bounded W by Mr. Kennestone's farm, S by Laurance Leach's, E by William Lord's, N by the woodland. **Signed**: Emanuel & Lucy Downing; **Acknowledged**: 2: 4: 1656 by Mrs. Lucy Downing; **Witnesses**: William Hathorne and William Flint; **Recorded**: 9: 11 mo: 1677.

HENRY STACY, Sr. to WILLIAM BROWNE – (4:510) On 8 November 1677, Henry Stacy, Sr. (husbandman), late of Marblehead, now of Salem, & wife Jane granted to William Browne (fisherman) of Marblehead for 9 pounds, 2¼ acres of land in Marblehead, bounded NW by land of Dorcas Peach, SE by land of Mark Pitman, SW by land of said Browne, NE by land of Thomas [Smea?]. **Signed**: Henry & Jane Stacy [by mark]; **Acknowledged**: 16: 9 mo: 1677; **Witnesses**: George Harvey [by mark] and Hilliard Veren, Sr.; **Recorded**: 20: 9 mo: 1677.

STEPHEN HASKETT to SAMUEL SHRIMPTON – (4:512) On 16 Nov 1677, Stephen Haskett (soap boiler) of Salem mortgaged to Samuel Shrimpton (merchant) of Boston, for 400 pounds sterling, ½ acre of land in Salem with his present dwelling house that he purchased of widow Sears & an adjoining half-acre with dwelling house, soap house & other outhouses he lately purchased of Francis Skerry, both bounded E by land of Widow Eastwick, N by land of Francis Skerry & John Williams, W by land of John Gardner, S by a highway by the south riverside; also 1¼ acres of land in Salem with one messuage or tenement he formerly purchased of Phillip Cromwell, bounded N by the highway near the north river side, E by land of John Gedney, S by land of William Bath, W by land of Joseph Wiles. If Haskett paid Shrimpton 400 pounds sterling by 31 May 1678 then the deed would be void. **Signed**: Stephen and Elizabeth Haskett; **Acknowledged**:

20: 9 mo: 1677 & wife Elizabeth yielded dower; **Witnesses**: Peter Joy and Michael Combs; **Recorded**: 21: 9 mo: 1677.

STEPHEN HASKETT to WILLIAM BATH – (4:515) On 2 October 1677, Stephen Haskett (merchant) of Salem granted to William Bath (fisherman) of Beverly, for 20 pounds sterling, 40 poles of land in Salem bounded S by land of Widow Eastwick, W by land of Nicholas Potter, N by land of said Haskett, E by land of Mr. John Gedney, with a 12-foot wide highway running down from the south end of the premises to the north river. **Signed**: Stephen & Elizabeth Haskett; **Acknowledged**: 20: 9: 1677 & wife Elizabeth yielded dower; **Witnesses**: Peter Joy & Michael Combes; **Recorded**: 22: 9 mo: 1677.

GEORGE KEASAR to THOMAS IVORY – (4:517) On 6 April 1666, George Keasar (tanner) of Salem granted to Thomas Ivory (wheelwright) of Lynn, for 20 pounds sterling, land in Lynn consisting of 2 10-acre lots that lay between Collins' Pond & the old pond, one formerly Jenkin Davis's & the other Thomas Parker's, bounded E by the range of 10-acre lots & including a common highway; also two adjoining 10-acre lots, one formerly Richard Brooks' & the other Richard Johnson's; bounded E by the common, W by the two aforesaid 10-acre lots, S by land of William Edmonds, N by land of Mr. Hanford. **Signed**: George Keaser; **Acknowledged**: 15: 1 mo: 1674; **Witnesses**: William Crofts & Allen Breed; **Recorded**: 26: 9: 1677.

JOHN HAWKES to ROBERT BATES – (4:520) On 10 December 1673, John Hawkes (yeoman) of Lynn with consent of his wife, granted to Robert Bates (husbandman) of Lynn, for 22 pounds, 60 acres of land in Lynn bounded S by a brook & land of Abraham Wellman, NE by Stone's meadow, W by Reedy meadow, NW by land of Henry Collins. **Signed**: John and Sarah Hawkes [by mark]; **Acknowledged**: 26: 9 mo: 1677; **Witnesses**: John Hathorne and Eleazer Hathorne; **Recorded**: 26: 9: 1677.

MARY ROPES to WILLIAM RUSSELL & THOMAS GREENE – (4:521) On 16 November 1677, Mary Ropes (relict & administratrix of George Ropes, carpenter, late of Salem, deceased) granted to William Russell & Thomas Greene, both of Salem, for 22 pounds, 20 acres of land in Salem that was given to said George Ropes by the town, bounded E by land of Thomas Greene, S by land of Mr. William Browne, Sr., W by land of Samuel Verry, N by land of Robert Wilson. **Signed**: Mary Ropes [by mark]; **Witnesses**: Hilliard Veren, Sr. and William Downton. Consented to by John, William & Samuel Ropes, sons of George & Mary Ropes, and by John Norman, their son-in-law. **Signed**: John Norman, John Ropes,

William Ropes & Samuel Ropes; **Acknowledged**: 19: 9 mo: 1677 by Mary Ropes; **Recorded**: 26: 9 mo: 1677.

ROBERT BRIDGES to ROBERT BURNAP – (4:524) On 24 February 1654, Robert Bridges of Lynn granted to Robert Burnap (husbandman) of Reading, Middlesex Co., for a competent sum of money, his 800-acre farm in Lynn & Reading, having Ipswich river running along the N or NE side, plus 25 acres on each side of Beaver dam in or near Reading, all originally granted by Lynn to the Right Honorable Robert Lord Brook, deceased, & since confirmed by the town to Robert Bridges. If it fell short of 825 acres when surveyed, Bridges surrendered his right & interest to Burnap so that he or we may recover what may be justly recoverable by law against the town of Lynn so far as justice requires that the town should make good the whole number of acres according to the original grant. **Signed**: Robert Bridges; **Acknowledged**: 20: 6 mo: 1656 with wife Mary yielding dower; **Witnesses**: Thomas Marshall, John Cotton & Hanah Hill; **Recorded**: 6: 10: 1677.

GEORGE CORWIN to ROBERT BURNAP – (4:527) An agreement was made between Capt. George Corwin (merchant) of Salem & Robert Burnap, to reserve to Burnap the 25 acres of meadow adjoining Beaver dam within or near the bounds of Reading from within named farm of 800 acres sold for 200 pounds by bill of sale 24 Feb 1662. **Signed**: George Corwin & Robert Burnap; **Witnesses**: Edward Norice & Thomas Burnap. Deed from Robert Burnap, Sr. of Reading (Middlesex Co.) to Capt. George Corwin (merchant) of Salem for a valuable consideration, right, title & interest [in the above parcel]. **Signed**: 10 Dec 1677 by Robert Burnap; **Acknowledged**: 10: 10 mo: 1677; **Witnesses**: Resolved White & Edward Norrice, Sec'y.; **Recorded**: 6: 10: 1677.

ELEAZER HATHORNE to Mr. KEASER (Deposition by Veren & Beadle) – (4:528) On 20: 12 mo: 1672, Hilliard Veren & Nathaniel Badle testified & said that they being present at Mr. Keaser's when Mr. Eleazer Hathorne signed to a deed he gave him for a small parcel of land before his house to the water sideward, Mr. Keaser, speaking to him concerning his wife's yielding up her thirds in said land, Mr. Hathorne replied "he was now going away his voyage & would not trouble his wife now, but when he returned, his wife should resign up her interest in the thirds," he should not question anything to the contrary, for he intended honestly there should be no stick there, but assured him without fail, at his return, his wife should do it & this he spake often when he gave possession of the land & afterwards, & in Mr. Keaser's house; & further Nathaniel Beadle testifies he owned he had received 10 shillings in money formerly, as part of the sum he was to have for the land, & 50 shillings paid to Isaac Williams, &

20 he paid in money at that time to Mr. Hathorne, & the remainder he was to pay in wood to his wife in his absence to make up the full of 8 pounds, 10 shillings which was the full of what he was to pay for the purchase of the said land, which also the said Hilliard Veren testified to the best of his memory, he engaged to Mr. Keaser that he should not be damnified or suffer, but his wife he engaged should deliver her thirds, & that he would make it good. **Signed**: 20: 12: 1672 by Hilliard Veren and Nathaniel Beadle; **Witnesses**: 29: 11 mo: 1677 by Samuel Symonds, Deputy Govr. and Daniel Denison.

ROBERT BURNAP & ISAAK BURNAP to Capt. GEORGE CORWIN – (4:529) On 24 February 1662, Robert Burnap (husbandman) of Reading and his son Isaak Burnap of Salem, with consent of both wives, granted to George Corwin (merchant) for 200 pounds, 800 acres of land in Reading & Lynn near Ipswich River, W by land of Capt. Walker, S Bear meadow & Willis's meadow. **Signed**: Robert & Isaak Burnap; **Acknowledged**: 22: 7: 1663, Robert Burnap, wife Ann yielded dower; 12: 8 mo: 1663 Isaak Burnap; **Witnesses**: Edward Norice & Isaak Williams; **Recorded**: 6: 10 mo: 1677.

ISAACK BURNAP to Capt. GEORGE CORWIN – (4:531) On 24 February 1662, Isaack Burnap signed a memorandum to deed 4:529, that included an additional 40 acres of land given by the town of Reading to said Isaak Burnap but not yet laid out. Capt. Corwin must take this land wheresoever the lot falls. **Acknowledged**: 12: 8 mo: 1663; **Witnesses**: Edward Norice & Isaack Williams; **Recorded**: 6: 10 mo: 1677.

SUSANNAH GOOSE to JOSHUA BUFFUM – (4:531) On 13 November 1677, Susannah Goose (widow) of Boston granted to Joshua Buffum (yeoman) of Salem, for 10 pounds, 5 acres of land in Salem bounded SE by the north river, SW by land now occupied by Jeremiah Neale, NW by the highway, NE by land of Jacob Pudeater. **Signed**: Susanna Goose; **Acknowledged**: 13 Nov 1677; **Witnesses**: John Hayward, Sr. & Eleazer Moody, serv't; Consented to and signed by Isaak Goose, son of Susanna Goose; **Recorded**: 6: 10 mo: 1677.

THOMAS COLE to JOSHUA BUFFAM – (4:534) On 10 November 1673, Thomas Cole (husbandman) of Salem granted to Joshua Buffam (carpenter) of Salem for 40 shillings, an acre of land in the north field of Salem lying against Trask's corn mill which Capt. Walter Price formerly bought of one Ingerson, bounded NW by land of said Joshua Buffam, SW by land of Widow Buffam, SE by land formerly Samuel Belknap's, NE by land of Richard Bishop. **Signed**: Thomas Cole & Ann Cole [both by mark]; **Acknowledged**: 10: 1 mo: 1675; **Witnesses**: Richard Croad & Sarah Wilkinson [by mark]; **Recorded**: 7: 10 mo: 1677.

JOHN CLEMENTS, Sr. to WILLIAM HATHORNE, Sr. – (4:537) On 2 November 1677, John Clements, Sr. (fisherman) of Marblehead granted to William Hathorne, Sr. (Esquire) of Salem for a valuable sum, 1 acre of land with dwelling house in Marblehead, bounded W by land of John Gatchell, Sr., N by a highway, E & S by common land. **Signed**: John Clements, Sr. [by mark]; **Acknowledged**: 2 Nov 1677; **Witnesses**: Thomas Flint & John Bullock; **Recorded**: 7: 10 mo: 1677.

Major THOMAS SAVAGE to GILBERT TAPLEY – (4:539) On 7 November 1677, Major Thomas Savage of Boston granted to Gilbert Tapley (fisherman) of Salem for 8 pounds, ½ acre of land near Winter harbor in Salem, bounded S by house & land of said John Tapley [sic] which he lately bought of Mr. Henry Bartholemew, NE by land of Mr. John Higginson, Jr., W & N by common land. **Signed**: Thomas & Mary Savage; **Acknowledged**: 3: 10 mo: 1677 by Thomas Savage & wife Mary; **Witnesses**: John Higginson, Jr. & Sarah Higginson; **Recorded**: 7: 10 mo: 1677.

JOHN TODD to JOHN ROBINSON – (4:541) On 26 September 1677, John Todd (husbandman) of Rowley, with consent of his wife, granted to John Robinson of Topsfield, for 2 cows, 8 acres of land in Topsfield bounded SW by John Goold's way, N or NW by land of Matthew Stanley, N or NE by land of said Robinson, E or SE by land of Sgt. Edmond Towne. **Signed**: John Todd; **Acknowledged**: 5: 9 mo: 1677; **Witnesses**: John Johnson & Joshua Poyntton; **Recorded**: 8: 10 mo: 1677.

LOTT KILLUM to JOSEPH FOSTER – (4:542) On 26 November 1677, Lott Killum (husbandman) of Salem and his wife Hanna granted to Joseph Foster (husbandman) of Salem for 10 pounds, 8 acres of land in Salem, bounded N by land of said Killum, W by the highway that Lott had laid out for his own particular use, S by land of Isaac Goodell, E by land of Zachariah Goodell. **Signed**: Lott Killum & Hanna Killum [by mark]; **Acknowledged**: 26: 9 mo: 1677 with wife Hannah yielding dower; **Witnesses**: Hilliard Veren, Sr. & John Black; **Recorded**: 8: 10 mo: 1677.

LOTT KILLUM to THOMAS FLINT – (4:545) On 26 November 1677, Lott Killum (husbandman) of Salem and wife Hanna granted to Thomas Flint (house carpenter) of Salem, for 28 pounds sterling, 28½ acres of land in Salem bounded N by land of John Buxton, S by land of widow Elizabeth Smith & Isaack Goodell, E & W by land of said Lott & Hanna Killum. **Signed**: Lott Killum & Hanna Killum [by mark]; **Acknowledged**: 26: 9

mo: 1677 with wife Hanna releasing dower; **Witnesses**: Hilliard Veren, Sr. & John Black; **Recorded**: 8: 10 mo: 1677.

NICHOLAS POTTER to son ROBERT POTTER – (4:547) Nicholas Potter (bricklayer) of Salem granted to his natural son Robert Potter of Lynn, for 4 pounds annually during the life of said Nicholas & 10 pounds on demand & 10 pounds payable to his sister Elizabeth Newhall, wife of Corp. Thomas Newhall, within one year after the death of said Nicholas, all his property in Lynn, a considerable part of which he had given Robert at his first marriage but had not then written a deed, his 6-acre houselot bounded S by the mill street & land of Burgis, N by land formerly William Knight's now in possession of Robert Potter, E by land of Robert Burges, W by land of John Hathorne, 3 acres in the neck where John Ramsdell lives which was formerly Henry Gaines, bounded N by land of Daniel Gott, S by land of Samuel Hart, E by salt marsh, W by the rocky hill; 3 acres formerly William Knight's bounded E by land of Robert Burgess, W by land of John Gillam, S by land of John Hathorne, Richard Hood & the aforesaid 6 acres, N by the common; 12 acres in the 1st division in Rumney Marsh bounded E by land of John Gillam, W by land formerly Capt. Bridges, N by the swamp, S by the river & land of Thomas Newhall; 2 acres in the same division bounded E & W by land of Francis Burnell, N by land of John Edmonds, S by the second division lots; 6 acres in the lower division of Rumney marsh bounded E by land of Goodman Collens, W by land formerly Abraham Belknap's, N by the second division lots, S by the river; 2 acres in the marsh below the town bounded E by land of John Fuller & Goodman Chadwell, W by the creek, S by land lately Thomas Coldum's, N by land of John Ballard; 1 acre in the fresh meadow bounded by land of Allen Breed, Daniel Gott, the other division of lots & the swamp. **Signed**: Nichols Potter [by mark] and Robert Potter; **Acknowledged**: 14: 4 mo: 1675; **Witnesses**: George Keaser, Sr. & Andrew Mansfield. It being understood that whereas in a will which he had made & left in the hand of Honor'd father Mr. Gedney, wherein he had given to daughter Elizabeth Newhall a parcel of land in the north field in Salem, do hereby make void the same & instead thereof give unto her 10 pounds to be paid by son Robert Potter, as is expressed in the writing in the former part of this paper, & likewise that neither of children at Lynn shall hinder any of dear children had by last dear wife of any part of estate which is not expressed in the writing in this paper. **Signed**: 26 May 1675 by Nicholas Potter [by mark]; **Witnesses**: George Keaser & Andrew Mansfield; **Recorded**: 11: 10 mo: 1677.

MEHITABLE COLLINS to JEFFRY PARSONS – (4:552) On 29 November 1677, Mehitable Collins, relict & administratrix of John Collins (mariner) late of Salem, deceased granted to Jeffry Parsons (husbandman) of Gloucester for 3 pounds, 2 acres of land in Gloucester, bounded W by common land, N by land of Thomas Verry, E by land of said Parsons & Samuel Doliver; S by land of said Parsons. **Signed**: Mehitable Collins [by mark]; **Acknowledged**: 29: 9 mo: 1677; **Witnesses**: Hilliard Veren, Jr. & Hilliard Veren, Sr.; **Recorded**: 11: 10 mo: 1677.

WILLIAM CLEAVES to DAVID PERKINS – (4:554) On 10 January 1676, William Cleeves (fisherman) of Beverly granted to David Perkins (blacksmith) of Beverly, for 6 pounds, 1 acre of land in Beverly bounded S by land of John Stone, W by land of Mark Haskall, N by land of Osmund Trask, E by the highway. **Signed**: William Cleeves; **Acknowledged**: 28: 9 mo: 1677, with wife Martha yielding dower; **Witnesses**: John Bennett & Samuel West; **Recorded**: 12: 10 mo: 1677.

EDWARD BERRY, Jr. to THOMAS CLARK – (4:555) On 18 October 1677, Edward Berry, Jr. (seaman) late of Painton, County Devon, England, now of Salem, with consent of his father Edward Berry, granted to Thomas Clark (tailor) of Salem, for 60 pounds, his dwelling house & land near the meeting house in Salem, lately made over to him by his father, who bought it from Abigail Lord, the executrix of William Lord (deceased) as by deed dated 1 October 1674, bounded N & W by the street or market place, S by land of said Abigail Lord (now Abigail White) & the housing parts as the 2 chimneys that run up together, one belonging to the bargained premises, the other to the tenement that Edward Winter lives in & the ground which lies on the E side of said house. **Signed**: Edward Berry, Jr. & Edward Berry; **Acknowledged**: 19: 8 mo: 1677; **Witnesses**: John Swinerton, Edward Bridges & Hilliard Veren, Sr.; **Recorded**: 12: 10 mo: 1677.

GEORGE CORWIN to JOHN CORWIN – (4:558) On 1 November 1677, George Corwin of Salem assigned to his son John Corwin, all his right in the bond endorsed in the back side of the deed [book 2: foll: 39]. **Signed**: George Corwin; **Acknowledged**: 1: 9 mo: 1766; **Witnesses**: Nathaniel Felton, Sr., Eleazer Hathorne & Edward Norrice, Sr. Assignment from the abovesaid John Corwin to John West & his son Thomas, all his right to the bond that was endorsed on the back side. **Signed**: 15 Nov 1677 by John Corwin; **Acknowledged**: 15: 9 mo: 1677; **Witnesses**: Eleazer Hathorne, Nathaniel Felton & Edward Norrice; **Recorded**: 25: 10 mo: 1677.

MATHEW PRICE to WILLIAM JAMESON – (4:559) On 28 December 1677, Mathew Price (tailor) of Salem granted to his son-in-law William Jameson (tailor) of Charlestown, Middlesex Co. and his daughter Sarah, William's wife, & to their lawful heirs, for love & affection, 24 rods of land in Salem being part of the land belonging to Matthew's dwelling house, bounded E by land of Joseph Miles, S by land of Thomas Ives, W by the street, N by his own land, reserving for himself the privilege of a highway through the front of the premises to his now dwelling house. **Signed**: Mathew Price; **Acknowledged**: 28: 10 mo: 1677; **Witnesses**: Hilliard Veren, Sr. & Phillip Veren; **Recorded**: 29: 10: 1677.

MEHITABLE COLLINS to JEFFRY PARSONS – (4:562) On 29 November 1677, Mehitable Collins, relict & administratrix of John Collins (mariner) late of Salem, deceased, granted to Jeffry Parsons (husbandman) of Gloucester for 3 pounds, 2 acres of land in Gloucester, bounded W by common land, N by land of Thomas Verry, E by land of said Parsons & Samuel Doliver; S by land of said Parsons. **Signed**: Mehitable Collins [by mark]; **Acknowledged**: 29: 9 mo: 1677; **Witnesses**: Hilliard Veren, Jr. & Hilliard Veren, Sr.; **Recorded**: 29: 10 mo: 1677.

RICHARD PRINCE to WILLIAM BROWNE, Jr. – (4:564) On 20 November 1677, Richard Prince of Salem, son of Richard Prince of Salem, deceased, granted to William Browne, Jr. (merchant) of Salem, for a valuable consideration, 27½ rods of land in Salem which his father had left him in his will, with a cellar now built in it, bounded E by land of said Browne, S by the street, W by land of Samuel Prince, N by land of Jonathan Prince. **Signed**: Richard Prince; **Acknowledged**: 31: 10 mo: 1677; **Witnesses**: John Pilgrim, Charles Readford & J. Murray; **Recorded**: 31: 10 mo: 1677.

SAMUEL WALTON to WILLIAM BROWNE, Jr. – (4:566) On 19 November 1677, Samuel Walton (fisherman) of Marblehead granted to William Browne, Jr. of Salem, his right & title to 2 parcels of land in Marblehead; the 1st being 6 acres near Robert Knight's water mill which he had bought of one Williams that went to England; the 2nd being ½ acre near his now dwelling house—these to secure payment of a debt of 28 pounds, 11 shillings & 8 pence to be paid in merchantable & good refuse fish. **Signed**: Samuel Walton; **Acknowledged**: 19: 9 mo: 1677; **Witnesses**: Richard More, Sr. & Charles Redford. [no recording date].

VINSON STILSON to JONATHAN BRIDGHAM – (4:568) On 2 August 1677, Vinson Stillson (cordwinder) of Marblehead, & wife Grace, mortgaged to Jonathan Bridgham (tanner) of Boston, for 54 pounds paid by Henry Bridgham, father of said Jonathan, all their messuage or tenement in Marblehead, with ½ acre of land, bounded S by the street that led to the water side, W by land of Robert Rowles, N by land of said Rowles & Richard Hanaford, E by land of said Hanniford. If Stilson paid 54 pounds on or before 1 August 1679, then the deed would be void. **Signed**: Vincent and Grace Stilson [both by mark]; **Acknowledged**: 23 Aug 1677;

Witnesses: Richard Way, John Hayward (servant) and Eleazer Moody (servant); **Recorded**: 2: 11: 1677.

JOHN WEST to ANTHONY BENNETT – (4:571) On 7 January 1671, John West of Beverly & wife Mary, who yielded dower thirds, granted to Anthony Bennett (carpenter) of Beverly, for a valuable sum, 5 acres of land on the back side of the great pond by the long beach between Manchester & Macnell Cove in Beverly, bounded S by the pond, W by land of Nicholas Woodberry. **Signed**: John West [by mark]; **Acknowledged**: 7: 11 mo: 1677; **Witnesses**: William Clark & John Clark [by mark]; **Recorded**: 7: 11 mo: 1677.

ANTHONY BENNETT to JOHN WEST – (4:573) On 7: 11 month 1677, Anthony Bennett signed a memorandum whereby he agreed to maintain forever a sufficient fence against great cattle & hogs, all the way so far as his land (bought from John West) that lay against the pond called Blackleeches pond & if he neglected to maintain the fence, the land would be forfeited to West. Further, if Bennett decides to sell the land he must offer it first to West. **Signed**: Anthony Bennett [by mark]; **Acknowledged**: 7: 11 mo: 1677; **Witnesses**: Eleazer Hathorne & Francis Collins; **Recorded**: 7: 11 mo: 1677.

MOSES MAVERICK to JOHN CARDER – (4:574) On 24 December 1677, Moses Maverick of Marblehead, with consent of wife Eunice, granted to John Carder of Marblehead, for a certain sum of money, 1 messuage or dwelling house with orchard, garden & ¼ acre of land in Marblehead adjoining Richard Norman's, also a cow's commonage. **Signed**: Moses & Eunice Maverick; **Acknowledged**: 9: 11 mo: 1677; **Witnesses**: Hilliard Veren, Sr. & Joseph Dolliber; **Recorded**: 9: 11 mo: 1677.

HENRY STACY, Sr. to JOHN HOLMES – (4:576) On 9 June 1677, Henry Stacy, Sr. (husbandman) of Salem & wife Jane, granted to John Holmes, for 15 pounds, 5 acres of land being all his part & interest that he purchased in the farm called Mr. Humfries farm, bounded W by land of Joseph Doliber, E by land of Nathaniel Walton, N by the highway that goes to George Darling's, S by the old way that went to Mr. King's. **Signed**: Henry Stacy [by mark]; **Acknowledged**: 9: 11 mo: 1677; **Witnesses**: Hilliard Veren, Sr. & Henry Skerry, Sr.; **Recorded**: 9: 11 mo: 1677.

ROBERT GOODELL to NICHOLAS MANNING – (4:578) On 7 June 1667, Robert Goodell (husbandman) of Salem granted to Mr. Nicholas Manning of Salem, for 29 pounds 10 shillings, 20 acres of land in the north field of Salem bounded N by land sometime of Thomas Reade, S by land of John Neale, W by land of Job Swinerton, E by land formerly Mr. Peeters, being parted from it by the highway. **Signed**: Robert Goodell; **Acknowledged**: 22: 5 mo: 1671; **Witnesses**: Edward Norice & George Thomas; **Recorded**: 10: 11 mo: 1677.

WILLIAM LONGSTAFF to BENJAMIN HOME – (4:580) On 9 January 1677, William Longstaff (cordwinder) of Salem, granted to Benjamin Home (tailor) of Salem, for 30 pounds sterling, half his now dwelling house in Salem with half of the land on which it stood containing about 1½ acres, which he bought of Ezekiell Fogg by deed dated 5 May 1676, bounded S by "a ridg of ground that was made by the digging of a ditch formerly by Ralph Fogg," N, E & W by the highway & the North river. **Signed**: William Longstaff [by mark]; **Acknowledged**: 10: 11 mo: 1677; **Witnesses**: Phillip Veren & Hilliard Veren, Sr.; **Recorded**: 10: 11 mo: 1677.

RESOLVED WHITE to JOSIAH WHITE – (4:583) On 9 January 1677, Resolved White & wife Abigail of Salem, executrix of the last will & testament of William Lord (deceased), granted to Josiah White, son of said Resolved, for love & natural affection, 4 acres & ten poles of land recovered by execution to settle a debt of about 50 pounds sterling owed by Nicholas Manning to said William Lord. The land was bounded E by land of Jonathan Pickering, S by the mill pond, W by land of Nicholas Manning & Francis Skerry or John Pickering, N by the highway. Said Josiah was to deliver yearly to said Abigail, for the term of her natural life, half the hay, corn, grain, or whatever else shall grow or be raised on said land, or the deed would be void. **Signed**: Resolved & Abigail White; **Acknowledged**: 14: 11 mo: 1677; **Witnesses**: Rebecka Wheeler & Hillard Veren, Sr.; **Recorded**: 15: 11 mo: 1677.

PETER MILLER to THOMAS HAWKINS – (4:586) On 15 January 1677, Peter Miller of Salem granted to Thomas Hawkins of Marblehead, for a certain sum of money, 1 acre of land with a house in Marblehead, bounded NW by land of William Potes, SE by land of William Nick. **Signed**: Peter Miller; **Acknowledged**: 18: 11 mo: 1677; **Witnesses**: John Blany, John Northy & Edward Humphreys; **Recorded**: 4: 12 mo: 1677.

ISRAEL PORTER (Deposition concerning boundary in Topsfield) – (4:588) On 30: 11 mo: 1677, Israel Porter, aged 32 or thereabouts, stated that about 18 or 20 years ago, his father was required by Topsfield, to show the bounds of his lands, which lay within the township, and, his being present, his father showed 3 bounds belonging to that part of Mr. Downing's farm, so-called, which lay within the Topsfield line. Also he showed 3 bounds belonging to his land in Blind hole (so-called) all which bounds were approved & accepted by Topsfield, & have so continued ever since for ought he had heard. **Sworn**: in Court at Salem, 30: 11 mo: 1677; **Witnesses**: Samuel Symonds, Dept. Gov'r. & Major Gen'll. Denison, Esq.; **Attested**: Hilliard Veren.

BENJAMIN PORTER to ISRAEL PORTER – (4:588) On 29 January 1676, Benjamin Porter (husbandman) of Salem granted to his brother Israel Porter, for some reasons & causes best known unto himself, ½ of a 9-score acre parcel of land in Salem commonly called Gott's corner, given him by the will of his deceased father & purchased by him from Mr. Gott, Jacob Barney, Jeffry Massey, William Watson & John Pickard, bounded E by land of Jacob Barney, S by land called Sharp's farm, W by land of Joshua Ray, N by land of Capt. John Corwin, which was formerly Mr. Peters. **Signed**: Benjamin Porter; **Acknowledged**: 30: 11 mo: 1677; **Witnesses**: Andrew Elliott & William Eliot; **Recorded**: 5: 12 mo: 1677.

JOHN WILD (Deposition concerning John Porter's land) – (4:591) On 30: 11 month: 1677, John Wild, aged about 62 years, testified that 20 years ago, or thereabouts, he was one of the men chosen by the town of Topsfield, to require farmer John Porter of Salem to show the bounds of his land that lay within Topsfield township. Farmer Porter then showed them 3 bounds belonging to that part of Mr. Downing's farm so called that lay within Topsfield line; also some years ago, upon the like occasion, the same bounds & no other were shown, belonging to the above said tract of land, which Topsfield town did both then & before approve of: & to the best of his knowledge, were the same bounds which were now claimed & held by Joseph Porter, son of the above said farmer John Porter. Likewise that tract of land of farmer Porter's in the place called Blind hole, being within Topsfield, he also showed them 3 bounds belonging to it, one on Smith's hill, another by a swamp side by Mr. Endecott's meadow, the other middle bound between these two, all which 3 bounds made the side next to Topsfield's common that then was. Likewise, from the bounds next to Mr. Endcott's meadow to William Nichols' bound tree, was the end of this tract of land, these & all these abovesaid bounds were approved of by Topsfield & are the same bounds now claimed & held by Benjamin Porter, to the best of his knowledge. **Sworn**: at Court at Salem, 30: 11 mo: 1677 before Samuel Symonds, Esq., Dept'y. Gov'r. & Maj. Gen'll. Daniel Dennison, Esq.

ISAACK WILLIAMS to JOHN HIGGINSON – (4:592) On 29 June 1672, Isaack Williams (shoemaker) of Salem, granted to John Higginson, Sr. of Salem for 8 pounds, ½ acre of land in Salem, which was half of what Samuel Williams (cooper) bought formerly of John Williams (cooper) bounded E & N by land of Daniel Rumboll & John Williams, W by land of Samuel Williams, S by the common called the pen. **Signed**: Isaack Williams; **Acknowledged**: 29 June 1672 by Isaack Williams & wife Margery yielded dower; **Witnesses**: John Higginson, Jr. & Samuel Williams; **Recorded**: 12: 12 mo: 1677.

JOHN HIGGINSON, Sr. to JOHN HIGGINSON, Jr. – (4:593) On 1 September 1676, John Higginson, Sr. of Salem granted to his son John Higginson, Jr. for natural affection, ½ acre of land in Salem bounded E by his own land which was formerly Daniel Rumbol's, N by land of John Williams (cooper), W by land of Samuel Williams, S by the common or highway. **Signed**: Mr. John Higginson, Sr.; **Acknowledged**: 1 Sept 1676; **Witnesses**: John Launder & Henry Higginson; **Recorded**: 12: 12 mo: 1677.

SARAH BROWNE to JAMES BROWNE – (4:595) On 16 November 1677, Sarah Browne (relict & executrix of James Browne, deceased) granted to James Browne (glazier) of Salem, for 90 pounds 4 shillings, 48 rods of land in Salem bounded by the lane that goes down to the north river, E by land of Mrs. Susanna Gedney, N by land of Joseph Hardy, Jr., S by her own land. **Signed**: Sarah Browne; **Acknowledged**: 8: 12 mo: 1677 by Sarah Browne, alias Healy; **Witnesses**: Abigaile Veren & Hilliard Veren, Sr.; **Recorded**: 15: 12 mo: 1677.

(4:597) On 26 January 1677, Samuel Browne (son of James Browne, deceased) and Sarah (his late wife & executrix) for good causes consented to deed of mother to his brother James Browne & yielded his right, title & interest in the parcel of land. **Signed**: Samuel Browne; **Acknowledged**: 26: 11 mo: 1677; **Witnesses**: Hilliard Veren, Sr. & Phillip Veren. [no recording date given].

SARAH BROWNE to JAMES BROWNE – (4:598) Sarah Browne wife of James Browne (glazier) of Salem, gave receipt to her son James Browne of Charlestown for 32 pounds 10 shillings in payment of the 1st 5 years rent which began 10 March 1672/3. **Signed**: 20 Mar 1672/3 by Sarah Browne; **Witnesses**: Samuel Pickworth & Elizabeth Price [by mark]; **Acknowledged**: 8 Feb 1677 by Sarah Browne alias Healy. Receipt from Widow Browne of Salem to her son James Browne in full satisfaction of 2 years rent due 1 Jan 1678 & 1 Jan 1679. **Signed**: 9 Nov 1677 by Sarah Browne; **Acknowledged**: 8: 12 mo: 1677 by Sarah Browne alias Healy; **Witnesses**: Nathaniel Beadle & Thomas Beadle; **Recorded**: 15: 12 mo: 1677.

ADAM WESTGATE (Bill of lading) – (4:599) On 18 May 1670 (dated in Barbados) a bill of lading, signed by Adam Westgate, stated: Shipped by the grace of God in good order & well conditioned, by Thomas Coddington, for account of the Ketch *Hopewell*, in & upon the good ship called the *Return*, whereof is master under God this present voyage, Adam Westgate, & now riding at anchor in the Carlisle Bay, & by God's grace bound for Boston to say 5 hhds. of Musco sugar, 2 hhds of rum, 4 hhdgs molasses, being marked & numbered as in the margin [in margin appears nos. 1, 2, 5-12], & are to be delivered in the like good order & well conditioned at the aforesaid port of Boston, the danger of the seas only excepted, unto Nathaniel Cary or in his absence to Mr. Richard Russell or to his assigne, he or they paying freight for said goods, 35 shillings per tun, money, with primage & average accustomed. In witness whereof the master or purser of said ship hath affirmed to 3 bills of Lading, all of this tenner & date, the one of which 3 bills being accomplished, the other 2 to stand void, & so God send the good ship to her desired port in safety, Amen. **Signed**: Adam Westgate [in a very scribbling manner]; Indorsed on back side of bill: Received the contents of the within specified bill of Lading in behalf of the rest of the owners of the Ketch *Hopewell*, 29 June, per Nathaniel Cary.

ALEXANDER LILLINGTON to Mr. JOHN HATHORNE – (4:600) On 4 August 1675, Alexander Lillington (planter) of Alabama Co. Carolina, now present in Salem, husband of Sarah James (only surviving child & lawful heir of Thomas James, late of Carolina deceased & formerly of Salem) granted to Mr. John Hathorne (merchant) of Salem for a valuable sum, 10 acres of land in the north neck of Salem that belonged to said Thomas James, bounded SW by land of Thomas West, NE by land of John Foster, SE by land of John Tompkins, NW by land of John Waters. **Signed**: Alexander Lillington; **Acknowledged**: 4: 6 mo: 1675; **Witnesses**: Samuel Crompton & Benjamin Gerrish; **Recorded**: 15: 12 mo: 1677.

JOHN GEDNEY (Executor of NICHOLAS POTTER), JOHN PITMAN & JOHN ARCHARD to JOHN BACHELOR – (4:602) On 20 December 1677, John Gedney (vintner), executor to the last will & testament of Nicholas Potter (deceased) and John Pitman & John Archard of Salem, granted to John Bachelor (yeoman) of Salem for 16 pounds, 10 acres near Bass river head in Salem that was formerly Thomas Wilkes (deceased), bounded S & W by common land, N & E by land of said Bachelor. **Signed**: John Gedney, John Archard & John Pickman; **Acknowledged**: 8: 12 mo: 1677 & 2: 10 mo: 1678; **Witnesses**: Hilliard Veren, Sr. & Nathaniel Pease [by mark]; **Recorded**: 8: 1 mo: 1677.

JOHN SHIPLEY to RICHARD KIMBALL – (4:605) On 24: 3 mo: 1656, John Shiply of Chelmsford granted to Richard Kimball of Wenham, for 100 pounds sterling, 3 parcels of land in Wenham: 100 acres of upland bounded E by land of Mr. Fiske, N by the pleasant road, W by land of William Welman, S by land of Thomas Browning & the great swamp; 10 acres of meadow bounded E by the great swamp, W by upland, S by land of Mr. Fisk, N by land of Mr. Bachelor – 50 acres of upland bounded E by the great pond, W by land of Mr. Lord, S by the "run" that leads to the great pond, N by land of Thomas Smith; 4 acres of meadow bounded W by land of William Lord, S by the island, E by land of Thomas Trusler, N by land of John Solart. **Signed**: John and Ann Shipley [both by mark]; **Acknowledged**: 31 May 1659 and 28 June 1659 by wife Ann who yielded dower; **Witnesses**: Thomas & Joan Fisk; **Recorded**: 19 Mar 1677.

RICHARD HUTTEN to RICHARD KIMBALL – (4:607) On 7 January 1656, Richard Hutten of Wenham granted to Richard Kimball of Wenham, for 14 pounds (for the first parcel) & 42 pounds 10 shillings (for the 2nd & 3rd parcels), 4½ acres of land in Wenham bounded E by the Swamp, W by land of Robert Morgan, 35 acres bounded N & E by land of James Moulton, NW by land of Richard Kimball, S by land of Mark Bachelor, W by meadow; 7 acres bounded E by land of Francis Uselton, S by upland, W by land of George Biam. **Signed**: Richard Hutten [by mark]; **Acknowledged**: 28 Dec 1676; wife Elizabeth yielded dower, 29: 10 mo: 1660; **Witnesses**: Charles Gott & Thomas Fiske; **Recorded**: 19 Mar 1677/8.

WILLIAM RAYNER to RICHARD KIMBALL – (4:609) On 2: 1 mo: 1658/9, William Rayner of Ipswich granted to Richard Kimball of Wenham, for 12 pounds 10 shillings, 2 parcels of land in Wenham, which said Rayner purchased from Mathew Edwards of Reading, who had received it by the last will & testament of his uncle Fairfield: 20 acres of upland bounded E by land of Mr. Newman, N by the great swamp; 2 acres of meadow which was part of 8 acres laid out to said Fairfield by the town of Salem, bounded E by the swamp, S by land of Richard Kimball, W by land of Robert Morgan. **Signed**: William and Elizabeth Rayner [by mark]; **Acknowledged**: 29: 10 mo: 1660, with wife Elizabeth yielding dower; **Witnesses**: Thomas Fiske & Caleb Kimball; **Recorded**: 19 Mar 1677/8.

JOHN FOSTER, Sr. to SAMUEL FOSTER – (4:610) On 25 March 1678, John Foster, Sr. (husbandman) of Salem, with consent of wife Martha, granted to his son Samuel Foster, for fatherly affection, his 3-acre estate in the north field or north neck of Salem, which had been in his possession many years & was part of what he had bought of Thomas Scudder, bounded E & N by land of his son John Foster, W by land of

Thomas Robbins, S by his own land. Samuel was not to sell the parcel without first offering it to him or his said son John. **Signed**: John Foster [by mark]; **Acknowledged**: 25: 1 mo: 1678; **Witnesses**: John Waters, John Foster, Sr., & Richard Croad; **Recorded**: 25: 1 mo: 1678.

JOHN RUCK, BARTHOLOMEW GEDNEY, JOHN HIGGINSON & GEORGE DEANE to JOHN GRIFFIN – (4:612) On 28 November 1677, John Ruck, Bartholomew Gedney, John Higginson & George Deane released claim to 15 acres of John Griffin's land at Bradford ferry delivered by execution to satisfy judgment, if Griffin delivered 15 bushels of wheat, 15 bushels of rye, 30 bushels of Indian corn, 1000 & ½ pine board, and what white oak stave he could procure to convenient landing place at Bradford on or before 30 April 1678, plus remainder of 31 pounds, 2sh. 3p. in neat fat cattle delivered to Salem before 31 October 1678. **Signed**: John Ruck, Bartholomew Gedney, John Higginson & George Deane; **Acknowledged**: 28: 9 mo: 1677; **Witnesses**: John Pickering & Edmond Bridges; **Recorded**: 26: 10 mo: 1667.

JOHN GRIFFIN to EDMOND BRIDGES (Attorney...) – (4:614) On 8 November 1677, in case of John Griffin, Bradford, & Edmond Bridges Attorney to John Ruck, John Higginson, Bartholomew Gedney & George Deane in action of debt of 31 pounds 2sh. 3p. Griffin acknowledged judgment & delivered 15 acres under attachment, front of land...at Bradford Ferry. **Signed**: John Griffin; **Acknowledged**: 28: 9: 1677; **Witnesses**: Edmond Bridges & John Pickering.

JAMES BROWNE to RICHARD PRICHARD – (4:615) On 23 February 1677, James Browne (glazier) of Salem, son of James Browne (deceased) granted to Richard Prichard (sadler) of Salem for 7 pounds 4 shillings, 16 poles of land in Salem, being part of the land James Browne had lately bought of his mother Sarah Browne & which adjoins her dwelling house, bounded S by land of Sarah Browne, E by land of Mrs. Susanna Gedney, N by his own land, W by the street. **Signed**: James Browne & Hannah Brown [by mark]; **Acknowledged**: 25: 12 mo: 1677; **Witnesses**: Phillip Cromwell & Hilliard Veren, Sr.; **Recorded**: 26 Mar 1678.

SAMUEL VERRY to CALEB BUFFUM – (4:617) On 21 March 1677/8, Samuel Verry (husbandman) of Salem, with consent of wife Alice, granted to Caleb Buffum of Salem, 7 acres in Salem bounded SW by river that comes out of Cedar Pond, N by land of Eleazer Giles, with privilege of a cart highway through his land. **Signed**: Samuel Verry; **Acknowledged**: 21: 1 mo: 1677; **Witnesses**: Richard Croade & Frances Croade [by mark]; **Recorded**: 27 Mar 1678.

EDWARD WALDRON to THOMAS BAKER – (4:620) On 15 March 1678, Edward Waldron of Wenham granted to Thomas Baker of Beverly, for 30 pounds, 10 acres of land in Beverly bounded N by land of George Hull, E, W & S by the common. **Signed**: Edward Waldron [by mark]; **Acknowledged**: 26: 1 mo: 1678; **Witnesses**: Thomas Fisk & Robert Herbert [by mark]; **Recorded**: 3: 2 mo: 1678.

THOMAS WEST to THOMAS TYLER – (4:621) On 11 March 1677/8, Thomas West (husbandman) of Salem granted to Thomas Tyler (seaman) of Boston (Suffolk Co.) for 5 pounds money, 10 pounds in wheat, rye & Indian corn & 28 acres of land at Bradford near Merrimac river (as appears by an instrument of sale of this date given by said Tyler), 2 parcels of land in Salem; his 1¼ acre homestead with his dwelling house, bounded W by the glass house field so called, S & W by the common, E by land of Samuel Gasking & Samuel Eborne, 10 acres in the north field bounded W by land that was Edward Burcham's, E by land that was Thomas James' now in the possession of Mr. John Hathorne. **Signed**: Thomas West [by mark]; **Acknowledged**: 1 Apr 1678 with wife Mary yielding dower 4: 2 mo: 1678; **Witnesses**: Edward Flint & Richard Croade. [see deed 4:630].

SARAH HEALEY to EZEKIELL CHEEVERS – (4:624) On 1 March 1677/8, Sarah Healey (sometime the wife of James Brown, Sr., deceased, sometimes living in Salem), with consent of her now husband William Healey, granted to Ezekiell Cheevers of Salem for a valuable consideration, land in Salem measuring 3 rods in the front & 8 rods in length, bounded W by the highway that leads to the North river, N by land of John Cromwell, E by land of Joseph Miles, S by land of Joseph Hardy. **Signed**: William & Sarah Healey; **Acknowledged**: 8: 4: 1677/8; **Witnesses**: William Boardman, Sr. & Samuel Green [by mark]; [no recording date].

EZEKIEL CHEEVER to HILLIARD VEREN, Jr. – (4:625) On 1 April 1678, Ezekiel Cheever, Jr. of Salem mortgaged to Hilliard Veren, Jr. of Salem for 130 pounds sterling, ½ acre of land with dwelling house bounded W by land of Joshua Ray, N by land of Thomas Jigels, E by the highway, S by land of Edward Norice. If Cheever were to pay 40 pounds on or before 5 Sept 1678, 30 pounds on or before 5 March 1678, 25 pounds on or before 5 March 1679/80 & 35 pounds on or before 5 March 1680/81, then the deed would be void. **Signed**: Ezekiel Cheever; **Acknowledged**: 1: 2 mo: 1678; **Witnesses**: John Price & Hanna Leach [by mark]; **Recorded**: 5 Apr 1678.

EZEKIEL CHEEVER, Jr. to HILLIARD VEREN, Jr. – (4:627) On 1 April 1678, Ezekiel Cheever, Jr. of Salem granted to Hilliard Veren, Jr. of

Salem, for 10 pounds, land in Salem being 3 rods in the front & 8 rods in length bounded W by the highway, N by land of John Cromwell, E by land of Joseph Miles, S by land of Joseph Hardy. **Signed**: Ezekiel Cheever; **Acknowledged**: 1: 2 mo: 1678; **Witnesses**: John Price & Hanna Leach [by mark]; **Recorded**: 5 Apr 1678.

JOHN ROW to HUGH ROW – (4:629) On 18: 1 mo: 1667, John Row signed an agreement [at Gloucester] with his brother Hugh Row, whereby John is to return Hugh's whole estate, both housing & land & all other necessaries, voiding the agreement of 13 October 1664 when John received Hugh's estate & Hugh came to live with him. John & Hugh further promised to confirm the agreement before a magistrate in a month or six weeks. **Signed**: John & Hugh Row [both by mark]; **Acknowledged**: by both before Samuel Symonds, 15 April 1667; **Witnesses**: Robert Elwell, William Coleman & Phillip Stainwood; [no recording date given].

THOMAS TYLER to THOMAS WEST – (4:630) On 11 March 1677/78, Thomas Tyler (seaman) at present of Boston (Suffolk Co.) granted to Thomas West (husbandman) of Salem, for a house & homestead in Salem & a 10-acre lot in the north field of Salem (as appeared by deed of sale that date), 28 acres of land in Bradford, which he lately purchased of Joseph Pike of Newbury & which was the land of John Griffin & Peter Nash, the highway from Haverhill to Andover excepted, bounded N by Merrimac river for 18 rods, E by land of Henry Kimball of Boston for 9 score rods, S by land of John Griffin for 32 rods, W by land formerly possessed by Peter Nash for 9 score rods. **Signed**: Thomas Tyler [by mark]; **Acknowledged**: 1: 2 mo: 1678, with wife Hannah yielding dower; **Witnesses**: Edward Flint & Richard Croade; **Recorded**: 5: 2 mo: 1678 [see deed 4:621].

EDWARD FLINT to GARTHRID POPE – (4:633) On 24 March 1676/7, Edward Flint (yeoman) of Salem, with wife Eliza yielding dower, granted to Garthrid Pope of Salem (widow) for a valuable sum, 28 rods of land in Salem on the W side of the bridge street near the houses of Joshua & Caleb Buffum, bounded NW by land of John Mecarter which he lately bought of said Edward Flint, NE by the street, SE & SW by Edward Flint's land. **Signed**: Edward & Elizabeth Flint; **Acknowledged**: 6: 2 mo: 1678; **Witnesses**: Ephraim Kempton & Richard Croade.

JOSIAH ROOTES, Sr. to JOHN LOVETT – (4:635) On 30 March 1677, Josiah Rootes, Sr. (husbandman) of Beverly, with wife Susanna yielding dower, granted to John Lovett, Sr. (cooper) of Salem, for 3 pounds, 3 acres of land bounded westerly with a white oak tree on the W end of said Lovett's house, & so to run to the westward corner of William

Hoar's land, wanting about a pole & a half, & so to take in all the land of said Roote's lying between William Hoare's land & the country road, the country road lying on NW from the abovesaid land; all which land above the 2 acres, before given with his daughter, he now makes a further confirmation of said 2 acres, together with the whole parcel of land before mentioned. **Signed**: Josiah & Susanna Rootes [both by mark]; **Acknowledged**: 3: 2 mo: 1678; **Witnesses**: Samuel Corning, Sr. & Nathaniel Hayward; **Recorded**: 30: 2 mo: 1678.

MARY HILLIARD to JOHN BROWN, Jr. – (4:637) On 28 June 1672, Mary Hilliard, relict & administratrix of husband Job Hilliard (mariner) of Salem, deceased, granted to Mr. John Browne, Jr. of Salem (mariner) for a valuable consideration, land in Salem near said Browne's now dwelling house, bounded W by land of said Browne, E by land of Thomas Jeggells, S by land of Joseph Swazy, N by land of Elizabeth Webb. **Signed**: Mary Hilliard [by mark]; **Acknowledged**: 22: 2 mo: 1678 & dower rights yielded; **Witnesses**: Richard More, Sr., John Ingerson, Sr. [by mark] & Edward Norrice, Sec'y.; **Recorded**: 1 May 1678.

SAMUEL PARSONS to GEORGE CORWIN – (4:639) On 8: 6th mo: 1659, Samuel Parsons of East Hampton, Long Island by order & appointment of his father Robert Parsons of Lynn & Johanna his wife, granted to George Corwin (merchant) of Salem for 5 pounds, 12½ acres of land in Salem being a quarter part of 50 acres formerly in the possession of John Pickering, 9½ acres of which are on the N side of the long pond between the land of Jenkin Davis & Gerard Spencer, & 5 acres of which are on the S side of the same pond next to Lynn bounds. **Signed**: Samuel Parsons; **Acknowledged**: 9: 6 mo: 1659 by Robert Parsons & wife Hanna; **Witnesses**: Edward Norrice, Jr. & John Hathorne; **Recorded**: 15: 3 mo: 1678.

ELIZABETH & JOHN PRICE to Major THOMAS SAVAGE – (4:640) On 20 December 1677, Elizabeth Price & John Price of Salem (executors of the last will & testament of Capt. Walter Price, deceased) granted to Major Thomas Savage (merchant) of Boston (Suffolk Co.) for a valuable sum, 2 parcels of land in Salem: 4 acres on Winter Island, bounded SW & SE by common land, N & E by the sea & Winter harbour, ½ an acre on the neck side N of Winter harbour, bounded S by house & land of Gilbert Tapley, N by land of Mr. John Higginson, Jr., W by common land. **Signed**: Elizabeth & John Price; **Acknowledged**: 17th: 2 mo: 1678; **Witnesses**: John Higginson, Jr. & Hilliard Veren, Sr.; **Recorded**: 15: 3 mo: 1678.

JAMES & SARAH ALLEN to FRANCIS NURSE – (4:643) On 29 April 1678, James Allen (minister) of Boston (Suffolk Co.) & his wife Sarah Allen, granted to Francis Nurse (yeoman) of Salem, for 400 pounds New England money, their 300-acre farm in Salem, bounded N by land of farmer Porter, Nathaniel Putnam, James Hadlock & Joseph Holton, W by land of said Holt [sic], E by land of Mr. Zerubbabel Endicott, S according to town grant. **Signed**: James & Sarah Allen; **Acknowledged**: 29 Apr 1678; **Witnesses**: Isaak Adington & Eleazer Phillips; **Recorded**: 16 May 1678.

HILLIARD VEREN, Jr. to EZEKIEL CHEEVER – (4:647) On 4 March 1677/8, Hilliard Veren, Jr. of Salem granted to Ezekiel Cheever of Salem for a valuable sum, ½ acre of land with his now dwelling house & outhouses in Salem, bounded W by land of Joshua Ray, N by land of Thomas Jeggles, S by house & land of Mr. Edward Norrice. **Signed**: Hilliard Veren, Jr. & Hannah Veren; **Acknowledged**: 1: 2 mo: 1678; dower yielded 10: 2 mo: 1678; **Witnesses**: Phillip Veren & Hilliard Veren, Sr.; **Recorded**: 16 May 1678.

SAMUEL ELWELL, Sr. to JOHN ROW – (4:648) On 21 June 1678, Samuel Elwell, Sr. of Gloucester, with consent of his wife Esther, granted to John Row of Salem for a certain sum of money, 2 acres of land in Starknaught harbour in Gloucester given him by his father-in-law Ormond Dutch, bounded NE & S by land of said John Row. **Signed**: Samuel & Ester Elwell; **Acknowledged**: 21: 4 mo: 1678; **Witnesses**: Robert Elwell & Isaack Elwell [both by mark]; **Recorded**: 21: 4 mo: 1678.

HENRY STACY to ALICE THOMAS – (4:650) On 20 June 1678, a promissory note was given by Henry Stacy (planter) of Lynn to Alice Thomas (widow) of Boston, for 18 pounds 6 shillings to be paid in 5 pounds silver at or before 1 October 1678 & the remainder in money within 15 months from the day of signing. [As collateral] Henry Stacy bound over 2 oxen, 1 cow, 1 horse, 8 ewes & 3 lambs. **Signed**: Henry Stacy [by mark]; **Acknowledged**: 22: 4 mo: [no year]; **Witnesses**: Thomas Hughson & Richard Croad; **Recorded**: 22: 4: 1678.

SAMUEL BENNETT to Capt. THOMAS MARSHALL – (4:651) Whereas Samuel Bennett (yeoman) of Rumney Marsh granted to Capt. Thomas Marshall 20 acres of land in Lynn Bennett lately purchased of Joseph Armitage, being the west end of Timothy Tomlin's four score acres given him by the town, Bennett bound over 20 acres of his own land lying in the field Thomas Stocker lives on, within the fence, to Marshall. But if Marshall enjoys the former twenty acres promised, then the bond would be void. **Signed**: 21 September 1673 by Samuel Bennett; **Acknowledged**: 6:

8 mo: 1673; **Witnesses**: John Fuller, John Hathorne and Thomas Newhall; **Recorded**: 9: 5 mo: 1678.

SAMUEL BENNETT to Capt. THOMAS MARSHALL – (4:652) On 13 September 1673, Samuel Bennett (yeoman) of Rumney Marsh (Suffolk Co.) granted to Capt. Thomas Marshall of Lynn, for 25 pounds, 20 acres of land in Lynn being part of a lot that was formerly Mr. Knowles', bounded N by a river or the ironwork's land, S by the common, E by the remainder of the aforesaid lot. **Signed**: Samuel Bennett; **Acknowledged**: 20 Sept 1673; **Witnesses**: John Fuller, Ralph King & Nathaniel Sharp. Joseph Armitage assigned over the contents of this bill unto Capt. Thomas Marshall as his own proper estate, being assignee of John Gifford, agent to Bex & Company. **Signed**: 5 July 1678 by Joseph Armitage; **Witnesses**: John Fuller & John Severne. This refers to a bill recorded in the 3d book, folio 141, 16: 2 mo: 1672, & this assignement endorsed on the back side of the original.

EZEKIEL NEEDHAM to DANIEL NEEDHAM – (4:654) On 21 June 1678, Ezekiel Needham (tanner) of Lynn granted to his brother Daniel Needham (husbandman) of Lynn for 32 pounds, 9 shillings, 6 acres of land in Lynn, formerly in the possession of Mr. Edmond Needham, father of said Daniel & Ezekiel, a small part of that land which was formerly John Farrington's said land divided into 2 pieces: 5 acres bounded SE & NW by land of Allen Breed, Sr. & the highway that goes from the ferry, W by land of said Daniel Needham, E by land of said Ezekiel Needham; 1 acre of sedge or salt grass bounded NW by the Saugus River, SE & SW by land of said Daniel Needham, NE by land of said Ezekiel Needham. **Signed**: Ezekiel Needham; **Acknowledged**: 8: 1 mo: 1678, with wife Sarah yielding dower; **Witnesses**: Thomas Laighton, Sr. & Thomas Laighton; **Recorded**: 10: 5 mo: 1678.

DANIEL NEEDHAM to EZEKIEL NEEDHAM - (4:657) On 13 August 1677, Daniel Needham of Lynn granted to his brother Ezekiel Needham, egress and regress through the 5-acre parcel of land referred to in deed 4:654. **Signed**: Daniel Needham; **Acknowledged**: 8: 5 mo: 1678; **Witnesses**: Thomas Laighton, Sr. & Samuel Hart; **Recorded**: 10: 5 mo: 1678.

WILIAM BARTRUM et al. to DANIEL NEEDHAM – (4:658) On 8 April 1666, William Bartrum (& wife Sarah) & Mary Burt & Sarah Burt (the natural daughters of Hugh Burt of Lynn, deceased) & William Bassett of Lynn (guardian of said Sarah Burt), granted to Daniel Needham (husbandman) of Lynn for 32 pounds, 3 parcels of land: 3 acres bounded W by land of Nathaniel Kirtland, E by land of Nathaniel Hanford, S by the common, N by land of William Clarke; [also] 2 acres of salt marsh bounded N by land of Mr. Needham, W by land of widow Thomas, S by the river, E by George Taylor; [also] 1 acre of salt marsh bounded N by land of Mr. Needham, E by land of George Taylor, W by land of John Newhall. **Signed**: William Bartrum, Sarah Bartrum [by mark], Mary Burt [by mark] & Sarah Burt [by mark] and William Bassett; **Acknowledged**: 30th: 8 mo: 1666 by all; **Witnesses**: Andrew Mansfield & Daniel Salmon.

JOHN MASON to WILLIAM HIRST – (4:661) On 1 Nov 1676, John Mason (merchant) of London (England), now resident in Boston, granted to his friend William Hirst (merchant) of Salem power of attorney to recover all his debts present & future. **Signed**: John Mason; **Witnesses**: William Gilbert, John Hayward. Scribe Hayward made oath that he & Gilbert witnessed the above. 28 May 1678; **Recorded**: 10: 5 mo: 1678.

CLEMENT COLDUM, GEORGE KEASER, EDWARD RICHARDS & WILLIAM EDMONDS – (Testamonies referring to deed 4:88) – (4:662) On 24 May 1678, Clement Coldum, aged about 55, testified that the grant of the old mill was in July 12: 1633 to Edmond Tomlins, which was the 2nd mill in the colony & that after that the town saw that the mill could not supply the town, they gave leave to build an overshoot mill upon the same water, with a sluice called by the name of the old sluice, being made by Mr. Howell, the second owner of the mill, & then Mr. Howell did sell the same mill to John Elderkin, & John Elderkind did sell it to Mr. Bennett & Mr. Bennett sold it to Goodman Wheeler, & Goodman Wheeler sold it to John Ballard, & John Ballard sold it to Henry Roads & the water to supply the mill with was granted to the mill before any meadow in the town was granted to any man, we mowing [?] all common then, & that he, Clement Coldum, kept the key of the old sluice for Mr. South, which was about 27 or 28 years ago. **Signed**: Clement Coldum. Taken upon oath, 3: 4 mo: 1678; **Recorded**: 11: 5: 1678.

On 3: June: 1678, George Keaser, aged about 60 years, testified that being at a town meeting in Lynn meeting house many years ago, Mr. Edward Tomlins made a complaint to the town of Lynn that there was not water enough in the great pond next to the town of Lynn to serve the mill to grind their grist in the summertime & he desired leave of the town to make a dam in the upper pond, to keep a head of water against the height of summertime so that he might have a supply of water to grind their grist in the drought of summer, & the town of Lynn granted him his request that he should make a dam there where the old trees lay for a bridge for all people to go over, instead of a bridge & the place was granted to him freely by the town of Lynn, for the use of the mill to Edward Tomlins that he might have supply of water to grind with. **Signed**: George Keaser. Taken upon oath 3: 4 mo: 1678; **Recorded**: 11: 5: 1678.

On 16 June 1678, Edward Richards, aged 62 or thereabouts, being in the town of Lynn for 45 years, testified that upon his certain knowledge, that upon the erecting of the old water mill, that Mr. Edward Tomlins had granted to him by the town of Lynn all the water & water courses & sluices were granted to him as his right, provided that he was not to stop or hinder the alewives to go up to the great pond & that the town of Lynn nor no man therein was to molest him or trouble him in his proper right. **Signed**: Edward Richards [by mark]. Taken upon oath 21: 4: 1678.

On 26 May 1678, William Edmonds, age 68, testified that the grant of the old mill was July 12th 1633, to Edward Tomlins, & after that the town saw that the mill could not supply the town, then they gave leave to build an overshoot mill upon the same water, with a sluice called by the name of the old sluice, being made by Mr. Howell the second owner of the mill, and had a supply of water for the mills from the old sluice & that the water was granted to the mill for the use of the town before the meadow was granted. **Signed**: William Edmonds. Taken upon oath, 3: 4 mo: 1678.

JOHN HALE to JAMES CONVERSE, Jr. – (4:665) John Hale (minister) of Beverly leased to James Converse, Jr. of Woburn (Middlesex County), representing his uncle Josiah Converse & his father James Converse, for 18 shillings annual rent payable in money after 20 May of each year for the term of 18 years, a parcel of meadow overflowed by the mill, late in the possession of the said Converses, which meadow belonged to the said Hale's lot & was to be returned unto him upon certain considerations mentioned in an act of arbitration, dated 20: 12: 1649, & signed by Edward Johnson & others, whereupon indentures were drawn between the abovesaid Josiah & James Converse & John Hale & signed 19 March 1677/8, about the time & manner of the said meadows being returned. It is further agreed that the said Josiah & James will lay down their mill pond & drain the meadow overflowed & shall have the use of the said Hale's meadow abovesaid together with all that upland of John Hales which now lyeth within the cross fence that now is set up by Samuel Richardson. At the expiration of the lease, the said land was to be returned to Hale with a fence (except on that side next to the river) round it sufficient against swine & great cattle in good tenantable repair. Hale is to repay 7 pounds, as expressed in the said indenture. If Hale places a tenant on the said lot within the 18 years, he will relinquish the 18 shillings of yearly rent & placing as much fence between the said upland & meadow as to go halves with the Converses, James Converse may resign up this lease within 2 weeks after the date hereof, otherwise to stand in full force & virtue.

Signed: 21 March 1677/8 by James Convers, Jr.; **Witnesses**: John Brooks & Israel Read [by mark]. It is further agreed that the upland now lying within Richardson's fence will be used by the Converses for pasturage but not for tillage. **Signed**: April 3, 1678 by Josias Converse & James Converse; **Witnesses**: Paul Thorndike & John Hill, who made oath at Salem court 26: 4 mo: 1678 they were present at above; **Recorded**: 9: 6 mo: 1678.

ZERUBBABELL ENDECOTT to JOHN ENDECOTT – (4:668) On 9 August 1678, Zerubbabell Endecott (gentleman) of Salem, with wife Elizabeth yielding dower, granted to his son John Endecott, for love & affection, 1 acre of land in Salem formerly belonging to his father John Endecott, Esq., Governor of the Massachusetts Colony, deceased, bounded E by the street, N & W by his own land, S by land of John Priest. **Signed**: Zerubabell & Elizabeth Endecott [by mark]; **Acknowledged**: 9: 6: 1678; **Witnesses**: William Browne, Jr., Charles Redford & William Murray; **Recorded**: 10: 6 mo: 1678.

Selectmen of Lynn to Mr. HENRY BARTHOLOMEW – (4:671) On 25: 12 mo: 1668, the Selectmen of Lynn granted to Mr. Henry Bartholomew (merchant) of Salem, for a valuable sum of money paid by Bartholomew on behalf of the town unto William Longly, "unto whome the town was indebted, upon an account of a judgment granted to him at Ipswich Court against the towne, about forty acres of land he sued for, which was given to one of his name as appeareth by the town records," 40 acres bounded E by land formerly in possession of Mr. Humphryes, S by Stones meadow, N by Popes meadow, W by a brook; also 2 acres in Stone meadow, bounded W by the meadow of Widow Fraile, S by upland, N by a brook, E by the meadow in the tenure of Capt. Marshall. **Signed**: Thomas Marshall, Thomas Laighton, Oliver Purchase, John Fuller, Allen Breed, Sr., Andrew Mansfield [by mark] & William Bassett. **Acknowledged**: 9: 1 mo: 1677/8 by Marshall & Laighton; **Witnesses**: John Gifford & Thomas Newhall; **Assigned**: to Francis Skerry of Salem, 23: 12 mo: 1669 by Henry & Elizabeth Bartholomew; **Witnesses**: William Dodge & Benjamin Balch; **Acknowledged**: 23: 12: 1669 by Henry, with wife yielding dower. **Assigned**: to Thomas Bancroft of Lynn, 10 Jan 1677/8; **Signed**: Francis Skerry; **Witnesses**: Edward Norrice, Sr. & Edward Norrice, Jr.; **Acknowledged**: 7: 6 mo: 1678 by Francis & wife Bridget; **Recorded**: 14: 6: 1678.

TRYPHENA GEERE to JOSEPH GERRISH – (4:673) On 15 May 1676, Tryphena Geere of Wenham (widow & administratrix of William Geere of Wenham, deceased) granted to Joseph Gerrish of Wenham (clerk) for 30 pounds, 12 acres of land with dwelling house in Wenham formerly purchased of Daniel Killam of Wenham, bounded N by land of Thomas Fisk, NW by land of said Fisk & land of Charles Gott, E by the common road, SW by land of Richard Hutten. **Signed**: Tryphena Geere [by mark]; **Acknowledged**: 15 May 1676; **Witnesses**: John Appleton & Samuel Appleton. James Moulton, Sr. & Richard Hutten, Sr. both of Wenham testified upon oath in court at Salem 24: 5 mo: 1678 that the lot which was the lot of William Geere (deceased) & the lot which was Goodman Rogers, his lying in Wenham, adjoining to Capt. Fisk's living, bounded on the N by Ipswich line, SW by the county road, have been possessed & improved by planting & otherwise, about 29 years. Deed allowed by the court: 24: 5 mo: 1678; **Recorded**: 14: 6 mo: 1678.

ARTHUR MASON to JOHN HATHORNE – (4:675) Assignment of a lease recorded in Book 2: folio 1:18 from Arthur Mason of Boston (as attorney for William Titherly) to John Hathorne (merchant) of Salem. **Signed**: 19: July 1678 by Arthur Mason; **Acknowledged**: 19: 5 mo: 1678; **Recorded**: 20: 6 mo: 1678.

ARTHUR MASON to JOHN HATHORNE – (4:676) 3 June 1673. Whereas Arthur Mason of Boston (Suffolk County) (biscuit-baker), attorney of William Titherly of Bidefolk (co. of Devon) England (mariner), assigned over unto John Hathorne in county of Essex (merchant) all right of said William Titherly in deed or lease of a parcel of land lying in Salem that Titherly bought of John Fogg of Barnstable (co. of Devon), merchant, by instrument dated 1 August 1665 and for securing Hathorne in peaceable possession he promised to save Hathorne harmless from all encumbrances from or by Mr. Edmond Batter or Capt. George Corwin & that William Titherly or lawful attorney in convenient time would give further legal assurance & for true performance bound himself in the sum of 140 pounds current money of New England. **Signed**: Arthur Mason; **Acknowledged**: 19: 5: 1678; **Witnesses**: Nathaniel Davenport & George Tite; **Recorded**: 20: 6: 1678.

JOHN TAPLEY to JOHN HIGGINSON, Jr. – (4:679) On 6 May 1678, John Tapley (fisherman) of Salem mortgaged to John Higginson, Jr. of Salem, for a valuable consideration, his dwelling house with ½ acre of land in Salem, bounded S by the highway, W by land of James Frude, N & E by the great cove. If Tapley were to pay Higginson 26 pounds, 6 shillings in refuse or merchantable dry fish at current price on or before 1 May 1683, then the deed would be void. **Signed**: John Tapley; **Acknowledged**: 7: 3 mo: 1678; **Witnesses**: Nathaniel Pease [by mark] & John Wilkeson [by mark]; **Recorded**: 21: 3 mo: 1678.

ROBERT GOODELL to ISAACK GOODELL – (4:681) On 10 February 1667/8, Robert Goodell of Salem granted to his son Isaack Goodell of Salem, for a valuable consideration, 2 parcels of land in Salem: 100 acres of upland near the great river, bounded NE by land of John Bachellor & John Pease, "the other side" by land of said Robert Goodell & Thomas Flint, deceased, "the next end" by said river, "the other side" by the land of Jonathan Walcott; also 7 acres of fresh meadow shaped in a triangle, bounded N by the great river aforesaid, W by land called Woodhill, "the other side" by the meadow of said John Pease. **Signed**: Robert Goodell; **Acknowledged**: 14: 6 mo: 1678; **Witnesses**: Job Swinerton & John Huchenson; **Recorded**: 12: 6 mo: 1678.

JOHN HATHORNE to MANASSES MASTONE – (4:683) On 27 May 1678, John Hathorne (merchant) of Salem, with consent of wife Ruth, granted to Manasses Mastone (blacksmith) of Salem for 5 pounds 10 shillings sterling, 2 acres of land on the south field in Salem bounded N & W by land of Lieut. Pickering, S & E by land of Elias Mason. **Signed**: John & Ruth Hathorne; **Acknowledged**: 29: 4: 1678, with wife Ruth yielding dower; **Witnesses**: John Ingerson [by mark] & Benjamin Gerish; **Recorded**: 22: 6 mo: 1678.

JOHN MASTONE, Sr. to MANASEH MASTONE – (4:686) On 24 December 1677, John Mastone, Sr. (carpenter) of Salem granted to his son Manaseh Mastone (smith) of Salem, for a valuable sum, land in Salem bounded about 50 foot front or thereabouts, to the highway as goes to the north river, opposite against Mr. Zerubbabel Endecott's field on the other side of the way westward, in the length of it northward, butting upon the land of Samuel Pickworth, deceased & upon Mrs. Susanna Gedney's where Mr. William Sweatland liveth, butting eastward, & upon his brother William Mastone's & his now dwelling house butting southward, about 25 or 27 poles nearest his barn, most of it standing upon said land. **Signed**: John Mastone, Sr.; **Acknowledged**: 23: 3 mo: 1678; **Witnesses**: Francis Neale & William Beale [by mark]; **Recorded**: 22: 6 mo: 1678.

RICHARD ADAMS to Capt. GEORGE CORWIN – (4:687) On 7 August 1678, Richard Adams of Salem (with consent of his wife) granted to Capt. George Corwin of Salem (merchant) for a valuable sum, 20 acres of land in Salem between the 2 ponds going to Lynn, bounded N by land formerly in possession of John Pickering, part of which belongs to the Widow More, deceased, S by Lynn bounds, E by spring pond, W by the common highway to Lynn. **Signed**: Richard Adams and Susanna Adams [both by mark]; **Acknowledged**: 7 August 1678 by Richard Adams; **Witnesses**: Thomas Bancroft & John Whiting, Jr.; **Recorded**: 22: 6 mo: 1678.

Essex Registry of Deeds, Southern District, Salem, Mass.; Oct 8 1875: The foregoing copy of the Fourth Book of Records of Deeds for Salem and vicinity was made in 1855 under the direction of the County Commissioners. It has now been examined and corrected and is a true copy of the original. **Attest**: Ephraim Brown, Reg.

***
Conclusion of Book 4 of Essex County Deeds
***

ABBOT/ABBOTT
George, 101, 102, 105, 115
Richard, 155
Sarah (___), 115
Thomas, 102
ABELL
Richard, 134
ABORN (see also EBBORNE)
Samuel, 202, 221
ACY
John, 276
ADAMS
___, Goodman, 16
John, 123, 261
Nathaniel, 320
Richard, 3, 12, 42, 63, 149, 221, 243, 347
Robert, 5
Susanna (___), 243, 347
ADDINGTON/ADINGTON
Isaac/Isaack, 275, 314, 341
AGER
Jonathan, 186, 236
ALDERMAN
___, Mr., 23, 59, 105
John, 292
ALFORD
___, Mr., 22
Benjamin, 285, 300
ALFORDS
John, 116
ALLEN (see also ALLING)
___, Mr., 68, 295
Abraham, 216, 255
Andrew, 116, 210
Eliza (___), 275
Elizabeth (___), 52, 275
Francis, 268-271
Henry, 295
Hope, 249
James, 67, 246, 275, 341
John, 309
Sarah (___), 341
William, 21, 52, 63, 212
ALLING (see also ALLEN)
Abraham, 202
John, 237
ALRED
Abraham, 154
Abram., 155
ANDREW
Daniel, 316
John, 69
Nicholas, 318
William, 284

ANDRE_/ES/ANDREWS
___, Capt., 215
Daniel, 190, 230, 234, 267, 316
John, 20, 69, 70, 222, 223, 308
Sarah (___), 69
Thomas, 309
William, 78
ANTELBY
Will, 228
ANTHROP/ANTROP
Thomas, 25, 29
ANTRUM
Martha (___), 163
Obadiah/Obadyah, 107, 109, 125, 163, 208
Thomas, 51, 52, 60, 87, 99, 193, 208, 209
APPLETON
John, 176, 196, 216, 236, 279, 305, 346
Samuel, 346
APPLEWHITE
Thomas, 155
ARCHARD /ARCHERD(see also ARCHAUD, ARCHER)
John, 97, 114, 134, 144, 193, 198, 275, 335
Samuel, 10, 11, 14, 30, 48, 65, 83, 95, 101, 134, 146, 182, 189, 192, 193, 196, 199, 217, 226, 235, 305
Susana/Susanna/Susannah (___), 134, 192, 193
ARCHAUD (see also ARCHARD, ARCHER)
Samuel, 225
ARCHER (see also ARCHARD, ARCHAUD)
___, Goodman, 30
Hannah, 185
Samuel, 32, 47, 58, 238, 256
ARMITAGE
Jane, 11
Joseph, 1, 3, 6-8, 11, 13, 25, 35-37, 39, 42-44, 89, 111, 141, 142, 144, 177, 180, 186, 196, 213, 226, 257, 275, 303, 341, 342
ASHBY
Abigail (___), 245
Anthony, 245
Benjamin, 280
ASLET/ASLETT
Andrew, 116
John, 102, 115, 312
ASPANE/ASPARE
Samuel, 178, 217

ASPINWALL
  William, 226
AUGER
  ___, Goodman, 189
  Jonathan, 193
AUSTIN, 155
  Richard, 257
AVERY
  Susanna (___), 41
  Thomas, 41, 307
AXEY/AXY
  James, 62, 78, 281
AYER
  Jonathan, 200

BABADG/BABADGE/BABBAGE/
BABBIDS/ BABIDGE
  Christopher, 221, 226, 234, 304
BACH
  Samuel, 120
BACHELDOR
  John, 74, 129
  Mark, 76
BACHELLER/BACHELLOR/
BACHELOR (see also BATCHELOR)
  ___, Mr., 336
  John, 24, 163, 190, 232, 250, 258, 287, 292, 301, 335, 347
  March, 190
  Mark, 41, 336
BACON/BACONS
  Daniel, 193
  Isaac, 46, 48
BADLE (see also BEADLE)
  Nathaniel, 325
BAILEY/BAILY (see also BAYLEY)
  Arthere, 150
  Henry, 170, 180
  Joseph, 245
  Theophilus, 144
BAKER, 296
  Edward, 70, 261
  Hugh, 303
  Priscilla (___), 265-267, 287, 311
  Thomas, 206, 265-267, 287, 311, 338
BALCH
  Benjamin, 37, 38, 64, 115, 166-168, 194, 211, 259, 345
  Freeborne, 64
  John, 64, 115
  Mary (___), 115
  Samuel, 211
BALDING
  Arrabella (___), 263, 264

John, 263
BALDWIN
  John, 176
BALHACK
  John, 94
  Nicholas, 94
BALLARD/BALLORD
  ___, Mr., 76
  Grace (___), 116
  John, 98, 142, 143, 204, 218, 219, 277, 328, 343
  Nathaniel, 98, 142, 143, 302
  Rebecca (___), 277
  William, 116
BANCROFT
  ___, Ens., 268
  Thomas, 202, 345, 347
BANK/BANKS
  Lidia (___), 33
  Stephen, 178, 217
BARBER/BARBOR/BARBOUR
  John, 24
  William, 271, 306
BARNARD
  Mathew, 322
  Robert, 115
  Thomas, 91
BARNES
  Jacob, 19, 22, 100
  Thomas, 23, 47, 75, 108, 217
BARNEY/BARNIE
  Jacob, 42, 133, 174, 175, 187, 316, 333
BARRY
  James, 155
  Richard, 155
BARTHOLEMEW/BARTHOLMEW/
BARTHOLOMEW, 300
  ___, Mr., 249
  ___, Mrs., 57
  Abraham, 142, 152
  Anna, 322
  Elizabeth, 262, 345
  Elizabeth (___), 117
  Hen./Henry, 10, 11, 13, 15, 21, 57, 99, 117, 141, 143, 145, 151, 162, 165, 166, 170, 176, 205, 213, 248, 256, 258, 272, 293, 301, 302, 306, 308, 316, 327, 345
  Mary, 205
  William, 7, 140, 181, 189, 204, 205, 212, 322
BARTLETT
  Elizabeth (___), 253
  Nicholas, 57, 117, 234, 253, 264, 321
  Robert, 305, 319

BARTOLL
John, 157, 207
Parnell (___), 157
BARTON
Edward, 63
J., 305
John. 310
Martha, 200
Mathew, 199, 200, 211
Robert, 300
BARTRUM
Sara/Sarah (___), 197, 342, 343
William, 89, 122, 162, 197, 342, 343
BASSETT
Sarah, 173
Sarah (___), 131
William, 131, 144, 173, 177, 180, 197, 295, 342, 343, 345
BASTOR
Joseph, 88, 89
BATCHELOR see also BACHELLER
John, 39
BATEMAN
Joas, 300
Joseph, 285
BATES
Francis, 265
Robert, 324
BATH
William, 323, 324
BATMAN
Jeremiah, 264
BATT
Paul, 316
BATTEN
___, Mr., 299
Edmond/Edmund, 137, 171, 197, 206
Mary (___), 206
BATTER/BATTERS
___, Mr., 5, 6, 9, 221
Edm./Edmond/Edmund, 10, 17, 18, 29, 51, 60, 69, 82, 87, 96, 102, 103, 106, 112, 117, 122, 130, 135, 141, 143-145, 153, 154, 167, 168, 187, 190, 192-194, 208, 214, 223, 256, 267, 268, 279, 286, 312, 346
Edward, 209
Sara/Sarah (___), 112, 153
Sarah, 51
BATTY
Nicholas, 81
BAYLES
John, 6

BAYLEY/BAYLY (see also BAILEY)
Guyde, 18
Henry, 57
William, 101
BEACHUM
Edward, 105
BEACHY, 148
BEADLE, 325 (see also BADLE)
___, Mr., 86
Hana (Leoman), 274
Hannah, 314
Hannah (Lemon), 279
Nathaniel, 194, 237, 245, 284, 325, 326, 334
Samuel, 245, 274, 279, 280, 304, 308, 311, 314
Thomas, 308, 334
BEALE/BEALL
William, 84, 116, 134, 249, 319, 321, 347
BECKELES
Thomas, 90
BECKET/BECKETT
John, 30, 42, 103, 136, 143, 149, 179, 184, 190, 192, 209, 251, 254, 286, 304, 309, 310
Margaret/Margarett (___), 309
Mary, 254, 309
Peter, 165
BELCHER
Andrew, 104
Jeremiah, 123, 261
BELKNAP
Abraham, 328
Joseph, 284
Samuel, 95, 137, 140, 144, 317, 326
Sara (___), 137, 140, 144
BELL
Abraham, 22
BELLINGHAM
John, 136
Penelope (___), 76, 77
Richard, 67, 76, 77, 147, 200, 232, 246, 278, 307
Samuel, 307
BENETT/BENNET/BENNETT
___, Mr., 343
Anthony, 331
John, 251, 329
Richard, 248
Samuel, 2, 8, 24, 28, 29, 181, 195, 204, 205, 213, 252, 261, 262, 341, 342
Sarah (___), 204, 261
BERRY
Edmond/Edmund, 278, 288, 289

Edward, 177, 289, 317, 323, 329
Elizabeth (___), 177
John, 90
BESSELL
John, 77, 146
BEST
John, 284
BETTE
James, 200
John, 124
BEX
John, 226
BIAM (see also BIHAM)
George, 336
BIGSBY
Joseph, 195
BIHAM (see also BIAM)
George, 239
BILES
Jonathan, 260
BIRDSALL
Henry, 7
Nathan, 31
BIRT, 23
BISHOP, 159, 317
___, Mr., 5, 100
Edward, 19, 22, 166, 207
Mary, 276
Nathaniel, 11, 13
Richard, 17, 31, 51, 163, 276, 288, 326
Samuel, 322
Thomas, 46, 78
Townsend, 3, 172, 275
BLACK
___, Goodman, 76
John, 108, 180, 224, 225, 327, 328
BLACKLEACH/BLACKLEECH/ BLACKLEICH
___, Mr., 107, 295
Elizabeth (___), 88
John, 23, 33, 88, 89, 239, 240
BLAISDELL
___, Wid., 11
BLANCHARD
Samuel, 210
BLANEY/BLANY
John, 203, 332
BLETHEN/BLETHIN
John, 58, 120
BLOOD
Isabell (___), 89
John, 28
Richard, 26, 46, 81, 89, 97, 162, 257
Robert, 28

BLOTE
William, 202
BLOTTS, 319
BOARDMAN
William, 338
BODBY
Thomas, 229
BOND
___, Mr., 215
Joseph, 322
BONFIELD
George, 123, 251, 319
BOOTEMAN see BOOTMAN, BUTMAN
BOOTH
Thomas, 214
BOOTMAN/BOOTEMAN (see also BUTMAN)
Hester, 190
Jeremiah, 176, 190, 209, 251, 310
BOUND
William, 298
BOURNE
John, 23, 77
BOUTWELL
James, 199, 242
BOWD
Joseph, 140, 196
BOWDEN
Michael, 292
BOWDITCH
William/Wm., 242, 246, 260, 261, 271, 310
BOWEN
Eliza, 65
Elizabeth (___), 65, 265
Joseph, 129, 212
Thomas, 65, 265
BOWING
Elizabeth (___), 231
Thomas, 231
BOWNE
Andrew, 228, 229
BOYCE
Joseph, 39, 52, 128
BRABROOK/BRABROOKE
Richard, 141, 237, 238
BRACKENBURY
John, 109
Richard, 207
BRACKET/BRACKETT
Mary (___), 317
Peter, 317

Thomas, 24, 76, 108, 156, 235, 244, 273, 297
BRADFORD
Robert, 190, 191, 207
BRADHOURNE
Edward, 155
BRADSTREET
___, Mr., 320
Ann (___), 51, 53, 118
Dudley, 115, 210
Humphry, 84
John, 84, 117
Simon/Symon/Symond, 1, 5, 6, 11, 40, 51, 64, 65, 70, 73, 115, 130, 210, 259
William, 265
BRAGG
___, Goodman, 283
Richard, 137
William, 155
BRANKER
Nathaniel, 120
BRATTLE
Thomas, 137
BRAY
Robert, 186, 218
Thomas, 125
BREED
Allen, 63, 69, 83, 97, 98, 104, 130-133, 139, 148, 159, 302, 324, 328, 342, 345
Elizabeth, 159
Elizabeth (___), 97, 98
John, 98, 143, 148, 219, 262, 275, 295
Miriam, 148
BREEDON
Thomas, 135, 136, 263
BRETT see also BRITT
Robert, 32
BREWER
Christopher, 173
John, 143
BRICE
James, 90, 92
BRIDGEMAN/BRIDGMAN
George, 47
John, 21, 86
BRIDGES
___, Capt., 5, 34, 62, 81, 148, 151, 152, 242, 281, 328
Edmond/Edmund, 195, 203, 237, 241, 266, 323, 337
Edward, 329
Mary, 132
Mary (___), 325
Robert, 63, 187, 204, 226, 283, 316, 325

Sarah (___), 195
BRIDGHAM
Henry, 330
Jonathan, 330
BRIDGMAN see BRIDGEMAN
BRIDMAN
John, 260
BRIMBLECOM/BRIMBLICOM
John, 83, 112
BRIMSDEN
Robert, 296, 297, 315
BRISCO/BRISCOE
Benjamin, 78, 79, 89, 162
Sara/Sarah (___), 162
BRITT see also BRETT
Robert, 32, 86
BROCK
John, 313, 321
BRONSDON
Robert, 195
BROOK
Robert, 325
BROOKES/BROOKS
John, 345
Richard, 324
Robert, 154, 174
BROUGHTON
Thomas, 70
BROWN/BROWNE
___, Mr., 24, 27, 79, 239, 240
___, Wid., 187, 310, 320
Abraham, 48, 317
Benjamin, 152, 176, 279
Cutting, 318
Elizabeth (___), 133
Elizabeth (Simpson), 129
Ephm./Ephraim/Ephrm., 66, 146, 247, 348
Hannah, 337
James, 117, 120, 134, 135, 150, 154, 187, 198, 208, 212, 245, 285, 291, 293, 294, 317, 334, 337, 338
John, 13, 27, 50, 64, 77, 87, 94, 95, 134, 151, 154, 163, 210, 293, 294, 306, 311, 340
Jonathan, 43
Mary, 281
Nicholas, 132, 133, 139, 141
Samuel, 317, 334
Sara (Cutting), 245
Sara/Sarah (___), 149, 285, 317, 334, 337, 338
Sarah, 184, 187
Sarah (Miller), 318
Thomas, 83, 122, 161, 281

Will/William, 4, 16, 19, 42, 48, 50, 53, 57, 59, 66, 74, 102, 103, 108, 109, 114, 118, 122, 127, 141, 143, 149, 152, 158, 161, 176, 180, 184-186, 188, 192, 193, 196, 198, 208, 211, 212, 216, 217, 221, 223, 233, 235, 236, 244, 252, 267, 275, 276, 279, 282, 301, 303, 305, 315, 318, 319, 323, 324, 330, 345

BROWNING
___, Goodman, 58, 185
Mary (___), 292
Thomas, 65, 76, 174, 184, 186, 205, 208, 217, 226, 243, 292, 301, 304, 336

BROWNS
Thomas, 73

BRYARES
John, 191

BUCKLEY/BUCKLY
Thomas, 286
William, 286, 304

BUFFAM/BUFFUM
___, Wid., 192, 195, 230, 276, 317, 326
Caleb, 302, 303, 337, 339
Joshua, 208, 292, 326, 339
Robert, 106, 276, 291
Tamsen (___), 208
Thomas, 36

BULFINCH
John, 22

BULL
John, 213

BULLARD
Ann (___), 178
Isaack, 177, 178

BULLOCK
Alce (___), 106
Alice (Flint), 43
Harry, 17
Henry, 11, 43, 93, 94, 106, 107, 263
John, 301, 327

BULTEEL/BULTEELE
John, 268-270

BUNKER, 207
John, 244

BURCH, 183
George, 55, 181, 229

BURCHAM
Edward, 34, 46, 65, 151, 338

BURCHETT
Thomas, 229

BURCHIN, 187

BURGES/BURGESS/BURGIS
Robert, 66, 82, 93, 104, 1123, 154, 173, 247, 328

BURNALL
___, Mr., 34

BURNAP/BURNUP
Ann (___), 107, 178, 326
Isaack/Isaak/Isack, 51, 52, 87, 99, 111, 154, 178, 326
Mary (___), 178
Robert, 107, 177, 178, 325, 326
Sara/Sarah (___), 178
Sarah, 177
Thomas, 177, 178, 325

BURNELL
Francis, 328
John, 120, 322
William, 58

BURNUP see BURNAP

BURRELL/BURRILL
Francis, 62, 69, 139, 151
George, 25, 26, 83, 132, 152
John, 73, 89, 242, 247, 277

BURROWS, 124
John, 37

BURT/BURTT
Edward, 93, 278
Hugh, 33, 34, 89, 93, 186, 197, 342
Mary, 197, 342, 343
Mary (Southwick), 289
Robert, 186
Sarah, 197, 342, 343
Thomas, 289

BURTON
Jacob, 252
John, 7, 23, 151, 260, 276

BURTT see BURT

BUSH
Edward, 200, 244, 297, 298

BUSHNELL, 188
John, 76, 108

BUTLER
Samuel, 312

BUTMAN/BUTTMAN (see also BOOTMAN)
Jeremiah, 192, 251

BUTTEN/BUTTON
___, Mr., 7
Robert, 274
Samuel, 274

BUTTMAN see BUTMAN

BUTTOLPH
Hannah (___), 219
John, 153, 219

BUTTON see BUTTEN

BUXTON
  Anthony, 170, 263, 268
  John, 183, 184, 243, 244, 307, 314, 327
  Thomas, 7, 16
BYAM/BYUM, 200
  George, 13, 39, 55, 56
  Susan (___), 55, 56

CALEY/CALIES/CALY/CALYES
  Mary, 158
  Thomas, 96, 157, 158, 205, 206
**CANTLEBERY/CANTLEBURRY/
  CANTLEBURY/CANTLEBURYE**
  John, 145
  Ruth, 145
  William, 47, 88, 108, 145, 183, 184
CAR
  James, 155
CARDER
  John, 331
CARRELL
  Anthony, 266
CARTER
  John, 198
  Obediah, 246
  Thomas, 104
CARY
  Nathaniel, 335
CASH
  William, 176, 264
CATT, 296
CAWLEY/CAWLYE
  Mary (___), 319
  Thomas, 303, 319
CHADWELL
  ___, Goodman, 328
  Abigail (___), 197, 315
  Benjamin, 247, 295, 302
  Elizabeth (___), 295, 302
  Moses, 197, 257, 262, 274, 275
  Sara (___), 275
  Thomas, 78, 81, 83, 197, 274, 315
CHANDLER
  Hannah, 115
  Thomas, 115
  William, 116
CHAPPELLMAN
  Michall, 182
CHARLES
  William, 33
CHARLES II
  King, 137, 244
CHARLESCROFT
  Richard, 154

CHASE
  Aquila/Aquilla, 161, 165
CHEEVER/CHEEVERS
  Ezekiel/Ezekiell, 330, 338, 341
  Peter, 301, 308
  Samuel, 251, 299, 304, 305, 319
  Peter, 308
CHESTER
  Sampson, 300
CHICHESTER
  ___, Mrs., 164, 170
  James, 30, 198
  Will/William, 14, 56, 101, 105, 164, 170
CHICKERING
  ___, Mr., 275
CHICKLY
  John, 120
CHILSON
  Walsing, 201
CHINGE
  John, 238
CHOATE
  John, 283
CHUBB
  Anis (___), 32
  Thomas, 32, 175, 179, 315
CHURCHMAN, 186
CLAP/CLAPP
  Edward, 200-292
  Ezra, 291, 292
  Nathaniel, 291, 292
  Nicholas, 291, 292
  Susanna (___), 200
CLARK/CLARKE see also CLEARK
  ___, Mr., 3, 209, 221
  Daniel, 266, 320
  Emanuel, 63, 140
  John, 251, 331
  Mary, 320
  Mary (___), 266
  Mathew, 159, 190, 197, 202
  Nathaniel, 245
  Samuel, 92
  Thomas, 323, 329
  William, 26, 90, 131, 132, 291, 331, 343
CLEARE
  John, 140
CLEARK see also CLARK
  William, 308
CLEAVES/CLEEVES
  Martha (___), 329
CLEMENCE
  John, 245

CLEMENT/CLEMENTS
  Aphia (___), 135
  John, 12, 25, 39, 135, 194, 216, 227, 327
  Joseph, 303
  William, 89
CLENTON
  Lawrence, 141
  Rachel (Haffield), 141
CLIFFORD
  Elizabeth, 305
  John, 141, 143, 234, 305, 319
CLOUTEMAN
  Thomas, 304
COALE see also COLE
  Thomas, 144, 288
COATE/COATES/COATS
  ___, Goodman, 135
  John, 155
  Thomas, 46, 142
COBBETT/COBBITT/COBBITTS
  ___, Mr., 73, 81, 152, 237
  Elizabeth, 132
  John, 320
  Thomas, 126, 130-132, 152, 159
COCKERELL/COCKERILL
  Elizabeth (___), 200
  William, 18
CODDINGTON
  Thomas, 335
CODNER
  Christopher, 38, 84
  Joane, 84
  Joshua, 227
  Mary (___), 84
  Robert, 65
COGGSWELL/COGSWELL
  John, 283
  Samuel, 283
  William, 322
COKER
  Robert, 161, 165
COLBOURNE
  Henry, 184
COLBY
  Miles, 90
COLDUM
  Clement, 343
  Thomas, 307, 328
COLE see also COALE
  Abraham, 282
  Ann, 326
  George, 228
  John, 205, 289, 306
  Peter, 71
  Thomas, 10, 19, 49, 317, 326
COLEBORNE
  Henry, 205
  Sara (___), 205
COLEFAX
  Venus, 234
COLEMAN
  William, 339
COLLACUT
  Thomasin, 200
COLLENS see COLLINS
  Frances, 200
  Hana, 200
  John, 148
COLLEY, 322
COLLINGS see COLLINS
COLLINS/COLLENS/COLLINGS
  ___, Goodman, 202, 328
  Edward, 198
  Frances/Francis, 50, 79, 130, 186, 188, 200, 249, 331
  Henry, 45, 78, 81, 142, 163, 164, 172, 295, 315, 319, 324
  John, 61, 78, 93, 149, 163, 172, 319, 328, 330
  Joseph, 164, 319
  Mehitable (___), 328-330
COLLINSWORTH
  Richard, 231
COMB/COMBE/COMBES/COMBS see also COOMBES
  Henry, 6, 305
  Michael/Michaell, 190, 324
  Richard, 268-271
CONANT
  ___, Mr., 207
  Elizabeth, 224
  Elizabeth (___), 246
  Exercise, 168, 194, 259, 295
  John, 259
  Lot/Lott, 102, 159, 166, 167, 190, 197, 224, 246, 305
  Roger, 37, 108, 121, 159, 166-168, 194, 245, 259
  Sara/Sarah (___), 166, 167
CONDE/CONDEY/CONDY
  Annis (___), 112
  Samuel, 65, 83, 102, 103, 112, 138, 144
CONKLIN
  Mary, 224
CONNELL
  William, 312
CONNEY
  John, 45, 263

CONVERS/CONVERSE
Allen, 108
Elizabeth (___), 108
James, 344, 345
Josiah, 344
Josias, 345

COOK/COOKE
___, Mr., 22, 214
___, Wid., 151, 268
Abraham, 214, 215
E., 211
Henry, 5-7, 15, 23, 31, 43, 51, 58, 71, 106, 107, 156
Isaac/Isaack, 107, 223, 263, 276, 318
John, 233, 246, 263, 290, 301, 307
Judith (___), 87, 107, 112, 156, 157, 263
Mary, 233
Richard, 70, 71, 135, 321
Samuel, 263

COOMBES/COOMBS/COOMES see also COMB
Barsheba (___), 119
Elizabeth (___), 210
Henry, 11, 79
Humfry/Humphrey, 119, 196, 199, 204, 310, 321
Michael, 209, 309

COOP
Timothy, 21

COOPER
Robert, 197
Thomas, 248, 289
Timothy, 78

COPP
John, 245, 246

CORE/COREE/COREY/CORY
Giles, 19, 49, 50, 59, 107, 113, 291, 292

CORNING
Samuel, 44, 55, 156, 207, 244, 257, 264, 265, 282, 283, 296, 340

CORTES
Zacheus, 60

CORTICE
Richard, 79

CORWETHIN see CORWITHEN

CORWIN/CORWINE
___, Capt., 124, 124, 205, 231, 278
___, Mr., 94
Abigail, 225
Elizabeth (___), 85, 86, 241
George, 41, 47, 49, 53, 56, 68, 72, 75, 77, 78, 85-89, 99, 104, 106, 123, 127, 129, 136, 138, 140, 141, 143-145, 150, 158, 176, 183-185, 189, 196, 211, 225, 241, 245, 246, 260, 261, 267, 279, 284, 294, 295, 307, 314, 315, 316, 318, 325, 326, 329, 340, 346, 347
John, 62, 188, 212, 225, 267, 294, 329, 333
Jon., 148
Jonathan, 59, 127, 150, 182, 189, 225, 288
Samuel, 6

CORWITHEN/CORWETHI/ CORWITHIE/CORWITHIN/ CORWITHY, 234
David, 7, 50, 79, 95, 96, 130, 188, 189, 200

CORY see CORE

COTHER
John, 90

COTTA
Robert, 173, 272

COTTER
Johannah, 125
Robert, 124, 125

COTTERILL
Benjamin, 155

COTTON
John, 325
William, 204

COWDREY/COWDRY
William, 44, 99, 107, 203

COYE, 175, 176, 240, 241
Richard, 64, 65

COYT/COYTE
John, 7, 217

CRADDOCK
Rebecca (___), 27

CRAFORD/CREFORD, 80
Edith, 77
Judith (___), 85, 216
Mordecai/Mordecae/Mordica, 16, 17, 35, 57, 77, 85, 146, 215, 216, 308

CRAFTS
William, 73

CRANE, 210

CREFORD see CRAFORD

CREVETT see CRAFORD

CROAD/CROADE
Elizabeth, 127
Frances, 306, 337
John, 54, 62, 63, 68, 70, 71, 86, 92, 112, 114, 122, 126, 127, 137
Richard, 209, 222, 230, 285, 286, 301, 306, 310, 327, 337-339, 341

CROE
Christopher, 135

CROFT/CROFTS
___, Mrs., 139
William, 28, 81, 132, 247, 281, 324
CROMPTON
Samuel, 311, 312, 335
CROMWELL, 121
Dorothie/Dorothy (___), 23, 37, 113, 124
Dorothy (Kenniston), 8
John, 104, 220, 291, 293, 297, 304, 338, 339
Mary (___), 304
Philip/Phillip, 4, 8, 10, 23, 36, 37, 48-50, 52, 75, 86, 87, 100, 103, 113, 114, 124, 137, 140, 150, 164, 171, 176, 184, 189, 191, 203, 209, 212, 222, 224, 234, 235, 237, 251, 262, 267, 296, 304, 310, 314, 315, 317, 318, 321, 323, 337
Thomas, 47, 96, 118, 222, 230, 249
CROOK
Henry, 34
CROSS/CROSSE
Robert, 141, 238
CULLEVEN
Richard, 185
CURTICE/CURTIS/CURTISE
Richard, 95-97, 200
Sara/Sarah (___), 96, 97
William, 105, 124, 179, 185, 196, 204, 321
Zacheus, 208, 209, 221, 309
CURTLAND
Nathaniel, 197
CURWIN
John, 174, 313
CUSHING
Jeremiah, 322
CUTLER
Samuel, 145
CUTTING
John, 245
Mary (___), 245
Sara, 245
CUTTS
John, 75

DANFORD
___, Capt., 101
DANFORTH
Thomas, 198, 314
DANIEL
Mary, 150
Nicholas, 150
DARLING
George, 203, 240, 241, 331

DAVENPORT
___, Capt., 72, 98, 129, 130, 160, 233
___, Lieut., 76
Nathaniel, 288, 346
Richard, 2, 23, 77, 82, 99, 100, 288
DAVID
John, 266
Laurance, 319
Thomas, 165
DAVIDSON see DAVISON
DAVIES see DAVIS
DAVIS/DAVIES
George, 69
Isaac, 224, 225
Jenckin/Jenkin, 46, 77, 78, 281, 324, 340
Lidea/Lidia, 225
DAVISON/DAVISSON/DAVIDSON
Nicholas, 20, 27, 53, 182
DAY/DAYE
John, 184, 234, 253, 321
Thomas, 172
DEACON/DEAKIN
Ann, 195
John, 79, 81, 82, 89, 130, 152, 195
DEAN/DEANE
___, Mr., 312
Elizabeth, 286
George, 47, 276, 285, 286, 337
DEANMAN
John, 239
DELBOE
Simon, 91
DELLY
William, 101
DENISON/DENNISON
___, Maj., 148
___, Maj. Gen., 50, 147, 333
Daniel, 65, 147, 148, 224, 237, 278, 326, 333
John, 132
Patience, 147, 148
DENMAN
John, 41
DENNIS
James, 292, 307
DENNISON see DENISON
DENTON
Daniel, 61
DEVEREUX/DEVERICK/DEVEROUX/DEVORIX
___, Mr., 319
John, 54, 84, 119, 157, 238

DEXTER
 Thomas, 1, 2, 29, 195, 294
DIAMOND
 Edward, 251
DICER
 William, 199
DICKENSON
 Richard, 155
DIKE
 Anthony, 205, 313
 Margery ( ), 313
DINSDAILE
 Tho., 155
DIVEN
 John, 69
DIX
 Thomas, 305
DIXEY/DIXIE/DIXY
 Thomas, 95-97, 158, 206, 210, 303
 William, 12, 18, 156
DODGE, 257
 Elizabeth ( ), 180
 John, 38, 188, 208, 250
 Mary ( ), 115, 135
 Richard, 32, 37, 38, 55, 115, 159, 166
 William, 2, 21, 37, 38, 41, 108, 115, 135, 142, 166, 168, 179, 180, 185, 194, 207, 239, 345
DOLE
 John, 310, 319, 320
 Richard, 310
DOLIBER/DOLIVER/DOLLIBER
 Joseph, 331
 Samuel, 271, 329, 330
DOOLITTLE
 John, 69
DOUNTEN/DOUNTIN/DOUNTON/DOWNTON
 Will/William, 128, 129, 147, 157, 161, 166, 181, 214, 220, 232, 238, 258, 324
DOVE
 Hannah ( ), 185
 Mathew, 185, 186
DOWNING
 , Mr., 16, 24, 33, 41, 46, 117, 209, 223, 332, 333
 Ann, 36
 Em., 101
 Emanual/Emanuel/Emanuell/Emmanuel, 1, 13, 36, 50, 52, 73, 151, 165, 182, 214, 323
 Lucie/Lucy ( ), 36, 51, 323
 Samuel, 48
DOWNTON see DOUNTEN

DRAPER, 23, 317
DRIVER
 Robert, 78, 83, 142, 278
DUDLEY
 John, 20
 Paul, 288
DUGGLES
 Allester, 252
DUMMER
 Steven, 245
DUNSTEN
 , Mr., 226
DURLAND
 John, 230
DUTCH
 Ormond, 341
 Samuel, 317

EARLY
 Abigail (Foot), 227
EASTON
 William, 107
EASTWICK see ESTWICK
EASTY see ESTY
EATON
 , Goodman, 301
 Daniel, 234, 235
 John, 268-271
EBBORNE/EBONNE/EBORN/EBORNE
 see also ABORN
 Samuel, 21, 48, 51, 128, 202, 221, 256, 260, 268, 276, 338
EDMONDS
 John, 328
 William, 46, 261, 324, 343, 344
EDSON
 Samuel, 108
EDWARD/EDWARDS, 5
 Elizabeth ( ), 7
 John, 283
 Marah ( ), 283
 Mary, 108
 Mathew, 107, 108, 336
 Rice, 25, 38
 Thomas, 7, 96
EGGINTON
 Jeremiah, 56
ELDERKIN/ELDERKIND
 John, 2, 3, 343
ELIOT/ELIOTT see ELLIOT
ELLINGWOOD
 Ralph, 20

ELLIOT/ELLIOTT/ELIOT/ELIOTT
  Andrew, 172, 175, 188, 208, 263, 274, 333
  William, 40, 251, 333
ELWELL
  Ester/Esther (___), 341
  Isaack, 341
  John, 305
  Robert, 339, 341
  Samuel, 341
ELWOOD
  Ralph, 21
EMERSON
  ___, Mr., 125
  John, 191, 225
EMERY/EMORY/EMORYE
  ___, Mr., 16, 252
  George, 32, 41, 53, 54, 62, 64, 83, 98, 101, 114, 116, 117, 118, 157, 193, 249, 256, 273, 315, 318, 320
  Mary (___), 256
ENDCOTT/ENDECOT/ENDECOTT/ ENDICOT/ENDICOTT
  ___, Mr., 46, 47, 53, 181, 183, 266, 284, 309, 333
  Elizabeth (___), 345
  John, 35, 40, 48, 57, 63, 68, 80, 85, 100, 110, 139, 147, 275, 304, 315, 345
  Zerubbabel/Zerubbabell/Zerrubbabel, 275, 341, 345, 347
ENGLISH
  Clement, 229
  Mary (Waters), 229
  Phillip, 303, 304
EPPS
  Daniel, 180, 259
ERINGTON
  Thomas, 10, 11
ESTE
  Isaac, 15
ESTIKES
  ___, Wid., 209
ESTWICK/EASTWICK
  ___, Wid., 323, 324
  Edward, 6, 179, 185
  Ester (___), 179, 185
  Stephen, 215
ESTY/EASTY
  Isaac/Isaack/Isack/Isaak, 22, 255, 265, 266
  Jeffrey, 11, 12
EVELEIGH
  Silvester, 125
EVERTON
  William, 212

EVESOME
  John, 89
FAIREFIELD/FAIREFIELDS/ FAIRFIELD
  ___, Mr., 336
  John, 108
  Walter, 112
  William, 203
FALLET
  Robert, 55
FARNSWORTH
  Mathias/Matthias, 79, 81, 162
FARR, 213
  George, 46, 142
  John, 203, 242
  Thomas, 35
FARRER
  Thomas, 261
FARRINGTON
  Edmond/Edmund, 21, 34, 81, 90, 93, 140, 141
  Elizabeth, 140
  John, 66, 98, 342
  Mathew, 66, 126, 140, 141
  Thomas, 9
FAULKNER
  Edmond, 44, 102
  Edward, 102
FEIRMAIES/FEIRMAYES/FERMAIES/ FERMAYES/FERMAYS
  ___, Wid., 86
  Benjamin, 86
FELCH
  Joseph, 268
FELLIES
  Richard, 189
FELTON
  ___, Mr., 137
  ___, Wid., 76
  Benjamin, 4, 60, 61, 77, 113, 124, 145, 162, 197, 208
  Ellinor, 18
  Mark, 61
  Mary (___), 85, 121, 249
  Nathaniel, 42, 43, 48, 76, 85, 121, 170, 176, 224, 249, 263, 268, 290, 318, 329
FERMAIES/FERMAYES/FERMAYS see FEIRMAIES
FEVERYEARE
  Edmund, 116
  Edward, 280
FIELD
  Alexander, 6, 14, 16, 145

FISH
Edward, 286
FISK/FISKE
___, Capt., 346
___, Mr., 207, 336
Joan, 336
John, 15, 124, 190, 239
Joseph, 281, 282
Phineas, 190
Remember, 190
Sara (___), 251
Thomas, 41, 55, 76, 108, 239, 251, 283, 336, 338, 346
William, 31, 250, 251
FITCH
___, Goodman, 78
FLETCHER
Ralph, 299
FLINDER
Richard, 192, 209, 251, 271, 310
FLINT
Alice, 43
Edward, 195, 338, 339
Eliza (___), 339
Elizabeth (___), 339
Thomas, 30, 43, 107, 113, 181, 214, 233, 271, 301, 307, 327, 347
William, 15, 16, 41, 43, 63, 149, 155, 171, 174, 175, 181, 189, 196, 217, 234, 235, 242, 243, 239, 323
FLOOD/FLUD
___, Mr., 78
Joseph, 46, 142
Obadiah, 142
FLYNT see FLINT
FOG/FOGG
Anna (___), 310
Dav./David, 155, 272, 273, 295
Ezekiel/Ezekiell, 264, 269-273, 302, 303, 310, 332
John, 9, 137, 272, 273, 302, 303, 310, 346
Ralph, 2, 3, 8, 25, 53, 60, 95, 100, 108, 136-138, 158, 210, 272, 273, 302, 303, 310, 332
Susanna (___), 272
Whittingham/Wittingham, 269-271
FOLLETT
Robert, 181, 229, 305
FOOT
Abigail, 227
Isaac/Isaack, 227, 248
John, 211, 284, 285, 300
Pasca/Pascha/Pasco, 22, 25, 133, 212, 227, 248

FOSTER
Andrew, 116
Bartholomew, 225
Christopher, 2, 35
John, 124, 151, 156, 182, 183, 202, 244, 272, 300, 335-337
Joseph, 327
Martha, 202
Martha (___), 272, 336
Samuel, 13, 14, 16, 55, 239, 336, 337
William, 158
FOX
Nicholas, 185, 188
FRAILE/FRAYLE
___, Wid., 218, 345
George, 39, 83
Samuel, 277, 289
FREKES
John, 134
FRIEND, 171
James, 15
John, 165, 258, 287
Samuel, 40, 45, 149
FROGMORTON, 116
FROUDE/FRUDE
James, 218, 346
FRY
John, 102
FULLER
Elizabeth (Farrington), 140
John, 27, 28, 81, 90, 97, 98, 126, 141, 152, 226, 262, 289, 328, 342, 345
Robert, 37
Thomas, 147, 191, 284
FURBISH/FURBUSH
John, 218, 238, 262, 299

GAFFEARDS/GAFFORD see GIFFORDS
GAGE
Joanna (Knight), 97
Thomas, 97, 98
GAINDFIELD
Robert, 291
GAINES
Henry, 328
GALE/GALLE/GALLY
Ambrose, 123, 149
Bartholomew, 152, 304
Edmond/Edmund, 19, 181, 190
Florence, 265
John, 170, 193, 216, 264, 265
Robert, 56
Sara (___), 190

GANSON
Benjamin, 311, 320
GARDENER/GARDNER
___, Mr., 10, 49, 271
Ann/Anne (___), 51, 53, 118
Ann (Downing), 36
George, 58, 94, 112, 120, 128, 193, 195, 199, 219, 231, 306
Hannah (___), 219
John, 24, 40, 65, 66, 77, 95, 104, 119, 145, 208, 245, 267, 296, 310, 311, 323
Joseph, 21, 36, 50-53, 118, 219, 268, 275, 276, 300, 311
Mary (___), 223
Priscilla (___), 296
Richard, 52, 53, 66, 161, 182, 295, 296
Samuel, 51, 52, 123, 124, 128, 137, 199, 219, 223, 231, 245, 306, 311
Sara, 161
Sara/Sarah (___), 182, 296
Thomas, 17, 46, 71, 94, 120, 161-163, 219, 226, 262, 263, 276, 304, 315, 319
GARFORD
Gervase, 10, 22, 293
GARNER
Thomas, 134
GARNETT
Richard, 249
GARRETT
John, 301
GASKILL
Edward, 46, 52, 57
GASKIN/GASKING/GASKOYNE, 317
Edward, 80, 137, 140, 144, 192
Samuel, 192, 230, 260, 276, 338
GATCHELL/GETCHELL
John, 7, 12, 84, 216, 227, 327
Jonathan, 227
Samuel, 84
Thomas, 227
Wibro, 227
GEDNEY/GEDNY/GIDNEY
___, Mr., 20, 34, 68, 72, 104, 221, 328
Bartholmew/Bartholomew, 109, 114, 153, 164, 188, 193, 228, 284, 285, 337
Eleazer, 125, 126, 163, 222, 280, 314
John, 8, 10, 17, 31, 32, 34, 35, 56, 57, 74, 86, 87, 95, 98, 103, 117, 118, 119, 124, 126, 153, 161, 162, 188, 198, 233, 256, 267, 268, 304, 308, 317, 323, 324, 335
Katheren/Katherine, 153
Katherin/Katherine (___), 35, 86, 162
Mary, 86
Susanna, 285

Susanna (___), 334, 337, 347
GEER/GEERE
Tryphena (___), 345, 346
William, 79, 345
GEGLES see **JEGELLS**
GERISH/GERRISH
Benjamin, 264, 268, 301, 320, 335, 347
John, 320
Joseph, 345
Mary, 310
Moses, 310
William, 5, 6, 73, 310, 314, 319
GETCHELL see **GATCHELL**
GIBBONS
___, Maj., 65
GIDNEY see **GEDNEY**
GIFFORD
John, 26, 135, 136, 226, 263, 264, 268-271, 295, 320, 321, 342, 345
GIFFORDS/GAFFEARDS/GAFFORD
___, Mr., 54, 177
GIGGELES see **JEGGLES**
GILBERT
William, 343
GILES
___, Wid., 58
Bridget/Bridgett, 42, 306, 307
Edward, 107, 306
Eleazer/Eliezer/Elizer, 231, 241, 306, 337
John, 231, 232, 307
Sarah, 231
GILL
John, 31
GILLAM see also **GILLUM**
John, 328
GILLO/GILLOW
John, 29, 65, 83, 106, 287, 290
Rose (___), 83, 106
Sarah, 290
Thomas, 106, 290
GILLUM see also **GILLAM**
Zachariah, 110, 111
GILMAN
Edward, 4
GINGELL
John, 68, 147, 248, 307
GINGEON/GINGION
John, 67, 76, 246, 278, 279
GIRDLER
Francis, 303
GISBOINE
John, 106

362

**GLANDFEILL/GLANDFELL/
GLANFIELD**
Robert, 154, 293, 294
GLOVER
Rebecca (___), 27
Steven, 257
GODFREY
George, 298
Hanah (___), 298
John, 105, 127, 128, 160, 161, 165, 178, 268-271, 299, 301
GODSOE
William, 289
GOITE see also GOYTE, 157
GOLDTHWAIT/GOLDTHWAITE
Thomas, 17, 41, 42, 52, 57, 60, 154, 178, 192, 241
GOLT
William, 105, 189
**GOODAL/GOODALE/GOODALL/
GOODELL**, 311
Elizabeth, 43
Isaac/Isaack, 327, 347
Margaret/Margarett/Margrett (___), 244, 307
Margery (___), 244, 307
Robert, 20, 39, 43, 86, 88, 104, 107, 113, 145, 150, 151, 153, 158, 182, 184, 244, 291, 307, 331, 332, 347
Thomas, 166
Zachariah, 307, 327
GOODHALL
Robert, 14, 23-25
GOOGE
___, Mr., 256
GOOKIN
Daniel, 198, 300
GOOLD
Elizabeth, 309
John, 203, 237, 241, 244, 288, 309, 320, 327
Sara, 237
GOOSE
Isaak, 326
John, 141, 143
Susannah (___), 326
William, 141, 143
GOOTCH see GUTCH
GOTT
___, Mr., 199, 333
___, Mrs., 27
Charles, 1, 17, 24, 25, 27, 53, 54, 60, 62, 79, 190, 336, 346
Daniel, 190, 295, 328

William, 32
GOULD
John, 163, 218, 284
Sara (___), 284
Sarah, 288
Zacheus, 15
GOULDING
Richard, 275
GOULT
Mary (___), 99
William, 99
GOWING
Robert, 20, 31
GOYTE see also GOITE
John, 121
GRAFTON
John, 45, 184, 226, 304
Joseph, 7, 13, 77, 96, 128, 162, 178, 184, 185, 196, 221, 226, 234, 253, 278, 300, 301, 304, 406, 321
Mary (___), 96, 234
Nathaniel, 126, 128, 162, 174, 178
Seeth (___), 226, 304
GRANT
Edward, 306
Francis, 210
GRAVE, 238
GRAVES
Elizabeth, 210, 312, 313
Mark, 66, 210, 312
Richard, 31, 34
GRAY/GRAYE
Abigail (___), 288, 289
Elizabeth (___), 80
Nathaniel, 312
Robert, 23, 28, 50, 57, 74, 80, 180, 181, 183
Samuel, 288, 289
GREATIAN
Thomas, 134
GREEN/GREENE, 135
Elizabeth (___), 293, 294
Henry, 204
Jacob, 205
John, 204
John, 301
Mary (Bartholomew), 205
Richard, 213
Samuel, 338
Thomas, 324
GREENFIELD, 171
Peter, 321
GREENOUGH
William, 306

GREENS
John, 232
GREGSON/GRIGSON
Richard, 126, 133
GRIFFEN/GRIFFIN
Humphry, 84
John, 337, 339
Richard, 155
GRIGSON see GREGSON
GROVE
Edward, 165, 176, 207, 217, 225, 314
GROVER
Edmond/Edmund, 172, 179
Edward, 188, 189
Jonathan, 263
Nehemiah, 172
GROVES
Edward, 156
GUILLAM
Edward, 20
GUPPI/GUPPY
John, 289
Ruben, 47, 53, 147
GUTCH/GOOTCH
Robert, 13, 17, 20, 50, 182

HACKER
George, 305, 319
HADLOCK
James, 341
HAFFIELD
Martha (___), 141
Rachel, 141
Richard, 141
HAGG
James, 219
HAINES see HAYNES
HALE
John, 170, 180, 193, 198, 216, 264, 265, 344
Tamsen (___), 108
Thomas, 47, 53, 57, 61, 62, 106, 136-138, 158
Thomasine, 158
HALGRAVE
John, 50
HALL
Edward, 97, 130, 132, 133
Isaac, 208
John, 151
Joseph, 302
HALSEY
James, 212

HALSTONE
William, 81
HAMMOND
Laur., 169
Samuel, 127
HAMPTON
James, 8
HANAFORD
Nathaniel, 151
Richard, 330
HANAVER see HANOVER
HANCOCK
Edward, 211
HANDFORD see HANFORD
HANDY
Joseph, 208
HANFORD/HANDFORD/HANFORTH/HANNIFORD
___, Mr., 34, 197, 324
Nathaniel, 3, 93, 287, 342
Richard, 330
HANKS
Adam, 29
HANNIFORD see HANFORD
HANOVER/HANAVER
Richard, 201, 224
HANSCOMBE
James, 259
HARDEE
Elizabeth (___), 22
HARDEN
___, Goodman, 125
HARDICK
John, 150
HARDING
Phillip, 159, 197
HARDY
___, Mr., 291
John, 196
Joseph, 40, 95, 104, 174, 193, 221, 291, 293, 296, 317, 334, 338, 339
Martha (___), 104
HARKER
William, 277
HARNET/HARNETT
Cecily (___), 41
Edward, 31, 41, 42
Eunis (___), 42
HARRIS
John, 149, 299
Joseph, 19, 57, 61
Samuel, 172, 173
Sarah (___), 299

364

HARROD
Henry, 61, 149, 162, 251
HART
___, Goodman, 58
Deborah, 283, 312
Isaac/Isaack, 202, 283, 284, 312, 315, 316
John, 52, 312
Jonathan, 315
Mary (___), 148
Samuel, 97, 98, 148, 162, 328, 342
Tho., 155
HARVEY
George, 323
Richard, 45, 273
HARWOOD
Elizebeth (___), 192
Henry, 8, 42, 77, 83, 84, 192, 217, 243, 310
HASCALL/HASCOL/HASCOLL/ HASKALL/HASKELL
Elizabeth (___), 177
John, 207
Patience (___), 207
Mark, 257, 329
Roger, 25, 32, 38, 54, 55, 166, 177, 179, 207
William, 40, 54, 55, 207
HASKETT
Elizabeth (___), 323, 324
Stephen/Steven, 124, 162, 209, 248, 256, 323, 324
HATHORN/HATHORNE/HAWTHORNE
___, Capt., 3, 13, 24, 25
___, Maj., 82, 191
___, Mr., 76, 77, 139, 326
Abigail (___), 237, 313
Abigail (Corwin), 225
Ann, 48
Ann (___), 101
Anna, 63, 124, 174, 179, 217, 223, 243, 250
Ele., 234
Elea./Eleazer/Eleazor/Elezer, 124, 137, 144, 155, 165, 203, 212, 225, 227, 228, 237, 250, 267, 311, 313, 324, 325, 329, 331
Elizabeth, 179, 235, 243
John, 13, 19, 43, 49, 50, 53, 56, 61, 84, 99, 100, 112, 117, 131, 142-144, 148, 172-174, 177, 181, 204, 219, 226, 233, 252, 257, 262, 282, 295, 302, 303, 324, 328, 335, 338, 340 342, 346, 347
Mason, 189
Nathan, 189
Nathaniel, 137, 155
Ruth (___), 347
Sara (___), 112, 301
Sarah, 295
William/Wm., 4, 5, 9, 31, 33, 36, 48, 51, 60, 62, 65, 68, 70-72, 93, 98-101, 113, 114, 121, 122, 124, 129, 141, 143, 147, 157, 160, 163, 172, 174, 176, 179, 192, 199, 211, 212, 216, 217, 222, 223, 226, 230, 234, 235, 237, 240, 243, 258, 295, 300, 301, 311, 323, 327
HAUGH
Samuel, 131, 133
HAVEN
Richard, 56, 79, 81, 112, 122, 142, 148, 162, 213
HAWARD see HAYWARD
HAWKES/HAWKS
Adam, 9, 29, 107, 135
John, 315, 324
Sarah (___), 324
HAWKINS
Abra./Abraham, 155, 249
George, 2
Thomas, 20, 332
HAWKS see HAWKES
HAWTHORNE see HATHORN
HAYDEN
James, 155
HAYLE
Thomas, 36
HAYNES/HAINES
Richard, 5, 6, 180, 195, 201
Robert, 180
William, 4-6, 85
HAYWARD/HAWARD
Edward, 150
Henry, 110
John, 244, 252, 295, 303, 318, 322, 326, 331, 343
Nathaniel, 340
Nehemiah, 59
HEALEY/HEALY
Sarah (___), 334, 338
William, 338
HEBBERT/HEBERT see HIBBERT
HENFIELD
William, 321
HERBERT see HIBBERT
HERMAN
Richard, 298
HERRICK
Edith (___), 172, 220

Henry, 40, 54, 55, 166, 167, 172, 188, 211, 219, 220, 251
Mary (___), 251
Zachariah, 115, 194, 207, 263
Zachary, 175, 211, 251
HIBBERT/HEBBERT/HEBERT/HIBARD HIBBERD/HIBBIRD/HIBERT/ HERBERT/HYBERT
Hanna, 252
Joane (___), 252
John, 35, 49, 129, 249, 252
Joseph, 252
Roberd/Robert, 41, 54, 55, 122, 156, 180, 185, 252, 338
HICKES/HICKS
Dorcas, 227, 233, 236
HIDE/HIDES
Isaac/Isack, 179, 185, 212
Richard, 19, 23, 59, 63, 80, 176, 187, 200, 249
HIGGINSON/HIGGENSON
___, Mr., 23, 30, 120
Henry, 334
John, 10, 114, 130, 138, 163, 174, 215, 219, 228, 229, 233, 243, 276, 284, 285, 300, 306, 308, 327, 333, 334, 337, 340, 346
Nathaniel, 215
Sarah, 327
Sara/Sarah (___), 215, 233
Sarah (Savage), 308
HILL/HILLS
Hanah, 325
James, 43
John, 80, 109, 113, 128, 225, 260, 282, 300, 311, 314, 345
Joseph, 120, 310
Zebulon, 76, 109, 282
HILLIARD
Edward, 80, 184, 188, 218, 221
Job/Jobe, 22, 189, 213, 248, 254, 294, 309, 340
Mary, 213
Mary (___), 189, 254, 340
HILLS see HILL
HILLYARD
Edward, 59, 80
Job, 162, 286
HIND/HINDS/HINES
James, 7, 8, 274
HIRST
William, 314, 343
HOAR/HOARE/HORE
Dorcas, 201

William, 11, 13, 156, 201, 340
HOBBS
Thomas, 101
William, 71, 73, 231
HODGE/HODGES
George, 176
William, 202
HOEMAN
Edward, 254, 255
HOLDING
Nicholas, 91
HOLDSWORTH
Joshua, 248
HOLEMAN
Edward, 121
HOLGRAVE
___, Mr., 1
John, 22
HOLINGWOOD
___, Wid., 110
HOLLARD
George, 318
Sarah (___), 318
HOLLINGWORTH/HOLLINGSWORTH HOLLINWORTH
___, Wid., 189, 190, 209, 254, 286
Elizabeth, 271
Elizabeth (___), 235, 263
Ellenor (___), 140, 234
Mary, 130, 140, 234
Richard, 35, 118, 163, 174, 219, 224, 235, 261, 263, 271, 299, 303
Susanna (___), 163
William, 56, 110, 111, 130, 134, 140, 141, 200, 234, 304, 305
HOLLIOKE see HOLYOKE
HOLLIS
William, 267, 278
HOLLYOKE see HOLYOKE
HOLMAN, 261
Edward, 260
HOLMES
John, 313, 331
HOLT/HOLTON
Joseph, 341
HOLYOKE/HOLLYOKE/HOLLIOKE
___, Mr., 151, 173, 181, 186, 202, 238, 290
___ (Pinchon), 69
Editha (___), 172
Edward, 35, 69, 142
Eleazer/Elizur, 69, 172
Samuel, 172

HOME
___, Deac., 311
Benjamin, 332
HOOD
John, 28
Richard, 83, 123, 328
HOOKE
William, 29, 195
HOOPER
Elizabeth (___), 127
John, 157, 227
Robert, 121, 127, 157, 159, 186, 260
William, 179, 183, 165
HORE see HOAR
HORMS
John, 289
HORNE/HORNES
Frances (___), 62, 117
John, 1, 17, 24, 32, 33, 56, 62, 68, 101, 117, 139, 145, 153, 156, 189, 268
HORNETT
Edward, 24
HORSMAN
Ankias, 164, 170, 171
Jane (___), 170
HOVY
John, 296
HOW/HOWE
___, Lieut., 76
John, 195, 206, 255, 266, 295, 296, 320
Joseph, 81, 130, 132
HOWARD
Mary, 68, 141, 162, 232
Nehemiah, 55, 74, 250
Nicholas, 39, 56, 74, 207, 250
Robert, 60, 61, 67, 68, 77, 84, 141, 162, 189, 232
William, 56, 196, 212, 297
HOWE see HOW
HOWELL
___, Mr., 343, 344
HOWLAND
Richard, 230
HOWLETT
Thomas, 147
___, Ens., 123, 195, 261
HUBBARD
James, 130, 139
John, 288
HUBBERT
John, 314

HUCHENSON/HUCHESON/ HUCHESSON/HUCHINSON see HUTCHENSON
HUD
Richard, 167, 168, 242
HUDSON
John, 5, 84, 126, 321
Jonathan, 81, 131, 262
Mary (___), 126
HUGHSON
Thomas, 341
HULL
George, 338
Isaac/Isaack/Isaak/Isack/Isak, 180, 188, 194
HUMBER
Edward, 137, 192
HUMFREY/HUMFRIES/HUMFRY/ HUMPHREY/HUMPHREYS/ HUMPHRIES/HUMPHRY/ HUMPHRYES, 157
___, Mr., 3, 78, 129, 209, 221, 242, 292, 331, 345
Edward, 210, 254, 332
John, 1, 2, 82, 165, 167, 240, 241
Joseph, 82, 177
Thomas, 322
HUNKINS
John, 266
HUNT
Katherine, 132
Samuel, 269-271
HUNTER
William, 45
HUTCHENSON/HUTCHESON/ HUTCHESSON/ HUTCHINSON/ HUCHENSON/HUCHESON/ HUCHESSON/HUCHINSON
Edward, 242, 274
Elisha, 59
Elizabeth, 233
John, 138, 271, 347
Joseph, 47, 85, 88, 138, 159, 160
Richard, 4, 6, 19, 66, 85, 86, 99, 100, 138, 139, 159, 160, 192, 233, 272
Samuel, 29, 58
Susannah (___), 192, 193
Thomas, 44
HUTCHINS
Nicholas, 313
HUTTEN/HUTTON
Elizabeth (___), 336
Richard, 273, 274, 336, 346
HYBERT see HIBBERT

INDIAN
Ned, 15
INGALLS/INGOLLS/INGOLS/INGULS, 243
___, Wid., 46
Edward, 45
Francis, 43, 177, 226
Henry, 45
John, 5
Robert, 45, 142, 277, 278
Samuel, 244
Sara (___), 277, 278
INGERSOLL
George, 17, 20, 76
John, 40, 80, 113
Nathaniel, 160
Richard, 2
INGERSON, 326
John, 187, 236, 340, 347
Nathaniel, 88, 218, 243, 244
Ruth, 236
INGOLLS/INGOLS/INGULS see INGALLS
IRELAND
William, 246, 248
IRESON
Edward, 142
John, 236
ISBELL
Robert, 11
IVERY see IVORY
IVES
Ele., 234
Martha (___), 321
Thomas, 113, 124, 150, 234, 235, 253, 316, 318, 321, 330
IVORY/IVERY
___, Wid., 130, 139
Thomas, 89, 122, 131, 162, 281, 324

JACKSON
___, Goodman, 61
John, 22, 30, 32, 42
JACOB/JACOBS
George, 71, 156, 157, 164, 169, 170, 258, 259, 316
Mary (___), 259
JAMES
___, Wid., 179
Erasmus, 74, 133, 142, 179, 237, 271, 309
Jane (___), 133, 142, 306
Sara/Sarah, 308, 335
Thomas, 15, 36, 52, 105, 111, 151, 291, 300, 308, 335, 338

JAMESON
Sarah (Price), 329
William, 329
JEGELLS/JEGELS/JEGGELLS/ JEGGLES/ JEGLES/JIGELS/JIGILS/ GEGGLES/ GEGLES, 243
___, Goodman, 77
___, Wid., 61, 104
Elizabeth, 154, 293, 294
Elizabeth (___), 134
Thomas, 20, 48, 134, 149, 154, 222, 233, 253, 291, 293, 294, 338, 340, 341
William, 48, 134, 149, 154, 294
JENCKES/JENCKS/JENKS
Joseph, 25-27, 36, 37, 40, 90, 98, 252
JENSEN/JENSON
Edward, 315
Samuel, 315
JEPSON
John, 155
JEWETT
Ann, 84
Joseph, 84
Nehemiah, 213
JIGELS/JIGILS see JEGELLS
JOANES
Edward, 154, 155
JOHNS
Alice, 14
Alice (___), 16
JOHNSON, 82
___, Mr., 15, 52, 221
Alce (___), 148, 149
Daniel, 149, 282, 287
Edward, 198, 344
Elizabeth, 144, 149, 313
Frances/Francis, 6, 60, 138, 140, 144, 151, 178, 201, 214, 216, 222, 224, 231, 254-256, 261, 300, 313
Hana (___), 201
John, 312, 327
Richard, 21, 26, 35, 65, 93, 126, 149, 167, 324
Samuel, 148, 149, 173, 186, 204, 226
Thomas, 23, 28, 115
JOLIFFE
John, 162
JOLLY
___, Mr., 197
JONES
Hugh, 156, 262, 268
Josiah, 300
Morgan, 73
William, 211

JOY
 Peter, 324
KEASAR/KEASER see KEYSER
KEAT
 Samuel, 125
KEAYNE/KEYNE/KEYNES
 ___, Capt., 152, 172
 Benjamin, 131, 132, 159
 Richard, 132
 Robert, 131, 132, 159
KEAYSER see KEYSER
KEBBEE/KEBEE
 Elisha, 223
KEISER see KEYSAR
KELHAM
 Alice (___), 27
 Austin, 24, 27
 John, 24, 27
KEMBALL/KEMBLE/KEMBOLL see KIMBALL
KEMP
 Edward, 239
KEMPTON
 Ephraim, 339
KENDALL
 Elias, 157
 Thomas, 30
KENISTON/KENESTONE/ KENNESTONE/KENNISTON
 ___, Mr., 100, 323
 Allen, 10, 113
 Dorothy, 8
 Dorothy (___), 113
KENNECOTTE
 Roger, 135
KENNESTONE/KENNISTON see KENISTON
KENNY
 Henry, 72, 79
 John, 225
KENT
 Samuel, 125
KENYS
 Henry, 59
KERRY
 Henry, 63, 64
KERTLAND see KIRTLAND
KESAR/KESER see KEYSAR
KETCHIN see KITCHEN
KETTEL/KETTLE
 Eliza (___), 125
 Elizabeth, 125
 John, 125
KEYNE/KEYNES see KEAYNE
KEYSAR/KEYSER/KEASAR/KEASER/ KEAYSER/KEISER/KESAR/KESER, 80
 ___, Mr., 325, 326
 Eliezer, 290
 Elizabeth (___), 30
 George, 28-30, 36, 39, 40, 65, 69, 83, 101, 106, 117, 124, 133, 146, 195, 197, 203, 208, 213, 217, 218, 223, 225, 237, 274, 277, 290, 324, 328, 343, 344
KILCUP/KILLCUPP
 William, 135, 321
KILHAM/KILLAM see KILLUM
KILLCUPP see KILCUP
KILLECOTT/KILLICOTT
 John, 178, 217
KILLUM/KILHAM/KILLAM/KULLUM
 Daniel, 346
 Hanna, 79
 Hanna (___), 327, 328
 John, 79
 Lott, 244, 307, 327
KIMBALL/KEMGALL/KEMBLE/ KEMBOLL/KIMBOLL
 Caleb, 336
 Charles, 260
 Henry, 209, 339
 John, 161
 Richard, 108, 124, 336
 Henry, 199, 204
 Thomas, 125, 315
KING
 ___, Mr., 139, 152, 177, 213, 331
 Daniel, 2, 3, 5, 21, 35, 78, 83, 84, 130, 133, 142, 168, 192, 203, 242
 Dorothy, 28
 Dorothy (___), 19, 23
 Elizabeth (___), 35, 78, 242
 John, 231, 241, 276, 307
 Katherin (___), 258
 Ralph, 78, 100, 136, 144, 180, 201, 203, 242, 342
 Sarah, 242
 William, 42, 71, 74, 154, 250, 258, 311, 317
KINSLEY
 Mary, 3
KIPPEN/KIPPIN/KIPPING
 Abigail, 185, 186, 253
 Arthur, 20, 186, 252, 253
 Mary, 253

KIRTLAND
  Alec, 148
  Alice (___), 56
  Hannah, 299
  John, 35
  Nathaniel/Nathanyell, 56, 93, 111, 112,
    141, 148, 195, 257, 262, 281, 342
  Parnell (___), 111, 262
  Phillip, 23, 130, 132, 139, 148
KITCHEN/KITCHIN
  John, 4, 40, 47, 53, 57, 106, 192, 244, 276,
    277, 296, 311
  Robert, 256
KITCUM
  William, 187
KNELL
  Philip, 315
KNIGHT/KNIGHTS
  Charles, 274, 279, 280
  Elizabeth (___), 97, 98
  Em/Eme (___), 136, 137, 273
  Francis, 126, 133
  Joanna, 97
  John, 10, 108, 136, 137, 199, 273, 277,
    296, 297, 310, 320
  Mary, 98
  Robert, 195, 206, 207, 251, 299, 330
  Sara (Lemon/Leoman), 274, 279
  William, 9, 97, 98, 126, 130, 328
KNOTT
  Richard, 265, 321
KNOWLES
  ___, Mr., 34, 45, 46, 82, 148, 201, 252,
    342
  Elizabeth (___), 126, 133
  Elizabeth (Willis), 316
  John, 126, 133, 226, 315, 316
KULLUM see KILLUM

LACYE
  Laurence, 210
LAFKIN
  Timothy, 23
LAIGHTON
  Thomas, 131, 342, 345
LAKE/LAKES, 113
  ___, Mr., 303
  Ann (___), 205, 206
  Anna (___), 138, 210
  John, 317
  Thomas, 136
  William, 114, 136-138, 158, 205, 206,
    210

LAMBERT
  John, 5780, 156, 193, 201, 252, 320
  Richard, 31
LANGLEY
  John, 155
LARKIN
  Hugh, 54
LASKIN/LASKINS
  Hugh, 25, 75
  Timothy, 28, 80
LATAMORE see LATTAMORE
LATHROP
  Thomas, 249
LATTAMORE/LATAMORE/
LATIMORE/LATTEMOR/
LATTERMORE/LATTERMORE/
LATTIMORE
  ___, Mr., 103
  Christopher, 65, 84, 121, 123, 157, 171,
    217, 238, 249, 260-262, 309
  John, 127
  Mary (___), 121, 123, 157, 217, 261, 309
LAUGHTON
  Thomas, 97, 149, 152, 173
LAUNDER
  John, 334
LAURENCE
  Thomas, 134
LAWES/LAWS/LAWSE, 118, 126
  ___, Goodman, 105
  Francis, 83, 112
LEACH/LEACHE/LEECHE, 22, 190
  Elizabeth (___), 208
  Hanna/Hannah, 237, 239, 338, 339
  John, 37, 40, 181, 188, 207, 208, 220,
    248, 258, 287, 301
  Laurence/Laurence, 42, 88, 93, 249, 323
  Richard, 37, 42, 93, 248, 249, 256, 272
  Robert, 37, 227
  Samuel, 191, 201, 202, 210, 222, 237-239,
    241, 246, 251, 255, 307, 309
  Sarah (___), 287
  Thomas, 137
LEADER
  Richard, 2, 9, 36, 37
LEE
  Richard, 283
LEECHE see LEACH
LEGA
  ___, Mr., 95
LEGG
  John, 45, 74, 83, 134, 245, 254

LEMAN
Robert, 200
LEMON/LEMONS/LEOMAN
Hana/Hannah, 274, 279
Mary (___), 274, 279, 280
Robert, 17, 57, 71, 76, 79, 108, 188, 274, 279, 280
Sara, 274, 279
LEONARD
Henry, 219, 237, 259
Nathaniel, 259
Thomas, 259
LEVERET/LEVERITT
John, 300, 314
LEVERMORE
William, 260, 263
LEWIS
Hana/Hanah (___), 200, 201
John, 81, 82, 104, 142, 168, 173, 201, 242, 243
Katheran, 186
LILLINGTON
Alexander, 308, 335
Sara/Sarah (James), 308, 335
LIND/LINDE see also LYNDE
Samuel, 292
Simond, 293
LINDALL
Timothy, 291, 293, 320
LINDE see LIND
LINDSEY/LINSEY
Eleazer, 278, 281
John, 238
LINSFORD
Frances, 126
LITTLE
Edward, 252
LIVERMORE
___, Mr., 170
LOGEE
Phillip, 241
LONGHAM, 38, 257
LONGLEY/LONGLY
Joanne (___), 123
Johana (___), 122
John, 111
William, 45, 122, 123, 130, 345
LONGSTAFE/LONGSTAFF
William, 310, 332
LOOK
Thomas, 142
LOOMES/LOOMIS
John, 80, 192

LORD,
___, Goodman, 16, 58
___, Mr., 336
Abigail, 209
Abigail (___), 170, 171, 174, 184, 185, 209, 278, 288, 289, 329, 332
Jane (___), 83
Richard, 90, 239, 240
Robert, 55, 83, 84, 117, 142, 148, 274
William, 13, 15, 18, 32, 36, 40, 45, 75, 82, 83, 103, 164, 170, 171, 174, 184, 185, 205, 207-209, 214, 233, 278, 288, 306, 323, 329, 332, 336
LOTHROP
___, Capt., 224, 225
___, Lieut., 76
Thomas, 100, 141, 143, 257
LOVEJOY
John, 116, 313
LOVET/LOVETT
John, 62, 156, 207, 258, 339
Mary, 62
LOWELL
___, Mr., 245
Isaack, 90
Percival, 5
LUFF
John, 5, 20, 41, 54
LUMMUS
Edward, 50
LUNT
John, 320
LYNDE see also LIND
Nathaniel, 293
LYON
John, 33
LYTEFOOT
Francis, 89

MABEE
Richard, 311, 315
MacMALLEN/MACKMALLEN/MACMALLEN
Allester, 113, 163, 175
Elizabeth, 312
MACNELL, 331
MAJEIRE
George, 267
MAN
John, 275
MANNERING/MANNING
Eliza (___), 304
Elizabeth (___), 311
Hanna (___), 156

Mary, 294
Nicholas, 171, 280, 304, 311, 214, 332, 332
Oliver, 119, 144, 145, 155, 156, 176
MANSFIELD
Andrew, 30, 33, 34, 35, 36, 62, 78, 79, 80, 90, 93, 104, 149, 151, 152, 164, 173, 180, 186, 187, 197, 199, 201, 238, 242, 275, 277, 278, 282, 291, 319, 328, 343, 345
Bethia/Bethiah, 79, 201
Damaris (___), 297, 298
Demaris, 287
Elizabeth (___), 33, 78, 79
Elizabeth (Needham), 152
John, 29, 30, 78, 79, 81, 148, 162, 187
Joseph, 123, 151, 152
Mary (___), 78, 79
Paul/Paule, 31, 74, 75, 182, 244, 287, 292, 297, 298, 318, 200
Robert, 8, 30, 33, 34, 78, 79, 81, 122, 151, 152, 162, 187
MAPES
William, 122
MARINER/MARRINER
Richard, 14
Thomas, 31
MARK
___, Wid., 40
MARRINER see MARINER
MARSH
John, 44, 49, 51, 56, 85, 87, 130, 161, 200
Susanna (___), 85
MARSHAL/MARSHALL, 153
___, Capt., 281, 345
___, Goodman, 66
Abigail, 105
Benjamin, 283
Edmond/Edmund, 10, 24, 39, 74, 250, 283
Peter, 175
Rebecca/Rebecka (___), 104, 105, 212, 213,
Thomas, 44, 45, 61-63, 66, 69, 70, 81, 82, 97, 103-105, 123, 131, 133, 182, 187, 204, 212, 213, 226, 283, 325, 341, 342, 345
MARSTON/MARSTONE/MASTON
Alce (___), 250
Alice, 198
Ephraim, 187, 286, 322
John, 46, 58, 117, 163, 164, 170, 197, 198, 250, 267, 306, 347
Manasseh/Manasses, 187, 193, 347
Mercy, 187

Nathaniel, 55
Sarah, 197
William, 18, 24, 46, 86, 117, 163, 198, 250, 347
MARSY
John, 186
MARTIN
Abraham, 299
John, 194
MARY
Peeter, 132
MARYON
John, 81
MASCALL/MASCOLL
John, 55, 88, 230, 312
MASON
Arthur, 346
Elias, 6, 15, 38, 75, 126, 149, 158, 177, 200, 243, 302, 347
Hanah/Hanna, 186, 290
John, 82, 103, 186, 214, 218, 289, 290, 343
MASSE/MASSEY/MASSY, 191
___, Goodman, 164
Elizabeth, 318
Jeffery/Jeffrey/Jeffry/Jefferie, 10, 20, 22, 38, 47-49, 58, 74, 76, 101, 108, 113, 157, 187, 191, 212, 248, 256, 293, 294, 301, 333
John, 112, 158, 169, 170, 287, 294, 302, 314, 318
Sarah, 294
Sarah (___), 169, 318
MASTERS
Nathaniel, 156
Ruth (___), 156
MASTON/MASTONE see MARSTON
MATHEW/MATHEWS
Abraham, 319
John, 69
Richard, 134
MAUL/MAULE
Edward, 198
Naomi/Naomie (___), 246, 271
Thomas, 189, 192, 213, 214, 233, 246, 254, 271, 285, 286, 317
MAUZUNE
Laurence, 252, 253
Mary (___), 252
Mary (Kippin), 253
MAVERICK
___, Mr., 143
Abigail, 159
Antipas, 213, 214

Elias, 197
Eunice/Unis (___), 222, 236-241, 251, 304, 305, 331
Martha, 237, 239
Mose/Moses, 32, 33, 62, 63, 86, 87, 121, 126, 129, 130, 149, 153, 157, 159, 165, 173, 174, 178, 179, 190, 197, 202, 206, 213, 214, 216, 222, 236-241, 251, 252, 260, 267, 271, 298, 299, 304, 305, 307, 318, 319, 331
Peter, 305
Samuel, 149, 154, 157, 222, 305

MAYE
George, 232

MEACHAM/MEACHUM/MEACHY
Jeremiah, 178, 194
Jeremy, 8
Isaack, 255, 292

MEADE
James, 293

MEASY
Samuel, 293

MECARTER
John, 339

MEEKES
Thomas, 180

MERRIAM
Elizabeth (Breed), 159
William, 70, 159, 261, 262

MERRITT
James, 188
John, 188
Nicholas, 127, 186, 188

MERRYWEATHER
Edward, 228

MICHELL
Edward, 107

MIGHILL
Nathaniel, 216

MILES
Joseph, 86, 87, 118, 124, 208, 232, 330, 338, 339

MILKE
John, 158, 210

MILLAR/MILLER
___, Mr., 245
Elizabeth (___), 189
John, 21, 32, 189, 318, 319
Mary (___), 318
Peter, 332
Sarah, 318

MILLETT
Thomas, 125

MILLS
James, 173

MOLDE/MOULD
Edward, 161, 182

MOODY
___, Lady, 81, 137, 242
Eleazer, 326, 331
Richard, 294
Samuel, 187

MOORE/MORE
___, Wid., 162, 347
Ann/Anna (___), 128, 178
Caleb, 296
Christian, 296
Christian (___), 206, 217
Hanna (___), 74, 142
John, 306
Katherne, 199
Richard, 8, 29, 47, 50, 56, 57, 99, 117, 150, 165, 166, 196, 204, 206, 217, 224, 242, 243, 256, 257, 290, 296, 302, 330, 340
Samuel, 120
Susana, 296
Thomas, 35, 176

MORGAIN/MORGAINE/MORGAINES
see also MORGAN
___, Goodman, 108
Daniel, 174
Samuel, 201, 262

MORGAN/MOGIN see also MORGAIN, 264
Evan, 179, 217
Robert, 170, 336
Samuel, 103, 197, 202, 231, 238, 251

MORIES, 161

MORRLY
Edward, 298

MORSE
Anthony, 310, 320

MOSES
Henry, 136, 184

MOSS
Jonathan, 251
Roger, 120

MOULD see MOLDE

MOULTON
James, 41, 124, 274, 336, 346
John, 311
Joseph, 311
Robert, 3, 291

MOUNTJOY/MUNJOY
John, 195
Walter, 305

MOWER
  Richard, 65
MOWLE
  Edward, 193
MOWSER, 292
MULFORD
  Friezwood/Friswid/Frizwid (___), 200
  John, 200
MUNJOY see MOUNTJOY
MURRAY/MURRY
  Benjamin, 204
  J., 330
  William, 345
MUZZY
  Benjamin, 262

NAILER
  Edward, 204
NANNY
  Robert, 4
NASH
  Peter, 339
NEAL/NEALE/NEEL
  Frances, 311, 314, 347
  Jeremiah, 246, 253, 326
  John, 153, 158, 171, 214, 239, 243, 258, 311, 332
NECK
  William, 27
NEEDHAM
  ___, Mr., 69, 343
  Anthony, 58
  Daniel, 274, 275, 342
  Edmond/Edmund, 152, 197, 242, 275, 342
  Edward, 152, 274
  Elizabeth, 152
  Ezekiel, 173, 203, 242, 342
  George, 91, 92
  Sarah (___), 342
  Sarah (King), 242
NEEL see NEAL
NEGRUS
  Jonathan, 57
NELSON
  Robert, 195
NEWALL/NEWELL see also NEWHALL
  ___, Goodman, 213
  John, 295
  Robert, 223
  Thomas, 82, 83, 204
NEWGATE
  John, 22
  Nathaniel, 22

NEWHALL see also NEWALL
  Elizabeth (Potter), 328
  John, 122, 123, 218, 277, 302, 343
  Thomas, 93, 130, 152, 281, 302, 328, 342, 345
NEWMAN
  ___, Mr., 107, 336
  Antipas, 200
NICHOLL/NICHOLS
  William, 7, 31, 68, 71, 73, 79, 171, 172, 231, 333
NICHOLSON
  Christopher, 129, 130
  Edmund, 129, 196
  Elizabeth (Simpson), 129
  Joseph, 129, 130, 318
NICK/NICKE
  Christopher, 129, 256, 262
  William, 63, 171, 196, 238, 246, 332
NIXON
  Mathew/Matthew, 71, 188, 202, 218
NORICE/NORISS see NORRICE
NORLAY
  John, 231
NORMAN, 8
  John, 170, 195, 280, 288, 324
  Richard, 11, 74, 102, 121, 142, 331
  Thomas, 136
NORRELL
  William, 300
NORRICE/NORICE/NORISS/NORRIS/NORRISS
  ___, Mr., 197, 307
  Dorothy, 111
  Edw./Edward, 6, 12, 13, 27, 45, 47-51, 54-55, 59, 60, 62, 68, 74, 78, 87, 88, 96, 97, 100, 101, 104, 106, 111, 112, 123, 127, 136-139, 144, 150, 151, 160, 176, 182, 184, 189, 190, 196, 202, 203, 208, 209, 232, 233, 242, 245, 246, 249, 260, 261, 271, 282, 284, 286, 296, 298, 300, 304, 306, 312, 313, 315, 325, 326, 329, 332, 338, 340, 341, 345
NORTHY
  Dorothy (___), 171, 238
  John, 6, 83, 123, 171, 238, 262, 332
NORTON
  George, 36, 44, 61, 124
  John, 59, 105, 194, 195, 279
  Mary (___), 105, 195, 279
  Thomas, 215
  William, 13, 17, 20, 73, 101, 182, 214, 215

NOWELL
Robert, 222, 308
William, 300
NOWLTON
John, 283
NOYCE/NOYES
John, 314
Nicholas, 73, 318
NURSE, 169
Francis, 97, 101, 156, 157, 164, 311, 341

OATLEY/OATLY/OTLEY
Adam, 2, 43, 226
OBER
Richard, 207, 274
ODIARNE
Henry, 155
OLIVER, 7
Bridget, 181
James, 20, 294
Nathaniel, 314
Richard, 321
Thomas, 11, 117, 180, 181, 183
ORMES
John, 55
ORNE
John, 208
OSBAND
___, Mr., 190
OSBORN/OSBORNE/OSBOURNE
Bezaleele/Bezaliell, 200
Joseph, 200
William, 200, 207, 226, 260
OSGOOD
John, 210
Steven, 102, 115
Thomas, 313
OTLEY see OATLY
OTTORRAY/OTTWAY
John, 252, 262
OXE
Robert, 319
OXENBRIDGE
___, Mr., 68
John, 67, 246
OXMAN
William, 196

PAGE
Isaac/Isaack, 44, 51, 80
PAINE see also PAYNE
John, 14, 15, 125, 136, 297
William, 6

PALFREY
Peter, 2, 20, 24, 74, 99, 103
PAMER
Richard, 308
PANLLY
Benjamin, 34
PARKER, 2
Hannaniah, 268
John, 322
Margaret (___), 322
Nathan, 116
Ralph, 168
Thomas, 324
William, 142
PARKMAN
Deliverance, 278
Elias, 177, 178, 209
Sara/Sarah, 302, 317
PARMINTER/PARMITER
Benjamin, 158, 210, 212, 303, 319, 321
PARNEL
Francis, 198
PARROTT
Francis, 276
Ralph, 155
PARSON/PARSONS
Hanna (___), 340
Jeffery/Geffery, 191, 328-330
Johanna (___), 340
Phillip, 321
Robert, 340
Samuel, 340
PARTRIDGE
John, 90
PASKE
Hugh, 176
PATCH
Edmond/Edmund, 37, 38, 55, 159
John, 207, 257, 258
Mary (___), 258
Nicholas, 207, 257
Thomas, 257, 258
PAYNE see also PAINE
William, 15, 84
PEABODY
Francis, 195
John, 312
Joseph, 312
PEACH
Dorcas, 323
John, 33, 45, 74, 118, 121, 142, 157, 158, 165, 206, 207, 241
PEARCE/PEARSE see also PEIRCE
Daniel, 310, 319

William, 88, 89, 135, 197, 204
PEARSEHOULL
William, 90
PEARSON
John, 93, 132, 173, 186, 238, 278, 283, 284
Madelen/Mauldin, 278
Mauldin/Mawdlin (___), 186, 238
PEASE, 159
___, Goodman, 160
Ann, 318
Gertrude (___), 38
Henry, 38, 84
John, 2, 7, 51, 107, 318, 247
Nathaniel, 335, 346
Robert, 14-16, 166, 202, 276, 311
Sarah, 318
William, 178
PECKANANNQUIT, 15
PECKER
James, 189
PECKETT
John, 80
PEDRICK
John, 309
PEETERS see PETER(S)
PEIRCE see also PEARCE
Daniel, 120
PEMBLETON
___, Mr., 76
PENNEY
George, 201
PEPIN/PEPPIN
___, Mr., 216
Samuel, 284
PERCY
Henry, 16
PERKINS
Abraham, 283
David, 329
Hanna (___), 283
Thomas, 203, 241, 255, 266, 309
PERLY
Thomas, 219
PERRY
Frances/Francis, 9, 10, 34, 53, 60
Jane (___), 34
PESTER
Elizabeth, 97, 306
William, 1, 48, 100
PETER/PETERS/PEETERS
___, Mr., 12, 33, 100, 104, 311, 332, 333

PETFORD
Peter, 12, 27
PETHERICK
John, 217
PETINGILL
Richard, 14, 16
PHELPS/PHEPHS
Christopher, 74, 182, 222, 279, 305
Edward, 115, 127
Hannah (___), 121
Henry, 46, 47, 113, 120, 121
John, 76, 128
Nicholas, 121
PHILLEN
Joseph, 280
PHILLIPS
Eleazer, 341
Henry, 67, 77
John, 31
William, 106
PHILLPOT
Thomas, 154
PHIPPEN
John, 183
Joseph, 112, 184, 189, 305
Samuel, 309
PHIPPENEY/PHIPPENY
Joseph, 253
PICKARD
John, 333
PICKERING
___, Lieut., 347
John, 10, 30, 112, 114, 124, 195, 235, 243, 280, 292, 301, 332, 337, 340, 347
Jonathan, 112, 126, 319, 332
PICKETT
John, 76
PICKMAN
John, 74, 165, 335
Lydea, 103
Nathaniel, 32, 74, 165, 193, 205, 208, 292, 313
Samuel, 40, 46, 99, 102, 103, 116, 118, 165, 174, 205, 314
PICKTON/PICTON
Ann (___), 170, 260, 264
Thomas, 121, 156, 170, 176, 260, 264, 265
PICKWORTH
Samuel, 197, 254, 334, 347
Sara (___), 254
Sarah (Marstone), 197
PICTON see PICKTON

PIGDEN/PIGDIN
　Thomas, 76, 86, 216
PIKE
　George, 112
　Joseph, 314, 339
　Robert, 112
PILGRIM
　John, 330
PINCHON
　___, Mr., 69
PIPIN
　___, Mr., 89
PITMAN/PITTMAN
　John, 203, 225, 275, 335
　Mark, 121, 206, 207, 323
　Nathaniel, 66, 240, 241
　Samuel, 124, 225
　Sara (___), 206, 207
　Thomas, 83, 121, 176, 201, 206, 249, 319
　William, 318
PITT/PITTS
　___, Mr., 121
　Susana (___), 249
　William, 7, 32, 33, 103, 123, 127, 157, 201, 211, 212, 217, 218, 238, 249, 262
PITTMAN see PITMAN
PITTS see PITT
PLAINE, 33
PLUMMER
　Samuel, 207
POMERY/POMERYE
　John, 279
　William, 279
POOLE/POOL
　John, 29, 130, 186
　Jonathan, 283
　Margaret (___), 131
POPE, 345
　Benjamin, 299
　Garthrid (___), 339
　Gertrude (___), 271
　Joseph, 21, 23, 31, 82, 88, 107, 120, 219, 268, 299, 302
PORINGTON
　John, 61
PORR
　Elizabeth (___), 298, 299
　William, 298, 299
PORTER, 265, 275
　___, Mr., 124, 266, 320, 341
　Anna (Hathorne), 223
　Benjamin, 333
　Elizabeth (___), 42
　Eunice (___), 30
　Israel, 219, 315, 332, 333
　John, 3-5, 9, 23-25, 72, 80, 85, 93, 98, 100, 101, 109, 110, 133, 135, 171, 172, 187, 214, 223, 231, 271-273, 323, 333
　Jonathan, 24, 30, 42, 76, 108, 244
　Joseph, 200, 209, 217, 223, 333
　Mary (___), 231
POST
　Abraham, 312
POTE/POTES
　William, 212, 322, 332
POTTER
　___, Goodman, 213
　Elizabeth, 328
　Em (___), 199
　John, 73
　Joseph, 73
　Mary (___), 72
　Mary (Gedney), 86
　Nicholas/Nichols, 29, 50, 65, 72, 81, 86, 87, 126, 132, 148, 198, 199, 273, 301, 311, 324, 328, 335
　Robert, 81, 148, 328
POUT, 284
POWDRILL
　Thomas, 155
POYNTTON
　Joshua, 327
PRATT
　William, 312
PREIST see PRIEST
PRESCOT/PRESCOTT
　___, Mr., 40
　Edward, 15
　John, 165
　Richard, 99
PRESTON
　Roger, 127
PRICE, 147, 191, 279
　___, Capt., 119, 160
　___, Mr., 47, 94
　Ann (___), 246
　Elizabeth, 306, 334, 340
　Elizabeth (___), 42, 263
　John, 112, 135, 188, 201, 202, 206, 223, 244, 237, 239, 253, 254, 263, 267, 277, 282, 284, 285, 287, 300, 306, 338-340
　Mathew, 117, 118, 122, 189, 208, 232, 236, 245, 329, 330
　Richard, 93, 101
　Sarah, 329
　Theoder/Theodere/Theodore, 64, 68, 79, 119, 135, 150, 233, 188

Walter, 12, 13, 19, 26, 29, 41, 42, 48-50, 54, 58, 62-64, 68, 70, 71, 73, 86, 87, 92, 103, 112-114, 119, 125, 127, 135, 141, 143, 156, 162, 178, 188, 206, 217, 221, 233-235, 243, 253, 264, 267, 282, 306, 326, 340
William, 273
PRICHARD/PRICHET/PRICHETT
John, 320
Richard, 337
William, 206
PRIDE
John, 1, 85, 216
PRIEST/PREIST
John, 304, 345
PRINCE
Jon., 114
Jonathan, 330
Richard, 20, 50, 66, 86, 118, 174, 205, 217, 221, 278, 292, 330
Robert, 47, 48, 79, 87, 88, 139, 191
Samuel, 330
Thomas, 225
PROCTER/PROCTOR
Benjamin, 283, 312
Deborah (Hart), 283, 312
John, 219
PROUT/PROUTE
Timothy, 150
PUDEATER/PUTDEATOR/PUDETER
Jacob, 235, 236, 248, 267, 277, 296, 297, 326
PUDNEY
Jno., 311
John, 256
PULLEN, 58
PUNCHARD
Abigail (Waters), 220
William, 220, 304
PURCHASE
Oliver, 62, 145, 212, 213, 252, 345
PUTNAM
___, Lieut., 107, 175
John, 21, 24, 25, 31, 47-49, 71-73, 79, 80, 82, 85, 86, 99-101, 106, 139, 147, 160, 233, 272, 284
Mary (___), 320
Nathan, 48
Nathaniel, 6, 19, 48-50, 71, 73, 85, 88, 100, 101, 138, 159, 160; 179, 181, 182, 191, 192, 233, 341
Thomas, 19, 33, 47-50, 66, 68, 71, 73, 82, 86, 88, 100, 101, 104, 112, 123, 139,

150, 160, 174, 191, 192, 256, 263, 277, 288, 302, 320

RAIMENT see RAYMENT
RAINES
William, 107
RAINSBERY
___, Maj., 311
RAMONDS see RAYMOND
RAMSDELL
John, 81, 148, 328
RAMSON, 316
RAND
Elizabeth (___), 163, 164
Robert, 45, 46, 123, 142, 163, 164, 173, 180, 181
Sarah, 278
RANDAL/RANDALL
Eliza, 161
Elizabeth (___), 161, 165
Samuel/Samuell, 59
William, 160, 161, 165, 301
RAWDON
John, 155
RAWSON
Edward, 126, 133, 315, 316, 321
RAY
___, Goodman, 30
Daniel, 23, 32, 82, 99, 100, 233
Joshua, 66, 187, 333, 338, 341
RAYMENT/RAIMENT
John, 37, 55, 115, 194, 207, 263
Judith (___), 263
Rachel (___), 115
Richard, 68, 87, 176
William, 219, 220, 231
RAYMOND/RAMONDS
Joshua, 95
Judith, 95
Judith (___), 144, 145
Nathaniell, 316
Richard, 6, 9, 40, 95, 144, 145
RAYNER
Elizabeth (___), 336
William, 13, 336
REA
Joshua, 87, 108, 147, 233, 246, 271, 286
Sara (___), 286
READ/READE/REED, 260, 312
___, Mr., 58
Abraham, 316
Aron, 202
Edward, 74
Esdras/Esdrass, 13, 79

Israel, 345
Mary, 256
Phillip, 148
Richard, 83, 103, 133, 138, 144, 171, 179, 206, 238, 262
Thomas, 40, 151, 256, 332
READFORD see REDFORD
READLE
Samuel, 124
REDFORD/READFORD
Charles, 304, 330, 345
REDKNAP
Benjamin, 287
Joseph, 35, 78, 126
REED see READ
Abraham, 243
Richard, 112, 179, 238
REEDY, 268, 324
REETH see REITH
REEVES
Elizabeth, 298
John, 15, 49
William, 244, 287, 297, 298
REITH/REETH
Richard, 222, 230, 279
REMINGTON
Mehitable, 276
Thomas, 276
RENOLDS see REYNOLDS
REVES see also REEVES
Thomas, 193
REY/REYE
Joshua, 233, 243
REYNOLDS/RENOLDS
Henry, 128, 147, 154, 223, 260
Sara/Sarah (___), 128
Thomas, 23, 28
William, 269, 271
RHOADES/RHOADS/RHODES/ ROADES/ROADS
___, Mr., 73, 123
Eleazer, 290
Henry, 27, 69, 90, 93, 173, 195, 277, 278, 281, 290, 343
John, 84, 216
Samuel, 238, 290
RIAL/RIALL/RYAL see also ROYALL, 39, 41, 42, 97
RICE
Marke, 90
RICESSONE
John, 298

RICHARD/RICHARDS
Ann (___), 90, 173, 177
Daniel, 286, 297
Edward, 3, 26, 27, 90, 97, 144, 173, 177, 196, 203, 213, 226, 247, 262, 273, 286, 287, 322, 343, 344
Elizabeth (___), 166
Mary, 297
Richard, 71, 73, 151, 166, 231
RICHARDSON/RICHESON/ RICHESSON, 345
Amos, 148
Amy (___), 180
Edward, 26
George, 2
Richard, 180, 181
Samuel, 198, 344
RICHMOND
John, 68
RIDDAN
___, Mr., 216
Thaddeus, 201, 292, 298, 307, 319
RIVEDOU, 89, 90
RIX
Margaret (___), 32, 34
Thomas, 14, 15, 18, 32, 34, 56, 72, 101, 117, 207, 317
ROADES/ROADS see RHOADES
ROBBINS
John, 284
Thomas, 97, 164, 223, 272, 285, 288, 302, 311, 317, 337
ROBBINSON/ROBBISSON see ROBINSON
ROBERTS
Lydea, 298
Timothy, 305
William, 231
ROBINSON/ROBBINSON/ROBBISSON/ ROBINSTON
___, Wid., 36, 279
Abraham, 257
Constance (___), 74, 182
Dorothy (___), 231
Eleanor/Ellenor, 208, 210
Elinor/Ellenor (___), 158, 214
George, 110
Jane, 71
John, 147, 202, 208, 214, 218, 219, 221, 231, 241, 244, 255, 266, 309, 320, 327
Mary (___), 257
Nathaniel, 211, 212
Samuel, 74, 75, 182, 223, 245
Timothy, 98

William, 43, 71, 263, 268
ROE/ROES see also ROW
Bartholomew, 204
John, 61
ROGERS
___, Goodman, 346
ROMBALL see RUMBALL
ROOPE
Anthony, 319
ROOT/ROOTE see ROOTES
ROOTEN/ROOTENS
___, Wid., 180
Richard, 10, 78, 142, 186, 278
Thomas, 59
ROOTES/ROOT/ROOTE/ROOTS
___, Goodman, 15
Joseph, 11
Josiah, 79, 156, 183, 201, 252, 339, 340
Susanna (___), 33, 340
Thomas, 11, 18, 39, 41, 45, 54, 114, 276
ROPES/ROPPS
George, 9, 22, 101, 113, 175, 190, 324
John, 324
Mary (___), 324, 325
Samuel, 324, 325
William, 232, 324, 325
ROSE
Richard, 236, 305
Ruth (Ingerson), 236
Thomas, 174, 318
ROSEWELL/ROSEWELS/ROSWELL
William, 90, 104
ROUNDIE
Deborah, 175
ROW see also ROE
Hugh, 339
John, 339, 341
ROWDEN
John, 18, 108
ROWLAND/ROWLANDS
Richard, 83, 158, 165, 174, 175, 199, 208, 230, 238, 241, 318
ROWLES
Robert, 238, 330
ROYALL see also RIAL, RYAL/RYALL, 19, 256
RUBTON
John, 231, 271
RUCK
___, Mr., 2, 49, 71, 157
Elizabeth (___), 280
Hanna/Hannah, 106, 230

John, 16, 31, 44, 68, 100, 105, 106, 109, 114, 116, 118, 119, 125, 126, 153, 163, 190, 191, 125, 126, 153, 163, 190, 191, 193, 195, 219, 231, 237, 241, 280, 284, 285, 287, 288, 300, 301, 308, 322, 337
Sara/Sarah (___), 109, 116, 119, 126, 193, 280, 287
Thomas, 16, 42, 43, 68
RUMBALL/ROMBALL/RUMBOL/ RUMBOLL/RUMB[ALL], 155
Daniel, 19, 23, 47, 53, 56, 62, 76, 93, 94, 98, 104, 114, 120, 122, 124, 134, 187, 198, 334
RUSH
Jasper, 61
RUSSELL
Henry, 121, 157, 260
James, 90, 257
Mary (___), 319
Richard, 1, 84, 233, 263, 320, 321, 335
William, 281, 289, 324
RYAL/RYALL see also RIAL, ROYAL, 129, 156, 164, 169, 248, 249, 287, 301, 316

SADLER, 30
___, Mr., 33
Richard, 34
SAFFORD
John, 261
Thomas, 123, 261
SALLARD
John, 25
SALLAS/SALLIS
John, 314
Thomas, 209
SALLENS
Alice (___), 155
Gregory, 155
SALLIS see SALLAS
SALLOES/SALLOW/SALLOWS/ SELLOES
___, Goodman, 283
John, 216, 225
SALMON
Daniel, 144, 172, 197, 343
George, 145
SALTONSTALL
Nathaniel, 314
SAMMOND
___, Mr., 45
SAMPSON
John, 73, 121

SANDEFORD see also SANFORD
  John, 155
SANDERS/SAUNDERS
  John, 106, 119, 192, 276, 277, 310, 311
SANDIES/SANDIN/SANDY
  Arthur, 33, 123, 188
  Margarett, 188
SANFORD see also SANDEFORD
  Elizabeth (___), 80
  Robert, 80, 275
SARGEANT/SEARGENT/SERGEANT/ SERGENT
  Abigail (___), 73
  Stephen, 261
  William, 73, 125, 139, 148, 257
SATCHELL
  ___, Goodman, 301
SAUNDERS see SANDERS
SAVAGE
  Ephraim, 216
  Mary (___), 216, 308, 327
  Perez, 216
  Sarah, 308
  Thomas, 4, 6, 8, 85, 215, 216, 308, 327, 340
SAWER, 263
SCARLETT
  ___, Wid., 72
SCOTT, 157
SCOTTOWAY
  John, 86
SCRUGGS
  Thomas, 37
SCUDDER/SCUTTER
  Elizabeth (___), 301, 302
  John, 129
  Thomas, 4, 272, 302, 336
SEARES see SEARS
SEARGENT see SARGEANT
SEARLE/SEARLES
  Humphrey, 321
  Mary, 196, 209
  Mary (___), 199, 321
  Stephen, 199, 321
  Thomas, 202, 274
SEARNAYES
  Marke, 57
SEARS/SEARES/SEERE
  ___, Wid., 323
  Alexander, 44, 45, 179, 185, 199
  Mary, 196
  Sander, 119, 145

SEASEAGE
  ___, Goodman, 312
SEDDON
  John, 155
SEDGWICK
  John, 95
SEERE see SEARS
SELARE
  John, 250
SELLOWES see SALLOES
SELMAN
  John, 322
SEMONS
  Robert, 314
SERGEANT/SERGENT see SARGEANT
SEVERANS
  Samuel, 315
SEVERNE
  John, 342
SEWALL
  Stephen, 282
SHAFFLIN/SHAFFLYN/SHAFLIN/ SHAPLIN
  Michael, 3, 16, 71, 153, 154, 214, 281
  Mighill, 58
SHAKERLY
  ___, Mr., 157
SHAPLIN see SHAFFLIN
SHARP/SHARPE, 333
  ___, Mr., 100, 303
  ___, Mrs., 87, 112
  Elizabeth, 106
  Hannah, 222
  Nathaniel, 176, 222, 279, 294, 342
  Rebecka, 222
  Samuel, 3, 279
SHATTOCK/SHATTUCK
  Hannah/Hanna (___), 53, 65, 66
  Samuel, 50, 53, 65, 161, 162, 182
SHAW
  George, 229
  William, 209, 214
SHEAFE
  Sampson, 295
SHEPARD
  Theophilus, 132
SHEPLEY see SHIPLEY
SHERMAID, 160
SHIPLEY/SHEPLEY/SHIPLY
  Ann (___), 336
  John, 31, 54, 336
SHIPWAY/SHIPWAYE
  John, 75

SHRIMPTON/SKRIMPTON
  Henry, 56, 57, 257
  Samuel, 256, 257, 323
SIBLEY/SIBLY
  Hana (___), 128
  Richard, 98, 128, 129, 288
SILSBY
  ___, Goodman, 172
  Henry, 46, 78, 142, 278
  Nathaniel, 308
SIMON/SIMONDS/SIMONS see also
  SYMONDS, 303
  ___, Goodman, 34
  James, 180, 288, 310
  John, 180, 282
  Samuel, 223, 224
SIMPSON
  Elizabeth, 129
  Francis, 130
  Francis/Frances, 129
  John, 230
SINDALL
  Austin, 204
SISCOM
  John, 119
SKELTON
  ___, Mr., 3, 100, 176
  Samuel, 2, 9, 109, 110
SKERRIE/SKERRY
  ___, Goodman, 58
  Bridget, 58
  Bridget (___), 345
  Ephraim, 194, 284
  Frances/Francis, 5, 20-22, 30, 32, 37, 40, 54, 55, 64, 76, 88, 98, 114, 135, 199, 323, 332, 345
  Henry, 32, 40, 56, 57, 62, 63, 72, 98, 189, 209, 213, 231, 236, 259, 262, 274, 303, 315, 316, 331
  Thomas, 209
SKIDWELL, 70
SKIPON
  Theophilus, 131
SKRIMPTON see SHRIMPTON
SLANTHER
  John, 144
SLATTER
  John, 103
SLAUGHTER
  John, 138
SMALE/SMALL/SMALLE
  Benjamin, 287, 316, 318
  Elizabeth, 155
  John, 72, 151, 156, 223

  Joseph, 202, 313
  Lidea (___), 313
  Ruth (___), 313
  Ruth (Cantlebury), 145
  Samuel, 198
  Thomas, 145, 146, 150, 183, 184, 313
SMEA
  Thomas, 323
SMITH, 78, 125, 333
  ___, Capt., 165, 240
  ___, Wid., 143
  Benjamin, 15, 103, 308, 317
  Elizabeth (___), 327
  Elizabeth (Goodell), 43
  George, 9
  James, 17, 156, 174-176, 189, 199, 224, 230, 241, 262, 292, 293, 306, 318
  John, 8, 43, 47, 53, 99, 104, 120, 158, 174, 187, 206, 239, 315, 320
  Mary, 230
  Mary (___), 306
  Michael, 84, 135
  Richard, 4, 267
  Temperence, 60
  Thomas, 42, 46, 100, 191, 251, 336
  William, 265
SOELL
  ___, Mr., 120
SOLART
  John, 336
SOLAS/SOLLACE/SOLLAS
  Grace (___), 136
  John, 57, 76, 224, 225
  Robert, 80
  Thomas, 42, 136
SOMERBY/SOMERSBY
  Abriell, 165
  Anthony, 161, 165
SONE
  Thomas, 134
SOTHERICK see SOUTHWICK
  John, 41
SOUDEN/SOUTONS/SOWDEN
  Pascah, 105
  Thomas, 127, 185, 212
SOUTH
  ___, Mr., 30, 343
SOUTHER
  Nathaniel, 43, 81
SOUTHWICK/SOTHERICK/
  SUTHERICK
  ___, Wid., 289
  Daniel, 58, 59, 120

John, 25, 43, 44, 58, 71, 106, 169, 181, 231, 232, 241, 260, 263, 268, 289, 303
Josiah, 46-48, 58, 120, 163, 276, 292, 300, 303
Laurence, 50
Mary, 289
Sarah (___), 71
SOUTONS/SOWDEN see SOUDEN
SPENCER
Garrard/Gerard/Jerard, 46, 172, 175, 340
Michael, 172
Roger, 22
SPOONER
___, Wid., 174, 260, 288, 317
Elizabeth, 230
Thomas, 8, 17, 34, 41, 57, 106, 230
SPRAGUE
Richard, 110
ST. CROIX
George, 267
STACEY see STACY
STACKHOUSE
Richard, 44
Susan (___), 44
STACY/STACEY
Ellen (___), 253
Ellenor (___), 127
Henry, 33, 252, 305, 323, 331, 341
Jane (___), 323, 331
John, 65, 127, 185, 253, 254
STAINWOOD/STANESWOOD
Phillip, 191, 339
STANBOROUGH
Josiah, 25
STANDISH
James, 18, 149, 212
STANESWOOD see STAINWOOD
STANLEY
Mathew, 266, 327
STARR
Mary (Conklin), 224
Richard, 224
Robert, 224, 234
Susanna, 224
STEEVENS see STEVENS
STEGGE
Thomas, 44, 45
STEVENS/STEEVENS
___, Mr., 136
Isaac, 169
James, 169
John, 110, 230
Phillip, 168
Phillip (___), 169

Timothy, 116
Will./William, 94, 95, 168, 169
STICKY, 195
STILEMAN
___, Mr., 19, 159, 160, 176, 278, 289
___, Wid., 114, 145
Eliah/Elias/Elyas, 3, 4, 17, 36, 46, 48, 51, 55, 75, 76, 95, 103, 111, 113, 114, 130, 138, 145, 174, 182, 208, 243, 276, 288
Mary, 51, 208
Richard, 3, 4, 52, 63, 75, 105
Samuel, 4, 75
STILLSON/STILSON
Grace (___), 330
Vinson/Vincent, 224, 246, 330
STOCKER
Thomas, 252, 341
STODDARD
Anthony, 67, 165, 307
James, 246
Solomon, 165, 240, 241
STONE, 199, 324, 345
___, Goodman, 180
Elener (___), 185
John, 18, 41, 80, 175, 179, 185, 262, 329
Nathaniel, 122, 245, 282, 283
Robert, 18, 71, 80, 154, 179, 209, 214, 258, 289, 298, 308, 311, 315, 318
STONEHIL/STONEHILL
Richard, 269, 271
STOUGHTON
William, 288, 314
STOW
Nathaniel, 142
STRAND
Robert, 12
STRATTON/STRATTONS
John, 65
William, 8, 84
STRICKER
Hanna (Waters), 304
Joseph, 304
STUDLEY
John, 12
SULARD
John, 13
SUTHERICK see SOUTHWICK
SUTTON
Richard, 102
SWARTON
Hanna (Hibbert), 252
John, 252

SWASY/SWAYSY/SWAZEY/SWAZY
John, 19, 23, 47
Joseph, 42, 141, 143, 209, 340
SWEATLAND
William, 347
SWEETE
Robert, 140
SWINERTON/SWINNERTON
Job/Jobe, 40, 48, 59, 79, 85, 86, 88, 139, 145, 151, 160, 166, 174, 175, 181, 183, 185, 192, 244, 260, 307, 311, 313, 332, 347
John, 88, 150, 175, 183, 184, 272, 287, 308, 323, 329
Ruth (___), 175
SYMONDS/SYMONSES see also SIMON
___, Goodman, 244
Herlackendine, 125
James, 287
John, 44, 47, 53, 63, 68, 76, 139, 153, 163, 180
Samuel, 125, 237, 245, 326, 333, 339
SYMPLE
Edward, 28

TABUTT
Martha, 309
TAINER
Thomas, 227
TALBY/TALEBYES
John, 26, 42, 217, 242
TALMAGE
___, Goodman, 199
TALY
Elizabeth (___), 320
John, 320
TAPLEY
Gilbert, 315, 327, 340
John, 186, 218, 346
TAPPEN
Isaac, 130, 134
TARBOX
John, 28, 39, 218, 277
TARREY
Mildmay, 127
TATE
Charles, 269-271
TAYLER/TAYLOR
___, Mr., 34
Ebenezer, 186
Edward, 283
Elizabeth, 242
George, 21, 34, 78, 151, 172, 186, 343
James, 315

TAYNOR
Thomas, 84
TAYNTON
Robert, 120
TEMPLE
Robert, 63, 68, 139
Tobias, 57
TENNEY
John, 276
TETHERLY
John, 137
THISTLE
Jeffrey, 274
Richard, 190, 201, 202, 246, 274
THOMAS
___, Wid., 278, 343
Alce/Alice (___), 83, 341
David, 80, 179, 183
Evan, 56
George, 195, 196, 199, 204, 332
Joane (___), 179, 183
THOMSON see also TOMPSON
Benjamin, 299
THORN, 195
THORNDIKE
___, Mr., 38, 160, 163
John, 187, 296
Mary, 225
Paul, 225, 264, 265, 274, 295, 297, 345
THORNEHILL
Timothy, 155
THROGMORTEN/THROGMORTON, 8, 54, 249
TIDCOMBE
Samuel, 155
TILER
Nathaniel, 35
TILTON
William, 46, 142
TING
Edward, 263
TITE
George, 346
TITHERLY
William, 137, 346
TOD/TODD
John, 179, 255, 327
TOLEMAN
Elizabeth (Johnson), 149
TOMKINS
John, 71, 219, 271
Ralph, 72, 315

TOMLIN/TOMLINS
___, Mr., 226
Edmond, 343
Edward, 70, 343, 344
Timothy, 69, 76, 175, 341
TOMMAS
David, 18
TOMPKINS
John, 124, 166, 202, 244, 260, 299, 335
Mary, 299
Ralph, 52, 318
TOMPSON see also THOMSON
George, 155
TOPEN/TOPPEN
Abraham, 147
Isaac, 146
TOURLAND see **TURLAND**
TOWN/TOWNE
___, Goodman, 262
Edmond, 76, 241, 244, 327
Jacob, 203, 241, 255
William, 17, 255
William Joseph, 255
TOWNSEND
___, Goodman, 58
Andrew, 290, 291
John, 186, 242
Mary, 186
Mary (___), 242, 290
Samuel, 291
Thomas, 29, 33, 35, 65, 111, 126, 242, 257, 290, 291
TRASK, 326
___, Capt., 4, 58, 100, 192, 303
Henry, 57, 58, 276
John, 230, 232
Mary, 244
Osman/Osmand/Osmond/Osmund, 19, 24, 54, 55, 108, 177, 188, 244, 252, 329
William, 48, 120, 301, 302
TRAVIS
James, 125
TREBBY/TREBEY
John, 127, 157, 224
TREVITT
Henry, 227
TREVYE
John, 246
TRUE/TREWE
Henry, 48, 58, 65
Israil, 58
TRUSKER
___, Goodman, 200

TRUSLER/TRUSTLER
Elianor/Ellenor (___), 27, 28, 121
Thomas, 121, 336
TUCK, 110
Thomas, 12, 32, 57, 61, 116, 117, 135, 173
TUCKER
Andrew, 237, 309
Elizabeth, 61
Robert, 61, 73
TURLAND/TOURLAND
Joshua, 42, 43, 47, 50, 52, 58, 64, 72, 94, 107, 296
TURNER
___, Mr., 216
Ephraim, 57
John, 11, 64, 178, 210, 217, 221, 222, 230, 254
Robert, 13
Thomas, 269-271
TUTTLE
John, 69
TWISLETON
Ezekiel, 300
TYLER
Hannah (___), 339
Jane (___), 23
Job, 101, 102, 105
Mary, 105
Mary (___), 101, 102
Nathaniel, 23, 126, 130
Thomas, 338, 339

UNDERWOOD
James, 12, 44, 45, 48, 58, 101, 274
UPTON
John, 93, 94, 219, 299
USELTON
Francis, 336
USHER
Hezekiah, 136

VAILE/VALE
Jeremy, 9, 12
VALLAT
Peter, 267
VANE
William, 306
VARNEY
Bridget/Bridgett (___), 191, 225
VENER/VENNER
___, Capt., 91
Samuel, 91, 92

VENUS
William, 14, 21
VEREN/VERIN/VERREN/VERRIN/ VERN
Abigail/Abigaile, 318, 334
Darcus/Dorcas/Dorckos, 9, 10, 16, 184, 219
Dorcas (___), 60
Hannah, 341
Henry, 233
Hillard/Hilliard/Hilloyard/Hillyard, 10, 42, 43-45, 47, 50-53, 55-61, 63-66, 68, 70-72, 74, 76, 77, 79, 80, 83, 84-90, 93-95, 97-99, 103, 105-110, 112-115, 117-119, 124-126, 128-130, 133-137, 140, 144-148, 153, 154, 156-159, 161-164, 166-168, 170-173, 176-179, 181-188, 190, 192, 193, 195, 197-199, 201, 202, 205-210, 212, 214, 215, 217-221, 223-233, 235-239, 241, 245, 248, 250, 252-254, 256, 258, 259, 263, 267, 268, 271, 273, 274, 276-282, 284, 285, 287-290, 292, 294, 296, 297, 299-305, 308-312, 314, 316-318, 320, 323-335, 337, 338, 340, 341
Johanah (___), 98
John, 166-168, 322
Joshua, 60, 221
Mary, 52, 65, 71, 79, 83, 99, 115, 140, 185, 194
Mary (___), 128, 129, 320
Nathaniel, 320
Philip/Phillip, 50, 53, 60, 80, 98, 128, 129, 151, 154, 194, 330, 332, 334, 341
VERIN/VERN see VEREN
VERNAZ
Alice (___), 32
VERREN/VERRIN see VEREN
VERRY/VERY/VERYE
Alice (___), 337
Samuel, 42, 51, 60, 61, 113, 154, 178, 324, 337
Thomas, 19, 329, 330
VIBERT
Julian, 267
VICKERY
George, 252
Rebecca/Rebecka (___), 252
VINSON
Nicholas, 172, 173
Sarah (___), 61
William, 61

W
Timothy, 307
WADES, 115
WAIMOUTH see WAYMOUTH
WAINWRIGHT
Francis, 224
WAIT/WAITE
Richard, 226, 263
WALCOTT
Jonathan, 191, 313, 347
WALDEN/WALDREN/WALDREY/ WALDRON/WALDRY
Dorothy (___), 119
Edward, 79, 338
John, 119, 129, 174, 196, 271, 318
Richard, 169
WALEN
Christopher, 217, 218
WALER see WALLER
WALKER
___, Capt., 69, 326
___, Lt., 151
Henry, 73
Richard, 192, 256
Susanna (___), 321, 322
Thomas, 321, 322
WALLER/WALER/WALLERS, 5, 174, 175
Christopher, 44, 46, 51, 54, 63, 80, 97, 113, 117, 118, 139, 150, 208, 249
Edward, 51
Margaret (___), 113, 117, 118, 208, 249
WALTHAM
William, 1, 222
WALTON
___, Mr., 33, 119, 201, 236, 271
Henry, 35, 242
Nathan, 188
Nathaniel, 224, 331
Samuel, 307, 330
Sarah, 307
William, 27, 104, 127, 159, 174, 190, 197, 202, 318
WARD/WARDS
___, Mr., 305
John, 108, 285
Joshua, 159, 192, 196, 217, 305
Michael, 31, 34
Samuel, 126, 165, 178, 214, 216, 230, 236, 272, 313, 319
WARE
___, Mr., 301
WARNER
Augustin, 150

William, 172
WARREN
Abraham/Abram, 56, 74, 232, 250, 258
Humphry, 261
Mary (___), 232
WATER
___, Goodman, 262
Christopher, 163
Richard, 42
WATERLAND
Nicholas, 200
WATERS
___, Goodman, 17
Abigail, 220
Ezekiel, 220, 221
Hanna, 304
John, 124, 272, 335, 337
Joyce (___), 71, 72, 220, 221, 229, 230, 304
Mary, 229
Richard, 26, 29, 71, 72, 181, 220, 221, 229, 230, 304
William, 122
WATSON
Joane (___), 235, 236
Nathaniel, 298
Thomas, 32, 36, 57, 62, 194, 235, 236, 248, 256, 284, 296, 297, 315, 318
William, 333
WATTS
Jeremiah, 250
WAY/WAYE/WEIGH
Aaron, 246, 248
Ester (___), 60, 61
Hester (___), 60
Richard, 10, 17, 29, 60, 61, 263, 331
WAYMOUTH/WAIMOUTH
Thomas, 153, 154, 173, 174, 318
WEB/WEBB, 157
___, Mr., 120
Elizabeth, 340
Elizabeth (___), 294
Henry, 59
John, 119, 186, 218
Jonathan, 294
Tho., 155
William, 321
WEEDEN
Richard, 269, 271
WEEKES/WEEKS
___, Goodman, 15
Bethia, 72, 136
Hanna, 72, 114, 135
Thomas, 11, 12, 15, 18

WEIGH see WAY
WELCH
Hannah (___), 266
Phillip, 266, 267
WELCOM/WELCUM
Peter, 235, 263
WELD
Daniel, 271, 321
WELLMAN, 107
Abraham, 315, 324
Thomas, 46, 103, 198, 199, 273
WELLS
Daniel, 301
Hanna, 294
WELMAN
William, 336
WESSEN/WESSON see WESTON
WEST
Adam, 236
Henry, 166, 168, 171, 172, 174, 185, 190, 197, 209, 225, 296, 303, 312
John, 88, 89, 273, 274, 294, 295, 329, 331
Mary (___), 254, 309, 331, 338
Mathew, 34, 78, 151
Samuel, 329
Thomas, 53, 105, 128, 139, 160, 161, 294, 300, 329, 335, 338, 339
William, 254, 309
WESTGATE
Adam, 20, 28, 35, 117, 118, 305, 335
Mary, 118
Mary (___), 305
WESTON/WESSEN/WESSON
Frances, 2
John, 55, 183, 268
Sarah (___), 183
WHARTON
Edward, 48, 75
Richard, 227, 228, 307
WHEELE, 195
WHEELER
___, Goodman, 343
Mary (___), 39, 45
Rebecka, 332
Thomas, 7, 24, 39, 45, 46, 61, 69, 142, 143, 186, 218, 219
WHELDON
Gabriel, 28
John, 28
WHIPPLE
___, Elder, 123, 261
WHITE
Abigail, 323
Abigail (___), 329, 332

387

Arthur, 321
Elias, 84, 227
Josiah, 332
Nicholas, 315
Resolved, 325, 332
Thomas, 141, 157, 158, 203, 273, 283
William, 105, 128, 133
WHITEERE/WHITTER/WITTER
Abraham, 212, 282
Edward, 282
Isaac, 282
Josiah, 213
William, 142
WHITEFORD see WHITFORD
WHITFIELD
Walter, 218
WHITFORD/WHITEFORD
Walter, 202
WHITING
___, Mr., 132, 159
Elizabeth, 73
John, 51, 96, 284, 347
Joseph, 73
Nathaniel, 172
Samuel, 73, 83, 93, 122, 130
WHITLOCKE, 46
WHITTAKER
Abraham, 301
WHITTER see WHITEERE
WICUM
Daniel, 276
WIGGIN/WIGGINS
Hannah, 115
Thomas, 39, 61
WILCOCK
Israel, 312
John, 312
WILD
John, 333
WILES
Joseph, 323
WILKES
Mary (___), 36
Robert, 119, 187, 306
Thomas, 36, 335
WILKESON see WILKINSON
WILKINS
Ann/Anna (___), 248
Bray, 67, 68, 76, 147, 246, 248, 278, 279, 284, 307
WILKINSON/WILKESON
John, 346
Sarah, 327

WILL
John, 223
WILLIAM/WILLIAMS, 330
___, Goodman, 7
___, Mr., 10, 207
Abraham, 12
Elizebeth (___), 192
George, 14, 71, 72, 262
Isaac/Isaack/Isaak/Isack, 63, 68, 72, 150, 182, 183, 190, 246, 325, 326, 333, 334
John, 51, 56, 57, 106, 110, 162, 192, 194, 209-211, 236, 244, 268-271, 294-297, 321-334
Joseph, 234, 253, 292, 313
Margery (___), 334
Mary, 233
Mathew, 104
Samuel, 56, 93, 103, 104, 108, 145, 156, 162, 173, 194, 210, 218, 223, 241, 248, 280, 281, 284, 287, 310, 333, 334
WILLIS, 303, 326
___, Mr., 25, 148, 151, 152, 242, 283
Elizabeth, 316
Thomas, 44, 126, 133, 316
WILLISTON/WILLISTONE, 58, 156, 248, 315, 316
WILLOUGHBY/WILLOWBY
Frances/Francis, 126, 168, 169
Nehemiah, 257
WILLOWES
___, Mr., 252
WILLS, 248
WILSON
Hanna (___), 45
John, 18, 45, 90, 208
Robert, 113, 324
Thomas, 200
WINCOLL
John, 70, 71
WINDOW
Richard, 73, 125
WING
John, 78
WINSLAD/WINSLADE
John, 135
WINTER
Edward, 289, 329
William, 148, 151
WISWALL
Ichabod, 322
John, 165
WITHERS
Jacob, 90

WITT
  John, 82, 83, 98, 105, 122, 123, 151, 152, 281
  Jonathan, 111
WITTAWOIES, 125
WITTER see WHITEERE
WOOD/WOODE
  Abigail, 119
  Daniel, 266
  Isaack, 178
  Mathew, 176
  William, 212, 322
WOODBERRY/WOODBERY/ WOODBURY, 166-168
  Andrew, 50, 57, 59, 111, 188, 189, 200, 202, 218
  Ann (___), 68
  Elizabeth, 207
  Humfrey/Humphrey, 18, 76, 108, 159, 163, 166, 181, 220
  Isaack, 188
  John, 159, 194, 210, 211, 295
  Martha (___), 256
  Mary, 163, 200, 225
  Mary (___), 50, 218
  Nicholas, 22, 76, 187, 207, 274, 331
  Peter, 168, 194, 219, 220
  Thomas, 256
  William, 135, 207, 296
WOODBRIDGE
  John, 310, 319
  Thomas, 314
WOODBURY see WOODBERRY
WOODCOCK/WOODCOCKE
  Hanna (___), 267
  William, 164, 267
WOODE see WOOD
WOODLAND see WOOLAN
WOODMAN
  Edward, 161, 165, 299
  Herculus, 187
WOODROW
  Benjamin, 133, 145, 183, 184, 244
  Rebecka (___), 145
WOODS
  William, 196
WOODWELL
  Mary, 109
  Mary (___), 222, 223, 308
  Mathew, 105, 109, 163, 222, 223, 272, 308, 114, 118
WOODY
  John, 30

WOOLAN/WOOLAND/WOOLEN/ WOOLLAND/WOODLAND/WOOLER
  Edward, 12, 122, 124, 152, 176, 178, 209, 234, 248, 253, 321
WOOLESTON/WOOLISTON, 249, 318
WOOLFE
  Peter, 163, 256
WOOLLAND see WOOLAN
WOOLLER see WOOLAN
WORMWOOD
  Henry, 98
WRIGHT/WRITE
  ___, Maj., 264
  George, 206
  John, 268-271
WRIGLEE
  John, 299
WRITE see WRIGHT

YEAMANS
  Fra., 126
  Francis, 133
YENEN
  Joshua, 208
YONGES/YOUNG/YOUNGES/YOUNGS
  Christopher, 13, 79
  John, 129
  Joseph, 7, 96, 105

www.ingramcontent.com/pod-product-compliance
Lightning Source LLC
Chambersburg PA
CBHW072130220426
43664CB00013B/2196